THE JAPANESE LEGAL SYSTEM

Colin P. A. Jones
Professor of Law
Doshisha University Law School

Frank S. Ravitch
Professor of Law and Walter H. Stowers Chair in Law & Religion
Director, Kyoto Japan Program
Michigan State University College of Law

HORNBOOK SERIES®

444 Cedar Street, Suite 700
St. Paul, MN 55101
1-877-888-1330

Printed in the United States of America

ISBN: 978-1-64242-537-6

To Akiko: thank you.

Colin P. A. Jones

To my wife Chika, my daughters Elysha and Ariana,
and my parents Carl and Arline.

Frank S. Ravitch

Preface

Japanese law is a field of great interest to many lawyers and law students around the world. Japan's role as a leading democracy and one of the world's largest economies makes the country a worthwhile subject of study. Yet it is also a subject that can seem impenetrable to outsiders. This is due in part to language, but also to the different roots of Japan's laws and legal institutions and sometimes to stereotypes and expectations about "Japanese culture" on the part of some foreign observers. Once one peels back the linguistic and contextual barriers to understanding the nation's legal system, Japanese law becomes a fascinating and rewarding field of inquiry for comparative law scholars and students, as well as for lawyers who plan to work in Japan or hope to serve clients who are Japanese or have Japan-related matters, whether individual, transactional or regulatory.

This book will teach you the structure of the Japanese government, the legal institutions that constitute a part of that government, and the foundation of law and practice that underpin them. Moreover, it will give you an inside look at how the Japanese legal system functions on the ground and in the day to day lives of those within the legal system and for the Japanese people. The chapters that follow will introduce you to many of the most important laws and regulations in Japan, give you an overview of the Japanese court system and legal professions, the Civil Code and the Criminal Code, the various parts of the Japanese government involved in law making and enforcement of laws, the Japanese Constitution, and Japanese legal history.

When you finish reading this book you will understand that most modern Japanese Law arose in recent times, from around 1868 to the present. You will also understand the important role that continental law, in particular German and French law, played in the formation of modern Japanese legal codes, and the role played by the United States in reshaping many laws and institutions (starting with the Constitution) during the post-war occupation. Most importantly, you will come to appreciate the ingenuity of Japan's leaders, jurists, lawyers and other citizens in adapting Western-modeled laws and institutions to their own needs and goals. The story of the modern Japanese legal system is connected directly to the story of the Japanese people over the last one hundred and fifty years.

June 2018

Acknowledgments

Colin P. A. Jones:

I would like to start by thanking my parents for being so encouraging when, at the age of seventeen, I first announced my plans to go to college in Japan, despite not knowing anyone there or a word of Japanese. Having parents who never doubted or discouraged me has been a tremendous positive in my life; without that quiet support and the self-confidence that comes with it, I probably never would have been able to persist in the path that made it possible for me to write this book.

During my two-plus decades in Japan, I have been the recipient of tremendous kindness from Japanese people from all walks of life. These include not only numerous scholarly and professional friends and associates, but numerous "regular" people—the Satō's and the Suzuki's—who opened their homes and treated me like family when I was still just a gawky kid who spoke their language haltingly and badly.

Special thanks are due to Kōichirō Fujikura, who taught me Japanese law when I was a student at Duke and then years later made it possible for me to become his colleague at Doshisha University. He has always been a kind and deeply insightful mentor, and everywhere I go in the world of academia I come across people who know him and speak of him in nothing but terms of the highest regard. Thanks also to Setsuo Miyazawa for encouragement and kindness, not only to me but to the community of Japanese law scholars in general. Gratitude is also due to my many present and former colleagues at Doshisha University.

Teaching is one of the best ways to force oneself to learn a subject, so I am thankful to all of the institutions that have given me the opportunity to teach Japanese law. This includes Doshisha University, of course, but also Osaka University, the University of Victoria, Duke Law School and Michigan State University College of Law. For this last opportunity I am grateful to Frank Ravitch both for the opportunity and for a friendship that ultimately led to this book.

I must also thank the University of Guam, in particular Dean Annette T. Santos of the School of Business and Public Administration, for providing a sabbatical destination amenable to the completion of this book. Special thanks are due to Professor Mari Hirayama for taking the time to read and comment on Chapter 8 and to Professor Tetsurō Hirano for his helpful feedback on parts of Chapter 10. Thanks also to Nicholas Benes for sharing his thoughts on the relevant portions of Chapter 11 not to mention accolades for his tremendous efforts in the field of Japanese corporate governance through the Board of Directors Training Institute. Some of the contents of Chapters 8 and 11 were derived from research supported by a grant-in-aid from Zengin Foundation for Studies on Economics and Finance.

Words cannot express the tremendous debt owed to my wife for her constant support and all the laughter and happiness we have shared. Love to my three children, who lost some paternal attention in the course of writing this book, but who are already a far greater legacy and source of pride and meaning than anything I can ever hope to publish.

Frank S. Ravitch:

First and foremost I thank Colin P. Jones for his incredible work as a co-author and his immense knowledge of the Japanese language and the Japanese legal system. To say that this book could not have been written without him would be the understatement of the century. This book is the culmination of his vision and depth of knowledge. It was an honor to add my small contributions to his vision.

I am grateful to Hiroyoki Ota and Taisuke Kamata who taught me a lot about Japan and the Japanese legal system when I had the pleasure of serving as a Fulbright Scholar on the Doshisha University Faculty of Law in 2001. I am also grateful to the Doshisha University Law School, my many wonderful colleagues at Doshisha, and my colleagues throughout Japan who have been so kind in their willingness to encourage me as I have struggled to learn the Japanese language and gain a better understanding of the Japanese legal system over the last decade or so.

I also thank my wife Chika, and my daughters Elysha and Ariana, whose brilliance, smiles and love make life better everyday. My parents, Carl and Arline Ravitch, who are a source of constant support and love, and who are an inspiration in everything I do. To my late Bubby and Pop Pop, who are always close to my heart, and who embodied all that is best in humanity. To my sisters Sharon and Elizabeth and their families, my Uncle Gary and Aunt Mindy, and my Aunt Jackie and Uncle Ken, who have been exceptionally supportive of all my work.

I am grateful to the Michigan State University College of Law, which supported my work on this book with a summer research grant, and to Dean Lawrence Ponoroff, and Charles Ten Brink, Hildur Hannah, Jane Meland, and the staff of the Michigan State University College of Law Library for their help and support. I would also like to thank Ryan Coy for his excellent research assistance, and Marie Gordon for her excellent secretarial support. I am especially grateful to Mac Soto at West Academic, who originally approached me about doing a book on Japanese Law and who supported both the book and my suggestion that Colin Jones should be my co-author because I did not feel qualified to undertake this project without someone of Colin's caliber and knowledge.

Summary of Contents

Table of Contents

WEST ACADEMIC PUBLISHING'S LAW SCHOOL ADVISORY BOARD

THE JAPANESE LEGAL SYSTEM

Chapter 1

INTRODUCTION

Analysis

A. JAPAN AND ITS IMPORTANCE IN THE WORLD

For all the talk of its decline, Japan has remained an economic, demographic and technological powerhouse well into the 21st century. Japan has the third largest economy in the world as measured by nominal GDP, which stood at $4.9 trillion in 2016. This is far out of proportion to its population which, despite decline of a different type, is still large. With 127 million people, Japan is the eleventh most populous nation on Earth. It is also one of the most well-educated and technologically advanced nations. Literacy rates are close to 100% and internet penetration exceeds 90%, higher than the United States. Japanese is estimated to be the 4th most commonly used language on the Internet.

The story of how Japan went from being an isolated island nation governed by feudal samurai overlords in the 19th century, to becoming a modern industrial power competing with Western nations on the world stage by the beginning of the 20th century, and then again rose from the defeat and ruin of World War II to become a different type of superpower, surely ranks as one of the great dramas of modern history. Despite it being fashionable to describe Japan as having a bleak demographic and economic future, it is and will likely remain a powerful and important country for decades to come.

Japan and its markets have become deeply enmeshed in the global economy. Japanese companies continue to buy, sell and invest around the world. Foreign companies have become increasingly adept at penetrating the still vast and potentially lucrative Japanese market for goods and services. According to JETRO, the Japanese government's international trade organization, Japan's exports in 2016 were valued at $644 billion while its imports were $607 billion.

Intercourse has not been limited to the commercial sphere either. In 2016 3.7% of marriages in Japan were between Japanese and foreign nationals. Spouses of Japanese nationals accounted for some, but not all, of the approximately two million foreign nationals living in Japan. Over 800,000 Japanese nationals were also recorded as being permanent or long-term residents of other countries. Globalization is thus a part of daily life for a significant number of Japanese people.

B. BARRIERS TO UNDERSTANDING JAPAN'S LEGAL SYSTEM

There are numerous instances where business interests or private life may touch upon Japan in a way that has legal significance, whether it is a cross border investment, a messy international divorce or a multi-jurisdictional estate plan. Yet compared to other developed nations, Japan's legal system may seem impenetrable and mysterious, even to lawyers or other professionals who have a sophisticated knowledge of at least one western legal system. This section will discuss some of the barriers likely to be encountered in trying to understand the Japanese legal system.

1. Language

Of the barriers to understanding language is probably the most obvious. Japanese is very different from English and other western languages and difficult to pick up or read casually. The written language is particularly complex and hard to learn. This is true even for people living in Japan, where the compulsory education system allocates significant classroom time to teaching students the nation's complex writing system.

Many primary and secondary sources on Japanese law are thus inaccessible to people who cannot read Japanese. Even for those who can, older laws and regulations—including some still in force—were written in *kanamajiribun*, an archaic version of the language that even some Japanese people may find cumbersome to read.

The good news is that the Japanese government has devoted significant energy and resources to both updating old laws in vernacular Japanese and making law-related resources available in English. Most national government institutions, including the judiciary and executive agencies, have English websites. A growing number of Japanese statutes have been translated into English and are available on-line (http://www.japaneselawtranslation.go.jp/?re=02). Moreover, important decisions of the Japanese Supreme Court are also translated and published on the court's official website (http://www.courts.go.jp/english/). There is also a growing body of secondary literature in English on Japanese law by scholars and practitioners, both Japanese and foreign.

These resources should be approached with some caveats. For example, the government's translation of a particular statute may not have been updated to reflect amendments to that statute. More often than not, the English version of Japanese government websites reflects the information the institution publishing it thinks or wants foreigners to know rather than being an exact translation of the corresponding Japanese website. Secondary literature, whether academic or professional, is often focused on a narrow area of law and written primarily for other academics or professionals.

2. Japan and the Civil Law Tradition

A more subtle barrier to understanding the Japanese legal system, at least for lawyers and law students in America and other common law jurisdictions, is that Japanese laws and legal institutions are heavily influenced by continental European legal traditions. In the somewhat arbitrary taxonomy of comparative law, Japan is sometimes described as having a "mixed" or "hybrid" system of law in that it combines elements of the Civil Law traditions prevalent in nations such as Germany and France, with later influences from the United States as well as native adaptations.

As a result, numerous aspects of the Japanese system may seem more familiar to a lawyer from a civil law jurisdiction. By contrast, to the American lawyer or law student unfamiliar with the civil law tradition, the Japanese legal system may seem particularly alien. There may be a powerful urge to attribute any differences to strange, alien "Japanese-ness" rather than continental Europe, and what are often actually quirks from the common law tradition. We thus recommend that interested readers refer to Glendon, Carozza and Picker's *Comparative Legal Traditions* in West's Nutshell series.

3. Assumptions

Another barrier to understanding the Japanese legal system—and explaining it—may be often unspoken assumptions about what is "normal." For example, American lawyers may be acculturated not to notice the extensive role common law courts play in the U.S. in seemingly mundane areas such as producing official documents relating to personal status, even in cases where there is no real dispute between parties. In most US jurisdiction, even an amicable divorce is still likely to be accomplished through a court decree which will also serve as proof of the change in marital status. This is not the only way of doing things.

For their part, Japanese lawyers may be mystified at how inheritance is handled in jurisdictions without a *koseki* family registry system (see discussion at Chapter 9) and find the involvement of courts in routine non-controversial estate cases inexplicable. Americans seeking to resolve legal issues in Japan may thus be inclined to think first in terms of what can be accomplished in court and consult with a lawyer (a loaded, misleading term to be discussed in Chapter 7). By contrast, someone in Japan seeking to resolve legal issues in the United States may find themselves stymied by the fact that their "official document" from Japan is looked at askance because it does not take the form of a court decree.

To understand how the Japanese legal system differs from those of the United States or other countries is thus not just a matter of understanding how laws are made, lawyers trained and courts make decisions. It is important to understand how the Japanese system of government as a whole is structured and how it functions, in addition to the role played by the courts and other institutions as part of that system.

4. (Lack of) Context as a Barrier

Another barrier to understanding Japan's legal system—possibly the most significant one—is contextual. Despite the availability of many statutes and precedents in English translation, readers may find them of limited use in understanding what is actually going on. Those who read the judgments of the Supreme Court in translation may find them either impenetrable or inexplicably brief. This is usually not a translation issue, but a reflection of the original text.

It is tempting to try to understand law from the text at hand, whether in the form of a written statute or a court judgment interpreting it. However additional context is needed to really understand the text. For example, to understand a judgment of the Japanese Supreme Court requires an understanding of prior judgments (including dissenting opinions) on the same or related subjects, the significance of particular phrases the court may have used in rendering its decision, the structure of the court and its approach to making decisions and other supplementary materials.

An additional contextual challenge can come from trying to understand why the Japanese legal system sometimes appears to function in a way that is not reflected in the law as it is written. Because of its history of adapting models from Western countries, Japanese laws and legal institutions can be described in terms which seem very familiar, despite operating in a very different way in practice.

Habeas Corpus—the "great writ" and proto-constitutional human rights remedy of Anglo-American jurisprudence—is a useful example. Japan has a *Habeas Corpus* statute that was enacted in 1948 by the Diet—the country's national assembly—during the American occupation, ostensibly to give life to the prohibition on arbitrary detention contained in Article 34 of the then-new Constitution.

This statute reads much as you would expect a *habeas corpus* statute to read. It refers to the ideals of the constitution and establishes a prompt remedy for anyone subject to unlawful detention. A court accepting a petition for *habeas corpus* may order the person responsible for detaining the person on whose behalf the petition is filed to bring the person to court for proceedings to determine the legality of the detention. Non-compliance with such an order can potentially trigger criminal penalties. If the court finds the detention to be unlawful, it can order the detainee to be immediately freed.

This should all seem familiar to the common-law attorney. However, *habeas corpus* in Japan has been largely relegated to the world of family law, where it offers a remedy in custody disputes where one parent "detains" a child by refusing to hand him or her over to the other. This usage is sometimes seen in common law jurisdictions as well, but in Japan it is almost the *only context* in which *habeas corpus* is regularly used. Japanese law students are usually surprised to learn that such a law even exists, and consciousness of its potential use as a possible remedy for human rights violations is limited.

Whether Japan needs a *habeas corpus* statute could certainly be debated, though as will be seen in Chapter 8, the country's criminal justice system is sometimes criticized for being heavily dependent on prosecutions based on confessions procured through prolonged detentions and for offering few prompt remedies for wrongful convictions. Here the important thing to appreciate is that while it would be correct to: (i) say Japan has *habeas corpus* and (ii) describe the *habeas corpus* statute as providing prompt judicial relief from wrongful detentions, these two correct statements would give a completely *misleading* impression as to how *habeas corpus* is actually used in practice, and what sort of judicial remedies someone could expect if they actually were wrongfully detained in Japan.

C. A CONTEXTUAL APPROACH TO THE JAPANESE LEGAL SYSTEM

The goal of this book is to provide primarily western readers with an overview of the Japanese legal system that imparts the context necessary to understand how it functions. It also offers Japanese and non-western readers insight into why American lawyers and law students may find the Japanese legal system difficult to understand, together with clues on how to explain it in terms they will understand. To these ends, the authors have followed three basic guidelines in approaching the subject matter.

1. Avoiding Cultural Explanations

Although it is common, possibly even fashionable to attribute the functioning of foreign legal systems to "culture," this book will actively avoid cultural explanations whenever possible. There are multiple reasons for doing so.

a. Definitional Problem

A basic problem with using "culture" to explain anything is that the term is vague and often used as a short-hand description of "the way things/people are." Describing "the way things are" in the legal system or any other aspect of Japanese society using "culture" as an explanation is thus tautological on a very basic level.

This is not to deny the usefulness of a term such as culture or suggest that Japanese culture (whatever it means) does not exist or have an influence on law and legal institutions. It is just not a particularly useful concept for explaining the Japanese legal system in practical terms and should perhaps be the last explanation looked to rather than the first.

On a more practical level, "the way we do things here"—another version of a cultural explanation—may be convenient for Japanese lawyers, officials or scholars who find themselves in the position of explaining some aspect of the Japanese system to foreigners in a second language, usually English. Yet such explanations may be mystifying rather than enlightening precisely because "culture" is used as a short-hand for a context that a foreign audience is unlikely to share. Foreign practitioners who accept such "this is the way things are" cultural explanations may also be effectively accepting an invitation to be led around by the nose if they do so without further inquiry.

b. Cultural Explanations Can Be Misleading

A basic failing of cultural explanations is that they can be seriously misleading, even wrong, at least once we start thinking in terms of law and legal institutions. For example, it is still common in the West to attribute the dismal treatment of allied prisoners of war by the Japanese military during World War II to the code of the samurai, or *bushidō* (the "way of the warrior"). Distilled to its most simplistic form, this explanation holds that under the dictates of *bushidō*, capture was a disgrace that an honorable samurai would choose death to avoid. This explanation is also sometimes tied to the samurai practice of *seppuku* or *hara-kiri*: ritual "suicide" by disembowelment and beheading. Thus, allied soldiers, sailors and airmen who allowed themselves to be captured were supposedly unworthy of humane treatment in Japanese eyes.

In reality, the samurai had ceased to exist decades before World War II. As discussed in the following chapter, part of the drama of the Meiji restoration was the *elimination* of the samurai class with its special legal status and monopoly on carrying weapons, and its replacement with a modern army based on conscripted peasants with firearms. Moreover, as was happening in other spheres of governance, by the 1880s, Japan's army and navy adopted French-modeled codes of military law, not the law of the *samurai*.

Certainly the Japanese military in World War II became famous for fighting to the death as symbolized by the dramatic, suicidal *kamikaze* suicide planes and *banzai* charges. The extent to which such practices reflect some sort of "samurai ideal" could probably be debated, but it is probably worth looking first to the 1882 Imperial Rescript to Soldiers and Sailors, effectively a form of law defining the Emperor's relationship with his military and what was expected of him. Significantly, this Rescript was written to affirm the reestablishment of direct Imperial control of the military after centuries of usurpation by the samurai class.

A more basic historical problem with the *bushidō* explanation is that Russian prisoners taken by Japan in the Russo-Japanese War of 1904–05 and German prisoners in World War I were actually treated comparatively well by their Japanese captors, even though the former conflict was led in part by generals and admirals born and raised as members of the samurai class. In this light *bushidō* ultimately fails to explain very much. The reality is that there are identifiable, modern, *familiar* legal, administrative and logistical reasons for why prisoners of war were treated a particular way in the various conflicts in which Japan was involved, though a detailed consideration of these is outside the scope of this book.

c. *Japanese "Uniqueness" and False Comparative Dichotomies*

Japan is the only non-western member of the G-7 group of advanced nations. As such it lacks the same long history of Judeo-Christian traditions, wars, political and economic linkages, and cultural traditions that are shared to some degree by most countries typically considered as "Western" (including those which geographically aren't, such as Australia and New Zealand). Thus, despite being a peer to economically significant western nations, Japan is in many ways more different from them than they are from each other.

Certainly, Japan is different. But there is a marked tendency in many popular western accounts of Japan to over-emphasize these differences, depicting it as a strange and alien place populated by inscrutable people. For those whose knowledge of the country is based primarily on news available in western languages and its portrayal in popular culture, Japan may summon up a mishmash of imagery; cutting-edge technology, samurai, geisha, *kamikaze*, clone-like *salariman* office workers, cherry blossoms, *anime* characters and so forth. Such a mixture may indeed be inscrutable, because it is not representative of reality.

Within Japan too, the theme of Japanese "uniqueness," enjoys enduring popularity in the media and can sometimes even be seen in academic or professional writing focused on ways in which Japan and the Japanese people are exceptional. For example, *Nihonjin no hōishiki* [*The Legal Consciousness of the Japanese People*], first published in 1967 by the late Professor Kawashima Takeyoshi, offers explanations of various ways in which the Japanese people (all of them!) have a different attitude towards law, many of which are based on contrasts to sometimes questionable characterizations of the "legal consciousness" of Western people.

Half a century later his book remains in print and widely read, being perhaps one of the most influential books on Japanese law. Professor Kawashima was also one of the first Japanese scholars whose work (including extracts of *The Legal Consciousness of the Japanese People*) was introduced in English translation, making him influential in the sphere of western comparative law scholarship relating to Japan as well (some of Kawashima's theories will be mentioned later in this book).

Yet many of Kawashima's characterizations of how both Japanese and western people are "conscious" of the law are based on tenuous anecdotal evidence and reflect a lack of practical focus. For example, in a chapter on the "consciousness of property rights," he describes the prevalence in America of signs saying "Private Property: Trespassing Prohibited" as evidence of the aggressive assertion of property rights by Americans, which he then contrasts with the Japanese attitude. However, a first year student at an American law school would (hopefully) jump to point out that such signs are not so much about the abstract assertion of property rights but the practical goal of limiting the tort liability of landowners to trespassers.

There is still a tendency on the part of some Japanese commentators to purport to speak authoritatively about how "we Japanese" think or feel about law, dispute resolution or other aspects of society. These may be a useful reference point but should be regarded with the same critical scrutiny that a legal practitioner should bring to any broad factual assertion about a large, complex population. Contrary to common characterizations of homogeneity, the nation's people comprise a broad range of backgrounds, attitudes and outlooks, something that can be readily confirmed through personal interactions as well as traditional and social media.

d. Ancient Culture, Modern Legal System

The idea of Japan as mysterious and unique is further compounded by an eagerness on the part of some commentators (both Japanese and foreign) to associate it with phrases such as "ancient culture" and "tradition." When compared to many other countries, Japan does indeed have a comparatively long history of being what might be called a relatively unified, homogeneous nation state, including continuity in the lineage of the imperial family that supposedly traces back unbroken to the deities who created the Japanese islands. Whether Japan is actually more "ancient" than European countries such as England, Italy or Greece is debatable to say the least. Still for some reason "tradition" is more readily accepted as an explanation for how things work in Japan in situations where they would be challenged if offered in London, Rome or Athens. In fact, when it comes to *written* history, Japan is actually a comparative latecomer with the *Kojiki*, the nation's oldest extant historical chronicle only dating back to the 8th century.

In the legal sphere, the tendency to characterize Japan as an "ancient" nation can be particularly misleading because its legal system is actually quite modern. This is particularly true when compared to the common law system, where the juries used in trials today have their roots in a method of proving cases that most litigants found preferable to trial by combat or compurgation, and *magna carta* and *habeas corpus* remain relevant despite predating the age of reason.

By contrast, with the possible exception of some of the institutions and practices directly related to the imperial system, virtually every Japanese law and legal institution postdates the Meiji Restoration of 1868. This history will be discussed in more detail in Chapter 2, but suffice it to say there is little that is ancient, traditional or mysterious about Japanese laws or institutions. These laws and institutions have been designed, administered and used by rational people seeking to accomplish rational goals. What constitutes "rational" is of course a contextual question, but one that can often be explained in terms more specific than "culture" or "the way things are done."

e. Language (Again)

Another culture theory offered by Kawashima and also commonly seen in other commentary on the Japanese legal system, is that Japanese laws are vague because the

Japanese language is itself vague. Having professionally translated Japanese legal texts into English for over two decades, one of the authors is highly skeptical of this explanation.

For example, in general terms, Japanese has numerous ways of expressing "you," which in writing include terms that specify the gender or type of institution addressed. By contrast, English is equipped only with "you" which does not even distinguish between singular or plural. Which is more vague? Similarly, in a family context Japanese has far more specific terms for "brother," "sister," "aunt," "uncle," and "cousin," in terms of clarity depending whether male, female, elder or junior, maternal relations or paternal. In the context of law, Japanese legal terminology can also be more specific. For example, there are multiple terms for custodial detention depending on the proceedings and the punishment.[1]

Some Japanese laws and regulations may indeed be vague. Americans may expect highly detailed statutory language because it is a way to clearly define what government can and cannot do. The absence of such language may simply reflect the desire to preserve greater flexibility for government actors, which would be unsurprising given that it is executive branch institutions that actually make most of the laws in Japan, as explained in Chapter 5.

f. Not Knowing It When You See It: When Culture Actually Matters

None of this is to say that culture doesn't matter. Cultural norms do have an effect on legal matters in every legal system. In any context preconceptions influence how we view and approach things, so of course Japanese law is influenced by elements of broader Japanese culture just like any legal system is influenced by broader culture. Some of what we see in the Japanese legal system actually do make sense in light of certain cultural norms. For example, the dynamics that apply within a particular group, whether a family, company or local community, and the desire to minimize conflict whenever possible due to expectations regarding those relationships. This is sometimes characterized as a particularly Japanese value using the term "*wa*" (loosely translated as "harmony"). In any case, the impact cultural norms such as these have on the Japanese legal system should not distract observers from the recent—and often continental—roots of that system. Such norms can, however, make things even more confusing for Westerners trying to understand why things are done, or decided, in certain ways.

2. An Instrumentalist Approach to Context

The second guideline followed by the authors is to focus on the practical aspects of the subject. For all of the theory and philosophy that goes into thinking about it, law is ultimately a practical discipline that is applied on a daily basis to the resolution of real world problems whether in courtrooms, legislative committee meetings or elsewhere.

Conceptually, this book is essentially based on the assumption that a random selection of humans from different countries and cultures stranded on a deserted island will all quickly discern that using rocks to break open coconuts works far better than trying to do the reverse. Our approach is thus shaped by trying to understand who is able to accomplish what through the legal system in Japan and why. This assumes law

[1] A possible exception might be the widespread use in statutes, contracts and court judgments of the catch-all "*tō*," which is commonly translated "*etcetera*."

and legal institutions are a tool. "A tool for whom, to accomplish what?—are often the questions that lead to better answers than seeking cultural reasons or focusing exclusively on the black letter law.

We believe that such an approach is helpful because part of the context in which the Japanese legal system needs to be understood is the very top-down nature in which many laws, regulations and rules manifest themselves to those who are expected to obey them. As will be discussed in more detail in the next chapter, an important thread in the story of Japan's legal system includes two periods of significant foreign influence: (1) the post-1868 adoption of foreign-modeled laws and institutions as part of an effort to fend off colonization through unfair treaties by showing western countries that imposed these treaties Japan was "civilized" (i.e., westernized) and (2) the post-war period of Allied occupation, during which significant changes were wrought as part of an effort to democratize and demilitarize Japan. This effort was very much influenced by the American occupation authorities, starting with the current Constitution, the first draft of which was prepared by them. This latter period was then followed by a period of more subtle and gradual retrenchment and even rejection of some of the imposed norms.

Historically, therefore, law in Japan has generally been something that comes from above, rather than being developed through grass roots democratic initiatives. This perception is likely still true for many Japanese people today, notwithstanding a long history of participatory democracy. Given the nature of the legislative process and the limits imposed on the ability of candidates for the national legislature to engage in effective dialogues with voters during elections (both subjects to be discussed in subsequent chapters), the average Japanese person may feel more isolated from the law-making process than in other countries. Add to this the more limited role and powers of courts in Japan than countries like the United States, and opportunities for the average Japanese person to play a role in some form of "rule making" through the assertion of rights in a judicial context may also more limited.

Thus, if one were to try to develop a theory of "Japanese legal consciousness," it should necessarily involve a consideration of if and when the (mythical) "average Japanese person" would rationally regard the Japanese legal system (broadly defined) as a potentially useful tool for resolving problems or accomplishing goals, whether personal or collective. This book will *not* seek to develop a theory of "legal consciousness," beyond trying to identify what may constitute rational behavior within a particular legal context. In adopting such a utilitarian approach to the subject matter it will focus not so much on "what is the law" but on "why is the law" and "who is it for;" these latter two lines of inquiry being more useful in appreciating the context in which the law and the institutions that administer it have developed in Japan.

3. Government as Legal System

On a very basic level, laws are tools by which people are told what to do or not to do, with varying degrees of force. "Told by whom" is part of the equation, but of course some of these tools include the rules by which government institutions are constituted and operated, and how those institutions make, interpret and enforce laws, regulations and rules.

In Japan and every other country, therefore, government and legal system are inseparable: law is a tool of governance. Courts themselves are a part of "the government" and play a particular role in the process of governing. Comparative law reveals that there a multitude of ways in which courts can be part of an overall system of government. This may seem obvious, but a problem with some accounts of the Japanese legal system directed at non-Japanese readers is they tend to focus on how the court system functions and how it resolves disputes (or doesn't).

The authors believe that such an approach can be misleading in a very fundamental way. First, to focus on "dispute resolution" immediately gives rise to the distracting temptation to think in socio-anthropological terms; how Japanese people approach conflict and its resolution as compared to people elsewhere. Second, based on such accounts alone, a reader in a country like the United States may feel that he or she has acquired an understanding of the different or similar ways in which Japanese courts deal with common types of litigation, yet never become aware of the very different—often more limited—role these courts play in society in the first place.

For example, it would be possible to compare the way family courts in Japan resolve divorce cases in a way that is amenable to comparisons with how American courts resolve them. Published Japanese cases can be compared with similar cases from U.S. courts. Yet this would likely be nothing more than a highly misleading exercise in comparative literary criticism if it failed to acknowledge the fact that in Japan approximately 90% of divorces are accomplished without any judicial involvement whatsoever through filings in the *koseki*—Japan's family registry system. This is administered at the top level not by the courts but by the Ministry of Justice.

While it may be interesting and valuable to ponder the sociological aspects of conflict resolution in different cultures, it is important to also be cognizant of the more basic role played by government structures that make recourse to the courts, whether for resolving disputes or official documents in avoiding or minimizing disputes in the first place.

Accordingly a part of this book—all of Chapter 3—will be devoted to providing an overview of the Japanese government as a whole and the role played by various institutions within the legal system, *other than the courts*. The authors believe that this context is critical to understanding the more traditional description of the "legal system"—the legislative process, the courts and the legal profession—that follows.

D. STYLISTIC NOTES

Throughout this book, key Japanese legal terms will be introduced where relevant. With the exception of place names and terms that western readers are likely to be familiar with (e.g., "Tokyo"), Japanese terms will be italicized and Romanized using the Revised Hepburn system, using macrons to denote elongated vowels. Personal names are expressed in the Japanese fashion, with family names first.

The names of Japanese statutes are presented based on the Japanese government's translations when available, though in some cases we have modified them slightly to make them easier to read. References to "the Act" or "the Code" are to whatever law or code was introduced in the text preceding it. Acronyms and other abbreviations for the names of statutes and regulations have also been used when appropriate. These are set forth in the glossary at the end of this book, as are some key Japanese legal terms that appear in the text.

Unless otherwise noted, English translations of statutes and language quoted from Japanese Supreme Court opinions are from the translations available at the websites introduced earlier in this chapter.

Court cases are cited in the most abbreviated fashion used in some Japanese treatises: the name of the court, the type of ruling (judgment or decision) and its date. More extended Japanese citation formatting also references the volume and page number of the reporter in which it appears (if any), but since these are only available in Japanese we have not done so. The "date only" form of citation we have used does mean that it is necessary to use context to identify which case is being referenced when the court in question issues more than one decision on the date in question, which is not uncommon. Where appropriate we have also included reporter citations but generally do not consider them necessary.

Problem w/ "dispute resolution" as comparison tool

←

Chapter 2

THE HISTORICAL CONTEXT

Analysis

A. OVERVIEW

Some Westerners who think about Japanese legal history may have visions of samurai and shōguns. As noted in the previous chapter, however, virtually all modern Japanese law and legal institutions were born after the Meiji Restoration of 1868. This does not mean that Japanese law lacks a longer history, but rather that most of what you will learn in this book about the Japanese legal system reflects developments in the Meiji Period and after the Meiji Period. Yet, earlier eras do subtly inform some aspects of the current Japanese legal system.

The history of the modern legal system can be divided into three rough periods. The first began with the Meiji Restoration of 1868 and saw the introduction of numerous European influences. The Meiji Period—the reign of the Meiji Emperor—ended with his death in 1912. However, what could be called the "Meiji system" of law rooted in the Meiji Constitution of 1889 continued until Japan's defeat in World War II and the establishment of the current constitution and system of government.

The second period is the post-war occupation and reform by the victorious allied powers led principally by the United States. This period goes from late 1945 to April 1952 when the Treaty of San Francisco was implemented. The Treaty of San Francisco is the peace treaty that officially ended hostilities between Japan and the allied powers, restored Japan's sovereignty and stripped it of its colonial possessions. During this period, many of Japan's basic laws and institutions—starting with the constitution—were drastically reshaped under direct or indirect American influence, with Japanese officials, politicians, jurists and lawyers also playing a key role in many of the changes. As you read this book, note how many basic statutes still in force today date back to this period.

The third period runs from the end of the occupation and continues through the present day. A number of themes dominate this period, not only economic reconstruction, but a political and bureaucratic leadership trying to come to grips with some of the changes imposed on them by the Americans. In some cases this involved simply undoing American reforms, such as the organization of the police or the elimination of the Cabinet Legislation Bureau. In others, however, this proved politically difficult; many Japanese people appreciated peace and the freedoms guaranteed by the new constitution, such as the freedom of assembly and expression and the right to unionize and strike. One aspect of the post-war development of the legal system could thus be characterized as an almost "passive aggressive" approach by authority figures to parts of the constitution and other laws left by the occupation, some of which, in fairness may have been unsuitable for Japan and its institutions in the first place.

The modern history of the Japanese legal system means that an American lawyer who looks at it may see things that look familiar and others that are strange. As noted in Chapter 1 and discussed further in this book, this is because of the mixture of German, French and other continental influences that trace back to the Meiji period, and the subsequent occupation era reforms. Yet, despite these familiar foreign influences the legal system remains very Japanese. Japan's Supreme Court has explained that the Constitution must be understood in the Japanese context and in that sense it is distinctly Japanese (Supreme Court, Grand Bench judgment of April 2, 1997, discussed in more detail at Chapter 6).

While the first two eras of Japan's legal system reform were dominated by foreign influences, some might see in the legal reform movement which began at the end of the 20th century the true beginning of a third era of reform, one where Japan for the first time began to develop its own truly native laws and institutions. These include a new system of legal education, a system of civic participation in criminal trials, a significant increase in the population of courtroom lawyers and a change in the way they are trained. These developments are described in Chapters 7 and 8.

Yet the history of Japan as a nation and a society goes back much further than the Meiji Restoration. Much older legal norms influenced by Buddhist and Confucian ideals that date back to the 7th century, as well as the rules imposed by the samurai overlords who dominated Japan for centuries until the Meiji Restoration, each have made their mark on Japanese law and society.

The next section will address the earliest known Japanese legal codes and the period through the twelfth century. This will be followed by sections covering the eras from the late twelfth century through the beginning of the Edo Period in 1603. The section after that will address the Edo Period, which ran from 1603 C.E. to 1868 C.E. The remainder of this chapter will focus on the period from 1868 to the present since it is this history that has had the greatest influence on the modern Japanese legal system. Historical context is also provided where relevant in some of the other Chapters.

B. EARLY JAPANESE LAW

Not much is known about Japanese law prior to the seventh century. Many of the earliest known legal concepts, along with the writing system that allowed them to be recorded, were influenced by Chinese Confucianism and Buddhism.

Japanese legal scholar and legal historian John Owen Haley wrote:

> Little is known about Japan's earliest legal order—to the extent one can be said to have existed at all—before the infusion of Chinese concepts and institutions. . . . As such it is likely that rule by arbitration based on kinship and customary norms supplemented by an occasional political command, if

necessary, cast as a deity inspired utterance, provided the essentials of rudimentary governance without written or institutional law.[1]

There is, however, some mention of political and legal organization in the *Wei Zhi*, a Chinese text from the Third Century that references *Wa* or *Wō* (the Chinese term at that time for Japan). Yet, as Haley explains, anything resembling a formal legal code is not known to have existed in Japan prior to the adoption of Chinese legal concepts in the seventh and eighth Centuries. Even then, Japanese social, religious, and political structures led to divergence from the Chinese model.

We do know that in 604 C.E. a set of seventeen "legal" norms, sometimes referred to as the "Seventeen Article Constitution," or *Jūshichijō Kenpō*, was created, and is generally attributed to the quasi-mythical imperial prince, Shōtoku Taishi. Although sometimes referred to as Japan's "first" constitution, it was not a constitution in the modern sense of the term, but it was designed to set basic, albeit broad and sometimes aspirational norms that were meant to be inculcated.

The first article of this charter declared "*Harmony is to be valued, and an avoidance of wanton opposition to be honored.*" Other values it extoled included revering Buddhist teachings and the Buddha, following the Emperor's commands, government officials behaving in an appropriate and tasteful manner, officials dealing impartially with legal complaints brought before them, promotion of a focus on the public good over private pursuits, and having multiple people involved in important decisions. These do not appear to have been formal legal norms. Some might say that things like a desire for harmony (*wa*) and preference for collective decision making remain hallmarks of Japanese society even today.

Beginning around 645 C.E. a set of legal developments known as the Taika Reforms was implemented. These reforms had an impact on control of land and helped to solidify power around the Emperor and reinforce centralized power vis-à-vis regional authorities. The reforms were modelled heavily on Tang Dynasty structures in China. They were implemented over a number of years and were not a formal legal code, but they did have some influence on the legal codes that were to follow.

In 702 C.E. a formal written code encompassing both administrative and penal legislation was promulgated by the Emperor Monmu. The code was referred to as the *Taihō Ritsuryō* or Taihō Code. The term *ritsuryō* is a combination of the term *ritsu*, which refers to penal law, and *ryō* which refers to administrative law. The *ritsuryō* were heavily influenced by Chinese law, as well as Chinese Confucianism and Buddhism, but adaptations were made for the Japanese system in which it was applied. This was not the first effort to create an imperial code, but it was the first comprehensive one.

Archeologists and legal historians have only been able to find segments of the *Taihō Ritsuryō*. In 718 C.E., however, the *Taihō Ritsuryō* was updated and amended by the *Yōrō Ritsuryō* (the Yōrō Code), which came into full force around 757 C.E. Thankfully much of the *Yōrō Ritsuryō* has been preserved for posterity. This includes the entire *ryō* section and enough of the *ritsu* portions that a detailed reconstruction was possible based on the Tang Dynasty models on which they were based. The *Yōrō Ritsuryō* is a rich source for understanding an aspect of Japanese legal history which remained until the Meiji Restoration. However, within two centuries of its promulgation the *Yōrō Ritsuryō*

---

[1] JOHN OWEN HALEY, AUTHORITY WITHOUT POWER: LAW AND THE JAPANESE PARADOX (Oxford Univ. Press 1991) at 29.

became less relevant as more of the population fell under the domain of military rulers, as well as increasingly powerful Buddhist institutions, each having their own codes and rules. Remnants of the *ritsuryō* live on in some of the internal rules and rituals of the imperial household, together with the system of imperial honors bestowed on noteworthy citizens (discussed in Chapter 3).

Substantively, the *Yōrō Ritsuryō* has a number of interesting facets. While much of it tracked Tang dynasty law there were significant differences based on Japanese culture. These include a lessening of the severity of the famously harsh punishments meted about by the law of Imperial China. Also, the Chinese political system allowed for the possibility of an emperor losing the "mandate of heaven." This could not be contemplated in Japan since the emperors supposedly descended in an unbroken lineage tracing back to the nation's founding deities.

Another feature of the Chinese system that was not adopted in Japan was the exam-based official bureaucracy. In the Chinese system one could rise in status based on merit so that even someone born as a peasant might raise their status. As a practical matter this was rare, but it did happen. By contrast, Japan's *ritsuryō* established a hereditary bureaucracy, which helped entrench the hereditary nobility. Noble families dominated by certain clans in the capitol benefitted the most, as did those acting as governors of provinces and other regions. Status and hierarchy were based on notional proximity to the Emperor, a system which lives on today in the low-key practice of honoring distinguished citizens with posthumous ranks.

The nobility's status was supported financially by taxes on land and the farming of land, which meant a system for determining and governing productive land was needed. The Japanese *ritsuryō* acknowledged far more interests in land than did the contemporary Chinese system. Farmers were awarded land and had what might now be called "ownership. However, increases in productivity generally failed to keep up with increases in taxation. Farmers found it increasingly difficult to pay taxes, with many being forced into a legal arrangement called the *shōen* system. Under this system *shōen* lords owned the land and the farmers lived on the land and farmed it. The *shōen* system spared the farmers from taxes as the lord was responsible for taxes, but it also reduced many farmers to the status of perpetual, hereditary tenants, a status which prevailed for many centuries up to the modern era.

Another notable difference between Japanese *ritsuryō* and their Chinese antecedents was the role of women. A person from China observing Japan between 757 and 1185 C.E. would likely have been most surprised by the status of women under Japan's *ritsuryō*. The status accorded women in the traditional Chinese Confucian system as reflected in the law of the Tang Dynasty (618–907 CE) was oppressive. In China at that time women could not inherit property and women lost all status in their ancestral clan when they married into their husband's clans. In Japan, however, women had inheritance rights, whether as daughters or spouses, and the woman's family continued to have a role after marriage.

Polygamy existed in both societies, especially among the wealthy, but in China second wives were considered chattels and could be sold. In Japan, second wives were not chattels and had rights of inheritance. In some families daughters were more valued than sons because a family could seek to increase its rank by "marrying up."

The comparatively higher status accorded to Japanese women by the *ritsuryō* is an example of the adjustments made to Chinese law to reflect Japan's cultural and political heritage at the time of their adoption. There were a number of female emperors, including, six who reigned between 593 and 770 CE, around the time when the *Taihō* and *Yôrō* codes were adopted.[2]

The *Ritsuryō* also adapted Tang Dynasty punishments for crimes to fit Japanese norms. Legal historian Carl Steenstrup has suggested the relatively light punishments in the Japanese *ritsuryō* compared to their Chinese corollaries may be due to the strong Buddhist influence on officials in Japan and fear of goryô (angry spirits) that also was influenced by native Shintō beliefs.[3] As noted in Chapter 7, the Emperor Saga banned the death penalty completely in 818 CE, a proscription which lasted for over three centuries, and saw politically inconvenient persons banished to remote islands rather than executed.

One aspect of the Confucian system of punishments retained from China , at least in part, was that the relative status of the offender and the victim played a significant role in determining criminal sanctions. For a son to assault his father was considered a far more reprehensible offense than a father hitting his son, which might not even be an offense at all. Elements of this remained in the Japanese Penal Code until recently. For example, article 200 of the Penal Code imposed more severe penalties for the murder of lineal ascendants than for other murders, until that provisions was found unconstitutional in 1973 (see discussion at Chapter 6).

The relative benevolence of the *ritsuryō* may be seen in other places as well. Some writers have suggested that some of Japan's modern social welfare policies have roots in principles enunciated in the *ritsuryō* mandating support and protection of the blind, infirm and elderly.

C. THE KAMAKURA PERIOD TO THE BEGINNING OF THE EDO PERIOD

The culture of Japan's imperial court in Kyoto, and possibly the imperial laws that came with it, flowered and peaked in the Heian Period which ran from 794 to 1185 CE. It was followed by a number of eras that bridged the period from 1185 C.E. to 1603 C.E., and which have been given various titles by historians. For purposes of this book we will consider them briefly as a single whole. This period is characterized by a number of trends, including the usurpation of political power by military rulers, unrest and civil war, the threat of foreign invasion, and the earliest contacts with Europeans and Christianity.

As noted in the preceding section, during this period the imperial *ritsuryō* were still technically in force, but became less important as the scope of imperial authority was reduced by the encroachment of the samurai warrior class, their rules and the local laws that developed in connection with the formation of a military feudal system. Buddhist temples and monasteries also became increasingly significant, as did their internal laws.

---

[2] These female emperors were ultimately succeeded by male members of other branches of the imperial lineage. Accordingly, the lineage has consistently been transmitted through the male children of male emperors. Male-only rules of succession are still reflected in the modern Imperial House Act, of 1947.

[3] CARL STEENSTRUP, A HISTORY OF LAW IN JAPAN UNTIL 1868 at 59–60 (E.J. Brill 1991).

The Kamakura Period (1185–1333) began when the samurai warlord Minamoto no Yoritomo was designated by the Emperor as "Shogun." Yoritomo established his capital at the location of his power base, the town of Kamakura near modern-day Tokyo, far from the imperial court at Kyoto.

The title "shōgun" requires some discussion because, while some western readers of a certain age may associate it with the James Clavell novel of the same name (or Japanese restaurants of questionable provenance), it actually has some bearing on more recent legal history. Under the *ritsuryō*, shōgun (which simply means "general") was a formal title granted by the emperor to a general of an army of a certain size, usually for a limited time and a specific purpose. In fact "shōgun" is only an abbreviation of a longer official title that expressed that purpose.

The full title of the shōguns from the Kamakura period up to the end of the Edo period in 1867 was actually *"seii tai shōgun,"* which literally means "Great Barbarian-Conquering General," and harked back to earlier times when imperial governments were still conquering those parts of Japan occupied by other tribes and races. The significance of this title was illustrated during the Kamakura Period, which saw Japan faced with existential threats from abroad—two separate invasion attempts by the Mongols, both of which were defeated by typhoons—the *kamikaze* divine winds. In addition to having titles that were intended to be temporary and for a limited purpose, the governments of the Shōguns were called *bakufu*. This term literally means "tent government," a reflection of their supposedly temporary character.

The coming of the Kamakura *bakufu* saw the Emperor relegated to more of a ceremonial and symbolic role. Minamoto no Yoritomo was an extremely bright and skilled leader. He created a legal and political system that was top down with his administration in Kamakura at the apex. This helped create stability after the era of civil war preceding his ascension.

Around 1225, the ruling Hōjō clan expanded on their Minamoto predecessors' creation of a top down type structure with real power centered in Kamakura rather than in the Emperor and Kyoto. There were some important legal developments at this time. The Hōjō leadership created the *Hyōjōsho* (High Court of Justice). Not long after that a lower court was also created. Many skilled bureaucrats and legal scholars were recruited from the imperial capital in Kyoto to Kamakura and eventually to the courts of local warlords during the Kamakura and later periods. While Kamakura era courts and laws have not continued into the modern period, these developments reflect the centralization of national political and administrative power in the Tokyo area of Japan, which has continued to the present day.

In 1232, a codification of administrative and civil law was promulgated based in the rights, positions, and duties of warriors. It was known as the *Goseibai Shikimoku* or *Jōei Shikimoku*. The term *shikimoku* reflects this code's origins as effectively a compilation of rules about and for warriors having its roots in existing rules but restated for the new political order. Subsequent Shogunates added to the *Goseibai Shimoku* which became one of the basic laws of the land until it was repealed in the Edo Period.

Additionally the rise of the samurai in the Kamakura Period coincided with the development of new schools of Buddhism such as the Zen and Jōdo Schools which appealed especially to the samurai and an increasingly literate populace. Buddhist ideals also impacted the legal sphere by influencing both those making and enforcing the law, and those most subject to it. Buddhist temples also developed into substantial institutions with their own internal rules that became increasingly important. These legal themes—the vastly increased role of warriors and the samurai class in political and legal dealings, the increasing role of local law, and the increased popularity and influence of new schools of Buddhism had a lasting impact on Japanese law until the Nineteenth Century.

Not surprisingly, as the number of courts grew questions of jurisdiction increased. Would courts in Kamakura, Kyoto, or local authorities decide a particular case? What about appeals? These questions were addressed by a growing body of legal rules and jurisprudence from legal scholars. As a result, various people and business/social institutions became more aware of their rights. During the Thirteenth Century litigation increased as groups and individuals asserted their rights in courtroom-like settings. Society became quite litigious and in a few cases groups of farmers or others successfully sued warriors, despite the latter being more powerful and having higher social status at that time. Many legal disputes were decided without ever going to court, through conciliation, decisions by village leaders, and settlements.

During much of this time period written copies were made of important decisions by courts. These copies were sent from the area where the court sat to major regional offices. As a result we have excellent records today of Kamakura Era case law. Additionally, many of the Shōguns' legal edicts, and some laws passed by regional rulers, have been preserved.

Over time local landowners gained more and more power over their areas and began assembling their own armies. Some became warlords. Eventually this localization of power and military loyalty led to what is known as the *Sengoku* (Warring States) Period, which lasted from the latter half of the fifteenth century to the end of the sixteenth. This period involved bloody conflict among regional military rulers called *daimyō*. It culminated in two unsuccessful military campaigns against Korea in the 1590s and the climactic battle of Sekigahara in 1600, which enabled the victorious Tokugawa Ieyasu to unify the country and establish a system of government that would last for over two centuries—the "Edo Period" discussed below.

During this prolonged period of strife that preceded the beginning of the Edo Period, however, Shogunal legislation in the form of the *Goseibai Shikimoku* as well as Imperial *ristsuryō* remained in force at what could be called a "national level." Yet the *daimyō* exercised almost complete discretion in matters such as punishment and control of land within their territories. Many established their own legal codes, though often based on existing models.

The rise of samurai rule saw the status of women decline, with the introduction of more repressive rules affecting their ability to inherit and dispose of property, and limiting their autonomy in marriage, divorce and domicile. The increased role of the warriors had other effects on the law as well. For example, the imposition of criminal penalties became more arbitrary and cruel and less dependent upon consistent procedures and clear rules. Execution as a form of punishment returned.

The Warring States Period also saw initial contacts with Europe. Portuguese traders first visited Japan in 1543, followed shortly by Catholic missionaries from Spain, and then by Dutch merchants. Portuguese merchants quickly alienated Japan's leadership by acquiring Japanese women as slaves. Christianity also proved to be a disruptive and unwelcome influence for Japan's leadership; Catholic missionaries were expelled, converts martyred and what was left of the Christian faith driven underground until the late 19th century. By 1641, the Dutch were the only European power permitted to have formal trading relations with Japan.

D. THE EDO PERIOD

1. Overview

The Edo Period lasted from 1603–1868 C.E. ending with the Meiji Restoration. After his climactic victory over rivals at the Battle of Sekigahara in 1600, Tokugawa Ieyasu—the first of the Tokugawa Shōguns—became the undisputed military ruler of Japan, and set about establishing a political system that would see his descendants rule for over two and a half centuries. The Edo Period was a period of peace, economic growth, flourishing of arts and culture, and isolation from the rest of the world. The impossibility of maintaining this isolation was a key factor in the Tokugawa regime's collapse.

Early on the Tokugawa authorities adopted a number of basic policies that came to define the Edo Period. Each of these is relevant to understanding how the Tokugawa period *ended* and the legal and political context in which the Meiji Restoration took place.

The first was *sakoku* ("closed country"), a term commonly used by historians to describe the isolationist policies that were one of the hallmarks of the period, though a term not actually used by Japanese until the 19th century, when the policy was still desired by some but was becoming untenable. In reality *sakoku* was the aggregate of a number of laws and policies adopted over the first few decades of Tokugawa rule: the prohibition of Christianity in 1612 (though missionaries and proselytizing had already been proscribed before the Tokugawa period began), the gradual restriction of access by foreign vessels to Japanese ports, several proscriptions on Japanese traveling abroad (which became a capital offense) and the lessening and ultimate termination of diplomatic and trading relations with most foreign countries. By the middle of the 17th century, intercourse with other nations was limited primarily to the Dutch and Chinese trading enclaves in Nagasaki, far from the Shogun's capital in what is now Tokyo. Contact also continued in Hokkaido (Russia), Tsushima (Korea) and Okinawa (China). The Dutch enclave was the principle source of information about the west (including law), which became the discipline of *rangaku* ("Dutch studies").

The second was to further strengthen the class structure with samurai at the top of the social order. It is common to characterize this period of Japan as having a Confucian modelled four-tiered class system, with merchants at the bottom, followed by artisans, then farmers and samurai at the top (in place of the scholars in the Chinese version).[4] In reality the key distinction—particularly the *legal* distinction—was between samurai and non-samurai. While in earlier periods there was some mobility between the non-samurai and other classes, in the Tokugawa period the barrier between *samurai* and the other classes became quite rigid. Here it should be remembered that notionally even the Shōguns were still inferior to the emperors, and the *ritsuryō*, were still in force. The Shōguns and *samurai* warlords below thus exercised legislative power in part through their authority to regulate how *samurai* should act, and, by extension defining who was and wasn't a *samurai*.

---

[4] Members of the imperial family, members of religious orders and the various "untouchable" communities existed outside this ordering.

Numerous rules and prohibitions went into defining and enforcing this distinction. For example, prohibitions against non-*samurai* carrying weapons had been imposed shortly before the Edo Period began, and were continued and further defined. Carrying two swords became the mark of the *samurai*. Other rules as to dress and hairstyles further served to identify who was who. It is sometimes mistakenly said that "regular" Japanese did not have surnames until the Meiji Period, but the reality is they fell into disuse through prohibitions on their use by anyone who was not a *samurai* or member of the Imperial court. Samurai were also removed from the lands from which their feudal stipends were derived. Thus, as between farmers and samurai, there was often even a geographical separation between the classes. Samurai were also subject to different, sometimes more stringent rules of conduct and punishments. One of the impressive accomplishments of the Meiji-era legal reforms was the relatively swift elimination of deeply-entrenched legally-defined class distinctions between the Samurai minority and the rest of Japanese society.

Third, a political system was established that saw fifteen Tokugawa shoguns rule Japan continuously for over two centuries. Despite his victory at Sekigahara, Ieyasu wisely realized that only so much land could be held by himself and his kinsman. As a result he allowed much of the land to be ruled by other feudal lords (*daimyō*). This resulted in the establishment of a feudal order in which the Tokugawas were the top overlords, with various rules and requirements intended to prevent the other *daimyō*—particularly those descended from the losers at Sekigahara—from ever being able to challenge the existing order. Domain lords were forbidden from importing weapons from abroad or building large ships or new castles, and were required to spend part of the year in the Shogunate capital in *Edo* (now Tokyo). They were also required to expend significant time and resources in elaborate processions traveling back and forth. Family members had to stay in the capital as hostage even when the *daimyō* returned to their domains. Feudal lords were prohibited from constructing castles.

Subject to these policies, however, the Edo Period saw continuity of law from earlier ages. The central power and legal authority of the Shogunate remained consolidated in a top-down legal structure with the Shogun at the top and local *daimyô* still holding significant power at the regional and local levels.

2. Edo Period Legal Culture

Tokugawa government was strongly neo-Confucianist in tone. This meant that, as Japanese legal historian Carl Steenstrup notes, the ruler "must be obeyed, as long as he rules well."[5] The laws of Ming Dynasty China (1368–1644 CE) also had a strong influence, and compared to the age of imperial rule penalties for violating criminal or tax laws could be quite harsh.

Edo Period local farmers often lived below subsistence level and were subject to the will of village authorities, samurai, *daimyō*, and the Shogun. Samurai themselves were often trapped in bureaucratic jobs in the new Capitol, Edo (Tokyo), or in regional towns and cities. Although being a *samurai* meant enjoying a stipend, inflation and other economic changes resulted in the impoverishment of those in the lower ranks. Some samurai found themselves in debt to the rising class of merchants, notionally at the

[5] CARL STEENSTRUP, A HISTORY OF LAW IN JAPAN UNTIL 1868 at 111 (E.J. Brill 1991).

Buke Shohatto

- gave daimyō power to create laws
- could not conflict
- "pre-emption"

bottom of the Confucian order but … fund a cultural renaissance.

In 1615, the Tokugawa Shog… …riors") and the *Kinjū Narabi ni Kuge Sho…* … former concerned the *daimyō* and other … …n that helped consolidate power under t… …ificant because it saw the Shogun purpo… …perial court. The first article defined t… … them primarily to cultural and artistic … …ted by additional rules over the course of t… …*hatto* were never amended.

Subject to the significant limit… …*imyo* was lord of his own fiefdom and co… …main. The buke shohatto was clear, howe… … their own domains (*han*) could not conflic… …y law promulgated by the Shogunate. Thus, at the start of the Meiji Period, Japan had no general uniform system of criminal laws with nationwide applicability, since each domain had its own penal codes, albeit many based on similar models.

Individual domains (*han*) had their own courts for resolving disputes and punishing crime. However, the Shogunate also had jurisdiction over cases involving matters between *daimyô* and between people from different territories, as well as any matters that were not purely local—a sort of feudal era diversity jurisdiction. Within domains village and city leaders were appointed who made sure laws and decrees were distributed and published, made sure each household met its tax duties, controlled access to irrigation water, and saw to local law enforcement and firefighting.

The Edo Period also saw the prohibition of Christianity and other groups viewed as a threat to the Shogun. The enforcement of these rules was brutal and those who refused to renounce prohibited faiths or affiliations were subject to death. The situation in Edo Period Japan was different from that in the West, where such persecutions were often based in religious animus by one religion against others. In Edo Period Japan the concern was about Western influence and any group that might be viewed as a threat to the Shogun's hegemony.

The Edo Period also saw much more government involvement in the administration of Buddhist temples and Shinto shrines, including the creation of a supervisory Temple and Shrine Commission. This was intended to prevent temples and shrines being used as tax havens.

Compared to prior periods, the taxation of farmers was excessive. Although some farmers were able to rise in status and develop landholdings in excess of what they worked, usually because they were village leaders or related to village leaders, most farmers existed at barely a subsistence level. In some regions starvation was not uncommon. Escape from this life was difficult, however, since farmers as a class were prohibited by law from selling or abandoning their lands and they were not allowed to travel outside of their village without permission. Still, worn down by starvation and horrendous working conditions some farmers escaped into larger cities where taxation was not as high. There they tried to blend in or join the merchant class, which was increasingly successful due, in part, to the lower taxes in cities and towns.

By 1742 many legal manuals and recorded precedents existed and these were compiled into a reasonably comprehensive set of written legal codes. One of these was called the *Kujikata-Osadamegaki*, or Laws Given by the Shogun for Litigation. Interestingly, the code was set up in a manner similar to *ritsuryô* with part dedicated to administrative law and civil matters and part dedicated to criminal law and criminal procedure. As a result we have a good centralized record of many of the laws and court decisions that were made between 1603 and 1742.

Notwithstanding the existence of such codes and the records of decisions, dissemination of the law outside of official circles was proscribed. As one saying at the time went: "The people do not need to know the law, but they must be made to obey it."

While officials were supposed to know, it was actually undesirable to the Shogunate authorities that the people (or people who assisted litigants for a living) should know what the rules actually were. Under the Tokugawa Neo-Confucian model of government, good leadership meant that there was harmony. The existence of litigation was inconsistent with this ideal. Although the Shogunate came to acknowledge the need to provide mechanisms for the resolution of civil disputes, it was regarded as shameful in a certain way. Moreover, parties would generally go to court uninformed about what the law actually was, with conciliation being the model used by officials. The apocryphal resolution by the highly idealized Edo-period *daimyō* and judge Oh'ōka Tadashi (Echizen) in a case between two parties over three dropped gold coins is illustrative. Both parties purported to *disclaim* any rights in the coins and Judge Oh'ōka resolved the case by adding one coin from his own purse so that each party could receive two. This was considered an ideal resolution because everyone—including the judge—lost out equally because of the dispute.

During the Edo Period, the merchant class grew in size and wealth. A sophisticated system of commercial customary law arose and these legal customs were often used to govern disputes among merchants. Even now, Japanese commercial law scholars are proud to point out that the world's first futures contracts (for rice) were supposedly developed in Japan during this period.

Although the social order made the merchants the lowest of the four classes, in practice they came to control a disproportionate amount of wealth, notwithstanding their relatively small numbers (less than 10% of the population). As a result, merchants also became important sources of credit and samurai were often the borrowers. This ultimately led to significant legal restrictions on interest rates as well as strict forms for loan documents, which would not be enforced by courts if the documents had any defects.

Edo Period law relating to families was more skewed in favor of husbands and male heirs. Abuse (and even killing) of a wife was sanctioned by some *daimyō* codes in certain situations, such as where the wife cheated or "wronged" the husband. Obviously, this was a terrible situation for many women because the husband had so much power over the wife and the threat of abuse, or even death, was real.

Moreover, unilateral divorce by the husband was allowed unless the husband was a samurai. If the husband unilaterally divorced the wife without adequate cause he would be obligated to return any dowry. If the husband was a samurai the families of the husband and wife would try to mediate the situation, and if things could not be resolved, the authorities had to report the divorce for it to become official.

A system of education was established at the local level—one of the first in the world available regardless of class. Literacy rates were high even among the impoverished farmers and villagers so teachers and local elders worked to teach school children moral lessons using literature and stories.

Edo Period criminal law could be brutal. During the early Edo Period executions were common, even for minor crimes. Cutting off criminals' noses or ears was also a standard form of punishment, as were other forms of corporal punishment such as severe beatings. Torture was sometimes used to coerce confessions from the accused or even testimony from witnesses.

Interestingly, samurai faced harsher penalties for some crimes than farmers. For some transgressions a samurai might be expected to commit *seppuku* (suicide by ritual disembowelment) even though a farmer might not be executed for the same crime.

3. The End of Isolation; Unequal Treaties and Collapse of the Tokugawa System

Although Japan was able to exist in highly-structured, peaceful isolation for most of the Edo Period, events elsewhere were to render this untenable. Through their interactions with the Dutch and the Chinese, Japanese authorities were aware of the gradual colonization of China and other Asian neighbors by European powers, particularly after China's defeat in the Opium War (1839–42). The evolution of the United States into a nation bordering the Pacific in the mid-19th century put Japan squarely between America and China, a huge potential market for American wares. The United States had already experienced Japan through its whaling fleet, whose ships occasionally wrecked on Japanese shores and saw their survivors treated badly—for violating Shogunate edicts on the exclusion of foreigners.

In 1853 after first calling at what is now Okinawa Prefecture and then the Ogasawara Islands Commodore Matthew Perry led a flotilla of naval vessels into Edo Bay. There he forced the Japanese authorities to accept a letter to the Emperor from US President Millard Filmore demanding "friendship, commerce, a supply of coal and provisions, and protection for our shipwrecked people." Perry also made a suitable display of his flotilla's military power. Announcing he would return the following year he then left.

By the time he returned in 1854 the Shogunate had decided to accept all of Perry's demands. This was memorialized in the Convention of Peace and Amity between the United States and the Empire of Japan (more commonly known as the Convention of Kanagawa), which opened the ports of Shimoda (near Edo) and Hakodate (in the Northern Island of Hokkaidō) and was responsive to the other demand's in Filmore's letter. It still only provided for limited intercourse between Japan and the United States, but opened the door for the treaties that followed.

In 1858 the United States was able to make Japan sign the more substantive Treaty of Amity and Commerce (also known as the "Harris Treaty"). This instrument increased the number of treaty ports, allowed Americans to establish permanent residences in them, and even engage in Christian practices within their confines. The Harris Treaty was similar to the treaties imposed on Qing China by Western powers after its defeat in the Opium Wars, which formed the legal basis for a process of colonization of parts of China that was already well under way when Japan was forced open.

Japan was soon forced to enter into similar treaties opening up to other Western nations. Since each contained a "most-favored nation clause" any newly negotiated benefit accrued to all existing treaty partners.

These treaties collectively came to be known as the "unequal treaties." This is because they significantly infringed on Japanese sovereignty by taking away its government's freedom to set tariffs, and gave westerners extraterritorial status. Under the treaties foreigners in Japan accused of crimes were to be tried in consular courts staffed by foreign judges. Similarly, commercial or other private law disputes between Japanese and western parties were also heard in these consular courts. Consular court judges were often staffed by unqualified diplomatic appointees who lacked formal legal training.

Getting rid of the unequal treaties through the adoption of laws and legal institutions familiar to westerners thus became a key driver of the legal reforms that followed the Meiji Restoration as well as the source of urgency with which such changes were made. Adopting western-style laws became part of an effort to stave off colonization by the western powers, a process that was already well under way on the Asian mainland.

Politically, Perry's arrival and the subsequent treaties sealed the fate of the Tokugawa system. The Shogunate revealed its powerlessness through the unprecedented act of seeking the views of leading *daimyō* as to how to respond to Perry's 1853 demands. This was followed in the years to come by further displays of weakness—seeking the consul of the Emperor Kōmei as to how to deal with foreigners. Kōmei became empowered enough that in 1863 he actually ordered the Shogun to expel the "barbarians." The failure of the Tokugawa Shogun to do so and live up to the terms of their ancient imperial mandate further damaged their legitimacy.

Meanwhile, members of samurai clans that had traditionally been excluded from political power saw an opportunity to use the Emperor's legitimacy and, when appropriate, foreigners and their superior military technology to seize control of the nation. A complex political game with numerous incidents of violence and limited warfare followed Perry's arrival. Whether on the winning or losing side, most of the Japanese involved probably recognized that Japan faced an existential threat from abroad, though they disagreed virulently on how to deal with it.

In 1867 Emperor Kōmei died and his son Mutsuhito succeeded to the throne. Mutsuhito became Emperor Meiji. With civil war breaking out and the defeat of Shogunate forces appearing inevitable, Tokugawa leaders formally returned political power to the Emperor in November of the same year. The Meiji Period officially began in 1868, though the Emperor's formal enthronement came later.

The rest of this chapter will focus on the Meiji Period and the post-World War II Period. Almost all Japanese law in force today comes from these periods, but it is important to note that some of the laws from earlier eras have had a lasting impact on the culture in which Japanese law functions, even if not on the law itself. As Carl Steenstrup so eloquently wrote in 1991 about ancient Japanese law:

> No other country has a history of law which is longer, or better recorded. It also provides the historian of Western law with a heuristic mirror. There is much more in this field yet to be investigated. The reason why one should do this is not just antiquarian interest, but *the fact that Japan's modern laws operate in*

a society whose facts and values are the products of Japan's old laws [emphasis added].[6]

E. THE MEIJI RESTORATION AND THE DEVELOPMENT OF THE MEIJI SYSTEM

1. Overview

The Meiji Restoration ushered in a period of profound societal, legal, political and economic change. In a strict sense the Meiji Period refers to the reign of the Emperor Meiji from his formal enthronement in 1868 until his death in 1912. It was followed by the comparatively short Taishō Period (1912 to 1926), and the much longer reign of Emperor Hirohito, known as the Showa Period, which went from 1926 to 1989). In terms of legal history, however, it is helpful to think of there as being a period in which something that could be called the "Meiji system," prevailed. This is the system of law and government which came into being after the Meiji Restoration, culminating in the establishment of the Constitution of the Empire of Japan of 1889, more commonly known as the "Meiji Constitution." This system prevailed until Japan's defeat and surrender in 1945, though elements of it remained until the new constitution came into force in 1947 during the Allied occupation.

Although it ultimately ended in disaster, the Meiji system made Japan a world power in a remarkably brief period of time. It also helped make Japan a colonial power. While Japan railed against the unequal treaties imposed on it by the west, it was quick to impose an unequal treaty of its own on Korea in 1876, It then acquired Taiwan from Qing China through military conquest in 1895, annexed Korea in 1910 and acquired Germany's territorial possessions in Micronesia as a reward for participating on the allied side in World War I.

The impact of Japanese-modeled laws and institutions adopted during their time as Japanese colonies can still be seen in various aspects of the legal systems of Korea and Taiwan since their independence after World War II. The Meiji Constitution also served as a model for the 1931 Constitution of Ethiopia.

As colonies, Korea, Taiwan and Japan's other territorial possessions were subject to a different, more authoritarian system of law that was nonetheless derived from the law of the Japanese home islands. Though a fascinating area of legal history, this is a subject outside the scope of this book.

2. Early Meiji Period Reforms

Immediately after the Meiji Restoration, the nation's new leaders had to struggle with numerous challenges: external threats, civil unrest—outright civil war at various junctions, not to mention the uneasy, shifting alliance between the new ruling factions themselves. Another was establishing their own legitimacy as rulers of what quickly needed to become a modern nation rather than a collection of feudal domains. Moreover, having delivered over two centuries of peace and prosperity, the Tokugawas were a tough act to follow, one that could only be outshone by the Emperor.

The teenage Emperor Meiji was immediately put into the public eye as the source of political authority. In 1868 a Charter was issued in his name in an effort to set the

---

[6] CARL STEENSTRUP, A HISTORY OF LAW IN JAPAN UNTIL 1868 at 159 (E.J. Brill 1991).

tone and help appease dissenters. Known in English as the Charter Oath, in Japanese it is the *Gokajō Goseimon* or "Oath in Five Articles," and contained the following commitments to the nation:

1. Deliberative assemblies shall be widely established and all matters decided by open discussion.
2. All classes, high and low, shall be united in vigorously carrying out the administration of affairs of state.
3. The common people, no less than the civil and military officials, shall all be allowed to pursue their own calling so that there may be no discontent.
4. Evil customs of the past shall be broken off and everything based upon the just laws of Nature.
5. Knowledge shall be sought throughout the world so as to strengthen the foundation of imperial rule.

The Emperor's religious role and divine lineage were also used to bind the people together through what became a politicized version of the Shintō religion that was imposed by the state (often referred to today as State Shintō), often at the expense of previously dominant Buddhist institutions. The *Gunjin Chokuyu* or Imperial Rescript to Soldiers and Sailors of 1882 was used to establish a direct relationship between the Emperor and his military.

The scope of legal changes wrought in the early Meiji period is astounding, though many of the laws and institutions from this time were superseded in the decades to come. The feudal domains (*han*) were converted to prefectures (*ken*) under more centralized control in 1871, and gradually consolidated, with former domain lords coopted as governors. In 1872, longstanding prohibitions on the alienation of land were removed, as were status-based restrictions on who could have interests in it. The government adopted its first national *koseki* (family register) system in 1872 (see discussion at Chapter 9), which among other things went on to help define who was Japanese and served as a source of demographic information about the national population to the government for policy purposes.

Conscription was introduced in 1873. Something the Japanese had learned quickly from western powers was that conscript armies equipped with firearms and a few months of training could massacre the bravest band of samurai swordsmen. The samurai monopoly on bearing arms was abolished, and in 1876 the wearing of swords—once a status symbol of the ruling class—was prohibited to all except for soldiers and policemen. The rapid elimination of the Edo Period class system with samurai at the top was extremely rapid. The *koseki* system played a role in this process too, since it inevitably ceased to show who had come from which pre-Meiji class group. Some of the samurai revolted, others went on to form the new class of intelligentsia and bureaucrats (which is what many of them had been before the Restoration anyway).

The old class system was replaced with a new one, a five-tiered system of titled hereditary nobility that was used to ensure the patronage and support of imperial courtiers, former *daimyō* (including those of the Tokugawa lineage) and other leading members of society. Under the 1884 Imperial edict that defined it, members of this aristocracy (known as *kazoku*) had certain privileges, including that of establishing formal family rules, participating in national affairs through the House of Peers after it was established in 1889, the ability to marry members of the imperial family (which was much larger than it is now) and protection of their hereditary lands from civil judgments. The aristocracy and much of the imperial family was abolished with the coming into force of the present constitution in 1947.

The new Meiji leadership also realized that they quickly needed to learn from the West about military technology, industry, government, law and other aspects of western society. This was a process that had already been started at the end of the Edo period, with the Tokugawa Shogunate relaxing its prohibition on foreign travel, and both the Shogunate and the individual *han* sending people abroad to learn. This effort accelerated in the Meiji Period, with the Iwakura Mission of 1871–1873 which saw a large group of leaders, officials, scholars and students visit the United States and a number of European countries. Although primarily a diplomatic mission ostensibly for the purpose of renegotiating the "unequal treaties" (an effort that was unsuccessful), the members of the mission also took the opportunity to observe all aspects of western society, including their legal systems. Thousands of government- and privately-sponsored students went abroad in the years that followed.[7]

The government and private institutions also engaged foreign experts of all sorts to visit Japan to teach a variety of subjects and disciplines, including law. For example, the American expert on the law of evidence John Henry Wigmore taught at Keiō University in Tokyo for several years and the German scholar Eduard Hermann Robert Techow helped draft Japan's first modern code of civil procedure. From France, the scholar Gustave Émile Boissonade de Fontarabie came to spend over two decades in Japan and played a key role in preparing drafts of Japan's Civil and Penal Codes. Similarly, the German diplomat Ottmar von Mohl was employed by the Imperial Household Ministry and advised the government on court protocols and honors. Although they did not come to Japan, the German scholars Rudolf von Gneist and Lorenz von Stein were consulted heavily in the process of drafting the Meiji Constitution.

As will be seen some western legal and governance concepts worked in Japan, but many were adapted to or improved by Japanese officials. By the end of the Meiji Period Japan had a strong bureaucracy and recognizably "western" legal system, a system of public education, an increasingly strong commercial and business environment, and a strong military. Continental—particularly German and French legal concepts and institutions—and to a lesser extent the common law, served as models for Japan and were adapted accordingly. In fact at one point factions developed within the Meiji government divided among those who favored French law and those who favored other options.

Some of these foreign concepts fit well with existing Japanese legal and social relationships, but others had to be adapted over time to fit within the Japanese social structure. In some cases there was an attempt to hammer square pegs into round holes, but in other cases the borrowed Western legal structures and concepts were easily adapted with some minor tinkering. In most cases, there was a bit of each as foreign legal concepts were implemented, and then slowly adapted, amended, and interpreted to work in the Japanese system. Regardless, the Western focus of much Meiji Period law

[7] The effort to learn from abroad remains an admirable feature of the Japanese legal system today. Significant legislative initiatives are often preceded by studies of how comparable laws or institutions work in what Japan considers to be its peer nations (such as the United States, France, Germany and other European nations).

was a sea change from earlier eras, and especially from the inward-looking Edo Period. As Professor John Owen Haley has explained:

> The Commitment of the Meiji leaders, whatever their motives, to full-scale legal reform is not in doubt. Nor should their achievements be slighted. The legal reformers of Meiji Japan undertook their task with deliberate care and without undue haste . . . . Despite the formidable obstacles of learning alien languages and adopting alien concepts and institutions, by the end of the [nineteenth] century the Japanese had established a modern legal system with independent courts, trained legal professionals, and an inclusive corpus of codified law. New institutions were created and new procedures introduced as courts and ministries were established and judicial and administrative practices developed. A new officialdom of professional judges, procurators, and police were selected and trained. Other careers in law became possible with recognition of the need for lawyers and legal scholars. Even the language of the law was almost completely rewritten. . . . An entirely new vocabulary was created, with new categories, new concepts.[8]

It is also important to appreciate that although under great pressure to modernize and Westernize, the Japanese essentially had the luxury of being able to choose from the most modern laws and legal institutions available to them as models, without being unduly restricted by traditions or vested interests, both of which were being uprooted. For example, Japan's Civil Code was originally based on the Napoleonic Code of France, but with improvements taken from the codes of Italy, the Netherlands, Belgium and other countries, and ultimately finalized with significant influence from the still more modern Prussian Civil Code, which at the time was still in draft form. The historical roots of some of the key codes and statutes that were adopted during the Meiji Period are discussed in other chapters.

3. The Meiji Constitution

It was the Meiji Constitution which came to define the basic form of Japan's modern government, and most of the enduring laws, codes and institutions that date back to the Meiji Period were brought into existence under the Meiji constitutional system. Examples include the Imperial Diet, which was established by the constitution, the (old) Court Organization act of 1890 which established the judiciary, the (old) Codes of Civil and Criminal Procedure (1890), the Civil Code (1896), the Commercial Code (1899), the Penal Code (1907), and so forth.

The early Meiji leaders—unelected oligarchs who cloaked themselves in the authority of the Emperor—were under pressure to establish some form of representative government. "Deliberative assemblies" had been promised by the Emperor in the Five Charter Oath, and Japan's intelligentsia was quickly learning how representative parliamentary systems in other countries worked. From early in the Meiji Period, there were increasing demands for a constitution and a parliament. In 1881 the oligarch Itō Hirobumi was appointed to head an imperial committee to study constitutions and the following year lead an overseas mission to study those of various countries.

---

[8] JOHN OWEN HALEY, AUTHORITY WITHOUT POWER: LAW AND THE JAPANESE PARADOX (Oxford Univ. Press 1991) at 69.

While Great Britain was the pre-eminent global power at the time and the Westminster parliamentary form of government was greatly admired, it was thought to be too dominated by partisan politics for the Japanese. It also gave too much power to Parliament. The Meiji leaders did not think Japanese were suitable for British-style democracy and wanted to isolate the Emperor from politics. The Japanese found much that was attractive in the constitution of the newly-emergent German federation (particularly Prussia), which had a monarch and a legislature but a constitution that isolated them from each other. The constitution that resulted from this prolonged effort in study, drafting and political maneuvering was an attempt to bring Japan firmly into the modern world. The Meiji Constitution was promulgated in 1889 and came into effect in 1890. The enactment of the document was a significant event in Japanese legal history (and Japanese history generally). Although it borrowed heavily from Western laws and constitutions, it was in many ways uniquely Japanese.

The new constitution was brought into the world as a gift from the Emperor. At the promulgation ceremony Emperor Meiji read out the introductory language to the charter before handing the document to the Prime Minister, a deliberate effort by the nation's leaders to create the impression that the text had actually originated from the Emperor himself. The fact that the minister of education was assassinated on his way to the ceremony illustrates that even two decades after the Meiji Restoration, political strife was still rampant.

The new charter created a bicameral legislature, the Imperial Diet, though only one chamber—the House of Representatives—was elective. The other chamber, the House of Peers was populated by imperial family members, aristocrats and appointees from other establishment constituencies. Its composition was also determined by an imperial edict rather than statute.

The Meiji Constitution also created a separate judicature and acknowledged that the Emperor's subjects had some basic rights, though subject to limitation by law. Yet it also made it clear that the source of all sovereign authority was the Emperor. This is illustrated by some of the provisions of Chapter I, which defined the imperial powers:

Article 1. The Empire of Japan shall be reigned over and governed by a line of Emperors unbroken for ages eternal.

Article 3. The Emperor is sacred and inviolable.

Article 4. The Emperor is the head of the Empire, combining in Himself the rights of sovereignty, and exercises them, according to the provisions of the present Constitution.

Article 5. The Emperor exercises the legislative power with the consent of the Imperial Diet.

Article 6. The Emperor gives sanction to laws, and orders them to be promulgated and executed.

Article 11. The Emperor has the supreme command of the Army and Navy.

Article 13. The Emperor declares war, makes peace, and concludes treaties.

The Emperor also existed outside the scope of the constitution. This is demonstrated by the fact that under the Meiji system what is now the Imperial House Act (which governs various aspects of the imperial household) was not a law that could be amended or repealed by the Imperial Diet, but effectively a separate constitution governing the Emperor and his family. Similarly, building on the Imperial Rescript to Soldiers and Sailors of 1882, which had helped cement the direct relationship between the Emperor and his military, article 11 of the Meiji Constitution made it clear the Emperor was "supreme commander" of the army and navy. Control over the Military was also kept largely beyond the influence of the constitutional civilian government, subject to the ability of the legislature to control the national budget. Moreover, according to the text of the constitution (including the examples given above), most of the powers of government were exercised directly by the Emperor. Even the legislative power was exercised by the Emperor "with the consent" of the legislature. That consent could be bypassed, however, in times of emergency through imperial decree.

In reality, however, the substantive powers of the Emperor were exercised by a cabal of imperial advisors and ministers on the civilian side and generals and admirals on the military side. The Meiji Constitution devotes sparse attention to these roles, with a single article making individual ministers of state responsible directly to the Emperor, and another acknowledging the existence of a Privy Council to advise his majesty on important matters of state.

Although not constitutional, there was also a financial aspect to this cabal. An oft-overlooked aspect of the development of the post-Restoration imperial system is that the Emperor went from being a teenager living on a Shogunate-approved stipend in Kyoto at the time of the Meiji Restoration, to the head of an extended family and vast bureaucracy controlling one of the largest concentrations of wealth in the country. By the end of World War II the Emperor, his family and the Imperial Household Ministry controlled vast holdings of lands and substantial shareholdings in countless Japanese companies (including being the largest shareholder in the Bank of Japan), wealth that was kept separate from and accounted for differently from the national budget. This wealth also represented one aspect of the power that could be exercised by the Emperor's advisors outside the formal scope of the constitution. Over time the centralization of power and prestige in the Emperor helped facilitate repression, militarization and war.

The Meiji Constitution established separation of powers of a sort, albeit one that still had the Emperor as the ultimate source of all sovereign powers. The Imperial Diet assisted the Emperor in exercising the legislative powers and the judicature dispensed justice in the Emperor's name. Yet subject to the article 4 undertaking to exercise the rights of sovereignty in accordance with the constitution, the executive powers of the Emperor—including the right to rule by decree in emergencies—was not open to legal challenge. The judges comprising the judicature were appointed by the Emperor and, as noted in Chapter 3, were under the administrative control of the Ministry of Justice. Courts offered limited means to directly challenge the exercise of state power outside the sphere of criminal prosecutions.

Article 57 did provide that "no judge [could] be deprived of his position, unless by way of criminal sentence or disciplinary punishment." Moreover, under Article 59 trials and judgments were required to be public, except when there was a "fear that, such publicity may be prejudicial to peace and order, or to the maintenance of public morality." This latter provision became highly problematic, especially during the Taisho and early Showa periods, as secret trials became more common, especially those involving political dissidents and others who opposed the power or actions of the military.

Meiji Constitution

created rights
- travel / relocation
- property
- religion
- freedom of speech
Article 22 & 27 & 28 & 29
created duties
- tax
- conscription
Article 20 & 21

In many respects the [illegible] modern eyes, though it should be compar[illegible]archies at the time, rather than republica[illegible]s. Moreover, it should also be remembered [illegible]mperor as the head of the nation after c[illegible]ship between monarch and subject that [illegible]titutional law never really had time to de[illegible]

The Meiji Constitutio[illegible]perial subjects (the people of Japan). Some [illegible] Japan. Others had existed *de facto* und[illegible] before been constitutionally enshrined [illegible]pelled out in articles 22–29. Articles 22 [illegible] and property rights, respectively are par[illegible]he Edo period, when most people were *n*[illegible]n of land was generally prohibited. Such [illegible]r in the Meiji Period, but their ratification in the Meiji Constitution is nonetheless noteworthy. Similarly, enshrining a freedom of religion in Article 28 represents a sea change from the harsh Edo-period proscriptions on Christianity, though as a practical matter the protection proved quite weak in the long run due to the imposition of State Shintō. The freedoms of speech, expression and assembly guaranteed by Article 29 proved severely limited when exercised by those who sought to speak out against imperial and military action or challenge the political orthodoxy.

Together, these rights enabled people, especially from rural areas, significant freedoms that had been denied them during the Edo Period. Moreover, a nationalized system of public education helped increase economic opportunity. Over time the education system combined with state Shinto and the Imperial Rescript on education helped further cement the status of the Emperor (and his advisors), while promoting an almost blind fealty to the Emperor and enabling the nationalism that followed.

The seemingly generous (compared to the Edo Period) grant of rights in the Meiji Constitution was also highly conditional since most of the rights granted were subject to further legislation. Virtually all of the rights were bounded by language such as "within limits not prejudicial to peace and order" and "within the limits of the law." Moreover, Article 31 made it clear that constitutional rights could not restrict the exercise of the Emperor's powers during war or national emergencies. Finally, the same chapter of the Meiji Constitution that granted rights, also imposed duties; to pay tax and serve in the military (articles 20 and 21), the latter being a burden not imposed on farmers during the Edo Period. Although the Imperial Diet was at least partially elective, the grant of the franchise was deferred to electoral laws (article 35). Initially the franchise was limited to males who owned property and paid a specified amount in annual taxes. This was not dissimilar from limitations on voting in Western countries at that time.

Another important element of the Meiji Constitution was that under article 48 the deliberations of both the House of Peers and the House of Representatives were required to be held in public, something not required of government bodies in prior eras. Yet, as with many seemingly forward-looking provisions in the Meiji Constitution there was a significant limitation since deliberations could be held in secret if demanded by the Emperor (*i.e.,* his advisors) or under resolution of the relevant House. Notwithstanding these limitations, the Imperial Diet became an important forum where the government could be publicly criticized, subject to suitable deference to the Emperor, of course. The limited parliamentary privilege accorded to Diet members for statements made in chamber (article 52) was also significant in this respect.

4. Meiji Period Legal Institutions and Codes

One of the earliest developments in the Meiji Period legal system came in 1871, just three years after Emperor Meiji assumed power. It was the establishment of the *Shihōshō,* the forerunner to the Ministry of Justice discussed in the next chapter. This quickly became the primary body controlling most facets of the legal system. Over the next few years it helped establish a system of courts.

This began with the establishment of local lower courts, but within a few years included a number of higher courts and prefecture level courts. Significantly, a high court was also established; although it was different from today's Supreme Court (*Saikosaibanshō*). The court was called the *Daishin'in,* and was modelled on some European high courts of the time. It could address issues of legal interpretation, but it could not decide factual questions. The development of the court system is discussed in more detail in Chapter 4.

The Department of Justice also helped establish a more formalized system for judicial training and training for lawyers. This included the establishment of a number of new law schools. The development of the legal profession is discussed in Chapter 7.

During the Meiji Period a system of formal legal codes developed based heavily on French, German and other continental European codes. Some of the individual codes such as the Civil Code and the Penal Code are discussed in the chapters that follow. However, since one of the goals of the Meiji leaders in implementing legal system reform was renegotiating the unequal treaties, it is worth noting that in 1890 codes of both criminal and civil procedure that would have been familiar to Europeans were adopted.

This still left Japan with a set of basic laws that were unfamiliar to many Japaneses and had to be adjusted and adapted through practice and amendment in the decades that followed. This ability of the Japanese legal system to adopt foreign law and adapt it to the realities of Japanese culture and social structures was put to the test during the Meiji Period. As cases came before courts, the foreign-modeled legal codes – some of which are still in force today - were often adapted to Japanese realities. As a result, a source of frustration to some foreign lawyers and legal scholars may be that Japan has many statutes and institutions that seem familiar but are actually interpreted or implemented very differently, reflecting not only different community norms, but the different way in which law has come to be used in Japan as a means of ordering society.

In some areas foreign innovations were introduced but proved unsuccessful. The jury system adopted in the Taishō Period and discussed in Chapter 8 is one example.

5. The Decay of the Meiji System

The Meiji program of legal reform was successful in achieving one of its driving goals. By 1911 all of the unequal treaties with western nations had been renegotiated and Japan came to be recognized as a growing regional power.

However, as Japan's population became further involved in the nation's economic development and overseas expansion through taxation and conscription, and became exposed to foreign political ideas of democracy and socialism, the nation's leadership came under growing pressure to permit greater participation. A law granting universal male suffrage was introduced in 1925 and resulted in the flowering of proletarian political parties (women did not receive the right to vote until 1945, during the early days of the post-war occupation).

At the same time, communism and organized labor were viewed as existential threats that challenged the notion of *kokutai*—the "body of the state," with the Emperor at the top of everything. For this reason, at the same time suffrage was expanded, the Peace Preservation Act of 1925 was passed. This formed the legal foundation for the surveillance and oppression that was necessary to counter balance the expansion of the franchise. The 1925 act built upon the Safety Preservation Law of 1894, an Imperial Ordinance, designed to limit protests and opposition to imperial rule. It was updated in 1900 by the even more draconian Public Order and Police Law. "Wa"—harmony—may have been a traditional value, but it was also a rigorously enforced policy, one coming at a time when Japan was experiencing profound social change and attendant disorder.

The Meiji constitutional system arguably started to decay after the death of Emperor Meiji in 1912. He had reigned long and acquired a mythical status befitting the role accorded to him by his constitution. His son the Taishō Emperor was sickly and incapable of maintaining the premise of imperial infallibility. At the same time, the oligarchs who had participated directly in the Meiji restoration and implementation of the changes that followed it had also mostly died off by this time. Political parties came into the ascendancy and pandered to populist demands.

Although it played a key role in Japan's development into a world power, the Historian Kawaguchi Akihiro has argued that the Meiji Constitution suffered from three basic flaws.[9] First, it could not be applied as written. This is because unlike most constitutional monarchies which operated under the fiction that the monarch was infallible but did not allow him or her to rule directly, the Meiji Constitution required the Emperor to be both infallible *and* be perceived as actually ruling. Those who clothed themselves in the Imperial authority at the time of the Meiji Restoration had no independent legitimacy of their own, and needed both Meiji's infallibility and the fiction of his direct rule to succeed.

Of course, the reality was that the Emperor did not rule directly and was not infallible. The constitution could thus not be applied as written; it had to be amended, even if only interpretatively. This was the second flaw. Paradoxically, this meant that movements seeking to *protect* the constitution rendered the Meiji constitutional system dysfunctional (the third flaw).

The events that led Japan into militarism, authoritarianism and disastrous war can be understood in this context. Assassinations of political leaders by military dissidents, and an outright coup attempt in 1936 can be characterized as an effort to protect the constitution as written from, politicians who used majority rule to stifle deliberation in the Emperor's Diet and interfere in his command of the military. Efforts by military modernizers and civilian technocrats to create a national security state uniting military and industrial resources also generally failed, criticized as "Tokugawa-like" usurpations of imperial power in violation of the constitution. The National Mobilization Act of 1938, which vested in the Cabinet vast powers to expropriate resources and take control of the

---

[9] KAWAGUCHI HIROAKI, FUTATSU NO KENPŌ TO NIHONJIN [Two Constitutions and the Japanese People] (2017)

economy was also criticized as an infringement by the Cabinet of the Emperor's constitutional powers to rule by decree in emergencies.

Even within the military there was disarray, since anyone of a rank high enough in the army or navy that they were commissioned directly by the Emperor could rebuff any attempted interference in their role as an infringement of his constitutional status as "supreme commander." As a result, military and civilian leaders alike in Japan could often do little but watch helplessly as high-ranking generals expanded the nation's disastrous war on the Chinese mainland.

A significant legal power held by the military arose from the fact that any Prime Minister was required to fill all Cabinet positions, including the Ministers of the Army and Navy, who were required to be officers still on active duty. The military could control who would fill these posts and by refusing to do so or by withdrawing their minister the military could cause a Cabinet to fail.

In 1940 the legislative branch of the Japanese government effectively "committed suicide" (in the words of Professor Kawaguchi) by forming the Imperial Rule Association. This was supposed to eliminate the baneful effects of partisan politics through the creation of a single unified party. Before the end of World War II virtually all Japanese people were part of a notionally unitary national organization that was deeply rooted in the family and the *tonarigumi* ("neighborhood grouping") system of mutual neighborhood cooperation and surveillance.

From the Tokugawa and earlier Shoguns the leaders of modern Japan had learned the dangers of defining powers delegated from the Emperor. The Meiji constitutional system, however, defied centralized leadership and made coherent decision-making difficult or impossible in times of crisis. The tension between the constitutional fiction of direct rule by the Emperor and the reality of his status as a figurehead came to a head when Emperor Hirohito had to demand that his prevaricating government accept the Allied terms of surrender after the atomic bombings of Hiroshima and Nagasaki in August 1945.

F. THE OCCUPATION AND BEYOND

World War II ended for Japan on August 15 when Emperor Hirohito took to the radio to announce to his subjects and the rest of the world that Japan would accept the Potsdam Declaration of July 26, 1945, which set forth the allied terms for the end of hostilities. In a sense the Potsdam Declaration is of constitutional significance—it is still included in most standard *roppō* statutory compilations sold in Japanese bookshops. Some constitutional scholars argue its acceptance was a form of revolution—the "August Revolution"—which resulted in a shift of sovereignty from the Emperor to the Japanese people. The formal conclusion of hostilities came two weeks later when Japan's military and civilian leaders signed the formal Instrument of Surrender on the US Battleship Missouri in Tokyo Bay on September 2. This instrument has not had the same lasting significance as a legal document as the Potsdam Declaration.

What followed was an almost seven year period of occupation, ostensibly by the allied powers (but mostly by Americans) led initially by General Douglas MacArthur in his role as Supreme Commander for the Allied Powers (SCAP). For the most part the Americans, operating out of SCAP's General Headquarters (GHQ) governed from behind the scenes, with the Japanese government being seen to take the lead in most of the post-war reforms that came about during the occupations. But the Americans were there, watching, advising and stepping in when necessary to ensure things went according to plan.

The American agenda in occupying Japan was well-planned and driven in part by the goal of implementing the Potsdam Declaration whose terms included: demilitarizing Japan and preventing it from ever becoming a threat to peace, stripping it of its colonies, the removal of "*all obstacles to the revival and strengthening of democratic tendencies among the Japanese people*" and the establishment of "*freedom of speech, of religion, and of thought, as well as respect for the fundamental human rights.*"

Constitutional amendment became a part of this agenda but was not foreordained, as discussed in Chapter 6. What was planned well in advance of the occupation was the abolition of the Peace Preservation Law, purging the government and educational system of militarists, abolition of State Shinto, and breaking up of the vast concentrations of wealth that had accumulated in the hands of a small privileged elite, including what at the time was a much larger imperial family.

(1)

A great deal of economic reform was thus wrought during the occupation, and a number of key economic and financial statutes date back to this era and show a distinctly American influence. The Anti-Monopoly Act of 1947 dates back to this period as do the Financial Instruments and Exchange Act of 1948 and the Corporate Reorganization Act of 1952.

(2)

The occupation also saw family law rendered more egalitarian, with the elimination of many of the provisions in the Civil Code and other laws that favored men, including the formal elimination of "head of household" status. The legal structure of the Japanese family was also significantly revised during this period as discussed in Chapter 9. The Americans had considered the pre-war family structure to have been part of the social system which had empowered militarism and oppression. Women were also quickly given the franchise, with the first election in which women voters and candidates participated taking place in April 1946.

(3)

The structure of Japan's government was also changed significantly. Some of this reflects the new constitutional system, but it also reflects American efforts to introduce government institutions they were familiar with, often with mixed success. Independent regulatory commissions are one example, and a few of these survive today. For example, the Fair Trade Commission, which is discussed in the next chapter. Others, such as standing legislative committees in both Diet Houses have been less successful, at least in terms of what the Americans intended.

It is also important to understand that the vast amount of legal reform that occurred in this period was carried out with the close involvement of, and sometimes active, sometimes passive aggressive participation of, Japanese officials, politicians, jurists and lawyers. Some of these participants were quite progressive and open to American suggestions. Some had even been imprisoned or subject to oppression by pre-war authorities, and many had been purged from government by Meiji period authorities.

In some ways the occupation period can be divided into at least two phases. The first is the early phase where the Americans were playing a more obvious and possibly idealistic role. This was when the constitution was promulgated, the prohibition on rearmament was maintained, and workers freed to unionize, strike and engage in political activities. Those who had supported the war were purged from numerous government institutions, the oppressive Home Ministry broken up, and the police localized.

The second phase began with the coming of the Cold War in 1948 followed by the Korean War in 1950. With these events the geopolitical importance of Japan as a US ally and logistics center began to take precedence. The spread of communism also loomed as an internal and external threat, and it became convenient for America that Japan begin to rearm. Some Japanese who had initially been purged but were subsequently deemed useful were rehabilitated. For example Kishi Nobusuke, who was prime minister from 1957–1960, initially spent three years in prison as a Class A war crime suspect, but was subsequently released by American authorities who saw him as a potentially useful political ally.

The governance of Japan during the occupation can seem schizophrenic in hindsight. On the one hand the constitution guaranteed a panoply of rights, including the right to free speech, collective labor action and property rights, while appealing to the nation's desire for peace. Yet criticism of the occupation was suppressed, censorship abounded, widespread confiscation and redistribution of property was official policy, unions became potential communist enemies, and Japan began to rearm. During this period, the nascent Supreme Court was thus forced to make some difficult decisions about whether some of these policies—the redistribution of farm land, for example—comported with the new constitution.

Japan regained sovereignty over its main islands on April 28, 1952 when the Treaty of San Francisco (executed in 1951) took effect and formally ended the state of hostilities between Japan and most of the allied powers. The military occupation by the United States arguably never ended, with American military bases remaining in various parts of the country to this day pursuant to the Treaty of Mutual Cooperation and Security between Japan and the United States of America of 1960 (which replaced a more one-sided treaty entered into at the same time as the Treaty of San Francisco). The return of sovereignty over Japan's national territory was actually a gradual process; The Anami Islands were returned in 1953, the Ogasawara Islands in 1968 and Okinawa in 1972. Russia still occupies four Japanese islands North of Hokkaido that it seized at the end of World War II.

The post-war period has seen Japan take the legacy of its two great periods of foreign-influenced legal system reform—the Meiji Restoration and the occupation—and develop more native laws and institutions from them. Some of the occupation-era reforms were speedily undone. The Cabinet Legislation Bureau, eliminated as a separate institution by the Americans, was re-established by the end of 1952. The American effort to prevent the police from becoming a tool of authoritarianism by reorganizing them primarily as municipal forces was also deemed unsuccessful and replaced with the current prefectural system discussed in Chapter 8. Other laws and institutions—including the constitution and the basic form of government—remain as created during the occupation but implemented and interpreted in an often different, Japanese way. The continental European underpinnings of many aspects of the Japanese legal system—including a number of basic statutes such as the Civil Code—also continue to strongly influence the nation's legal culture, having started to make their mark decades before the Americans did.

The view of many is that despite the purge of the militarists from governance, for the most part the civilian bureaucrats who ran the country before the war—including in particular the judges and MOJ officials who mostly survived the purge—continued to run the country after the war, cooperating as necessary with the occupation authorities until that phase was over. The continued status of many spheres of law as regulatory fiefdoms where legislators and courts often seem reluctant to tread may be a reflection of this history, and the deeply embedded nature of Japan's technocratic elites.

Chapter 3

THE STRUCTURE OF THE JAPANESE GOVERNMENT

Analysis

A. INTRODUCTORY REMARKS

This chapter will provide an overview of the structure of the Japanese government, as well as descriptions of those institutions that are worth noting in the context of the legal system, which of course exists within a much larger system of government. The judiciary is discussed in the next chapter.

Constitutional theory would suggest that the totality of this system consists of the legislative, executive and judicial branches. Yet in reality, the various parts of the Japanese government operate and interact in ways that may seem surprising given the formal, American-style (and arguably American-imposed) tripartite separation of powers articulated by Chapters IV, V and VI of the Constitution.

An interesting manifestation of this can be found in the criticism directed at Prime Minister Abe Shinzō for describing himself in May of 2016 as "head of the legislative branch." It was probably an impolitic thing for the head of the executive branch to say openly. Yet as the leader of the political party controlling a majority of seats in both houses of the Diet, he was arguably simply describing the reality of Japan's parliamentary system, which has historically had more in common with Westminster-style models than anything American.

People making this criticism consistently failed to identify who actually *was* the head of the legislative branch. Each of the two Diet chamber has a Speaker who is notionally its head, but neither is head of the Diet as a whole. Moreover, as we shall see the majority of legislation passed by the Diet is actually drafted by executive branch agencies and submitted by the Cabinet. As head of both the Cabinet and the political party controlling both houses of the legislature, Mr. Abe may thus have simply been stating political and institutional reality.[1]

[1] That said, the minutes of the meeting in question were revised to have him describing himself as "head of the executive branch."

B. THE LEVELS OF JAPANESE GOVERNMENT

Japan has three tiers of government: national, prefectural and municipal. For the most part, the national government is the only one relevant to the legal system. Japan has a unitary system of national law. Constitutionally only the Diet can make "laws," with the lower tiers of government severely limited in their authority to make rules compared to, for example, states in federal systems such as the United States. Japan's courts are also national institutions. For this reason only a brief summary of the other levels of government is necessary.

Japan has 47 prefectures and approximately 1700 municipalities. Both have their own assemblies and chief executives—governors for prefectures and mayors of municipalities. The nation's capital, Tokyo is often described as a city but is technically a prefecture comprised of 23 special wards, 26 cities, 5 towns and 8 villages. Moreover, unlike Osaka and Kyoto which are both prefectures that include a number of municipalities, including Osaka City and Kyoto City respectively, there are no cities or towns within Tokyo Prefecture named "Tokyo."

The constitution and many statutes refer to both lower levels of government collectively using the term "local public entities." Under article 93(2) of the constitution, both the chief executives and assemblies of such entities must be elected. This makes local politics somewhat different from the national level and its Westminster-style system of cabinets formed from the party controlling the Diet.

By contrast, prefectural and municipal governments are similar to a "presidential" system where the chief executive is elected separately from and may thus be from a different party from the party that controls the assembly. Their democratically-elected character also makes prefectures and municipalities different from the pre-war system under which prefectural governors were typically bureaucrats appointed from the Home Ministry and mayors were chosen from a limited range of acceptable candidates.

Historically the lower tiers of government were the means through which national government policies were implemented. Prefectural and municipal governments were used to administer national programs with minimal autonomy as to the details of implementation. Amendments to the Local Autonomy Act of 1947 (LAA) that took effect in 2000 were intended to lessen the "top-down" character of governance by giving local governments more autonomy (and responsibility) over their internal affairs, though as to key programs centralized control remains.

Many regulatory statutes give the authority to grant licenses or other approval to mayors or prefectural governors. However, administering nationally-mandated programs remains a significant role of local governments in which they still appear to enjoy limited autonomy. For example in 2013 Akashi City attempted to use a form of birth report that did not require parents to check a box indicating whether the child was legitimate or not, but was quickly overruled by the Ministry of Justice which oversees the *koseki* family registration system nationwide.

Prefectural and municipal governments are constituted under the LAA. Under article 94 of the constitution, local public entities may "enact their own regulations within the law." Such ordinances are discussed in Chapter 5.

Municipalities are further subdivided into cities, towns and villages. This distinction is based on population but not rigidly so. Tokyo is unique in that it includes

23 "special" wards (*ku*) comprising the metropolitan core and which are similar to municipalities.

Twenty cities—essentially every major Japanese metropolitan center—are "specially designated cities" (*seirei shitei toshi*). Such cities are designated by cabinet order and have assumed many of the programs (and associated budgets) that would otherwise be performed by prefectural authorities. However, in certain key areas of governance—notably the police and management of public school personnel—the prefectures retain control. They are also able to establish administrative subdivisions known as *ku* (wards) which perform many of the functions that, in smaller municipalities would be performed out of the city, town or village hall.[2]

Most interactions between the people and government take place at the level of municipal authorities through the systems of family and residence registration, as well as for schooling, benefit and most tax purposes. Criticisms of the current system of local government include that the prefectural governments are an unnecessary additional level of bureaucracy, and that there are too many local assemblies and governments in general. In recent decades there has been a concentrated effort to merge municipalities. As a result the current number of cities, towns and villages is approximately half that which existed at the end of the 1980s. The government has also been studying the possibility of moving to a "federal" system in which about a dozen "states" would perform more government functions with greater autonomy.

With this brief summary of the lower tiers of government out of the way, the remainder of this chapter will focus on the structure and institutions of the national government, excluding the judiciary.

C. THE EMPEROR

1. Introduction

At the time of writing the current Emperor of Japan was Akihito, the 125th in a lineage asserted to go back unbroken to the Emperor Jimmu, who earliest extant records credit with founding the nation and being a direct descendent of Japan's founding deities. The Emperor is thus by far the oldest institution of the Japanese government.

The governmental role played by the Emperor is small and low key but complicated for a variety of political, religious and historical reasons.

After the Meiji Restoration, the emphasis on the Emperor's divine roots through the development of a state-sponsored and created form of Shintō was used to unify the nation, arguably with disastrous consequences. In his current role under the present Constitution, the Emperor remains a much more gentle unifying force, one that is perhaps highly fitting as a symbol of the Japanese character.

2. Constitutional Role

The first eight articles (Chapter I) of the Japanese constitution define the status and role of the Emperor. It can be instructive to compare these provisions to Chapter I of the Meiji Constitution which effectively attributes all powers of government to the Emperor. In the current constitution most of these powers are allocated to the three

[2] Confusingly, unlike the *ku* in Tokyo (which are technically "special wards" or *tokubetsuku* under the LAA) wards in smaller cities do not have elected executives or assemblies.

branches of government, with the Emperor playing a strictly symbolic role in the performance of "acts in matters of state," in accordance with the "advice and approval" of the Cabinet.

While the provisions of Chapter I are rarely a source of dispute today, the seemingly benign article 1 ("*The Emperor shall be the symbol of the State and of the unity of the People, deriving his position from the will of the people with whom resides sovereign power*") was a cause of serious contention between the Japanese government and American occupation authorities when the charter was being negotiated in draft form. Given the prior constitutional system, the transfer of "sovereignty" from the Emperor to the Japanese people was nothing short of revolutionary.

Similarly, the English version of Article 2 ("*The Imperial Throne shall be dynastic and succeeded to in accordance with the Imperial House Law passed by the Diet*") disguises another profound change from the prior constitutional regime; the clear subjugation of the Emperor to the Diet. In Japanese, the "Imperial House Law" (*kōshitsu tenpin*) is not expressed using the term for "law" (*hōritsu*); under the Meiji Constitutional system the rules of the Imperial Household were notionally established by the Emperor himself without formal involvement of the legislature. The old Imperial House Law was thus co-equal with the Meiji Constitution itself and much more extensive than under the post-war system. It once contained rules regarding litigation involving imperial family members as well as mandating certain types of religious ceremonies, no longer possible due to the constitutional separation of religion and government.

Article 2 of the Constitution thus clearly subordinates the Emperor to the Diet. Similarly, Article 8 subjects the Emperor to the financial control by the Diet, reflecting the fact that under the pre-war system the imperial family became one of the most significant *zaibatsu*, concentrating tremendous wealth in the hands of a small group of people.

Other provisions of Chapter I are devoted to defining the constitutional roles of the Emperor, referred to as "acts in matters of state." These consist of appointing the Prime Minister and Chief Judge of the Supreme Court (article 6), promulgating laws and regulations, convoking and dissolving the Diet, announcing elections, attesting appointments to high-level executive and judicial positions, attesting the ratification of treaties, receiving foreign ambassadors, granting amnesties, bestowing honors and performing ceremonial functions (article 7). Article 3 subjects all of these acts by the Emperor to the advice and consent of the Cabinet, rendering his role truly symbolic.

Article 4 makes it clear that the Emperor has no other role in acts of state outside the constitution, and has no "powers related to government." Although the text of article 4 appears to limit him to only clearly enumerated functions, the Emperor also engages in a wide range of other activities that one would expect from a constitutional monarch; giving speeches at public and private events and entertaining and corresponding with foreign heads of state and other similar activities.

It is also not even clear whether the Emperor can be properly described as a "monarch;" Constitutional law scholar Shigenori Matsui has suggested that he cannot and that "Japan should be viewed as a constitutional republic."[3] Similarly, while the Emperor is often described in foreign reference sources (such as the CIA's online "World

---

[3] SHIGENORI MATSUI, THE CONSTITUTION OF JAPAN: A CONTEXTUAL ANALYSIS 58–59 (2011).

Fact Book" data base) as the "head" or "chief" of state, and the Cabinet Legislation Bureau and Supreme Court have made occasional oblique references to the Emperor being *genshu* (head of state), there is debate among constitutional scholars about whether this is appropriate. After all, the Emperor is not described as such in the Constitution, and such a characterization would have been incompatible with a charter that purportedly vests sovereignty in the Japanese people. Yet for most intents and purposes he is treated by everyone in the Japanese government and abroad as the head of state, particularly with respect to diplomatic protocol.

3. The Imperial Family, Proxies and Succession

As an institution the Emperor also includes the other members of the Imperial Household. At the time of writing this consisted of the Emperor and 18 other members from four different generations, including the Emperor himself. Members of the Imperial Family have a special status—they are technically not included within the universe of "Japanese people" (*kokumin*). They do not have voting rights and are registered in a special registry the *kōtōfu*, not the *koseki* (family registry) system in which regular Japanese families are registered (see Chapter 9). Under the Imperial House Act (IHA), members of the Imperial Family are subject to various legal restraints not applicable to regular Japanese people: they may not enter into adoptive relationships (IHA, article 9), and marriages by princes and princesses are subject todeliberations by a committee comprised of other members of the Imperial Family, the Director of the Imperial Household Agency, and the Prime Minister, the Speaker and Vice-Speaker of both chambers of the Diet, the Chief Judge and one other member of the Supreme Court.

In the pre-war period, the Imperial Household was much larger, and given the wealth it came to accumulate, constituted one of the *zaibatsu* (financial conglomerates) that the Americans sought to break up after the war. In addition to subjecting imperial finances to Diet control, the American occupation stripped all but the core members of the household of imperial status, thereby drastically reducing its size. They may have cut it back too much, since the family has been shrinking, and could potentially be reduced to a single nuclear family within two generations.

Article 2 of the IHA limits succession to legitimate male members of the Imperial Family according to seniority. In other words, the throne cannot be transmitted through a female member. The possibility of amending the law to permit has been discussed, but it is likely to be politically unacceptable; the lineage of the imperial family has been transmitted exclusively through male members (there have been the occasional female emperors in the distant past, but the lineage has not been continued through their offspring). The IHA (article 12) also mandates that a princess born into the Imperial Family who marries a commoner loses her status, being removed from the *kōtōfu* and being reflected in a *koseki* just like regular Japanese people. Since the youngest generation of the family consists of three princesses and one prince, the youngest of the family. If all three princesses marry, the prince will be the only one left in his generation.

The shrinking imperial family has potential constitutional implications. Although they are largely symbolic, the functions performed by the Emperor entail a significant amount of paperwork, including signing and sealing notices of promulgations and attestations of appointments. In the first 29 years of his reign Emperor Akihito executed approximately 30,000 such documents.

At the time of writing Akihito was in his 80s, and had been hospitalized for various ailments. Under article 4 of the Constitution the Emperor can delegate his constitutional roles to proxies, which according to the applicable statute can be chosen from other members of the Imperial Family. Having an imperial family with only a few adult members would thus be potentially problematic. Article 5 of the constitution provides for the appointment of a regent if the Emperor is a minor or severely incapacitated.

In 2016 Emperor Akihito caused a stir by announcing his desire to abdicate. There were no provisions in existing law for him to do so—death being the only means recognized in the IHA by which the imperial title could succeed. In essentially advocating for a particular type of law, he was regarded by some as overstepping his role as a completely apolitical symbol of the nation. In 2017 the Diet passed a law creating a special amendment to the IHA allowing Akihito (but not subsequent emperors) to abdicate. At the time of writing this was scheduled to take place on May 1, 2019. At that time the current Crown Prince, Naruhito, will assume the throne.

4. Religious Roles of the Emperor

Although the Japanese constitution relegates the Emperor to a symbolic role in the nation's governance, it should be remembered that he also has a much older role as an important figure in the hierarchy of the Shinto religion. He is thus involved in numerous religious ceremonies as well. While much of the Shinto religion is focused on family ancestors, local shrines, *kami* (often poorly translated into English as gods, but more appropriately meaning a spirit being or spiritual force), and aspects of animism, there is also an element of Shinto focused on the Emperor and his ancestors as a link to the nation's founding Shintō deities.

While his role as a religious figure is generally kept separate from his constitutional role, there are numerous areas where these dual roles are potentially problematic under Articles 20 and 89 of the constitution, which prohibit state involvement in religion and expenditure of public funds for religious institutions, respectively. For example the death of one Emperor and the enthronement of a new one both involve the performance of Shinto rituals confirming the Emperor's connection to the founding deities of Japan. Government involvement in some of the ceremonies relating to the enthronement of the current Emperor Akihito and the funeral of the late Emperor Hirohito were justified on the grounds that they were "cultural" events of historical significance. Other religious elements of the Emperor's status have been retained as being within the realm of the "private affairs" of the Imperial Household.

Some critics have also associated the Imperial system with the militarism and totalitarianism that led to Japan's disastrous involvement in World War II. This was particularly true during the post-war reign of Emperor Hirohito, on account of his direct involvement in the government before and during the war. In addition to the religious dimension of the Emperor's reign, there are also areas of controversy arising in the anachronism of having an emperor in the first place.

One area of controversy is the National Anthem, *kimigayo* which is essentially a paean to the imperial system. Constitutional litigation has arisen in the case of public school teachers disciplined for refusing to perform or sing the anthem on the grounds that it violates their freedom of conscience. The results in these cases have gone against the teachers, except when the discipline imposed by the school was too severe.

Some of the constitutional issues arising from the Emperor and his involvement in the Shintō religion are discussed in Chapter 6.

5. Regnal Years

The use of reign titles for official dates is another subtle influence of the imperial system. Emperors are referred to not by their names but by the reign title that is created when they accede to the throne. The emperor at the time of writing (Akihito) is known as the Heisei Emperor. He acceded to the throne in 1989, so 2018, the year in which this book was published was the 30th year of Heisei. While many Japanese people are now more accustomed to the western system of dating, official documents are still dated using regnal years.

6. The Emperor and the Public Service

An interesting aspect of the Emperor's role is his relationship to high-ranking government officials. Under the Meiji Constitution such officials (including judges) were regarded as servants of the Emperor. Now, however, Ministers of State are appointed by the Prime Minister and the civil service is controlled by the Cabinet,. However, under article 7 of the Constitution the Emperor "attests" (*ninshō*) the appointment of Ministers of State and "other officials provided by law" as well as ambassadors to foreign countries. Within the public service there is thus a distinction between those officials whose appointments are attested by the Emperor (*ninshōkan*) and those who are not. Currently those whose appointments are attested are:

1. Ministers of State (other than the Prime Minister, who is appointed by the Emperor based on the designation of the Diet
2. The three Deputy Secretary Generals of the Cabinet Secretariat
3. The three commissioners of the National Personnel Authority
4. The vice ministers (*fukudaijin*) to each of the ministries, the Reconstruction Agency and Cabinet Office
5. The Grand Steward and Grand Chamberlain of the Imperial Household Agency[4]
6. The Chairman of the Fair Trade Commission
7. The Supreme Prosecutor, Deputy Supreme Prosecutor and eight high prosecutors.
8. Ambassadors and special ambassadors
9. Chairman of the Nuclear Regulatory Commission
10. The three Inspectors of the National Board of Audit
11. The 14 judges of the Supreme Court (other than the Chief Judge, who is appointed directly by the Emperor with the advice and consent of the Cabinet)
12. The chief judges of the eight high courts

[4] The special act allowing Emperor Akihito to abdicate also creates a Chamberlain for the retired emperor which is also a *ninshōkan* position.

What is noteworthy about this list is the absence of any top-level officials from Japan's Self Defense Forces.

7. The Emperor and the System of Honors

One obscure but interesting area where the long history of the imperial system interacts with what by comparison is a very recent constitution, is in the nation's system of honors. Under article 7 of the Constitution, "awarding of honors" is one of the "acts in matters of state" performed by the Emperor.

The Meiji period saw the establishment of a modern system of honors based on the existing system of official rankings dating back to the 7th and 8th centuries and based on notional proximity to the Emperor. The modern system sought to balance the aspirations of larger imperial household, the hereditary aristocracy and officials and military personnel. The Meiji system of honors created a system of rewards for service to the nation, and in some cases these came with lifetime pensions. It also enabled Japan to participate in reciprocal diplomacy through awards honors to the royalty of other nations.

The occupation saw Japan's aristocracy eliminated and the system of granting honors and rankings to the living suspended as militaristic and inegalitarian (the need to honor war dead meant the system of awarding *posthumous* rankings quietly survived and remains in effect today). In 1960 a bill was proposed to revive the system of honors, but it was defeated. In 1963 the Cabinet re-established certain aspects of the old system through a Cabinet order, thereby resuscitating a system of awarding people honors and medals with (non-hereditary and substantively meaningless) ranks attached. In 2003 the system of honors to the living was also amended to eliminate the numerical rankings, though the various categories of award still exist within a clear hierarchy.

The primary beneficiaries of the honors system appear to be public servants. Achieving a certain level in government service creates a reasonable expectation that an honor of commensurate stature will be received after retirement. A former Supreme Court judge can expect to receive a higher level of honor than a former high court judge, and so forth. This is worth mentioning because it is one possible factor influencing official behavior that is rarely mentioned in western accounts of Japan.

D. THE DIET

1. Introduction

Japan's system of parliamentary government has a history of over 120 years. Although there have been periods when the political process was subverted by militarism and oppression, the fact remains that the Diet, Japan's national legislature, has been convened annually since it as established, with regular elections being held as required by law notwithstanding war, attempted coups, privation, conquest and other turmoil. This record is impressive when compared to the political histories of many other countries of the world. Perhaps it is because of this long history that, despite having been significantly reconstituted under the current constitution, certain aspects of post-war legislative practices and procedures governing the electoral process retain a surprising degree of continuity with the pre-war Diet system.

Under the Meiji Constitution, the Diet—the Imperial Diet, as it was called—was comprised of two houses, the House of Representatives and the House of Peers. The

House of Representatives was constituted from representatives chosen by election. Initially the franchise was limited to male citizens paying a certain amount of taxes, with universal male suffrage being introduced in 1925.

The House of Peers consisted of members of the imperial family, hereditary aristocrats, appointees, and other members elected by very select constituencies from amongst their members, such as lower-ranking aristocrats, scholars from the imperial university system and top taxpayers. A few members from the elites of Japan's colonial possessions were added in 1945, shortly before the institution ceased to exist.

As originally envisioned by the American occupation authorities, a reformed legislature—no longer the "Imperial" Diet—was to become a unicameral body through the simple elimination of the House of Peers. The Japanese advocated for retaining the second chamber, now known as the House of Councillors, which the Americans accepted subject to it being elective. The result is a bicameral system in which both chambers effectively represent the same constituency: Japanese voters. Although members of the two chambers are chosen from different electoral districts and serve different terms, the most meaningful difference in the composition of the two may be that whichever has most recently experienced an election is more likely to reflect the current national sentiment.

The remainder of this section will offer an overview of the structure and functioning of the Diet as an institution. The legislative process is discussed in Chapter 5.

2. Constitutional Dimensions and Composition

The basic features of the Diet are set forth in Chapter IV of the Constitution. Article 41 declares the Diet to be the "highest organ of state power." This is regarded by most scholars as a largely meaningless statement, though it does mean the three branches of government delineated by the constitution are not co-equal and is arguably one of the reasons why the judiciary is highly deferential of the Diet.

Article 41 also establishes the Diet as the "sole law-making organ of the State." As noted at the outset of this chapter and discussed in Chapter 5, in reality much of the legislation passed by the Diet is actually drafted by the executive branch agencies.

The Diet is comprised of two chambers: the House of Representatives (HOR) and the House of Councillors (HOC). In English these are sometimes also referred to as the "lower" and "upper" houses, respectively. This is misleading since the HOR is constitutionally superior. First, it can choose a prime minister, approve a budget and ratify a treaty over the objections of the other chamber (articles 67, 60 and 61). Second, upon a vote of 2/3 of its member the House of Representatives can pass legislation over the objections of the House of Councillors (article 59). A practical manifestation of the HOR's superiority and importance can be seen in the fact that all prime ministers and most cabinet ministers have been members of that chamber.

HOR members are elected for terms of four years, but the chamber is subject to dissolution (article 45), which is common. By contrast, the HOC is not subject to dissolution and it members serve for six year terms, staggered so that 1/2 are up for re-election every three years (article 46).

The number of members of the two chambers and details as to electoral districts are left to legislation (article 43). At the time of writing, the House of Representatives has 465 members. Of these, 289 were elected from single-seat electoral districts. The remaining 176 were chosen based on proportional voting from multiple seat districts comprised of regional groupings of prefectures. For example, together with Okinawa the island of Kyushu comprise a single multi-seat HOR district.

The HOC has 242 members; 146 from multi-seat electoral districts based on prefecture. The remaining 96 seats are drawn based on proportional voting from candidates running nationwide on party tickets. For these seats, voters can either vote for a candidate or the party. The mixture of electoral districts and proportional voting helps ensure minority parties reliably obtain some seats in the Diet. However, it also means some political parties may field candidates whose principal qualification is that they are famous, since the proportional voting system means they can be expected to obtain a seat based on name recognition alone.

Malapportionment in Diet seats has been a persistent problem in Japan. This is due both to demographic shifts which have caused rural seats representing far fewer voters than those in urban seats, but also to the methods used to draw up electoral districts. Efforts to distinguish the constituency of the House of Councillors by making it more of a "regional" representative body through prefectural electoral districts also makes a certain amount of malapportionment unavoidable. The Supreme Court has developed a significant body of equal-protection jurisprudence on malapportionment. Challenges have also been brought to various other methods of choosing Diet members, and voting rights has been one of the areas where the judiciary can be said to have been active, as discussed in Chapter 6.

Diet members standing for election are subject to numerous restrictions imposed by electoral laws which greatly restrain their ability to interact directly with or communicate with voters other than in the manner permitted by law. These are also discussed in Chapter 6, but it is worth noting at this juncture that during the electoral process the nation's law makers are seriously restrained in their ability to have meaningful discussions with voters about what the nation's laws should be. The principal goal of much electioneering activity by individual candidates often appears to be devoted to getting the electorate to remember his or her name. The value of name recognition in both houses may also be a factor in the dynastic nature of Diet politics, with some seats being held by several generations of the same family.

In terms of gender, the Diet does a poor job of representing the population. Globally, Japan ranked in the bottom quartile in terms of female representatives in the national legislature, with only 10% of Diet seats held by women as of April 2018.

3. Diet Sessions

There are four types of Diet sessions. First is the emergency session of the House of Councillors convoked by the Cabinet at a time when the House of Representatives has been dissolved (article 54(2)). There have only been two examples of such sessions, both in the 1950s and neither for what most would consider "emergency" reasons.

Ordinary sessions of the Diet are required to be convoked at least once per year (article 52). Under article 10 of the Diet Act of 1947, the length of an ordinary session is 150 days unless: (i) the term of the members of one of the chambers expires earlier or (ii) both houses move to extend the session, which can only be done once (Diet Act, article 12(2)). Ordinary Diet sessions are usually convoked in January and continue into the summer, though occasionally extensions may take them into the fall.

If the House of Representatives is dissolved before the expiry of the four year term of its members, the Constitution (article 54(1)) requires a session of the Diet be convened within 30 days of the election. By custom this is referred to as a "special" session and is usually quite short, lasting just the few days required to appoint a prime minister, constitute a Cabinet and appoint the speakers of the two houses.

Under article 53 of the Constitution, an extraordinary session of the Diet can also be convened by the Cabinet, and the Cabinet must do so if requested by more than 1/4 of either chamber. Although it is common for extraordinary sessions to be called by the Cabinet and granted by the Diet, the Cabinet has also repeatedly ignored requests for such sessions by opposition party Diet members satisfying the 1/4 membership threshold. While constitutionally dubious, this problem does not arise until the fall, after the ordinary session has expired. It is also considered "resolved" by the start of a new ordinary session in January of the following year, meaning there are few remedies for what otherwise appears to be a clear constitutional breach.

Although only the HOR is subject to dissolution, the HOC also closes when this happens, unless summoned for an emergency session (article 54(2)). The powers of the Diet are not affected by the type of session; the difference is more one of practice and practicalities. The appointment of the Prime Minister and other key figures would not take place in an ordinary session. By contrast, ordinary sessions of the Diet will necessarily be devoted to the recurring business of government, including consideration of the annual budget. Extraordinary sessions tend to get more attention because they are often convened to address controversial legislation when there is not enough time left in an ordinary session to pass it.

Regardless of type, each Diet session is independent. This is true even though the composition of both chambers may remain unchanged across several sessions. For reference, details of the Diet sessions from 2013 through 2017 are set forth in Table 3-1 below:

TABLE 3-1 RECENT DIET SESSIONS

Session number*	Type	Date	Length in days (extensions)
195	Special	November 1–December 9, 2017	39
194	Extraordinary	September 28, 2017	1
193	Ordinary	January 1–June 18, 2017	150
192	Extraordinary	September 26–December 17, 2016	83 (17)
191st	Extraordinary	August 1–3, 2016	3
190th	Ordinary	January 4–June 1,2016	150
189th	Ordinary	January 26–September 27, 2015	245 (95)
188th	Special	December 24–26, 2014	3
187th	Extraordinary	September 29–November 11, 2014	54* (63 scheduled but cut short due to dissolution of HOR)
186th	Ordinary	January 24–June 22, 2014	150
185th	Extraordinary	October 15–December 8, 2013	55(2)
184th	Extraordinary	August 2–7, 2013	6
183rd	Ordinary	January 28–June 26, 2013	150

SOURCE: House of Representatives home page.
* Diet sessions are counted from the first session convened under the current constitution (a special session lasting from May 20 to December 9, 1947).

The compartmentalized nature of Diet sessions also imposes constraints due to certain well-established operating principals, some of which are based on precedent than law. One of these is the principle of *fusaigi*, not re-opening debate on a particular matter during the same session. If the Diet decides on a matter it may not be again raised for consideration during the same session.

In addition, there is the *fukeizoku no gensoku* (the principle of non-continuity). Under this principle (which *does* have a legal foundation in article 68 of the Diet Act), any legislative or other proposal that is still pending when a Diet session expires and must be reintroduced in the next session. It is possible to commit some matters to one of the Diet's standing committees so that they are carried over to the next session, but this is the exception rather than the rule. The principle encourages legislators to focus on closing out important government first. But it also gives opposition parties the opportunity cause procedural delays and run out the clock, thereby forcing concessions from the majority party or coalition.

In looking at the functioning of the Diet it is important to remember that both chambers have been controlled by the same party—the conservative Liberal Democratic Party (LDP)—for most of the seven decades since the constitution was promulgated. The LDP has thus been able to generally conduct much of the substantive legislative process behind closed doors in the party mechanism, with the legislative procedures established by the constitution and the Diet Act being reduced to bothersome formalities or opportunities for opposition parties to grandstand, complain and stall. Some of the problems with the current system—the decline in importance of the Diet's formal legislative committees and the limited amount of debate over policy that actually takes place in formal Diet proceedings—are a reflection of this history. Some observers have pointed out there may have been more debate under the Meiji Constitution than under the current constitution. For example, under the Meiji Constitution there was a UK-style "prime minister's question time" but there is no such practice in the current Diet.

The fact that the LDP has controlled both houses has also meant that instances where the use of the legislative override by the House of Representatives has been necessary have been rare even when the LDP has enjoyed such dominance. Since 1955, there have only been a few comparatively brief periods when the two chambers were controlled by different parties (1989–1990, 1998–1999, 2007–2009, 2010–2012), and only one period during which the LDP and its allies did not control the HOR (2009–2012). The comparative rarity of *nejirekokkai* (literally, "screwed up Diet," the term used to describe the situation when the Diet's two chambers are controlled by different parties or coalitions) can result not only in legislative gridlock, but can stall other aspects of government as well. Among other things, by statute various leadership roles at important government institutions—the Bank of Japan and the National Personnel Authority, for example—can only be filled upon the consent of both houses.

4. Diet Institutions

Under article 16 of the Diet Act, each chamber has a Speaker (Presiding Officer) and a Vice Speaker (Deputy Presiding Officer). A Provisional Speaker (Presiding Officer) may also be appointed if the Speaker and Vice Speaker are unavailable or have not yet been chosen. In addition, each of the permanent committees discussed below has a chair. All of these roles are filled from the members of the applicable chambers Finally, each chamber has a secretary general who is *not* a Diet member, but is in charge of the administrative apparatus of the applicable house.

Article 41 of the Diet Act establishes in each chamber 17 standing committees devoted to specific areas of policy such as foreign affairs, the judiciary and education as well as discipline and administration of the chamber itself. Special committees can also be established as necessary (Article 45).

Each chamber also has a Legislation Bureau that assists members prepare draft legislation. These are different from the Cabinet Legislation Bureau discussed later in this chapter. Their staffs may include personnel on secondment from executive branch agencies or the judiciary.

The National Diet Library was originally established in 1890 under the Meiji Constitution. It exists to accumulate and make available to Diet members as well as policy makers and citizens information necessary to inform the legislative function.

5. Other Diet Powers

The principal roles of the Diet are to choose the Prime Minister, approve the budget, ratify treaties and pass legislation. However, the Constitution also vests in the Diet certain other powers that are both relevant to the legislative process but can also be used as a political weapon and to keep the executive branch in check.

a. *Control of Imperial Household Finances*

An obscure but historically significant power of the Diet is its ability to control the re-accumulation of excessive wealth by the imperial family through the requirement that all transfers of property and gifts to the imperial household be approved by the Diet (Constitution, article 8) and that all appropriations for the household also be approved by the Diet (article 88).

b. *Budgetary and Financial Controls*

Although the budget is prepared and submitted by the Cabinet (article 86), it must be approved by the Diet (article 60), as must all expenditures and incurrences of debt by the state (article 85). The Diet also receives the audit of the national accounts from the Board of Audit (article 90; see discussion later in this chapter). Either chamber of the Diet or individual committees may also request the BOA audit and report on areas of specific areas of concern (Diet Act, article 105; Board of Audit Act, article 30–3).

c. *Investigative Powers*

Under article 62 of the constitution each Diet chamber is empowered to "demand the presence and testimony of witnesses, and the production of records" in connection with the conduct of "investigations in relation to government." The Diet Act (article 104) provides the details of the process by which the Diet chambers or their committees may demand information from the Cabinet or other government bodies. A separate law, the Diet Testimony Act of 1947 sets forth the details of the process and establishes penalties for bad behavior such as failure of witnesses to appear despite a summons and perjury.

In reality, the formal Diet investigation process has rarely been used to challenge the government. This is perhaps unsurprising given the prolonged periods of control of both the Diet and the Cabinet by the LDP.

There is a largely academic debate over whether the ability to conduct investigations is a power of the Diet separate from its legislative function, or one that is merely intended to facilitate its performance of that function.

In light of the limited use of the investigative powers given the dominance of the government powers in successive Diets, in 1997 the HOR rules were amended to make it possible for preliminary investigations to be ordered upon the request of at least 40 of the chambers' members (HOR Rules, article 56–3).

d. *Interpellations*

Under article 63 of the constitution, Diet members may require the Prime Minister or other ministers of state appear and answer questions. There are no formal penalties for the failure of a minister to refuse to do so. With the consent of the speaker of their chamber, individual Diet members may also submit questions to the Cabinet which must in principle provide a response within seven days (Diet Act, articles 74 and 75). For those Diet members whose parties are perpetually in opposition, the use of such questions may be one of the key tools they have to hold the government to account and appeal to voters. Formal written responses to these written questions (*shitsumon shuisho*) are approved by Cabinet resolution and published in the official gazette (*kanpō*) thus may have a certain interpretive value regarding the law, regulation or policy being questioned.

e. Non-Confidence Motions

Under article 69 of the Constitution the HOR may pass a resolution of non-confidence against the Cabinet. If it is passed (or a resolution of confidence fails to pass), the HOR is dissolved and the Cabinet must resign. This has never happened.

While not anticipated by the constitution and having no legal significance, the HOR may occasionally move for a vote of non-confidence against individual Cabinet members or other top government officials. These motions are occasionally successful and politically significant. Similarly, the HOC may also pass motions calling for individual cabinet members or officials (including the Prime Minister himself) to take responsibility for a failure. These also pass occasionally but are less significant politically. Votes of non-confidence are also occasionally brought by a chamber against its own officers but are rarely successful.

f. Impeachment

Finally, a special court is established in the Diet for the purpose of initiating and conducting impeachment trials in cases involving judicial misconduct (constitution, article 63; Judicial Impeachment Act of 1947). This process is discussed in more detail in Chapter 4.

National Personnel Authority commissioners may also only be removed through impeachment by the Diet, pursuant to the procedures set forth in the National Personnel Authority Commissioner Impeachment Act of 1949. This has never happened.

E. THE CABINET AND THE EXECUTIVE BRANCH

1. Historical Background

As a government institution, the Cabinet dates back to 1885, with Meiji oligarch Ito Hirobumi serving as the nation's first prime minister. The Meiji Constitution, however, does not even mention cabinets or prime ministers. Instead, it contains a few sparse references to "ministers of state," who were charged with advising the Emperor (Meiji Constitution, article 55(1)). The Emperor being infallible, they were also required to take responsibility for such advice. Ministers of state also signed any laws, Imperial Ordinances or Imperial Rescripts regarding matters under their jurisdiction (article 55(2)).

The Meiji Constitution contained no requirement that ministers of state be members of either chamber of the Imperial Diet and often they were not. This was by design; the drafters of the Meiji Constitution wanted to isolate the Emperor from the pettiness of party politics, particularly given the view that the Japanese people were not really "ready" for a full-blown Westminster-style parliamentary system. Yet political parties did become an important force in Japanese system of government and came to dominate cabinets until all were disbanded in 1940 in furtherance of the nation's war efforts.

Cabinets under the Meiji Constitutional system suffered from a number of handicaps. First, the prime minister had no special powers, being nothing more than a first among equals. Second, each minister of state was responsible directly to the Emperor, meaning that it was easy for cabinets to fall into disunity. Third, cabinets were unable to exercise significant control over the military, which constitutionally answered directly to the Emperor and nobody else (they were technically the "Imperial" not "Japanese" army and navy). Both the Army and Navy Ministries were represented in cabinets, but before 1913 and after 1936 their ministries were required by cabinet regulations to be on active service. This meant either branch of the military could cause a cabinet to fail by withdrawing its minister and refusing to appoint a new one.[5] The average life of cabinets under the Meiji system was little more than a year, though with some exceptions the lifespan of cabinets in the post-war system has not proved dramatically longer.

2. The Cabinet Under the Current Constitution

The Cabinet is now a constitutional institution, clearly vested with defined powers of government. Many of the powers vested in the Emperor under Chapter I of the Meiji Constitution were effectively transferred to the Cabinet under Chapter IV of the current one. The role and powers of the prime minister are also set forth; (s)he is no longer merely a first among equals but a clearly superior creature, having the power to appoint and remove other ministers of state (Constitution, article 68).

There is significant overlap between the Diet and the Cabinet. The constitution requires that the prime minister and at least half of the ministers of state comprising the Cabinet be selected from the ranks of Diet members (articles 67 and 68). Typically all are, and primarily from the HOR.

The English version of article 65 of the Constitution describes the Cabinet as being vested with the "executive power." In Japanese, however, the term is *gyōseiken* or "administrative powers" (to add to the confusion, in the English version article 73 tasks the Cabinet with "administer[ing] the law faithfully" whereas the Japanese is *shikkō*, which is typically translated "execute"). This may just be quibbling over language, but Americans readers who think of separation of powers as including an "executive branch" should be aware that in Japanese the Cabinet is not actually described as such. Nonetheless this book will sometimes use the term to describe the administrative apparatus under the control of the Cabinet.

Article 66(2) of the Constitution requires all Cabinet members to be civilians. This was a requirement added late in the drafting process and a new word—*bunmin*—had to be invented to express the concept of a "civilian" in Japanese. Insofar as article 9 of the constitution ostensibly prohibits Japan from having a military, it is unclear how anyone could be anything other than a civilian. Constitutional scholars generally regard the

[5] The failure to provide for adequate controls over the military is sometimes described as a defect of the Meiji Constitutional system. It should be remembered, however, that the historical experience of the Meiji leaders who designed that system, was that a clearly defined military figure—the Shōgun—could usurp political power from the Emperor.

requirement as being meaningless, though "civilian control" of Japan's extensive self-defense forces remains an important concept politically.

In another rejection of the Meiji Constitutional system, article 66(3) holds the Cabinet collectively responsible to the Diet, rather than individual ministers being responsible to the Emperor. However, the Constitution also provides only limited means for the Diet to actually hold the Cabinet responsible—the non-confidence motions discussed in the preceding section.

Under article 72 of the Constitution, *"the Prime Minister, representing the Cabinet submits bills, reports on general national affairs and foreign relations to the Diet and exercises control and supervision over various administrative branches."* The punctuation in the Japanese renders it uncertain whether the "representing the Cabinet" refers only to submitting bills or to all of the other enumerated roles, meaning there are potentially significant interpretive disputes over the powers vested in the Prime Minister. Article 6 of the Cabinet Act of 1947 specifies that the Prime Minister supervises the administrative branches in accordance with policies decided through cabinet decisions, indicating a preference for the collective interpretation.

Under Article 73, in addition to "general administrative functions" the Constitution also charges the Cabinet with responsibility for: (i) administering the law faithfully, (ii) conducting affairs of state, (iii) managing foreign affairs, (iv) concluding treaties (with the approval of the Diet), (v) administering the civil service (which is understood to refer to the national civil service, excluding that portion working in the legislative and judicial branches), (vi) preparing the budget and submitting it to the Diet, and (vi) enacting cabinet orders and (vii) deciding on amnesties and commutations. Of these, cabinet orders are discussed in greater detail in Chapter 5.

3. The Cabinet and Ministers

The Cabinet is comprised of the Prime Minister and ministers of state (*kokumu daijin*), a term that is both constitutional and confusing. Even within the constitution the term is used in contexts that either excludes or includes the Prime Minister (Article 68 being an example of the former and Articles 63 and 66 of the latter). Article 75, which says "[t]he Ministers of State, during their tenure of office, shall not be subject to legal action without the consent of the Prime Minister" is the most paradoxical provision in this respect, since it either means that the Prime Minister is *not* a minister of state, or that he is but may only be prosecuted by his own consent.

The term "minister of state" is confusing in English in part for linguistic reasons: in Japanese the term *daijin* (minister) has no relationship to the term for ministry (*shō*). It is thus possible to be a minister of state without having a ministry.

In fact there are several other government roles bearing the title "minister" (*daijin*) which are not constitutional, but overlap with the "minister of state." First there are *gyōsei daijin* ("administrative minister") or *shumu daijin* ("minister having primary responsibility"), the latter term frequently used in statutes delegating authority to a minister. These are the ministers of state appointed to the head of the ministries, such as the Ministry of Finance.

Second, there are "ministers of state for special missions (*naikakufu tokumei tantō daijin*) who sit in the Cabinet Office, and who are usually referred to in English as "Minister of State for xx." Such ministerial posts are provided for in a statute, and although their occupants do not sit atop a ministry they are empowered to get information from other government institutions and make policy recommendations within their remit.

Third, there are *tantō daijin* or "Ministers in Charge" who generally sit in the Cabinet Secretariat (discussed below). These can be created by the Prime Minister for emergency or other special purposes without enabling legislation.

In addition, there are ministers of state who sit in the Cabinet but whose roles involve oversight of institutions that are not ministries. " These are the Chief Cabinet Secretary and the Chairman of the Public Safety Commission.

All of the above four categories are "ministers of state" and collectively referred to as "*kakuryō*" or cabinet members. They are appointed both as ministers of state and with orders to perform one or other roles (e.g., Minister of Finance). Article 74 requires that statutes be signed by the *shunin daijin* (competent minister of state).

Under the Cabinet Act (Article 2(2)) the Cabinet is comprised of a maximum of 14 ministers of state, but this can be expanded to 17 if necessary. However a confusing set of supposedly temporary amendments relating to the 3/11/2011 earthquake, tsunami and nuclear disaster, and the 2020 Tokyo Olympics meant that at the time of writing the maximum number of ministers of state is 19, not including the Prime Minister. Even this, however, is not enough to fill all of the positions for which a minister of state is designated (there being dozens of "minister in charge" and "special mission portfolios"). It is thus common for a single minister of state to be responsible for both a ministry and one or more other portfolios.

The Cabinet also functionally includes four members who are not ministers of state: three vice secretaries to the Cabinet Secretariat (one each appointed from the membership of the HOR and HOV, and one from the bureaucracy) and the Director General of the Cabinet Legislation Bureau, which is discussed later in this chapter.

The Cabinet formally conducts business through twice-weekly cabinet meetings (*kakugi*). Most government actions, including cabinet legislative proposals, cabinet orders, high-level official appointments and other matters (including the numerous other acts in matters of state notionally performed by the Emperor with the advice and consent of the Cabinet) must be approved through a unanimous cabinet decision (*kakugi kettei*). Although matters of great importance are decided at them, cabinet meetings are largely formalities, often lasting less than fifteen minutes. The brief twice weekly meetings are usually not enough to address all government business, so additional matters are approved through the execution of circular cabinet resolutions.

4. The Prime Minister

The Japanese Prime Minister does not have significant powers compared to many other heads of government. His ability to appoint people to official roles has traditionally been limited to the members of his Cabinet and a few others. His ability to interfere in the staffing of individual ministries—even the appointment of the administrative vice ministers—has traditionally been limited. Staffing of even the Cabinet Secretariat is under the control of the Cabinet as a whole and for the most part allocated to career bureaucrats on secondment from the various ministries. Similarly, the majority of the Prime Minister's seven official secretaries are dispatched from the key ministries, providing a pipeline between those ministries and the Prime Minister. The Prime

Minister also has almost no ability to create organizations through which to govern; the composition and operation of administrative bodies being left to statutes such as the National Government Organization Act of 1999 (NGOA). And although the term *shushō kantei* is sometimes used in the press to refer to the Prime Minister's Office or as a synonym for the Japanese government power (in the same manner as "the White House"), the term technically refers to the Prime Minister's official residence and the location where Cabinet Meetings are held. It is not an official governmental institution and its administration is under the Cabinet Secretariat.

In addition to a ministerial designation, one member of the Cabinet is typically also designated the Deputy Prime Minister. This is not, however, a post formally named in the constitution or any statute.

5. The Cabinet Secretariat

The Cabinet Secretariat or *Naikaku Kanbō* is established under article 12 of the Cabinet Act and is charged with managing the affairs of the Cabinet, helping to formulate important national policies and coordinating the efforts of the various Ministries and other national government agencies. The head of the Cabinet Secretariat—the Chief Cabinet Secretary, is a Cabinet post filled by a minister of state. It is one of the most powerful positions in the Cabinet and often viewed as a proving ground for future prime ministers.

The Cabinet Secretariat is also where crisis management is supposed to take place. Laws under its jurisdiction include the Cabinet Act, various statutes relating to national security policy, the Basic Act on Cyber-security, the Basic Act on Intellectual Property, the Basic Maritime Law, various laws about urban planning, the Basic Space Act, and a number of laws relating to the national public service and their compensation. The Cabinet Secretariat is where national strategy is formed, and one of the places where the upper ranks of the bureaucracy interact with the political process directly.

The Cabinet Secretariat is also responsible for submitting legislation to be proposed by the Cabinet to the Cabinet Legislation Bureau for formal review, and then formally proposing the same to the Diet once the Cabinet processes have been completed.

In 2014 the Cabinet Act was amended to establish within the Cabinet Secretariat the Cabinet Personnel Bureau, which exercises more centralized control over top-level bureaucratic appointments within national government institutions. While a recent development, this appears to have has achieved greater centralized control over top level ministerial and agency appointments as well as generating concern that it will result in increased politicization of the bureaucracy.

6. The Cabinet Legislation Bureau

Together with the Budget Bureau of the Ministry of Finance, the Cabinet Legislation Bureau (CLB) is considered to be one of the most post powerful executive branch institutions. Any ministry that wishes to pass legislation through the Cabinet must undergo the vigorous vetting process imposed by the CLB. The CLB also provides legal advice to the Cabinet and other branches of government, including constitutional interpretations. In areas where the Supreme Court has not yet expressed a view or, as in the case of Article 9, declined to do so, the CLB's interpretation of the constitution is effectively final.

The CLB predates the existence of cabinets, with roots going back to 1875 and the establishment of the first modern Japanese government bureau devoted to researching and drafting legislation. This became a part of the cabinet infrastructure when the first cabinet was established in 1885. After World War II, the American occupation authorities considered it inappropriate to have an executive branch agency so intricately involved in preparing legislation and under their influence the CLB was disbanded. However it was re-established almost immediately after the occupation ended in 1952.

According to its enabling statute (the Cabinet Legislation Bureau Establishment Act of 1952), the CLB performs the following functions: (i) reviewing, commenting on and amending proposed laws, Cabinet orders and treaties to be submitted to the Cabinet for approval, (ii) drafting laws and Cabinet orders for presentation to the Cabinet, (iii) giving opinions on legal issues to the Cabinet, the Prime Minister and other Ministers; (iv) researching domestic, foreign and international law; and (v) other matters relating to the legal system.

For all its power the CLB is a small institution with just a few dozen personnel. It is comprised of four departments and a secretariat. The First Department is most important, as it is charged with giving legal advice to the rest of the government, including on constitutional matters. It also maintains a constitutional archive. The Second, Third and Fourth Departments are allocated responsibility for drafting and reviewing laws for specific Ministries.

Key CLB staff are elite "career" bureaucrats sent by the various ministries, through an informal allocation of posts. Their ranks also include prosecutors and judges on secondment.

There is said to be an unwritten rule that only officials originating from the MOJ, the MOF, the MIC and METI may serve as heads of one of the CLB's four departments. Moreover, despite notionally being appointed by the Cabinet, from its re-establishment in 1952 the head of the First Department has always gone on to become the Director General of the CLB. Prime Minister Abe Shinzō broke this long-standing practice in 2013 to appoint a complete outsider (a former MOFA bureaucrat) to the post in order to force the CLB to change its longstanding view that Article 9 of the constitution prohibits Japan's Self Defense Forces from participating in collective self-defense operations abroad with allies such as the United States. The desired change in interpretation was issued by the CLB and the appointment of the next Director General reverted to longstanding practice.

It is indicative of the degree to which the CLB (and perhaps the national bureaucracy as a whole) is isolated from the political process that Abe was widely criticized for riding roughshod over well-established practices to force a particular constitutional view on the institution and, by extension, the nation. Yet by law the CLB is subordinate to the Cabinet, which notionally appoints its Director General. An American president using her appointment powers to install heads of executive departments (or even federal judges) whose views of the law are consistent with her own would raise few eyebrows, yet for the Japanese Prime Minister to do the same was viewed as controversial. In fact, the CLB has a history of frustrating Prime Ministers seeking to do even slightly adventurous things abroad with the Self Defense Forces, such as participating in the American-led wars in Iraq and the Global War on Terror.

Compared to many top-level bureaucratic posts, CLB Directors General have comparatively long tenures (up to 3–5 years), and may survive several changes of Cabinet, though the practice is for the CLB Director to submit a proposed resignation every time a Cabinet resigns. Including benefits, the Director General is also said to be the most highly-compensated of all bureaucrats.[6]

It is also not uncommon for ex-CLB Director Generals to be appointed to the Supreme Court. For example, Yamamoto Tsuneyuki, the Director General displaced by Prime Minister Abe's 2013 appointment was subsequently appointed to the Court (where, ironically, given its reluctance to rule on article 9-related controversies, his views on the subject were unlikely to trouble conservatives like Abe).

The Director-General of the CLB is also one of the five top bureaucrats permitted to "assist" the Prime Minister and other Ministers of State when they appear before Diet plenary sessions or committee meetings (Diet Act, article 69; the other four are the President of the National Personnel Authority, the Chairman of the FTC, the Chairman of the Nuclear Regulation Authority and the Chairman of the Environmental Disputes Coordination Commission). Under article 63 of the Constitution the Prime Minister and other minister of state must "must appear [before the requesting Diet chamber] when their presence is required in order to give answers or explanations." The "assistance" of the CLB Director-General involves answering questions about the interpretation of the constitution or other laws presented to the Prime Minister or other Cabinet Ministers. This practice has been criticized as undemocratic and indicative of how much control over government is actually exercised by bureaucrats rather than elected representatives. When the Democratic Party of Japan came into power in 2009 they ceased the practice, but it was revived again in 2012.

Leaving aside the political dimensions of this practice, as already noted, providing constitutional and legal opinions to and, by extension on behalf of the government is part and parcel of the CLB's role in government. In the past it issued written opinions that were published and referenced almost as a source of law, though this practice was terminated in the 1960s. The CLB now focuses more on oral opinions and supposedly arrived at its historic 2013 decision to change its longstanding interpretation of article 9, through meetings at which no notes were supposedly taken.

The limited role played by the Supreme Court in interpreting certain parts of the constitution, particularly the "no-war" provisions of article 9 but also those provisions relating to the scope of executive powers, the interpretations enunciated by the government—whether by the CLB Director-General, the Prime Minister or some other Cabinet Minister (reading from an answer prepared by the CLB or other bureaucracy)—have significant weight and are cited as a form of quasi-law by scholars and practitioners.

In the legislative sphere, the CLB process for vetting legislative proposals submitted by Ministries and other executive branch agencies is extremely rigorous. The CLB has well-established rules for the style, formatting and language used in statutes. A ministry bureaucrat who submits a poorly-drafted proposal for review can expect a hard time.

[6] An interesting indicator of the balance between bureaucrats and legislators at the time the current constitutional system was established in the early postwar period is Article 35 of the Diet Act, which requires all Diet members to be paid no less than the highest-paid member of the national bureaucracy.

Because it essentially functions as a central clearing house for Japanese laws and regulations, part of its review also includes the use of consistent terminology across statutory regimes, and ensuring that new legislation does not result in conflicts with subsequent legislation. Something as innocuous as a Ministry changing the title of one of its own Bureaus may be quite complex because the CLB will require that every law and regulation referencing the title of that Bureau be identified and also amended. As a result of this process, instances of litigation resulting from the interpretive difficulties caused by different statutes using the same term in different ways as sometimes occur in the US system are rare, if not unheard of in Japan.

7. Ministries, Agencies and Commissions: An Overview

a. Introduction

As per the National Government Organization Act, most national government institutions are organized as a ministry (*shō*), agency (*chō*)[7] or commission (*iinkai*). As a general rule, ministries are headed by ministers of state and represented directly in the Cabinet, while agencies and commissions generally are not, with the exceptions being the National Public Safety Commission and the Reconstruction Agency which each have their own dedicated minister of state. This is a significant difference, since it means ministries are able to directly propose legislation and negotiate their budget through the Cabinet process, while non-ministries are not. Similarly, not being directly represented in the Cabinet the judiciary is said to be dependent on the MOJ for representation for such matters.

Note that until a wholesale reorganization of central government institutions in 2002, there were twelve ministries and ten agencies. The current structure thus reflects a restructuring at the turn of the century which resulted in ministries and agencies being combined. Prior to this there had been a Ministry of Labor that was separate from the Ministry of Health and Welfare, a Ministry of Transportation separate from what was once the Construction Agency, a stand-alone Ministry of Local Government and so forth. Also, both the environment and defense portfolios were held in agencies for much of their existence. Defense was not upgraded to ministry status until 2007. This history is helpful in understanding some of the jurisdictional boundaries that exist within and between Ministries today.

(i) Ministries

At the time of writing there were eleven Ministries. Together with their common abbreviations (as reflected in their website URLs), these are:

- the Ministry of Internal Affairs and Communications (MIC)
- the Ministry of Justice (MOJ)
- the Ministry of Foreign Affairs (MOFA)
- the Ministry of Finance (MOF)

---

[7] *Chō* is also the term used by local government bodies to describe parts of their administrative apparatus. This can lead to confusion. For example the *keisatsuchō* is the *National* Police Agency, while the very similar-seeming *keishichō* refers to the Tokyo Metropolitan Police Department. For those who spend most of their time in Tokyo and see the Metropolitan Police personnel patrolling in front of the Diet, the Prime Minister's residence and other key government buildings, the distinction may be particularly confusing!

- the Ministry of Education, Culture, Sports, Science and Technology (MEXT)
- the Ministry of Health, Labor and Welfare (MHLW)
- the Ministry of Agriculture, Forestry and Fisheries (MAFF)
- the Ministry of Economy, Trade and Industry (METI)
- the Ministry of Land, Infrastructure, Transport and Tourism (MLIT)
- the Ministry of the Environment (MOE)
- the Minister of Defense (MOD)

The role of each ministry in the legal system is discussed in more detail in the following section.

(ii) Agencies

There are also 21 national government agencies. With some variations, agencies generally exist and function as largely independent institutions with a particular jurisdictional remit but are nonetheless technically subordinate to another organization, whether the Cabinet Office, a ministry or commission. Some agencies (the Reconstruction Agency, the Financial Services Agency) may have a special minister (*tokunin daijin*) who is titular head, but will also have a Director (*chōkan*). With some exceptions, agency directors are appointed by the head of the institution they are a subsidiary of (usually a ministry) and, unlike ministers, may be career bureaucrats or even government outsiders. The following table lists the agencies and the institution which they are an external department of.

TABLE 3-2 NATIONAL GOVERNMENT AGENCIES

Agency	Affiliation(s)
Imperial Household Agency	Cabinet Office
Reconstruction Agency	Cabinet Office
National Police Agency	Cabinet Office → National Public Safety Commission
Financial Services Agency	Cabinet Office
Consumer Affairs Agency	Cabinet Office
Fire and Disaster Management Agency	MIC
Public Security Intelligence Agency	MOJ
Prosecutors Agency (Agencies)	MOJ
National Tax Agency	MOF
Cultural Affairs Agency	MEXT
Sports Agency	MEXTA
Forestry Agency	MAFF
Fisheries Agency	MAFF
Agency for Natural Resources and Energy	METI
The Small and Medium Business Agency	METI
Japan Patent Office*	METI
Japan Tourism Agency	MLIT
Japan Meteorological Agency	MLIT
Japan Coast Guard	MLIT
Secretariat of the Nuclear Regulatory Authority	MOE → Nuclear Regulatory Authority

* The use of "office" rather than "agency" is a quirk of the English naming convention; in Japanese the same term as the other Agencies (*chō*) is used. Similarly, the use of "Japan" in the English name of this and certain agencies is not reflected in the Japanese language titles.

** Here again, despite the English name, the Japanese same term (*chō*) is used as with all of the other agencies listed. Even more confusingly, the Nuclear Regulatory Authority has jurisdiction over what in English is called the "Japan Atomic Energy Agency" but which in Japanese is described as a research institute rather than a chō for NGOA purposes.

(iii) Independent Administrative Commissions

A third category of national government institution that should be mentioned consists of what are generally referred to in statutes such as the NGOA using the surprisingly generic (in both English and Japanese) term: *i'inkai* (commission or committee). To distinguish them from other types of *i'inkai* (such as Diet committees), the term *gyōsei i'inkai* (Administrative Commission) or *dokuritsu gyōsei i'inkai* (Independent Administrative Commission) is sometimes used. This book will refer to them as Independent Administrative Commissions or IAC.

The "Independent" in Independent Regulatory Committee refers to the fact that for the most part they are structured so as to be isolated from the politics of Cabinet changes, being comprised of commissioners all or most of whom serve for fixed terms. For this reason, despite its name, the National Personnel Authority (discussed below) is considered to be an IAC.

There are two types of IAC. First, there are those established under articles 49 and 64 of the Cabinet Office Establishment Act of 1999 and currently consisting of the Fair Trade Commission (discussed later in this chapter), the National Public Safety Commission (described in Chapter 8) and, since 2016, the Personal Information Protection Commission.

The second type consists of those established under Article 3 of the NGOA and sometimes referred to as "Article 3 Commissions" to contrast them from bodies whose statutory basis lies elsewhere. Each Article 3 Commission is attached to particular a Ministry, but its Chairman and Commissioners are appointed for fixed terms by the Prime Minister with the consent of both houses of the Diet. Currently this category of IAC includes:

- **The Environmental Dispute Coordination Commission** (under the MIC), which provides out-of-court dispute resolution mechanisms for environmental disputes.
- **The Public Security Examination Commission** (under the MOJ), which oversees the designation of and render dispositions regarding destructive or murderous organizations as defined under the Subversive Activities Prevention Act of 1952 and the Act on the Control of Organizations Which Have Committed Acts of Indiscriminate Mass Murder of 1999 (which was passed in response to the 1995 sarin gas attack perpetrated by the Aum Shinrikyō doomsday cult).
- **The Central Labor Relations Commission** is under the MHLW and discussed later in this chapter.
- **The Japan Transport Safety Board** under the MLIT and is tasked with investigating train, airplane and marine accidents and safety issues.
- **The Nuclear Regulatory Authority** (under the MOE) was established after the March 11, 2011 Fukushima nuclear disaster starkly demonstrated the detrimental impact of the collusive relationship that had existed between the nuclear power industry and the prior regulators under the MEXT (which was effectively charged with the sometimes conflicting goals of advancing the cause of nuclear power and regulating its safety). It is assisted by the Secretariat of the Nuclear Regulatory Authority.

b. *Leadership and Organizational Structure of the Ministries*

Before looking at the significance of each individual ministry within the legal system it will be helpful to identify some common characteristics applicable to all the Ministries. Many of these traits also apply with other executive branch agencies but are most easily understood within the context of the Ministries.

The principal law governing the organization of the ministries and most other central government organizations is the National Government Organization Act The NGOA establishes the basic rules of organization and jurisdiction of the Ministries and Agencies under the jurisdiction of the Cabinet, other than the Cabinet Office itself. Further details of the establishment and organization of each ministry are provided for in statutes specific to each ministry (e.g., the Ministry of Justice Establishment Act of 1999).

The basic structure mandated by the NGOA is as follows. Each ministry is headed by a minister *(daijin)* appointed by the Prime Minister (NGOA, Art. 5; occasionally the Prime Minister may "double hat" as minister for a particular ministry). In addition to the minister, each ministry also has one to three vice ministers *(fukudaijin)*, who are nominated to the Cabinet by the relevant minister for appointment (NGOA, Art. 16). Vice ministers are typically Diet members, though this is not a requirement. Vice ministers are not "ministers of state" for constitutional purposes.

Below the vice minister the NGOA also allocates to each ministry one to three parliamentary secretaries *(daijin seimukan* or sometimes just *seimukan)* who are appointed by the Cabinet at the request of the minister (NGOA, Art. 17). Parliamentary secretaries are also typically appointed from the ruling party Diet membership, and such an appointment is likely to be a common career path for an up and coming relatively junior member.

A 2014 amendment has also made it possible for Ministers to appoint a single special assistant *(daijin hosakan)* to work on special projects or areas of focus (NGOA, Art. 18). Such appointments are also made by the Cabinet upon the request of the minister, and area also typically Diet members.

The trinity of minister, vice minister and parliamentary secretary are commonly referred to the "three political roles" *(seimu sanyaku)*. Together they represent the titular political leadership of the ministry and, unless a *daijin hosakan* has been appointed, may also be the only part of the ministry structure that is both democratically accountable (all must resign when the Cabinet is dissolved, NGOA, Art. 16(6), 17(6)).

The degree to which any of these roles is able to exercise meaningful leadership is debatable. Cabinet posts are a source of political patronage for a prime minister, so changes are frequent, with Ministerial postings often lasting about a year. For example, from January 2000 through August 2016 no less than *27* different people had served as Minister of Justice. The MOJ may be an extreme example, but even the seemingly crucial post of Minister of Finance was held by 14 different persons over the same period.

The top career official in each ministry is the *jimujikan* or "administrative vice minister." As discussed later, in reality some ministries may have a more complicated hierarchy.

The NGOA provides a framework for the internal organization of the ministries (as well as of agencies and commissions). At the top is the *kanbō* or secretariat. All ministries are required to have a *kanbō* and they may be created within agencies if deemed necessary (NGOA, article 7). In the case of commissions, the secretariat is a *jimukyoku* or *jimusōkyoku* (NGOA Art. 7(7)(8), terms which are best also translated "secretariat" or "general secretariat," but which suggests a lower-ranking organization when compared to a *kanbō*,

Ministerial secretariats provide the administrative functions (accounting, legal, personnel, etc.) for the ministry and also centralize policy-making and execution for the areas within its jurisdictional remit.

Ministries must also establish internal bureaus (*kyoku*) to facilitate the performance of their respective statutory functions (NGOA article 7).[8] These may consist of two types of bureau: those which are subdivisions within the central apparatus of the ministry, and regional bureaus that enable the ministry to perform its functions nationwide. Most of the ministries have local bureaus (and in some cases branches of those bureaus) covering broad regions of Japan and providing nationwide reach. For example, the MOF has nine regional Local Finance Bureaus which. Any company engaged in a business that is subject to regulation by one or more ministries (which is likely to be most businesses), will likely interact with the national government through such local or regional bureaus.

Ministries, agencies and commissions may further subdivide their internal organizations into *bu* (departments), *ka* (sections) and *shitsu* (literally "rooms," though they may not physically be in separate rooms). This is left to other legislation or regulations (NGOA, article 7).

Another category of official body established by ministries and some Agencies and Commissions is the *shingikaitō,* which will be referred to in this discussion as a "Council" but the translation of which literally means "deliberative council (*shingikai*), etc." Councils include a wide variety of bodies established "*for taking charge of the study and deliberation of important matters, administrative appeals or other affairs that are considered appropriate to be processed through consultation among persons with the relevant knowledge and experience, pursuant to the provisions of an Act or a Cabinet Order*" (NGOA, article 8).

There is a tremendous variety of councils, some of which go by other names (hence the "etc."). A common feature is that they are generally composed of outsiders, academics, representatives of key stakeholders and other people whose views may be deemed relevant to their mandate. Some councils are large, with subcommittees and various study groups, and assist the relevant Minister with research, setting policy and considering legislation. Others provide initial dispute resolution mechanisms within specialized areas. The MIC's Telecommunications Dispute Resolution Committee and National-Local Dispute Resolution Committee, and the MOF's Customs Duties Appeals Board are examples of these. Others may control or review professions involving special professions: the MOJs' National Bar Examination Committee and the FSA's Chartered Accountant and Auditor Oversight Board are examples. More detail on some of the councils considered particularly relevant to the legal system is provided in the Ministry-specific overviews below.

---

[8] Agencies or commissions under a ministry are sometimes referred to as an "external bureau" (*gaikyoku*) of that ministry.

There is skepticism as to the degree to which some Councils actually provide independent advice or oversight rather than merely rubber-stamping the pre-ordained conclusions of the ministry they sit under. There is often little transparency regarding how their members are chosen and the agendas tend to be set by the bureaucrats. With respect to those bringing academic expertise to the remit of the Council, a common disparaging phrase sometimes used in the popular press is "*goyōgakusha,*" which implies a privileged relationship with government based on saying/delivering what those authorities want. Accordingly, the degree to which these Councils function in the way intended as opposed to providing a consultative window dressing that largely rubber stamps the plans of the bureaucracies that effectively control them (by providing the all-important *jimukyoku* or secretarial function that organizes the meetings and sets the agendas), may depend upon the specific body.

8. The Ministries

a. Overview

We can now turn to an overview of each of the individual ministries. For the most part it will be necessarily brief, since our interest is limited to understanding the basic organization, jurisdiction and the role it may play in the legal system. However, understanding the legal system as a whole, particularly in the field of business regulation, requires appreciating that in most spheres of activity there is a very clear system of vertically-integrated regulation, with specific silos falling under the jurisdiction of a particular ministry. In the past this was even more pronounced, but it is still possible to link individual types of financial institution, corporate form, legal forms of gambling, accounting rules and forms of gambling that effectively attach to a particular ministry.

To understand the ministries as they are today it helps to be aware of two significant events in the post-war history of the Japanese government. The first it the occupation era restructuring which resulted in the elimination of the Army and Navy Ministries, the dismantling of the Home Ministry into a number of constituent parts, the separation of the judiciary from the MOJ, and the "demotion" of the Imperial Household Ministry to the Imperial Household Agency. The second is the significant restructuring that took place at the beginning of the 21st century.

Note that the Ministry of Finance is typically considered the most important of all ministries. However, the discussion that follows puts the Ministries in the *kenseijun* (ordering protocol) used by the government itself, which reflects the age of the Ministry or a predecessor governmental institution that has been subsumed within it.

Finally to give some idea of the relative size of the ministries and some of the other agencies, the following table gives the number of employees authorized as of March 31, 2016.

TABLE 3-3 STATUTORY HEADCOUNT BY MINISTRY AT 3/31/2016

Category	Authorized Headcount*	Notes.
Cabinet institutions	1,175	Includes 16 "special" employees
Cabinet Office	13,934*	Includes 47 special employees Cabinet Office Total includes the following breakdown of agencies and commissions
Imperial Household Agency	1,004	Includes 47 special employees
Fair Trade Commission	480	(number of administrative staff)
National Public Safety Commission	7,797	= the number of employees of the National Police Agency, including 2,149 police officers
Personal Information Protection Commission	78	(number of administrative staff)
Financial services Agency	1,571	
Consumer Affairs Agency	320	
Reconstruction Agency	197	
MIC	4,816	Includes 1 special employee
MOJ	52,809	Includes 1 special employee and 11,799 prosecutorial agency employees
MOFA	5,959	Includes 163 special employees
MOF	71, 193	Includes 1 special employee
MEXT	2,115	Includes 1 special employee
MHLW	31,700	Includes 1 special employee
MAFF	21,661	Includes 1 special employee
METI	7,991	Includes 1 special employee
MLIT	58,573	Includes 1 special employee
MOE	2,953	Includes 1 special employee
MOD	21,062**	Includes 21,033 special employees
Total	296,138	

SOURCE: Gyosei Shokui Teiinrei (Cabinet Order Regarding the Headcount of Administrative Institutions).

* Actual number of workers may be less.

** "Civilian" component only; does not include approximately 230,000 uniformed members of the Self Defense Forces.

b. *The Cabinet Office*

In addition to the Cabinet Secretariat, there is also a *naikakufu* or Cabinet Office and even some Japanese people may find it difficult to differentiate the role of the two institutions. The Cabinet Office is the newer of the two, having been added to the Cabinet in 2001 to greater centralize control by the Cabinet and the Prime Minister. By law (the Cabinet Office Establishment Act of 1999), the Cabinet Office is charged with assisting the Cabinet and the Cabinet Secretariat implement important policies. It also performs a miscellany of oversight and coordination functions encompassing the system of honors, the imperial family, advancement of gender equality, food safety and consumer protection, financial regulation, disaster preparedness and numerous other areas of governance.

Although not a ministry by name, the Cabinet Office is often treated as such for various purposes. Although its titular head is the Prime Minister, it also has several ministers of state for special missions as discussed above. The Cabinet Office Establishment Act of 1999 currently requires the appointment of special ministers for Okinawa and the Russian-occupied Northern Territories, financial regulation, gender equality and demographic crisis, and food safety and consumer protection.

The Cabinet Office organizational chart is exceptionally complex. In addition to a number of internal departments responsible for various aspects of policy and governance, attached to it are several significant independent agencies and other bodies, including the Imperial Household Agency, which manages the affairs of the Emperor and the Imperial Family (and under the Meiji Constitution was a separate Ministry). It also has five external bureaus, the Financial Services Agency, Fair Trade Commission, Consumer Affairs Agency and the Personal Information Protection Commission, as well as the National Public Safety Commission (which is separately represented in the Cabinet through its chairperson). These are discussed later in this chapter, except for the NPSC, which is coveredin Chapter 8. The Cabinet Office is also assisted by a number of deliberative councils and regulatory commissions of various types.

(i) *The Fair Trade Commission*

The Fair Trade Commission (FTC) is Japan's principal competition regulator. It is an external bureau of the Cabinet Bureau that also still bears the occupation era stamp of an American-style independent regulatory commission set up to break up the wealth concentrated in the *zaibatsu* financial conglomerates that dominated the pre-war economy.

Established under Chapter 8 of the Anti-Monopoly Act of 1947 (AMA), the FTC is comprised of five members: four commissioners and a chairperson, all of whom who are appointed by the Cabinet with the approval of both houses of the Diet (AMA, article 29).

Commissioners serve a fixed term of five years, with eligibility for reappointment subject to a mandatory retirement age of 70 (AMA, article 30). Appointments made to a mid-term vacancy serve out the remainder of the term, and there are provisions for "recess appointments" if the Diet is not in session to approve an appointment (article 30). The chairperson is usually an ex-MOF official, but ex-prosecutors and former BOJ officials have also served in this role. One commissioner is likely to be a prosecutor and another a judge on secondment from the judicial branch. Lower level employees may also include personnel on secondment from the judiciary, the prosecutors agency and the

MOF (article 35 of the AMA requires the appointment of a prosecutor or lawyer to the FTC secretariat).

The principal laws under the FTC's remit are the AMA and the Subcontractor Act (technically, the Act against Delay in Payment of Subcontract Proceeds, Etc. to Subcontractors of 1956), which, as the name suggests is intended to protect subcontractors from abuse practices by general contractors. These are discussed in Chapter 11.

(ii) The Financial Services Agency

Until 1998 the Ministry of Finance acted as the nation's financial regulator. However, the collapse of Japan's economic bubble earlier in the decade followed by the high-profile failures of a number of banks and other financial institutions revealed an harmfully close relationship between regulators and regulated. The financial institution oversight function was placed in the newly-created Financial Services Agency which is now an agency of the Cabinet Office, with a Special Minister for Financial Affairs as well as the head of the Agency. Despite having been separated from the MOF, most of its personnel are former MOF officials and there are still exchanges of personnel between the two organizations. The FSA also performs some of its supervisory functions through the MOF's Regional Finance Bureaus. From 2012 until the time of writing the Minister of Finance Asō Tarō also controlled the Minister of State for Financial Services brief.

The FSA has jurisdiction over most laws and regulations relating to the financial industry, including the Financial Instruments and Exchange Act, the Trust Act, the Insurance Act, the Foreign Exchange and Foreign Trade Act, the Moneylending Business Act, the Banking Act and the laws governing the patchwork of other financial institutions which in the past would have been under a specific ministry (e.g., agricultural cooperatives under the Ministry of Agriculture and so forth). Some of these laws are discussed in more detail in Chapter 11.

The FSA also has jurisdiction over two important bodies. The first is the Securities and Exchange Surveillance Commission (SESC). Under the FSA Establishment Act of 1998 (Art. 6), the SESC is technically a *shingikai*, a deliberative body established to assist the agency set and implement policy, but is actually vested with various powers under the Financial Instruments and Exchange Act and certain other statutes. Its three commissioners, including one who acts as chairperson, are appointed for three year terms by the Prime Minister with the approval of both Diet Chambers (FSA Establishment Act, articles 12–13). The SESC plays an important role in protecting the integrity of capital markets and investigating misconduct and recommending sanctions in cases where they are warranted.

The second is the Certified Public Accountants and Auditing Oversight Board which, as the name suggests oversees the accounting profession. It also oversees the qualifying exam for becoming an accountant, and is responsible for administering the Certified Public Accountants Act.

(iii) Consumer Affairs Agency

Within the context of the legal system, the Consumer Affairs Agency deserves some additional attention. Japanese economic and business regulation has tended to be vertically-integrated based on ministerial fiefdoms. This has resulted in protections accorded to consumers being a patchwork of rules that depended upon what area of business was being regulated by whom; mobile phone contracts regulated by the Ministry of Internal Affairs and Communications, electronic products by the Ministry of Economy Trade and Industry, food safety by the MAFF and so forth. Moreover, regulators may have sometimes been perceived as caring more about advancing the interests of their regulatory constituents than the public in general.

The CAA was established in 2009 and, according to its enabling statute, is charged with ensuring proper labelling and other aspects of protecting the rights and interests of consumers across a wide range of industries, business practices and regulatory statutes. While it acts as a clearing house for consumer-focused information and a point of contact for consumer complaints, it has few powers and appears limited in its ability to do anything contrary to the interests of the primary regulators of specific economic sectors. That it is held in low esteem is suggested by the fact that in 2016 it was proposed that the agency be relocated to the regional city of Tokushima on the island of Shikoku.

Consumer protection regulations are discussed further in Chapter 11.

(iv) Personal Information Protection Commission

The PIPC overseas data privacy and offers a mechanism for resolving complaints over the misuse of personal information, which is protected by the Personal Information Protection Act of 2003. It is a so-called "article 3" commission, comprised of eight members and a chair.

c. *Ministry of Internal Affairs and Communications (MIC)*

The MIC is the primary descendant of the Home Ministry, which was established in 1873 but dismantled in 1947 by Allied Occupation Authorities. One byproduct of this was the Ministry of Local Government (*jichishō*), which in 2001 was amalgamated into the MIC together with the Ministry of Post and Telecommunications and a number of other miscellaneous agencies and institutions. As a result, the MIC now has jurisdiction over an eclectic range of government functions. It can become involved in a surprisingly broad range of activities, as is reflected in a PR campaign it ran on the theme of "The MIC is everywhere." The MIC also performs the role as administrator for the entire government apparatus, which gives it certain powers over other ministries.

Currently the MIC is comprised of its Secretariat, nine internal bureaus, two external bureaus and various other units. Broadly stated, with respect to the legal system, the MIC has jurisdiction over how prefectural and local governments are organized, and many of the taxes that help fund those governments, and the elections by which they are constituted (as well as national elections). It is also the nation's telecommunications and broadcasting regulator. It also administersthe Telecommunications Business Dispute Committee, which offers an initial forum for disputes among telecommunications business operators over issues such as colocation and access to facilities, and the National-Local Dispute Resolution Committee which seeks to resolve disputes between the national and regional/local governments. The MIC also oversees the postal system.

Key statutory regimes falling under the domain of MIC include: The Local Government Act, the Public Offices Election Act, the Constitutional Amendment Referendum Act, the Political Funding Act, The Local Public Finance Act, The Telecommunications Business Act, the Radio Waves Act, the Broadcast act, and a wide range of broadcast and telecommunications laws and regulations. Depending on the law (e.g. the Telecommunications Business Act), businesses in the regulated industry will most likely interact with the MIC through one of its regional bureaus.

The MIC also has a Policy Review Bureau. New legislative programs often contain requirements that they be reviewed after a certain number of years. Through this bureau the MIC thus sometimes gets to second-guess the legislative efforts of other ministries.

d. Ministry of Justice (MOJ)

(i) Overview

Of all the institutions of the executive branch, the MOJ deserves the most attention in connection with the functioning of the legal system. It is arguably as important as the court system itself. Accordingly, this chapter will devote considerably more attention to the MOJ than it does to any of the other ministries.

First let us begin with the name. In Japanese it contains no reference to "justice." *Hōmushō* is the Japanese term, but *hōmu* simply means "legal affairs." The regional *hōmukyoku* under the MOJ's jurisdiction and discussed later in this section are referred to in English as "Legal Affairs Bureaus" and in corporations the *hōmubu* is the legal department. The English term persists for historical reasons that are relevant to understanding the MOJ and its relationship to the judiciary.

The MOJ has its origins in the *Shihōshō* which was established in 1871. *Shihō* means "to administer the law," but is also used to express terms such as *shihōseido*, which is commonly translated "justice system." *Shihōshō*—the MOJ's original name—is still used today as the Japanese translation for the US Department of Justice. The English name "Ministry of Justice" thus traces its roots back to this original Japanese title, because until the formal separation of powers established in the post-war constitution, the MOJ actually administered the courts—the justice system—and the judiciary was effectively subordinate to it as to matters of personnel and administration.

The post-war separation of powers enforced by the new constitution thus meant removing from the MOJ the judicial part of its mandate. Confusingly, in Japanese the Constitution uses *shihō* to refer to the judicial branch of government, even though it is commonly used more broadly to refer to the justice system as a whole, including a number of components administered by the MOJ.

(ii) The MOJ, Prosecutors and Judges

The MOJ has its own personnel hired through the process described later in this chapter and its organizational chart typically shows public prosecutors agencies (*kensatuchō*) as being subordinate to the Minister of Justice. However, the reality is that the MOJ is run by prosecutors. This can be confirmed simply by asking a Japanese prosecutor or, if one is not handy, by referring to commercially-published directory of government institutions, which will show that most bureau-chief and other top positions at the MOJ are occupied by prosecutors, or even judges on secondment to the MOJ. Historically, every administrative vice minister of the MOJ in Japan's post-war history has been a former prosecutor, and as noted previously in this chapter, within the MOJ hierarchy the *jimujikan* is actually considered to be below several top prosecutorial officials.

As will be discussed in Chapter 4, there are significant personnel interactions between the judiciary and the MOJ, which can seem inconsistent with notions of constitutional separation of powers. The judiciary is also said to be reliant on the MOJ for negotiating its budget with the MOF. The MOJ also has primary jurisdiction over laws relating to the judiciary, including judicial compensation.

(iii) Personnel and Organization

The MOJ does not oversee vast public infrastructure spending or have regulatory jurisdiction over significant industry sectors. As Table 3-3 shows, however, it is one of the larger Ministries by personnel, reflecting its responsibility for prisons and other detention/correctional facilities. Corrections officers alone account for over 1/3 of MOJ personnel.

Organizationally, the MOJ is comprised of its secretariat and six internal bureaus. It also has two external bureaus, the Public Security Examination Commission and the Public Security Intelligence Organization. The MOJ website also lists as a "special" organization, the Public Prosecutor's Agency. The MOJ also has its own research and training institute (the "Research and Training Institute of the Ministry of Justice") at which MOJ personnel are trained.

(iv) Civil Affairs Bureau

The Civil Affairs Bureau oversees the civil justice system and has jurisdiction over many basic institutions relevant to it. These include the system of corporate and real estate registration, nationality and the family registration system. In addition it has primary responsibility for the administration and, when necessary, amendment of many key codes and statutes, including the Code of Civil Procedure, the Civil Code and laws relating to family and property.

The Civil Affairs Bureau has a national presence through eight regional Legal Affairs Bureaus and another 42 Regional Legal Affairs Bureaus, with 262 additional branches and 106 smaller outposts (all usually referred to just as "legal affairs bureaus"). The legal affairs bureaus are one venue where citizens interact directly with the national government through the system of registering corporations and interests in real estate. The legal affairs bureaus also deal with nationality issues, offer consultations on possible human rights violations and provide guidance to municipalities in the same geographic location with respect to the family registration system. They also function as regional outposts through which the MOJ can conduct litigation and other MOJ business.

The Civil Affairs Bureau derives some of its staff—including its head—from judges seconded from the judiciary. Serving as Civil Affairs Bureau Chief is said to be one of the key posts that can take a judicial career to an appointment to the Supreme Court.

(v) Criminal Affairs Bureau

The Criminal Affairs Bureau has jurisdiction over the criminal side of the justice system. It administers the Penal Code, the Code of Criminal Procedure and various other criminal statutes and thus has significant control over amendments made to them. The career path of a prosecutor who becomes administrative vice minister or Supreme Prosecutor will often have involved time as head of this bureau.

(vi) Corrections Bureau

The corrections bureau oversees the nation's prisons, juvenile detention facilities, training schools for juvenile offenders, and other criminal detention facilities. It also oversees a separate training facility for correctional workers.

(vii) Rehabilitation Bureau

The reintegration into society of criminal offenders is a central goal of the Japanese criminal justice system. One indicator of this is the existence within the MOJ of a separate Rehabilitation Bureau. As the name suggests, is devoted to the supervision and rehabilitation of paroled convicts, persons who have been given suspended sentences and juvenile delinquents. The Rehabilitation Bureau sits atop a nationwide system of 50 regional parole bureaus, one corresponding to each judicial district.

(viii) Immigration Bureau

The first experience most visitors to Japan will likely have with the nation's officialdom will likely be with the MOJ, through the Immigration Bureau (the next being the MOF (Customs Agency) officials in the baggage claim area). The English name is misleading as Japan does not actively encourage immigration, and the Japanese name *nyūkokukanrikyoku* would actually be more accurately translated "Entry Control Bureau." The Immigration Bureau controls the system for regulating the entry and residency status of non-Japanese in Japan. This bureau also regulates the nation's famously unwelcoming system of asylum for refugees and operates three detention facilities (two at the nation's principal international airports in Tokyo (Narita) and Osaka, and one in Nagasaki prefecture). These are where foreign nationals who enter the nation illegally or are being held awaiting deportation or action on applications for refugee or asylum applications are detained when necessary.

The Immigration Bureau has eight regional bureaus, which have several sub-bureaus and branches through which non-Japanese residents make visa-renewals and other changes of status. Note that the system of residence visas is separate from the requirement that resident aliens register in the municipality in which they reside (which is an extension of the same requirement that applies to Japanese people).

(ix) Litigation Bureau

Under article 1 of the Act on the Authority of the Minister of Justice in Litigation Affecting the Interests of the Nation, the Minister of Justice represents the state in litigation in which it is a party or otherwise participates (non-criminal litigation, that is; *all* criminal litigation being handled by the state through the public prosecutors offices). If the litigation involves another ministry or agency, an independent administrative corporation, local government or a variety of public or quasi-public corporations such as pension funds, Japan Post and even such quasi-governmental bodies as the Japan Horseracing Federation, the minister may allow the litigation to be handled by personnel from the applicable institution. However, in all cases the Minister of Justice retains ultimate control over the direction of the case and the government's involvement in it.

The Litigation Bureau is primarily responsible for the state's involvement in litigation. It was re-established in 2015 after a decade hiatus during which its functions were performed out of the MOJ Secretariat. The Litigation Bureau has its own lower level secretariat and a number of sections including three devoted to the principal types of litigation in which the Bureau becomes involved: civil, administrative and tax.

It is not uncommon for some of the personnel involved in this role at the MOJ to also be judges on secondment. The MOJ being run by prosecutors whose expertise and training is weighted on the criminal side, the judiciary is considered a source of expertise and experience in civil and administrative litigation. As has happened in certain well-known examples of administrative litigation, judges who perform this role on behalf of the government may go back to the judiciary and hear similar types of cases as judges, giving rise to questions about impartiality and separation of powers.

(x) Human Rights Bureau

The Human Rights Bureau is charged with investigating human rights problems, spreading awareness of human rights, consulting with victims of human rights violations, and related activities. As already described, however, the MOJ has jurisdiction over many of the instrumentalities of state power which in any system of government are most readily associated with the possibility of human rights abuse. This includes not only prisons and other detention facilities, but also the death penalty and the family registration system which, as discussed elsewhere, institutionalizes various forms of discrimination in the sphere of family and personal status. The MOJ also administers the asylum process for people fleeing human rights abuse elsewhere in the world. Finally, as already noted, through the Litigation Bureau the MOJ acts as defense counsel in cases brought against the state asserting violations of constitutional rights.

Perhaps unsurprisingly, therefore, when the Human Rights Bureau performs its role of advancing and expanding awareness of human rights, it does so in a way which almost completely disassociates them from the text of the constitution or the numerous human rights conventions that Japan has joined. Instead the Bureau tends to focus on the elimination of various forms of discrimination by private parties rather than human rights violations by government actors. Eliminating discrimination is a worthwhile government goal, of course, but the bureau's approach necessarily involves ignoring discriminatory systems embedded in law and policy, such as the various forms of legal discrimination based on gender, nationality and birth status embedded in the family registry system. Prolonged detention and coercive interrogations, long identified as a persistent and problematic feature of the Japanese criminal justice system as discussed in Chapter 8, also do not feature in human rights discourse led by the Human Rights Bureau.

(xi) Public Prosecutors Agencies

See discussion at Chapter 8.

(xii) Public Security Intelligence Agency (PSIA)

As its name suggests, the PSIA is one of the nation's intelligence agencies, and devotes particular energy to countering subversive organizations. It has been described as the closest Japan has to an FBI, though being much smaller in scale and jurisdiction, the comparison may not be appropriate. The PSIA maintains a regional presence in locations corresponding to the eight regional legal affairs bureaus. It has its own training institute.

(xiii) Public Security Examination Commission (PSEC)

The PSEC oversees the designation and supervision of organizations that have been deemed problematic under specific statues, such as the Subversive Activities Prevention Act and the Act on the Control of Organizations Which Have Committed Acts of Indiscriminate Mass Murder, which was passed after the 1995 sarin gas attack by the Aum Doomsday cult.

(xiv) Legislative Council of the Minister of Justice

While there are various legislative councils spread out through the ministries, the Legislative Council of the Minister of Justice bears special mention. It has existed since 1949 and its approximately 20 members (scholars and other people of suitable expertise and experience) assist the Minister in considering changes to the laws forming the foundation of the civil and criminal justice systems.

(xv) National Bar Exam Commission

The MOJ has oversight over the administration of the national bar examination (NBE), passage of which is generally necessary to become a judge, prosecutor or *bengoshi* lawyer (see discussion at chapter 7). Through the NBE system the MOJ exercises control over entry to the elite legal professions.

(xvi) Legal Aid Evaluation Commission and Hōterasu Legal Aid Centers

The nationwide system of *Hōterasu* legal aid centers that provides defense counsel to criminal suspects and defendants unable to afford their own, and various other forms of legal aid, is placed partially under the jurisdiction of the MOJ through this commission which evaluates the services performed by these centers. Some defense lawyers have pointed out the inherent conflict of what is essentially a system of providing defense counsel through a system under the jurisdiction of a ministry controlled by prosecutors. *Hōterasu* is also discussed in Chapter 7.

(xvii) Prosecutorial Fitness Commission

Pursuant to the Prosecutors Agency Act, prosecutors are subject to evaluations every three years, and may be subject to additional evaluations if they suffer from physical or mental impairments that prevent them from performing their duties. Its members include six Diet members, a Supreme Court judge and the president of the federation of bar associations. It also has the ability to remove prosecutors for misconduct.

(xviii) Commission for Special Appointments of Public Notaries and Prosecutors

This commission oversees the appointment of assistant prosecutors as prosecutors, and of public notaries (who are often former judges, prosecutors or other MOJ officials, as discussed in more detail in Chapter 7).

e. *Ministry of Foreign Affairs (MOFA)*

Japan gets along with most of the world, and has diplomatic relations with 194 of the world's 196 countries. The Ministry of Foreign Affairs dates back to 1869 and has existed for longer than any other ministry or agency without experiencing any change of its name. Because it encompasses all of the ambassadors and special ambassadors that are appointed, it has more *ninshōkan* (public officials whose appointments are attested by the Emperor) than any other ministry.

One of MOFA's bureaus is devoted to international legal affairs, with divisions devoted to the Law of the Sea, international judicial proceedings, treaties (general), economic treaties and social treaties MOFA has primary responsibility for negotiating treaties that are submitted to the Diet and for participation in international organizations. However, to the extent treaties or treaty bodies relate to specific industries or policy areas under the jurisdiction of another ministry, personnel from that ministry may well also play a key role. It is not uncommon for judges or prosecutors to be seconded to key consular posts.

One of the judges on the Supreme Court is usually a former MOFA bureaucrat. This is intended to ensure the court always has someone with expertise on international law. At the time of writing this judge was Keiichi Hayashi, who had previously been head of both MOFA's Treaty Bureau and its International Legal Affairs Bureau.

f. Ministry of Finance (MOF)

The Ministry of Finance is generally regarded as the most powerful of all the ministries. This is unsurprising given its control over both tax revenues and the process of preparing the budgets that are submitted by the Cabinet to the Diet. Any policy that another ministry wishes to implement or continue requires a negotiation with the MOF regarding the necessary budget allocation.

While its English name has remained the same, as with the MOJ its Japanese name has changed over time. Since 1869 until 1998 in Japanese it was known as the "*Ōkurashō*" which literally means "Ministry of the Large Warehouse" and first appeared as a term of law and government in the *Taihō Ritsuryō* of 702. The change in 1998 to the more mundane *zaimushō* (literally, "Ministry of Finance") was thus controversial, at least to some MOF bureaucrats. But they probably had little ability to block it given that it was driven in part by the transfer from the MOF to the newly-created FSA of regulatory authority over the financial industry after a number of high-profile bank failures that contributed to the nation's prolonged financial malaise, as well as high profile scandals involving unseemly entertainment of MOF regulators by bankers.

Through its powers over the national income and expenditures the MOF becomes involved in all aspects of governance. Even in connection with the financial industry, there is still a great deal of interaction between FSA and MOF personnel (at the time of writing the Director of the FSA was a former MOF bureaucrat), and the FSA is reliant on the MOF's regional finance bureaus to perform its financial regulatory functions. The MOF is responsible for managing national assets, and the Minister of Finance appears as the shareholder of record in the registers of those companies in which the national government still maintains direct stakes (including Japan Tobacco and telecommunications giant NTT).

The MOF has surprisingly few internal bureaus: the International Bureau, the Financial Bureau, the Customs and Tariffs Bureau, the Tax Bureau and the Budget Bureau. The last is widely acknowledged to be the most powerful ministerial bureau in the government. It also has the obligatory secretariat.

The MOF also has Regional Finance Bureaus which facilitate the nationwide reach of the MOF in its regulatory roles, such as confirming budgetary performance and managing national property.

Sitting under the MOF as an external bureau is the powerful National Tax Agency which administers most of the nation's tax regimes (except the local tax system, which is under the MIC). The close relationship between the MOF and the NTA is illustrated by the fact that the top official of the NTA, the Commissioner, has with a few exceptions always been a former head of one of the MOF's bureaus.

The NTA's "Large Enterprise Examination and Criminal Investigation Department" is able to conduct criminal examinations and make arrests in malicious tax evasion cases (and was made famous in the 1987 movie "A Taxing Woman" by renowned director Jūzō Itami). Within the NTA is the National Tax Tribunal, which has branches around the country and acts as the initial forum for disputes between taxpayers and the NTA, though panels comprised primarily of NTA officials but also a smattering of lawyers, tax professionals, and university professors as well as judges and prosecutors on secondment.

The MOF is also involved in various vices. Through the regime for taxing alcohol, the NTA effectively regulates that industry, and tobacco is regulated through both the taxation regime but also through the special legal regime governing Japan Tobacco, the former tobacco government monopoly and now a semi-private company. Among other things, Japan Tobacco has a statutory mandate to buy the entire crop of tobacco from domestic producers, which puts MOF in the odd position of regulating a small slice of the agricultural sector.

The MOF has jurisdiction over the laws relating to tax (other than local taxes, which are under the MIC), national finance, tobacco and alcohol. It also has an extremely close relationship with the Bank of Japan. Some might say "too close," the past practice of the *jimujikan* of the MOF becoming the BOJ Governor raising some questions about the BOJ's independence. Several policy-related government financial institutions—Japan Finance Corporation, Japan Bank for International Corporation and Development Bank of Japan—also fall under the MOF's jurisdiction.

The MOF also controls two key IAA: Japan Mint, which manufactures the nation's coinage, and the National Printing Bureau, which produces the nation's paper currency, passports, stamps and other similar items. It is also responsible for publishing the *kanpō*—the official gazette—and official compilations of laws and regulations.

g. *Ministry of Education, Culture, Sports, Science and Technology (MEXT)*

The Japanese government has had a Ministry of Education since 1871. The current sesquipedalian name dates back to the government reorganization of 2001 that resulted in a number of other institutions and functions being folded into its mandate.

In addition to its Secretariat, MEXT has six internal bureaus: the Lifelong Learning Policy Bureau, Elementary and Secondary Education Bureau, Higher Education Bureau, Science and Technology Bureau, Research Promotion Bureau and Research and Development Bureau.

The MEXT's jurisdiction touches upon a number of basic constitutional mandates. Article 26 of Constitution gives children the right to an education and obliges those caring for them to provide it. It also requires compulsory education to be free. The MEXT thus oversees the performance by the state of these constitutional duties and has broad jurisdiction not only over the system of compulsory education, but also over kindergartens (pre-K day care facilities being under the jurisdiction of the MHLW), universities and graduate schools.

Although public schools are for the most part organized and operated at the prefectural and municipal levels, the MEXT exercises a tremendous unifying influence over what is taught. The constitutional requirement that basic education be made available to all at no cost enables it to dictate what children eat (school lunches being provided and thus mandatory) and the textbooks that can be used to teach them. Textbooks are also subject to certification by the Minister of Education (etc.). Such mandates have been a recurring source of controversy, particularly with respect to descriptions in history texts of Japan's conduct during its wars as well as its colonial policies. This certification process generated what at one point was certified by the Guinness Book of World Records as the longest-running civil lawsuit. This was commenced in 1965 by Historian Saburo Ienaga, who had been ordered by the Ministry to change and delete descriptions of Japan's wartime conduct as part of the certification process. He argued this violated article 26 of the Constitution and constituted censorship prohibited by Article 21. In 1997 the Supreme Court broadly acknowledged the authority of the government to oversee the contents of public school textbooks (Supreme Court, 3rd Petty Bench Judgment of August 29, 1997).

The MEXT is also able to control what is taught at public schools through national curricular guidelines it establishes and revises regularly. Although not technically of a legal or regulatory nature, the Supreme Court has found these guidelines to have a law-like character by upholding the official sanctioning of a public school teacher for fail to teach in accordance with them (Supreme Court, 1st Petty Bench judgment of January 18, 1990).

Article 23 of the Constitution also guarantees academic freedom, and while this has been deemed not to apply to compulsory education, it applies at the university and graduate school level. However, many universities—including most of the elite universities such as Tokyo University and Kyoto University, whose law faculty graduates fill the ranks of the bureaucratic elite—are national universities (now "national university corporations") and thus fall squarely under the jurisdiction of the MEXT.

Since even private universities must be established and accredited under the School Education Act and the Standards for the Establishment of Universities (which despite its title, is actually a MEXT ordinance), higher education in Japan takes the form of a highly regulated industry, imposing numerous compliance burdens on faculty and administrators alike. In areas of graduate or professional education that impact the regulatory jurisdiction of other ministries—law and medical schools, for example—the regulatory systems can seem byzantine and intrusive.

The MEXT also has two external bureaus, the Japan Sports Agency, which was established in 2015 in anticipation of the 2020 Tokyo Olympics, and the Agency for Cultural Affairs. The latter agency has jurisdiction over, *inter alia* copyright and the system of designating buildings, traditional arts and even people as cultural treasures (see Chapter 11).

h. Ministry of Health, Labor and Welfare (MHLW)

As with the MEXT, the MHLW can be linked to a number of specific constitutional mandates, including the article 25 guarantee of "minimum standards of wholesome and cultured living," and the provisions of articles 27 and 28 relating to labor standards and organization. Compared to the ministries described above, the MHLW is comparatively new, having roots going back to the Bureau of Health Services of the Home Ministry before it was dismantled during the Allied occupation, with one of the fragments becoming the Ministry of Health. The freeing of workers to unionize and strike also saw the establishment during the occupation of the Ministry of Labor. These were ultimately combined in into the current MHLW in the 2001 government reform.

The MHLW has jurisdiction over a vast system of public welfare and benefits programs encompassing *inter alia*, the Welfare Act the national health insurance scheme, disability benefits and so forth. The day to day administration of many of these programs (the public income assistance system, for example) is performed by local governments. The MHLW also regulates health care, the system of licensing doctors and other medical professionals and the approval of drugs and medical devices. Because of its involvement in medical and pharmaceutical regulation, the MHLW is different from other ministries in having a significant body of elite cadres who are also qualified medical professionals.

Its Pharmaceutical/Food Safety Bureau is also involved in food safety. In this respect it has overlapping (possibly competing) jurisdiction with the MAFF and the new Consumer Affairs Agency.

As shown in the Table 3-3, the MHLW is one of the larger ministries in terms of personnel. This is reflected in its ten central bureaus as well as a nationwide network of Health and Welfare Bureaus that oversee and coordinate the implementation of relevant policies. These bureaus are also the home of Narcotics Agents, the approximately three hundred specialized law enforcement officers under the MHLW dedicated to drug-related offenses. They are the only category of law enforcement personnel who can legally conduct "sting" operations.

The MHLW also controls the nation's complex system of employment regulation. Its network of prefectural labor bureaus provides nationwide oversight. These also coordinate with the network of local "Hello Work" employment security offices (which provide employment support for the unemployed) and Labor Standards Inspection Offices. Labor Standards Inspections Offices enforce employment rules and have on their staff Labor Standards Inspectors, who have broad powers to investigate criminal violations of employment laws, including powers of arrest (which are rarely used).

— *Labor Relations Commissions*

An external bureau of the MHLW worth mentioning in the context of the legal system is the Central Labor Relations Committee (CLRC) and the system of subsidiary Prefectural Labor Relations Committees (PRLC) under it. Labor relations committees were established as a way to resolve disputes between unions and management, though major disputes of this sort are relatively uncommon today.

This system of Labor Relations Committees was set up pursuant to the Labor Union Act of 1945 (LUA) in the immediate aftermath of World War II at a time when there was widespread unemployment and poverty, millions of demobilized war veterans returning to Japan and mass strikes by newly-organized workers. While most visitors to Japan find it to be extremely peaceful and well-ordered and Japanese people themselves are likely appreciative of this aspect of their society. However, it is important to be cognizant of the fact that at various times in the not too-distant past the nation was wracked by widespread, disruptive, sometimes highly politicized strikes and other actions by organized labor. This experience has informed the Japanese response to dealing with these types of disputes and the roles of the labor relations commissions.

Under the LUA, labor relations commissions perform three basic functions: (1) conducting investigations to ensure that employers are respecting workers' rights to unionize, (2) mediating disputes between unions and employers over wages and other working conditions and (3) resolving disputes between individual workers and employers.

Although the CLRC and PLRC were established at a time of widespread labor unrest, over time a combination of economic growth, a shift from blue collar to white collar jobs, privatization (some of the most disruptive strikes were by employees of the national railway system which was broken up and privatized in 1987), decreased union membership in general, and the transformation of many unions into comparatively docile "in-house" unions, have resulted in many commissions having a small case load. While a decline in union vs. management disputes has seen a parallel increase in disputes between individual workers and management, these are now more likely to be resolved through the comparatively new (established in 2004) system of Labor Tribunals discussed at Chapter 10.

The CLRC is comprised of 45 commissioners who are appointed by the Prime Minister for two year terms (LUA, art. 19–3, 19–5). Commissioners are supposed to be drawn equally from representatives of labor, management and the public interest (15 each). PLRC commissioners are appointed by the governor of the applicable prefecture, and while these may have fewer members, the requirement of equal representation by the three stakeholder groups is the same.

Initial dispute resolution functions are provided at the prefectural level by panels of commissioners drawn primarily from those representing the public interest but with participation from those representing labor and management as necessary. When acting in its capacity as a forum for dispute resolution the PLRCs have quasi-judicial powers to demand the production of evidence and hear testimony. Appeals from PLRC decisions are made to the CLRC, which also hears disputes involving certain categories of government employees.

i. Ministry of Agriculture, Fisheries and Forestry (MAFF)

As its name suggests the MAFF has jurisdiction over Japan's system of agriculture, as well as forestry and fisheries, much of the administration of the two latter domains being conducted through two external bureaus, the Forestry Agency and the Fisheries Agency. To the extent visitors to Japan encounter the MAFF at all, it would be through the agricultural and animal quarantine desks at the nation's international airports.

The MAFF oversees Japan's agricultural regulation which involves a byzantine system of subsidies, production restraints, import restrictions and other mechanisms designed to control agricultural production, food availability and pricing. In addition, it effectively has top-level oversight over agricultural land regulation that depends in part on designating some land "farm land" and some individuals as "farmers." Agricultural land is a special category of land subject to a special system of tax benefits and transfer restrictions.

The MAFF also plays a significant role in administering what is collectively a massive part of the financial industry, the JA system of agricultural cooperatives, which because of their role in acting as a full-service provider of business services to agricultural communities, are the only significant financial institutions not subject to the same restrictions on other businesses imposed on banks. These are discussed in Chapter 11.

j. Ministry of Economy, Trade and Industry (METI)

After MOF, METI is probably the most economically significant of all the ministries. In the past its predecessor, the Ministry of International Trade and Industry (MITI) was identified by some western scholars as playing a key role in implementing the industrial policy behind Japan's period of spectacular economic growth. Its name was changed in 2001 with the restructuring of the central government agencies.

Together with the standard ministerial secretariat, METI has six internal bureaus: (i) Economic and Industrial Policy, (ii) Trade Policy, (iii) Trade and Economic Cooperation, (iv) Industrial Science and Technology Policy and (v) Manufacturing Industries and (vi) Commerce and Information Policy. In addition it is represented nationwide through its eight Regional Bureaus of Economy, Trade and Industry.

As its name and internal organization suggest, METI is a key regulator in many areas of business and the economy, including energy, mining, manufacturing, small to medium enterprises (SME) and most forms of intellectual property through the Japan Patent Office (discussed below).

METI also seems adept at extending its jurisdiction into areas of interest of other ministries. For example, although the Companies Act is under the jurisdiction of the MOJ, the METI has also sought to play a role in reforming Japanese corporate governance. Similarly, although the Civil Code and the basic rules of contract are under the MOJ and most telecommunications and Internet-related laws are under the MIC, METI has jurisdiction over the law on electronic signature of contracts, IT security and certain other related areas.

Being heavily involved in fostering exports and international trade generally, METI also has a significant presence overseas parallel to that of the MOFA. The most significant is through the Japan External Trade Organization, an IAC that sits under METI's. Another related IAC under METI is NEXI, Japan's export insurance provider.

METI also sits atop three very significant external bureaus: the Agency for Natural Resources and Energy, the Japan Patent Office, and the Small and Medium Enterprise Agency (brief summaries of these are given below). METI also used to have authority over nuclear power regulation but this was transferred to MOE after the March 11, 2011 Fukushima nuclear disaster exposed an unhealthy incestuous relationship between METI regulators and the nuclear power industries that may have compromised the safety of Japan's nuclear plants.

(i) Agency for Natural Resources and Energy (ANPE)

The ANPE acts as regulator for almost all aspects of Japan's energy and natural resource policies including mining, fuel imports, power generation and transmission.

Although regulatory authority over nuclear power has been moved to the MOE, ANPE is still closely involved through its general oversight over and close relationships with the nation's electrical utilities.

(ii) The Japan Patent Office (JPO)

The JPO has jurisdiction over most intellectual property matters in Japan, with the exception of copyright, which is under the MEXT's Agency for Cultural Affairs, as already noted. The JPO oversees the system for applying for patents (*tokkyo*), which protect inventions involving new or improved technologies, utility model (design) patents (*jitsuyōoshin'an*), which protect a more limited range of innovations relating to design and functionality, as well as that for design rights (*ishōken*) which relate to physical appearance of a product. The JPO also administers the system for registering and protecting trademarks. Intellectual property is summarized in Chapter 11.

(iii) The Small and Medium Enterprise Agency (SMEA)

Over 99% of Japanese companies are SMEs and thus fall under the jurisdiction of the SMEA.

The Basic Act for Small and Medium Enterprises together with other laws provide a variety of definitions of what constitutes an SME. These definitions are generally tied to capitalization and/or number of employees, but may also apply (or not) depending upon the nature of the business a particular company is conducting and with whom.

Various benefits may accrue to SMEA status, including both subsidies and protections from the abuse of superior bargaining power by larger companies. However there are various thresholds which apply and which may vary depending upon the type of business in which a company is engaged. Typically a threshold of less than JPY 300 million in capitalization and/or fewer than 300 employees applies in manufacturing or construction with lower thresholders for wholesalers, retailers and service providers. Note that these thresholds do not actually distinguish between "small" enterprises and "medium" enterprises. The Companies Act also provides a separate definition of "large company" which applies for corporate reporting and other requirements. These topics are also discussed in Chapter 11.

k. Ministry of Land, Infrastructure, Transport and Tourism (MLIT)

Created in the 2001 restructuring out of the combination of two Ministries: Transport, the National Land Agency and the Hokkaido Development Agency, the MLIT is one of the largest ministries (by personnel). Through its 13 internal bureaus and its network of regional bureaus it exercises jurisdiction over transportation (although traffic regulation falls under police authorities). The MLIT has top level supervision over most infrastructure (transportation-related and otherwise) and urban planning. The northern island of Hokkaido having once been a frontier subject to special development programs that have been inherited by the MLIT mean it, rather than the Cultural Affairs Agency, has jurisdiction over various policies relating to the protection of the Ainu people and their culture. The Ainu were once the dominant indigenous population of the island.

Given its mandate, the MLIT has jurisdiction over a wide range of economically significant regulatory regimes, including construction standards, zoning, urban planning, maritime laws, and acts as the principal transportation regulator. It is also oversees the system of registering automobiles, as opposed to the licensing of drivers, which is administered by prefectural police.

The MLIT also sits over four external bureaus, the Japan Tourism Agency, the Meteorological Agency, the Japan Transport Safety Board and the Japan Coast Guard. This last agency is worth mentioning since it performs the role of the "police of the sea" with powers to investigate crimes and make arrests in connection with matters under their jurisdiction.

A niche part of the legal system under the MLIT is Japan's system of maritime accident tribunals. Nine such tribunals are located in key port cities around the nation. While the task of investigating the cause of shipping accident now falls to the Japan Transport Safety Board (and the Japan Coast Guard), the tribunals conduct quasi-criminal trial-like proceedings for purposes of determining fault in maritime accidents. The tribunal in Tokyo has jurisdiction over particularly serious accidents resulting in multiple deaths. Tribunal proceedings are conducted by a panel of three experts and a *rijikan* assuming the role of prosecutors and *hosanin* acting as defense counsel for the mariner whose responsibility as issue. A tribunal is empowered to issue administrative punishments—loss of a seaman's license or other qualifications. Appeals from tribunal decisions can be made to the judiciary.

l. Ministry of the Environment (MOE)

The MOE was created in the reorganization of 2001 by elevating what was at the time the Environmental Agency to a ministry and transferring jurisdiction over industrial waste from the Ministry of Welfare to it. In 2012, after the Fukushima Nuclear Disaster, regulatory authority over nuclear power was transferred to it in the form of the Nuclear Regulation Authority (technically an IAC) and its Secretariat.

The MOE has four internal bureaus, as well as regional bureaus. As a relatively new ministry with comparatively limited budgetary or regulatory clout it is generally regarded as one of the weaker parts of the national government.

m. Ministry of Defense (MOD)

(i) Overview

The MOD is the newest ministry, the defense portfolio having been elevated to such status only in 2007 through combination of its predecessors, the Defense Agency and the Defense Facilities Agency. It is the largest ministry by headcount, if SDF uniformed personnel are included (See Table 3-3).

Japan's military dates back to the establishment of a heavily armed "Police Reserve" in 1950 and the National Safety Agency. The former evolved into the Self Defense Force and the latter the Defense Agency. However, post-war pacifism and constitutional constraints meant that for decades the national defense establishment was not directly represented in the Cabinet and was constrained in its rule-making power. Elevation to a ministry means it is now able to negotiate its budget directly, request cabinet decisions and propose legislation directly, pass ministerial regulations and of course participate directly in cabinet decisions.

The MOD is comprised of a secretariat, four internal bureaus providing strategic planning, personnel training and management and "back office" functions such as finance with regional bureaus providing national oversight as well as administering military bases in Japan. The Acquisition, Technology and Logistics Agency is an external bureau of the MOD responsible for procurement and logistics. The MOD also controls two universities: the National Defense University and the National Defense Medical University.

Through the US-Japan military alliance, the MOD plays an important role in the nation's diplomacy. This alliances has seen US military bases on Japanese soil continually since the end of World War II, with what was essentially an occupying army being converted into an allied military presence after the end of the occupation in 1952.

(ii) The MOD and the Self Defense Forces

The MOD administers Japan's Ground, Air and Maritime Self Defense Forces. These are collectively referred to as the *jieitai* (self defense forces or SDF in English). Many people likely consider the SDF to be a separate institution subordinate to the MOD. In reality they are effectively the same institution, with article 2 of the Self Defense Forces Act of 1954 (SDFA) defining "SDF" as including the entire MOD organizational structure from the Minister of Defense down. The SDFA also makes it clear that the role of commander in chief of the SDF is performed by the Prime Minister, representing the Cabinet.

The relationship between the uniformed and civilian components is complicated in many democracies. In Japan there are a few additional twists. The first is the problem of trying to understand what the distinction between "civilian" and "military" even means in a country which constitutionally is not supposed to have a military. In the Japanese context it is common to talk of conflict between the *seifukugumi* (the uniformed component) and the *sebirogumi* (the suit-wearing component). The principal difference is a legal one, with the SDFA defining those categories of personnel who must wear uniforms. Most MOD personnel of both categories are *tokubetsushoku* (special) public servants under the NPSA (see Table 3-3).

Historically, the *sebirogumi* have generally been dominant—consistent with the concept of "civilian control" enshrined in the constitution, though not without a certain amount of mumbling for the lack of respect shown to the uniformed services. This is reflected by the relatively low-key role accorded to general staff, the completely absence of any *ninshōkan* (personnel whose appointments are attested by the Emperor) in the uniformed services and, by some accounts, the comparative scarcity and low grade of official honors bestowed on ex-military personnel as compared to ex-suit-wearing career bureaucrats.

(iii) Constitutional Issues

A major influence on the development, organization and activities of the MOD/SDF has of course been article 9 of the Japanese constitution and its interpretation. This is discussed at greater length in Chapter 6.

9. Incorporated Administrative Agencies

The taxonomy of national government institutions also includes a large number of what are generically called "incorporated administrative agencies" [9] (IAAs) but individually may be called Research Institutes (*kenkyūjo*), Centers (*sentā*),

---

[9] The Japanese term—*dokuritsu gyōsei hōjin*—would be more accurately translated "independent administrative corporation."

Organizations or Institutes (*kikō*), Associations (*kyōkai*), Funds (*kikin*) or other names. For historical reasons two—the Bureau of Printing and the Mint under the MOF, confusingly, are called "bureaus" (*kyoku*) in Japanese, though they are different from the internal ministry bureaus discussed above. The National Archives, National Art Museum, NEXI (Japan's export insurance provider), the National Cancer Institute, the Civil Aviation College and various other institutions also fall under the rubric of "IAA."

As of April 1, 2017 there were 87 such entities Each IAA is established and operates under its own implementing statute and secondary regulations, and falls under the jurisdiction of a particular ministry. There is thus a broad variety in the way in which they are organized and the purposes they serve.

A basic feature of IAA is that they perform one of three broad categories of public function—research, management of medium-term policy objectives or execution of administrative functions—but are isolated to a degree from government. They are, nonetheless, usually clearly located under the jurisdiction of a particular Ministry or Agency. The variety of IAA and their complex relationships with other parts of the government, and the status of people working for them make it confusing to an outsider whether they were part of the government or not, particularly as a good number have the word "National" in their name.[10]

IAAs have been the source of criticism for a number of reasons, including that at least some may enable Ministries to use their independent status and special, often more flexible rules to evade the strict scrutiny and restrictions that apply to national public servants in areas such as retirement age, policy-making, record keeping and so forth. Some observers have noted the accumulation within some IAAs of huge asset portfolios, including real estate, investment securities and massive retirement reserves (arguably unnecessary for entities that are funded from taxes) that, because of the IAA's separate corporate status, do not accrue to the benefit of the Japanese people in general.

On the other hand, to the extent some IAA's are purportedly "independent" corporate bodies, there are questions about whether their governance structures adequately isolated them from meddling in furtherance of political or bureaucratic interests. For example, one noteworthy IAA is GPIF (Government Pension Investment Fund), which operates the world's largest pension fund by assets has in the past been criticized for having inadequate governance, a lack of professional asset managers and being subject to political influence.

Some IAA perform roles relating to the legal system. For example the Environmental Restoration and Conservation Agency under the MOE) administers pollution-related health damage compensation systems. These include financial assistance to persons suffering from asbestos-related health problems, as well as pollution-related programs.

10. The National Personnel Authority and the Public Service

a. *The National Personnel Authority*

The National Personnel Authority is established under Chapter 2 of the National Public Service Act of 1947 (NPSA) and oversees the national public service, the

[10] A useful indicator is that the URLS for the websites of most (but not all) IAAs share the same ".go.jp" top-level domain indicator as Ministries and other government bodies.

administration of which is also governed by the same act. The universe of prefectural and municipal public servants is much larger and governed by a separate law, the Local Public Service Act of 1950 (LPSA). The MIC has primary jurisdiction over the local public service. The discussion in the remainder of this section will be primarily about the national public service.

The NPSA delegates to the National Personnel Authority broad authority to make rules governing the national public service, their compensation, appointment and dismissal. The National Personnel Agency also administers the national public service exams and conducts some of the training received by national bureaucrats over their careers. Some of these roles overlap with the jurisdiction of individual ministries and other national government institutions which generally have broad discretion to choose who they hire out of those who pass the appropriate exam.

Nominally under the jurisdiction of the Cabinet, the National Personnel Authority is one of the structural features of Japan's government intended to by isolate the bureaucracy from politics. Its establishment having been strongly advocated by occupation authorities, it retains some of the hallmarks of the US-style independent regulatory commissions that were introduced into the Japanese government system during the occupation but for the most part abandoned after the occupation ended, with the National Personnel Authority being one of the few survivors.

The National Personnel Authority is headed by three Commissioners, one of whom is designated President. Commissioners are appointed by the Cabinet with the consent of both houses of the Diet. They serve a fixed term of four years, subject to reappointment for a maximum term of service of twelve years. They are not subject to removal during their term except through an impeachment process initiated by the Diet and conducted by the Supreme Court, or if other circumstances apply (such as reaching the mandatory retirement age).

Commissioners may not be from the same political party or have held any significant roles in a political part during the five years prior to their appointment. article5(5) of the NPSA prohibits the appointment of two or more commissioners who graduated from the same faculty of the same university, a reflection of occupation authority's concern over the domination of the national bureaucracies by graduates of the University of Tokyo Faculty of Law (which persists nonetheless). At the time of writing the President of the National Personnel Authority was a former high court judge.

b. *The Public Service*

(i) *Constitutional Dimensions*

Japan's public service encompasses a wide variety of government and quasi-government employees. Before getting into some of these varieties, however, it should be noted that in Japan "public servant" or "public official" (*kōmuin*) is a term that has several constitutional dimensions.

The most important are probably those set forth in the first two paragraphs of article 15 of the charter:

> *(1) The people have the inalienable right to choose their public officials and to dismiss them.*

(2) All public officials are servants of the whole community and not of any group thereof.

In addition, those harmed by public servants are entitled to seek compensation from the state (article 17, State Redress Act of 1947). Article 36 of the Constitution also protects individuals from torture by public officials.

As noted later in this section, public officials are also subject to restrictions on their constitutional rights to engage in collective labor actions. Finally, under article 99 public officials are subject to a duty to "respect and uphold" the Constitution.

Article 73 of the Constitution charges the Cabinet with administering the "civil service." The Japanese word used here is *kanri*, a somewhat obscure term which under the Meiji Constitution referred to officials (and military officers) appointed through the exercise of the Emperor's prerogatives; essentially elite officials. The term is rarely used in formal contexts today but still carries a connotation limiting its ambit to only high level national government officials. Article 93 of the Constitution uses an even more obscure term "*ri'in,*" to refer to "local officials."

(ii) Definition

So what is a "public official (*kōmuin*)?"

There are several categories. First, as already noted a basic distinction is between national public servants (*kokka kōmuin*) and local (*i.e.,* prefectural and municipal) public servants (*chihō kōmuin*). The former are governed by the NPSA, the latter by the LPSA. *Most* national public servants are subject to the rules made by the National Personnel Authority, while local public servants are under the jurisdiction of the local government body they work for, as well as the MIC through its jurisdiction over local government.

Another distinction is between *gengyōshoku* and *higengyōshoku*, terms that might best be translated "non-managerial and managerial." *Gengyōshoku kōmuin* are those performing mostly "blue collar" roles such as driving, maintenance and so forth, and who although paid from public funds do not exercise any meaningful governmental authority. *Higengyōshoku kōmuin* are essentially "white collar" managerial workers who actually exercise some (possibly miniscule) form of governmental authority.

The NPSA (Art. 2) also provides for two broad categories of national public servants: *ippannshoku* (general) and *tokubetsushoku* (special). The "special category" includes the Prime Minister, Ministers of State, heads of agencies and various other "political cadre" level positions, SDF personnel and certain categories of MOD employees. It also includes the employees of other branches of government: judges, judicial clerks and other court employees as well as employees of the Diet. There are separate laws for such categories of special public servants, but for the most part they are subject to a regime similar to that of executive branch public employees.

Interestingly, Diet members themselves are not included in the statutory definition of public servant and were actually clearly *excluded* from the ambit of even "special public official" when the NPSA was first enacted. Although unequivocally a type of public official (Paragraphs 3 and 4 of article 15 of the Constitution referring to the election of public officials), they are not covered by the NPSA in part because article 1(2) declares that it provides "*exclusively for the standards for the administration of the civil service referred to in Article 73 of the Constitution of Japan.*" Inclusion of Diet Members here would thus imply they were subordinate to the Cabinet.

Under article 2(2) of the NPSA, "general" workers are defined as all national public servants who are not in the special category. Such workers will be the principal focus of the discussion that follows.

(iii) Public Service Exams

Historically, despite its many borrowings from Chinese legal models, pre-modern Japan never really adopted the system of public officials chosen through an elaborate system of examinations; officialdom was reserved for the samurai class and thus, essentially hereditary. After the Meiji period, however, Japan made up for lost time and now has an elaborate system of public service examinations designed to isolate government jobs from political patronage and nepotism.

The names and contents of the public service exams have changed periodically over time, a reflection in part of a never-ending struggle by politicians to "reform" the civil service, or at least render it less insular and/or amenable to centralized control. Rather than attempting to explain the details of the testing regime at the time of writing (which are likely to change), a few enduring characteristics of the system and broad categories of testing regimes will be noted.

There are national exams and local (prefectural and municipal exams). The latter may involve local content. Depending on the local government body holding them, they may also be held later in the year in recognition of the fact that many applicants will likely try first for the more prestigious national, prefectural and large municipality exams.

National public service exams consist of three different categories. The exam through which a person enters the national public service will be determinative of the category of public servant they become and how their career will likely progress.

The first category of exam might best be called the "cadre exam," though it is currently called the "*sōgōshoku*" (comprehensive worker) exam, and in the past the "Level 1" exam. Second, there are several *ippanshoku* (general worker) exams, which qualify passers to join the national public service as a general worker, but not in the elite category. Finally there are a variety of exams for positions with specific roles like emergency services workers, as well as those for general workers in the other branches of government, such as court and Diet clerical and managerial staff.

Note that passing the requisite exam does not guarantee government employment: it merely renders the successful candidate eligible to be hired by the relevant government institution(s). That said, the number of people who are allowed to pass the exam is based on anticipated hiring needs. Each ministry or agency has its own selection process and criteria for choosing people from those who do pass the exam.

As discussed in chapters 4, 7 and 8, most judges and prosecutors pass a separate qualifying exam, the National Bar Exam.

(iv) "Career" and "Non-Career" Officials

In the national public service one of the most commonly-made distinctions is between *kyaria* and *non-kyaria* officials. Confusingly, these are Japanized versions of the English terms "career" and "non-career," though both refer to career tracks in the public service. The former are the elite bureaucrats who have passed the top level "cadre" exam and go on to form the managerial class of the ministry they join or related agencies or institutions. The ranks of the "career" bureaucrats are dominated by graduates from Tokyo University, particularly its law faculty. By way of example, as of September 2016 of the eleven ministerial *jimujikan* administrative vice ministers, seven were graduates of Tokyo University's law faculty, and two were graduates of its economics faculty.

"Career" bureaucrats are typically taken on as part of an entering class that may consist of only a few dozen people, depending on the ministry or agency. They can expect to then go through a special career course that will see them moved through various roles within their ministry or agency, including postings to regional branches, secondments to other ministries, agencies or local governments, study abroad and other advanced training. They will participate in policy making, drafting laws and regulations and develop an extensive network of relationships with other bureaucrats as well as politicians. Although they will initially be promoted with the rest of their classmates in lock-step and can at least be expected to reach the level of *kachō* (section head), beyond that the competition for the few top level leadership roles, such as bureau or department head, becomes intense. Although mandatory retirement age for most public servants is 60 (with the possibility of remaining on in non-managerial roles at reduced compensation to the age of 65), those who do not make the cut are expected to resign to clear the field for their more successful peers. Giving them a financial incentive to resign is part of the *amakudari* system described later in the next section.

Officially, the top career bureaucrat in a ministry is the *jimujikan* or "administrative vice minister," Reality may be different depending on the ministry and pay grade. For example, because the MOJ is effectively controlled by prosecutors, the *jimujikan* is said to be only number four in rank after the Supreme Prosecutor, the Tokyo High Prosecutor and the Osaka High Prosecutor, each of whom receives a higher salary than the *jimujikan*. Part of this may be a function of the fact that prosecutors have a higher retirement age than most other public servants and will thus naturally be more senior than the *jimujikan*. Similarly, in the Ministry of Foreign Affairs the Ambassador to the United States is said to be above the *jimujikan*, and in fact the ambassadorship is often the next appointment for a MOFA bureaucrat who has made it to the administrative vice minister. This may also be a function of the higher retirement age for ambassadors, but it creates the odd situation where an ambassador is senior to the bureaucrat notionally above all ambassadors in the official MOFA hierarchy.

"Non-career" bureaucrats also typically serve out their entire working lives at their ministry or agency, but without the same breadth of experience or opportunities as those in the "career" category. It is theoretically possible for "non-career" bureaucrats to rise to leadership positions and even happens occasionally. Recent changes to the National Public Service Exam regime are also said to be driven in part to both reduce the "non-career/career" distinction and help break down barriers between ministries. For the most part, however, it appears that the career/non-career distinction will persist.

Finally, when discussing the careers of bureaucrats, particularly those in the elite category, it is important to be aware of their role in politics at both the local and national levels. Due to the comparatively early retirement age, many former bureaucrats continue to remain active in government and industry. It is not uncommon for retired officials to seek public office, both in the Diet and also at the prefectural level. The connections with the Liberal Democratic Party and other political parties they develop through their careers may render them attractive candidates. Nine of Japan's post-war prime ministers were former bureaucrats (the most recent example being Kiichi

Miyazawa, 1991–1993). At the prefectural level, a 2014 study revealed that 28 of 47 prefectural governors were former national government bureaucrats.

Involvement in prefectural and municipal politics may also begin before a bureaucrat even leaves government service due to the widespread practice of ministries seconding personnel to governments at these levels. Under the pre-war system prefectural governors were generally appointed from the ranks of Home Ministry officials, the constitutional requirement that both executives and assemblies of local governments be elected. However, this does not prevent the seconding of elite officials from ministries to local governments as vice-governors and vice-mayors. As of October 1 2017, 1,794 national officials were on secondment to prefectural and local governments, with hundreds in high level positions including scores of vice-governors and vice-mayors. Such arrangements were dominated by the MIC (which has jurisdiction over local government affairs) and the MLIT (which has jurisdiction over vast amounts of infrastructure spending). Local government personnel may also be seconded to ministries as a reciprocal part of these arrangements.

(v) Restrictions on the Constitutional Rights of Public Service Workers

Significant efforts have gone into isolating the public service from politics, at the expense of some of their basic constitutional freedoms. For example, article 28 of the Constitution guarantees the rights of workers to "to organize and to bargain and act collectively." Public servants, however, are limited in their ability to unionize and engage in collective bargaining and outright prohibited from striking (NPSA, articles 108–2, 105–5 and 98; LPSA Arts. 52, 55 and 37). Such prohibitions have been consistently upheld by the Supreme Court over the years on public interest grounds (e.g., Grand Bench judgments of April 8, 1953, Nov. 27 1963, Oct. 26, 1966, and Apr. 25, 1973). Ostensibly the National Personnel Authority plays a role in mitigating these restrictions on the constitutional rights of public service workers by issuing recommendations regarding salary increases and other benefits that national and local government employers are expected to follow as part of the bargain. Through these mechanisms, the possibility of Japanese public servants using strikes as a political tool as happens in other countries has largely been foreclosed.

Public servants are also subject to stringent prohibitions on other political activities, except, of course voting (NPSA, article. 102, LPSA, article 36). A significant difference between local and national public servants in this respect is that local public servants are not subject to criminal penalties for violations, whereas national public servants are (NPSA, article 110(1)(xix)). Moreover, the NSPA delegates to agency broad rule-making authority to define the types of political activity subject to such penalties (National Personnel Authority Regulation 14–7). This broad delegation of the power to restrict the exercise by public servants of the rights to speech, association and other constitutionally-protected freedoms was challenged and upheld in a case known as the *Sarufutsu Case* (Supreme Court Grand Bench judgment of November 6, 1974).[11]

The courts have continued to uphold such restrictions and the punishments used to enforce them. In 2012, however, the Supreme Court vacated the conviction of a low-level social insurance agency employee who had been arrested and prosecuted for delivering

[11] The case involved a postal worker prosecuted for putting up election posters for a communist party candidate.

Akahata, the communist party newspaper in his free time (Supreme Court, 2nd Petty Bench Decision of December 7, 2012).[12]

In addition to complying with the restrictions of the NPSA, national public servants are required to follow the National Public Services Ethics Code of 2000.

c. *Amakudari—Descent from Heaven*

Japan's government consistently receives high marks for government transparency and lack of corruption from organizations such as Transparency International. It is extremely rare to hear of instances of public servants demanding or being paid bribes to exercise their authority in a particular way.

One reason for the lack of corruption may be that public servants are generally well compensated and assured "lifetime employment" (a misnomer discussed in more detail in Chapter 11). Public service careers remain one of the top choices of college and high school graduates in Japan. While job security is an obvious attraction, another factor may be that some public service careers may prove to be as or even more lucrative in the long term than private sector employment. While government salaries may be somewhat lower than the private sector they are generally isolated from economic fluctuations. Moreover, those in the elite category may enjoy a variety of perks including subsidized housing in fashionable neighborhoods, opportunities to study abroad at elite universities and a system of benefits that compare very favorably to the private sector when contributions are compared to pay-outs.

Finally, for those who have served their ministry faithfully, there are reasonable assurances of post-retirement positions that will continue to provide an income until the age of 65 or even 70. Such positions may be made available to "career" bureaucrats in their fifties as a way of encouraging them to leave due to a lack of opportunities for advancement within their ministry.

This is called "*amakudari*" and literally means "descent from heaven." A related practice is called "*watari,*" which refers to the transition through a succession of different *amakudari* posts, each one resulting in a generous retirement package so that by the end of a *post*-bureaucratic career, an ex-Ministry cadre can expect to enjoy a moderately wealthy "real" retirement.

In the past, *amakudari* was quite open and readily facilitated by the private sector. Elite bureaucrats would retire into the boards of leading corporations, serve a few years and then leave to make room for the next retiree (after receiving a nice retirement pay out). The popular press reveals an understandable resentment of *amakudari* on the part of at least some Japanese people who may regard it as a form of endemic, institutionalized corruption (which it arguably is). It is also common to attribute *amakudari* as an ulterior motive of government policies.

Some private sector employers may of course see value in having former government insiders on the payroll, but it is also difficult to evaluate whether any particular arrangement involves any perceived coercion by the regulator. When a company or other institution is subject to highly-publicized regulatory sanction, it is sometimes rumored

---

[12] Efforts by the police and other government authorities to suppress communism and punish its practitioners whenever possible is a subtle but recurring them in Japanese politics and constitutional jurisprudence. The arrest of this particular individual reportedly followed a month of surveillance and reportedly involved over 150 police officers.

that one of the reasons why this particular instance of wrongdoing was "made an example of" is because of the institution's failure to accept *amakudari*. This may be exaggerated, of course, and is often impossible to verify but it is illustrative of perceptions of the practice.

Unsurprisingly, purporting to combat *amakudari* is politically popular, resulting in what seems to be a constant game of cat-and-mouse (or perhaps "whack-a-mole" is the better analogy) between elected politicians and the bureaucracy to stamp out the practice. Various restrictions that have been imposed include prohibitions on bureaucrats retiring directly into an industry they have previously been regulating. It is also less common to see them on corporate boards. However, since a great deal of the law-making process is heavily dependent on the bureaucracy, the ministries generally seem to succeed in developing new and different methods of *amakudari* that evade whatever restrictions are put in place. *Amakudari* into the private sector now seems to take place below the board levels through "advisory" or "consultancy" roles, or into non-public companies or financial institutions, making it difficult to obtain relevant information.

Ministries are also able to secure *amakudari* through IAA or a variety of other ostensibly private foundations or "public interest" entities that are in fact captive to a particular ministry or agency and may rely on it for funding either through subsidies, the outsourcing of work (policy-related research, marketing campaigns and so forth) or the embedding into the law of a role for that entity, as will be discussed shortly.

The retirement of elite officials into high-level posts outside government is the aspect of *amakudari* that received the most attention, but the practice also extends to lower level "non-career" officials who may end up doing more mundane jobs. A highly-politicized audit conducted by the Democratic Party of Japan during its brief tenure in power from 2009–2012 resulted in a highly-politicized audit and publication of extensive details regarding the manner in which such arrangements benefitted former government insiders. For example, the audit revealed that the photocopy services available at the nation's courts were being provided by an ostensibly private foundation that was actually full of retired court workers.

Amakudari has a number of baneful influences. It is identified as one of the factors involved in the accumulation of huge portfolios of assets in what are essentially government assets, but accruing to *tokubetsu kaikei*—the "special budgets" under the control of a particular ministry rather than the general budget. Much is made of Japan's burgeoning public debt, but less attention is given to the significant asset side of the balance sheet, many of these assets having been moved into *de facto* fiefdoms under individual ministries.

Also, because *amakudari* involves the creation of foundations ostensibly devoted to some quasi-public purpose, another result of the practice is said to be a stunted non-profit sector. Since the *amakudari* based public-interest foundations that do exist are ultimately beholden to the government and include former bureaucrats on their boards, they are generally unable to pursue the public interest by openly challenging government policies.

For example the Center for Human Rights Education and Training is, as its title suggests, devoted to expanding awareness of human rights in Japan. However its website reveals a characterization of what constitute human rights problems in Japan based almost entirely on various forms of private discrimination, rather than the more widely accepted view of human rights violations as things that happen in prisons and other aspects of the criminal justice. This makes perfect sense once one appreciates that the Center is essentially under the jurisdiction of the Ministry of Justice, which as already noted runs the prisons and the criminal justice system. A review of their board of directors conducted several years ago revealed former MOJ bureaucrats.

Since the unspoken goal of many *amakudari* systems is to ensure continued employment of people in their 50s and 60s, it also appears to have the result of reserving opportunities for people in that demographic group, at the expense of restricting new entrants (generally young people). As noted in Chapter 7, many of Japan's legal professions can be entered by passing highly competitive exams that limit entry (mostly by young people) while at the same time offering a largely unrestricted *amakudari* entry route for older people with suitable government experience.

More significantly, perhaps, given the key role they play in much of the law making process, bureaucrats are able to include in statutes or requirements that ensure *amakudari* systems generate suitable revenues for their intended beneficiaries. For example, the Companies Act requires the articles of incorporation of a new company to be attested by a notary. This entails the payment of a significant notarial fee (currently JPY 50,000) to a public notary, a legal profession comprised almost exclusively of retired judicial and MOJ officials (see discussion at Chapter 7). A special act on the copyrighting of software requires registrations of this sort to be made to a foundation designated by the Director of the Cultural Affairs Agency, and so forth.

Other examples involve requirements embedded in industry regulations that certification or accreditation from an ostensibly private body. For example, the *pachinko* machines used in one of Japan's leading past-times (and unofficial forms of gambling) are required to be certified for use by a body accredited by the National Public Safety Commission. The leading certifying body has a board that is full of former police officials. Collectively these subtle requirements can make some aspects of life and business in Japan strangely complicated and/or expensive.

F. THE BOARD OF AUDIT (BOA) AND NATIONAL FINANCES

An obscure government institution that nonetheless plays a constitutional role is the Board of Audit (*kaikeisensa'in*). Under article 90 of the Constitution, "[f]inal acconts of the expenditures and revenues of the State shall be audited annually by a Board of Audit." The BOA thus checks whether expenditures have been made in accordance with the budget.

In its current form the BOA is established under the Board of Audit Act of 1947(BOAA), though together with the CLB, it is one of the oldest parts of the Japanese government, having been first established as an independent institution in 1880. In fact, article 90 of the Constitution is very similar to article 72 of the Meiji Constitution in terms of the role envisioned by both charters for the BOA. Moreover, even under the Meiji Constitution the organization and powers of the BOA were decided by the laws passed through the Diet, rather than imperial decrees as was the case with other administrative bodies under that system. The BOA was also one of the few institutions in the Meiji system of government that could criticize the military—for poor bookkeeping, at least.

The BOA today is still an odd creature; an administrative agency it is independent of the Cabinet (BOAA, article 1) and, perhaps more importantly, the Ministry of Finance. It is headed by three Commissioners who are appointed by the Cabinet with the approval of both houses of the Diet (BOAA, articles 2, 4), unless the HOR has been dissolved in which case the Cabinet can make an interim appointment that lasts until a new Diet has been fully constituted (BOAA, article 4). Commissioners themselves choose which one of them will be President, the formal appointment to that role being made by the Cabinet (BOAA, article 3).

As with the National Personnel Authority, in order to isolate the BOA from politics and changes of administration commissioners are appointed for a fixed term (of seven years), with the possibility of a single reappointment. Commissioners cannot be removed mid-term unless convicted of a crime, however they are subject to mandatory retirement at the age of 65 (BOAA, articles 5(3), 7). If a vacancy occurs during the middle of a Commissioner's term, then the Commissioner appointed as a replacement only serves out the remaining term of the person (s)he is replacing (BOAA, article. 5(2). This is worth noting because as we will see in the case of other key appointments (Supreme Court judges, for example), despite roles at the top of some government institutions having terms of office that are either long or undefined, the combination of mandatory retirement age and the practice of appointing people already well into their sixties to them means there is often a significant amount of churn. In the case of the BOA, historically its presidents have only sat for a term of one or two years before retiring.

The BOA has broad statutory powers to enable it to perform its constitutional role of auditing the expenditures and revenues of the state, as well as other roles accorded to it by law. Its mandate includes identifying sloppy accounting practices by government institutions, improper expenditures and determining when indemnification should be sought in connection with misused public funds (BOAA, articles32(3),(4)). While it technically audits national finances, this extends to the use of national government subsidies, which means that essentially all prefectural and local governments may be required to account for the use of funds to the BOA. The audit process may also encompass private companies that do business with government entities as well.

Under article 22 of the BOAA, the BOA is required to audit a variety of basic aspects of national finances, including monthly expenditures and receipts, the books of any corporation in which the government owns more than a 50% stake, and funds, precious metals and securities handled by the BOJ on the nation's behalf. Under Article 23 the BOAA can also conduct discretionary audits on a much broader range of areas in which national finances or assets are implicated. Since 2005 the BOA has been empowered to report on problem areas outside the context of its audit of the annual fiscal report. (BOAA article 30–2)

Under article 11 of the Finance Act of 1947, the Japanese national fiscal year begins on April 1 and ends on March 31 of the following year. Most companies and other institutions follow suit.

Under articles 37 to 41, of the Act, after the fiscal year closes, each Minister and head of other national government agencies must submit to the Minister of Finance accounting reports for their areas of jurisdiction. The Minister of Finance, then prepares a consolidated accounting report (the "closing books") for that fiscal year for approval by the Cabinet. This process is typically complete by the end of August (by statute, the Cabinet must submit the closing books to the BOA by November 30; Finance Act Art.

39). The BOA typically conducts its audit from September through November, generally submitting it to the Cabinet in early November, which then submits it to the Diet later in the month.

Although the Constitution has the BOA submitting its audit report to "the Diet" what actually happens is it is submitted to each chamber by the Cabinet, and each chamber votes on it independently. The HOC has a permanent committee devoted to the closing books that reviews the report. Since 1998 the HOR has also had a permanent committee devoted to both reviewing the reports of the BOA but also supervising the national bureaucracy generally.

By some accounts, the BOA has been neutered in its ability to provide financial oversight on ministerial spending has been neutered by the development generous *amakudari* positions for BOA officials.

Chapter 4

THE JUDICIARY

Analysis

A. INTRODUCTION

Superficially, Japan's court system is very much a product of the current constitution. Together with the occupation-era Court Act of 1947, the charter appears to create the judiciary anew from whole cloth. Closer scrutiny of the main text of the Act appears to acknowledge little in the way of continuity between the current judicial system and the courts that existed under the Meiji Constitution. Even the building in which Japan's Supreme Court is located—an oddly angular, ultra-modern structure across the moat from the Imperial Palace—suggests a complete break from the past, and offers an interesting contrast to the headquarters of the MOJ, which offers one of the few surviving examples of a prominent pre-war government building in central Tokyo).

Yet there are numerous threads that tie the two different systems together. First and foremost being the judges who largely survived the occupation-era purge of government officials unscathed. This fact was a source of criticism from certain quarters (such as the Japanese Communist Party) who regard the judiciary as having been complicit in the rise of the militarism and authoritarianism that led Japan into disastrous military conflict.[1]

The Court Act Implementing Regulations of 1947 also provided detailed rules for the transition of cases pending under the old court system into the new, as well as the transition of judicial employees. Article 19 of these Regulations also contains interpretive rules for how statutory references to specific types of court under the old system should be read in light of the new courts established under the Court Act. One consequence of this was to equate references to the highest level of appellate court under the old system, the Supreme Court of Judicature (*Dai shin'in*) with those to the Supreme Court under the new system.

As a result, precedents of the Supreme Court of Judicature are still effectively binding as to interpretations of laws predating the Constitution where the Supreme Court has not yet issued a differing view. Article 5 of the Regulations specifies that Supreme Court of Judicature decisions are to be treated as decisions of the Supreme Court. Furthermore, under the current Code of Civil Procedure (e.g., article 318) and the

---

1 Continuity of judges may also have resulted in what might appear to be resistance on the part of some of them to the legal norms enunciated in the new constitution. In reality it may have often been a matter of busy judges who studied the pre-war laws and administered them for years or decades before the new regime was put in place doing things the old-fashioned way.

Code of Criminal Procedure (article 405) failure to follow such precedents can constitute grounds for an appeal.

Because of this continuity a brief overview of the salient features of the pre-war judicial system are in order. As with other aspects of the current constitutional system, the modern Japanese judiciary is based in many ways on a rejection of what existed before it.

B. HISTORICAL BACKGROUND

Chapter 5 (articles 57 through 61) of the Meiji Constitution contained the charter's relatively sparse provisions on the judicial system. The English translation of that charter describes the "judicature" as being exercised by the courts in accordance with the law, in the name of the Emperor (article 57).

Another thread of continuity with the post-war constitution can be found in the terminology used in the Meiji charter: "*shihō*" and "*shihōken*" both of which are translated in English as "judicature." *Shihō* means the "administration of law," and refers to the court system and the administration of justice (*shihōken* technically refers to the authority or power to administer the law). The administrative aspect of this term is significant. Under the Meiji system, the Ministry of Justice was named the *Shihōshō,* a term closer to the English title than is the case with the MOJ's current Japanese title (*hōmushō*), as already noted in Chapter 3. Thus, although the English version of the current constitution uses "judiciary" and "judicial power" as translations for *shihō* and *shihōken*, respectively, the Japanese terms used are the same as in the Meiji Constitution.

Not being a separate branch of government, the courts and judges had a lower status under the Meiji Constitution. Administrative authority over them was exercised by the Ministry of Justice, and within the universe of public officials even judges on the Supreme Court of Judicature were of a comparatively lower stature when compared to that of Supreme Court justices today. Judges also had less security in their positions, the constitution providing that they could only be removed for criminal convictions or disciplinary punishment but the rules of punishment left to statutory law (article 58).

The scope of jurisdiction of the regular courts was also more limited, with the Meiji Constitution specifically anticipating the existence of special courts (article 60) and providing for a special Court of Administrative Litigation to deal with claims of infringements of rights by the government (article 61). Examples of special courts including military tribunals and the special tribunals established within the Imperial Household Ministry under article 49 of the old Imperial Household Act for civil litigation between members of imperial family (but not the Emperor).

The Court of Administrative Litigation was established in Tokyo under an 1890 statute which allowed its judges to be chosen from the ranks of experienced officials and judges. That last presiding judge of that court went on to be a judge on the post-war Supreme Court, another example of continuity. This Court of Administrative Litigation was also limited in its jurisdiction to those cases set forth in separate laws or imperial edicts, and it was specifically not permitted to hear claims for damages brought against the government. Under a separate act, the court was also given jurisdiction over taxes and tariffs, the denial or cancellation of business licenses, water use, public works and demarcation of public and private lands. There was no system of appeals from its judgments.

The regular court system consisted of a four-tier structure organized under the now defunct Court Organization Act of 1890. At the bottom were the Ward Courts which had jurisdiction over minor civil disputes and criminal offenses that were decided by single judges.

Above the ward courts were the district courts, which had appellate jurisdiction for cases heard in the Ward Courts and initial jurisdiction over most other civil and criminal cases. The district courts also had bankruptcy jurisdiction and cases were generally heard by panels of judges. Above the district courts were the courts of appeal at which panels of judges heard appeals arising from cases below. An exception to its appellate jurisdiction was that it had initial jurisdiction over civil cases involving litigation against members of the imperial family (other than the Emperor, which was impossible, of course).

Finally there was the above-mentioned Supreme Court of Judicature which, having been established in 1875, actually predated the Meiji Constitution and the Court Organization Act. Modelled after the French Court of Cassation, it can be misleading to think of it as a "supreme court" in the model of the US or the current Japanese supreme courts. It actually consisted of over a hundred judges in Civil and Criminal Divisions. Most appeals to it were decided by panels of five judges, but an entire Division could sit *en banc* if necessary to prevent different panels from making differing interpretations in similar situations. The Supreme Court of Judicature also had initial and final jurisdiction over cases involving *lese majeste* or other crimes against the Emperor and criminal prosecutions of members of the imperial family.

In addition to this four-tiered structure there were other quasi-judicial institutions. For example police chiefs were also able to dispense summary justice in cases of certain minor infractions (which, conveniently, police authorities were also able to define using their own regulatory authority), essentially acting as judge in the trial of first instance. There was also a system of juvenile tribunals for young offenders, and departments within district courts devoted to conciliating family disputes.

C. THE ORGANIZATION OF THE POST WAR JUDICIARY

1. Constitutional Dimensions

Article VI (articles 76 through 82) of the Constitution provide for the judiciary. As with the Meiji Constitution, the terms *shihō*, and *shihōken* are used again but this time rendered in English as as "judiciary" and "judicial power," respectively.

By declaring the "whole" judicial power to be vested in the Supreme Court and such other courts as are established by law, article 76 can be seen as a rejection of the Meiji system under which certain types of cases were resolved through special courts as described above. Article 76 makes this clear by also explicitly prohibiting the establishment of extraordinary (special) tribunals or the exercise of *final* judicial power by any executive branch institution. One ramification of Article 76 in conjunction with article 9 of the Constitution is that despite having a large military in the form of the Self Defense Forces, Japan currently lacks a system of courts martial or special rules of criminal justice that apply only to uniformed service personnel.

Article 82 of the Constitution requires trials to be held in open court with certain limited exceptions for special types of cases. Article 37 also guarantees defendants in criminal trials a "speedy and public" trial.

Compared to the Meiji system, the Constitution also establishes greater protection for judges, who can only be removed by impeachment or judicial declaration of incapacity (article 78). A special process for impeaching judges through a court established within the Diet (article 64) exists as a form of check and balance, and is discussed in more detail later in this chapter.

Judges other than those on the Supreme Court serve for a term of ten years with "privilege of reappointment," subject to statutory retirement age (article 80). Constitutionally, such judges are nominally appointed by the Cabinet, but only from a list of candidates nominated by the Supreme Court. This suggests that in theory the Cabinet could decline to appoint individual judges nominated by the Supreme Court. In practice this has never happened, meaning that what appears superficially to be a constitutional "check and balance" between the branches of government does not actually function as such. The judiciary effectively controls the appointment and reappointment of its own personnel, other than Supreme Court judges.

That said, the appointment/reappointment process for lower court judges (other than summary court judges, whose appointments are discussed below), involves the supreme court administrative apparatus receiving recommendations from a Lower Court Judge Nominating Committee comprised of 11 members representing the bar, the prosecutors, judges and relevant "people of learning." This body receives relevant information about candidates for appointment/reappointment from eight regional committees (one for each high court district) comprised of five members, one from each of the three key legal professions, and two "people of learning."

Compared to the Meiji system, the present constitution also raised the status of the judiciary by establishing the Chief Judge of the Supreme Court as equal to the Prime Minister through the requirement that both be appointed directly by the Emperor. This equality of status is further reinforced by the Chief Judge receiving the same salary as that of the Prime Minister. The 15 judge composition of the Supreme Court, though not mandated by the Constitution, is also said to have been set so that there would be rough parity with the number of ministers of state in the Cabinet.

The Supreme Court is also vested with rule-making powers (article 77) in connection with the conduct of trials, as well as over prosecutors and lawyers, though it has not exercised these latter powers.

The Supreme Court is the only court specifically provided for in the constitution, and the Chief Judge of that court the only judge. Most of the finer details of the court system and the judges who populate it are set forth in the Court Act of 1947 as described in the following section.

2. The Court Act and the Organization of the Lower Courts

a. Overview

The Court Act establishes a four tier system comprised of five types of court: summary courts, district courts, family courts, high courts and the Supreme Court.

As the following table shows, the number of courts in Japan is impressive. Collectively they provide a judicial presence throughout the nation, including not just all major metropolitan centers on the four main Japanese islands, but on smaller islands with relatively small populations (and possibly a *bengoshi* attorney population of zero).

TABLE 4-1 JAPANESE COURTS

Court	Number
Supreme Court	1
High Courts	8
High Court Branches	6
Intellectual Property High Court*	1
District Courts	50
District Court Branches	203
Family Courts	50
Family Court Branches	203
Family Court Local Offices	77
Summary Courts	438
* Technically a "branch" of the Tokyo High Court	

What is equally impressive about the number of courts and branches is that this network of just over 1,000 courts and branch courts was, as of 2017, served by just under 3,850 judges (of whom approximately 700 were women). They were assisted by approximately 22,000 judicial employees of various types. Other than Supreme Court judges, whose numbers are established in the Court Act, the number of judges and other judicial employees is set by the frequently-amended Act on Number of Court Officials of 1951.

This body of approximately 26,000 people in roughly 1,000 courts handled an impressive docket. According to the Supreme Court's judicial statistics for 2015, the number of new cases and cases at all levels of the judiciary resolved were as follows:

TABLE 4-2 COURT CASES FOR 2015

Type of Cases (all courts)	New Cases	Cases Cleared
Civil/Administrative (other than family)	1,432,279	1,424,983
Criminal	1,032,791	1,030,590
Juvenile Crime (family courts)	94,889	97,825
Family (divorce, adoption, inheritance, etc.)	969,953	958,527
Total	3,529,912	3,511,925
SOURCE: Supreme Court Judicial Statistics.		

Simply dividing the number of cases by the number of judges (before taking into account those engaged in administrative roles as discussed later in this chapter), or even the total number of judicial employees suggests a judiciary subject to a burgeoning, perhaps even excessive caseload. The problem may be particularly acute in rural areas served by branch courts which can only deal with a limited range of cases, and may have only a single overworked judge, or no full time judge at all. Expanding access to justice through greater functionality of branch courts is one of the many agendas advocated by the JFBA.

b. Summary Courts (and Summary Court Judges)

A great volume of cases are handled through Japan's summary courts. The nationwide network of 438 summary courts accounted for over half (803, 626) of the civil cases and over two thirds (743,386) of the criminal cases cleared in 2015.

For those judges who have passed the NBE the mainstream judicial career discussed later in this chapter may involve postings at summary courts either as practical experience or a form of punishment. However, there is also a special category of judges who serve only in these courts. Under the Court act, summary court judge positions are open to persons having at least three years as assistant judges, prosecutors and assistant prosecutors, judicial clerks, family court investigators, MOJ administrators and certain other personnel in teaching roles at Supreme Court or MOJ training institutes.

Many of the nation's approximately 800 summary court judges appear to be chosen from the ranks of judicial and MOJ bureaucrats at or near their mandatory retirement age in those roles, which was set at 60 for most public servants until recently. Under article 50 of the Court act, summary court judges have a mandatory retirement age of 70 rather than the 65 that applies to most other judges. This suggests that it is a judicial role intended for well-experienced but non-elite members of judicial system officialdom near the end of their careers, a different approach from countries were small-claims court might serve as a training ground for young lawyers seeking to move into judicial positions.

Accordingly, when the subject of Japanese judges is discussed it is important to appreciate that not all of them have passed the NBE. Confusion can be compounded by the tendency of even the judiciary or other official sources to omit summary court judges when counting judges, particularly if the discussion involves the National Bar Exam and the process of qualifying as a *hōsō* legal professional (see discussion at Chapter 7). The Judicial Compensation Act of 1948 also establishes a completely different pay scale for summary court judges.

Just as with other judges, summary court judges are appointed by the Cabinet for a ten year term based on nominations by the Supreme Court. The Supreme Court has a "Summary Court Judge Selection Committee" comprised of representatives of each of the three *hōsō* legal professions, as well as "people of learning" (Supreme Court Rules on Selection of Summary Court Judges, article 3). This Committee in turn receives nominations for appointments to summary courts within each of Japan's 50 judicial districts from Summary Court Judge Nomination Committees established at each district court and composed of the chief judge of the district court, two other judges from the same court, the chief judge of the family court in the district, the chief prosecutor for the district, the head of the local bar association and two "persons of learning" (Supreme Court Rules, articles 15, 18).

There is also a law-based testing component to the selection process, though information on it seems deliberately sparse and it may exist as much to exclude undesirables than to ensure qualified people become summary court judges. Anecdotal evidence suggests there are actually two testing tracks; one involving a law-based exam that may enable eligible court, MOJ employees or other qualified hopefuls to move to summary court judgeships mid-career, and another that is putatively exam-based but is essentially a reward for judicial employees who have devoted much of their career to administrative roles within the court system rather than helping manage trials. Since these latter category of employees are much less likely to have accumulated the knowledge of trial procedure necessary to pass the exam, there are occasional allegations that this part of the process is "managed" to ensure they pass anyways. There is also a largely undefined role accorded to the chief judge of the high court having jurisdiction over the applicable appellate district being involved in approving nominees.

Cases in summary court are heard before a single judge. Under the Court Act summary courts have jurisdiction over minor criminal cases. Many of these result in the payment of fines, and summary courts may only impose punishments involving imprisonment or imprisonment with labor for three years or less for a narrow range of specific offenses such as theft or breaking and entering (article 33). A great deal of a summary court's criminal docket involves summary *(ryakushiki)* non-trial proceedings, as discussed in Chapter 8.

Summary courts also have jurisdiction over civil disputes (other than administrative claims) where the amount in dispute is JPY 1.4 million or less. As discussed in Chapter 7, specially-qualified judicial scriveners (a category of licensed legal profession) are able to represent clients in civil proceedings in summary courts. The jurisdictional threshold of JPY 1.4 million thus also represents a boundary between this legal profession and the *bengoshi* attorneys who have the authority to represent clients in any Japanese court. In 2016 the Supreme Court ruled that this jurisdictional threshold also applied to out of court settlement negotiations involving amounts in dispute in excess of JPY1.4 million (even if the settlement resulted in the client receiving less than that amount), thereby potentially excluding judicial scriveners from a significant part of the lucrative market for debt resolution services (Supreme Court 1st Petty Bench decision, June 27, 2016).

c. *District Courts*

District courts are the backbone of the judicial system. Japan is divided into 50 judicial districts, each of Japan's 47 prefectures constituting a judicial district, with the exception of the Northern island of Hokkaidō which is divided into four districts due to its size. With Hokkaido and Tokyo being exceptions, the district court for each prefecture is located in and named after the municipality serving as the administrative capital of that prefecture. Thus, the district court having jurisdiction over cases within Hyōgo prefecture is named the Kōbe District Court rather than the Hyōgo District Court.

District courts are the courts of initial jurisdiction for most cases, other than those clearly allocated to summary, family or high courts. Much of their docket time is devoted to resolving cases under the Code of Criminal Procedure, the Code of Civil Procedure, and other major procedural statutes such as the Administrative Case Litigation Act and the Bankruptcy Act.

District courts also have appellate jurisdiction over appeals from most civil summary court decisions. They are also the court of first instances in most administrative litigation. In special types of cases there are also geographical limitations on which court the case may be brought. For example patent cases may only be brought in the Osaka or Tokyo district courts (CCP, art. 6 and 6–2). Similarly, a 2015 amendment to the Antimonopoly Act transferred initial adjudicatory authority over anti-trust cases previously exercised by the Fair Trade Commission to the exclusive jurisdiction of the Tokyo District Court. As discussed in Chapter 10, large insolvency cases may also be brought in Tokyo or Osaka regardless of the location of the headquarters of the filing company. Branches (*shibu*) of district courts in other municipalities also have more limited jurisdiction than that of the main court (*honcho*), though this may be a function of the number of judges staffed to it (some branches lacking even a single full-time judge, meaning they cannot handle cases requiring a panel).

District courts are also an important part of the organization of the judiciary. Under the Supreme Court's Rules for Administration of Lower Courts (the "Lower Court Rules"), district courts are required to establish "departments" (*bu*) (article 4). The number of departments each district court will have is determined by the Supreme Court based on consultations with the chief judge of the court as well as the chief judge of the high court having appellate (and administrative) jurisdiction over it. There will usually be a certain number of civil departments and criminal departments, with each department typically staffed with 3–5 judges, enough to staff at least one three judge panel.

Most matters coming before district courts are resolved by a single judge, except for trials for serious crimes, appeals from summary court dispositions and certain other special cases, in which case panels of three judges are used (Court Act, article 26). At trial, the senior judge of the relevant department is the *sōkatsu* or the head of that department, and sits in the center of the panels of that department as presiding judge (*saibanchō*). The judge sitting to the right (called the *migibaiseki*) will typically have at least five years' experience while the one to the left (the *hidaribaiseki*) will typically be a "judge in training" with less than five years' experience.

Some civil departments may specialize in certain types of cases (e.g., bankruptcy, corporate). On the criminal side, there are a certain number of criminal departments but there will also be a *reijō gakari*, a judge or judges responsible for handling requests for arrest, search, detention and other types of warrants from police and prosecutors.

By way of example, at the time of writing an organizational chart and description of the Kyoto District Court showed seven civil departments. All but one of these were shown as handling "regular" civil cases. Only one department was shown as also handling administrative litigation, with another apparently devoted exclusively to bankruptcy, corporate reorganization, civil enforcement and other similar proceedings. Another department handled labor cases, and another intellectual property. On the civil side there was also a separate office (*shitsu*) devoted to receiving the initial filings and maintaining the court records. On the criminal side there were three criminal departments, a *shitsu* performing the same functions as on the civil side, and a *reijō gakari* for warrants.

The organizational chart also shows the summary courts and district court branches within the judicial district and under the court's administrative jurisdiction. According to the court's website this organization was populated by 54 judges at the main court and 8 at branches elsewhere in the district.

The various judicial departments of a district court come together under a "judicial division" of the court which is distinguished from its administrative division. Under article 20 of the Lower Court Rules, the Judicial Conference of the court is supposed to designate one or more judges of the court to be responsible for the administrative affairs of the court. In practice this is likely to be the chief judge of that court. The Chief Judge of the court is in any case is vested with authority to caution judicial employees of the court in connection with the performance of their duties (Lower Court Administrative Rules, article 21). Under article 24 of the same Rules, each district court is required to have a secretariat comprised of a general affairs department and an accounting department, with smaller administrative organs mandated for branch courts and summary courts under the jurisdiction of the district court.

The administrative aspects of the organization of the district and other courts, the role played by judges acting as administrators in this administrative apparatus, and the significance of such roles within the career system described in more detail later in this chapter are important to understand. They make the judiciary a very different institution than in countries such as the United States. The fact that the court system is as much a bureaucratic institution as any ministry described in chapter 3 is also important to appreciate in order to understand how courts decide cases, particularly those having an impact on other parts of the government.

Although notionally each district court is independent and equal to others, there is a well-established and clearly understood, hierarchy of district courts. The Tokyo District Court is by far the most important district court in the country, the Osaka district court second and so forth. Not only does the Tokyo District Court have jurisdiction over the most populous area of Japan (as well as the city where many leading Japanese companies have their headquarters), but with Tokyo being the seat of the national government it is also where a great deal of important administrative litigation and high profile political prosecutions are brought. As discussed elsewhere, certain types of actions can only be brought in the Tokyo District Court, with the Osaka District Court also being an additional option in some.

From the standpoint of judicial administration too, the Tokyo District Court is particularly important. With more than 500 judges staffed to it and its branches, it accounts for a significant percentage of the entire population of Japanese judges. In fact the number of judges staffed to the Tokyo District Court is greater than that of all the district courts within some appellate districts in other parts of the country. Moreover, although not technically staffed to the court, those judges on secondment to the MOJ or other executive branch agencies would also be under the administrative jurisdiction of the Tokyo District Court. Accordingly, the chief judgeship of the Tokyo District Court is one of the most important and prestigious *administrative* posts in the judicial hierarchy. This was illustrated by the 2017 promotion of the judge holding that role directly to the position of Chief Judge of the Tokyo High Court, a common stepping stone to a seat on the Supreme Court.

District courts are also where enforcement of civil judgments takes place, including those issued by family courts. Under article 62 of the Court Act, each district court has one or more *shikkōkan* or "court enforcement officers" (they are sometimes referred to in English literature on the Japanese courts as bailiffs, which makes it easy to confuse them with the different category of judicial administrative personnel who maintain order within individual courtrooms). Court enforcement officers are a special category of public servant who are compensated by the fees charged to litigants seeking enforcement of judgements. Civil enforcement is discussed in more detail in Chapter 10.

Court enforcement officers are chosen through a law-based testing regime, eligibility to sit for which requires at least ten years relevant experience. While it might sound like a job requiring youth and vigor, it has traditionally been a post-retirement job for judicial clerks. The statutory retirement age for court enforcement officers is set at 70, which is higher than the traditional retirement age of judicial clerks and other court administrators (60, more recently 65, subject to some limitations).

d. Family Courts

Unlike district courts, which existed in the same name under the Meiji constitutional system and performed many of the same basic judicial roles (deciding civil and criminal cases), family courts are a post-war creation. They represent the amalgamation under the Supreme Court of two very different institutions—the domestic relations tribunals that had previously existed as branches of the district courts, and the juvenile criminal tribunals that had existed under the MOJ. It is thus an odd institution having jurisdiction over an extremely broad category of civil cases—family and inheritance cases—as well as criminal jurisdiction in cases involving juvenile offenders.

One noteworthy feature of family court proceedings is that they are not open to the public. While this a common feature of family court and juvenile criminal trials in many countries, in Japan this treatment had to be reconciled with constitutional mandates regarding public trials.

With respect to family disputes, the Supreme Court has reconfirmed through a number of rulings that in most case the family court's role is an administrative, paternalistic one involving primarily private affairs through proceedings that did not need to be conducted or resolved as a "trial," and thus did not need to be conducted in open court (Supreme Court, Grand Bench decision of June 30, 1965).

With respect to juvenile criminal trials a similar rationale—that the process of arriving at decrees in such cases is not a "trial" subject to constitutional open court requirements—has prevailed. The non-public character of juvenile criminal trials has been criticized in recent years—particularly in cases involving serious crimes such as murder where victims or their family wish to participate. In 2008 the Juvenile Act of 1948 was amended to allow victims and surviving family members to observe proceedings in such cases, at the discretion of the court.

Family courts deal principally with cases arising under different procedural regimes than the district courts: the Juvenile Act, the Domestic Relations Case Procedure Act of 2011 (DRCPA), and the Personal Status Litigation Act of 2003 (PSLA). Under a special procedural statute the Tokyo and Osaka family courts (only) also have jurisdiction over cases arising under the Hague Convention on the Civil Aspects of International Child Abduction, which Japan ratified in 2014. Family court proceedings are discussed in more detail in chapter 10.

Family courts are also different in the composition of their personnel. There is no discrete category of "family court judges," though some judges may end up spending much of their careers in the family court system. However, a great deal of fact-finding at family courts is conducted outside the scope of courtroom proceedings by family court investigators (discussed at Chapter 7), who may be appointed by the judge if it is deemed necessary in connection with a conciliation and the issuance of a decree. The family court investigator report may be the most determinative piece of evidence relied on by a judge in issuing a decree on child custody or visitation matters. Family courts also have on staff doctors and other medical personnel.

Since a great deal of the family court caseload on the civil side consists of conciliation proceedings, much of it is actually handled by the family court conciliators (*chōteiin*) comprising a part of the panel. Under article 248 of the DRCPA, a family court conciliation panel is comprised of the judge who heads it and two conciliators. In reality, in many courts the judges may be too busy to sit in every conciliation session meaning the bulk of the work falls on the conciliators, together with the court employees involved, a judicial clerk and, if appointed to the case, a family court investigator. Article 250 of the DRCPA also allows the Supreme Court to appoint *bengoshi* lawyers with at least 5 years' experience to act as what are essentially part-time family court judges (though without actually calling them *saibankan*—"judges").

Family court conciliators are engaged on a part-time basis by the family courts from the community and chosen for their experience and social standing. Some are lawyers, law professors or retired family court personnel, part of the intent behind the system being to ensure that parties have access to legal knowledge relevant to the conciliation process—and possible consequences of its failure—without needing to hire a lawyer. It is now more common to hire counsel for family court proceedings.

Family courts and their branches are located throughout Japan based on the same judicial districts and organization as district courts. Some family courts also have local offices in summary courts to provide additional coverage. As with district courts, family courts have administrators and a chief judge. Family courts are located in Japan in the same fashion as district courts, though in some instances they may be in different locations within the same city as the corresponding district court. Although theoretically equal to district courts within the tiers of the judiciary, family courts are widely viewed as "lesser" courts. They lack any appellate jurisdiction, handle few "important" or newsworthy cases, and will typically have fewer judges than the corresponding district court in any case. For example at the time of writing the Kyoto Family Court had eight judges compared to 54 at the Kyoto District Court.

Within the family court system there is a further hierarchy, with the Tokyo Family Court being at the top. Hierarchy is also apparent in other administrative details. For example certain important family courts have a supervising family court investigator, and the supervising family court investigator of the family courts in the location of the high court of appellate jurisdiction (*i.e.*, Sapporo, Sendai, Tokyo, Nagoya, Osaka, Hiroshima, Fukuoka and Takamatsu) are responsible for supervising family court investigators at other family courts within the jurisdiction.

e. *High Courts*

There are eight high courts having appellate jurisdiction over the judicial districts within their geographical boundaries. The Northern island of Hokkaido has the Sapporo

High Court, the Southern island of Kyushu the Fukuoka High Court, the island of Shikoku the Takamatsu High Court. On the main island of Honshū there are the High Courts of Sendai, Tokyo, Nagoya, Osaka and Hiroshima. There are also six branch high courts, the Kanazawa Branch of the Nagoya High Court, the Okayama and Matsue Branches of the Hiroshima High Court, the Miyazaki and Naha (Okinawa) Branches of the Fukuoka High court, and the Akita Branch of the Sendai High Court. There is also a specialized branch of the Tokyo High Court that handles intellectual property matters and referred to in English as the Intellectual Property High Court.

High courts have appellate jurisdiction over cases arising from the family and district courts under them and offer an avenue of further appeal from decisions of summary courts within their respective domains (Court Act, article 16). They also have initial jurisdiction in certain "treason-like" offenses as defined under the penal code, though prosecutions are virtually unheard of.

Article 17 of the Court act also anticipates high courts being given initial jurisdiction over other particular types of cases under specific statutes. Examples include optional initial jurisdiction over *habeas corpus* petitions as well as mandatory initial jurisdiction over a wide range of claims brought under electoral laws, election-related litigation. Certain regulatory regimes also vest in the Tokyo High Court (only) initial jurisdiction over challenges to adjudications or dispositions by administrative bodies, such as the MIC (as to dispositions in connection with its jurisdiction over the radio spectrum under the Radio Act) and the JPO as to patent filings (Intellectual Property High Court only). Under articles 16 and 61 of the Attorneys Act, the Tokyo High Court is also the first court to hear appeals from decisions by the JFBA as to the denial of registration or disciplining of *bengoshi* attorneys.

Unlike lower courts where many cases are decided by a single judge, proceedings in high courts are usually conducted before a panel of three. In a limited category of specific types of cases, panels of five may be used. (Court Act, article 18). As with decisions of district court panels, there is no practice of high court judges issuing dissenting opinions.

High courts also play an important role in the administration of the district, family and summary courts within their jurisdiction. The chief judges of Japan's eight high courts thus play an important role within the national judicial bureaucracy, both with respect to the administration of judges but other judicial employees as well (as is evidenced by the fact that their appointments are attested by the Emperor, the same as supreme court judges other than the chief judge). As with district courts, in addition to having a judicial division comprised of criminal, civil and other departments handling trials, high courts have an administrative arm including not only a general affairs and accounting department, but a personnel department that plays an important role in the personnel evaluation of judges discussed later in this chapter.

Of the high courts, the Tokyo High Court is by far the most important. First and foremost its jurisdictional remit covers approximately 30% of the Japanese population, as well as the majority of leading Japanese companies. Moreover, as the court of appeals from the district court in the nation's capital, it also handles appeals from most important administrative and other government-related litigation. As noted above it also has exclusive or near-exclusive jurisdiction over specialized types of litigation including patent and antitrust.

As an administrative subdivision of the national judicial bureaucracy, it is by far the most important, having personnel management authority over approximately half of the judges in Japan, including virtually all on secondment to other parts of the government. As discussed in the section that follows, a posting to the Tokyo High Court can be a sign of a successful judicial career, one that may lead to a seat on the Supreme Court. One consequence is that despite being in a cosmopolitan and international city, the Tokyo High Court is reliably one of the most conservative courts in the nation. As noted later in this chapter, the chief judges of the eight high courts comprise a separate category of judge for statutory purposes.

3. The Supreme Court

a. Overview

Although described in singular terms, "the" Supreme Court is actually several things. First and foremost it is a court, of course, but even this aspect is complicated by its division into three panels called "Petty Benches" and occasional sittings *en banc* as the "Grand Bench." Second, it is also an administrative apparatus that sits atop the national judicial bureaucracy.

In fact, when scholars or legal practitioners speak or write of "the Supreme Court" more often than not they may be referring to it in this latter capacity; as an administrative institution. In this aspect it can be helpful to think of the Supreme Court as an additional "ministry"—a "ministry of dispute resolution" perhaps—as it may have more in common with the executive branch agencies described in Chapter 3 than the courts in many common law countries.

The Supreme Court also performs an educational function. It operates the Legal Research and Training Institute (LRTI) where judges, prosecutors and *bengoshi* attorneys who have passed the NBE receive their finishing training as well as the Training and Research Institute for Court Officials, where court administrators, judicial clerks and family court investigators received training.

This multifunctional aspect of the Supreme Court—which can be readily discerned from the organizational chart found on its English website—makes it very different from supreme courts in countries such as the United States.

FIGURE 4-1

Organization Chart of the Supreme Court

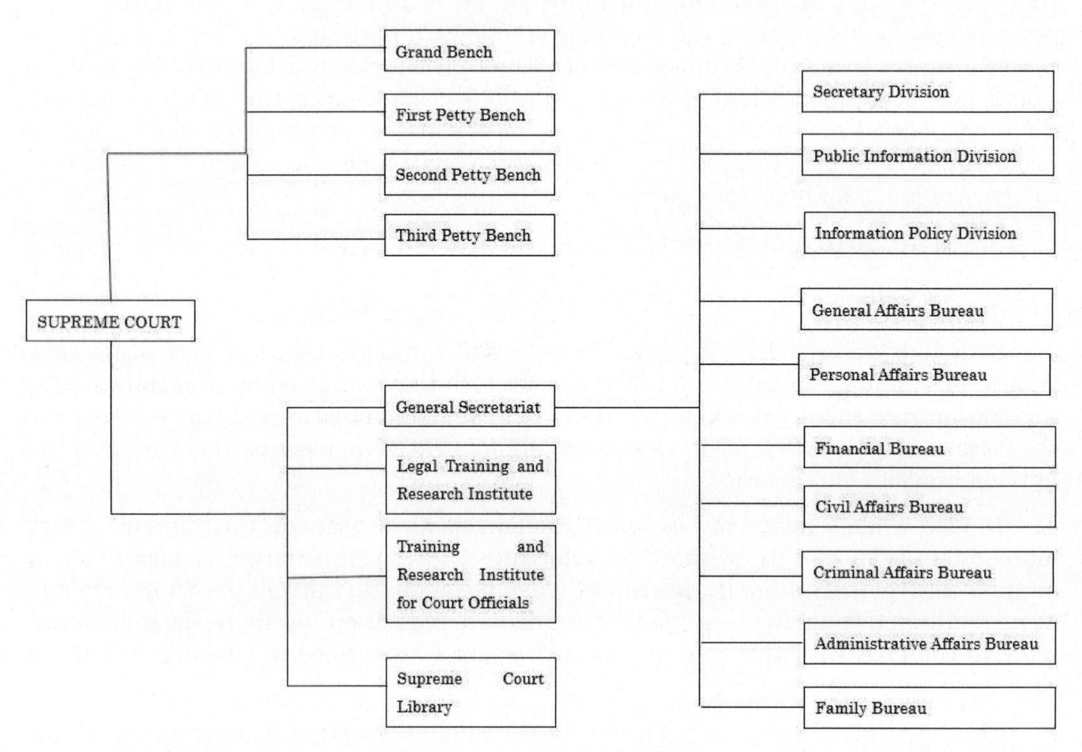

Source: Japanese court system English website at www.courts.go.jp.

b. Supreme Court Judges

The Chief Judge of the Supreme Court is a constitutional role (Constitution, article 79) appointed directly by the Emperor as designated by the Cabinet (article 6). Paragraph (2) of article 39 of the Court Act vests in the Cabinet the authority to appoint other Supreme Court judges, while paragraph (3) provides that both the appointment and removal of all the court's judges must be attested by the Emperor.

The Constitution defers to legislation the number of other judges on the court. Article 5 of the Court Act sets this at 14, for a total bench of 15. The constitution does not mandate any qualifications for appointment as a Supreme Court judge, though does permit the Diet to subject them to mandatory retirement at a certain age (Constitution, article 79). Currently this age is set at 70 (Court Act, article 50). The Court Act also imposes certain eligibility requirements on Supreme Court judges: they must be at least 40 years old and at least ten of them must be *hōsō* legal professionals (see Chapter 7) having at least ten years' experience as a full judge or twenty years' experience as an assistant judge, prosecutor, *bengoshi*, law professors and/or summary court judges or a combination of these roles (article 41).

Within this very broad legal framework, a variety of additional informal rules and practices have also become firmly entrenched in the Supreme Court appointment process. For example, despite a statutory minimum age of 40, for the past half century all appointees have been in their sixties. The court has also been overwhelmingly male—it was not until 1994 that its first female judge was appointed (Takahashi Hisako, a former MHLW official). At the time of writing, over 174 people had served on the Supreme Court since its establishment but only six had of these were women. Graduates of the law faculties of Tokyo University and Kyoto University have also been predominant among appointees.

Another practice that has developed results in the allocation of Supreme Court seats amongst key legal system stakeholders, subject of course to being acceptable to the Cabinet. Of the fifteen seats on the court, typically six are made from the ranks of the judiciary (usually former high court chief judges), two from former prosecutors, two from those who served in executive branch agencies such as the CLB and the MOFA, four from members of the bar (*bengoshi*), and one from legal academia.

These categories are not always as clear as they seem and further practices appear to have developed within them. For example, the four seats allocated to *bengoshi* typically rotate among former presidents of one of Tokyo's three bar associations or the Osaka Bar Association.

Even those appointed from the judiciary may actually have spent much of their careers as administrators or at the MOJ, the most famous example being Kagawa Yasukazu, who spent 29 of his 37 years as a judge on secondment to the MOJ before returning to an appointment within the judiciary.

Research by Professor Nishikawa Shin'ichi suggests that a career within the judiciary offers four identifiable "routes" to the Supreme Court. Each involves a combination of postings as chief judge of a high court (with the Tokyo High Court and, to a lesser extent, the Osaka High Court overwhelmingly being by far the dominant path) and time in at least one of four key non-judicial posts (i) head of the Supreme Court Secretariat, (ii) Director of the Legal Research and Training Institute, (iii) Chief Research Judge, and (iv) Head of MOJ's Civil Affairs Bureau.[2]

The existence of well-established paths to the Supreme Court also indicates that to a certain extent substantive decisions regarding at least some appointments to its bench are being made not by the Cabinet, as implied by the constitution, but by the Supreme Court itself. The government has acknowledged that the "opinion" of the Chief Judge is extremely important to making appointments, including that of his successor. The Chief Judge and the judicial administration supporting him can thus been seen as playing a determinative role in the court's composition.

It has also become well-established practice that the Chief Judge of the Supreme Court is almost always appointed from those existing members of the Court who had also previously been career judges. At the time writing 18 persons had held the post of Chief Judge since 1947; of them, all were male and all but three were graduates of the faculty of law at Tokyo University (the remaining three were from Kyoto University). Almost all were also former members of the career judiciary.

---

[2] SHIN'ICHI NISHIKAWA, SAIBANKAN KANBU JINJI NO KENKYU "KEIREKITEKI SHIGEN" WO TEGAKARI TO SHITE [RESEARCH IN THE PERSONNEL MANAGEMENT OF CADRE JUDGES USING "RESUME RESOURCES" AS CLUES] (2010).

c. *Supreme Court Judicial Retention Elections*

By constitutional mandate (article 79), the appointment of each Supreme Court judge must be ratified by the electorate at the first House of Representatives Election after his or her appointment. The details of this ratification process—which was modelled after the Missouri Plan system of judicial retention elections that had started to be used in some U.S. states in the decade before the Japanese constitution was promulgated—are set forth in the Law of the People's Examination of the Supreme Court Judges of 1947.

However, this carefully constructed, constitutionally required system of judicial retention elections been reduced to a largely meaningless formality for several reasons. First, the combination of appointing judges who are in their mid-sixties and the statutory mandatory retirement age of 70 means there is constant churn in the court's composition and judges have often retired before they can leave any meaningful impression on the public mind. Article 79 of the constitution anticipates additional retention elections for Supreme Court judges ten years after their initial approval by voters, but the last time a judge was on the Court long enough for this provision to apply was 1963. Thus, unlike the United States Supreme Court, the membership of Japan's top court is constantly anonymous to most Japanese people. Even some law professors and lawyers would probably struggle to name all fifteen members at any given time, and the average voter may not be able to name even one judge from the entire history of the court, let alone its current slate.

Thus, expecting the electorate to cast meaningful votes about specific judges in a retention election is arguably questionable. Nonetheless, discontent with the government generally or the judiciary specifically results in a small but significant part of the electorate voting *against* retention. For example, those judges on the court as of March 2017 who had been evaluated through the electoral process received a "thumbs down" vote from approximately 8–9% of voters. There have also been PR campaigns to vote down specific judges who in the past have upheld voter disparity in malapportionment cases (see Chapter 6), though with limited results.

Yet judicial retention elections have arguably been rendered even more meaningless by the Supreme Court itself through its decisions interpreting this aspect of the Constitution. To the extent that some voters who do not recognize any of the names of the judges on retention election ballots simply leave them blank, how those votes should be treated has in the past been the subject of dispute. This in turn depends on how the system of retention elections is characterized—*i.e.*, is it a vote to retain or a vote to remove? In a 1952 decision the Supreme Court held that blank ballots could effectively be treated as votes in favor of retention on the grounds that: (i) elections were not a process that completed the appointment of judges to the court, but were rather a decision by the voters about whether to remove a specific judge who had already been duly appointed, (ii) treating blank ballots the same as votes *against* removal did not violate the constitution, and (iii) failure to provide detailed information about the types of opinions judges had made did not violate the electoral rules (Supreme Court, Grand Bench judgment of February 20, 1952).

In a 1972 decision, the court reconfirmed that treating ballots indicating neither a clear expression of intent for or against the removal of a Supreme Court judge the same as a vote *against* removal did not violate the constitutional guarantees of freedom of conscience and expression. (Supreme Court 3rd Petty Bench judgment of July 25, 1972). Thus,a judge can only be removed when a majority of ballots are cast in favor of removal.

The constitution is unclear as to whether an additional retention election is required in the case of a Supreme Court judge who is subsequently appointed as Chief Judge. The issue has not been litigated but the CLB view has expressed the view that a second retention poll is not required.

d. The Supreme Court as a Court

As a court, the Supreme Court is actually comprised of three panels of five judges each. These are called "petty benches." The membership of each panel is fixed, subject to retirements and replacements. Each has its own courtroom within the court's building in central Tokyo and together they perform much of the court's judicial work. The composition of the petty benches typically seeks to achieve a balance in background and expertise. The chief judge sits on one of the petty benches (typically the one he was already on before elevation), though is usually busy with administrative tasks.

Occasionally all 15 judges sit together *en banc*—which is called the "Grand Bench"—to decide particularly important cases. Article 10 of the Court Act grants the Supreme Court discretion to establish further rules as to when cases are heard by the Grand Bench, but does *prohibit* petty benches from deciding:

(i) Cases in which a determination is to be made on the constitutionality of law, order, rule, or disposition, based on the argument by a party (except the cases where the opinion is the same as that of the judicial decision previously rendered through the full bench in which the constitutionality of act, order, rule, or disposition is recognized).

(ii) Cases other than those referred to in the preceding item when any law, order, rule, or disposition is to be decided as unconstitutional.

(iii) Cases where an opinion concerning interpretation and application of the Constitution or of any other laws and regulations is contrary to that of a judicial decision previously rendered by the Supreme Court.

Put more succinctly, the Grand Bench must be convened if the court is going to rule on a constitutional question for the first time, is going to issue a ruling of unconstitutionality *or* is going to reverse a prior precedent of the court on the constitution or any other law or regulation. Article 9 of the Supreme Court's "Rules on the Administration of Supreme Court Trials" (Supreme Court Rule No. 6 of 1947, as amended) also permit Petty Benches to refer cases for trial by the Grand Bench if its members are of diverse opinions or it is otherwise deemed appropriate to do so. Separate Supreme Court rules also require the Grand Bench to be convened for a trial for the impeachment of a National Personnel Authority Commissioners (which has never happened). Articles 3 and 4 of the Judges Status Act of 1947 also designate the Grand Bench as having original jurisdiction over proceedings relating to the competency or disciplining of high court or Supreme Court judges, and appellate jurisdiction over appeals from similar proceedings involving other judges.

Grand bench proceedings take place in a large imposing courtroom, images of which often accompany news of their decisions. Yet Grand Bench judgments are rare, and those requiring oral arguments or other courtroom proceedings other than the rendering of the court's judgment are even rarer.

In the Court's history there have been years in which the Grand Bench did not sit at all. In more recent years it has been slightly more active, though according to the Supreme Court's on-line search engine there were only 25 Grand Bench judgments/decisions during the ten year period from January 1, 2007 to December 31, 2016. Of these, five were issued in 2015, making it a comparatively busy year. Judicial statistics show that during the same year all of the benches of the Court collectively handled appeals in 7,233 civil and administrative cases and 3,606 criminal cases.

One odd ramification of the bifurcation of roles between the Grand Bench and Petty Benches is the result of the case can be telegraphed before the court makes a decision because of the composition of the court hearing it. If a Petty Bench accepts a constitutional challenge to a law or regulation on an issue where the Grand Bench has previously found the matter to be constitutional, it can be expected to reaffirm the constitutionality. By contrast, if the Grand Bench takes such a case it is a sign of a possible reversal.

Similarly, since most Supreme Court decisions are rendered based on the pleadings of the parties, the likely decision of the court is also telegraphed by its decision to hold oral arguments. Article 319 of the Code of Civil Procedure and Article 408 of the Code of Criminal procedure allow an appellate court to reject appeals without a hearing, oral arguments being ordered in a Supreme Court case are indicative of at least the possibility of a reversal. One exception, however, has developed in death penalty appeals for which the court always holds a hearing even when it rejects the appeal.

As a judicial body, the Supreme Court is formally comprised of its 15 judges. However it is also supported by approximately 40 research judges (*chōsakan*) whose existence is anticipated under article 57 of the Court Act. Research judges play an important role in the court's function and are members of the career judiciary who have passed the NBE and have at least ten years' experience. Time as a *chōsakan* is generally considered a sign of a successful judicial career, and the Chief Research Judge (*shuseki chōsakan*) is identified by Professor Nishikawa in his research as one of the four "key posts" that often leads to a seat on the Supreme Court. Research judges are selected within the context of the overall judicial career system (discussed below), and are very different from the judicial clerks hired by individual judges in the US system.

Research judges play a crucial role in assisting the court's 15 judges, doing research, recommending dispositions and writing draft opinions of the court, though this assistance reportedly does not extend to judges wishing to write concurring or dissenting opinions. Although under article 75 of the Court Act deliberations of individual Supreme Court benches are, like those of all discussions by judicial panels, supposedly subject to strict secrecy (Court Act, article 75), the involvement and collaboration of research judges appears to be an unspoken exception. This was demonstrated by the slightly embarrassing issuance on the same day in 2007 of judgments of separate petty benches in two similar cases that contained a paragraph of almost identical language.

With just fifteen judges—all in their sixties—serving as both the nation's constitutional court and final court of appeal on all other matters of Japanese law, the Supreme Court is overworked. This becomes starkly apparent when the court is compared to its predecessor, the Grand Court of Judicature which had a narrower jurisdictional and administrative mandate, but two to three times as many judges. Research judges thus make it possible for the court to handle its burgeoning docket. At the same time, however, there is criticism that the bulk of the court's work is being done behind the scenes by anonymous research judges rather than those formally appointed to the Court.

The Supreme Court is the only court in the Japanese system in which individual judges issue separate concurring or dissenting opinions. Occasionally a minority view expressed in dissenting opinions in a Supreme Court judgment can come to be the majority view expressed in a subsequent opinion reversing it. For example, in 1995 the court upheld the constitutionality of article 900 of the Civil Code, which at the time accorded inferior inheritance rights to children born out of wedlock (Supreme Court, Grand Bench decision of July 5, 1995). This decision was rendered over a strong dissent by five judges. Subsequently petty benches of the court affirmed the constitutionality of that decision on five separate occasions, the last in 2009. However in 2013, the Grand Bench reversed itself, finding the provision to violate the equal protection guarantee (Supreme Court, Grand Bench decision of September 4, 2013). The provision deemed unconstitutional was subsequently excised from the Civil Code.

e. The Supreme Court as an Administrative Body

As a bureaucracy the Supreme Court represents the apex of an administrative system that reaches down through the appellate districts of the high courts and their administrative arms into the individual district, family and summary courts around the nation. Apart from the Chief Judge, Supreme Court judges do not appear to become intimately involved in this side of the court's activities, which are in any case conducted by largely anonymous career judges serving in administrative roles and non-judge career judicial public workers.

As Figure 4-1 shows, the administrative side of the Supreme Court is comprised of four key branches: the General Secretariat, the LRTI, the Training and Research Institute for Court Officials, and the Supreme Court Library. Of these the head of the General Secretariat and the LRTI are regarded as two of the four "key posts" that can take a career judge to a seat on the Supreme Court itself.

Of the court's two training institutes and its library little more needs to be said. The bulk of the administrative function is performed through the General Secretariat, which is comprised of ten bureaus. The heads of these bureaus are career judges, and postings to them are signs of a successful career. However, some bureaus are more important than others, particularly the Personnel Affairs Bureau, which has tremendous power over the careers of judges and other court personnel around the country.

Also noteworthy is the existence of four bureaus devoted to particular types of litigation and other disputes handled by the courts: civil, criminal, family and administrative. While the bureaus may not interfere in the conduct of individual cases, they may provide "guidance" to the nation's judges regarding particular types of cases. For example the family bureau might circulate a directive to family courts around the country to pay particular attention to a particular piece of legislative history in applying a statute in a specific category of cases. In the past these bureaus might also hold study groups for judges likely to handle a particular category of cases to discuss the best way of handling similar issues arising in similar cases in different courts In this capacity the administrative side of the court has the ability to subtly encourage uniformity of interpretation without the "court" side of the Supreme Court issuing an opinion.

One of the interesting facets of the Japanese system is that the Supreme Court is able to exercise a high degree of control through its General Secretariat *in spite of* provisions of the Court Act intended to preserve the administrative autonomy of individual courts. Under articles 20, 29 and 31–5 of the Act, the administrative affairs of each high, district and family court are supposed to be conducted through a "judicial assembly" comprised of all of the full (*hanji*) judges on that court and presided over by its chief judge. Insider accounts describe the proceedings at these assemblies as now meaningless formalities where administrative policy is announced rather than deliberated.

4. Judges and the Judicial Career

a. *Categories of Judges*

Judges in Japan are very different from their counterparts in common law jurisdictions such as the United States where judges are usually appointed or elected to a specific position on a specific court role and may remain there for a prolonged period of time, potentially for life in the case of federal judges appointed under Article III of the U.S. Constitution. Moreover, judges in the common law system are typically chosen from the ranks of practicing lawyers, which may include government lawyers such as prosecutors. By contrast, as in some European systems, Japanese judges are a highly specialized form of national bureaucrat involving a very different career path from private sector attorneys.

First it is helpful to understand some terminology. Generically, all judges are referred to as *saibankan* (literally "trial official")—judges. However, the Court Act distinguishes between six different categories of judge. The first two categories sit on the Supreme Court: the Chief Judge and the 14 other Supreme Court judges.

The remaining four categories fit under the constitutional rubric of "judges of inferior courts." These are appointed for ten year terms by the Cabinet "from a list of persons nominated by the Supreme Court" (article 80). The first category of these judges is comprised of summary court judges (*kan'i saibansho hanji*). As discussed earlier in this chapter, such judges are often drawn from the ranks of experienced judicial employees and have not necessarily passed the NBE (note, however, that it is still necessary to distinguish summary court judges as a category of judge, from "career" judges who may spend part of their time acting as judges in summary courts). Unless otherwise noted, they are not included in the discussion that follows.

The next category consists of high court chief judges (*kōtōsaibansho chōkan*). These are the only judges other than those on the Supreme Courts whose appointments involve action by the Emperor. There are only eight of them and, although the Court Act anticipates a broader range of qualified individuals, in reality they are drawn exclusively from those who have passed through the remaining two categories, which comprise the bulk of the career judiciary: *hanjiho* (assistant judges) and *hanji* (judges).

b. *The Judicial Career*

The judicial career for those who enter the profession by passing the National Bar Exam begins with an appointment as an assistant judge (*hanjiho*). Although theoretically anyone passing the bar and entering the Supreme Court's Legal Research and Training Institute (see Chapter 7) can apply to be so appointed, the judiciary is generally able to discourage those who it deems unqualified or undesirable from formally applying in the first place. The foreign nationals who occasionally succeed in passing the NBE are also not eligible for appointment as judges (or prosecutors).

Iitial appointments as *hanjiho* and subsequent reappointments after the constitutional ten year term are first vetted by the Lower Court Nomination Consultative Committee before recommendation to the Cabinet. The reality, however, is that the judicial bureaucracy chooses its own new recruits.

Under article 27 of the Court Act, *hanji-ho* may not conduct single-judge proceedings and only one may sit on a three judge panel. However, under the Act concerning the Exceptions to the Authority of Assistant Judges of 1948, assistant judges with five years' experience and who have been designated by the Supreme Court may act as full judges (though they remain assistant judges in title). Virtually all *hanji-ho* receive this designation after five years.

After ten years an assistant judge can expect to be reappointed (a constitutional requirement) as a *hanji* (full judge). They will generally retain this status until retirement at the mandatory retirement ages (for *hanji*) of 65.

Assistant judges, judges and summary court judges are subject to annual personnel reviews. The reviews are generally conducted by the chief judge of the court to which they are posted (or, in the case of summary court judges, the chief judge of the district court having jurisdiction over their court) with further input and adjustments from the chief judge of the high court in which the court is located, and centralized coordination through the Personnel Bureau of the Supreme Court's General Secretariat.

The criteria on which judges are evaluated are not fully publicized, and judges have long grumbled about the opaque nature of their evaluations. Factors that are considered are widely understood to include rendering "correct" decisions (*i.e.*, not being overturned on appeal) and docket clearing. Generating bad press, complaints from parties or other subjective factors may also play a role. Some scholars have suggested that issuing decisions supportive of the policies of the ruling LDP is also a success in judicial career success.

Comparing the number of cases shown in Table 4-2 with the number of Japanese judges suggest why docket-clearing is an important criteria for evaluation. Depending on the court a judge may have two hundred matters on his or her plate with dozens of new ones coming in every week, requiring clearance of that number just to stay above water. While a preference for settlements is sometimes attributed to a Japanese cultural predelicition for "harmonious" conclusions, a more mundate but equally plausible reality is that settlements require less effort by judges, enabling them to dispense with some or all evidentiary proceedings, avoid drafting judgments and forestall appeals. The docket-clearing imperative (which is hardly unique to Japanese judges, of course) is also sometimes blamed for judges relying on formulaic decisions, with language copied from other judgments that may not actually apply to the case at hand.

Personnel evaluations affect judges in their careers in at least two principal ways. First is the timing of their next salary increase. One aspect of the judicial hierarchy is in pay grades, with the Act on Judicial Compensation of 1948 establishing 24 grades for judges from assistant judge to chief judge of the Supreme Court, with an additional 17 grades just for summary court judges.

While the burgeoning caseload of many judges is a common subject when the judiciary and access to justice are discussed, there seems little appetite for increasing the number of judges, other than from *bengoshi* attorneys who see the sclerotic judiciary as a problem for the pursuit of justice, or at least their business. Cynical observers have suggested the judiciary may be reluctant to change the status quo because increasing the number of judges would invite a reconsideration of judicial pay, which is quite high compared to other public servants—particularly at the senior ranks. Typically the administrative vice minister of a ministry or the head/ director general of an executive branch agency is the highest-paid member of that agency, and there is only one of each. By contrast, according to one estimate, as of 2015 there were approximately 160 judges *below the supreme court* level being paid the same or more than *jimujikan* administrative vice ministers or agency heads.

Another way in which personnel evaluations impact judges is manifests itself in postings. Being a member of the career judiciary involves frequent transfers, typically every three years. Most young assistant judges will experience various parts of the nation's court system—tours in family courts and summary courts, experience in a smaller city and so forth. But over time, some judges will gravitate to posts in the Tokyo and Osaka areas and possibly managerial roles within the administrative apparatus of the judiciary whether at the Supreme Court, in the high courts. Some will also be appointed prosecutors and seconded to the MOJ where they may act as counsel for the government when the state is involved in litigation, or seconded yet again to other executive branch agencies (where they are reportedly appreciated because, not coming from a different Ministry with competing interests, they provide good, objective legal services). There are also various programs for young judges to obtain experience in "the real world" such as by spending time at a law firm working as a *bengoshi*.

Just like other Japanese bureaucratic institutions with long-term employment, the judicial career system imposes a huge managerial task on those who administer it. Imagine a map of Japan with 3,000 holes, each representing a judicial position and containing a marble. Every year dozens of marbles are removed (deaths and retirement) and approximately 90 marbles representing freshly-minted *hanjiho* marbles are added every year. Marbles are moved to fill vacancies, but only some are suitable for some holes (e.g. chief judge posts, or other roles where full *hanji* status and possibly suitable years of experience are required).

At the same time, repeat postings to family courts in smaller cities or branch courts far from Tokyo may be regarded as "punishment" postings. Article 48 of the Court Act protects individual judges from transfers, suspensions or pay cuts against his or her will, but judges who wish to see any improvement in their career prospects are unlikely to refuse a posting.

A practical ramification of the judicial career system is that it in longer trials it is not uncommon for the presiding judge (or one of the judges on a panel) to change in the middle of them. A judge who has heard witness testimony in court may be replaced by one who ends up rendering judgment based on the transcripts. A judge may also be tempted to delay reaching a resolution in a bothersome case so that it is taken over by his or her replacement.

Because of the negative impact the career system has on judicial autonomy (as discussed in more detail in the following section) Japanese lawyers have long advocated the elimination of the three separate *hōsō* legal professions (see Chapter 7), and its replacement with a system in which judges are chosen from the ranks of suitably-experienced trial lawyers as in the United States. Though the Court Act anticipates that lawyers can be appointed to all levels of the bench, and an increasingly formalized system for making such appointments based on negotiations between the JFBA and the Supreme Court has been in existence since 1991 it has had limited impact. The number of judges appointed from the practicing bar annually remains in the single digits, and over 1/3 of those who apply are reportedly rejected by the Supreme Court. There is also little evidence that those appointed from the ranks of lawyers are allowed to proceed through the "elite" course described above and ultimately participate in judicial administration. The impact of this system on the judiciary as a whole can be said to be negligible.

As noted in Chapter 3, judges are also seconded to other branches of the government typically after first being appointed a prosecutor. Some prosecutors may also spend time in the judiciary on secondment as judges. This arrangement is referred to as *hanken kōryū* (literally, "interchanges between judges and prosecutors"), and is a source of frequent criticism from those who feel it leads to an overly cozy relationship between the courts and a frequent party in court proceedings—the executive branch. Since 2012 the secondment of prosecutors to the judiciary to act as criminal trial judges was reportedly stopped.

Given the small total population of career judges (*hanji* and *hanjiho*), the number on secondment elsewhere at any given time is surprisingly large. As of December 2016, 157 judges were on secondment to other government agencies, primarily the MOJ (97) but also including two each at the Cabinet Legislation Bureau and the legislation bureau of the House of Representatives. At the MOJ judges dominated the litigation bureau, filling both the bureau chief post as well as providing the heads of several of its sections. At a 2013 HOC Legal Affairs Committee, a representative of the Supreme Court also acknowledged having one judicial employee on secondment to the secretariat of the Judicial Impeachment Committee, which is discussed later in this chapter. The fact that any given time career judges are performing roles in the executive and legislative branch should be borne in mind when considering what "separation of powers" means in the Japanese context.

Judges are subject to the NPSA and the National Public Service Code of Ethics. Under article 52 of the Court Act they are further prohibited from certain political activities or engaging in other employment. Under article 49 of the Act they may be subject to disciplinary action if they violate their official duties, neglect their jobs or "degrade themselves."

5. Judges and Judicial Autonomy

Although article 76(3) of the constitution declares that "*All judges shall be independent in the exercise of their conscience and shall be bound only by this Constitution and the laws,* in reality this guarantee may not extend to protecting judges from the judicial administrative apparatus. The career system for Japanese judges and the control it gives the judicial bureaucracy is regarded by some scholars and practitioners to have had a deleterious effect on the autonomy of *individual* judges. It is regarded as having made many judges conservative bureaucrats who almost always decide in favor of government interests in criminal, administrative or constitutional trials, and prefer institutionally convenient results even in civil litigation (such as favoring mediated settlements which do not require formal fact findings or legal research and will not be appealed). The phrase *"hirame saibankan"* (literally, "flounder judge") is often used as a derisive metaphor to describe judges who, like the fish, have eyes that only look up, worried about how their actions will be viewed by those higher up in the judicial hierarchy.

It is important to understand, however, that Japan has never had a tradition of judges being highly autonomous. Under the Confucian legal tradition Japan borrowed from China prior to opening to the world, judges who made the wrong decisions were supposed to be punished. As noted at the start of this Chapter, under the Meiji constitutional system judges were subject to administration by the MOJ. Textbooks often cite as an example of budding judicial independence the *Ōtsu* incident of 1891. In that case despite tremendous political pressure judges refused to sentence to death a policeman who had attacked and injured the crown prince of Russia during a state visit to Japan, such a sentence only being possibly by applying a statute that on its face applied in the case of attacks on members of the Japanese imperial family. However, subsequent examples are rare.

Moreover under the current constitution the judiciary as an *institution* has in the past been subject to severe criticism, even attack from other parts of the government. The prime example is the *Urawa Incident* of 1948, which involved a woman who caused the death of her husband and three children by burning down her house. Her husband had dragged the family into debt and in desperation she caused the death of her three children but survived herself in a failed attempt at *shinjū* a form of familial murder/joint suicide that is not uncommon in Japan as means escape from impossible situations. She was thus a sympathetic defendant and received a sentence from the Urawa District Court so lenient that it sparked public criticism.

The legal affairs committee of the House of Councillors used its investigatory powers under article 62 of the Constitution to call the woman, her husband, and the prosecutor who handled the cases as witnesses and issued a report criticizing the judiciary and the prosecutorial authorities for their handling of the case. This included commentary to the effect that, in evaluating the case emotionally in accordance with "traditional" Japanese values the court had ignored the rights of the dead children and their father and demonstrated an attitude that was not conducive to the process of democratization. In response the Supreme Court issued a statement complaining about this improper use of the Diet's powers of investigation, which in turn generated a response from the legislative committee criticizing the Supreme Court for opining on constitutional matters outside its remit.

The social upheaval of the 1950s and 1960s also saw the growth of labor movements and leftist opposition to conservative ruling forces and the military alliance with the United States. Within the legal community, this saw the creation in 1954 of the Japan Young Lawyers Association (JYLA) whose membership was initially drawn from all three of the elite legal professions as well as legal scholars and other constituencies. Taking positions in opposition to many government policies, the organization became the focus of severe criticism from right wing quarters as did the fact that its members included judges, coming at a time when lower courts were issuing progressive rulings. In 1970, petitions were brought to impeach the over 200 judges who were members of the group. The petitions were unsuccessful, but in what came to be known as the "Blue

Purge," the Supreme Court made a concentrated effort to drive left-leaning judges out of the judiciary.

Another famous incident implicating judicial autonomy is that of the so-called "Hiraga Letter." In a 1969 constitutional challenge resulting from change in designation of national forest land for purposes of installing anti-aircraft missile facilities (the so-called "Naganuma Nike Case"), Hiraga Kenta, the chief judge of the Sapporo District Court gave a "personal letter" to Fukushima Shigeo, the senior judge on the panel hearing the case (and a member of the JYLA) "advising" that a ruling in favor of the state would be appropriate. Judge Fukushima's panel nonetheless found the existence of the SDF to be unconstitutional, citing the existence of a "right to peaceful existence" derived from the preamble to the constitution. This was overturned on appeal by the Sapporo High Court and the Supreme Court avoided the constitutional issue entirely by finding that the plaintiffs lacked standing (Supreme Court, 1st Petty Bench judgment of September 9, 1982).

Hiraga was issued a formal warning both by the conference of judges of his court as well as the Supreme Court Secretariat on the grounds his letter infringed on the independence of judges protected under article 76 of the constitution. Yet it was Fukushima who was arguably punished more severely, being subsequently condemned to a series of unglamorous postings, mostly at regional family courts. Both judges were also subject to petitions for impeachment, though neither resulted in a trial.

Judicial autonomy has also been called into question in other instances. For example, research into US archives has revealed that while the *Sunagawa* case (discussed in Chapter 2) challenging the constitutionality of American military bases in Japan was under consideration by the Supreme Court, Chief Judge Tanaka Kōtarō was secretly discussing the state of deliberations with US ambassador, Douglas MacArthur II. More recently, a 2015 book by ex-judge Segi Hiroshi revealed that political pressure from dominant politicians resulted in the Supreme Court changing the way it instructed judges to calculate damages in defamation suits, resulting in higher awards particularly for politicians and others likely to be aggrieved by freedom of the press.[3] Note that the bureaucratic character of the court makes lower-level lobbying of this sort readily possible: a politician may summon the head of the relevant bureau of the Supreme Court Secretariat to complain (or facilitate third party complaining) about the way the courts handle particular types of cases.[4]

6. Impeachment and Other Forms of Judicial Discipline and Control

The law and administrative powers of the Supreme Court provide a number of means for disciplining judges. These are discussed below.

a. *Impeachment*

Article 78 of the constitution declares that:

> Judges shall not be removed except by public impeachment unless judicially declared mentally or physically incompetent to perform official duties. No

---

[3] HIROSHI SEGI, NIPPON NO SAIBAN [Japan's Trials] (2015).

[4] One of the authors has first-hand experience watching such lobbying take place in the office of a leading opposition politician and directed at the head of the family bureau of the Supreme Court.

disciplinary action against judges shall be administered by any executive organ or agency.

Under article 64 of the constitution, a judicial impeachment court is established in the Diet and comprised of members from both chambers. The details of impeachment are left to a statute, the Judicial Impeachment Act of 1947 (JIPA). Under article 2 of the JIA a judge can be removed for serious breach or dereliction of duties or conduct unbecoming a judge.

The JIA establishes a Judicial Impeachment Committee comprised of ten members each from the House of Councillors and House of Representatives, respectively (article 5). By statute, anyone can file with the committee a demand that a judge be impeached (article 15), though the Committee's website indicates that complaints brought by non-Japanese are treated differently. The Committee investigates such complaints and, if merited, will issue articles of impeachment to the Judicial Impeachment Court (articles 11 and 14). Records of committee deliberations are not public (article 10(3)).

In recent years several hundred complaints have brought to the committee annually. Cumulatively, the number of complaints brought from 1948 to 2016, was 19,220. However, very few have been successful, with the committee only requesting formal impeachment proceedings against only 9 judges and deciding upon a suspended impeachment[5] of 7 more in its entire history. Since the vast majority of petitions asserted "wrong decisions" as their principal grounds, this is perhaps unsurprising.

When impeachment is requested the trial is conducted by the Judicial Impeachment Court, a court of record comprised of 7 members from each Diet chamber (article 16). Proceedings are held in public and the judge being impeached may be represented by counsel (articles 22 and 26). Impeachment trials are rare; as noted in the preceding paragraph, only nine impeachments have ever been initiated by the Judicial Impeachment Committee. Of these only seven resulted in the judge being removed from office, though the two examples of the court deciding against removal are from 1948—the year in which the system was established. In every instance in the decades since, initiation of impeachment proceedings has resulted in removal.

The Judicial Impeachment Court also hears petitions for reinstatement from judges who have been removed through impeachment five or more years previously (JIA, article 38). The principal reason for such proceedings is likely not to restore impeached judges to the bench, but to enable them to register as *bengoshi* lawyers, since impeachment disqualifies former judges from practicing law (Attorney Act, article 7). The Judicial Impeachment Court has received seven such petitions in its history and has ordered reinstatement in four cases.

In two separate incidents in 2014 and 2016 judges were convicted of surreptitiously taking pictures of women (one by installing a secret camera in the women's restroom in the MOJ building). They were spared impeachment because at the time they were on secondment to the MOJ and thus technically prosecutors, not judges.

One interesting aspect of the judicial impeachment system is that article 15(3) of the JIA requires the Supreme Court to file a petition with the Judicial Impeachment Committee if it becomes aware of impeachable behavior on their part. Although this has

---

[5] Article 13 of the JIA permits the committee to suspend the prosecution of impeachments where circumstances render it unnecessary to proceed, even when impeachable behavior may have taken place.

only occurred eight times by 2016, the number of instances where a judge has been impeached is almost identical to the number of times the Supreme Court has been a complainant (the records published by the JIA do not indicate who the complainant is in the cases resulting in impeachment).

b. Judicial Status Proceedings and Other Disciplinary Measures

Article 78 of the cCnstitution does not prohibit disciplinary proceedings against judges other than impeachment; it only prohibits such proceedings being brought by the executive branch. Article 78 also clearly anticipates judges being removed without impeachment if "judicially declared mentally or physically incompetent."

The processes for removing mentally or physically incompetent judges as well as disciplining others are set forth in the Judicial Status Act of 1947 (JSA). Under this law, disciplinary or competency proceedings involving summary, family and district court judges are conducted at the high court having jurisdiction over the court to which they are posted, and the Supreme Court has appellate jurisdiction over appeals from such proceedings, as well as original (and final) jurisdiction over proceedings involving supreme court and high court judges.

There have only been two cases of JSA proceedings being used to remove judges for incapacity. There are rather more instances of judges being disciplined, though the only formal punishments that disciplinary proceedings can result in are a formal warning or a fine of no more than JPY 10,000 (JSA article 2). Unsurprisingly, there are rather more instances of judges being formally sanctioned under the JSA than through the impeachment process. Examples of transgressions resulting in disciplinary action under the JSA include losing trial records on a train, drunk driving, being drunk on the job, failure to account for travel expenses properly and shoplifting. The most infamous example is the 1998 case of Teranishi Kazushi, an assistant judge who was disciplined for engaging in political activities. He had attended a symposium about pending anti-organized crime legislation and publicly expressed objections to the proposed legislation after identifying himself as a member of a judiciary.

Outside the scope of these formal mechanisms, article 21 of the Supreme Court's rules on the administration of lower courts allows the chief judge of a court to caution the judicial employees of that court (which would include other judges) regarding the state of their duties. This can also be used as a means of issuing formal cautions to judges for inappropriate behavior. From 2014–2016 Judge Okaguchi Kiichi was given formal warnings by the chief judge of the Tokyo High Court. A heavy Twitter user with a large and devoted following, Judge Okaguchi tweeted a picture of himself in bondage as well as half naked. At the time of writing he continued to tweet, including posting articles critical of the judiciary and the government, pointing out errors in Supreme Court judgments and occasionally making fun of his own formal warnings.

In addition to the formal and informal mechanisms for disciplining and controlling judges discussed in this chapter, a final mechanism can be found in the appointment process. Under article 80 of the constitution judges are appointed for 10 year terms. Although the article refers to a "privilege of reappointment," judges are occasionally not recommended for reappointment (or encouraged to resign at the end of a term). The Lower Court Judicial Nomination Committee described above thus provides a mechanism for complaints about judicial behavior to be reflected in the reappointment process.

Finally, as noted earlier in this chapter, postings to unimportant regional courts can also be a means of disciplining troublesome judges, or at least preventing them from becoming involved in important trials.

7. The Judicial Power

Constitutionally, Japanese courts are vested with the "whole judicial power" (article 76). Yet what does that mean?

Under the Meiji Constitution (article 57(1)) the "judicature" was "exercised by the Courts of Law according to law, in the name of the Emperor." Moreover, the judicial power exercised by the law courts was clearly limited, not extending to the matters handled by the administrative and special courts anticipated by articles 60 and 61. Consistent with the practice in some European systems, under article 2 of the Meiji-era Court Organization Act the ordinary courts were charged with hearing "criminal and civil trials," except when special courts had jurisdiction by law.

The reference to the "whole" judicial power in the current constitution represents an express rejection of the limited jurisdiction accorded to the law courts under the Meiji system and a strengthening of the judiciary in comparison to other branches of government. Yet this still leaves unanswered the question of what constitutes the judicial power.

Constitutional scholars have offered various definitions. Those of Miyazawa Toshiyoshi ("State action in trying suits at law") and Shimizu Tōru ("Action in cases where there is a dispute in a specific case between parties who are assumed to bring suit, and independent courts deriving sovereign power using certain litigation procedures for the purposes of resolving such dispute by adjudicating what the law is and ensuring its correct application.") are two of the most widely cited "classical" definitions. Both arguably raise more questions than they answer, and in the type of intellectual effort that only law professors seem capable of, subsequent generations of constitutional law experts have pondered the question and proffered alternative definitions (translations in this paragraph by Colin Jones).

One can also point to the much more succinct parameters offered by the Court Act, article 3(1) of which declares the courts to have jurisdiction over "all legal disputes." While this may also not seem particularly helpful, it provides a good segue into another approach, which is to consider the question in more concrete terms; the proven attributes of the judicial power—its characteristics and limits in practice.

In a 1952 case challenging the constitutionality of the establishment of the National Police Reserve—the predecessor of the current Self Defense Forces—the Supreme Court declared that "for judicial power to be invoked a concrete legal dispute must be brought before the courts" (Supreme Court, Grand Bench Decision of Oct. 18, 1952). This was further clarified the following year in a case brought by a party challenging the validity of a 1948 joint Diet resolution declaring the Imperial Rescript on Education void, the Supreme Court further clarified its stance by holding that:

> . . . our nation's courts, except where especially provided for in the constitution, are invested with the power to judge all suits at law but such suits at law must be disputes between parties relating to the existence of concrete rights or obligations or legal relations and which disputes can further be resolved with

finality through the application of the law. (Supreme Court, 3rd Petty Bench Decision of November 17, 1953).

Thus, from early in its history the Supreme Court has bounded the judicial power with a "case and controversy" requirement analogous to that found in U.S. constitutional law. It has also developed a set of precedents that effectively unify the concept of "judicial power" in article 76(1) of the constitution, the notion of what constitutes a "trial" for purposes of article 32 (which guarantees "access to the courts."),[6] the article 82(1) requirement that trials be conducted in open court, and the jurisdictional statement contained in article 3(1) of the Court Act.

In developing the parameters of the judicial power, the Supreme Court has had to rule on the validity of various aspects of the nation's system of dispute resolution, including many that predate or otherwise seem inconsistent with the current constitution. These include the vaguely oxymoronic concept of the "non-contentious case" (handled under the Non-Contentious Case Act of 2011) and a system of family courts where mandatory conciliation before litigation is required and most proceedings are not conducted in open court. Both of these are discussed in Chapter 10.

There are a number of spheres to which the judicial power does not extend. These include matters clearly set forth in the constitution: disputes about the eligibility of Diet members for their seats (article 55) and judicial impeachment proceedings (article 64, but note the discussion in the proceeding section).

Through adjudication the Supreme Court has also identified other realms where the judicial power does not extend. One is to the acts of foreign sovereign. This was confirmed in a 2002 case in which residents around the US air force base at Yokota sought damages and injunction in connection with the noise pollution caused by night landing practices (Supreme Court 2nd Petty Bench judgment of April 12, 2002). Under the US-Japan Status of Forces Agreement (SOFA), Japan has also surrendered primary jurisdiction over offenses committed by US service personnel in Japan meaning that Japanese courts typically do not hear such cases.

The Supreme Court has also been reluctant to become involved in the internal workings of the Diet. In 1962 it declined to adjudicate whether a controversial piece of legislation was duly passed in accordance with the procedures mandated by the Diet Act (Supreme Court, Grand Bench judgment of March 7, 1962).[7] The court is also generally reluctant to use the judicial power to question or challenge the exercise of legislative discretion granted to the Diet except in the rare instances where it finds a law to be unconstitutional, as discussed in chapter 5.

When it has openly challenged the Diet it has frequently been in the context of a charge of legislative nonfeasance—the Diet *failing* to take legislative action mandated by the constitution (including in response to changes in social conditions and sometimes warnings from the court in prior cases on the same issue). It has used some version of this rationale on the two occasions it ruled malapportionment in the allocation of the House of Representatives to be unconstitutional (Supreme Court, Grand Bench

---

[6] Note that the English version of article 32 is poorly rendered as it fails to capture the "right to receive a trial in a court" nuance of the Japanese version.

[7] Given that the law in question was the Police Act of 1954 which drastically altered the organizational structure of the nation's entire police system and that the Court issued its decision six years later, it is questionable what other decision it could have arrived at.

judgments of April 14, 1976 and July 17, 1983), as well as to overturn laws denying the rights of Japanese living abroad to participate in elections (Grand Bench judgment of September 14, 2005), and *partially* invalidate a 180 day restriction on women remarrying after dissolution of a prior marriage (Grand Bench judgment of December 16, 2015).

In two instances, the Supreme Court has also declined to use the judicial power to involve itself in "political questions." The first was the 1959 *Sunagawa Case* (discussed previously in this chapter and in Chapter 2), in which the court declined to rule on the constitutionality of the Japan-US security alliance. The other was in 1960 when, in the so-called "*Tomabechi Case*," it refused to decide whether article 7 of the Constitution alone provided grounds for the dissolution of the House of Representatives without a vote of non-confidence pursuant to article 69 (Supreme Court, Grand Bench judgment of June 8, 1960).[8] Such dissolutions are now a well-established practice.

Outside the scope of national government, the courts have also declined to extend the use of the judicial power to adjudicating disputes arising within specific types of institutions or communities having a high degree of internal autonomy. This is said to be based on a "social unit theory" (*bubun shakai ron*); that certain types of institutions, organizations or communities within society have a high degree of internal autonomy and that disputes arising amongtheir constituent members should not be resolved through the judicial process unless they are likely to affect the rest of society.

This theory was first articulated in a suit challenging the disciplinary action taken by a municipal assembly against one of its members. On appeal the court declared:

> The scope of contentions in law is broad and there are some matters which should, by their nature, be left outside judicial power. This is because in a society or an organization which has an autonomous system of legal norms, there may be instances where the realization of such norms is better left to be dealt with through autonomous measures than by resorting to adjudication.
>
> (Supreme Court, Grand Bench judgment of October 19, 1960)

Although not always applied consistently, the court has issued decisions based on a similar reasoning in connection with political parties expelling members (Supreme Court, 3rd Petty Bench judgment of December 20, 1988), national universities in the context of granting academic credit (3rd Petty Bench judgment of March 15, 1977), and the legitimacy of sacred items in the context of disputes within religious organizations (3rd Petty Bench judgment of April 7, 1981) and in connection with disputes over status within religious organization (2nd Petty Bench judgment of September 8, 1989). Note that although framed in terms of particular types of organizations or communities, each of these instances implicates other provisions of the constitution: local self-government, freedom of religion, academic freedom and freedom of association.

---

[8] It is worth noting here too that the Court rendered its decision eight years and several elections after the dissolution in question.

Chapter 5

JAPANESE LAW: WHAT IT IS AND WHERE IT COMES FROM

Analysis

In this chapter we will review the categories of Japanese laws and regulations and how they are made. Some consideration will also be given to the subject of precedent and the extent to which courts—the Supreme Court in particular—play a role in "making law." Precedents in other institutions will also be discussed.

A. THE TAXONOMY OF JAPANESE LAWS AND REGULATIONS

According to the Ministry of Internal Affairs and Communications, as of March 1, 2017 Japan had exactly 8,307 laws and regulations. It further categorizes them as follows.

TABLE 5-1 JAPANESE LAWS AND REGULATIONS IN FORCE AS OF MARCH 1, 2017

Constitution (*kenpō*)	1
Laws (*hōritsu*)	1,967
Cabinet Orders (*seirei*)	2,157
Imperial Edicts (*chokurei*)	73
Ministerial Ordinances (*furei/shōrei*)	3,759
Cabinet Edicts (*kakurei*)	11
Rules (*kisoku*)	339
Total	8,307
SOURCE: MIC	

This list does not include a number of important items: treaties, prefectural and municipal ordinances, and numerous forms of lower order regulation that can actually be quite important and will be discussed below. Nonetheless, the exactitude of Table 5-1 is impressive.

The following sections will discuss each of the categories in Table 5-1.

1. The Constitution

There is of course only one constitution, which is discussed in other parts of this book, including Chapter 6 in particular.

2. Laws

Hōritsu (Laws) are the laws passed by the Diet in accordance with the procedures set forth in the Constitution (article 59) or which were passed earlier and survived the transition to the new constitutional system. As noted in prior chapters, some current laws such as the Civil Code and the Penal Code are much older than the current constitution. The oldest law still on the books, the Explosives Control Ordinance was passed by the Grand Council of State in 1884 and predates even the Meiji Constitution.

The legislative process under the current constitution is discussed later in this chapter. At this juncture, it will first be worth discussing different ways of categorizing statutory law.

a. Laws and Legislation

Most of the laws passed by the Diet are actually amendments to existing laws. Some bills passed into law by the Diet may actually consist exclusively of minor amendments to a large number of existing laws. Thus, when we speak of a law as part of the legislative process, it is often referred to by a name that will cease to exist after it has been passed, such as "An Act to Amend Part of the Civil Code." Similarly, controversial bills may be referred to in the press by a simplistic name that reflects its essence but is not technically accurate. For example, in 2017 the Diet passed what was commonly referred to as a "conspiracy law," but was actually a set of amendments to a number of existing laws. Examples of completely new laws being added to the books are thus comparatively rare.

Outside the scope of the legislative process, laws are referred to by their specific title (e.g., the "Civil Code" or the "Hotel Act") as it is currently in force, subject to whatever recent amendments have been made. Sometimes laws are replaced by completely new laws with the same title as the old one, the current Bankruptcy Act of 2004 having replaced the Bankruptcy Act of 1922.

b. Cabinet Legislation vs. Diet Legislation

Most legislation passed by the Diet is actually drafted by ministries or other executive branch institutions and submitted to the Diet by the Cabinet. Only about 10% of laws passed by the Diet actually originate from within the Diet. The legislative process is discussed in greater detail later in this chapter.

c. Basic Laws

Some laws establish basic frameworks for government policies. These are called "basic laws" (*kihonhōō*"). Often consisting of broad statements of principle and vaguely-defined mandates for national and sometimes local governments, these laws often figure in discourse but rarely seem to directly impact daily life. They do not generally create new rights or obligation and the details of implementation are left to further legislation and regulations. Basic laws are sometimes considered to be a bridge between some of the broad mandates articulated in the constitution and specific legislation. Currently Japan has about 50 basic laws, covering areas of policy as diverse as nuclear power, the handicapped, food safety and cybersecurity. Basic laws are usually initiated by the Diet.

d. *General Laws vs. Special Laws*

It is common to distinguish between *ippanhō* (general laws) and *tokubetsuhō* (special laws). The former are laws that establish general rules of wide applicability in a particular sphere. The latter establish special rules that apply in certain circumstances or to certain actors within that sphere. For example the Civil Code is considered a general law, in that it establishes the basic rules for civil society including most commercial transactions. The Commercial Code is considered a "special law" in that it creates special rules—some at variance with the Civil Code—that apply to merchants and other special types of business in transactions that would otherwise be governed by the Civil Code. To the extent a special law conflicts with a general law, the former will generally prevail.

For some well-established statutory regimes such as the Civil Code, which are the foundation for numerous other laws, it is often easier to legislate through special laws than amending the underlying general law, which could trigger the need to make numerous other conforming amendments.

Another category of "special" law is a *tokureihō* (literally "law for a special case") which provides an exception to another law for special circumstances or even individuals. A recent example was the 2017 law passed allowing a special exception to the Imperial House Act to allow Emperor Akihito to abdicate (see Chapter 3).

e. *Laws Affecting Only Certain Territories*

Another type of "special law" is anticipated by article 95 of the Constitution, under which a law that applies only to a single prefecture or municipality cannot be passed unless the consent of the affected voters is also obtained in a local referendum. Less than two dozen laws of this type have been passed, all early in the post-war period. Interpretation has also led to unusual results. For example the 1950 act providing for special construction in the nation's capital was passed with a referendum of the citizens of Tokyo, though the law which replaced it in 1956 was not. Nor did the 1950 Hokkaido Development Act involve a referendum, despite clearly being applicable to a single prefecture.

In 1996 the Supreme Court rejected challenges to the condemnation of private land in Okinawa for use by the US military on a number of grounds, including by finding that the article 95 requirement did not apply. The court reasoned that the law permitting the government to appropriate land for use by US military bases applied everywhere in Japan, even though the concentration of bases in Okinawa meant the burden of the law fell primarily on that prefecture (Supreme Court, Grand Bench judgment of August 28, 1996).

3. Cabinet Orders

Seirei (cabinet orders) are a form of delegated legislation anticipated by Article 73 of the Constitution, which empowers the Cabinet to issue orders "*to execute the provisions of th[e] Constitution and of the law.*" Cabinet orders are vetted by the Cabinet Legislation

Bureau and must be approved by a unanimous cabinet resolution. They must also be jointly signed by the responsible minister of state and the Prime Minister. They are promulgated in the name of the Emperor (constitution, articles 74, 7). Cabinet orders may be used to impose criminal penalties, but only if authorized by law (article 73).

The wording of the Constitution suggests that cabinet orders could be used to directly implement the constitution without delegating primary legislation. However, this would run afoul of the charter's designation of the Diet as the "sole" law-making organ of the state and no cabinet orders have been passed without enabling legislation. One possible exception can be seen in the system of honors described in Chapter 3. These are bestowed on noteworthy citizens and foreign dignitaries, pursuant to an 1881 ordinance that was abolished during the occupation but revived through a 1955 cabinet order without legislation. At the time there was significant populist opposition to reviving a system deeply rooted in pre-war militarism and aristocracy. Some scholars grumble about the constitutionality of this arrangement.

Some cabinet orders issued during the occupation under the direction of occupation authorities have a special character, similar to that of the "Potsdam Edicts" described in the next section. One example can be seen in the current Immigration Control and Refugee Act, the principal act governing the entry and status of non-Japanese in Japan. It began as a so-called "Potsdam Cabinet Order" (officially "Cabinet Order Number 319 of 1951) titled the Immigration Control Order, but it surivived pursuant to transitional legislation passed at the end of the occupation which gave it the effect of a law. It was amended in 1982 at which time it was given its current title as a "law," but is still formally referred to as "Cabinet Order No. 319 of October 4, 1951." Supplementary provisions added with amendments refer to "this cabinet order" or "this law" depending on when they were passed.

4. Imperial Edicts

Surprisingly, the corpus of Japanese laws and regulations still includes a number of pre-war *chokurei* (imperial edicts). Under the Meiji Constitution the powers of government sprang from the Emperor and the use of imperial edicts as a tool of regulation was common. Those which have remained in force through the postwar period do so through a combination of occupation-era law and cabinet orders (such as the "Law in Connection with the Effectiveness of the Provisions of Orders in Effect at the Time of Implementing the Constitution of 1947" and the "Cabinet Order in Connection with the Effectiveness of the Provisions of Orders in Effect at the Time of Implementing the Constitution of 1947"), which converted various imperial edicts not repugnant to the new constitution into cabinet orders under it. Some of the edicts included the so-called "Potsdam Edicts" which were orders issued by American occupation authorities through the Japanese government in the form of imperial edicts issued under Article 8 of the Meiji Constitution. Most of these expired at the end of the occupation, but a number of mostly obscure rules were preserved in force through additional legislation taking effect.

5. Ministerial Ordinances (Rules)

Ministerial rules (*shōrei,* or *furei* if issued by the Cabinet Office) are the most common form of delegated legislation and are typically the means by which a ministry implements legislation within its remit, pursuant to a legislative authorization. These are not formally approved by the Cabinet and are promulgated in the name of the relevant minister of state rather than by the Emperor. As with laws and cabinet orders, promulgation is through publication in the *kanpō* official gazette.

Some ordinances of this type are referred to as "*kisoku*" (rules), but are technically orders (*rei*) of the ministry. Ministerial ordinances includes rules of the Cabinet Office, which it should be recalled from Chapter 3 is in many ways another ministry-like institution under the Cabinet that may thus issue rules in connection with matters under its remit. These, however, are *not* cabinet orders (*seirei*) discussed in subsection 3 above. Agencies may also issue rules (*chōrei*)

Many regulatory regimes have multiple tiers of delegated regulation including both cabinet orders and ministerial ordinances. For example the Telecommunications Business Act of 1984 establishes the basic regulatory framework for telecommunications in Japan. The Act anticipates that some details of implementation will be left up to cabinet orders while more detailed areas of regulation (particularly technical matters requiring subject matter expertise) will be dealt with in MIC rules. These are manifested in the Telecommunications Business Act Implementing Order of 1985 (the cabinet order), and the Telecommunications Business Act Implementing Rules of 1985 (the MIC rules).

Ministerial rules may not impose penal sanctions or otherwise limit the rights of or impose duties on the people unless permitted by the relevant delegating legislation (Administrative Organization Act, article 12(3)). The passage of ministerial ordinances or rules to implement laws or cabinet orders relating to matters within a ministry's jurisdiction is specifically anticipated in article 12 of the NGOA.

6. Cabinet Edicts

Kakurei (Cabinet Edicts) were orders issued by the Prime Minister under the Meiji constitutional system. As with Imperial Edicts a small number have survived, though most deal with obscure subjects. For example, a 1912 cabinet edict regarding the manner of flying flags during periods of national mourning remains in force today.

7. Other National Government Rules

A separate category of *kisoku* (rules) are a form of delegated legislation issued by agencies, committees and other national government institutions that are not Ministries or the Cabinet Office. Examples include the large body of rules passed by the National Personnel Authority in connection with administering the national public service as well as rules of the National Public Safety Commission and the National Board of Audit.

Rules of this category are also promulgated through publication in the official gazette. The primary authority for establishing such rules is in article 13 of the NGOA.

8. Supreme Court and Diet Rules

The term *kisoku* also include the rules of the individual Diet chambers passed pursuant to article 58(2) of the Constitution, and rules passed by the Supreme Court under article 77. The Supreme Court rules has issued a variety of rules relating to the conduct of civil and criminal litigation, as well as judicial administration. Insofar as Supreme Court and Diet chamber rules are specifically anticipated by the Constitution, there is some academic debate over whether they are inferior to Diet legislation. Since instances of conflict resulting in judicial resolution are rare, the question is mostly academic. One example may be the rules passed by the Supreme Court to implement the

Habeas Corpus Act (discussed in Chapter 1). These have had the effect of narrowing the scope and availability of relief under the Act. This has been criticized by some scholars, but seems unlikely to be remedied through judicial proceedings.

Supreme Court and Diet chamber rules are also published in the Official Gazette.

9. Prefectural/Municipal Ordinances and Rules

Under Article 94 of the constitution, local public entities (the constitutional term for both prefectures and municipalities) "have the right to manage their property, affairs and administration and to enact their own regulations within law." Under article 14(1) of the Local Autonomy Act of 1947, municipal and prefectural assemblies may pass ordinances (*jōrei*) in connection with matters under their jurisdiction, so long as they do not conflict with national law. Unless otherwise permitted by applicable law such assemblies may only impose duties or limit rights through ordinances (article 14(2)).

Prefectural and municipal ordinances may be backed by penal sanctions of less than 2 years imprisonment or fines of JPY 1 million (article 14(3)), unless otherwise authorized by law.

Interestingly, there are instances of ordinances of a similar character being passed by all or most of the prefectural assemblies taking the place of or supplementing national penal statutes. For example, all prefectures have adopted ordinances prohibiting dealings with organized crime groups. In some cases local ordinances can thus develop into a form of shadow national regulation.

Because of its size and status as a political and business center, ordinances passed by the Tokyo prefectural assembly can have an inordinate impact, given its large population and the many companies headquartered there. For example, Tokyo ordinances restricting certain types of publication deemed harmful to minors may be easier to pass and receive less publicity than if the Diet sought to impose similar restraints through legislation, yet because most major publishers are headquartered in Tokyo the impact may be effectively national (see discussion at Chapter 6).

The executive of a local public entity (prefectural governors or mayors of municipalities) may also issue rules (*kisoku* again) that are backed by non-penal fines of no greater than JPY 50,000 (article 15). Since the police are a prefectural institution, municipalities that establish ordinances with criminal penalties may not always be in a position to ensure they are enforced.

Prefectural and municipal ordinances and rules are promulgated through the notification process established by the rules of the applicable prefecture or municipality. They do *not* appear in the *kanpō* official gazette.

10. Treaties

Treaties are a type of law. Under article 98(2) of the constitution, ". . . treaties concluded by Japan and established laws of nations shall be faithfully observed." However, this is understood to be an expression of ideals intended to address international opprobrium towards Japan's perceived flaunting of international norms at the time of the Constitution's drafting rather than a statement according treaties the force of domestic law.

That said, academic theory holds Japanese treaties to be self-executing unless the treaty by its terms requires further legislative action. Some would likely question whether this is actually the case in reality, particularly with regard to conventions on human rights or gender equality. Japanese courts have generally been reluctant to recognize claims based on treaties or international human rights conventions, though a counterargument might be that this is because the Japanese constitution provides adequate grounds for addressing human rights violations.

Treaties are negotiated by the Cabinet subject to approval of the Diet (Constitution, article 73). What constitutes a "treaty" is a matter of interpretation and is not dependent on the title of the instrument. The official government view is that a treaty requiring Diet approval is (i) an international promise including legal components, (ii) an international promise including financial components or (iii) any other important agreements with other countries of a nature requiring ratification. This circular definition means that what constitutes a treaty is somewhat elastic and may not be consistent with its treatment by treaty partners. For example, the Status of Forces Agreement with the United States relating to military bases in Japan is a treaty for Japanese law purposes, but not for US law purposes. The constitutional requirement that the Diet approve agreements (which would by their nature be public) has not prevented the government from negotiating various secret agreements with other countries, the United States in particular. For example a secret agreement with the United States regarding the payment of certain expenses in connection with the reversion to Japan of sovereignty over Okinawa was not presented to the Diet for ratification.

International treaties signed by Japan are ratified through the same mechanism as budgets. This means the House of Representatives can ratify a treaty with a simple majority vote notwithstanding the objections of the House of Councillors (Constitution, article 60). In that respect it is easier to ratify treaties than it is to pass domestic legislation.

11. Other Rules and Interpretive Guidance

While the above description covers the principal categories of form legal rules, a great deal of regulation, particularly in business and industry, may take place at a lower level. Additional types of rules in this category may take many forms and include guidelines, notices, manuals and directives. The authority for national government institutions to issue rules can be found at article 14 of the NGOA.

An example of such a rule can be found in the Personal Information Protection Act, which provides for data protection generally. In the context of the telecommunications business, companies must follow the MIC's Guidelines for the Protection of Personal Information in the Telecommunications Business. This is technically a *kokuji*, an official notification from a government institution to the public at large.

Similarly, companies in some industries may be expected to conduct their business in accordance with an official manual or guidelines. For example, businesses licensed to provide temporary office staff or other "dispatched workers" are required to conduct their business in accordance with a 400 page operating manual prepared by the MHLW, in addition to the laws and regulations governing this highly-regulated industry.

In practice, obtaining a license, permit or registration to engage in a particular business subjects that business to extremely broad regulatory authority that may sometimes seem to exceed that anticipated by the underlying laws and formal regulations. For example, in 2015 the Worker's Dispatch Act of 1985 (which governs the business of supplying temporary labor, as described in Chapter 11) was amended to add a requirement that employers of dispatched workers provide a certain amount of free training every year so that such workers can enhance their skills and advance their careers. What such workers needed to be paid while being trained (*i.e.,* the amount they received while being deployed to clients, or minimum wage) was a financially significant questionthat was not answered through formal law or regulation. Rather a "rule" was effectively imposed through the MHLW website's FAQs (*i.e.,* one of the questions on the website guidance relating to the new statutory requirement was "What rate should workers be paid while receiving training?" The MHLW's answer was that it should be the deployment rate, not minimum wage; a *defacto* rule).

One form of regulation that bears particular attention is the *tsūtatsu* or "directive." These are instructions by higher level regulatory authority (e.g., a ministry or one of its bureaus) to the lower level officials who must implement specific laws and regulations. The General Secretariat of the Supreme Court also uses *tsūtatsu* to issue instructions to lower tiers of judicial administrators and judges.

Tsūtatsu often provide detailed interpretive advice to local administrators as to how to deal with particular types of situations not clearly addressed in a statute or regulation. For some in government jobs or related industries, a form of "legal practice" may involve developing great familiarity with such directives, and specialty publishers sell books comprised mostly of the directives relevant to particular regulatory fields.

Although not directed at the public, *tsūtatsu* can have a tremendous impact on people generally because they offer authoritative guidance on the interpretation of law or regulation, and may sometimes be used to *change* such interpretations. For example, a 1952 MOJ directive relating to the nationality and family register treatment of Japan's former colonial subjects after the San Francisco Treaty of Peace took effect resulted in them losing their nationality and many Koreans in Japan being rendered effectively stateless.

An interesting example of regulatory authorities using *tsūtatsu* to effectively amend the law can be found in the application of article 772 of the Civil Code which contains a presumption that a child born within 300 days after the dissolution of a marriage is the child of the former husband. This has been the bane of some women and their children for decades and may result in the child being registered in the family registry as the child of a man he or she has no biological connection with, or not being registered at all. Conservative sentiment has made it difficult to change the law. However, in 2007 the MOJ's Civil Affairs Bureau issued a *tsūtatsu* to family registry authorities around the nation instructingthat for women able to provide medical certification establishing that their children had been conceived *after* marital dissolution, those children did not need to be registered as children of the ex-husbands, even if born during the 300 day period specified by the law. Since article 772 does not contain such an exception, the MOJ was clearly bending black letter law—but not breaking it.

Those negatively impacted by dispositive regulatory actions, including the issuance of *tsūtatsu*, may theoretically be able to seek relief through the Administrative Case Litigation Act, discussed in Chapter 10). However, the fact that the government institutions are able to impose significant regulations on businesses and individuals through rules such of these which are effectively established outside of (or "below") the formal legislative and regulatory processes can probably be attributed in part to the extremely limited role actually played by courts in second-guessing regulatory decisions, particularly at the national level.

12. A Note on Administrative Rule-Making

As Table 5-1 makes clear, there are far more cabinet orders and ministerial rules than actual legislation. While the MIC categories are based on the authority issuing the rules (cabinet, minister, other), within the sphere of legal scholarship they are also commonly characterized in another way.

At the level below laws and ordinances (*i.e.* rules that are established by a democratically-elected assembly, whether at a national or local level), the wide range of Japanese regulation can be divided into *hōki meirei* or *gyōsei meirei* (administrative orders) and *gyōsei kisoku* (administrative rules). This distinction can be made with respect to both national and local regulations.

Administrative orders are regulations having direct effect outside the regulatory authority issuing them, in that they may create or restrict the rights of people, or impose obligations on them. Under the Administrative Procedure Act of 1993, such regulations are supposed to be prepared through a process in which the public has an opportunity to comment (article 38). Administrative orders can be further categorized as *shikkō meirei* (execution commands) and *i'nin meirei* (delegated commands). The former are issued to implement the fine details of a law or cabinet order (e.g., mandating the sort of form that must be filled out to apply for a license) but may have little substantive impact. The latter type are more likely to impact the people in a significant way. Theoretically, regulations of this latter type are only considered permissible pursuant to a clear delegation of regulatory authority in primary legislation passed by the people's representatives.

The Supreme Court has occasionally invalidated administrative rules that exceed the scope of authority delegated to the rule-making institution. For example, article 4 of the Child Welfare Allowance Act of 1961 establishes a number of categories of single-mother households eligible for a child welfare allowance from the government. One of these categories includes "other similar situations as determined by cabinet order."

Initially the relevant cabinet order also made women with children born out of wedlock eligible, but rendered them ineligible if the father acknowledged paternity. The Supreme Court found this aspect of the cabinet order to be void as contrary to the purpose of the primary legislation and outside the scope of the delegated regulatory authority (Supreme Court, 1st Petty Bench judgment of January 31, 2002). In an earlier case, however, the court upheld the NPSA's *carte blanche* delegation to the National Personnel Authority of the authority to establish regulations defining types of political activities which, if engaged in by public servants, could subject them to criminal penalties (the so-called *Sarufutsu* case; Supreme Court, Grand Bench judgment of November 6, 1964).

In contrast to administrative orders, *gyōsei kisoku* (administrative rules) are rules that are essentially only directed internally, to those who administer the higher level laws and regulations. They may include formal rules, guidelines, directives or other mandates discussed above. The more formal of these may involve a public comment process before their issue, but many do not. In theory they do not bind anyone outside the regulatory body, but as the earlier discussion shows, they may have significant impact on people's lives or business activities by imposing a particular interpretation or procedural requirement on administrative officials.

The solicitation of public comments on secondary legislation and other official rules and orders is required by Article 39 of the Administrative Procedure Act of 1993, though there are numerous exceptions. However the solicitation period for comments is sometimes so short as to be render meaningful comments impossible.

13. Official Positions

In some areas of constitutional or public law, particularly those which by their nature generate little litigation or are not amenable to judicial resolution, the government's "official position" (*seifukenkai*) may have a law-like character. Such positions are articulated in various ways, but often come in the form of the official response to questions submitted by Diet members. The answers (and, by some accounts, sometimes the questions) may involve significant research and interpretation by the relevant government authorities (including the CLB) before they are formally announced by the appropriate minister in the Diet. Formal responses to questions from Diet members are prepared by the appropriate ministries, vetted and approved by the Cabinet. They can thus be quite authoritative.

With respect to specific regulatory statutes and regulations, the ministry or other authority having jurisdiction over it may also issue interpretive guidance. These interpretations may not be conclusive and are subject to judicial challenge, but the judiciary is often reluctant to second-guess ministries' areas under their jurisdiction.

14. A Special Case: The U.S.-Japan Status of Forces Agreement

Special note should be made of the Status of Forces Agreement (SOFA) between Japan and the United States, an agreement made pursuant to Article VI of the 1960 Treaty of Mutual Cooperation and Security between the two countries. Modeled after SOFA's executed by the United States with NATO partners, the US-Japan SOFA effectively creates US military bases as islands of extraterritoriality within Japanese territory. It also gives US authorities primary or concurrent jurisdiction over crimes committed by US personnel and their dependents in Japan. While the SOFA is drafted in a way which suggests Japanese authorities would have jurisdiction over US military personnel who violate Japanese law, implementation has often been different. If an offending soldier or sailor is able to return to their base, Japanese authorities may find it difficult to access them for questioning and arrest. Since the SOFA also allows the entry and exit of military personnel outside the scope of Japanese immigration regulations (including through air and sea ports controlled by the US military), it is also possible for an offending service member to be removed from the country before Japanese authorities can take formal action. Rape and other crimes by US military personnel against Japanese citizens are a recurring source of friction, particularly in Okinawa where US bases are concentrated.

The SOFA also constrains Japanese sovereignty in other ways. For example, US military aircraft are not subject to Japan's Aviation Act, and much of the airspace around Tokyo is under the jurisdiction of US military air traffic control at Yokota Airbase rather than Japanese civilian aviation authorities.

The SOFA also extends US Jurisdiction to any US military property located anywhere in Japan. This has been interpreted to include the sites where US military aircraft have crashed, even if they are not on a military base.

Administration of matters arising under the SOFA are determined by a joint committee comprised of the US ambassador to Japan and top military officials on the American side, and key officials from the MOF, MOFA, MOJ, MAFF and MOD on the Japanese side. Under it there are over two dozen subcommittees dealing with specific areas impacting the SOFA, including a subcommittee on civil trial jurisdiction and another on criminal procedure. The proceedings of these minutes are outside the scope of normal Japanese government processes and decisions made and matters discussed not subject to public scrutiny. Some Japanese commentators have suggested the committee constitutes a second, "secret" government largely unbounded by democratically-accountable constitutional structures.

B. THE LAW-MAKING PROCESS

Article 41 establishes the Diet as the "sole law-making organ of the state." This is in sharp contrast to the Meij Constitution under which the legislative power was exercised by the Emperor "with the consent of the Imperial Diet" (article 5), except in times of emergency when rule by Imperial decree was possible (article 8). Under the Meiji Constitution the affairs of the Emperor and his family, as well as his relationship with the military in his capacity as supreme commander of the army and navy (articles 11 and 12) were also outside the rule-making jurisdiction of the Imperial Diet.

To understand the true significance of the current constitution's designation of the Diet as the "sole law making organ" requires consideration of what "law-making" (*rippō*) actually means. The standard understanding has been that a "law" (*hōritsu*) is a rule that limits the rights of, or imposes a burden on the people either directly or through duly delegated regulatory authority. Beyond this, there is also general acceptance of the view that laws may also include "framework" legislation—such as the "basic laws" discussed earlier in this chapter. These do not necessarily create clear rights or duties in the people but establish a conceptual foundation (e.g., for example, the principle of a gender equal society) on which more specific laws and policies will or should be established.

Notwithstanding article 41, as already noted earlier in this book much of the legislation passed by the Diet is actually drafted—made—by executive branch agencies and proposed to the Diet by the Cabinet. Moreover, article 11 of the NGOA specifically anticipates that ministries, through their minister, can propose to make, amend or abolish laws (or cabinet orders) in their regulatory sphere by submitting a proposal to the Prime Minister for consideration by the Cabinet.

Note that while the ability of the Cabinet to propose legislation may seem non-controversial based on the English version of the constitution (article 72 of which says, in part that "Prime Minister, representing the Cabinet, submits *bill*s, reports on general national affairs and foreign relations to the Diet" (emphasis added)), the Japanese version does not actually use the term meaning bill (*i.e., hōritsuan,* literally "proposed law," the term used in Article 59, which describes the legislative proposal). Rather it uses the more generic *gian* ("matter for consideration"). Although this more general term is understood to include draft legislation, the lack of an unambiguous legislative role for the Cabinet is an odd constitutional omission. In the past, a "US-style" approach whereby the bills proposed by the Cabinet were submitted to the Diet through friendly Diet members was experimented with, but quickly abandoned. Today few if any scholars question the authority of the Cabinet to submit legislative proposals directly to the Diet, it having become a well-established practice.

Of course each chamber of the Diet can and does propose legislation. However, the Diet Act actually imposes numerous restraints on legislative initiatives by Diet members. This reflects the early history of the post-war Diet when the lack of such restrictions resulted in individual members flooding the legislature with *omiyage hōan*, "gift bills" intended to curry favor with constituents. To prevent such behavior, article 56 of the Diet Act requires that in order for a member of the HOR to submit a proposal (s)he must receive the support of 20 other members of the chamber, 50 if the proposal would require budgetary action. For proposals in the HOC, the thresholds are 10 and 20 respectively.

In addition, in the HOR a member proposal will not be accepted unless it has also been approved by that member's political party. In 1997 the legality of this practice was challenged in a case where a proposal to adopt a national referendum for important policy matters failed because, although it had the support of the requisite number of HOR members, it was not approved by the moving member's party. The Tokyo District Court held that the HOR practice was within the scope of the Diet's internal autonomy and not amenable to judicial oversight (Tokyo High Court judgment of June 18, 1997, 1618 Hanji 71).

Not only does the Cabinet propose a great deal of legislation to the Diet, but such proposals account for a great majority of legislation actually passed into law. As shown in Table 5-2, the success rate for Cabinet legislative proposals is much higher than those initiated from within the Diet. The following table gives a picture of the makeup and success rate for legislative proposals initiated by the Cabinet and the Diet, respectively.

TABLE 5-2 COMPARATIVE SUBMISSION AND SUCCESS RATE DATA FOR CABINET- AND DIET-INITIATED LEGISLATIVE PROPOSALS

	Cabinet-Initiated		Diet-Initiated	
Diet Session	Number*	Number passed/Success rate (%)*	Number *	Number passed/ Success rate (%)*
193rd Diet (Ordinary Session) Jan. 20–June 18, 2017	(6) 66	(3)/(50%) 63/95%	(50) 136	(0)/(0%) 10/7%
192nd Diet (Extraordinary Session) Sept. 26–Dec. 17, 2016	(11) 19	(6)/(54%) 18/95%	(54) 126	(4)/7% 13/10%
191st Diet	(11)	(0)	(54)	(0)

	Cabinet-Initiated		Diet-Initiated	
Diet Session	Number*	Number passed/Success rate (%)*	Number *	Number passed/ Success rate (%)*
(Extraordinary Session) Aug.1–3, 2016	0	0	0	0
190th Diet (Ordinary Session) Jan. 4–June 1, 2016	(9) 56	(4)/44% 50/89%	(28) 72	(2)/(7%) 18/(25%)
189th Diet (Ordinary Session) Jan. 26–Sept. 27, 2015	(0) 75	(0)/NA 66/(88%)	(4) 72	(0)/(0%) 12/(17%)
188th Diet (Special Session) Dec. 24–26, 2014	(0) 0	(0)/NA 0/NA	(0) 4	(0)/NA 0/(0%)
187th Diet (Extraordinary Session) Sept. 29–Nov. 21, 2014	(2) 31	(2)/(100%) 21/68%	(43) 28	(3)/(7%) 8 /29%
186th Diet (Ordinary Session) Jan. 24–June 22, 2014	(4) 81	(3)/(75%) 79/98%	(42) 75	(0)/(0%) 21/28%
185th Diet (Extraordinary Session) Oct. 15–Dec. 8, 2013	(8) 23	(7)/(88%) 20/87%	(28) 45	(2)/(7%) 10/22%
184th Diet (Extraordinary Session) Aug. 2–7, 2013	(8) 0	(0)/(0%) 0/0%	(28) 0	(0)/(0%) 0/0%
183rd Diet (Ordinary Session) Jan. 28–June 26, 2013	(0) 75	(0)/NA 63/84%	(0) 81	(0)/NA 10/12%

	Cabinet-Initiated		Diet-Initiated	
Diet Session	Number*	Number passed/Success rate (%)*	Number *	Number passed/ Success rate (%)*
182nd Diet (Special Session) Dec. 26–28, 2012	(0) 0	(0)/NA 0/NA	(0) 2	(0)/NA 0/0%
181st Diet (Extraordinary Session) Oct. 29–Nov. 16, 2012	(33) 10	(2) 5/50%	(52) 6	(2)/(4%) 1/17%
180th Diet (Ordinary Session) Jan. 24, Sep. 8, 2012	(23) 83	(6)/(26%) 55/66%	(35) 77	(0)/(0%) 31/40%

*For each session, the upper values in parenthesis refer to bills carried over from the prior Diet session. The lower values refer to those newly submitted during that session. See Chapter 3 for a discussion of Diet sessions and the limitations on continuing legislative proposals past their expiry.

The comparative success of Cabinet legislation is not a recent phenomenon; the average passage rate for legislation submitted by the Cabinet has consistently exceeded 80% for the entire history of the post-war constitutional system. This is surprisingly similar to what prevailed in the Imperial Diet, where the average success rate was about 83% for legislation submitted by the government over 92 sessions from 1890 to 1947. This compared to an average success rate of about 16% and 9% for proposals by the House of Peers and House of Representatives respectively.

Under the current constitution distinction between legislation initiated by the Diet and that initiated by the Cabinet involves some subtle interplay between the two branches. For example, there may be instances where for political reasons or due to the Diet calendar, it may still be occasionally more convenient for the Cabinet to have a piece of proposed legislation submitted by a a Diet member. Furthermore, customs have developed whereby certain types of legislation are expected to be initiated by the Cabinet or the Diet, depending on their substance. Those submitted by the Cabinet include laws relating to government institutions (other than the Diet) and the matters within their jurisdiction as well as those relating to budgetary matters (the budgeting process being controlled in the first instance by the Cabinet). Laws that custom holds should be initiated by the Diet include those relating to the Diet itself, electoral laws, laws relating to the oversight of administrative institutions, and the so-called "Basic Laws" discussed earlier in this chapter.

Regardless of the intent, legislation goes through a very different process depending upon whether it is initiated by the Cabinet or the Diet. Legislation submitted by the Cabinet will typically originate from whichever ministry has (or wants) jurisdiction over the matter being legislated and commences the process by seeking a cabinet resolution to make, amend or rescind a law (NGOA, article 11). If more than one ministry might have jurisdiction over the matter, then there is a process for resolving potential turf disputes). The ministerial drafting schedule takes place within the framework of a recurring legislative and budgetary cycle, the latter of which must be typically taken into account in legislation that requires appropriations.

Ministries are staffed with professional technocrats well accustomed to the intricacies of crafting legislation. Depending upon the area of policy, a ministry will likely have or need to establish deliberative council of experts, industry representatives and other constituencies who can be consulted for area-specific insights, though the actual influence of such councils and consultations is sometimes debatable.

After various internal checks have been cleared, the proposed legislation is sent to the Cabinet Legislation Bureau for a preliminary review. Further consultations may also be required with other Ministries; the Ministry of Finance for any budgetary impact, the Ministry of Justice if the proposed legislation includes any criminal penalties or would involve the commercial or corporate registry system and so forth. Consultations with relevant ministries may also be suggested by the Cabinet Legislation Bureau. With inter-ministerial consultations out of the way, the proposed legislation can then be socialized with the dominant political parties and, if necessary opposition parties as well.

The Minister(s) in charge of the legislation then requests cabinet approval of the legislative proposal. This involves a second submission of the law to the CLB, which returns it to the Cabinet with an opinion. Since the purpose of the preliminary consultation with the CLB is to prevent any hurdles arising at this stage in the process, this consultation is typically a formality, though at this stage of the process the CLB may still propose amendments. The bill is then submitted to the Cabinet for approval which, if given, is unanimous.

Once approved by the Cabinet, the law is explained to the party in power at its legislative committee, a number and code is attached to the Bill denoting it as having initiated from the Cabinet and it is distributed to the members of each Diet chamber. Which chamber shall consider the bill first is up to the Diet, but the Cabinet may indicate a preference. Despite the tight control exercised over the drafting process up to its submission by the Cabinet to the Diet, once it has been submitted even the Prime Minister retains no formal control over the process that follows including amendments, other than through his status as head of the dominant political party.

Legislation initiated by Diet members goes through a different process. Many Diet members may lack the technical skills necessary to draft legislation competently either personally or through their staff. Each chamber of the Diet has a legislation bureau staffed with bureaucratic professionals, including officials on secondment from other branches of government. The process of crafting Diet-initiated bills may be more iterative, with the legislative staff helping Diet members with research and drafting in order to express their policy wishes in legislation that will not conflict with other laws. The procedural hurdles that need to be cleared in order for this type of legislation to succeed have been discussed above.

Whichever route it takes, once a bill is in the Diet, such substantive deliberation as does take place occurs mostly within the relevant committees of the two houses. Question time is allocated to each committee member but questions must be submitted in advance so bureaucrats can help prepare the appropriate answers. Follow-on questions are possible, but the deliberative aspects of the legislative may sometimes be highly scripted. Final approval of the full session of the relevant chamber is required. Questions are also allowed at this stage but subject to even more restrictions. The result is a process where there may be little actual deliberation. In fact the ruling party may use its majority control of both houses to rush through controversial legislation, a tactic that may be necessitated by the pressures of the Diet calendar and days remaining in the present session.

Legislation that is passed first by the HOC is sent to the HOR for approval. The HOC may also initiate legislation, though such instances represent the minority case and are the bills least likely to succeed. If the HOR approves the bill first, it is sent to the HOC. If the HOC refuses to approve the matter or gives no response, the HOR may deem the proposal rejected after 60 days (Constitution, article 59(4)). If the HOR is able to muster a 2/3 majority, it can pass the legislation over the objections of the HOC (Art. 59(2)) or call for a joint committee of both houses (Art. 59(3)).

In addition to legislation, the joint committee process is intended to resolve disagreements over the budget, ratification of treaties and choice of prime minister as well (Articles 60, 61 and 67) before the HOR exercises its override powers. Joint committees were held on a number of occasions early in the history of the current constitution, prior to the development of the so-called "1955 system" of almost constant rule by the LDP. Since then, however, there has only been instance of a joint committee being held, in 1994.

Because of prolonged LDP control of both houses for most of the history of the current constitutional system, instances of the HOR using a 2/3 majority vote to overcome the resistance of the HOC have been rare. As with the joint committees, a number of instances of this happening occurred in the 1950s, and then five decades intervened before the measure started to be used again in 2007 when the LDP lost control of the HOC (which it subsequently regained a few years later).

While the general rule is that the approval of both chambers through a simple majority of the required quorum is required to pass a measure into law, subject to the ability of the HOR to use its 2/3 as explained above, the constitution provides for two exceptions where special procedures are required. First, a constitutional amendment must be approved by 2/3 of the full membership of both houses before being submitted to a national referendum (Article 96). This considered by some to be an excessively high threshold. At the time of writing the constitution had never been amended. The second are laws affecting a specific area and require a local referendum, as described earlier in this chapter.

How a proposed law will fare in the Diet is generally known before it is put to a vote, particularly if it originates from the Cabinet. This is because Diet members are generally required to vote in accordance with the mandate of their party. Parliamentarians who ignore such instructions are subject to various forms of punishment by their party, which may include being expelled from their party which in turn may result in them losing their Diet seat. Such treatment has been challenged on a number of constitutional grounds but has always been upheld, since the judiciary has long held political parties as essential to the functioning of a parliamentary democracy and been reluctant to interfere in their internal affairs. It has also been noted that this tradition goes back to the pre-war time when strict party discipline was necessary to stand up to the militarists and bureaucrats. In the case of proposals that have a significant moral component or where the party lacks a unified view, it may permit members to vote their consciences without sanction.

Sometimes in the course of approving a bill, the relevant HOC or HOR legislative committee may pass an ancillary resolution (*futai ketsugi*) expressing views as to how the law should be interpreted or implemented. While these do not become a part of the law when passed, the government is expected to respect them when executing the law.

Once legislation is passed by the Diet it is submitted to the Emperor. While the Emperor's assent is not required for legislation to take effect, the promulgation of the laws is one of formal roles accorded to him under Article 7 of the Constitution. Under Article 66 of the Diet Act, laws submitted to the Emperor must be promulgated within 30 days. Promulgation is accomplished through publication in the *kanpō* (Official Gazette). Interetingly, though there is no formal legal basis for this part of the process: the Meiji-era rules on official documentation practices were repealed during the American occupation but never formally replaced. The current use of the *kanpō* to promulgate laws is thus a matter of official custom.

The default rule under Article 2 of the Act on General Rules for Application of Laws of 2006 is that laws take effect twenty days after promulgation, unless the law itself provides differently. Some laws may have a very long lead time between promulgation and taking effect, if they need time to be socialized properly or significant secondary legislation is required for implementation. The Supreme Court has also upheld laws taking effect immediately upon promulgation, at least with respect to the applicability of amendments imposing enhanced criminal penalties (Supreme Court, Grand Bench judgment of October 15, 1958).

C. STATUTES AND STATUTORY LANGUAGE

1. The Structure and Character of Japanese Statutes

Because of the discipline imposed through the CLB vetting process on much of the legislation passed by the Diet, Japanese statutes and higher order regulations demonstrate a high degree of consistency in their structure, organization and use of terminology. Instances of litigation arising because of conflicting terminology across different statutes and regulations or other defects are rare.

Statutes are identified by the year in which they are passed and a number indicating the order in which they were passed. Regulations similarly identify the regulatory authority issuing them, the year of issuance and the number.

Large statutes such as the Civil Code, the Companies Act or the various procedural codes are divided into multiple parts, chapters, subchapters or sections depending on their size and organization. Regardless of this organization statutes contain numbered articles. Within articles there are paragraphs and clauses.

Laws are generally formatted consistently. Article 1 of many statutes sets forth its purpose. Article 2 oftain contains any necessary defined terms. Penal sanctions for violations generally come towards the end. Supplementary provisions (*fusoku*) at the end of the statute may deal with transitional matters, specify when the law will come into force and identify prior laws being repealed. If a law has been amended multiple times the *fusoku* may be extensive. Easily overlooked, the the *fusoku* can occasionally contain important language.

Long statutes and codes may have a preliminary subsection containing *sōsoku* or general rules of interpretation that apply throughout. Some statutes or regulations have schedules (*beppyō*) which are updated regularly (e.g., those relating to the authorized number of public servants and their salaries). Drafters generally seek to avoid renumbering articles, so when an amendment deletes an article, the article in question is usually left in place with "deleted" in lieu of other text. Amendments that add language can be accomplished by adding an article with a hyphenated number at the appropriate place. For example, between articles 817and 818 of the Civil Code, there is an entire subsection dealing with Special Adoption (and numbered articles 817–2 through 817–11) which was added in 1987.

Statutory drafting manuals are commercially available and readily illustrate the structure, logic and terminology used in the creation of Japanese law. The ability to draft legislation is a high-order skill acquired by central government officials through years of devotion to the craft. The results are apparent in laws that are generally very well-ordered and constistently-structured.

The fact that most of the laws actually passed by the Diet are initiated by the government means that a great deal of it is drafted in a very "pro-government," even subtly authoritarian, fashion. In business-related area of laws, the laws may be drafted so as to delegate authority to fill in the final details through secondary legislation back to the Ministry that drafted the legislation. Accordingly, particularly in business-related areas of law one of the most important things to understanding the law is to identify which ministry has jurisdiction over the law in question. This is easy to do since each Ministry's website contains a link to the laws and regulations under its jurisdiction. Moreover, these links will include not only legislation in effect, but bills submitted to the Diet, giving the impression that the Ministry itself is proposing legislation, which is actually not far from the truth in many cases.

Laws initiated by the Diet do not benefit from the same degree of expertise and this sometimes shows in the results. Most of the small number of statutory provisions found unconstitutional by the Supreme Court have originated from the Diet rather than the Cabinet.

2. Statutory Language

One of the significant innovations to written law that came with the post-war constitution was its rendering in vernacular Japanese. Previously, statutes and regulations had been rendered in *kanamajiribun*, a form of what is essentially "classical" Japanese, with different rules of grammar and punctuation and written using a different character set to express grammatical elements. While this form of statutory drafting is succinct and elegant in its own way, the average Japanese person might find it difficult to read, similar to the way that many native English speakers may generally understand the works of Shakespeare but struggle with some of the nuances and specific terms and phrases he uses.

Laws passed after the draft constitution was announced on April 17, 1946 were drafted in the vernacular, a decision made not by the Diet but at a meeting of top bureaucrats held the next day. The first statute written the new way was an amendment to the Postal Act. Since then, the Japanese government has made an effort to modernize the language of those laws that predate the Constitution. This has been a gradual process; the Penal Code was not rewritten in the vernacular until 1995, and the process of modernizing the language of the Civil Code was not completed until 2005. While there is a body of commentary about the supposed "legal consciousness" of Japanese people that attributes to them a "cultural" or "traditional" lack of interest in law or legal remedies, it is rarely mentioned that for much of the post war period the law was rendered in a textual form that many average people might have found bothersome to read.

Today *kanamajiribun* looks positively archaic and, when appearing in a *roppō* statutory handbook, is usually a sign of one of a shrinking number of statutes of a purely pre-war vintage. This is not always the case, however. The Public Notary Act of 1908 was amended in 2000 to reflect the role of notaries in dealing with electronic commercial registry records but the language was left in *kanamajiribun,* making it look rather odd, like a software license written in Latin.

D. CUSTOM AND CUSTOMARY LAWS

As noted at the outset of this book, Japan's legal system is comparatively modern and quite rational as a result. The early rules for trials first established in 1875 called on judges to settle cases first based on written law and custom if written law was lacking, and logic/reason (*jōri*) if there was no custom or written law. However, written law has supplanted a great deal of custom since then. Today custom plays little role in Japan as formal legal norms, though in some sectors of Japanese society—the world of Sumo, for example—long-held customary rules may govern those who participate voluntarily.

A possible role for custom is still recognized in some statutes. For example, article 3 of Japan's choice of law statute, the Act on General Rules for Application of Laws of 2006 provides that "*Customs which are not against public policy shall have the same effect as laws, to the extent that they are authorized by the provisions of laws and regulations, or they relate to matters not provided for in laws and regulations.*" As discussed in Chapter 9, in the private law context article 92 of the Civil Code also acknowledges that the intent to follow custom can prevail over some non-mandatory private law provisions. Local customs were surveyed when the Civil Code and Japan's other modern statutes were drafted in the Meiji Period, and in some instances customs were recast as laws.

E. THE ROLE OF PRECEDENT

1. Precedents of Non-Judicial Institutions

As in other places, precedent has long had a role in Japanese institutions. For example, many Diet practices and procedures are based on precedents (*senrei*—literally "previous instances/examples") and recorded in a book of precedents maintained by each chamber. The 2013 edition of the House of Councillors *senreiroku* (Record of Precedents) ran to over 800 pages and included precedents such as the well-established practice of numbering Diet sessions, the Emperor delivering an opening address at Diet convocations and the protocol for greeting him on the occasion.

Administrative institutions may also be bound by precedent though these may be presented in the form of *tsūtatsu* (directives) or other types of "rules" discussed earlier in this chapter, as examples of recommended practice. *Zenrei ga nai* ("there is no precedent for it") is a stock bureaucratic phrase ushered in response to the prospect of doing something new or different not clearly anticipated by regulations.

2. Judicial Precedent (Hanrei)

a. *Historical Background*

Edo Period proscriptions on the dissemination of information about the law also made a precedent important. Local officials who had to apply what rules were known in criminal cases could not always be sure about sentencing and feared the perception of being unfair by applying different punishments in similar cases. This led some officials to create collections of sentencing precedents that their successors could use to ensure consistent application of the law. This practice was eventually accepted by the Tokugawa authorities.[1]

In the early Meiji period when law was changing as part of a transition to both a more centralized form of government and western-based legal models, there was tremendous uncertainty among judges as to what the law was, which law should be applied to a particular case and how. This would have been particularly frustrating since under the system of *ritsuryō*, a judge who punished an offender incorrectly was himself potentially subject to punishment. A desire for certainty saw the use of the Tokugawa-era practice of *ukagaisho* written inquiries by judges to higher judicial authorities regarding how to handle particular cases. Collections of these inquiries and the responses became their own form of precedent, though one that faded in importance as Japan developed a modern system of courts.

Precedents continued to be important for administrative purposes into the Meiji Period and beyond. By the Taishō Period, some legal scholars were going further and asserting court precedent as a source of law, albeit different from the statutes passed by the Diet.

At the same time, however, Japan has never had clear statutory rules adopting case law as a form of law, such as the reception statutes of many common law jurisdictions. Moreover, the idea of judges "making" law through precedent in individual cases was affirmatively rejected very early in the Meiji period with the passage of "Understandings Regarding Trial Administration," an 1875 proclamation of the Grand Council of State. Article 4 of this proclamation mandates that decisions of judges in trials could *not* become rules of general applicability in future cases. This would seem a perfectly rational rule for a central government trying to establish a uniform system of laws established by national authorities rather than judges who at the time were effectively local officials. Interestingly, articles 3, 4 and 5 of Understandings Regarding Trial Administration are still treated as valid law, to the extent they are included in the government's "e-gov" on-line database of laws and regulations.

A more recent law—article 4 of the Courts Act—mandates that "a conclusion in a judgment of a higher instance court shall bind the lower instance courts *with respect to the case concerned.*" (emphasis added). This formulation can also be read as implicitly denying any broader general applicability of higher court decisions in other cases.

---

[1] The Supreme Court today has also established a database of sentencing precedents in furtherance of the same goal, as discussed in Chapter 8.

References to judicial precedents do appear in some Japanese statutes. The earliest example being the post-war a Code of Criminal Procedure of 1948, article 405(ii) and (iii) of which specifies "inconsistency with Supreme Court precedents" or, if such precedents are lacking, inconsistency with high court or Supreme Court of Judicature precedents as grounds for appeals from a lower court judgments. Similar provisions are found in the Code of Civil Procedure (articles 318 and 337).

Yet it would be a stretch to say that these references to *hanrei* render court decisions other than those of the Supreme Court a form of case law. As a basic matter they only establish rules to guide judges as to a category of judgments that are likely to be overturned on appeal, rather than creating rules of law having a normative effect outside of the judiciary. In that sense the role that precedent has come to play in the legal system is arguably consistent with the bureaucratic character of the judiciary as described in Chapter 4.

b. Hanrei—An Overview of Precedent Today

More often than not judicial precedents, particularly lower court decisions but sometimes even those of the Supreme Court, seem to function primarily as examples of the court dealing with a particular issue in the context of a particular statutory provision. In that sense they can be seen as similar to other forms of precedent, particularly in connection with basic laws such as the Civil Code or Penal Code.

That said, judicial precedents are referred to using a different term than is used when describing precedents in an administrative or legislative context. Here the term is not *senrei* but *hanrei* (an "example of a judgment"). When discussing common law countries the term *hō* (law) is added to the end to create the term "*hanreihō*"—case law—but this formulation is rarely if ever used when discussing Japanese court precedents.

The constitutional designation of the Diet as the sole law-making organ of the state would seem to foreclose any role for Japanese courts in creating "case law" in the same manner as appellate courts in common law jurisdictions. Whether Japanese courts "make law" depends entirely on how the term "law" is defined. As the preceding discussion in this chapter illustrates, it is by no means a simple definition. That said, it is not—or should not—be an entirely theoretical discussion either. Under article 76(3) of the Constitution judges are supposedly bound *only* by the Constitution and the laws (*hōritsu*). One could argue this means precedent *cannot* be binding on judges (absent laws to such effect), but the accepted view is that "law" in this clause has a much broader meaning than just legislation passed by the Diet.

Under Article 81 of the Constitution the Supreme Court is clearly vested with the power to review the constitutionality of laws, orders, regulations and dispositions. Article 10 of the Court Act and related Supreme Court rules provide clarity as to when cases must be heard by the Grand Bench in both constitutional and other cases. In this sense Supreme Court decisions—particularly those of the Grand Bench—can be seen as having a precedential value in presenting a conclusive interpretation of the constitution and other statutes that lower courts must follow.

Leaving aside the question of whether judicial precedents constitute a separate type of positive law, *hanrei* are an important *element* of Japanese law. *Hanrei* are critical to understanding what statutory law means and how cases are brought and resolved through the litigation processes. Precedents are also an important part of constitutional law, broadly defined, with decisions of the Supreme Court playing an important interpretive role, one that tends to be overlooked by those who focus primarily on the small number of instances where the court has found laws or regulatory actions to be unconstitutional.

In the field of civil law, precedent has played an important role in turning the often brusque provisions of older statutes like the Civil Code into something that can be used to litigate specific cases. As discussed in Chapter 9, Japanese tort law is based largely on Article 709 of the Civil Code, which merely articulates the general principal that one who negligently or intentionally causes injury to another is liable for compensation. It is necessary to look to precedent for greater details such as standards for determining negligence, issues of causation, apportionment of liability among joint tortfeasors and so forth.

Supreme Court precedents (and in some areas of law, pre-war decisions of the Supreme Court of Judicature) play an important role in filling in interpretive gaps or even supplementing the law where it does not address situations. In that sense, the court can be seen as playing a role in "making" law. It also sometimes expressly or implicitly reverses prior precedent. While a detailed examination is not possible, some examples will hopefully give a flavor of the type of "law-making" conducted by the Supreme Court:

(a) Article 1(3) of the Civil Code contains a general prohibition on the "abuse of rights" which has been applied by courts to specific instances such including finding it as a limiting the ostensibly absolute powers of the head of households in the prewar family system (Supreme Court of Judicature judgment of June 20, 1901) and a source of liability of steam train operators for damages caused by smoke (Supreme Court of Judicature judgment of March 3, 1919).

(b) In the past provisional registrations of title in real estate were a common form of collateral taken by lenders, exposing borrowers and tenants to the risk of the lender asserting ownership when the intent was a form of lien for borrowings worth far less than the value of the property. In a November 1967 judgment the 1st Petty Bench prohibited lenders from retaining the value of the property beyond the amount of the loan, and subsequent decisions further clarified the rules relating to this form of secured lending.

(c) Courts have also been largely responsible for the development of rules involving spouses in *defacto* marriages. For example an October 6, 1918 judgment the Supreme Court of Judicature held that the wife in an unregistered (and thus not legally-recognized) marriage was entitled to seek damages in connection with the death of her husband at a railway crossing.

(d) The Supreme Court has made numerous important decisions on the subject of who has standing to bring suit in various contexts. For example, in a November 25, 1999 judgment, the 1st Petty Bench held that persons who lived, worked or went to school near a road expansion project but did not have affected property rights did not have standing to bring suit to invalidate the permit issued under the Urban Planning Act. However in a December 7, 2005 judgment the Grand Bench effectively reversed this finding by recognizing a broad category of stakeholders as having standing to challenge a permit for a different project authorized under the same law.

Supreme Court decisions have often led the law by providing needed structure where it is lacking or applying doctrines such as "abuse of rights" which amount to a change of seemingly clear statutory provisions. The legislature sometimes follows up and develops statutory rules that confirm them. For example, in the example of (b) above, in 1978 the Diet subsequently passed a law relating to contracts for using provisional title registrations as a form of collateral. Similarly, as noted in Chapter 11, some significant employment law has been developed first by court decisions and subsequently codified in legislation.

In light of the importance of *hanrei*, mastering them is a basic feature of legal studies. No law school student could hope to graduate or hope to pass the NBE without a firm understanding of the key precedents in the areas of law tested on it.

As already noted, most significant *hanrei* are Supreme Court precedents. The Supreme Court receives thousands of appeals per year. Most are rejected perfunctorily with a standard form judgment stating the appeal fails to assert a constitutional claim or other grounds for Supreme Court review. Some of the comparatively small number of cases that go on to be reviewed by a Petty Bench and virtually all of the even smaller number decided by the Grand Bench become precedents.

However, even at the Supreme Court level, what makes a case a "precedent" as opposed to just a final resolution of a particular dispute is somewhat subjective. In some cases even dissenting or concurring opinions may have a precedential value as an indicator of a possible future direction of the court.

Brief mention should be given to the precedential value of lower court decisions. One difference between Japan and common law systems such as the United States is the in significance of judgments rendered by appellate courts other than the Supreme Court. Japanese High Court judgments may be persuasive indicators of the interpretation of a statute or even the constitution, but have little if any *stare decisis* value in terms of binding lower courts, even those within its appellate and administrative jurisdiction.

Lower court decisions may also be indicative of a trend in a particular area of law and may be noted and discussed by scholars and practitioners active in the field. However, it may be nothing more than a trend and possibly a misguided one at that; the Supreme Court may subsequently decide to set things right with a decision. For example, for decades Japan's *habeas corpus* law was used by lower courts as a means of promptly resolving disputes over the custody of children arising between estranged married couples. In 1993, however, the Supreme Court issued a decision holding that as between parents who were still married, the remedy should generally not be used as it was preferable to resolve such matters not in district courts, but through the procedures and expertise available in family courts (Supreme Court, 3rd Petty Bench judgment of October 19, 1993).

In areas where the Supreme Court has declined to articulate a view, high court decisions and even occasionally lower court decisions may be the only precedents available and are thus useful indicators of a judicial view of a particular interpretive issue, though they are not conclusive. On some issues, even high court opinions are missing and occasionally lower court opinions are referenced by default, though their significance may be greater as educational materials rather than indicators of legal norms.

By way of example, a type of study guide used by most law students is legal publisher *Yūhikaku*'s "100 Precedent" (*hanrei hyakusen*) series of case sumarries: the current edition (2013) of the two volume set of constitutional precedents in this series together contain summaries of 215 of the leading constitutional precedents. Most are Supreme Court Grand or Petty Bench precedents, but also included are eight high court precedents, 15 district court cases and even a summary court precedent.

To the extent the Supreme Court renders a perfunctory rejection of appeals in a case decided by the lower court, this could be interpreted as a tacit acceptance of the lower court ruling, but it could also just be a matter of the Court avoiding the issue. In any case, an undisturbed lower court decision on an issue obviously does not have the same significance as a Supreme Court judgment.

c. *Judgments, Decisions and Orders*

To understand *hanrei* it is also important to appreciate the distinction between a judgment (*hanketsu*), decision (*kettei*) and order (*meirei*).

A judgment (*hanketsu*) is rendered by a court based on oral argument (*kōtō benron*)—a full trial (or *saiban*). This is a term of constitutional significance, article 32 of the constitution preserving the right to a trial in a court (a nuance which is not evident from the English version, which refers only to the "right of access to the courts").

Some exceptions to the oral argument requirement apply. For example the Supreme Court may render judgment without oral argument if it deems the appeal without merit. Judgments are generally delivered in court, though it is not necessary for the parties to be present in the case of civil trials (CCP. article 342, CCivPro article 251). Once confirmed through the waiver and exhaustion of appeals, *hanketsu* have *res judicata* effect on the parties and the court.

By contrast, a *kettei* ("decision") is a ruling by a court without oral proceedings and under a procedural regime that may not constitute a trial. The court may at its discretion hold proceedings comparable to them but this is not required. *Kettei* may include various procedural decisions or determinations of law that can be rendered without consideration of evidence or evidentiary proceedings that are not subject to the formal requirements of the CCivP. Also included in the ambit of *kettei* are *shinpan* (decrees), which are made by family courts in divorce or other matters when conciliation has failed but typically in advance of formal litigation (see Chapter 10).[2]

Meirei (orders) are another type of dispositive action. Unlike a *kettei* which is usually rendered by a court (which may consist of a panel of judges), a *meirei* is issued by the presiding judge (who may also be the only judge, depending on the case). Confusingly some *kettei* decisions are described as "orders" since they involve a decision by the court to order a party to do something (e.g., a court order to disclose documents in civil litigation under CCivPro, article 223). Similarly confusing, a *hanketsu* judgment may include an order to a party to do something, such as pay damages, but are considered part of the judgment.

---

[2] The term *shinpan* is also used to describe decisions made by administrative agencies such as those of JPO in respect of patent applications.

Kettei and *meirei* may be rendered by an assistant judge, while *hanketsu* judgments require the involvement of a full judge. Although generally the rules that apply to *hanketsu* are also supposed to apply to *kettei* and *meirei* whenever appropriate (CCivP article 122), the procedural approach on appeal is different for the two types of disposition. This is thus relevant to which types of disposition are more likely to become precedents. *Hanketsu* judgments are appealed through the *kōsō* and *jōkoku* processes described at chapters 8 and 10 in criminal and civil criminal trials, respectively. *Kettei* and *meirei* are appealed through *kōkoku* process described in the same chapters.

Put simply judgments (*hanketsu*) are usually the result of a more rigorous evidentiary and procedural process. *Kettei* and *meirei* may involve trial-like procedures, but may also result from discrete procedural dispositions or proceedings that do not constitute "trials" for procedural or constitutional purposes. For example, this latter category includes most family court and bankruptcy proceedings.

Of the 215 constitutional precedents annotated in the "100 Constitutional Precedents" series described above, all but 17 came in the form of appeals from *hanketsu* judgments. The remainder were *kōkoku* appeals or decisions involving procedural orders. The most famous of these is probably the 2013 Grand Bench decision finding unconstitutional the Civil Code's grant of inferior inheritance rights to children born out of wedlock discussed earlier in this chapter. It took the form of a *kettei* decision because it rose to the Supreme Court as a special *kōkoku* appeal from a *shinpan* decree by a family court, which deals with inheritance matters. Similarly, in the 3 volume *hanrei hyakusen* Civil Code Precedents in the same series (7th edition, 2015) of the 306 Civil Code precedents covered, only eleven were *kettei* decisions, all in the area of family and inheritance.

Which cases become precedents may also be driven by requirements as to the form that judgments and decisions take. Under Article 253 of the CCivPro, a *hanketsu* judgment must include: (i) the *shubun* (dispositive portion), (ii) facts, (iii) reasoning, (iv) the date of final arguments, (v) identification of the parties and their counsel, and (vi) identification of the rendering court. The statement of the facts must make the claims at issue clear and be adequate to justify the result. Judgments in criminal cases follow a similar format and contain a *shubun*, a statement of reasons, the applicable provisions of the penal code or other criminal statute and the findings of fact indicating the elements of the offense. *Kettei* and *meirei* may follow a similar format though the formal requirements are not as rigid.

The *shubun* is the dispositive portion of the judgment. It is typically very short—in a civil trial it may either order the payment of damages or, reject a plaintiff's claims and apportion liability for court costs. In a criminal trial it will typically declare the defendant guilty or acquitted (usually the former). In appellate cases, the *shubun* may consist of a statement dismissing the appeal, vacating the lower court judgment and remanding for further proceedings, or replacing the lower judgment with the appellate court's own judgment.

The *shubun* portion of a judgment or other decision is not what makes a case a precedent. Rather, it is the reasoning that leads to and justifies the result announced by the *shubun*. This part of a judgment can sometimes be very long and complicated. Fortunately, the Supreme Court has developed the practice of underlining the key portions of the reasoning parts of its judgments. These portions of the judgment are often what get repeated in annotations, textbooks, as well as subsequent court decisions citing the precedent.

The reasoning part a judgment that becomes a precedent may also be surprisingly short, as may the judgment itself. Some Supreme Court judgments—particularly those of the Petty Benches—may be just a few pages long. For example, what is considered one of the principal Supreme Court precedents on the subject of the rights of foreigners in Japan is just one page long and the key (underlined) language simply declares that the holding in an earlier Grand Bench judgment makes it clear the constitution does not guarantee foreign residents in Japan the right to temporarily travel abroad (the so-called "Kathleen Morikawa Case," Supreme Court 1st Petty Bench judgment of November 16, 1992, citing Supreme Court Grand Bench judgments of June 19, 1957 and October 4, 1978).

This is true outside the sphere of constitutional litigation also. The Supreme Court is often able to use sparse judgments to add definition to equally sparse statutory provisions. For example, in a two page 1992 ruling the 2nd Petty Bench added definition to article 234 of the Penal Code, which proscribes the forcible obstruction of business, by finding that the act of putting dog excrement in the pocket of a fire chief's uniform and a dead cat painted red in his desk drawer constituted "force" (Supreme Court, 2nd Petty Bench judgment of November 27, 1992).

However it is not always necessary to rely solely on its text (and prior precedents) to understand a Supreme Court judgment. The role of research judges (see discussion at Chapter 4) has become institutionalized to the extent that it has become a common practice for the *chōsakan* primarily responsible for helping the court with a particular judgment to write an article (called a *hanrei kaisetsu*) explaining the rationale behind it. Some legal scholars will go so far as to say it is impossible to truly understand a Japanese Supreme Court precedent without also reading the *hanrei kaisetsu*. For example on May 1, 2000 the 1st Petty Bench issued a decision (*kettei*) on the issue of whether a court could order visitation in cases of parents who are separated but not divorced (the relevant provision of the Civil Code—article 766—only referring to *post-divorce* custody-related dispositions). The official ruling was only one page long but the research judge's *hanrei kaisetsu* was much more voluminous, and contained a great deal of reasoning not immediately apparent from the judgment itself.

The structure of *hanrei* means that a particular Supreme Court judgment or decision may become important because it contains language indicating the court's views on a particular facet of law, rather because of its dispositive result. Those who focus on the limited role the Supreme Court has played in finding statutes or government acts unconstitutional (see Chapter 6) may thus be missing the significant body of constitutional precedents created by the court in the course of ruling in favor of the government, or avoiding the constitutional question altogether.

A byproduct of the formal structure of *hanketsu* judgments is that courts lower courts can use them to make a significant statement without giving it any dispositive effect. For example, occasionally high courts have issued what are sometimes called *dasoku hanketsu* (literally, "snake leg judgments"), judgments that are not controversial in the actual result (the dispositive *shubun* portion) but which generate publicity because of statements (*dicta*) in the reasoning portion.

For example, in 2005 the Osaka High Court issued a judgment finding the visit by then Prime Minister Koizumi Jun'ichirō to the Yasukuni Shrine (where those who died in Japan's military services are enshrined) was unconstitutional (Osaka High Court judgment of September 30, 2005). Similarly, in a 2008 appeal from three lower court cases the Nagoya High Court ruled that the dispatch of Japan's Air Self Defense Forces to Iraq to support the American-led war on terror was also unconstitutional (Nagoya High Court judgments (3) of April 17 2008).

Both judgments generated significant news, but had no real dispositive effect. This is because in each case the high court panel rejected the appeals of the plaintiffs, citizens groups seeking nominal damages and, in the case of the SDF case, an injunction. The *shubun* part of the judgments rejected the appeals on the grounds the plaintiffs had not suffered any actual damages. However in the reasoning part of the judgment, the courts engaged in a long analysis of the facts and the law and declared as *obiter dicta* that the constitution had been violated. The plaintiff appellants were presumably reasonably happy with a ruling of unconstitutionality, while the government, having won, could not appeal but was also not subject to a dispositive ruling that required it to change its behavior. Notwithstanding the Nagoya High Court ruling, the dispatch of SDF to Iraq continued unabated. This aspect of the role and structure of *hanrei* helps explain why it is not uncommon for activists to bring constitutional challenges fully expecting to lose but hoping that in its judgment a court will make statements favorable to their cause that also generate headlines.

For purposes of understanding the law, therefore, much of the import of *hanrei* is not in the dispositive result of the case but in a particular statement or declaration made in the reasoning that leads to it. This means that a precedent cited as supporting a particular view of the law—that unwarranted use of GPS tracking devices by police may violate article 35 of the Constitution (see Chapter 8)—may not see that view reflected in the substantive result of the case (*i.e.,* the conviction of the defendant being upheld on other grounds). This means that academic commentaries on precedent can make the Supreme Court seem more progressive than it actually is in practice.

Finally, before leaving the subject of *hanrei,* brief mention should be made of how *hanrei* are referenced. Some Western writers on Japanese law use U.S.-style case names that set forth the names of the parties to identify *hanrei.* For example, the 1976 *House of Representatives Malapportionment Case* finding and election law unconstitutional, discussed in Chapter 6, is sometimes referred to in English scholarship as "*Kurokawa v. Chiba Election Commission.*" This is not particularly helpful since such denotations are never used in Japanese and it may often be difficult to identify the actual parties in action in many cases, since many reported cases (particularly criminal and family cases) have identifying information removed before publication. Typically well-known cases are referred to by a descriptive title (e.g., the "Overseas Voting Rights Case"), with enough information about it (court, date of judgment) to be locable.

F. ACCESS TO INFORMATION ABOUT THE LAW

1. Roppō and Other Statutory Compilations

That Japan has a unitary legal system based primarily on statutory sources of law means that it is comparatively easy to *find* the law. Today virtually all national laws and most regulations, rules, directives and interpretations are available on the Internet.

The unitary and statutory nature of the law also means that it is easier to compile it into a comparatively small volume. Whereas the US CODE ANNOTATED in paper form takes up several bookcases, the entire corpus of Japanese statutory law and some key regulations can be fit into a brick-like two volume compilation called the "*Roppō Zensho*," which is published annually by *Yūhikaku*, one of Japan's leading legal publishers. Junior associates at Japanese law firms could once be identified because they were the ones lugging these heavy volumes into a conference room.

Virtually all statutes and most regulations are also available on line. Notwithstanding this, there is still a tremendous market for paper-based, commercially-published compilations of statutory and regulatory materials. These are collectively referred to as "*Roppō*," which literally means "Six Laws," a reference to what were once considered the six foundational codes of Japan: the constitution, the Civil Code, the Penal Code, the Commercial Code, the Code of Criminal Procedure and the Code of Civil Procedure (in the 19th century the term was actually first used to refer to the *French* versions of these laws which early Japanese officials and jurists used as a reference).

Through *Roppō* the law has long been more accessible to the average person than it would be in the United States. For example, a student or businessperson might find it useful to spend $15–$20 ever year or two to procure a current small *Roppō* containing the six codes and various other statutes relevant to daily life, such as the Labor Standards Act, the Child Welfare Act and even the UN Charter.

A practitioner active in a particular industry would also be able to procure a more specialized volume containing all the laws, regulations and other administrative rules and interpretations relevant to that industry. For example there are specialized *Roppō* for the railway industry, telecommunications, government finance, social welfare, fisheries, and so forth. There are also a variety of annotated *roppō*, which also contain short summaries of court decisions interpreting specific statutory clauses.

The publication of *roppō* involves editorial decisions. Interestingly, even the most basic *roppō* will usually contain the text of the Potsdam Declaration of 1945, the Treaty of San Francisco, key extracts of the US-Japan Security Treaty and various international human rights conventions to which Japan is a party.

The editing involved in producing a *roppō* can also have a subtle impact on interpretation. For example, those who only read the Japanese constitution in a *roppō* will likely think that the constitution was promulgated with descriptive headers and paragraph numbers, which is not the case as these have been added by editors. For example in one *roppō* Article 9 of the constitution appears with the header "Abandonment of War, Rejection of War Potential and the Rights of Belligerency" when in fact the language relating to war potential is much more nuanced than a simple rejection. Similarly, many *roppō* contain headers referring to the "superiority of the HOR," though no such language is used anywhere in the constitution.

In the past private publishers offered English translations of Japanese statutes. These have been largely eclipsed by the Japanese government's own effort to produce English translations of many of its laws, which are available at its Japanese Law in Translation website (www.japaneselawtranslation.go.jp). Some translations which are not available here may be available on individual ministry/agency websites. For example, at the time of writing a translation of the Imperial House Act is not available at the above website but could be found on the English web page of the Imperial

Household Agency. Similarly, detailed guidelines and regulations about competition regulation may be found at the English website of the Fair Trade Commission.

2. Publication of Hanrei

Significant Supreme Court decisions and judgments (other than those which involve a simple rejection of a petition for appeal) are published in official paper reporters and available on line at the official court website. *Keishū* and *Minshū* are the principal reporters for the Supreme Court's judgments in criminal and civil cases respectively, but less significant rulings may appear in more obscure reporters.

Some *hanrei* of lower courts in specific areas such as intellectual property, labor disputes or family law are also available in official reporters. However, the process by which some lower court precedents are chosen for publication in these official reporters while others are not is opaque. Translations of important Supreme Court opinions are also available on the court's English website.

Publication of judgments and decisions is complicated by the fact that case records in criminal cases—including the judgment itself—are not available to the public under the Act on Criminal Case Records of 1987. Similar constraints apply to most family court cases.

Private publishers also offer a number of edited case reporters where lawyers or scholars can submit cases for publication. Family or criminal cases can be published this way subject to the removal of identifying information about the parties involved (which takes place in officially published precedents as well). Private, fee charging databases are also available.

The respect for the privacy of parties, defendants and victims of crime that supposedly drives this is admirable. However, it also means that there is a significant difference in the ability to access non-public case information as between legal system insiders and outsiders. It would seem very difficult for an outsider to do comprehensive research based on court decisions—when defamation crosses the threshold from tortious conduct to a criminal offense, for example—due to constraints on access to the relevant case records. While the records of civil court cases are kept by the courts those of criminal cases are maintained by the prosecutors. The Final Criminal Case Records Act of 1987 severely restricts public access to criminal trial records, including final judgments that have not been published.

3. Note-Taking in Courts and Open Courts

The surprisingly tight control over access to legal information once extended even to conduct by persons observing trials. Although article 82 of the Constitution requires trials to be conducted in open court, for the first four decades of the post-war period spectators in Japanese courtrooms were prohibited from taking notes about what transpired. Journalists accredited to the courts press club were permitted to do so, but the press club system would prevent them from writing anything negative or controversial.

In 1987, Larry Repeta, a young America frustrated by the constraints the note-taking prohibition imposed on his ability to do research on Japanese white collar criminal trials filed suit challenging it on constitutional grounds. In 1989 the Supreme Court ruled against him, finding inter alia that there was no constitutional right to take notes in a courtroom and that allowing just accredited journalists to do was not an equal protection violation. However, in the course of reaching these conclusions the court noted that "note-taking by spectators in the courtroom is worth respecting and should not be hindered without due reasons." (Supreme Court, Grand Bench judgment of March 8,1989). Although procedurally a loss for Repeta, substantively the case was a victory, as evidenced by the Supreme Court's General Secretariat's issuance of a directive to courts around the country to allow note taking.

It is still not permitted to make audio or video recordings of trial proceedings. Courts may do so for their own purposes (e.g., to facilitate the judicial clerk's preparation of the formal trial record) but these appear to be inaccessible to litigants or other interested parties.

G. LEGAL SCHOLARS AND LEGAL SCHOLARSHIP

Law professors play a number of roles in "shaping" the law. Establishment-friendly legal scholars often participate in the legislative process by consulting with relevant ministries and sitting on the various study groups and legislative committees.

Most legal scholars in Japan are true academics who studied law as undergraduates and then went on to pursue advanced degrees, just as in other disciplines. This is changing with the new Law School system described in Chapter 7, which has seen more legal practitioners moving into teaching positions. However, most law professors lack the practice background more common to their American counterparts. In the past, law professors were able to avail themselves of the registration privilege accorded under the Attorneys Act before it was amended in connection with the introduction of the law school system.

Law professors can also be influential, particularly if they teach at the law faculty of Tokyo University or a few other top national or private universities and thus have some influence over the views of students who graduate and pursue careers in law or government. Legal scholars are also a source of learning about foreign legal systems, a subject that receives significant attention in the legislative process today. Most Japanese law professors are also comparativists to some degree or another; they are expected to go abroad for their sabbaticals and many incorporate comparative information about foreign legal systems into their writings and lectures. Because of the deep German and French roots of many aspects of Japanese law and institutions, many law professors can read German and/or French, as well as English.

Including through the introduction of knowledge from abroad, scholars can also provide a conceptual framework for possible interpretations in areas of the law where courts have not made clear decisions or are unlikely to. Article 9 of the constitution is an area rich with this sort of academic theory as are various aspects of the imperial system, such as whether the Emperor could be allowed to abdicate.

The names of a few great scholars—mostly deceased—live on in association with some highly revered texts, some dating back decades and updated periodically by disciples. The constitutional textbook first published in 1993 by Ashibe Nobuyoshi (1923–1999) is now in its 6th edition and considered the standard work on the subject. Wagatsuma Sakae (1897–1973) is still one of the most highly-regarded scholars of the Civil Code with numerous books and a current annotation of the Code carried on in his name. Kawashima Takeyoshi (1909–1992) is another leading scholar of the Civil Code and related subjects, but also widely known because of a widely-read, controversial mass-market non-fiction book called "The Legal Consciousness of the Japanese People" which was first published in 1978 but remains in print today(see discussion in Chapter 1). Kawashima is also one of the first legal scholars whose work was introduced to foreign audiences in English. Dandō Shigemitsu (1913–2012) is a name deeply linked to criminal jurisprudence and multiple well-known texts. Professor Dandō is also an example of another way in which legal scholars affect the legal system, by going on to become Supreme Court judges.

Chapter 6

CONSTITUTIONAL LAW

Analysis

A. INTRODUCTION

The Japanese Constitution (*Nihonkoku Kenpō*) shares some superficial similarities with the United States Constitution. As we will see, this is an understandable reflection of its history. It would be a mistake, however, to make assumptions based on the U.S. experience about how the Japanese Constitution is interpreted and applied. As noted in other chapters, Japan's laws and institutions have historically been influenced primarily by European models as well as the Japanese historical experience. This was also true of the Meiji Constitution, which the current Constitution replaced.

It is essential to remember that, whatever its origins, the Constitution is distinctly Japanese in practice. This is especially true for issues such as judicial review, legislative power, and the characterization of human rights.

It is also important to remember that the Constitution was to a degree imposed on the nation. There is a healthy debate about the degree to which the Japanese were able to influence its ultimate form and subsequent implementation, as will be discussed later in this chapter. Yet the manner in which the Constitution is understood and interpreted reflects its unusual history. In some cases one can even discern what might be called a "passive aggressive" attitude towards what the Constitution says and means, at least on the part of some of the government actors it is supposed to restrain. In any case, even if it was originally "imposed" to a degree, it's implementation and interpretation have been exclusively Japanese for decades.

It should also be noted that although every sentence is different, the current Constitution is technically an *amendment* of the Meiji Constitution of 1889. This is also reflected in its similar structuring and order; Chapter I of both charters is about the Emperor, and so forth.

That the Constitution is an amendment of its Meiji predecessor is not just an interesting piece of procedural trivia. Much of the current Constitution can be understood at a basic level as a dialogue with and a rejection of the Meiji Constitution and many aspects of the Meiji system of government. Notwithstanding the new Constitution there is, in fact, a significant degree of continuity between the Meiji and current systems, one that becomes more apparent when turning from the field of constitutional law to the other laws and institutions discussed in this book.

This chapter will first address the history of the modern Japanese Constitution. This will be followed by sections addressing judicial review, the legislative branch, the executive branch, local governments, individual rights, equal protection, and the famous renunciation of war clauses contained in Article 9.

Japanese constitutional law is a subject about which a significant body of English-language literature is available. Accordingly, the coverage in this chapter is intended to give readers a flavor of the subject rather than a comprehensive overview. Moreover, those provisions of the Constitution relevant to the structure of government, the law making process and the judiciary are discussed primarily in the chapters on those subjects. The constitutional aspects of criminal law and justice are discussed in Chapter 8.

B. ORIGINS OF THE CONSTITUTION

1. From Defeat to Draft

As noted in Chapter 2, World War II ended for the Japanese people on August 15, 1945 with the acceptance of the Potsdam Declaration. This was followed by the US occupation and administration by Supreme Commander for the Allied Powers (SCAP), US General Douglas MacArthur, and his administration (commonly referred to as GHQ). Early on SCAP realized that it was important to implement a constitutional framework that severely limited imperial and military power, created a democratic government structure, gave the people broader rights than had previously existed, and put an end to government support for State Shintō. That said, the Constitution was not imposed without Japanese input or consideration of Japanese society.

In October, 1945 MacArthur told the newly-appointed Prime Minister Shidehara Kijurō that significant "liberalization" of the Meiji Constitution would be necessary. The Japanese government formed a committee on Constitutional reform led by the commercial law scholar Matsumoto Jōji. This committee ultimately created two drafts of a new Constitution. The one favored by Matsumoto himself, Draft A, made only limited changes to the Meiji Constitution. It kept significant power in the Emperor and it allowed the use of military force so long as it was supported by the Ministers of State. The other draft, Draft B, was more progressive, but did not clearly state that military force could never be used.

Famously, the contents of Draft A were obtained by the press and published on February 1, 1946. This generated a negative reaction from some Japanese people and created a problem for the committee, since SCAP was concerned about the lack of desire for real change evidenced by Draft A.

This led MacArthur to order Brigadier General Courtney Whitney, commander of GHQ's Government Section, to draft a new Constitution that achieved the goals of demilitarization and limiting imperial power. MacArthur enunciated three general principles to be reflected in the new Constitution: (1) the Emperor would be the dynastic head of state with defined powers and duties and would be responsive to the will of the people, (2) Japan would renounce war and be prohibited from having military forces, and (3) Japan's "feudal system" and nobility would be eliminated. Almost as an afterthought, "*pattern budget after British system*" was also included at the end of this directive.

Whitney put Colonel Charles Kades, also a lawyer, in charge of a team of Americans who would produce the first draft of a completely new constitution. Kades' committee had only one week to prepare the draft, in English, with limited access to reference materials. The team included one woman, Beate Sirota Gordon, who was the only member who could read Japanese and to whom the inclusion of the gender equality provisions in article 24 of the Constitution is attributed.

On February 13, 1946 the American draft—commonly referred to as the "MacArthur Draft"—was given to Japan's foreign minister as a counterproposal to what had been presented a few days earlier as the Japanese government's draft, Matsumoto's Draft A. The surprised Japanese demurred, but the Americans threatened to take the MacArthur Draft directly to the Japanese people who they thought were likely to support the expanded rights it guaranteed. In early March Japanese government officials submitted an alternative draft, which SCAP found unacceptable because it made too many changes and did not guarantee enough rights. Two days of intense, secret negotiations followed between GHQ and Japanese government representatives, with the American occupiers generally having the upper hand. A final draft was agreed upon on March 5 and submitted to MacArthur who approved it. An outline of this draft was then announced the following day as the government's own creation, with no mention of American involvement.

While the timeline leading up to this part of the process may give the impression of American occupiers running roughshod over the government of a defeated nation, MacArthur actually had an agenda that was arguably at least partially in the interests of the Japanese. At the end of December 1945, representatives of the victorious allied powers agreed to the formation of The Far Eastern Commission (FEC). The FEC was to oversee the Allied Council of Japan, through which the allies would participate in overseeing the governance of Japan. Some of the allied powers represented on these bodies wanted to try Emperor Hirohito for war crimes and execute him, which would have made the task of peacefully governing Japan significantly more difficult for MacArthur. In this sense, the American and Japanese representatives in the constitutional drafting process shared a common interest and became "Partners for Democracy," the title of one of the best English accounts of the Constitution's birth.[1]

Thanks to the quick and secretive efforts of both the American and Japanese sides, by the time the Council met for the first time in April of 1946, MacArthur could point to a draft Constitution that had been "produced" by the Japanese government and was being widely debated by the Japanese people.

2. From Draft to Debate to Promulgation

Another timing issue relevant to the Constitution was Japan's first post-war national election, held on April 10, 1946. Although it was the last Diet election under the Meiji Constitution, the occupation had already resulted in suffrage for Japanese women who participated as both voters and candidates. The outline of the new Constitution was announced before the election, and the Diet (HOR) resulting from it would be charged with debating and passing it.

---

[1] RAY A. MOORE & DONALD L. ROBINSON, PARTNERS FOR DEMOCRACY: CRAFTING THE NEW STATE UNDER MACARTHUR (2004). There are several other useful English accounts of the constitution's birth, and the National Diet Library's English web page on the subject is very useful, including access to all relevant documentation.

Before this happened, the outline published in March was turned into a proper draft by a small committee of Japanese government officials. One of the interesting innovations incorporated into this draft was its rendering in vernacular Japanese rather than the more classical *kanamajiribun* Japanese that had previously been used for legal drafting (see discussion in Chapter 5). This would make it easier for the average person to read and, perhaps conveniently, it helped to minimize the fact that it was a a document originally drafted in English and translated into Japanese.

The draft was presented to the Emperor for approval and then announced on April 17, 1946. After being discussed by the Privy Council, it was then presented by the Emperor to both houses of the Imperial Diet for deliberation in the form of a proposed amendment to the Meiji Constitution. Even though the new Constitution clearly rendered the Emperor a symbolic figure and completely rewrote the national charter, the people were more likely to accept the Constitution if it had imperial support and came into existence through the existing required procedures. The records of the deliberations on this are an important part of the history of the current Constitution, showing how representatives of various sectors of Japanese society viewed the proposed charter (albeit, within the context of being subject to military occupation).

Although many of the nation's legislators may have felt that given their defeat and occupation they had little choice but to pass the proposed draft, this part of the process also shows the people's representatives had an impact on the final product. For example, the guarantee of the right to seek compensation from the state under articles 17 and 40, and the constitutional duty to work and pay taxes under articles 27 and 30 were added at this stage of the process. Similarly, the "right to maintain the minimum standards of wholesome and cultured living" under article 25 was also added during the Diet deliberation under the strong insistence of its newly elected socialist members. A key change was also made to article 9, which became highly important to Japan's ability to re-establish a military, as discussed later in this chapter. Some changes were also requested by SCAP and the FEC, such as the addition of the requirement that Cabinet members be "civilians."

On October 7, 1946 the Japanese Diet overwhelmingly voted in favor of the new Constitution. After being approved by the Emperor on October 29 (a requirement of the Meiji Constitution for its amendment), it was promulgated on November 3, 1946, the birthday of the late Emperor Meiji. The new Constitution came into force on May 3, 1947, which is now a national holiday—Constitution Day.

3. The Linguistic Legacy of the Drafting Process

The MacArthur Draft was originally written in English and then translated into Japanese. Throughout the process leading to the charter's promulgation, the American and Japanese sides worked through translations. Legal drafting, interpretation and translation are challenging tasks even under the easiest of circumstances. In some instances the Japanese sought to use their linguistic advantage and superior knowledge of Japanese legalese to tweak the *Japanese* version. Many of these changes were caught by SCAP officials and rejected. A few others were either approved or not noticed, or if noticed, not rejected. Perhaps the most notable of the changes not rejected by SCAP was translating the English term "the people" to the Japanese term *kokumin*, which effectively means "the Japanese people."

When reading the Constitution in English it is thus important to appreciate that it is not simply a direct translation of the Japanese version. Rather it is the end result of two very similar but not always identical versions.[2] As the example in the preceding paragraph demonstrates, the English version does not always capture all of the nuances of the Japanese, which is of course the controlling version.

4. The Constitution Since Its Birth

After the allied occupation formally ended on April 28, 1952 and Japan fully regained its sovereignty, there was naturally an interest in amending the Constitution. In 1956 the Commission for Investigating the Constitution was established under the Cabinet to consider amendment. The records of the Diet session at which the enabling legislation for this commission was considered offers a useful window into the attitudes towards the Constitution of the various politicians at the time.

Since that time, constitutional amendment has been a constant subject in political debate, particularly in connection with article 9 and the role of Japan's military in international security and the nation's mutual defense treaty with the United States. In April 2012, on the 60th anniversary of the coming into force of the Treaty of San Francisco, the conservative LDP (then in a rare period of opposition) issued a comprehensive proposed amendment to the Japanese Constitution. Other amendments have also been proposed over the decades.

Yet the Japanese Constitution has never been directly amended. The document in force today is the same document that was promulgated in 1946, at least in its textual form. Some constitutional provisions have been "reinterpreted," especially in relation to "collective self-defense," a concept discussed later in this chapter.

One of the interesting things about the LDP's 2012 draft is that at least some of the many proposed amendments, if passed, would have simply rendered the text of the Constitution consistent with the way it is already interpreted and understood. For example, the proposed amendments would add language clearly empowering the Prime Minister to dissolve the House of Representatives, but this is already a well-established practice despite the lack of clear constitutional authorization. Other proposed changes, however, would have been significant, imposing new obligations on the people, restricting their freedoms and clearly authorizing the existence and active use of the armed forcese. At the time of writing the amendments seemed unlikely to pass in their entirety despite the LDP regaining power. They are nonetheless a useful indicator of the dominant party's view of the current charter.

Needless to say, constitutional revision has long been a goal of conservative members of Japanese society, such as the LDP, which has controlled the Diet and thus the Cabinet almost uninterrupted from the 1950's to the present day. This means that a succession of governments whose leadership (ministers of state, Diet members and other public officials) have an obligation under article 99 to "respect and uphold" the Constitution have frequently sought to change it, occasionally openly criticizing it in the process.[3] Conceptually, the LDP may have found it a struggle to advocate constitutional

---

[2] During the occupation there was an English verion of the *kanpō* (official gazette), so the English version of the constitution is that promulgated in the English gazette, while the Japanese is from the Japanese *Kanpō*.

[3] In December 2012, shortly before becoming Prime Minister for the second time Abe Shinzō described the constitution as *mittomonai* – "shameful.".

revision in a way that does not invite criticism of their decades of controlling the government and the policy-making process.

Constitutional amendment is not easy. Under article 96, amendment requires the approval of supermajorities in both houses of the Diet followed by a national referendum. Throughout most of the post-occupation period LDP and its allies have not held the necessary supermajority in both houses Even in recent years when LDP and its conservative allies have managed to obtain a supermajority, some of those allies have had different views on constitutional revision. Polls reveal a significant percentage of the population support the Constitution and the peace it advocates, though others reveal support for at least amending it to reflect the reality of the SDF. In any case, until recent years the nation's fractious opposition parties have been able to retain enough seats in the Diet to block change, in part by appealing to voters through opposition to any form of constitutional change, with a particular focus on protecting article 9. One reflection of this is the fact that it was not until 2007 that the Diet was able to pass a law (the Constitutional Amendment Procedures Act) establishing the procedures for the national referendum that is a necessary part of the amendment process.

In 2014 Prime Minister Abe Shinzō proposed amending article 96 to make amendment easier. Discussion of the "real" amendments would occur later under his proposal. The proposal was met with a significant backlash, as were other "limited" amendment trial balloons , such as one to give the Cabinet clearly-stated emergency powers, which are currently lacking.

Another factor in the lack of constitutional amendments may be that, with some notable exceptions such as military capabilities and their use in foreign affairs, LDP-controlled governments have generally been able to achieve most of their goals through legislation and interpretation without amending the Constitution for most of the period during which it has been in effect. One of the interesting features of the party's 2012 proposed amendments is that they would generally leave the judiciary untouched, the LDP apparently not regarding the courts and their application of the Constitution as having been problematic enough to merit changing.

To the LDP constitutional amendment may be as much about ideology as law: they released their draft on the 60th anniversary of the coming into effect of the Treaty of San Francisco, which formally ended the occupation and restored full sovereignty to the Japanese people in the main islands. Amendment may also be about having a charter which empowers the government to proactively tell the Japanese people what to do more than it can now. Given that constitutional revision is controversial and ideologically unpopular with some members of the public, a continued policy of reinterpretation may prove to be a safer path for LDP.

C. JUDICIAL REVIEW AND CONSTITUTIONAL INTERPRETATION

The power of judicial review under the Japanese Constitution is a fascinating topic. This section will approach the topic of judicial review by exploring three interrelated issues. First, the textual basis for the power of judicial review will be addressed. Second, and perhaps most importantly, the practical realities of judicial review will be addressed, including the reasons for significant judicial deference to the legislature. Finally, some of the cases where the Japanese Supreme Court has found laws or their application in a particular case to be unconstitutional will be addressed. The discussion will also include the remedies which have been, and have not been, ordered by the Court. Readers might find the remedies portion of this equation to be quite odd from a U.S. perspective.

1. The Textual Basis for Judicial Constitutional Review

The Meiji Constitution did not provide for judicial review of legislation or regulations. There were academic theories in favor and against the courts having such powers, but both sides were framed in terms of the powers of the Emperor. In other words, could courts protect the Emperor by preventing the legislature from abusing its powers, or did the Emperor's involvement in the legislative process make the laws unassailable? These debates remained academic, since in 1913 the Supreme Court of Judicature held that the judicial power did not extend to evaluating the constitutionality of laws or regulations (Supreme Court of Judicature judgment of July 11, 1913).

Significantly, the power of judicial review is expressly given by the present Constitution in Article 81, which reads:

> The Supreme Court is the court of last resort with the power to determine the constitutionality of any law, order, regulation or official act.

This is different from the U.S. Constitution where the power of the Supreme Court to overturn federal or state legislation or executive action that conflicts with the Constitution was established through precedent.[4]

The Japanese Supreme Court's first discussion of the power of Judicial Review came in 1948, in a case involving an appeal against an evidentiary ruling in a criminal trial arising before the Constitution took effect and before the Supreme Court existed. In many ways a transitional case, it nonetheless saw the court accept a broad interpretation of Article 81, expanding "official acts" (*shobun*) to include judgments (*hanketsu*) of lower courts (Supreme Court, Grand Bench judgment of July 8, 1948).

The language of article 81 says nothing about whether lower courts have a power of constitutional review. In a 1950 case the Supreme Court held that the wording of article 81 only established that the Supreme Court has the final word in constitutional interpretation and did not preclude lower courts from also exercising the power of constitutional judicial review (Supreme Court, Grand Bench judgment of February 1, 1950). The Supreme Court also acknowledged the possibility of lower court judicial review when it made its Rules of Criminal Procedure in 1948 and amended its rules of Civil Procedure in 1954.

Even without interpretation or rules Article 81 is a remarkably clear statement of the power of judicial review. One might be forgiven for assuming that after the early decisions described above, the judiciary would have gone on to assert its broadly-interpreted power of judicial review to challenge constitutionally suspect government acts and laws in the manner of the U.S. federal courts. But this has not been the case. At the time of writing, the Japanese Supreme Court has only found provisions of laws to be unconstitutional in ten instances. Although most are discussed in greater detail elsewhere in this or other chapters, for convenience these cases are listed below.

[4] Marbury v. Madison, 5 U.S. (1 Cranch) 137 (1803); Martin v. Hunter's Lessee, 14 U.S. (1 Wheat.) 304 (1816); McCulloch v. Maryland, 17 U.S. (4 Wheat.) 316 (1819). Interestingly the provision in the MacArthur Draft that eventually became article 81 initially included language allowing a 2/3 majority of the Diet to overturn a Supreme Court ruling, suggesting the Americans involved may have had some reservations about U.S.-style judicial review. That provision was eliminated in the process that followed.

TABLE 6-1 INSTANCES OF THE SUPREME COURT FINDING A STATUTORY PROVISION UNCONSTITUTIONAL

Case and Citation	Summary
Lineal Ascendant Homicide Case (Grand Bench judgment of April 4, 1973)	Article 200 of Penal Code providing for heavier punishments for those murdering lineal ascendants than apply to murders involving other victims violate the equal protection guarantee of article 14(1). See discussion at subsection C.3. of this chapter.
Pharmacy Proximity Restriction Case (Grand Bench judgment of April 30, 1975)	Prohibitions on opening a pharmacy within a defined distance from an existing one infringe the freedom to choose one's occupation guaranteed by article 22(1). See discussion at subsection C.3 of this chapter.
House of Representatives Malapportionment Case (1) (Grand Bench judgment of April 14, 1976)	Disparity in number of voters represented by different seats in the House of Representatives based on the allocation in the Public Officials Election Act violate the equal protection guarantee of article 14(1), as interpreted through articles 15(1) and (3), and article 44. See discussion at subsection C.1 of this chapter.
House of Representatives Malapportionment Case (2) (Grand Bench Judgment of July 17, 1985).	Disparity in number of voters represented by different seats in the House of Representatives based on the allocation in the Public Officials Election Act violate the equal protection guarantee of article 14(1) and article 44. See discussion at subsection C.1 of this chapter.
Restriction on Partitioning Forest Land Case (Grand Bench judgment of April 22, 1987).	Restriction in the Forestry Act on the right to seek partition of joint interests in forest land violates the guarantee of property rights under Article 29. See discussion at Chapter 9(C)(1).
Postal Act Liability Exemption Case (Grand Bench judgment of November 11, 2002).	Exculpatory provision in Postal Act rendering postal employees immune from negligence liability violates the right to seek compensation from the state guaranteed by article 17. See discussion at subsection C.3 of this chapter.
Overseas Voting Rights Case (Grand Bench judgment of September 14, 2005.	POEA provisions restricting the right of Japanese living overseas to participate in Diet elections violates the right to choose public officials and the guarantee of universal adult suffrage under article 15(1), and violates the provisions of article 43(1) and 44 relating to Diet elections. See discussion at Chapter 10(F)(5)(c) and subsection C.1 of this chapter.
The Birth Out of Wedlock Nationality Case (Grand Bench judgment of June 4, 2008).	Provision in Nationality Act which had the effect of treating children born out of wedlock to a non-Japanese mother and a Japanese father differently depending on whether the father acknowledged paternity before or after birth violated the equal protection guarantee of article 14(1). See discussion at Chapter 4(C)(3)(d); Chapter 6(E)(2)(b) and subsection C.2 of this chapter.
The Legitimacy-Based Discrimination in Inheritance Case (Grand Bench decision of September 4, 2013).	Provision in Civil Code according children born out of wedlock only 1/2 of the inheritance rights of children born in wedlock violates the equal protection guarantee of article 14(1). See discussion at subsection C.1 of this chapter.
The Women-Only Remarriage Restriction case (Grand Bench judgment of December 16, 2015, 69 Minshū 2427)	Provision in Civil Code prohibiting women (but not men) from remarrying for a six month period after dissolution of a prior marriage was unconstitutional as to the period of restriction greater than 100 days. See discussion at subsection C.2 of this chapter.

Apart from these *horei iken* ("unconstitutional law or regulation") rulings, there are about a dozen other instances where the court has found a law or regulation to be constitutional, but its application in a particular situation to be unconstitutional. These are known as *tekiyō iken* ("unconstitutional application") cases. A few are discussed later in this chapter.

In addition to the relative infrequency with which the Japanese Supreme Court has overturned national legislation, the lack of remedies offered in some cases where national legislation has been overturned may surprise those who assume the power of judicial review is similar to that under the U.S. Constitution. In this respect, one feature of both constitutional and administrative litigation are *jijō hanketsu* (rulings accounting for circumstances). In a *jijō hanketsu* the court may recognize a constitutional or other violation by government authorities, but decline to do anything about it beyond acknowledging it happened because of the circumstances of the case (e.g., the building subject to a legal challenge to the issuance of its building permit has already been largely completed by the time the litigation is resolved).

An example of *jijō hanketsu* in constitutional law is provided by the two *House of Representatives Malapportionment Cases* (see Table 6-1). In each of these the Grand Bench found the electoral districts and resulting allocation of Diet seats under the Public Offices Election Law unconstitutional. The reason for this is that the law allowed for different weight to be given to votes in different locations, a violation of the Constitution's equal protection guarantees. Yet, the Court did not go so far as to invalidate the elections themselves. In other words, the election was based on an unconstitutional legislative electoral scheme, but would stand. This may seem an odd result, but of course for the Court to invalidate the entire election and thus delegitimize the resulting Diet and everything it did several years after the fact, would have been a recipe for chaos.

In a similar vein, the 2013 *Legitimacy-Based Discrimination in Inheritance Case*, the court found the Civil Code provisions granting a smaller share of inheritance to children born out of wedlock to violate the equal protection guarantee, but applied it retroactively only as to those cases involving estates that had not yet been settled. A ruling which had not been so limited in effect would potentially have resulted in countless new disputes being brought into court.

2. The Reality of Judicial Review and Interpretation

Some American scholars have pointed to the paucity of cases as an indicator of the court being "conservative," though Americans may be more inclined to regard frequent judicial intervention in the legislative process as normal and even a good thing. There are a number of reasons why the Japanese Supreme Court has rarely used its power of judicial review to invalidate legislation or other government acts. Japanese constitutional law scholars for their part have advanced a number of reasons for the court's seeming reluctance to issue rulings of unconstitutionality, many of which are interrelated.

First, as already noted, article 41 of the Constitution clearly denotes the Diet as "the highest organ of state power" and the "sole law-making organ of the State." Thus, unlike in the United States where the three branches of government are notionally equal in stature, in Japan the legislature is clearly accorded superior status. As discussed in Chapter 5, Japan lacks a common-law style tradition of judges making positive law, but

Article 41 also clearly limits the Supreme Court's ability to do so. Unsurprisingly, the Supreme Court is highly solicitous of the legislative branch, and in a judgment will occasionally acknowledge that a particular statute is problematic while indicating it is a problem for the legislative branch to fix.

Second, the modern nature of the Japanese Constitution itself can be said to have caused judicial review to move in a different direction than the United States. The catalog of extensive and, when compared to the US Constitution or the Meiji Constitution, modern rights enunciated in Chapter III includes some that are used for interpreting other clauses of the Constitution but are so vague that they alone are considered inadequate grounds for concrete judicial relief.

The "right to the pursuit of happiness" in article 13 is an example of a Japanese constitutional right that can rarely if ever be used alone as a basis for seeking concrete judicial relief. It may, however, be used to bolster claims based on other more specific provisions of the constitution. The right to the pursuit of happiness also forms the conceptual basis for certain other rights, such as the right to privacy, reputation and self-determination and tort liability for the infringement of these rights has been recognized in civil litigation.

With respect to some of the other enumerated constitutional rights, the prevailing view is that the right is considered to be protected primarily through "systemic guarantee" (*seido hoshō*) rather than as actionable rights. For example, the guarantee of academic freedom in article 23 is a highly abstract one that is considered to be assured primarily through the autonomy of universities, which is considered a corollary protection of the provision.

Some other rights provisions are interpreted as being effectively mandates to the legislature rather than a source of concrete rights that can be asserted directly by individuals through the courts. In some cases this is clear from the text of the Constitution. For example, article 10 states that "the conditions necessary for being a Japanese national shall be determined by law" and article 27 mandates that "standards for wages, hours, rest and other working conditions shall be fixed by law."

An early example of the court addressing the justiciability of provisions such as these is a 1967 case known as the *Asahi Case* (Supreme Court, Grand Bench judgment of May 24, 1967). The *Asahi* case was brought by an impoverished plaintiff suffering from tuberculosis who claimed the amount of welfare payments he received from the government pursuant to standards set by the MHLW were so small as to constitute a violation of article 25, which reads:

> All people shall have the right to maintain the minimum standards of wholesome and cultured living. In all spheres of life, the State shall use its endeavors for the promotion and extension of social welfare and security, and of public health.

Article 25 describes a fascinating right since it seems to guarantee that the state will work to maintain an adequate social safety net. It is commonly cited as an example of a "program provision" (*puroguramu kittei*), a constitutional or legislative provision articulating a policy program that anticipates further law-making, rather than enunciating concrete rules itself. Article 1 of the Public Assistance Act of 1950, the statute at issue in the *Asahi Case* clearly states the law's purpose is to give life to article 25 of the Constitution.[5]

The *Asahi Case* also presents an interesting and possibly rare example of the Supreme Court making a special effort to address a constitutional issue when it didn't have to, albeit in favor of the government. Since the plaintiff died while the appeal to the Court was pending, procedurally the judgment consisted of rejecting the appeal by the plaintiff's heirs on the grounds that the claim was not heritable. But in famous dicta beginning with, "As a matter of further elaboration" (*nen no tame*), the court offered a supplementary opinion as to the nature of article 25 rights.

Acknowledging that article 25 gave broad discretion to the legislature and administrative agencies, the court declared judicial review of decisions about welfare payments should be available "[o]nly in cases where such decision is made in excess of, and by abuse of, the power bestowed by the law."

The view that at least some provisions of the Constitution are effectively interpreted by the court as grants of legislative discretion, and judicial review for constitutional purposes involves considering whether the Diet has breached its legislative discretion in passing a law or failing to amend one that has been rendered inappropriate by social change. For example, in December of 2015 the Grand Bench issued two judgments on separate provisions of the Civil Code. One was the *Women-Only Remarriage Restriction Case* (Table 6-1 above), the other a challenge to the Civil Code requirement that married couples share the same legal surname (Supreme Court, Grand Bench judgment of December 16, 2015; 69 Minshū 2586). Both challenges were based on a number of constitutional provisions including article 24(2), which mandates, *inter alia*, that "*with regard to. . .matters pertaining to marriage and the family, laws shall be enacted from the standpoint of individual dignity and the essential equality of the sexes.*" Although western readers might take this as a fairly clear mandate for gender neutral family laws, in both cases the court referred to the provision as the Constitution according the Diet legislative discretion, which apparently includes the discretion to have gender-discriminatory laws if necessary.

In the *Remarriage* case the court found the Diet's discretion had been exceeded to the extent the remarriage-only prohibition was greater than 100 days, while in the other case the court found the same-surname requirement to be within the scope of the Diet's discretion, but also used dicta to suggest legislation might be in order. The *Remarriage* case was also interesting in that although it rejected the claim of legislative nonfeasance, it bolstered its conclusion about the partial unconstitutionality of the Civil Code provision with a reference to legislative history—*unsuccessful* legislative history (a 1996 Diet effort to shorten the prohibited period to 100 days that was never passed into law).

With the Constitution interpreted not only as a check on legislative and executive power, but also as imposing on the Diet positive obligations to make or change legislation needed to implement the Constitution in accordance with social change, constitutional litigation and judicial review take on a very different character from that of the US Supreme Court. In Japan, it is not uncommon for constitutional litigation to be brought

---

[5] Unlike in the U.S. system it is not necessary to identify a specific constitutional provision as the basis for the Diet's ability to pass a particular statute. Nonetheless, despite the concept of the "program provision" being a standard topic covered in Japanese constitutional law texts and classes, statutes such as the Public Assistance Act which contain a clear statement linking legislative purpose to a specific constitutional provision are rare.

in the form of a damage suit for legislative nonfeasance (*rippō no fusakui*); essentially arguing that the Diet has failed to fulfill a constitutional mandate. The *Remarriage Case* and the *Overseas Voting Rights Case* were both brought in this fashion. Though the Court may not find the plaintiffs to have suffered any actual damages, this form of action provides an opportunity to rule on the constitutional issue. At the same time, if the Court does not want to deal with the constitutional issue it can simply find that the legislature has not had enough time, or dismiss the case for lack of damages.

This state of affairs means that the Supreme Court can use its judgments to signal the Diet that legislative action is required, without invalidating the law at issue in a case, though it is not clear the Diet always listens. Voting right malapportionment is a prime example. In addition to the two *House of Representatives Malapportionment Cases*, there are numerous other cases involving large disparities in the representation of voters in both Diet chambers. In some of these cases the court found the disparities to be an "unconstitutional situation" but fell short of holding the legislative apportionment to be outright unconstitutional or void. For example, in a 2011 decision the court held that the disparity in electoral districts "had become contrary to the Constitutional requirement of equality in the value of vote" but because the Diet had taken some remedial action it did not rise to the level of a violation of article 14(1)'s equal protection guarantee (Supreme Court, Grand Bench judgment of March 23, 2011).

Another textual factor in judicial review and constitutional interpretation lies in the two separate "public welfare" qualifiers contained in article 12 and 13, which read as follows:

> Article 12
>
> The freedoms and rights guaranteed to the people by this Constitution shall be maintained by the constant endeavor of the people, who shall refrain from any abuse of these freedoms and rights and shall always be responsible for utilizing them for the public welfare.
>
> Article 13
>
> All of the people shall be respected as individuals. Their right to life, liberty, and the pursuit of happiness shall, to the extent that it does not interfere with the public welfare, be the supreme consideration in legislation and in other governmental affairs.

These apply to all the rights in the Constitution, making them subject to limitation in the interests of the public welfare. Since most legislation is presumptively in the public interest, the result is that a great deal of judicial review takes place based on what American constitutional scholars would consider a "rational basis" standard. Some Japanese scholars have suggested a subtle, higher standard of review is actually being applied in cases involving certain categories of rights.

The use of the public welfare qualifier to justify legislation that constrains or restricts the exercise of constitutional rights and freedoms is sometimes criticized as being similar to the Meiji Constitution, which granted the Japanese people certain fundamental rights, but subjected them all to possible limitations imposed by law. Note also the article 12 concept of "abuse of freedoms and rights" as another potential limitation. There does not appear to be any significant jurisprudence on this language, however.

A third difference can be seen in the role of the Cabinet Legislation Bureau in reviewing legislation before it is passed. As discussed in Chapters 3 and 5, the CLB serves a number of functions, including reviewing Cabinet legislative proposals before their submission to the Diet. This ensures a certain amount of quality control is exercised before Cabinet-initiated laws are passed, and helps ensure such laws are consistent with the Constitution, or at least the CLB's interpretation of it. Most of the rulings of unconstitutionality in Table 6-1 above have involved statutory provisions that originated from the Diet rather than the Cabinet. Professor Satō Jun'ichi and other scholars have argued that the Supreme Court's deference to the legislature is in part due to the fact that the Cabinet Legislation Bureau has pre-vetted the laws that are passed.[6]

These scholars suggest that for a number of reasons the CLB's evaluation of these laws is not an appropriate basis for the sort of significant deference to the legislature that the Japanese Supreme Court has exhibited. These reasons include a CLB interest in maintaining the executive branch status quo and the moral hazard involved in eschewing the power of judicial review in deference to the views of an executive branch agency that produces and/or reviews the statutory provisions at issue.

Fourth, institutional factors relating to the judiciary's position in a larger system of government may also be a factor in the Supreme Court's apparent "conservatism." The judicial career track and process for selecting Supreme Court judges (see Chapter 4) ensures that judges with progressive constitutional views are sidelined and never make it to the top. Lower court judges who find laws unconstitutional have found their careers side-tracked, being relegated to a series of postings at small regional courts away from the power center of Tokyo. This conservatism starts at the top with Supreme Court judges who are appointed by the Cabinet, and thus the ruling party, but extends to the bottom where the selection of new assistant judges from candidates at the LRTI has also served to exclude the "wrong sort" of people. Note also that as discussed in Chapters 3 and 4, some judges may spend time on secondment to the MOJ acting as defense counsel to the government in constitutional and administrative litigation before returning to the court system. The Diet also controls the judicial branch's budget, and the Supreme Court is reportedly dependent to an extent on the MOJ for representing it in budget negotiations. There are thus numerous institutional factors which would seem to mitigate in favor of the judiciary not "rocking the boat."

Fifth, like the US Supreme Court, Japan's Supreme Court has developed numerous doctrines and techniques for avoiding constitutional decisions whenever possible. These include what amounts to a "case or controversy" requirement, as well as doctrines of mootness and ripeness. In the past the court has also used highly restrictive notions of standing to procedurally frustrate both administrative and constitutional litigation.

Sixth, as was already touched upon in the discussion of the scope of the judicial power in Chapter 4, the Supreme Court is limited in what it can do even if it does find a law or state action unconstitutional. Malapportionment cases are long and complicated and often not decided until several years after the election at issue is finished. The court's limited powers to change reality also mean that little may happen if other government actors ignore its decisions, which arguably has happened after some of the

[6] Jun-ichi Satoh, *Judicial Review in Japan: An Overview of the Case Law and an Examination of Trends in the Japanese Supreme Court's Constitutional Oversight*, 41 LOY. L. A. L. REV. at 604–605, 624–25, 627 (2008).

malapportionment cases, as well as the *Lineal Ascendant Homicide* case discussed in the next section.

3. Some Examples of the Court Issuing Rulings of Unconstitutionality

In order to give a flavor for the Supreme Court's constitutional jurisprudence, in this section we will summarize some of the instances where the court has found a statutory provision or its application in a particular case to be unconstitutional.

Although the first instance of a statute being found unconstitutional did not arise until 1973, the first ruling in which the Supreme Court found a constitutionl violation was issued in 1948. In that ruling the court vacated a conviction based on a confession procured after an unreasonably long and unjustified detention (Supreme Court, Grand Bench judgment of July 19, 1948).[7]

A more famous case in the criminal sphere is the *Third Party Property Confiscation Case* (Supreme Court, Grand Bench judgment of November 28, 1962). In that case, the Court found that the application of a provision of the Customs Act in the confiscation of a ship used by smugglers without giving its owner notice or an opportunity to be heard violated both article 29 (which makes the right to own and hold property inviolable) and article 31 (which prohibits the imposition of penalties without due process of law).

The first example of the Court actually invalidating a statutory provision on constitutional grounds was the *Lineal Ascendant Homicide Case*. In it the court found that the higher range of punishments for murder of a lineal ascendant in Article 200 of the Penal Code (imprisonment with labor for an indefinite term to the death penalty), than those applicable to other types of murder under Article 199 (at the time, three years imprisonment with labor to the death penalty), and the correspondingly more limited scope for reductions due to mitigating factors violated the equal protection guarantee of article 14(1).

The case involved a defendant who killed her father to escape a terrifying history of physical and sexual abuse at his hands. Repeated rapes had resulted in her bearing five of his children and aborting six other pregnancies. She committed the homicide after ten days of confinement at his hands. The quandary for the judges at each level of the proceedings was that the law would not let them give a very sympathetic plaintiff a suitably lenient sentence. The Utsunomiya District Court tried to do so by finding article 200 unconstitutional and giving her a light sentence for excessive self-defense. The Tokyo High Court found article 200 constitutional, but gave her the lightest possible sentence with credit for pre-judgment detention.

It may seem strange that the first instance of a statute being found unconstitutional involved an equal protection violation based on distinctions between victims. However, the court did not find that the distinction in sentencing by itself violated the equality principle. Rather, the distinction was applied in a way that resulted in only those who killed lineal ascendants even with mitigating circumstances being ineligible for suspended sentences (which the Supreme Court ordered).

---

[7] As discussed in Chapter 8, prolonged pre-trial detentions remain a common feature of the criminal justice system.

The aftermath of the case illustrates the potential limitations on the judiciary when it *does* exercise its powers of judicial review to strike down legislation, Despite being found void on constitutional grounds, article 200 remained on the books for two decades, until it was quietly deleted when the Penal Code was converted to vernacular Japanese in 1995. During this period prosecutors reportedly avoided the constitutional issue by simply not bringing charges under it.

The next example was the *Pharmacy Proximity Restriction Case* (citation in Table 6-1), in which the Court found a provision of the Pharmaceutical Affairs Law unconstitutional. The basis for the ruling was the guarantee in Article 22 of the Constitution giving every Japanese citizen the right to choose his or her occupation unless that decision interferes with the public welfare.

The law in question in the *Pharmacy* case placed geographic limitations on where pharmacies may be located, ostensibly to prevent pharmacists from selling substandard drugs. The Court found, however, that the law did not serve its stated purpose of preventing the sale of substandard drugs, and in fact, interfered with the pharmacist's right under Article 22 to be free to choose "the form and content of occupational activities." The Court was clear that the government does have a strong interest in occupational licensing laws to protect the public welfare. The law in question, however, was not even rationally related to the government's stated interest in preventing the sale of substandard drugs.

In the *Postal Act Liability Exemption Case* (citation in Table 6-1), the Court found unconstitutional a provision of the Postal Act which exempted the postal service for liability even for gross negligence or willful misconduct in the handling and delivery of mail, including registered mail. The court found that the liability exemption violated article 17's guarantee of the right to seek redress from the state or public entities, at least as it applied to gross negligence or intentional conduct in the delivery of registered mail.[8] This may seem an oddly particular ruling, but the court may have had a special interest in registered mail since that is the method used for delivery of court documents. The case was brought by a party who was a plaintiff in a civil action and suffered a significant loss due to the mis-delivery of a court order freezing the bank account of the defendant in the action, who consequently had the opportunity to remove funds from the account.

D. SEPARATION OF POWERS

The Constitution has a system of separation of powers or *sankenbunritsu*, but this does not mean that the system functions in the same way as in the U.S. system. The legislative branch in Japan has even more power than does Congress in the U.S. There are also, of course, similarities. The Japanese legislature known as the Diet (or *Kokkai*) is bicameral, like the United States Congress, but as mentioned above the Japanese Constitution makes the Diet "the highest organ of state power" and "the sole law-making organ of the State."

Perhaps the most significant difference between the Japanese Diet and the U.S. Congress, however, is the fact that the Diet determines who will be Prime Minister, and that the Prime Minister must come from the Diet. As discussed in Chapter 2 the Prime

---

[8] Article 17 reads: "Every person may sue for redress as provided by law from the state or a public entity, in case he has suffered damage through illegal act of any public official."

Minister appoints cabinet ministers, the majority of whom must also be members of the Diet. Thus, the connection between the legislative and executive branches in Japan more closely resembles a European parliamentary system. In the Japanese system, the ability of the executive branch to directly check (as opposed to indirectly check) the legislature is almost non-existent as a matter of constitutional design, but the actual relationship between the two branches is far more complex than the constitutional text suggests, a topic discussed in depth in Chapters 3 and 5.

Constitutionally the executive branch is a fascinating amalgamation of European parliamentary concepts and Japanese political reality. Compared to the US system, the Japanese executive branch is weaker, with a Prime Minister vested with far fewer formal powers than the US president. Yet, as a practical matter the Japanese executive branch still has a great deal of power.

Unlike the Diet, the executive branch has a national presence through the various regional offices of the ministries, as well as direct relationships with prefectural and municipal governments through the national programs administered by them. Although the Diet must approve the national budget, it is the executive branch that negotiates and prepares it. The executive branch is also responsible for foreign relations. Moreover, the executive branch plays a leading role in much of the lawmaking that actually takes place. See Chapters 3and 5 for further discussion. The Prime Minister is also the leader of the party in power, and along with its coalition parties, holds the majority in the Diet.

As noted in Chapters 3 and 4, there are also numerous well-established interactions in the form of exchanges of personnel between the judicial branch and other branches of government. This also makes the concept of separation of powers more nuanced.

E. RIGHTS AND DUTIES OF THE PEOPLE

1. Overview

The Constitution provides a wide range of individual rights and freedoms, most of which are set forth in Chapter III. It also imposes three duties on the people: the duty to educate children, the duty to work and the duty to pay taxes (articles 26(2), 27 and 30).

Some of the rights and freedoms guaranteed by Chapter III, such as criminal procedure rights and labor rights are addressed in other chapters of this book. Others are discussed below. Unsurprisingly, some rights and freedoms have been the subject of more judicial and academic attention and interpretation than others. As noted earlier in this chapter, some of the provisions of Chapter III enunciate rights but also contain interpretive language that has the effect of limiting them, such as the article 12 requirement that freedoms and rights not be abused and that they be utilized "for the public welfare."

A non-exhaustive list of the rights and freedoms enunciated in the Constitution (not including criminal procedure protections) include the rights to:

- respect as individuals; life, liberty and the pursuit of happiness (article 13);
- equality under the law (article 14);
- choose and dismiss public officials; universal suffrage; secrecy of voting (article 15);

- peacefully petition the government (article 16);
- sue for redress from state or public entities (article 17);
- freedom from bondage and involuntary servitude, except as a criminal punishment (18);
- thought and conscience (article 19);
- freedom of religion (article 20);
- freedom of assembly, association and speech; privacy of communication (article 21);
- freedom to choose occupation and residence; freedom to move to a foreign nation and divest oneself of nationality (article 22);
- academic freedom (article 23);
- marriage based on mutual consent; family legislation based on gender equality and individual dignity (article 24);
- a minimum standard of wholesome and cultured living (article 25);
- receive an equal education correspondent to their ability (article 26);
- right (and obligation) to work (article 27);
- workers to organize and act collectively (article 28);
- own and hold property, subject to public welfare; just compensation for property taken for public use (article 29);
- access to the courts (32);
- equal treatment in qualification for members of the Diet and their electors (article 44); and
- public trials (article 82).

Linguistically, some rights are formulated as rights of the (Japanese) people (*kokumin*). Others are formulated as relating to "any/no person" (*nanpito*), which lacks the nuance of Japanese nationality of *kokumin*. However the title of Chapter III describes its contents as the "rights of the Japanese people."

Accordingly, a basic question of constitutional interpretation has been the extent to which the constitutional guarantees extend to non-Japanese.[9] The seminal case on this issue, known as the *McClean Case*, involved an American named Ronald McClean. He came to Japan as an English teacher in 1969 but also participated in anti-Vietnam war and other demonstrations at the American Embassy in Tokyo and other places. When he applied for a renewal of his working visa it was denied because of his political activities. He brought suit claiming he was punished for exercising rights guaranteed by the Constitution.

McClean lost, but in its ruling the Supreme Court held that:

the guarantee of fundamental rights included in Chapter Three of the Constitution extends also to foreign nationals staying in Japan except for those

[9] Note that in the private law sphere, Article 3(2) of the Civil Code states that "[u]nless otherwise provided by applicable laws, regulations or treaties, foreign nationals shall enjoy private rights."

> rights, which by their nature, are understood to address Japanese nationals only. This applies to political activities, except for those activities which are considered to be inappropriate by taking into account the status of the person as a foreign national, such as activities which have influence on the political decision-making and its implementation in Japan (Supreme Court, Grand Bench judgment of October 4, 1978).

It qualified this holding with the following language:

> [The] guarantee of fundamental rights to foreign nationals by the Constitution should be understood to be granted only within the scope of such a system of the visa status of foreign nationals and does not extend so far as to bind the exercise of discretionary power of the state. . .in renewing visas.

In other words, foreign nationals in Japan ostensibly enjoy most of the constitutional rights and freedoms guaranteed by the Constitution, but only within the framework of the broad discretion granted to immigration authorities by immigration legislation. The standard Japanese textbook description of the *McClean Case* is that it establishes that foreigners in Japan enjoy essentially the same constitutional protections as Japanese people, subject to some exceptions. However, non-Japanese who actually have to live with this interpretation might be forgiven for concluding it means the opposite, since constitutional protections that are subject to immigration legislation and administrative discretion do not seem very "constitutional." Furthermore, it is not clear how foreigners in Japan are supposed to know *a priori* whether their activities might "inappropriately" affect policy decisions or implementation (affecting policy arguably being the point of *all* political activity).

Despite the holding in the *McClean Case*, non-Japanese parties have generally lost in other cases where their rights have been at issue. Examples include cases where non-Japanese have unsuccessfully sought eligibility for managerial-level public service jobs and welfare benefits (Supreme Court, Grand Bench judgment of January 26, 2005 (the *"Tokyo Prefectural Worker Nationality Case* discussed below), and 2nd Petty Bench judgment of July 18, 2014). It is also worth noting that even in the *Birth Out of Wedlock Nationality Case* (see Table 6-1), in which a fractious court issued a majority opinion as well as several concurrences and two separate dissents, virtually all of the Justices seemed to be able to agree on the basic notion that:

> Japanese nationality means a lot to people in order to enjoy the guarantee of fundamental human rights and other benefits in Japan.

Ronald McClean might have had better luck had he been a Japanese corporation. In the *Yawata Steel* case—Japan's version of *Citizens United v. FEC*[10]—the court held that, despite not having articles of incorporation with a statement of purpose allowing such activities, corporations could nonetheless make donations to a political party (the LDP). This conclusion was based in part on the court's view that, to the extent possible, the rights and obligations of the people in Chapter III of the Constitutions should also be enjoyed by domestic corporations (Supreme Court, Grand Bench decision of June 24, 1970).

A detailed exposition of the full panoply of constitutional jurisprudence being beyond the scope of a work such as this, the following sections will explore two rights in

---

[10] 558 U.S. 310 (2010).

depth to give readers a feel for how some of the most important rights have been understood and interpreted. These rights are freedom of speech and freedom of religion.

2. Freedom of Speech Under Article 21

This section addresses freedom of speech under article 21 but will also touch on the freedom of conscience under Article 19, which has been implicated in some free speech cases (particularly in the context of the freedom from compelled speech).

Article 19 reads:

> Freedom of thought and conscience shall not be violated.

Article 21 reads:

> Freedom of assembly and association as well as speech, press and all other forms of expression are guaranteed. No censorship shall be maintained, nor shall the secrecy of any means of communication be violated.

If one were to only consider the text of these provisions, the freedom of speech and expression appear to be very broadly defined. The reality, however, is that freedom of speech is far more limited than the text would suggest. This does not mean that Japan lacks speech protections, but those protections are not nearly as robust in practice as they are in the text of the Constitution. Significantly, freedom of the press and the freedom of speech in the context of elections have been construed in a manner that may be surprising to those unfamiliar with the Japanese system. In fact, one can contrast the freedom of speech with the freedom of religion (and the freedom from religion) discussed in the next section. The religious freedom guarantee of the Constitution is remarkably strong as a practical matter when compared to the freedom of speech.

When addressing freedom of speech in Japan it is helpful to consider the situations in which it is threatened or restricted. This is because there is no coherent doctrine used by the courts to address free speech separate from where and how that speech manifests itself. There are also no instances of the Supreme Court finding regulation of speech outright unconstitutional.

However, two things are abundantly clear. First, speech can be regulated in many contexts where doing so promotes the public welfare and public harmony from the perspective of those doing the regulating. Second, regulation of speech does have its limits, but those limits are generally exceeded only when a government action cannot be justified on some reasonable (in the view of the courts)-basis.

The rest of this section will explore free speech in a variety of contexts where claims have arisen: elections, obscenity, hate speech, private speech on public property (including public demonstrations), compelled speech by public employees, and content neutral restrictions on speech. One theme that is common throughout the speech cases is that the Court often balances the free speech interest with the government's interest, but in a manner that gives far more deference to the government interest than is generally given in U.S. free speech cases. Additionally, government interests in public welfare and public harmony often override free speech rights, even when the interests asserted are not well documented.

Before moving on it is worth noting that a certain amount of speech regulation takes the form of quasi-self-regulation. For example most government institutions (including the courts) have a *kisha kurabu* or press club. Members of the press accredited to the club get special access to press releases and other information from that institution. However, those who write anything too critical of it may find their access revoked. One of the complaints made by Larry Repeta in the note-taking case described in Chapter 5 was that members of the judicial press club were allowed to take notes during trials, while members of the general public were not.

a. Electoral Laws

To those familiar with U.S. style electoral campaigns, one of the most surprising aspects of the Japanese Supreme Court's free speech decisions arises in the context of election laws. The Public Office Election Act of 1950 contains numerous limitations on the ability of candidates for public office to appeal to the electorate. Direct polling of voters is prohibited, and it wasn't until 2013 amendments to the POEA that restrictions on campaigning by individual candidates over the Internet were relaxed. Yet the POEA still restricts campaigning to only a short window of time prior to the election, controls the distribution or broadcast of election materials, and limits the type and quantity of posters and other materials that can be used to solicit votes. These restrictions make it nearly impossible for citizens to get significant information about individual candidates from sources other than the media, and difficult for candidates to appeal to voters on any basis other than name recognition and party affiliation.

Anyone who has been in Japan around election time has probably heard trucks with loudspeakers going down the street. The messages broadcast are not substantive, however, and are generally just the name of the candidate and a request that people vote for that candidate. This is a result of these restrictive laws.

These restrictions would likely be unconstitutional in most constitutional democracies, but the Japanese Supreme Court has upheld them. An example of the Court's reasoning arises from a 1955 case that approved dramatic limitations on the distribution or broadcast of election materials (Supreme Court, Grand Bench judgment of April 6, 1955). The 1955 case, and a later case decided by a Petty Bench in 1982, accepted the government's justifications for these restrictions on the distribution of campaign literature because such distribution might cause unseemly competition, and ironically, because distribution of these materials could impact the fairness of elections (Supreme Court, 3rd Petty Bench judgment of March 23, 1982).

The result is a situation where voters are kept remarkably uninformed about the differences between candidates (other than party affiliation) unless the voters themselves become politically involved and seek out that information. On a basic level, the restrictions seem to make it almost impossible to engage voters in discussions about what the law should be at the stage at which they choose their lawmakers.

b. Obscenity

Application of article 175 of the Penal Code's prohibitions on the distribution of obscene materials is also interesting. In a 1957 case the court upheld the conviction of a publisher for distributing a translation of D.H. Lawrence's classic work, *Lady Chatterly's Lover* (Supreme Court, Grand Bench judgment of March 13, 1957). In that case, the Court held that the government can ban materials it deems obscene to promote a minimum standard of sexual morality. The Court held that this is true even if the work that is banned has literary value. Courts have also upheld laws that ban photos or video showing male or female genitalia or pubic hair, which has resulted in an odd situation where sex acts can be shown on video or in photography so long as the genitalia are not visible.[11]

As suggested by the constitutional law scholar Shigenori Matsui, there are signs that the Court is becoming more willing to deny the government's ability to ban material that could be deemed obscene if that material has literary or artistic value.[12] However, in 2016 the Japanese artist Megumi Igarashi was convicted of violating obscenity laws for distributing electronic data that made it possible to use a 3D printer to create a model of her vagina. At the time of writing her case was under appeal.

Like most countries Japan prohibits the creation or possession of child pornography under the Child Prostitution and Child Pornography Act, and the courts have upheld these restrictions (Supreme Court, 3rd Petty Bench judgment of February 20, 2006). At the time of writing, the law did not yet apply to anime, comics or other virtual depictions of children engaged in sexual behavior but not involving actual children.

An interesting but little-noted aspect of restrictions on speech actually comes from lower tiers of government. In 1964 the Tokyo Prefectural assembly passed the "Ordinance Relating to the Healthy Upbringing of Youths" that, *inter alia*, empowers the prefectural governor to designate books as "good" and "harmful" to youth. Designation as the latter effectively results in a book not being carried by mainstream bookstores. Amended several times, the ordinance now also includes requirements relating to the blocking of juvenile access to pornographic and other "unhealthy" websites and calls for "self-regulation" in the sale and promotion of things such as comics or cartoons depicting prohibited forms of sexual intercourse. While only applicable to Tokyo, since most publishers and telecommunications companies are located in the prefecture, it may have a practical impact similar to national law, despite imposing more stringent restraint than any legislation passed by the Diet. In 1988 the Supreme Court upheld the prohibition on selling magazines officially designated as "harmful" via vending machines under a similar ordinance in another prefecture, and found that it did not constitute "censorship" prohibited by article 21(2) of the Constitution (Supreme Court, 3rd Petty Bench judgment of September 19, 1988).

c. *Hate Speech*

Hate speech is also a fascinating area of Japanese speech regulation, and one that has garnered a great deal of attention in recent years with the Supreme Court creating hate speech jurisprudence that is both fascinating and progressive, drawing a line between the U.S. system's significant protection for hate speech and many European systems' toleration of complete bans on hate speech.

In December, 2014 the 3rd Petty Bench of the Supreme Court of Japan upheld a ruling against *Zaitoku-kai,* a hate group that targets ethnic Koreans living in Japan. Both the Kyoto District Court and the Osaka High Court had held *Zaitoku-kai* liable in tort for 12.2 million yen in damages due to its inflammatory demonstrations aimed at a school for Korean residents living in Kyoto (Osaka High Court Judgment of June 3, 2014, affirming Kyoto District Court). Moreover, the courts enjoined the hate group from picketing within two hundred meters of the school.

---

[11] See Shigenori Matsui, THE CONSTITUTION OF JAPAN: A CONTEXTUAL ANALYSIS, at 206 (Hart Publishing 2011).

[12] *Id.* at 205–206.

The case arose after *zaitoku-kai* held loud protests and marches outside the school, which included racist and hateful rhetoric. The group used loudspeakers so that it disturbed and scared the children inside the school. They also posted videos of their hate marches online. The group argued it had a free speech right to protest outside the school. The lower courts disagreed because the protests were targeted in a manner that disturbed the school, victimized the students, and interfered with their education.

All five Justices on the 3rd Petty Bench of the Supreme Court of Japan affirmed the lower court decision. Yet, unlike in the U.S. where the Supreme Court has held that hate speech is a protected form of speech,[13] the Japanese Supreme Court found that hate speech can be penalized through civil sanctions when it causes trauma to its victims and is designed to do so.

Subsequently in 2016 the city of Osaka passed Japan's first hate speech ordinance, the Osaka City Ordinance on Dealing with Hate Speech. The ordinance uses a shaming approach as its primary tool, providing a regime for publicizing the names of those found to have engaged in hate speech in violation of the ordinance. At the time of writing a lawsuit has been filed in the Osaka District Court challenging the ordinance. The suit was filed by a plaintiff who used an assumed name to post videos of a hate rally online and is seeking to keep the city from publishing his real name.

On May 25, 2016, the Diet passed the national Hate Speech Act of 2016. That Act, however, does not ban hate speech. Rather it only applies to threats of bodily harm or threats to people's lives, and has no penalty for those who engage in hate speech.

d. Public Demonstrations

The question of speech and assembly on public property also raises a number of issues. The Court has upheld government requirements that demonstrations or gatherings in public parks and other public places be conducted after receiving permits (Supreme Court, Grand Bench judgment of July 20, 1960; Supreme Court Grand Bench judgment of September 10, 1975). In these cases the Court held that public safety and management concerns are adequate to allow the denial of a permit.

As Professor Shigenori Matsui has explained the government may have less leeway in denying access for gatherings at civic centers if the government builds them and makes them available to the public.[14] For example, in a case brought under the State Compensation Act, the Court held that the denial of an application by a labor union to use the Ageo City Welfare Center for the funeral of a union leader was wrongful, citing the freedom of assembly guarantee in article 21 (Supreme Court, 2nd Petty Bench judgment of March 15, 1996). The Welfare Center's management had refused a request to use the center because it could result in alleged property management issues due to the possibility of violent union-related protests. The Court found that the asserted reason was inadequate to deny the right to use the center because any concerns asserted as the basis to deny access must be specified and supported by objective facts. This would include a showing that any disruption could not be properly addressed by local law enforcement.

---

[13] Snyder v. Phelps, 562 U.S. 443 (2011); R.A.V. v. City of St. Paul, 505 U.S. 377 (1992).

[14] Matsui supra note 46, at 209–210.

e. *Compelled Speech*

The court has also upheld compelled speech or expressive behavior that advance government interests, including that of the judiciary. Courts occasionally order defendants to publish apologies as a remedy in civil defamation cases. In 1956 the Supreme Court held that this did not constitute a violation of either article 21 or the guarantee of freedom of conscience in article 19 (Supreme Court, Grand Bench judgment of July 4, 1956). A similar issue that has received more recent attention from the courts and the media are claims of compelled speech by public school teachers who do not want to sing or play the music for the national anthem. Some teachers have objected to the idea that their status as public servants means their superiors can require them to engage in expressive behavior they do not agree with and be punished for refusing to participate.

In one case that also implicated the freedom of conscience guaranteed by article 19, a public school teacher was disciplined for refusing to play the national anthem on the piano at a school event. The Court's opinion in that case focused heavily on the freedom of conscience issue, finding that playing the piano for the national anthem did not violate the teacher's freedom to think and believe what she wanted to, since she just had to go through the motions of playing the tune. The Court, did not however, address in detail the related argument that requiring her to play the piano for the national anthem would be compelled speech (Supreme Court, 3rd Petty Bench judgment of February 27, 2007).

In a more recent case the Supreme Court held that punishing teachers for not standing for the National Anthem is constitutional, but that the sanctions imposed cannot be excessive from the perspective of school regulation and the need to maintain order. The Court held that sanctions may be excessive if they go beyond a reprimand and involve things such as "a major salary reduction or yet more severe measures." The Court held that enforcing suspensions could "have deleterious effects on (teachers') execution of their duties, their salaries and can also influence future raises. If such disciplinary measures accumulate with every school ceremony," the negative effects would be greatly compounded (Supreme Court, 1st Petty Bench Judgment of February 9, 2012). Thus, some of the penalties imposed on the teachers, such as suspensions or significant salary reductions, were too harsh.

3. Religion and Articles 20 and 89

This section will discuss freedom of religion and the separation of religion from government under articles 20 and 89 of the Constitution. Article 20 reads:

> (1) Freedom of Religion is guaranteed to all. No religious organization shall receive any privileges from the state, nor exercise any political authority.
>
> (2) No person shall be compelled to take part in any religious acts, celebration, right or practice.
>
> (3) The State and its organs shall refrain from religious education or any other religious activity.

Article 89 reads:

> No public money or other property shall be expended or appropriated for the use, benefit or maintenance of any religious institution or association, or for

any charitable, educational or benevolent enterprises not under the control of public authority.

On their face these articles seem to provide a strong barrier against government support for religion and strong protection for the free exercise of religion. The latter has generally been true, but the state of the former is more complex, as we shall see.

The immediate concern of articles 20 and 89 at the time of drafting was State Shintō, the politicized version of the Shintō religion used after the Meiji Restoration as a political tool for unifying the nation around the Emperor and enhancing his legitimacy. State Shintō also helpedto justify military conquest. State Shintō came to be promoted by the prewar government in schools, at public events, as well as through gifts from Imperial Shrines to Japanese homes. It also led to persecution of non-conforming individuals and non-cooperating religious officials, who were forced to participate in Shintō ceremonies regardless of their actual religious beliefs.

Despite this history, articles 20 and 89 are drafted in neutral terms and apply to any religion. However, at a grass roots level many Shintō and Buddhist practices have become established cultural practices that have identifiable religious roots and trappings but for many Japanese people (many of whom engage in both) lack any significant nexus to deeply-held religious beliefs. At a higher level, retention of the Emperor as a symbolic institution within the apparatus of government has meant accommodating his role in the Shintō religion and the various devotional duties that come with that role. Courts have thus had to deal with distinctions between cultural practices passively rooted in religious tradition and active participation or furtherance of religion in a number of contexts.

The *Tsu City Groundbreaking Ceremony* case is the most famous of what will be referred to as the, "Shintō as culture" cases (Supreme Court, Grand Bench judgment of July 13, 1977). The case is interesting, because the Court adopted a test very similar to that adopted by the U.S. Supreme Court in *Lemon v. Kurtzman*,[15] but then held that traditional Shintō practices can be interpreted as a cultural practice and therefore government funding of, or other involvement in, such practices was not problematic under article 20, paragraph 3.

The facts of the *Tsu* case are quite interesting. In Japan it is common before breaking earth on a construction project to hold a Shinto ceremony to appease the spirits who will be disturbed by the process. Such rites were performed at a city-sponsored groundbreaking ceremony for the construction of a municipal gym. The ceremony and offerings were paid for by the city. A case was brought by a local citizen alleging that the public sponsoring and funding of the ceremony violated article 20.

On appeal the Supreme Court held that the State must be religiously neutral, but that did not mean all state connection with religion was prohibited; only state connection with religion that, when considering Japanese social and cultural conditions and the "purpose and effect" of the state action, exceeds a reasonable standard consonant with the objective of religious freedom, is unconstitutional. In other words, a violation of article 20(3) only occurs when government conduct has a purpose with religious

[15] 403 U.S. 602 (1971). The "Lemon Test" requires that any legislation concerning religion must have a secular legislative purpose, must not have a primary effect that advances or inhibits religion, and must not result in excessive government entanglement with religion.

significance or the effect of the government conduct is to subsidize, promote, suppress, or interfere with religion.

In the *Tsu City Groundbreaking Ceremony Case,* although the rites were obviously connected to religion, they were deemed not to be unconstitutional when considering the totality of the circumstances. The ceremony had the secular purpose of "marking the start of construction by a rite performed in accordance with general social custom to pray for a stable foundation for the building and accident-free construction work." According to the Court, the effects of the ceremony did not subsidize or promote Shinto or have the effect of suppressing or interfering with other religions. Therefore, government support for, and involvement in, the ceremony was not a religious activity for purposes of articles 20 or 89.

The reasoning from the Tsu City case was followed in several other cases. For example, the *Minoh War Memorial* case decided by the Supreme Court in 1993 involved a challenge to both the use of public funds to procure a site for the relocation of a memorial to war dead in connection with the construction of a public school and participation by local officials in Buddhist and Shinto memorial services. In that case the court rejected the challenge to official participation in memorial services on the grounds that it was "*to show courtesy in society toward war-bereaved families in memorial services dedicated to consoling and commemorating the souls of the war dead in their hometown, and such attendance cannot be regarded as having an effect of supporting, encouraging or promoting, or suppressing or interfering with any particular religion.*" Similarly, the use of public funds to procure the relocation site was upheld on the grounds that the memorial was devoted primarily to the war dead rather than a particular religion (both Shinto and Buddhist memorial services were performed there), that it was necessary for the construction of the public school, and because the association that administered the memorial was not a "religious organization" for purposes of article 89 (Supreme Court, 3rd Petty Bench judgment of February 16, 1993).[16]

In a similar vein, the Court upheld the participation of the governor of Kagoshima Prefecture in the "*Daijōsai*" *Shintō* ceremony held in 1990 in connection with the succession to the throne of Emperor Akihito. As described in its ruling, this was a "*ceremony in which the emperor gives thanks to the ancestors and the gods in heaven and the land for peace and the harvest of various crops and, for the state and the populace, prays for peace and the harvest.*" The *Daijōsai* was provided for as part of the succession process in both the ancient *ritsuryō* as well as the pre-war Imperial House Act. The Supreme Court, however, found the participation of the governor to be for the purpose of extending "*a social courtesy to the emperor who is the symbol of the integration of the nation and the populace. . . and its effect does not comprise assistance, promotion or enhancement of a specific religion, or suppression of or interference with it*" (Supreme Court, 1st Petty Bench judgment of July 11, 2002).

In 1997, the Supreme Court issued a significant opinion that continued to follow, and augmented, the legal framework set forth in the *Tsu City* case, but which drastically departed from the prior case's understanding of, and application of, that framework. The *Ehime Tamagushi Case* saw the court strike down the use of public funds by government officials from Ehime Prefecture and Tokyo for offerings to Shintō shrines, including the

[16] An important part of the context underlying this case is that during the occupation, public schools were ordered to remove war memorials from their grounds.

controversial Yasukuni Shrine, where Japan's war dead and service personnel are enshrined (Supreme Court, Grand Bench judgment of April 2, 1997). It is one of the small number of *tekiyō iken* (unconstitutional application) holdings of the Supreme Court.

The offerings cost relatively small sums of money and consisted of twigs from a specific type of tree, the sakiki tree, wrapped with folded white papers. This sort of offering to a Shinto Shrine is called *tamagushi.* The offerings were paid for using government funds and given by representatives of the government at the behest of the prefectural government.

Significantly, the Court explicitly held that, "*the Constitution should be interpreted as striving for a secular and religiously neutral state by regarding the total separation of state and religion as its ideal.*" The Court held this approach helps protect the freedom of religion. The Court recognized, however, that total separation between religion and state is impossible, because any time government regulates social norms it can impact religion indirectly. It argued that the test to determine whether religious neutrality is violated is the "purpose and effects" test used in the *Tsu City* case, but with an endorsement gloss; *i.e.*, considering whether the government action under review favors a religion in the eyes of the public. The Court applied this analysis to the case under both Article 20 and Article 89, and found that paying for and giving the offerings violated both the purpose and effect elements of the test and endorsed religion.

The Court held that the offering of *tamagushi,* in the name of the local government, directly supports the religious activity of the Shintō shrine. The Court also noted that government officials may give *saisen* (small offerings of cash made to temples or shrines) from their own pockets because this would not constitute government action. The governor was ordered to repay the government for all the expenditures made in support of the offerings because he had ordered the other defendants to make the offerings by invoking his power under relevant municipal laws.

Recently, in two separate Grand Bench opinions and a related Petty Bench opinion, the Court followed, and further elaborated on the analysis of the *Ehime Tamagushi* case. The results were not the same in the two Grand Bench cases, but the factual distinctions are significant. This is especially so because the same local government in Hokkaido was involved in both.

In *Sunagawa City Shrine I,* one of the court's most recent *tekiyō iken* (unconstitutional application) rulings, the issue was that the city of Sunagawa had granted a neighborhood association the use of city-owned property, located in and near a municipal meeting hall, for a Shintō Shrine without requesting any compensation (Supreme Court, Grand Bench judgments of January 20, 2010, 64 MINSHŪ 1 (gyo-tsu No. 260)). The shrine consisted of a *torii* (a gate to a Shintō Shrine), a *jishingu* (stone monument to the deity that is seen as protecting the local area), a *hokora* (small Shintō Shrine), and a sign noting that the shrine was located in the building. A religious association called the Ujiko managed the property and performed festivals and rituals, but paid no compensation to the city for the use of the property.

The Court applied the endorsement analysis from the *Ehime Tamagushi Case*—how this situation would be viewed from the public's perspective—and held that the city's actions violated both Article 20 and Article 89. The fact that the shrine was originally taken on by the city at the request of a local citizen who had donated the land (for tax reasons) did not change this analysis. The Court acknowledged the religious nature of

Shintō shrines and the problems raised by perceived government favoritism toward the shrine. The Court held that the use of a government meeting building to house a religious shrine, especially without any compensation, would be viewed from the public's perspective as favoring religion; in this case, Shintō.

The Court noted, however, that it would be inappropriate to require the mayor to remove the shrine immediately because it would make it hard for the Ujiko group to carry out its religious activities, which in turn would harm the religious freedom of members of the group. Thus, the Court remanded the case to see whether any "*rational and realistic alternative means*" other than total removal of the shrine was possible. The Court suggested several possible alternatives, including a grant, transfer for compensation, or lease at fair market value. The Court itself seemed to favor a remedy that involved compensation or a lease at fair market value, but since it also mentioned a grant, it is not clear what would be required. A Petty Bench of the Court subsequently approved a lease at fair market value and some related measures (Supreme Court, 1st Petty Bench judgment of February 16, 2012).

In another judgment involving a different shrine in Sunagawa City, but with facts somewhat distinguishable from *Sunagawa City Shrine I*, the Court upheld a transfer by the local government to a neighborhood association of a Shintō shrine and the small parcel of land on which it sat (Supreme Court, Grand Bench judgment of January 20, 2010, 64 MINSHŪ 128 (gyo-tsu No. 334) "*Sunagawa City Shrine II*)). The transfer of the land and shrine was challenged under article 20(3) and article 89. Interestingly, in *Sunagawa City Shrine II* the Court noted that given the religious nature of a Shintō shrine, the city might have been viewed by the public as favoring a particular religion. The Court found, however, that the land had originally belonged to the predecessor of the same neighborhood association and the purpose for which it was given to the city—apartments for schoolteachers—was no longer being served because the apartment building was no longer there. As a result, the land transfer was viewed by the Court as a return of land given by the association to the city for a specific purpose that was no longer being served. The land transfer was thus a constitutional way to avoid problems under Article 20 and Article 89 that would have existed had the city continued to allow the shrine on its land free of charge. Thus, the facts of the case are different, in an important way, from the facts in *Sunagawa City Shrine I.*

In the free exercise context, one of the most famous cases is the so-called *Jehova's Witness Kendō Refusal Case* (Supreme Court, 2nd Petty Bench judgment of March 8, 1996). In that case, which has become famous among constitutional law and law and religion scholars around the world, a municipal technical college in Kobe was the defendant in a suit brought by a student whose faith (Jehovah's Witness) prevented him from engaging in Kendo, one of the college's physical education requirements. This resulted in the student being unable to graduate and ultimately being expelled for failing to satisfy the requirement. The Court reasoned that for everyone to have free exercise of religion as expressed in the Constitution, accommodations are appropriate because for some people a seemingly neutral law can interfere with freedom of religion, and that the college should have provided such an accommodation in this case. The court held that such accommodations must be balanced against the interests of others and society, but that the government must have a very good reason to infringe on the interests of the religious individual. The court also explained that accommodations are a way to prevent a negative impact on the religious person resulting from the law. The Court also held that to the extent an accommodation allows the religious person to avoid a requirement or a hardship the government may require an equally demanding alternative.

There is, however, debate among Japanese scholars over whether the case was primarily decided under the Constitution or under the education laws. The court's judgment does reference article 20 of the Constitution, but has more extensive references to the School Education Act of 1947 and its implementing regulations. The side supporting the argument that the Constitution played at least an important role in the decision seems to have the stronger argument and that position has garnered a great deal of support among Japanese constitutional law scholars.

Another case that illustrates the complex relationship between religion—*Shintō* in particular—and the constitution is the *SDF Officer Enshrinement Case* (Supreme Court, Grand Bench judgment of June 1, 1988). In that case the widow of a Christian officer in the Self Defense Forces who had died in an accident while on duty brought suit objecting to his enshrinement in the local *Gokoku* shrine (a Shintō shrine dedicated to the spirits of military and public safety personnel who die in the line of duty). The suit was brought against the SDF and the non-governmental veteran's association for their role in the enshrinement and sought damages for infringement of "religious rights of personality" and asserted violations of article 20(3) of the Constitution. The court found that although the SDF had indirectly participated by cooperating with the veteran's association in performing clerical work, the actual enshrinement was carried out by the association and the government could not be considered to have engaged in religious activities. The court went further to reject the "religious rights of personality" argument, noting that the freedom of religion guaranteed by the Constitution also included the freedom of others to engage in religious behavior that the plaintiff might find objectionable in the context of her own beliefs.

F. EQUAL PROTECTION

The Constitution addresses the equal protection of law in several places. Article 14(1) contains a specific equal protection guarantee, article 15(2) mandates universal adult suffrage, article 24 requires gender equality in family law, and article 44 prohibits discrimination in eligibility to vote or stand for Diet seats. As with the U.S. Constitution and other charters containing similar guarantees, the details matter and in some contexts constitutional equal protection is much stronger than in others.

Article 14(1) of the Japanese Constitution reads:

> All of the people are equal under the law and there shall be no discrimination in political, economic or social relations because of race, creed, sex, social status or family origin.[17]

Article 44 contains a similar prohibition on "discrimination because of race, creed, sex, social status [or]] family origin" but also includes "education, property or income." There are various academic views as to the meaning of the categories and bases of discrimination enumerated in articles 14(1) and 44, but courts have not identified them as having any special significance. In a 1964 ruling in a case asserting age discrimination, the Supreme Court opined that the categories of discrimination enumerated in article 14(1) were indicative rather than exclusive (Supreme Court,

[17] The other two paragraphs of article 14 are devoted to eliminating the hereditary nobility and prohibiting awards or honors that are heritable or accompanied by special privileges.

Grand Bench judgment of May 27, 1964). As noted in Chapter 3, the Human Rights Bureau of the MOJ has embraced very broad categories of discrimination for its own activities, including discrimination against people with criminal records and discrimination based on sexual orientation.

Article 14 naturally raises the question of what standard should be applied when government is alleged to have violated the equal protection rights contained therein. Interestingly, many Japanese legal scholars have argued that a heightened standard of review should apply to at least some forms of discrimination prohibited by article 14, including a form of strict scrutiny similar to that used in United States constitutional jurisprudence. The Japanese Supreme Court, however, has applied a rational basis type standard to most equal protection claims under Article 14, and has given a great deal of deference to the government.

A well-known example of equal protection jurisprudence is the *Tokyo Prefectural Managerial Exam Case* (Supreme Court, Grand Bench judgment of January 26, 2005). That case involved a member of Japan's ethnic Korean population born and raised in Japan. She was a permanent resident of Japan holding special permanent resident status (see discussion in Chapter 9). This population now includes several generations of people who were not eligible for Japanese citizenship at birth and for various reasons were unable or reluctant to go through the process of naturalizing.

The plaintiff in the action was employed by the prefectural government but was denied the opportunity to take a test that would have qualified her for promotion to a management level position. The denial was based on the ground that such positions were only open to Japanese citizens. Her argument was that she was a medical professional and the positions to which she would have sought promotion had she been allowed to take the test did not involve tasks that should require citizenship.

The prefecture argued that its policy was required for it to properly administer its management system, which allows any employee who reaches particular levels of management to be eligible for a variety of senior management positions within the government. It also alleged that some of these senior positions require the performance of tasks exercising "public authority" (*kōkenryoku*), for which only citizens should be eligible, and argued that it needed to draw the line where it did in order to maintain its system in a consistent way. The Court found the "difference in treatment of Japanese vs. non-Japanese employees is not in violation of article 14(1) of the Constitution if it is based on reasonable grounds."

In numerous other cases, the court has also found a rational basis for legislation that has the effect of discriminating between people based on various attributes. Examples include the inability of salaried employees to deduct expenses compared to the self-employed and the differing treatment accorded students and workers by the national pension system (Supreme Court, Grand Bench judgments of March 27, 1985 and September 28, 2007). In an early case the court also upheld the differing regional rules that naturally result from the ability of prefectural and municipal governments to pass ordinances within the scope of existing law (Supreme Court, Grand Bench judgment of October 15, 1958).

With respect to public law, the court has generally left it to the legislature to implement gender equality. Although it found the women-only remarriage prohibition partially unconstitutional in 2015, it had previously upheld it (Supreme Court, 3rd Petty

Bench judgment of December 5, 1995). In the *Spousal Surname Case*, the court upheld an ostensibly gender-neutral legal requirement while acknowledging that it overwhelmingly affected women (all three of the female judges on the court at the time dissented). In a pair of 1982 decisions, the Tokyo High Court acknowledged that provisions in the Nationality Act which made children of mixed marriages where the father was Japanese eligible for Japanese nationality by birth, but not those involving a Japanese mother and a foreign father (leaving the child potentially stateless, depending on the nationality laws of the father's country) was defective, but declared it could not provide a remedy (Tokyo High Court judgments (2) of June 23, 1982). The law was amended in 1984.

In the private law sphere the courts (including the Supreme Court) have been more active in policing gender discrimination in areas such as employment or other areas of private regulation. However, in such cases this has been done through article 90 of the Civil Code which renders juristic acts against public policy void (although the Constitution is generally understood to require state action, it is of course a useful indicator of public policy). An interesting example, involves a village in Okinawa where by custom villagers had *iriaiken* common rights (see chapter 9) to use a neighboring forested area. These rights vested primarily in male members of the community, and women who married out of the village could not enjoy the rights unless they divorced and resumed their maiden name. In 2006, the Supreme Court found this customary rule void under Article 90 of the Civil Code (Supreme Court, 2nd Petty Bench judgment of March 17, 2006).

At the time of writing there were no Supreme Court cases on discrimination based on sexual orientation. The leading case in this area is a Tokyo High Court ruling that found the refusal by a lodging facility established and operated by Tokyo Prefecture to accept reservations from a gay rights group was unlawful (Tokyo High Court judgment of September 16, 1997).

Yet the numerous instances where the Supreme Court has upheld discriminatory laws and regulations do not mean its jurisprudence has rendered article 14(1) toothless. After all, the majority of cases in Table 6-1 where it has overturned statutory provisions on constitutional grounds have involved article 14(1) violations. Although cases where the court arrives at an unconstitutionality ruling are rare, the court has been particularly active in equal protection cases involving of voting rights. This would be consistent with its view that law should be made by the legislature, since the composition of the legislature should naturally reflect that of the voting population.

G. ARTICLE 9 AND THE RENUNCIATION OF WAR

Japan's constitution is famous for article 9, whose provisions ostensibly renounce war and the possession of military potential. The text of article 9 reads:

> (1) Aspiring sincerely to an international peace based on justice and order, the Japanese people forever renounce war as a sovereign right of the nation and the threat or use of force as means of settling international disputes.

(2) In order to accomplish the aim of the preceding paragraph, land, sea, and air forces, as well as other war potential, will never[18] be maintained. The right of belligerency of the state will not be recognized.

The pacifist nature of the constitution is further emphasized through the charter's preamble, which contains several references to peace and a resolution that the nation should never again "be visited with the horrors of war." However, as an abstract statement of principle, the preamble lacks the same concreteness and normative potential as Article 9.

Article 9 originated in the MacArthur Draft (as article 8) and was intended to prevent Japan from remilitarizing and posing a threat to international security. Language similar to that of the MacArthur Draft was ultimately included in the final version of the Japanese Constitution, subject to some amendments, including the "*Ashida* amendment" discussed below.

Perhaps the most fascinating aspect of the history of article 9 is how rapidly it seems to have been embraced. The people of Japan were weary from the ravages of war, so from the start the Constitution's pacifist principles had obvious appeal to some. Some within the government were also happy with article 9. The reasons for this varied, but one major factor was that rebuilding Japan's infrastructure and economy became a central focus of the government and there would be far more funding for those tasks if there was no need to fund a military.

To the extent article 9 is now generally accepted as only prohibiting offensive war, Japan's constitution may not be as unique as some Japanese like to think. Other countries (e.g., the Republic of the Philippines, the Republic of Korea) also have constitutional prohibitions on wars of aggression. Similarly, some countries simply have no militaries without having a constitutional prohibition to that effect.

Japan by contrast, has managed to develop one of the largest and most well-equipped military forces in the world, notwithstanding the seemingly significant constitutional restraints imposed by article 9. The reality is that article 9 was a reflection of the wartime goal of the principal allied powers to demilitarize Japan, a goal announced in the Potsdam Declaration and reflected in the initial policies of the post-war occupation, policies reflected in the Constitution. Yet with the outbreak of the Cold War and subsequently the Korean War, the constitutional restraints on Japan defending itself proved inconvenient before the occupation even ended. The creation in 1950 of the National Police Reserve which was transformed into the SDF in 1954 was as much a reflection of American policy as of Japanese.

On the Japanese side, the pacifist provisions were likely unwelcome to some of those in government from the start. The so-called "Ashida amendment"—the addition of the language "[i]n order to accomplish the aim of the preceding paragraph" to the MacArthur Draft's unqualified prohibition on military forces and other war-making potential, has helped provide an interpretive loophole through which many tanks, fighter aircraft and missile frigates have been driven.

Grossly oversimplified, the language of the Ashida amendment makes it possible to argue that Article 9 only prohibits the possession of military forces used to exercise the

[18] Yet another example of the dangers of relying on the English version of the constitution is the fact that the "never" part of this formulation is not clearly stated in the Japanese.

sovereign right of war or resolving international dispute. That said, there is also a view that even without this interpretation, article 9 should not be a suicide pact, and nothing about it prohibits Japan from defending itself. Arguably, the other rights and freedoms guaranteed by the constitution would be meaningless if the government was unable to protect the infringements that would result from the nation being invaded or controlled by foreign enemies.

At the same time, however, it has never been politically acceptable to assert that article 9 is completely meaningless. Many Japanese people suffered terribly during the war and the desire to avoid being involved in conflict again has resonated widely amongst Japanese people for decades, as was evidenced by the widespread popular opposition to the execution of the new US Japan Mutual Security Treaty of 1960, and more recently in demonstrations against the relocation of a US Marine Base within Okinawa.

During the Cold War, Japan was able to focus on the threat of a direct attack by the Soviet Union and thus focus on territorial self-defense within the scope of its alliance with the US. The Cold War's end, followed by the post-9/11 expansion of the Global War on Terror resulted in greater attention on the restraints imposed by Article 9 on the use of the SDF abroad, whether in peace-keeping operations or in conjunction with US-led military operations. Moreover, changes in regional circumstances, including both the development of nuclear weapons and ballistic missiles by North Korea as well as the aggressive pursuit of territorial claims in the South China Sea by China have made it increasingly necessary for Japan's leaders to think about the possibility of participating in preemptive strikes on other countries. Interpretive and legislative changes during the second administration of Prime Minister Abe Shinzō have significantly expanded the range of activities the SDF can engage in outside of Japanese territory, including engaging in hostilities.

The "interpretive change" in the preceding sentence was possible in part because the Supreme Court of Japan long ago effectively abdicated any role in interpreting Article 9. In a 1959 case known as the *Sunagawa Case*, the Supreme Court overturned the acquittal of a group of defendants prosecuted for trespassing on a US military base. The district court had based its acquittal on the grounds that the US military forces in Japan constituted "war potential" prohibited by Article 9 and that the law criminalizing trespassing on US bases was thus void. The Supreme Court rejected this interpretation, noting that:

> The [US Japan] Security Treaty . . . is featured with an extremely high degree of political consideration, having bearing upon the very existence of our country as a sovereign power, and any legal determination as to whether the content of the treaty is constitutional or not is in many respects inseparably related to the high degree of political consideration or discretionary power on the part of the Cabinet which concluded the treaty and on the part of the Diet which approved it. Consequently, as a rule, there is a certain element of incompatibility in the process of judicial determination of its constitutionality by a court of law which has as its mission the exercise of the purely judicial function. Accordingly, unless the said treaty is obviously unconstitutional and void, it falls outside the purview of the power of judicial review granted to the court. It is proper to construe that the question of the determination of its constitutionality should be left primarily to the Cabinet which has the power to conclude treaties and

the Diet which has the power to ratify them; and ultimately to the political consideration of the people with whom rests the sovereign power of the nation. (Supreme Court, Grand Bench judgment of December 16, 1959).

Although this case was about the constitutionality of U.S. forces in Japan, the idea that national defense is a high-order political matter in which the courts should not involve themselves has also informed the understanding of the constitutionality of the SDF. Constitutional scholars who possibly want Article 9 to mean more than it actually does appear to seek comfort in noting that while the Supreme Court has never found the SDF to be unconstitutional, it has never found it to be constitutional either. Since the SDF has existed for over six decades this type of reasoning seems purely academic.

Moreover, when presented with the opportunity to stake out a clear position on the subject, the Court has avoided doing so. In the 1982 *Naganuma Nike Case*, the court was faced with a district court decision clearly declaring the SDF to be unconstitutional and a High Court decision doing the opposite. The Supreme Court avoided the constitutional issue by finding the plaintiffs in the original action lacked standing (Supreme Court of Japan, 1st Petty Bench, judgment of September 9, 1982).

One consequence of the Supreme Court's non-involvement in constitutional interpretation in disputes implicating article 9 and the SDF is that by default the Cabinet Legislation Bureau has long had the final word on interpretation in these areas. Surprisingly, despite being notionally subordinate to the Cabinet and the Prime Minister, successive generations of CLB leaders have stymied prime ministers seeking to use the SDF more assertively abroad. Until Prime Minister Abe Shinzō engineered a change of interpretation in 2013, the CLB had long opined that Article 9 prohibited the SDF participating in "collective self defense" activities abroad in conjunction with allies such as the United States.

Despite its seemingly broadly elastic interpretability, article 9 together with the still powerful currents of Japanese pacifism that it has come to symbolize, have a powerful influence on the development and use of the SDF. This legacy means that the SDF and Japanese defense policy in general are still subject to restraints that may not apply to "normal" militaries in other countries. For example, until 2014 Japan lacked a general act prohibiting spying or the dissemination of sensitive information relevant to national security, other than the confidentiality obligations contained in the NPSA, the SDFA and certain other specific legislation. When such a law—the Designated National Security Act—was passed in 2013 (taking effect the following year), some Japanese observers regarded it as one of the many signs of the resurgence of pre-war style fascism. For those in countries contemplating greater military ties with Japan, however, such an act would likely be a basic condition to sharing any sort of sensitive information (the passage of such an act being, for example, a condition to any country seeking to join NATO).

Similarly, the SDF lacks many of the attributes of a "true military" in other countries. For example, there is no system of military justice or courts martial (which would likely be unconstitutional under Article 76 of the constitution) and other than the special non-penal disciplinary procedures provided for under the SDFA, SDF personnel are essentially treated as other public servants. In a similar vein, article 3 of the Japanese Penal Code makes offenses such as murder punishable when committed by Japanese nationals abroad. Accordingly, sending SDF personnel abroad in situations where they may be required to use lethal force—even in self defense—requires special legislative dispensations to ensure that they are not violating Japanese law while abroad.

Chapter 7

THE LEGAL PROFESSIONS

Analysis

A. INTRODUCTORY REMARKS

When discussing the Japanese legal system it is common to contrast the size of its attorney population with that of the United States. A typical comparison made as of 2017 would yield approximately 1.3 million attorneys registered in the US as against 39,000 for Japan. Differences such as these—two orders of magnitude, or one order of magnitude if you adjust for population—have long been used for those wishing to derive broad, simplistic contrasts between Japanese and American society. Before Japan's two (going on three) "lost decades," when the nation was still regarded as an economic superpower utilizing a seemingly new and unbeatable political and economic paradigm, some admirers of the "Japanese model" used such comparisons to explain Japan's success. Japan focused on training engineers; Americans on lawyers—no wonder Japanese cars were better!

In reality, however, such comparisons were and still are meaningless for a number of reasons. First, they fail to account for the far greater complexity of the American legal system, with its fifty plus states and territories each with its own laws and system of courts with an overlay of federal law and courts. Second, as discussed elsewhere in this book, the Japanese system of government obviates the need to use the courts (and thus lawyers) in various instances such as non-contentious divorce, adoption and probate where in common law systems such as the United States courts have historically played an important role.

Most importantly, however, the comparison ignores an even more basic reality—that United States has a unitary legal profession while Japan does not. In the US, virtually everyone engaged in the practice of law whether as an attorney in private practice, a government or in-house lawyer, prosecutor or judge, has gone through the same basic system of training and is subject to the same basic licensing regime albeit, on a state-by-state basis. By contrast Japan has a surprisingly heterogeneous legal services industry populated by a complex taxonomy of professionals, including a number of other licensed professions some of which actually refer to themselves as "attorneys" or "lawyers"—in English. As suggested by the title of one of the earliest articles to point out this basic difference, comparing the entire American lawyer population with only a small subset of Japan's multifarious legal professions—courtroom lawyers—is akin to comparing "apples and persimmons."[1]

When the American and Japanese "lawyer/attorney" professions are compared, on the Japanese side of the comparison is usually only a single category of legal professional known as *bengoshi* who, together with most judges and prosecutors, obtain their qualifications by passing one of the nation's most competitive qualifying exams—the National Bar Exam (NBE). *Bengoshi* have a monopoly on representing clients in all Japanese courts and are also able to provide the broadest range of other legal services including those not directly related to litigation.

The latter half of this chapter will discuss *bengoshi* and the way they are trained. However, it is equally important to understand how they fit into Japan's highly balkanized market for legal services, as well as the way the demand for legal professionals within key governmental institutions such as courts are met. Finally, another feature of the Japanese legal services industry is that a large number of law-related roles in government and private industry are filled by people having no formal qualifications whatsoever.

Accordingly, the first half of this chapter will focus on Japan's *other* legal professions before turning to the subject of *bengoshi*. Judges and prosecutors are also included within the definition of "legal professionals" but are discussed in Chapters 4 and 8 respectively.

B. UNLICENSED PROFESSIONS

The unlicensed practice of law is an offense under the Attorney Act of 1949, article 72 of which says that no one but an attorney (*bengoshi*) or a Legal Professional Corporation, shall "*for the purpose of obtaining compensation, engage in the business of providing legal advice or representation, handling arbitration matters, aiding in conciliation, or providing other legal services in connection with any lawsuits, non-contentious cases, or objections, requesting for re-examination, appeals and other petitions against administrative agencies, etc., or other general legal services, or acting as an intermediary in such matters.*" Other provisions of the same law prohibit champerty and unlicensed persons holding themselves out to be *bengoshi*.

This language may seem a fairly comprehensive prohibition, but article 72 of the act ends with a caveat—". . . *provided, however, that the foregoing shall not apply if otherwise specified in this Act or other laws.*" Among other things, this exception anticipates that other licensed professions will practice within their area at least within the scope of their respective licensing statutes. But even where this *proviso* does not apply, there are numerous interpretive questions about what the individual components of the general prohibition actually mean—*engage in the business of*, for example—that a significant amount of legal work is done by unlicensed professionals (or licensed professionals with the wrong license).

Being unlicensed this category of legal professionals is difficult to define and quantify. Accordingly, it should be borne in mind that this is largely intended as a "catch-all" category. That said, four identifiable categories within this category bear mention.

---

[1] Richard Miller, *Apples v. Persimmons: The Legal Profession in Japan and the United States*, 39 J. OF L. ED. 27 (1989).

1. Corporate Legal Department Employees

The most well-known category of unlicensed Japanese legal professional are the thousands of white-collar workers in corporate law-related roles. Some Japanese companies may have a legal department dedicated to contract review and litigation management, while others may deal with such matters through a subdivision of the "general affairs" department. Other companies may also have separate sections dealing with tasks such as managing intellectual property or regulatory compliance. Finally, most companies of any size will have a personnel department that deals with employment and labor law issues.

While the undefined nature of these roles means comprehensive data on the people performing them is unavailable, some indicator is available through the questionnaire-based surveys of corporate legal departments conducted every five years by legal publisher *Shōji Hōmu*. The results of the 2015 survey (in which 960 of 6,193 companies surveyed responded) show about 2/3 of large Japanese companies having a dedicated legal department or section. Together with prior survey results it also shows a historical trend of companies gradually increasing the number of employees focused on the legal role. Nonetheless, a small but significant number of firms still lacked even a single employee dedicated exclusively to the legal function.

The dedicated legal departments of those companies having them would likely be staffed with employees having at least an undergraduate degree in law. Unlike the frequent shifts from posting to posting associated with the lifetime employment system, a job in the legal department may also involve an extended or even permanent posting, prolonged training and experience being needed to develop the skills of a true (albeit unlicensed) "corporate counsel."

In recent years companies have also started to hire licensed professionals. There is also a small but growing community of *bengoshi* lawyers working within corporate legal departments. Large multinationals may also have U.S.-qualified lawyers, or at least employees who have obtained an LL.M. from a U.S. or other foreign law school. The 2015 *Shōji Hōmu* survey revealed 206 companies employing 530 Japanese-qualified *bengoshi* attorneys. Interestingly, 133 companies employed a total of 405 US-qualified lawyers, suggesting that in many cases the corporate legal role is particularly focused on the firm's international operations.

2. Government Legal Roles Requiring No Special Qualifications

All three levels of government (national, prefectural and municipal) have departments or institutions where at least some of the employees are involved in compliance, preparing legal documents, policy and rule (or law)-making, and dealing with legal disputes. Just as with companies, someone who succeeds in joining the public service as a general worker will likely be transferred through a variety of roles in his or her career, and some of these may involve a significant legal component. As indicated by the discussions in Chapters 3 and 5, some public servants working in ministries, the CLB or other national government institutions may develop a deep knowledge of at least those laws and regulations under their remit, not to mention the legislative process.

Other than the ability to pass the general public service exam, which requires some basic knowledge of law, these roles involve no formal training or qualifications. For purposes of this book they are distinguished from judges, certain judicial employees and other special forms of government employment that involve passing a special-law based exam and receiving a particular skill-based title (e.g., judicial clerks). These more defined law-based governmental professions are discussed below.

3. Law Professors

In the United States and some other countries, most law professors will likely have gone through the process of qualifying as lawyers. Some will even have at least a few years of practice experience before joining academia.

By contrast, in Japan law has traditionally been like any other academic discipline—those interested in the subject do graduate research in the subject and enter the academic track. Some law professors may become highly influential figures, and provide expert legal opinions in trials involving complex questions of law (e.g., international bankruptcy). As described further in this chapter, those in the relevant subject areas may be involved in the administration of the national bar exam. Those who do not espouse anti-establishment views and are not overly critical of government policy may find themselves on government legislative or other committees of the type discussed in Chapter 3, considering legislation or government policies. However many legal academics lack practice experience, and may have never passed the NBE, though they may participate in administering and grading it.

Before the Attorney Act was amended in 2004 in connection with the introduction of the law school system and the new qualification regime discussed later in this chapter, law professors with suitable experience could register *bengoshi* without passing the NBE. This back-door into the profession has been closed, subject to a transitional period during which some who could have done so under the old act could still register for a period after the amendment.

As of the time of writing, over 150 universities had undergraduate faculties of law, and some of these also had traditional academic graduate programs leading to master's or Ph.Ds. Approximately 45 universities also had graduate professional law schools, which are discussed in more detail below.

4. "Consultants"

A wide variety of consultants or other businesses may engage in what amount to some form of the unlicensed practice of law under the rubric of consulting or other services. For example "*seiriya*" are a form of unlicensed bankruptcy consultants who help businesses and individuals resolve their debts. "Management consultants" may help companies incorporate or prepare and review contracts or legal documents for submission to government agencies. Other service providers may be experts in niche regulatory regimes. To the extent conducted as a business this may violate the Attorney Act and/or other laws governing the activities of other licensed professions. However, there are numerous gray areas in this area of the law and enforcement is sporadic.

C. GOVERNMENT LEGAL ROLES INVOLVING SPECIAL QUALIFICATIONS

In addition to the unspecific law-related government jobs described in B.2 above, within at least some government and judicial institutions there are law-specific job qualifications that involve passing a qualifying exam that leads into a specialty career track within the public service. Public servants of this category may be accorded special roles and authorities under various statutory regimes. For example, judicial clerks are accorded various dispositive roles under the civil and criminal procedural regimes. Thus, although these are in essence a form of "licensed" legal profession, they involve qualifications that are only meaningful within the government and, with the exception of judges and prosecutors who have passed the NBE, do not confer any special practice privileges in the private sector. However, government service may facilitate qualification as one of the licensed legal professionals discussed later in this chapter.

1. Judges and Prosecutors

As noted later in this chapter, together with *bengoshi* attorneys, the judges and prosecutors who have passed the prestigious NBE form a triumvirate of elite legal professions collectively referred to as *hōsō*. Judges have been discussed in Chapter 4 and prosecutors are discussed in Chapter 8.

2. Specialized Court Employees

As noted in Chapter 4, the number of Japanese judges is very small given the nation's overall population. The smooth functioning of the judicial system is thus heavily dependent on the availability and expertise of court officials in addition to judges. As of 2015 the total number of non-judge judicial employees was about 22,000 and was comprised primarily of three basic categories: (1) court administrative workers (*saibansho jimukan*), (2) judicial clerks (*saibansho shokikan*) and (3) family court investigators (*kateisaibansho chōsakan*).

Little more will be said of the approximately 9,500 court administrative workers. Although they work within the judicial system and need some degree of knowledge of court rules and procedures to do their jobs, they represent the general administrative arm of the judicial bureaucracy. Also, little will be said here of some of the other categories of miscellaneous personnel, including some of the specialized (and in some cases part-time) categories of employees mentioned in Chapter 3, such as family court conciliators and court enforcement officers. Accordingly this section will focus on judicial clerks and family court investigators.

a. *Judicial Clerks*

Judicial clerks (*saibansho shokikan*) are critical to the functioning of the courts. Under the Court Act they are vested with special responsibilities, including the preparation of court documents, legal research and interfacing with parties to litigation and their counsel (Court Act, article 60). Examples of their other special roles include the service of process necessary to start civil litigation (CCivPro, articles 98 and 100) and the preparation of documents necessary to enforce judgments after it is over (articles 382 and 383). Although the English term "clerk" might be fitting for those at an early stage in their career, very experienced members of this profession might be more appropriately referred to as "magistrates" in that they may play a very significant role in managing the litigation process except for conducting the trial and similar proceedings. "Magistrate" may also be appropriate since some judicial clerks go on to become summary court judges at or before retirement.

Becoming a judicial clerk is a distinct career path that involves first passing the appropriate Judicial Public Servant exam and subsequently being admitted to the Supreme Court's Training and Research Institute for Court Officials. Completion of a two year program of education and practical training at the Institute qualifies one to be a judicial clerk. Judicial clerks will advance through various roles (usually within the same appellate court district) until reaching retirement age. Just as with judges, there is a hierarchy of judicial clerks, with chief clerks at each court as well as a cadre of clerks devoted to keeping the Supreme Court running.

As of 2015 the population of judicial clerks stood at about 9,700.

b. Family Court Investigators

Although "family court investigator" is a more accurate translation, English language documents prepared by the courts somewhat confusingly refer to them as "family court probation officers." This reflects the role they play in juvenile criminal cases. This book will use the term "family court investigator."

As of 2015 there were approximately 1,600 of these professionals. Family court investigator is another specific career path. Similar to judicial clerks, successful aspirants must first pass the appropriate Judicial Public Service Exam and then gain entry to the Judicial Employee Training and Research Institute for a two year training course. Compared to judicial clerks they can be seen as playing roles devoted more to substance than procedure. Although the testing and training process ensures they have adequate legal expertise, they are also required to learn psychology, sociology and other skills useful to investigating, understanding and mediating family disputes as well as reasons for juvenile criminal behavior and methods of rehabilitation. They may play a decisive role in family disputes. For example they produce the custody evaluations used by judges to make decisions about visitation and parental authority in connection with divorce. Some family court investigators also go on to become summary court judges.

3. Assistant Prosecutors and Other MOJ/Prosecutorial Personnel

Just as with judges, for a country with a population as large as Japan, the number of Japanese prosecutors (*kenji*) seems tiny; approximately 1,845 as of 2015. Prosecutors and other prosecutorial personnel are discussed in more detail in Chapter 8.

4. The Police

While the police are not considered legal professionals and are discussed in much more detail in the following chapter, they bear brief mention in this chapter for the simple reason that the local *kōban* police box (see Chapter 8) may be the first place many average Japanese people turn to for legal advice of any type, civil or criminal.

D. LICENSED LEGAL PROFESSIONS (OTHER THAN *BENGOSHI* ATTORNEYS)

1. Introductory Remarks

To appreciate the role within the Japanese legal system of *bengoshi* attorneys—*i.e.,* those legal professionals whose testing and training assumes that they will be engaged primarily in representing clients in court—it helps to first be aware of the much larger universe of other licensed professions providing a wide variety of mostly non-contentious legal services. Even if one ignores the unlicensed and governmental professions discussed previously in this chapter, the market for legal services in Japan is served by a bewildering menagerie of licensed professionals who, for the most part offer a much narrower range of services within their respective spheres. This is quite different from countries such as the United States where there is a single, unitary legal profession. Moreover, there is significant overlap in the services some of these Japanese professions provide—preparation of legal document or corporate secretarial services, for example.

Some might reasonably question the inclusion of some licensed professions—customs brokers, for example—in a list of "legal professionals." The reason for doing so in this book is because almost all of the statutes defining the various professions and the scope of the services they may provide include an exception that allows *bengoshi* attorneys (and in some cases other licensed professionals) to also provide those services. Thus, *bengoshi* are the closest corollary to lawyers in the United States and other countries in having the ability to provide the broadest range of legal services. Moreover, the other providers of these various categories of legal services are in competition with *bengoshi* within those narrower bailiwicks, and may actually go through a qualification process that makes gives them an advantage in doing so.

In any case, the reality is that a great deal of the needs of Japanese people for legal services is met by licensed professionals other than *bengoshi*. This was likely more true in the past when the artificial scarcity of *bengoshi* meant that towns or cities with populations in the tens of thousands might not have even one. Other legal professions naturally filled the void.

Another consequence of Japan's heterogeneous legal services market is that the average Japanese person may have only a dim appreciation (if any) of the difference between the various licensed professions and the range of services each can provide. Given that there is a great deal of overlap in some areas where multiple professions can compete to provide the service, there may be confusion at a very basic level. It is not uncommon to see advertisments in trains and print or other media from different professions offering what are essentially the same services. Even the names of the place of business where these professions practice may be confusing: *bengoshi* lawyers practice in *hōritsu jimusho* (literally "law offices") while administrative scriveners (discussed below) typically call their offices as *hōmu jimusho* ("legal affairs offices").

In addition, once these other licensed professions are added to the mix of what might be analogous to "attorneys" in the US context, Japan may actually have something in the order of a quarter of a million legal service professionals. Together with the unlicensed and governmental professions discussed above the total number of legal professionals it much closer to parity with the United States and other countries.

Before turning to the individual categories of licensed legal professions, a few general observations are in order.

a. Relationship with Government Compared to Bengoshi

First, with a few exceptions each profession (other than *bengoshi*) exists within a sphere of regulation under the control of a particular ministry or agency of the national government. Accordingly, it is perhaps easiest to think of most of the legal professions as existing within the system of vertically-integrated regulation described in Chapter 3.

In fact, at risk of oversimplification it may be helpful to think of most of the ministries as having their own captive legal profession. With the exception of *bengoshi* attorneys, each profession is governed by a specific statute under the jurisdiction of that ministry/agency and is entered through an official testing and/or appointment process ultimately under the controlof that authority. Moreover, although the qualifying exams are highly competitive (virtually all have a lower pass rate than even the most difficult US bar exam), most have testing waivers or direct registration schemes for persons with suitable government experience, usually the supervising ministry or agency. In other words, the professions have an aspect of the *amakudari* systems discussed at Chapter 3.

Similarly, although many of these professions have to register with regional or national associations and are subject to rules of professional conduct established by those bodies, they are ultimately also subject to discipline by the government institution having statutory jurisdiction over the profession. *Bengoshi* attorneys are thus special in being the only autonomous, self-regulating legal profession.

b. Titles and Terminology

When these other professions are mentioned in English it is common to refer to theme using demeaning terms such as "scriveners," "paraprofessionals" or "paralegals." This condescension is belied by the difficulty of passing the qualifying exam and the high level of legal knowledge and, in some cases, experience that may be required of them to be eligible to practice. Moreover, it is inconsistent with the fact that at least some of these professions have taken to referring to themselves as "attorneys" or "lawyers"—in English (doing so in Japanese would be a violation of the Attorneys Act). That said, for the sake of consistency this book uses the English titles found in the Japanese government's translation of the relevant statutes or terms.

Many of the private licensed legal professions discussed in this section are collectively referred to in Japanese as *"shigyo."* This is because their professional title ends in the word *shi*, a character meaning "scholar" and commonly used to denote certain learned professions (*gyō* meaning "business"). The same is true of *bengoshi.*

c. Professional Corporations

As is the case with *bengoshi* attorneys, most of these professions can be practiced either by individuals or through special professional corporations, with the statute defining the profession also defining the details of its particular type of corporate entity. For purposes of this chapter the details of the various types of corresponding professional corporations will be ignored.

d. Mandatory Registration

Just as with *bengoshi* attorneys, the laws governing most (but not all) of these professions make registration with a national or regional professional association a mandatory requirement for practice. The costs associated with this requirement can impose an additional hurdle to new entrants in addition to the very rigorous qualification regimes. Depending on the profession, initial registration fees may be over one thousand dollars with additional monthly fees of several hundred dollars. Based on a 1996 Supreme Court decision, the mandatory registration requirement imposes limits on the ability of professional associations to make political contributions using member funds (Supreme Court, 3rd Petty Bench judgment of March 19, 1996).

2. *Shihōshoshi* (Judicial Scriveners)

Judicial scriveners are one of Japan's oldest legal professions, dating back to 1872 and the government's initial efforts to create a modern system of courts that involved three defined professions. These were: *shōshonin*, who prepared evidentiary documents (and went on to become the public notaries discussed later in this Chapter), *daigennin* (literally "person who speaks on behalf of someone else) who are the forbearers of today's *bengoshi* lawyers, and *daishonin* ("person who writes on behalf of someone else"), who prepared documents on behalf of clients for use in court and elsewhere.

Judicial scriveners evolved from this last profession, though they are no longer formally involved in preparing court documents, except at the summary court level as discussed below. Today they feature prominently in what in some common law jurisdictions would be called "conveyancing"; the documentation and registration of real estate transactions and other services related to the corporate and real estate title registries maintained by the MOJ through its nationwide network of Legal Affairs Bureaus.

Judicial Scriverners can also provide services relating to the system of escrow that is also administered through these bureaus. Those who receive additional training and otherwise meet qualification requirements are also permitted to represent clients in civil litigation at the summary court level, provide certain ADR services and represent and advise clients in boundary-confirmation procedures.

With a pass rate of around 4% (2017 results), judicial scriveners may have one of the most competitive qualifying exams of any legal profession in the world. However, under article 4(2) of the Judicial Scriveners Act of 1950 (JSA), former court employees, judicial clerks and MOJ and prosecutorial officials with at least ten years' experience are eligible to register as judicial scriveners without sitting for the exam.

At the time of writing there were about 22,000 judicial scriveners, approximately 6,000 of whom were also qualified to provide summary court representation services. As required by the JSA, each judicial scrivener is registered with one of the 50 judicial scriveners associations, which are organized on the same geographical basis as the district courts (*i.e.,* one for each prefecture except for Hokkaidō, which has four). Some judicial scriveners may also be members of one of 20 regional associations that are qualified to conduct real estate registration for government entities. Japan's extensive public works projects mean that such public authorities are heavy users of real estate registry services.

Misbehaving judicial scriveners are subject to disciplinary actions by their professional association, as well as sanctions from the MOJ.

3. *Gyōseishoshi* (Administrative Scriveners)

Administrative scriveners have the same roots as judicial scriveners, in the *daishonin* of the early Meiji period. Those who prepared documents on behalf of others for submission to police or other local authorities came to be subject to separate practice regulations imposed by those authorities. This ultimately put them under the jurisdiction of the Ministry of the Interior. The post-war dismantling of that ministry and other related reforms was followed by the passage of the Administrative Scrivener Act of 1951 (ASA) and the establishment of a separate profession in its current form. Its history and practice before municipal and prefectural governmental institutions puts it under the jurisdiction of the MIC and prefectural governments.

Entry into the profession is possible through a number of routes, the most common of which is passing the qualifying exam, which in 2017 had a pass rate of 17%. *Bengoshi* lawyers, patent attorneys, certified public accountants and certified tax accountants are also eligible to become administrative scriveners (ASA, article 2) without passing the exam. There is also an *amakudari* route for a wide variety of national and local public servants with suitable experience to join the profession without passing the exam.

Administrative scriveners are authorized to charge fees for the preparation and submission of regulatory documents to *most* government bodies on behalf of clients. Since 2015 those who have gone through an additional qualification process to become "designated administrative scriveners" can also represent clients in first level (non-judicial) dispute proceedings with such bodies, such as filing objections or petitions for reconsideration in connection with unfavorable administrative dispositions (see discussion at Chapter 10). They can also prepare contracts and other legal documents, except those which by law are reserved to other professions. (ASA, article 2).

Their ability to prepare legal documents for a fee means that in addition to contracts and administrative filings, they can help parties engaged in *pro se* litigation by preparing documents for litigants to file in court (a service that may also be offered by judicial scriveners). There are, for example, administrative scriveners who purport to specialize in divorce. Even though they cannot represent clients in court they can prepare the relevant documents. Since many offer services relating to visa applications and immigration law, they are also one of the professions most likely to interact with Japan's foreign population.

Administrative scriveners seem more circumspect about titles; individual members of the profession may refer to themselves in English as "administrative lawyers" or as working in "administrative law offices. In advertising, their professional associations refer to their members as "*machi no hōritsuka,*" which could best be translated "your neighborhood legal professional," possibly sowing further confusion among people who primarily associate *legal professional* with *bengoshi* and going to court.

The ability of administrative scriveners to represent clients in filings with administrative agencies is subject to some important exceptions. Since many of the ministries atop these agencies have their own captive professions it is unsurprising that they seek to maintain practice monopolies in certain spheres. For example, administrative scriveners are not supposed to represent clients before the various registry systems administered through the Legal Affairs Bureaus, this being the province of judicial scriveners as already discussed. Similarly, there is an ongoing dispute over whether administrative scriveners can perform filings with Labor Standards Bureaus, formally the territory of Labor and Social Security Attorneys.

At the time of writing there were approximately 46,300 administrative scriveners, including 2,400 qualified as designated administrative scriveners. They were registered in one of 47 prefectural professional associations.

Administrative scriveners are subject to discipline by their professional association, and by the governor of the prefecture in which they are registered.

4. Shakai Hoken Rōmushi (Labor and Social Security Attorneys)

Labor and social security attorneys are a comparatively new profession born from the postwar expansion of labor and employment rights. Established under the Labor and Social Security Attorney Act of 1968 (LSSAA), the profession added a level of specialization to a sector of the legal services market previously served mostly by administrative scriveners. Entry into the profession is achieved primarily by passing an exam on the relevant areas of law and which in 2017 had a pass rate just under 7%. The LSAA contains a wide range of exemptions for various subjects tested on the exam for persons having relevant experience in government employment regulation roles. *Bengoshi* lawyers can also act as labor and social security attorneys.

This profession is under the jurisdiction of the MHLW. Focusing on Japan's complex system of labor, employment and social welfare benefits regulation, labor and social security attorneys authorized to prepare relevant documents and represent clients before Labor Standards Bureaus and other relevant bodies. They can also assist *bengoshi* in employment-related litigation. Those who receive additional training and pass a further qualifying exam can become "designated" (*tokutei*) labor and social security attorneys. Designated labor and social security attorneys may represent clients in employment-related ADR proceedings.

At the time of writing there were approximately 40,000 labor and social security attorneys registered with one of 47 prefectural associations. Members of the profession are subject to discipline through their associations and from the MHLW.

5. *Benrishi* (Patent Attorneys)

Patent attorneys are another profession with a long history.

As a workable system for registering patents and similar rights came into shape over the decades following the Meiji Restoration, there also developed a need for special professionals competent to handle the relevant procedures. In 1921 a specific law governing the patent attorney profession was passed. In 2000 a new Patent Attorney Act (PAA) was passed which completely revised and modernized the rules governing them.

Under the PAA, patent attorneys can represent clients before the JPO and METI in connection with registrations for patents, utility models, designs or trademarks, or international applications. With respect to such intellectual property rights they can also provide licensing and other documentation-related services as well as ADR-related services. Those with suitable knowledge and experience can act as co-counsel with *bengoshi* in specific types of intellectual property litigation (PAA article 6–2). Finally, they have practice rights before customs authorities in connection with the import of trademarked and patented items. (PAA, articles 4 and 5).

As with other professions, entry is achieved primarily through passing an exam, the Patent Attorney Exam (PAA article 7). Portions of the exam may be waived for persons having a suitable academic background or government experience (article 11). The 2017 Patent Attorney Exam had a 6.5% pass rate. *Bengoshi* lawyers and persons with at least seven years' experience as a patent examiner at the JPO are qualified to practice without taking the exam (article 7).[2]

At the time of writing there were approximately 11,000 patent attorneys. Unlike many of the other legal professions there is only a single professional association, the "Japan Patent Attorneys Association" (JPAA). Registration with the JPAA is mandatory. Headquartered in Tokyo, the JPAA has nine regional branches for national coverage.

---

[2] Oddly the exemption for *bengoshi* means that they can apparently practice as *benrishi* without any formal requirement that they study patent law first.

However, the vast majority (approximately 7,000) of patent attorneys practiced in metropolitan Tokyo.

Patent attorneys are subject to sanctions from the Minister of Economy Trade and Industry under the PAA (articles 32–36) and the disciplinary rules of the JPAA.

6. *Kaiji Dairishi* (Marine Procedure Commission Agents)

Sometimes referred to as the "judicial scriveners of the sea," Marine Procedure Commission Agents provide maritime law-related services. They are involved the documentation and registration of conveyancing transactions relating to ships, as well as a wide range of licensing and qualification requirements relating to boats, ships and the workers who operate them.

Under the jurisdiction of the MLIT, entrance to the profession is achieved by passing a test or through suitable government experience (Marine Procedure Commission Agent Act of 1951, article 2). There is a professional association—the Marine Procedures Commission Agent Association—withnine regional branches nationwide, but registration with it is not required by law as is the case for most of the other professions. At the time of writing the Association had 355 members. It appears common for someone with this qualification to also have another license, such administrative scrivener.

7. Zeirishi (Certified Public Tax Accountant)

Zeirishi are the most populous of the licensed professions. At the time of writing they numbered approximately 75,000. Although the official translation of their name is "Certified Public Tax Accountant," some who target foreign clients seem to get away with calling themselves "tax lawyers" in English. As the name suggests, *zeirishi* help clients with tax-related matters, including preparation of relevant documents and representing them before the tax authorities. Under the rubric of "ancillary services" they may also provide various finance-related documentation and bookkeeping services. As a result, *zeirishi* are one of several legal professions that provide incorporation and corporate secretarial services. *Zeirishi* can act as assistant counsel to *bengoshi* lawyers in tax-related litigation before courts (Certified Public Tax Account Act of 1951 (CPTAA), articles 2, 2–2).

Entry to this profession can be achieved through a combination of testing and professional experience, with a wide range of testing exemptions available for persons with suitable academic or practical experience. *Bengoshi* lawyers and chartered public accountants are also able to become *zeirishi* without further training or testing (CPTAA, article 3).[3]

There are 15 regional *zeirishi* associations overseen by a national federation. Registration with the national federation through one of these associations is mandatory for a *zeirishi* wishing to practice. *Zeirishi* are under the overall jurisdiction of the MOF, and are subject to disciplinary actions by the National Tax Agency and other tax authorities. *Zeirishi* appear to be one of the few professions originating from the Kansai area of Western Japan, having their roots in efforts first by Osaka prefecture (in 1912), then Kyoto prefecture to regulate the conduct of professional "tax-challengers." The establishment of a nationally-regulated profession did not occur until 1942.

---

[3] Again, the law seems to permit *bengoshi* attorney to hang out a shingle as a tax accountant without ever studying or demonstrating any knowledge of tax law or accounting.

The influence of *amakudari* (retirement into the profession by former tax officials) may be particularly noteworthy for *zeirishi*. Anecdotal evidence suggests that there is a significant difference in *zeirishi* who qualify through the testing process and those who do so through *amakudari*. In other words, a former official can build his practice based on the perception of having inside connections. Moreover, some clients of this type of *zeirishi* may be afraid to take their business elsewhere out of the (possibly unwarranted) fear that doing so will trigger a tax audit.

8. *Kōnin Kaikeishi* (Certified Public Accountants)

As in other countries, Japan's certified public accounts are one of the principal professions involved in advising businesses, particularly the exchange-listed public companies for which they perform annual audit services. Some might question their inclusion in a list of "legal professions," but overlap and competition between the legal and accounting professions has been a constant theme in the development of the two professions elsewhere in the world. In addition, in Japan a licensed CPA license is also eligible to practice as both a *zeirishi* and register as an administrative scrivener, meaning the profession is able to provide a range of legal services broader than may be permitted of CPAs in other countries.

Entry to the CPA profession is generally achieved through the CPA exam, which had a pass rate of around 10% in 2016. However, the law recognizes a wide range of exemptions for various test subjects for those having the requisite academic background or professional experience (Certified Public Accountants Act of 1948 (CPAA), articles 3, 8–10). There is also a procedure for registration by accountants qualified in other countries, but this is exceptionally rare.

By law CPAs are required to register with the JICPA, the Japan Institute of Certified Public Accountants (CPAA, articles 17, 19). Although a national institution, it has 16 regional associations which correspond roughly with the geographical boundaries of the MOFs Regional Finance Bureaus.

As of October 2016, there were 29,191 CPAs registered with the JICPA as well as a grand total of 3 registered foreign CPAs. CPAs are subject to oversight by the Certified Public Accountants and Audit Oversight Board which is under the Financial Services Agency. By statute, CPAs are subject to discipline from the Prime Minister (CPAA, articles 29 *et seq.*), though this role is actually performed by the FSA.

9. *Tochi Kaoku Chōsashi* (Land and House Investigators)

Tochi kaoku chōsashi are a profession that has not appeared in previous English accounts of Japan's legal professions. However, in Japanese they are typically included in the ambit of *shigyō* when the professions "peripheral" to *bengoshi* and *hōsō* are debated. However, their remit is not one in which *bengoshi* are able to practice.

Land and house investigators are focused on land surveys and work closely with the real estate registration system. Unlike judicial scriveners, however, they specialize more in confirming the metes and bounds of property and its correct registration. Although just as with judicial scriveners they work closely with the real property registration system, they are focused on that part of the system that describes tracts of land, whereas judicial scriveners are focused on the registration of rights and interests in land and other real property.

Land and house investigators may also provide services relating to boundary disputes, including boundary-related ADR services. Judicial scriveners can also advise on boundary issues involving property having a value below a certain threshold. This reflects a compromise that was made when the two separate systems for recording land and interests in it were combined into one, threatening to put many judicial scriveners out of work.

Land and building investigators are under the jurisdiction of the MOJ. Entry into the profession is through a law- and geometry-based exam (pass rate, approximately 8%), with an alternate route allowing registration for those having suitable experience working in a Legal Affairs Bureau (Land and Building Investigator Act, article 4). Members of the profession must register with the prefectural association where they practice (Land and Building Investigator Act, article 47). At the time of writing there were approximately 17,000 members of this profession registered in prefectural associations. Disciplinary actions against misbehaving Land and Building Inspectors may be brought by their professional association or by the appropriate Legal Affairs Bureau.

10. *Tsūkanshi* (Registered Customs Specialist)

A *tsūkanshi* (registered customs specialist) is generally required in order to engage in the business of representing clients in clearing goods through customs (Customs Business Act of 1967, articles 3(1) and 13). This profession is entered through a qualifying exam which mostly tests knowledge of customs-related laws (but also of the US-Japan SOFA). There are waivers for persons demonstrating adequate customs-related experience (Customs Business Act, articles 23 and 24). Registered Customs Specialists are under the jurisdiction and disciplinary authority of the Director of Customs. At the time of writing there were around 16,000 *tsūkanshi* registered with Japan's nine regional customs authorities.

This is another profession that has typically been excluded from English accounts of Japan's legal professions. It is also typically excluded from the *shigyō* peripheral professions when those are discussed in Japanese. We have chosen to include them in this chapter, however, because the Customs Business Act (article 3(5)) grants special dispensations to *bengoshi* lawyers and, with respect to certain types of activities, patent attorneys in the performance of duties that would other need to be performed by a *tsūkanshi*. They are thus another profession whose scope of services overlap with *bengoshi* attorneys.

11. *Kaiji Hosanin* (Maritime Counselor)

Less a "profession" than a role, *kaiji hosanin* (literally, "marine affairs assistant") act as counsel for maritime personnel whose culpability for maritime accidents is being adjudicated before a maritime accident tribunal (Maritime Accident Tribunal Act of 1947). Under the jurisdiction of the MLIT, Maritime Counselors do not pass a test, but eligibility to register can be achieved through suitable experience in various maritime-related positions *or* by being a *bengoshi* lawyer (Maritime Accident Tribunal Act Regulations, article 19). It is thus another example of an area of legal services where *bengoshi* lawyers can naturally practice, but where there is also competition from professionals having very different, often much more specialized, qualifications and experience.

12. *Kōshōnin* (Public Notary)

To American readers who associate notarial services with a minor functionary verifying the identity of a person signing a document and administering oaths, Japan's "public notaries" may seem quite alien. To those having experience with continental European-style public notaries they will likely seem more familiar.

Of course, verification of identification and signature is one of the services a Japanese *kōshōnin* (public notary) can perform for a fee. Though if this is required for a legal document to be used in another country, the notarial service provided by the consular authorities of that country in Japan may be a better bet. In any case, public notaries in Japan are few in number and, unlike those in America, have extensive legal knowledge and experience and (supposedly) perform a much more sophisticated role than simply verifying signatures (which, as discussed in Chapter 9, are not commonly used to execute legal documents in any case).

Japan's public notaries are based on continental European models. The nation's first Public Notary Act was passed in 1886 and based on the French system, but this was replaced by the current German-inspired Public Notary Act of 1908. Just as in continental legal systems, public notaries perform a wide and much deeper variety of services, which entails a great deal of experience and the ability to understand and explain to clients the legal documents before they proceed with executing them

Public notaries are appointed by the Minister of Justice and are subject to geographical restrictions on their practice. They are essentially tied to the Legal Affairs Bureau having jurisdiction over their notarial district (Public Notary Act, article 10). At the time of writing there were approximately 500 public notaries at around 300 notary offices around the country.

Under article 12 of the PNA, public notaries are supposed to be appointed from the ranks of those passing a notarial exam, with article 13 providing that lawyers, judges and prosecutors who have passed the national bar exam can also be appointed without passing the notarial test. In reality, however, the notarial test was not even held for decades, with public notary appointments widely understood as serving as a form of *amakudari* position for judges, prosecutors and MOJ bureaucrats. Public notaries are subject to a statutory retirement age of 70, which ensures a steady churn while still being later than that of most other public service jobs.

Public notaries are technically a form of public servant, though their compensation is derived solely from fees paid by clients. However, some fees are built into the system by incorporation into laws under the primary jurisdiction of the same ministry that has jurisdiction over public notaries. As noted in Chapter 3, the Companies Act (administered by the MOJ) requires notarial attestation of the articles of incorporation of a new company (the actual preparation of the articles would be performed by one of the other professions described above). The statutory fee is JPY 50,000. With close to 90,000 *kabushiki gaisha* (joint stock corporations, the most common corporate format) newly incorporated in 2016 this works out to an average income of close to JPY 9 million (roughly $90,000) per notary.

As public servants, public notaries are immune from personal liability for professional negligence. If they commit malpractice (such as invalidating a will by allowing a beneficiary to act as a witness, as has happened in at least one instance), the remedy of the aggrieved party is to sue the state under the State Redress Act.

E. THE LEGAL ELITE: *HŌSŌ* AND *BENGOSHI* LAWYERS

1. Introductory Remarks and Terminology

Having introduced much of the population of the crowded jungle in which they operate, we can now turn to the profession most people are actually referring to when they talk about "Japanese lawyers"—the *bengoshi* attorneys who have passed the National Bar Exam (NBE) and have a monopoly on representing clients before all Japanese courts, as well as the ability to provide the broadest range of other legal services.

The term *bengoshi* is a compound of three Chinese ideographs (i) *ben* which has numerous meanings, but in this context would best be rendered "to advocate", (ii) *go*, which means to "protect" and (iii) *shi*, the suffix introduced earlier in this chapter meaning "learned profession."

Although the Japanese constitution guarantees a right to counsel in criminal prosecutions (articles 34 and 37), the term used in the Constitution and other statutes such as the code of criminal procedure is "*bengo'nin*" which is translated "counsel" and in Japanese does not contain the same connotation of a learned profession (*nin* simply meaning "person"). In the criminal context *bengonin* and *bengoshi* are synonymous, and any possibility of discrepant meaning is resolved by article 31 (1) of the Code of Criminal Procedure of 1948 (CCP), which requires *bengonin* to be chosen from the ranks of *bengoshi*. However it is possible in summary and family court proceedings for a non-*bengoshi* (*i.e.*, an unlicensed person) to act as *bengonin* if the court gives leave (e.g., CCP, article 31(2)).

Another term introduced earlier is *hōsō*. There is no real English equivalent for this term; sometimes "legal profession" is used as a translation, but in the context of all the other professions discussed in this chapter it is likely to cause confusion. The "*hō*" means "law" and "sō" is a comparatively obscure character that in ancient times referred to lower level palace officials and in modern times is still used as a component in terms describing ranks of non-commissioned military personnel such as "sergeants." Today *hōsō* refers to the triumvirate of elite legal professions—judges, prosecutors and *bengoshi* attorneys—who have achieved their status by passing the NBE.

Judges have already been discussed in chapter 4, and prosecutors are covered in more detail in chapter 8. For purpose of the discussion that follows it should just be remembered that not all Japanese judges or prosecutors have passed the NBE and those who have not are generally not included within the ranks of *hōsō*.

As of 2017 Japan's *hōsō* population stood at just under 44,000, with a breakdown of approximately 3000 judges (those who passed the NBE; this number does not include summary court judges), 1800 prosecutors and 39,000 *bengoshi*.

As these numbers show, the vast majority of *hōsō* are *bengoshi* in private practice. Morever, as the discussion that follows will show, *bengoshi* account for most of the recent dramatic increase in the number of *hōsō* as well as the resulting angst within and about the profession. Thus, when policy-makers and the media discuss *hōsō*—often in the context of its "population problem"—more often than not they are talking mainly about *bengoshi*.

Although *bengoshi* are by far more numerous than the two other categories of *hōsō*, for historical and institutional reasons it is the governmental *hōsō*—the judges and prosecutors—who are more important in understanding how *bengoshi* are trained and qualified. As discussed in the next section, in the past judges and prosecutors were trained differently and the term *hōsō* itself contains a connotation of officialdom.

Each of the three professions also has their own governing statute. The basic features of the judicial profession are set forth in the Courts Act, the prosecutors are governed by the PPOAA and *bengoshi* by the Attorney's Act of 1949. As public servants prosecutors and to a lesser extent judges are also subject to the National Public Service Act.

While the three *hōsō* branches are separate professions, there is a certain amount of interchange. As discussed in Chapter 3 and 4 judges and prosecutors have *hanken kōryū* exchanges of personnel and there is also a mechanism for appointing experienced *bengoshi* to the bench, though such appointees only account for a small fraction of sitting judges. But the most common interchange is likely one way, with prosecutors and judges registering as *bengoshi* when they leave government service. This may be a common path chosen by those reaching mandatory retirement age or growing weary of the civil service rat race.

2. *Bengoshi*: A Historical Overview

a. *The Pre-War Legacy*

As discussed in Chapter 2, during the Tokugawa period there was an official proscription on the dissemination of knowledge about law and most other behavior that fostered litigation, the occurrence of which was taken as a sign of disharmony, immorality and thus bad government. People who specialized in assisting litigants for a fee did exist but were not held in high regard.

The Meiji Restoration resulted in some disenfranchised samurai using their education and literacy to become involved in the practice of law. This also enabled them to participate directly in the widespread and often fierce debates about how Japanese society should be restructured.

During the Meiji Period, the first officially recognized class of what could be considered "lawyers" was established in 1872, the *daigennin* discussed earlier in this chapter. This profession was initially modeled after the French *advocat*. However there were no rules about formal qualifications and *daigennin* were limited to representing clients in civil litigation. In 1876 a testing regime was added to prevent unqualified people from practicing. The tests were implemented at a prefectural level with graduates of the elite law faculty of Tokyo Imperial University being exempt from this requirement. The test became a national examination in 1880 and *daigennin* were freed of geographical restraints on where they could practice. This came at the price of being required to join professional organizations that eventually evolved into today's prefectural bar associations. *Daigennin* also came to be permitted to represent defendants in criminal prosecutions, an innovation that was due in part to a certain basic unfairness in favor of non-Japanese. Defendants from countries which had agreed to renegotiate the unequal treaties and thus accept the jurisdiction of Japanese courts over their nationals were entitled to defense counsel, while Japanese defendants were not, until this change.

In 1893 the first Attorney's Act was passed and the profession came to be referred to by its current title—*bengoshi*, though that term had already been introduced in 1890 in the Code of Civil Procedure. At this time *bengoshi* were still limited to representing clients in court proceedings, subject to qualification testing by the Ministry of Justice, and were required to join regional bar associations that were subject to the oversight and disciplinary authority of the MOJ.

In 1914 the testing requirements for *bengoshi* were combined with those for judges and prosecutors, a development that enhanced the private profession's social status. In 1923 the testing exemption for Tokyo University law graduates was eliminated. In 1933 a new Attorney's Act was passed. For the first time *bengoshi* were officially authorized to provide legal services other than in connection with court proceedings. The profession was also formally opened to women, though there had been female advocates before this development.

b. The Postwar Era

The postwar history of *bengoshi* and *hōsō* can be divided into two distinct periods. The first is the period of roughly five decades running from the end of the Allied occupation to the turn of the 21st century. The second begins with the program of legal system reform first conceptualized in the late 1990s and implemented in the opening years of the new millennium.

(i) The First Fifty Years

The occupation-era democratic reforms brought changes that enhanced the status of *bengoshi*. This included the current Attorney's Act of 1949, which among other things removed the profession from the supervisory and disciplinary authority of the MOJ. Although article 77 of the Constitution gives the Supreme Court the power to make rules governing *bengoshi* (and prosecutors) it has generally refrained from doing so.

Another change was that b*engoshi* were generally required to go through the same qualification process as the two governmental *hōsō* professions. This meant successful completion of a course of training at the LRTI. Collectively therefore, hōsō became (and remain) a body of legal professionals who must all pass through a judicial training institute but only a small minority of whom actually become judges (or prosecutors). *Bengoshi* represent the majority of LRTI trainees who either did not satisfy the somewhat opaque selection criteria of the governmental *hōsō* constituencies, or never aspired to such jobs in the first place.

The period at the LRTI has always been a critical part of the *hōsō* training and qualification practice, particularly in the past when it was a full two years and there were no formal educational prerequisites to sitting for the NBE. *Hōsō* and *bengoshi* in particular commonly identify themselves with their class at the LRTI. For example, someone from the class of 53 would have started their training at the LRTI in April of 1999. The sunflower-emblem lapel badges issued to *bengoshi* as a form of professional education bear a unique registration number, from which can be derived the year its owner entered the LRTI.[4]

---

[4] This badge is issued by the *bengoshi*'s bar association and obtaining a replacement if lost involves publication of a notice in the official gazette. It used to be the only form of official identification of the *bengoshi*'s status and practice rules technically require it to be worn when a *bengoshi* is acting in such capacity. Some of the other licensed legal professions also have special lapel badges, but most use some form of symbol, such as

The role of the LRTI in the process of qualifying as a *bengoshi* is also important to understand because the Institute's capacity has always dictated the number of people who can pass the NBE. As Table 7-1 shows, for quite some time—roughly the three decade period from the 1960s to the 1990s the number of NBE passers was stable at just under 500 per year. Although the 1–3% pass rate shown for this period suggests the exam was exceptionally "difficult," the more accurate term would be "competitive," since the NBE's pass rate was (and still is) essentially a function of the ratio of people sitting for the exam to the number allowed to pass every year. This number is still notionally based in part on the capacity of the LRTE. In short, the government-controlled NBE/LRTI qualification process has had the effect of strictly limiting the number of new entrants to the ranks of *bengoshi* lawyers.[5]

In 1998 the course of study at the LRTI was shortened from two years to 18 months, and then again to 16 months in 2006 for passers of the old NBE before that exam regime was phased out completely. Under the new NBE and law school regime described in the following pages, the training at the LRTI has been further shortened to 1 year, much of which actually involves internships at law firms, courts and prosecutors' offices around the country. However, the LRTI capacity remains a notional constraint on growth in the profession.

---

a chrysanthemum petal motif, reflecting their closer relationship with government authority (the chrysanthemum being the symbol of the Emperor and thus government, particularly under the Meiji constitutional system).

[5] An interesting byproduct of this exceptionally competitive NBE regime was that for a Japanese person graduating from a law faculty and having adequate English skills, it might be easier to qualify in the United States by getting an LL.M. from an American law school and sitting for the New York bar exam.

TABLE 7-1(OLD) NATIONAL BAR EXAM PASS RATES:

Year	Taking Exam	Number passing[1]	Pass Rate (%)	Year	Exam takers	Number passing	Pass Rate
1949	2,570	265(3)	10.31	**1980**	28,656	486(49)	1.70
1950	2,806	269(3)	9.5	**1981**	27,816	446(33)	1.60
1951	3,668	272(2)	7.42	**1982**	26,317	457(48)	1.74
1952	4,761	253(7)	5.31	**1983**	25,138	448(44)	1.78
1953	5,138	224(3)	4.36	**1984**	23,956	453(52)	1.89
1954	5,250	250(10)	4.76	**1985**	23,855	486(45)	2.04
1955	6,347	264(10)	4.16	**1986**	23,904	486(59)	2.03
1956	6,373	297(14)	4.41	**1987**	24,690	489(60)	1.98
1957	6,920	286(6)	4.13	**1988**	23,252	512(61)	2.19
1958	7,109	346(11)	4.87	**1989**	23,202	506(71)	2.18
1959	7,858	319(8)	4.06	**1990**	22,900	499(74)	2.18
1960	8,363	345(15)	4.13	**1991**	22,596	605(83)	2.68
1961	10,909	380(17)	3.48	**1992**	23,435	630(125)	2.69
1962	10,762	459(26)	4.27	**1993**	20,848	712(144)	3.42
1963	11,686	496(28)	4.13	**1994**	22,554	740(157)	3.28
1964	12,698	508(25)	4.00	**1995**	24,488	738(146)	3.01
1965	13,644	526(25)	3.86	**1996**	25,454	734(172)	2.88
1966	14,867	554(18)	3.73	**1997**	27,1746	746(207)	2.75
1967	16,460	537(24)	3.26	**1998**	30,568	812(203)	2.66
1968	17,727	525(35)	2.96	**1999**	33,983	1,000(287)	2.94
1969	18,453	501(37)	2.72	**2000**	36,203	994(270)	2.75
1970	20,160	507(34)	2.51	**2001**	38,930	990(223)	2.54
1971	22,336	533(28)	2.39	**2002**	45,622	1,183(277)	2.59
1972	23,425	537(26)	2.29	**2003**	50,166	1,170(275)	2.33
1973	25,339	537(24)	2.12	**2004**[2]	49,991	1,483(364)	2.97
1974	26,708	491(23)	1.84	**2005**	45,885	1,464(350)	3.19
1975	27,791	472(36)	1.70	**2006**[3]	35,782	549(118)	1.53
1976	29,088	465(39)	1.60	**2007**	28,016	248 (57)	0.89
1977	29,214	465(33)	1.59	**2008**	21,994	144(39)	0.65
1978	29,390	485(32)	1.65	**2009**	18,611	92(16)	0.49
1979	28,622	503(40)	1.76	**2010**[4]	13,223	59(6)	0.45

SOURCE: Ministry of Justice.

(1) Bracketed number represents the number of female passers.

(2) Year in which new law school system commences operations (see discussion in subsection (ii) following)

(3) Year in which first sitting of "new" bar exam was held (see Table 7-2).

(4) Final year of "old" bar exam.

The qualification regime under the old NBE was on its face exceptionally egalitarian. There were few formal educational prerequisites to sitting for the annual NBE. Talented individuals might pass the exam while still in university, and being a university graduate was not required in any case. A few exceptionally talented people might struggle with the dilemma of having passed both the similarly competitive top-level national public service exam and the bar exam, in which case they had the option of serving as a public servant first and then going to the LRTI and qualifying as a lawyer after retirement. Nonetheless, despite the facially egalitarian regime, as Table 7-1 shows, women have long been seriously underrepresented among the ranks of bar passers.

Though egalitarian, its brutal competitiveness meant passing the NBE could involve a significant investment of time. *Juku* cram schools taught law as a subject to be regurgitated in the format required by the NBE. Even those who were ultimately successful in passing the exam would likely have done so after having devoting several of the productive years of their lives to studying for and repeatedly failing the exam. The average *bengoshi* was said to have passed on his or her fifth attempt, and many takers might never pass at all. This system also meant the pool of desirable candidates for service as governmental *hōsō* (those who were young, unpolluted by real world experience and ideally passed the NBE on their first attempt) came to be crowded out by the ranks of those who had only managed to pass after years of repeated failures.

Another facet of the *bengoshi* profession during this period is that it had a highly anti-establishmentarian bent. Perhaps this is only natural given its freedom from government regulation, and the fact that *bengoshi* are the only profession charged with helping people by directly challenging government conduct through criminal, constitutional and administrative litigation. Morever, someone with the ability to pass the bar exam—particularly while still in college or soon after graduating—would also typically be eligible for a good corporate or government job. Unless, that is, they had rendered themselves ineligible through political activities, were members of disadvantaged communities or demographics, or pursued the legal profession for ideological reasons. Thus, any particular bar association was likely to have included a significant component of communist or socialist lawyers. In a 1989 book titled "*Bengoshi,*" lawyer Uchida Masatoshi describes what to him was a "typical" week in the life of a practicing attorney. Among other things it included a gathering that ended in the participants singing *L'internationale*, the international socialist anthem. It was not until the 1980s that a significant business bar began to develop and the strong anti-establishment streak in the *bengoshi* community began to be diluted.

This background explains one of the seemingly counterintuitive arguments made by some members of the *bengoshi* community in opposition to increasing their numbers: that having more *bengoshi* would result in *less* public interest litigation. In other words, to the extent many *bengoshi* chose the profession for ideological reasons—to help the weak and disadvantaged and challenge the wrongful exercise of state power through the courts—they needed the bread and butter legal work that was readily available thanks to the artificial scarcity of their numbers in order to support at least a middle-class lifestyle. Greater competition among lawyers for fee-earning cases would thus make it harder for them to devote time and resources to *pro bono* public interest work.

(ii) *The 21st Century: Law Schools and the New NBE*

(a) *The JSRC Recommendations*

At a time when westerners were still admiring Japan for having so few courtroom lawyers, Japanese policy makers were arriving at a different conclusion; the country needed more. Not only that, but it needed a different *type* of *bengoshi*. One of the pillars of legal system reform recommended by the Cabinet's Justice System Reform Council (JSRC) was to increase the number of *bengoshi* and change the way they and their *hōsō* colleagues were trained.

In its December 21, 1999 interim report entitled "*The Points at Issue in the Justice Reform*," the JSRC identified a number of issues facing Japanese society in the 21st century, including a longstanding shortage of *hōsō* legal professionals, particularly lawyers. Perhaps the more significant issue, though, was a perceived distance between the people and the judicial system, a lack of trust in the courts by the citizenry.

> . . . we hear the following criticisms that are pointed out at our justice [sic] malfunction: "The administration of justice is not open and it is distant from the people," "Both lawyers and the court of justice give us awkward feelings. They lack warmth," "The system of administration of justice is hard to understand and difficult for the people to utilize it," "When the society/economy rapidly changes, administration of justice cannot fully meet the expectation of the people with regard to speed and expertise," "It has failed to exercise the check-function against administration," etc. Plainly speaking, the Japanese administration of justice (the legal profession) is not accepted as a familiar or reliable existence because of their unknown character to people.

Internationalization was also identified as a key factor in the need for a new, different legal profession:

> We are faced with issues such as how to protect safety and rights of individuals and businesses deployed around the world, how to construct a fair and energetic global market and how to participate in it with effective trade strategies, and moreover, how to cope with universal issues such as human rights, environment and international crime."

Nonetheless, the primary focus of the JSRC *Points at Issue* was domestic. The JSRC thought that *bengoshi* should become like "doctors for social ills." There should thus be more of them, and they needed to be more evenly geographically dispersed. Although not mentioned in detail in the *Points at Issue*, most *bengoshi* were concentrated in Tokyo, Osaka and a few other major metropolitan centers (as is still largely the case today; see Table 7-4). At the time some prefectural bar associations might have had only two or three dozen members, and it would not be unusual for a city with a population of a few hundred thousand to have only three or four lawyers, or even none for smaller municipalities. People in such communities got by using other legal professions or had one come in from elsewhere if litigation was absolutely necessary. As noted by *Points at Issue*, this was an obstacle to getting the people and the judicial system more engaged with each other and, by extension, changing the way the country was governed.

After 61 meetings over a two year period, on June 12, 2001, the JSRC issued its formal Recommendations, entitled *For a Justice System to Support Japan in the 21st*

Century (referred to below as *Recommendations*"). Those recommendations relevant to the *hōsō* legal professions are summarized below:

- An increase in the number of NBE passers to 1500 per year under the current system of qualification, to be achieved in part by shortening the training period at the LRTE to 18 months (LRTE capacity still being a constraint).
- The establishment of a new system of graduate professional law schools to train *hōsō* candidates.
- The gradual replacement of the current NBE with a "new" NBE open only to graduates of the new law schools, with the number of passers gradually increased to 3,000 per year by 2010.

The JSRC's recommendations for changing the way lawyers were trained and the reasons for doing so are worth quoting at length because they tacitly acknowledge the deficiencies of what is now the "old" system of becoming a *hōsō*, which resulted in *bengoshi* whose principal qualifications consisted of the ability to regurgitate legal knowledge on a highly competitive exam and whatever training they received at the LRTI.

> "A new legal training system should be established, not by focusing only on the "single point" of selection through the national bar examination but by organically connecting legal education, the national bar examination and legal training as a "process." As its core, law schools, professional schools providing education especially for training for the legal profession, should be established.

The JSRC also identified a basic failure in the relationship between academic legal education and the legal profession under the existing system:

> While the current [i.*e.*, old] national bar examination system has the advantage of being open to anyone, it is still very hard for candidates to pass the examination, although the number of successful candidates has been gradually increasing. For this reason, candidates have become more prone to give priority to acquiring techniques for passing the examination. . . .
>
> On the other hand, conventional legal education at universities has not necessarily been sufficient in terms of either basic liberal arts education or specialized legal education. Moreover, partly because at the undergraduate stage (law faculties of universities), the major purpose of education has been to send people with a certain level of legal education into various sectors in society, while at the postgraduate stage (postgraduate schools), the major purpose has been to train academic researchers, it has been pointed out that there exists a gap between education and actual legal practice. Accordingly, it is difficult to say that law faculties and postgraduate schools have played a proper role in fostering the legal profession as a profession.

The JSRC thus articulated an admirable goal; devoting significant governmental and academic resources to the establishment of a comprehensive, structured system for training the elite legal professions as a replacement for the old system which actually encouraged students to *sacrifice* opportunities to learn the academic theory of law in order to attend bar prep courses and learn how to package a limited range of legal knowledge into a format that was pleasing to those grading the NBE (a skill clients do not necessarily evaluate highly).

The JSRC nonetheless still seemed to assume there was a "correct" number of bar exam passers (and thus *bengoshi*), and that this number could be identified and adjusted as necessary. As already described, for many years the "correct" number of bar passers had been a little under 500 per year. In in its recommendations JSRC decided the new "correct" number would initially be 1,500 until gradually increased to 3,000 per year. This goal was to be achieved by 2010 and was based on the goal of Japan eventually having a *hōsō* to population roughly comparable to France.

The JSRC's were then expressed in a wide range of legislation, including amendments to the Attorney's Act and the National Bar Examination Act of 1949. The MEXT acquired a large new jurisdictional mandate, and used it to establish standards for a new class of graduate professional schools—the law schools recommended by the JSRC.

(b) The Establishment of Law Schools and the "Correct Number" of Bar Passers

During what was understood to be a limited window of opportunity, many Japanese universities rushed to apply for licenses to establish law schools. The entire system started operation in April 2004. Suddenly Japan had dozens of law schools with thousands of students.

Although it had originally been envisioned that there would be about twenty law schools whose graduates would be eligible to take a new NBE with a pass rate of 70–80%, the MEXT used its new jurisdictional mandate to grant licenses to no less than 74 law schools. The result was that the first class of law school graduates sitting for the new NBE (which remains under the control of the MOJ) saw a pass rate of only 48%. The pass rate quite predictably went down in subsequent years, as each new class of graduates competed with those who failed in prior years for a relatively fixed number of passing slots (see Table 7-2).

Another problem that quickly arose was that before the first class of law school graduates had even qualified to practice at the end of 2007, the existing *bengoshi* community began to complain about the sudden increase in new lawyers, which was already taking place due to the increase in the number of those passing the *old* NBE. Since an apprenticeship with an experienced lawyer remains a practically (even if not formally) necessary part of a young lawyer's training in most jurisdictions, the sudden rapid increase in bar passers has meant firms with openings for new associates were being overwhelmed.

In addition, complaints soon began to circulate in the mainstream media about the *quality* of law school graduates, even those who passed the NBE. These complaints invariably took it for granted that *hōsō* who qualified the old way were of "high quality," even though a basic premise of the new law school/NBE regime was that Japan needed qualitatively different *bengoshi*.

These questionable qualitative concerns, together with the lower than expected—and declining—bar pass rate were soon rightly or wrongly characterized as a problem attributable to deficiencies in law school education. This was despite law schools and their programs having all been rigorously vetted by the MEXT upon establishment and on a continuing basis both directly and through the periodic accreditation reviews required by MEXT regulations. Moreover, MEXT regulations prohibited law schools from devoting too much curricular time to bar exam subjects or blatantly "teaching to the bar."[6] The whole point of the new system was to have law schools that did more than just teach students how to pass the bar exam, but bar pass rates were the only metric anyone—including the MEXT which set the system up, used for evaluating them.

The sudden "problem" of law school quality was deemed so urgent that MEXT had established a committee to study how to improve the quality of law school education before a single law school graduate had qualified to practice, indicating that whatever "quality" meant in the context of the problem, it had nothing to do with the views of end users of legal services.

The "qualitative failure" of law school education trope likely proved a useful excuse for the MEXT to respond to what was quickly perceived a policy failure. It did so by forcing law schools to reduce their class sizes, engage in increasingly stringent grading or even shut down. While framed in qualitative terms, all of these measures appeared to have the same basic goal: reducing the number of people graduating from law school and sitting for the bar exam. This in turn would cause the pass rate to go up (unless the government adjusts the "correct" number of passers downward, which it did).

The core issue remained that, just as under the old system, the number of people allowed to pass the NBE was an arbitrary one that can be and has been reset based on political pressure government caprice. Faced with a sudden increase in new, inexperienced and supposedly inferior new *bengoshi* as well as complaints from the established lawyers about a sudden decline in their earnings, there quickly developed a consensus amongst legal system stakeholders that the planned 3,000 bar passers per year was unachievable; it was officially abandoned by a 2013 cabinet resolution.

The sometimes surreal debate about what the "correct number" of passers should continues but that number appears likely to remain at around 1,500 for the foreseeable future. Certainly Table 7-2 below shows a progression in that direction, though some bar associations are still calling for a further reduction to 1,000 per year. All of this has been an unfortunate set of developments for the universities that hired faculty and built facilities based on a government commitment to expand the number of bar exam passers to 3,000 per year, not to mention the early classes of law school applicants who invested time and tuition based on the same set of expectations.

---

6 For this reason *Juku* cram schools (under the jurisdiction of METI) which dominated bar preparation under the old NBE regime have done fine under the new systems as well.

TABLE 7-2 NEW NATIONAL BAR EXAM PASS RATES

Year	Number of people sitting	Number passing	Pass rate (%)
2006	2,091	1,009	48.3
2007	4,607	1,851	40.2
2008	6,261	2,065	33.0
2009	7,392	2,043	27.6
2010	8,163	2,074	25.4
2011	8,765	2,063	23.5
2012	8,387	2,102	25.1
2013	7,653	2,049	26.8
2014	8,015	1,810	22.6
2015	8,016	1,850	23.1
2016	6,899	1,583	22.9
2017	5,967	1,543	25.8
SOURCE: Ministry of Justice.			

At the time of writing at approximately half of Japan's law schools had stopped accepting new students or already closed down. Many of those still surviving were having trouble filling their entering classes, and it remains to be seen whether the system will survive. A particularly disturbing trend has been plummeting law school applicant numbers, which dropped from 72,800 in 2004 to 8,274 in 2016.

Despite tremendous ministerial energy devoted to supposedly "improving" the quality of law school education, the end result has been to make going to law school—and thus becoming a *hōsō*—an unattractive option for many of the talented, intelligent people the system was intended to attract. In fact, the "decline in quality" of law school graduates voiced early in the system's history may prove to be a self-fulfilling prophecy, with many law schools struggling to fill entering classes by lowering standards.

Ultimately, the most basic problem facing the Japanese law school system today and thus, the manner in which *bengoshi* are trained, seems to be the inability of policymakers to be honest about the true purpose of the NBE. It is unequivocally about imposing what are essentially arbitrary numerical limits on the number of people entering the legal professions—particularly *bengoshi* going into private practice—and is openly discussed in such terms. Yet the law school system was designed for the express purpose of training lawyers who had skills beyond the ability to pass exams, and law schools continue to be subject to regulatory and curricular mandates that assume qualitative goals outside the scope of bar exam performance.

(c) *Law Schools and the Law School Equivalency Exam*

Prior to the introduction of the law school system, law was an academic discipline taught primarily at the undergraduate level, with graduate programs primarily for those seeking to advance into academia. Japanese universities are a mixture of public and private universities, with most public universities being "national" universities, including Tokyo and Kyoto Universities which are renowned for their law faculties.

Confusingly, law schools were an addition to, not a replacement for this system. This meant that universities establishing law schools would also still have their preexisting undergraduate and graduate law faculties. MEXT regulations restricting the ability of law schools to intermingle their classes and teaching resources with these other law faculties made the situation complex.

Law schools were established based on high ideals. As envisioned in the JSRC's *Recommendations*:

> With regard to the system for legal training, in order to secure legal professionals with suitable quality to undertake the administration of justice in the 21st century, the system shall not consist of selection based upon the "single point" of the national bar examination. Rather, a system for legal training shall be established that consists of a "process" that organically connects legal education, the national bar examination, and apprenticeship training. As the core of the system, graduate schools specialized in training of legal professionals (hereinafter referred to as "law schools") shall be established.
>
> And:
>
> Law schools should provide educational programs that, while centered on legal theory, introduce practical education (e.g., basic skills concerning how to determine the required elements and fact finding), with a strong awareness of the necessity of building a bridge between legal education and legal practice.

Unfortunately, ideals have fallen to the wayside through the rigidity of the NBE and its use as a tool for limiting entry to the *hōsō* legal professions.

In some ways Japanese law schools were modeled on the US system. Graduates receive what is typically referred to in English as a J.D., a "doctorate" of law, though there is no requirement to write a thesis in order to graduate. While undergraduate law classes in Japan may see professors lecturing to hundreds of students, law schools are limited in the maximum number of students in class, and instruction is supposed to involve teacher-student interactions and the Socratic Method.

Similar to the US system, Japanese law schools were also supposed to enrich the legal professions by facilitating entry by people with a broad range of backgrounds, particularly graduates from non-law academic disciplines and people with work experience or other professional qualifications. At the same time, however, many prospective law school students were graduates of the undergraduate law faculties which remain in existence. Accordingly, law schools offer two programs—a three year program for those with no law background, and a two year program for those able to demonstrate an adequate foundational understanding of the basic areas of law tested through each law school's entrance examination.

While most law schools drew the bulk of their faculty from their existing law programs, MEXT regulations require that 1/3 of a law school's full-time faculty members be "practitioners," and that most of those be *hōsōi*. One could look at this requirement cynically as a way of ensuring a certain number of *amakudari* posts for retiring judges and prosecutors, but it also reflects a concern that the academics from law faculties were too. . . academic and might not be able to help students pass the NBE (many law professors having not passed it or practiced themselves).

Although most law schools seek to differentiate themselves, the combination of MEXT regulations, accreditation requirements (essentially a form of additional indirect MEXT regulations) and the grim prospects of passing the NBE forces both law students and law school faculties to focus as much as possible on the core subjects that are tested on the bar exam and, to a lesser extent, their chosen optional subject. Although mandated by regulations and curricular requirements, other program offerings intended to ensure law students get the broad, practical education that was the intent of the law school program—courses in other subject areas (such as foreign law), clinics, internships and study abroad offerings may be regarded as tempting diversions that nonetheless threaten to distract students from the primary goal of passing the NBE.

Within the universe of bar exam subjects, in order to avoid professors focusing on their own interests or advancing unorthodox views of the subject, law schools are all expected to teach towards common curricular objectives established by the law school community as urged by the MEXT.[7]

Under the current system, being a graduate of a law school became a prerequisite to sitting for the new NBE. The old problem of people perpetually sitting for and failing the NBE (and thereby driving the pass rate further down) was "solved" by introducing a rule that only permits graduates to sit for the exam during the five year period after graduation.[8] As a result, some law schools receive applications from people who have already graduated from law school once, seeking to do so again in order to requalify to sit for the NBE.

Another option, however, is to sit for the *yobishiken* which literally means "preparatory exam" but is essentially a Law School Equivalency Exam (and will be referred to as such in this book). Also under the jurisdiction of the MOJ, the LSEE is an exam which, like the old NBE, has no significant educational prerequisites. Passing the *yobishiken* gives one the same status as a law school graduate—the entitlement to sit for the NBE (but without going to law school). It is an odd test in that it merely entitles those who pass it to take another test on essentially the same subject matter.

First held in 2011, the LSEE was, according to the MOJ, intended to ensure that even those without the financial means to attend law school would be able to join the ranks of *hōsō* if they were talented enough. There are, however, no financial need prerequisites to sitting for it. Although it was originally expected that about 50 people would be allowed to pass the equivalency exam each year, the number has quickly been expanded so that in 2017 444 people passed.

---

[7] That one result of this is the government effectively telling what areas of constitutional law should be taught and how surprisingly does not seem to bother anyone.

[8] This was initially a "three strike" rule that permitted law school graduates to only sit for the NBE three times during the five year period following graduation.

TABLE 7-3 LAW SCHOOL EQUIVALENCY EXAM RESULTS

Year	Number sitting	Number passing	Pass Rate (%)
2011	6,047	116	1.79
2012	7,183	219	3.05
2013	9,224	351	3.81
2014	10,374	356	3.44
2015	10,334	394	3.81
2016	10,442	405	2.7
2017	10,743	444	4.1
SOURCE: Ministry of Justice.			

The LSEE is suspiciously like the old NBE in both its pass rate and the way it is implemented, including having a final component consisting of an oral exam. Despite its intended purpose of providing an alternative for those unable to attend law school, a significant number of those passing it are law students. For example 1/3 of those passing in 2015 were reportedly law school students who had not yet graduated.

One might reasonably suspect the MOJ of keeping the LSEE in place as a means of quickly restoring the old bar exam system in the event the law school system fails completely, and possibly even as a means of hastening that result. The LSEE also risks splitting the ranks of *hōsō* into those who went to law school and a "superior" elite caste who did not need to. Some top law firms now reportedly refuse to hire *bengoshi* who did not pass the LSEE. In fairness, those who pass the LSEE have an exceptionally high NBE pass rate compared to law school graduates (72.5% in 2017 compared to a national average of 22.5% for law school graduates). However, the LSEE is also effectively subverting the JSRC's original goals of fostering a legal profession with various skills beyond the ability to pass highly competitive exams.

3. Qualifying as a *Bengoshi* Lawyer

While the law school system will doubtless undergo more dramatic change (with some predicting its collapse and abolition), the process of qualifying as a lawyer remain similar to that which has prevailed for decades. With some minor exceptions, one must pass the NBE, complete a course of training at the LRTI and then register as a *bengoshi* attorney.

a. The NBE and the LSEE

The NBE and the *yobishiken* (Law School Equivalency Exam) are administered by the National Bar Examination Commission, an MOJ *shingikai* deliberative council (see discussion at Chapter 3) established and administered through the National Bar Examination Act of 1949 (NBEA, articles 12 *et seq.*). The Commission is comprised of seven members representing each of the three *hōsō* professions as well as academia and other constituencies. Commissioners serve for two year terms.

Under the Commission are the two committees that do much of the actual work of preparing and grading exam questions; the NBE Testing Committee and the LSEE Testing Committee. These Committees are comprised of subcommittees of scholars in the applicable fields (e.g., public law, criminal law, etc.) as well as representatives of the three *hōsō* constituencies. There is overlap between the two committees, but the total membership of NBE Testing Committees is larger (approximately 250 compared to approximately 175 for the LSEE Testing Committee), in part because the former requires involvement of experts in the NBE's optional subjects, which are not tested on the *yobishiken*. Having law school professors involved in preparing bar exam problems arguably creates a conflict of interest in that they can advantage their own institution's graduates (or specific favored students) by revealing problems or simply indicating particular areas of their subject matter to focus on. Blatant instances of this actually happening have been rare, however, and offending scholars have been dealt with harshly in the few instances when it has.

The NBE is a grueling four day exam held over a five day period in mid-May of every year. As with most academic programs in Japan, law school graduation is in March, meaning students sitting for the NBE for the first time must begin preparing for the NBE well in advance of that date. The exam can be taken in one of seven testing locations: Sapporo, Sendai, Tokyo, Nagoya, Osaka, Hiroshima or Fukuoka.

The NBE consists of multiple choice and exam questions in the core subjects of Public Law (constitutional and administrative law), Civil Law (the Civil Code, Code of Civil Procedure, Commercial Code, Company Law and related subjects) and Criminal Law (the Penal Code and Code of Criminal Procedure). In addition, those sitting for the exam must also answer an essay question in one of the following "optional" subject areas of their choice: labor law, bankruptcy, intellectual property, economic law (e.g. anti-trust, etc.), tax law, environmental law, international private law and international public law. Labor law and bankruptcy are typically the most common choice every year. The introduction of optional subjects to the NBE was one of the innovations that came with the new law school system intended to contribute to the development of more specialized lawyers.

Being graded by computer, the results of the multiple-choice portion of the NBE are announced in June, with about 1/3 of test takers typically failing. The essay answers of those who pass the multiple choice portion are then graded by the appropriate Testing Committee subject matter experts, and the final results of the NBE are announced in early September.

The LSEE is held over a bifurcated schedule similar to the old NBE. First there is a multiple choice component held in May, shortly after the NBE. Those who pass this component are eligible to sit for the essay exams portion in July. Those who pass the essay portion must then sit for an oral examination in October. The subject matter of the exam is essentially the same core areas of law as the NBE (minus the optional subject areas). Unlike the NBE, the equivalency exam also includes a "general knowledge" component the scope of which encompasses famous works of literature, famous historical events as well as the ability to read English or identify correct protein sequences! The final results of the exam are announced in November.

b. The Legal Research and Training Institute

Passing the NBE makes one eligible to become a *shihōshūsei* or Legal Apprentice. This involves entering the Supreme Court's Legal Research and Training Institute for a one year course in practical skills.

Formal induction into the LRTI takes place at the end of November, after a brief introductory training session in December, Legal Trainees then spend the next eight months dispersed around the country, where they spend two months with a law firm, two months with a prosecutor's office, two months at the criminal division of a district court, and two months at the civil division of a district court. After receiving exposure to the realities of the four principal areas of *hōsō* practice, Legal Trainees then spend approximately one month in focusing on optional programs intended to help them develop areas of interest. Legal Trainees gather at the LRTI for a two month finishing program focused on practical training in civil trial skills and criminal trial skills.

Finally, in November there is a graduation exam that Legal Trainees must pass in order to complete their training. In the past this was largely a formality, with most trainees passing. However, the increase in the number of Legal Trainees failing this exam has been another area of grumbling attributed to the "poor quality" of law school education (rather than any problems with training at the LRTI, of course).

As the final stage through which most people qualifying as a *bengoshi* pass, the LRTI's training program illustrates yet another subtle gap between the ideals underlying the law school system and its reality. That is, even for those who wish to become corporate lawyers or otherwise practice outside litigation, the qualification entails devoting significant time and energy to the practice of law in Japanese courtrooms. Given the existence of other legal professions focused on other areas of legal practice, the focus on litigation skills may make sense in context. Yet it means that the system of legal education and qualification offered through law schools and the NBE regime will likely continue to be inherently limited in its ability to produce a broad-based legal profession.

c. *Registering as a* Bengoshi

Under the Attorneys Act, successful completion of the LRTI training course renders one eligible to become a *bengoshi* (art. 4). However it is also possible to become a *bengoshi* merely through becoming *eligible* to enter the LRTI (*i.e.,* by passing the NBE), but instead acquiring practice experience in one of a variety of law-related jobs in government or the private sector for the designated number of years (five or seven, depending on the job) and then receiving supplemental training as designated by the MOJ (art. 5) and provided by the JFBA. This provides a route for qualifying to practice as a *bengoshi* without going to the LRTI. However, only a small number of NBE passers have availed themselves of this route.

As discussed earlier in this chapter, in the past it was possible for some law professors to qualify as a *bengoshi* without taking the NBE, but this exception has been phased out. Under the current Attorneys Act the only exceptions to the requirement that *bengoshi* have passed the NBE is for ex-Supreme Court judges (art. 6), most of whom will have passed the NBE anyways and for those qualifying as *tokunin kenji* prosecutors, as discussed earlier in this chapter and in Chapter 8.

Under the Attorneys Act (articles 8 and 9) the final step in qualifying as a *bengoshi* is joining a bar association and registering on the list of lawyers maintained by the Japan Federation of Bar Associations.

4. Bar Associations and Law Firms

Japan's bar associations are established geographically in concordance with the location of district courts, of which there is one in each prefecture, with Hokkaido being an exception (see Chapter 3). Another exception of a different sort is Tokyo, which is a single judicial district but for historical reasons has three bar associations. Note that not all bar associations follow the naming conventions of the corresponding district courts. For example, while the district court for Hyogo Prefecture is the "Kobe District Court," the bar association is the Hyogo Prefectural Bar Association. On the other hand, some prefectural bar associations (Miyagi, Ishikawa) are named after the principal city (Sendai, Kanazawa) where the District Court is located.

As Table 7-4 below shows, despite the intent of the JSRC in expanding their population, *bengoshi* remain heavily concentrated in a few small urban centers—Tokyo, Osaka and, to a lesser extent Nagoya (Aichi Prefecture) and Fukuoka. The small population of registered foreign lawyers is concentrated almost exclusively in Tokyo.

TABLE 7-4 BAR ASSOCIATIONS AND POPULATION DATA BY PREFECTURE

Bar Association	Number of Members as of January 1, 2017*	Number of registered foreign lawyers	Prefectural Population (est., as of October 1, 2015)
Tokyo	8,022 (1,575)	76	13,515,000
Tokyo First	4,981 (988)	138	
Tokyo Daini	5,211 (1091)	167	
Kanagawa	1,576 (303)	3	9,126,000
Saitama	832 (133)	0	7,267,000
Chiba	772 (133)	0	6,223,000
Ibaraki	283 (48)	1	2,917,000
Tochigi	219 (33)	0	1,974,000
Gunma	281 (34)	0	1,973,000
Shizuoka	463 (84)	1	3,700,000
Yamanashi	119 (15)	0	835,000
Nagano	244 (42)	0	2,099,000
Niigata	277 (44)	0	2,304,000
Osaka	4,445 (767)	10	8,839,000
Kyoto	753 (149)	0	2,610,000
Hyogo	907 (179)	2	5,535,000
Nara	169 (27)	0	1,364,000
Shiga	144 (30)	0	1,413,000
Wakayama	146 (19)	0	964,000

Bar Association	Number of Members as of January 1, 2017*	Number of registered foreign lawyers	Prefectural Population (est., as of October 1, 2015)
Aichi	1,934 (374)	5	7,483,000
Mie	191 (31)	0	1,816,000
Gifu	194 (36)	2	2,032,000
Fukui	103 (13)	0	787,000
Kanazawa (Ishikawa)	172 (27)	0	1,154,000
Toyama	121 (14)	0	1,066,000
Hiroshima	581 (91)	0	2,844,000
Yamaguchi	171 (18)	0	1,405,000
Okayama	393 (82)	0	1,922,000
Tottori	65 (11)	0	573,000
Shimane	85 (20)	0	694,000
Fukuoka	1,240 (217)	3	5,102,000
Saga	102 (12)	0	833,000
Nagasaki	163 (22)	0	1,377,000
Oita	160 (24)	0	1,166,000
Kumamoto	270 (42)	0	1,786,000
Kagoshima	206 (24)	0	1,648,000
Miyazaki	142 (15)	0	1,104,000
Okinawa**	265 (40)	2	1,434,000
Sendai (Miyagi)	441 (63)	0	2,334,000
Fukushima	201 (25)	0	1,914,000
Yamagata	101 (11)	0	1,124,000
Iwate	103 (10)	1	1,280,000
Akita	78 (12)	0	1,023,000
Aomori	119 (14)	0	1,308,000
Sapporo (Hokkaido)	777 (112)	0	5,382,000
Hakodate (Hokkaido)	57 (6)	0	
Asahikawa (Hokkaido)	75 (11)	0	
Kushiro (Hokkaido)	76 (9)	0	

Bar Association	Number of Members as of January 1, 2017*	Number of registered foreign lawyers	Prefectural Population (est., as of October 1, 2015)
Kagawa	173 (24)	0	976,000
Tokushima	97 (9)	0	756,000
Kochi	92 (15)	0	728,000
Ehime	166 (18)	0	1,385,000
TOTAL	**38,954 (7,165)**	**411**	**127,095,000**

SOURCES: Sources: lawyer data, JFBA; prefectural population: Japanese government.

* Okinawa lawyer number includes 9 "special" members who obtained their licenses during the period of US administration pursuant to a different qualification regime than applied in Japan. Table 7-4 ignores JFBA, which *bengoshi* also join when they join their local association. The table does not include 1,005 professional corporations and 4 foreign law professional corporations.

Most lawyers practice in law offices. According to the 2016 edition of the *Bengoshi Hakusho* (the "Lawyer White Paper," published annually by the JFBA), there were a total of 15,829 law firms in Japan as of 2016. Most of these firms were small; 9,404 were operated by solo practitioners, 2,934 had two lawyers, and 2,489 had three to five. Only ten firms had more than 100. Of the top ten firms, nine were located in Tokyo and one in Osaka. The largest—Nishimura Asahi, had 508 lawyers. The career path for many lawyers—and the business model of many small firms—is to take a young lawyer on as a salaried apprentice for a few years, until they develop enough experience and clients to start their own practice.

A comparatively recent trend has been for *bengoshi* to work in corporate legal departments. According to the Japan In-house Lawyers Association, Japan went from having 66 such in-house *bengoshi* in 2001 to 1,707 in 2016. Of these, the vast majority (1,460) were registered with one of Tokyo's three bar associations.

Finally, an even more recent trend—one that may be attributable in part to the rapid increase in the *bengoshi* population, is their employment by governments, both at the national level and the prefectural and municipal level. The Attorney Act made it difficult for registered *bengoshi* to take public employment until it was amended in 2004. This change plus increased flexibility in public employment have resulted in a small but growing number of *bengoshi* being employed on a fixed-term contract basis by national, prefectural and municipal government institutions. According to a 2015 report by the JFBA, there were 131 *bengoshi* working in such capacities in national government institutions and a further 56 worked for municipal and prefectural governments. Given the total number of public servants in Japan, these numbers are vanishingly small. Moreover, the fixed-term aspect of their employment means that such *bengoshi* are unlikely to advance into positions of influence through the career track described elsewhere.

5. *Bengoshi* Regulation

In addition to the Attorneys Act, the principle source of rules governing attorneys is the Rules of Professional Conduct produced by the JFBA. These rules are similar to professional conduct rules elsewhere, though some might find them more focused on lawyers than on clients when compared to jurisdictions such as the United States. For example, rather than a duty to "zealously represent clients," article 21 of the Rules requires *bengoshi* to endeavor to realize the rights and *valid* interests of their clients, but requires the *bengoshi* to follow his or her own conscience (*ryōshin*) in doing so. Similarly, conflict of interest rules may seem quite different, reflecting the manner in which many small firms permit their salaried *bengoshi* to engage in moonlighting—in other words such *bengoshi* may be permitted to have their own clients outside the scope of the firm's business, so long as it doesn't interfere with the duties they must perform for firm clients.

Anyone can bring a complaint against a *bengoshi* or a *bengoshi* professional corporation. As in many jurisdictions, *bengoshi* are expected to comport themselves in an exemplary fashion, and Article 56 of the Attorneys Act mandates disciplinary action against a *bengoshi* (or professional corporations) who:

> . . . violates [the Attorneys Act] or the articles of association of the bar association to which he/she or it belongs or of the Japan Federation of Bar Associations, or damages the order or reputation of said bar association or misbehaves in a manner impairing his/her or its own integrity, whether in the conduct of his/her professional activities or not.

Complaints are handled in the first instance through the Bar Association in which the *bengoshi* is registered. Article 58 of the Attorneys Act establishes a two stage process for the resolution of complaints, first by having them reviewed by a preliminary disciplinary committee (*kōki iinkai*) which determines whether a further investigation is required. In that case the complaint is referred to a separate disciplinary committee (*chōkai iinkai*) of the same Bar Association, which decides whether disciplinary action is merited and if so what it should be. Appeals to from JFBA determinations regarding discipline are made to the Tokyo High Court.

Article 57 of the Attorneys Act provides for four types of disciplinary action: a formal warning, a suspension of practice for two years or less, an order to withdraw from the bar association where the *bengoshi* is registered, and being stricken from the rolls (disbarred). An increase in disciplinary actions against *bengoshi* has been another source of grumbling about the new law school system and the sudden influx of new lawyers—that it will lead to more immoral lawyers. That said, reported incidents of serious disciplinary actions often involve *bengoshi* who qualified prior to the law school system.

By law, *bengoshi* are "entrusted with the mission of protecting fundamental human rights and achieving social justice" (Attorneys Act, article 1). Although this may seem like nothing more than a well-intentioned hortatory statement of purpose, many *bengoshi* take it quite seriously and devote some or all of their time to public service and the protection of human rights.

As the only self-regulating legal profession and, indeed, one of the few sectors of the economy that is not subject to the jurisdiction of a ministry or executive branch agency, *bengoshi* are a potentially disruptive force in Japan. *Bengoshi* are the only one of Japan's many legal professions that can seek to protect human rights by directly challenging state action in criminal, administrative, constitutional and civil court proceedings. It is thus fascinating that they are also the only legal profession about which there is an impassioned debate over how *few* of them there should be.

Another interesting aspect of the rules of professional conduct in Japan are that they apply only to *bengoshi*. The rules applicable to other *hōsō* judges and prosecutors are the ethical rules applicable to public servants generally, and what few mandates are provided in statutes such as the Court Act and PPOA, as well as in the procedural code rules for recusal of judges or other judicial personnel.

6. *Gaikokuhō Jimu Bengoshi* (Registered Foreign Attorneys)

Since the passage of the Act on Special Measures Concerning the Handling of Legal Services by Foreign Lawyers of 1986 (the "Foreign Lawyers Act") it has been possible for attorneys qualified in other jurisdictions and who meet the requirements of the law to register with a Japanese bar association and engage in the business of advising clients on the law of their home jurisdiction. Such registered foreign lawyers are referred to as *gaikokuhojimubengoshi* (literally "foreign law affairs attorney") or "*gaiben*" for short.

Although the number of lawyers holding this qualification is small—just a few hundred (see Table 7-4 for details), the existence of this qualification has made it possible for large foreign international firms to establish Japanese offices in their own names and to establish joint practices with Japanese *bengoshi* (though initially the practice rules were so restrictive that this was exceptionally difficult).

The Foreign Lawyer Act (article 10(1)(i) is also somewhat exclusionary in qualifying eligibility for registration as a *gaiben* with practice *outside* of Japan for at least two years. While this requirement annoys some foreign lawyers, the principal intent of the restriction seems to prevent Japanese people who fail to qualify as Japanese *bengoshi* from going to the United States, qualifying as a lawyer there and immediately returning to Japan to practice in non-litigation fields.

7. *Hōterasu* and Other Legal Aid Systems

Another part of the government's millennial legal reforms was the establishment of a comprehensive government-funded legal aid system. While the current constitution (article 37(3)) has always imposed on the state an obligation to provide criminal defendants counsel, the system of appointing them had previously been *ad hoc*. In addition there had not been a system of legal aid for low-income people seeking to protect their rights through the civil justice system. The ability to ensure criminal defendants in areas with few if any *bengoshi* were adequately represented was another issue.

In 2006 the Japan Legal Support Center, an independent administrative corporation under the jurisdiction of the MOJ was set up. Operating under the name *hōterasu*, the JLSC has offices throughout the country. Through salaried lawyers on fixed term contracts, the JLSC offices offer legal services to those unable to afford them. It also provides (either directly or by coordinating with local bar associations) counsel to indigent detainees and criminal defendants, as well as referrals to cooperating *bengoshi* and judicial scriveners in civil matters.

The system is subject to some criticism. Overall funding is an issue, and on the civil side the standards for taking cases may be very demanding. Although its president is a *bengoshi*, it is ultimately under the jurisdiction of the MOJ which is both run by prosecutors and operates facilities in which *hōterasu* clients may be detained; criminal defense lawyers who work through it are on a certain level required to sign an engagement contract with their opponents in court. The *hōterasu* mandate also extends to providing assistance to victims of crimes, resulting in another potential conflict with its role in defending accused criminals. Grumbling from lawyers about the parsimonious compensation *hōterasu* offers is common. Finally, it is said to be exceptionally rare for *hōterasu* to assist with administrative or constitutional litigation against government entities.

The JFBA and local bar associations or regional bar federations have a program of fixed-term subsidies for the establishment of what are called *himawari* law offices. These have generally been established in areas with few if any *bengoshi*. *Bengoshi* working for such law offices are expected to provide criminal defense and other public interest legal services to the community.

Finally, it should be noted that the small but growing number of municipalities hiring staff *bengoshi* can use them to provide a form of legal aid, by making them available for consultations at municipal offices, another one of the first places the average Japanese may turn for legal advice.

Chapter 8

THE CRIMINAL JUSTICE SYSTEM

Analysis

This chapter will describe the institutions that enforce Japanese criminal law and impose punishments, as well as the process by which that happens. An overview of substantive criminal law is also given.

A. LAW ENFORCEMENT ACTORS AND INSTITUTIONS

Other than the courts and defense lawyers, the principal actors in the criminal justice system can be divided into three basic categories: police, prosecutors, and correctional institutions. Each of these is discussed below. To fully appreciate this chapter it may be helpful to first read the description of the Ministry of Justice in Chapter 3.

1. Police

a. Historical Background

In the Tokugawa period urban law enforcement was carried out by *machibugyō*, the feudal local officials vested with extremely broad powers both administrative and adjudicatory in character. These included not only the authority to investigate crimes and make arrests, but to engage in a wide range of activities that would now be considered community surveillance. They also conducted trials and administered punishments.

After the Meiji Restoration, policing was another area where the nation's leaders looked to western countries for inspiration. Japan's first modern police force, the Tokyo Metropolitan Police, was established in 1874 based and on French models. The police soon came to be under the jurisdiction of the powerful Home Ministry.

The police also came to include the *tokkō* or "special high" police. Initially established in 1911 in response to an anarchist plot to assassinate the Emperor, the *tokkō* became a nationwide network of secret police whose remit included identifying and stamping out communists, labor activists and other internal threats. The military also had their own police, the *kenpei*, who not only had jurisdiction over soldiers and naval personnel, but could also enforce the Peace Preservation Act and other national security laws against civilians.

During the post-war occupation, the Home Ministry was dismantled and the *tokkō* and *kenpei* abolished. American-led reforms included reorganizing the police as municipal rather than prefectural forces. However, the financial burden of maintaining individual police forces was too much for most municipalities, and corruption was also a problem. This American "innovation" was quickly undone after the occupation ended, with the passage of the current Police Act of 1954 which established the current system of police organized primarily at the prefectural level.

b. The Police Today

Under the Police Act, the remit of the police is defined in terms of protecting the life persons and property of individuals, preventing, suppressing and investigating crime, arresting suspects, managing traffic and other activities aimed at preserving public safety and order (article 2(1)). The Police Act creates a two-tiered system of policing: a small national cadre under the National Police Agency (NPA) and the prefectural police.

(i) National Institutions: The National Public Safety Commission and the National Police Agency

(a) The NPSC

The NPA is formally under the control and supervision of the National Public Safety Commission (Police Act article 15). The NPSC is in turn directly under the Prime Minister (article 4).

The NPSC is comprised of a chairman and five commissioners. The chairman is a minister of state who sits in the Cabinet (see Chapter 3). The five commissioners are appointed by the Prime Minister with the consent of both Diet chambers. Unlike the chairman, commissioners are appointed for fixed and staggered terms of five years, thereby insulating them to a degree from changes in cabinets and, in theory, electoral politics. This insulation is further bolstered by a prohibition on having more than three commissioners who are members of the same political party. A person may not be appointed as a commissioner if they have served in a police or prosecutorial role within the past five years (article 7).

The members of the NSPC are busy people. The day-to-day administrative functions are performed by the NPA, which the NPSC is supposed to be overseeing (Police Act, article 5(4)). For much of the postwar period, the chairman of the NPSC was usually also the Minister of Local Government, reflecting that ministry's origins in the pre-war Home Ministry. This practice stopped after the government reorganization which saw jurisdiction over local government transferred to the newly-created MIC.

(b) The NPA

The National Police Agency is Japan's elite, "national" police force. Dominated by graduates of the law faculty of Tokyo University, the NPA consists of approximately 2,100 police officers, 4,700 administrative staff and the 900 strong Imperial Guard. The NPA is headed by a Commissioner General who is appointed and removed by the NPSC with the consent of the Prime Minister and who is the only police officer who exists outside the formal ranking system established by the Police Act(article 62).

The NPA is comprised of a secretariat and five bureaus: the Community Safety Bureau, the Crime Bureau, the Traffic Bureau, the Security Bureau and the Information and Communications Bureau. The Security Bureau is the headquarters of the NPA's "public security" policing infrastructure, which overseas many aspects of counter-intelligence and surveillance of foreign spies and suspicious domestic groups. Although headquartered in Tokyo the NPA has a national presence through seven regional bureaus.

Also attached to the NPA are: (i) the National Police Academy, which provides training for senior police officers, (ii) the National Research Institute of Police Science, which does forensic testing and other analytical services and research, and (iii) the Imperial Guard, who provide security for the Emperor and members of the imperial family.

The Police Act charges the NPA with a wide range of responsibilities over the nation's police system, including planning, budgeting, maintaining crime statistics, interfacing with foreign law enforcement institutions and so forth. Although prefectural police account for the vast majority of actual police personnel and activities, the top-down guidance from the NPA means that their equipment, approach and organizations all seem very similar. In many ways, the current system thus represents the "renationalization" of the police force, despite the occupation-era efforts to localize law enforcement.

The Police Act (article 62) establishes a uniform nine-tiered system of ranks. All police officers (except the top police official, the Commissioner General of the NPA) fit within this ranking system and there is no formal legal distinction between NPA officers and those of the prefectural police forces. However, while prefectural police personnel are members of the relevant prefectural public service, NPA officers are national public servants who may expect to advance through the ranks much more rapidly than their prefectural counterparts. An NPA officer is generally promoted to Assistant Commissioner (the fourth highest rank) after 15 years of service, whereas a prefectural officer might spend 25 years achieving the same status.

The combination of a single system of ranks in an overlapping prefectural and national policing system creates an interesting dichotomy. NPA officers will typically start their careers the same way as all Japanese police officers, working at the coal face of the local police box as a lowly constable under the supervision of more senior prefectural officers. Yet these senior officers will know the NPA rookie is likely to go on to become a influential figure in the national police bureaucracy which oversees them and must treat their young charges accordingly.

(ii) Prefectural Police

The prefectural policing system in many ways duplicates the national system at a regional level under the jurisdiction of prefectural governors. Each prefecture has its own Public Safety Commission with 3 or 5 commissioners appointed by the governor with the consent of the prefectural assembly. As with the NPSC, the prefectural commissions notionally oversee the prefectural police, but administrative functions are performed by those same police.

The internal organization of prefectural police forces is to a degree left to secondary legislation and prefectural ordinances, though functional divisions (traffic, security, etc.) generally mirror the organizational structure of the NPA. The organizational structure of prefectural forces also includes their headquarters and the police stations, substations, local police boxes and other outposts that create an extremely broad police presence. Or at least the appearance of one; some of Japan's famed *kōban* police boxes are empty some or all of the time, containing either a phone or a retired police officer for guidance. Prefectures also have their own police colleges. Above the prefectural level, individual prefectural systems fall under the jurisdiction of one the NPA's seven regional districts. Because of the prefecture's size, the organization of the Hokkaido police is somewhat more complicated with geographical subdivisions that do not exist in other forces.

With some exceptions discussed below, prefectural police officers are members of the local public service. However, those who advance to the rank of Assistant Commissioner become national public servants and, with certain exceptions, their appointment and removal is conducted by the NPSC with the consent of the applicable prefectural Public Safety Commission. However, there has never been an instance of a prefectural commission refusing such consent. In essence, therefore, the police ranking system is structured to place the upper tiers of even prefectural police under the control of the NPA.

Broad national cooperation between the police is also anticipated by the Police Act (articles 59 through 61–3) and police officers are not necessarily restricted by prefectural boundaries in conducting investigations or arrests. Large contingents of riot police can also be marshalled from various locations to provide security for international meetings or to disperse protestors. This means police bussed or flown in for such purposes are less likely to be influenced by local sentiments when they are helping implement national policy over local objections. This was illustrated in 2016 when a member of a riot police squad in Okinawa clashing with protestors opposing the construction of a US military base was recorded on camera using a derogatory term to refer to the local people. It was soon discovered that the officer was from a unit of the Osaka prefectural police dispatched to the island in response to the protests.

For historical and political reasons the name given to the police force of Tokyo (which it should be remembered is technically a prefecture, not a municipality)—the Tokyo Metropolitan Police—is different in some ways from the organization of other prefectural police forces. Because of the location of the concentration of central government institutions, there is a much tighter relationship between the TMP and the national bureaucracy.

This is reflected in the fact that the highest rank in the police is that of Superintendent General and only a single person holds it, the head of the Metropolitan Police Department; the top police officials in other prefectural police forces are one or two ranks lower. The role of Superintendent General has also always been filled by someone who has risen through the elite national career track rather than the prefectural police. And although there are no officials within the police system whose appointments are formally attested by the Emperor under article 7 of the Constitution, by tradition a retiring Superintendent General and his successor are invited to the imperial palace for tea with his majesty.

According to the 2015 Police White Paper the authorized number of police for all prefectures was 258,875 police officers of all ranks. The number of police stations, police boxes and other police outposts was approximately 14,000 organized primarily around 1,166 police stations.

(iii) Key Statutes and Regulations Governing the Police

The principal statutes governing the police are the Police Act, the Code of Criminal Procedure and the Police Duties Execution Act of 1948 (PDEA). Although not law, police investigatory activities are also governed by the NPSC's Criminal Investigation Protocols (CIP), which were first adopted in 1957.

The Police Act establishes the organizational structure of the police force nationally and locally, as discussed in the following section. The CCP imposes restraints on police in connection with arrests and investigations, though other acts may also be relevant in connection with (for example) electronic surveillance and organized crime groups. The PDEA establishes some of the basic parameters of conduct by individual police officers in the course of performing their duties. Article 7 sets forth the circumstances under which police officers may use their weapons, for example. As discussed later in this chapter, at the same time the PDEA almost seems to expand the scope of police activities beyond the scope of what is permitted by the constitution. For example, notwithstanding the broad prohibitions on warrantless apprehensions and detentions contained in articles 33 and 34 of the constitution, article 3 of the PDEA permits police officers to take persons into "protective custody"—a form of detention—in certain circumstances.

The Act on Punishment of Organized Crimes and Control of Crime Proceeds of 1999, as well as prefectural ordinances relating to organized crime groups further empower police in connection with organized crime groups as discussed below. The Act on Wiretapping for Criminal Investigation of 1999 (Wiretapping Act) defines the procedure to be followed by law enforcement when intercepting private communications for purposes of a criminal investigation.

2. Other Law Enforcement Agencies

While the police are the largest and most ubiquitous law enforcement institution in Japan, police-like powers are exercised for more limited purposes by other national government agencies or personnel. These include narcotics agents and labor inspectors under the MHLW, the Japan Coast Guard under the MLITT, corrections officers under the MOJ, fisheries inspectors under the MAFF, mine inspectors under METI and the military police contingents of the Self Defense Forces.

These other categories of law enforcement officials are sometimes collectively referred to as "special judicial police officers" (*tokubetsu shihōkeisatsuin*) for purposes of the CCP and may only exercise some police powers. For example labor standards inspectors have the power to investigate labor code violations and make arrests in connection with those amounting to criminal offenses, but do not carry weapons. The most significant category of other law enforcement personnel are the public prosecutors, discussed in the following section.

3. Public Prosecutors

a. Historical Background

In defining the structure of the ancient imperial government and its actors, the *ritsuryō* (see Chapter 1) established a *danjodai* as an institution with police and prosecutorial powers. The subsequent creation outside the scope of the *ritsuryō* of the *kebiishi*, which also came to exercise broad judicial, prosecutorial and police-like powers both diminished the significance of the *danjodai* and became one of the means by which the warrior caste came to control government institutions.

In 1869, the Meiji government re-established the *danjodai* as a prosecutorial and police institution. This was soon replaced in 1873 by a prosecutorial system based on

French models, though still applying *ritsuryō* derived criminal laws. As the adoption of western models progressed, the Meiji precursor to the current system was established through the now-defunct Court Organization Act of 1890. This law established prosecutorial bureaus within the courts and broadly defined the role and powers of prosecutors themselves, including a strict prohibition on prosecutors trying to influence judges in any ways or being involved in trial administration (article 81).

b. Modern Prosecutors

(i) Overview

With the constitutional separation of the judiciary from the executive branch, prosecutors are now governed primarily by a separate statute, the Public Prosecutors Office Act of 1947 (PPOA).[1] Under article 1 of that law, prosecutors are charged with conducting prosecutions, seeking the correct application of the law by the courts, overseeing the conduct of trials, and communicating with the courts regarding other matters under the jurisdiction of the courts.

Although the day-to-day role of most prosecutors is in the criminal sphere, they may become involved in civil affairs as representatives of the public interest or in other roles through other statutory schemes. For example, the Civil Code accords various roles to prosecutors in areas such as termination of custody proceedings, management of the property of minors, management of property whose owner is unascertainable and the appointment and oversight of adult guardians. In some cases these may be "default" roles for when directly interested persons such as parents or family members are not available. As noted in Chapter 3, some prosecutors are also engaged in the heady business of running the MOJ and participating in other aspects of governing the nation.

(ii) Organization and Ranks

The PPOA establishes a nationwide network of public prosecutors offices that correspond in location and hierarchy to the judicial system. There is the Supreme Public Prosecutors Office corresponding to the Supreme Court, below that eight High Public Prosecutors Offices (corresponding to the high court districts), then 50 District Public Prosecutors Offices (corresponding to district and family court districts), and 438 at Local (*ku*) Prosecutors Offices corresponding to the summary courts (PPOA, article 1). There are also branch offices corresponding to the various branches of the courts.

Article 3 of the PPOA establishes a five-tiered ranking of prosecutors: the Prosecutor General, Deputy Prosecutor General, Superintending Prosecutor, Public Prosecutor and Assistant Prosecutor. The Prosecutor General oversees the entire prosecutorial system from the Supreme Public Prosecutors Office and is assisted by the Deputy Prosecutor General. Eight Superintending Prosecutors oversee the prosecutors within the jurisdictions of the High Public Prosecutors Offices they head. The appointments of these ten prosecutors are made by the Cabinet and attested by the Emperor.

---

[1] Note that in the English version of the Constitution (article 77) the term *kensatsukan* is rendered as "public procurator." While this term may be familiar to those with experience in continental legal systems and is used in some literature on the Japanese legal system, translations of other statutes (such as the CCP) use the English term "public prosecutor." This book uses the latter term or just "prosecutor" throughout (there being no private prosecutors).

As noted in Chapter 3, the Prosecutor General is the top bureaucrat at the MOJ in all but name only. This status is also a function of the later retirement age for prosecutors compared to other public servants. The Prosecutor General is also one of the highest-paid public servants, receiving the same level of compensation as ministers of state (other than the Prime Minister) and judges of the Supreme Court (other than the Chief Judge).

The primacy of the Tokyo High Public Prosecutors Office within the prosecutorial service mirrors that of the Tokyo High Court within the judiciary and discussed in Chapter 3. Despite the existence of a notionally superior Deputy Prosecutory General, the Superintending Prosecutor of the Tokyo High Public Prosecutors Office is understood to be the *real* number two prosecutor, as is reflected in his higher pay as well as the fact that, with a single exception, every Prosecutor General since 1970 has been promoted from that role. The post of Deputy Prosecutor General—the second highest rank—thus appears to be a sort of consolation prize for the prosecutor who didn't quite make it to the top.

Below the three leadership levels, article 3 of the PPOA provides for only two other formal ranks of prosecutor—prosecutor and assistant prosecutor. The reality is more complicated and involves a much more gradated hierarchy based on pay grade, title, posting and other attributes.

In addition to the five ranks of prosecutors, the PPOA also establishes two classes of prosecutors; first and second. Second class prosecutors are the junior ranks of the service, and include both junior *kenji* prosecutors who are *hōso* who have passed the NBE and assistant prosecutors (*fukukenji*) who have not.

Although the PPOA envisions that prosecutors of both classes can be appointed from a broad range of legal system stakeholders including *bengoshi* and law professors, in practice the talent pool from which their ranks are drawn is narrower. Second class *hōsō* prosecutors are appointed from the ranks of those who passed the NBE and have completed a course of training at the LRTE (PPOA, article 18(2)). They can then be promoted to the first class after eight years of service, similar to the way that assistant judges are reappointed full judges after ten years (PPOA, article 19).

Assistant prosecutors (*fukukenji*) are appointed from the ranks of those passing the qualifying exam administered by the MOJ's Public Prosecutors and Notaries Public Appointment Examination Committee (PPNPAEC). Those who are eligible to sit for the exam consist of a wide range of mostly law-enforcement related public service jobs, including prosecutorial administrators, police and other law enforcement officers, judicial clerks (PPOA implementing order of 1947, article 2). The primary source of assistant prosecutors is prosecutorial administrators (*kensatsujimukan*).

After three years, an assistant prosecutor is eligible to sit for an additional qualifying exam (also administered by the PPNPAEC) to become a full *kenji* prosecutor (second class), and then proceed through the ranks of prosecutor in the same fashion as those who have passed the NBE. However, they probably cannot expect to rise to the same heights as the elite who did. They are also distinguished in practice through use of the term *tokunin kenji* (specially-appointed prosecutor), though this is not a formal title used in the PPOA. The qualifying exam to become a *tokunin-kenji* is extremely competitive, and subject to additional qualifying procedures those who pass it may ultimately be able to register as *bengoshi* lawyers after leaving the prosecutorial service—a rare back door into the practice of law that does not require passing the NBE.

At the time of writing the official headcount for the public prosecutors offices nationwide consisted of approximately 1,900 *kenji* prosecutors, 900 *fukukenji* assistant prosecutors and 9,050 public prosecutor's assistant officers (*kensatsujimukan*). When one takes the number of prosecutors and, after accounting for those who are busy running the MOJ, divides the remainder by the number of public prosecutors offices and branches around the country, it becomes apparent they are spread extremely thin.

The scheme envisioned by the PPOA is that assistant prosecutors can act as prosecutors only at local public prosecutors offices (PPOA article 16(2)), in other words dealing with matters arising in the summary courts. "Real" (*kenji*) prosecutors would handle the work of the higher level public prosecutors offices and thus matters in other higher courts. However, even just dividing the number of *fukukenji* by the number of summary courts (438) shows there are probably not nearly enough of them.

The reality is that a significant amount of prosecutorial duties—investigating suspects, even making charging decisions in minor cases—are actually performed by the *kensatsu jimukan*—prosecutorial administrators. The CCP, for example, grants a wide variety of investigatory and other police-like powers to *kensatsujimukan*.

The empowerment of administrative personnel originated as an effort to address a temporary shortage of suitably-qualified personnel at the time the PPOA was enacted in 1947. A transitional *fusoku* provision (supplemental article 36) of the law declares that "for the time being" the MOJ could cause *kensatsujimukan* administrators to perform the duties of prosecutors at the lowest level of public prosecutors offices. Seventy years later, this "temporary" practice has been institutionalized and helps explain why Japan's prosecutorial service is able to function with so few fully-qualified prosecutors.

In 2013 the JFBA issued a formal opinion calling for the abolition of the now long-standing practice of allowing essentially unqualified personnel to act in prosecutorial roles. Unlike prosecutors and assistant prosecutors who pass highly competitive exams requiring knowledge of criminal law and procedure, *kensatsujimukan* are only required to pass a lower level national public service exam and are thus not formally trained for prosecutorial roles.

Also, unlike *kensatsujimukan*, prosecutors and assistant prosecutors enjoy heightened job security. This is intended to preserve their autonomy.

Under article 25 of the PPOA, qualified prosecutors may not be removed or suspended or have their compensation reduced except under specific circumstances or unless terminated for cause. These include impeachment-like proceedings by the Public Prosecutors' Qualifications Examination Committee (PPQEC), a committee under the MOJ. Prosecutors and assistant prosecutors are also subject to review every three years by the PPQEC, or whenever requested by the Minister of Justice or deemed necessary by the PPQEC itself.

(iii) Investigations and Arrests by Prosecutors

Public prosecutors work closely with the police who do the bulk of the nation's criminal investigatory work. To a degree they also have the power to direct the police in doing so. However, prosecutors also have extremely broad powers of investigation and arrest that they can exercise independently of the police. In theory all prosecutors have these powers, but the Tokyo, Osaka and Nagoya District Public Prosecutors Offices have departments devoted to special investigations without police involvement. Having the combined ability to investigate crimes, arrest, detain and question those suspected of them and then conducting the prosecution at trial makes the public prosecutors unusually powerful. There are also obvious conflicts of interest that arise from these combined roles. In political corruption cases or corporate scandals the prosecutors may handle both the investigation and arrests themselves, in addition to the subsequent prosecutions. This practice has been criticized for enabling prosecutors to use their coercive investigative powers to force suspects and witnesses into corroborating the version of events the prosecutors *speculate* has happened, rather than what actually did happen. Criminal investigations conducted directly by prosecutors are often very high profile cases. Some are even described by the media as *kokusaku sōsa*—"national policy" investigations, which may be intended to crush politically inconvenient personages in which the required result of the investigation (*i.e.*, the target is convicted of something) seems predetermined.

(iv) "Civilian Control" of Prosecutors

The degree to which Japanese prosecutors should be insulated from political influences is a hotly-debated subject in Japan, particularly when they pursue cases that clearly seem to be politically motivated. Since prosecutors are all appointed career bureaucrats, there is some question about whether they are (or should be) accountable in some way to more democratic institutions.

Under article 14 of the PPOA, the Minister of Justice has the power to supervise and direct prosecutorial affairs, but with respect to the conduct of individuals may only give directions to the Supreme Prosecutor. This is intended to keep the Minister from interfering directly in the conduct of individual cases, though this could theoretically be done through the Supreme Prosecutor who has the power to direct those below him in the hierarchy. In fact, the article 14 powers of the Minister of Justice are only known to have been used once, in 1954, resulting in the indefinite suspension of the arrest for bribery of the politician Eisaku Satō (who went on to become prime minister).

In 2012 Minister of Justice Toshio Ogawa sought the approval of Prime Minister Noda to use the power in connection with a questionable prosecution of Ozawa Ichirō, a well-known politician. He was refused and resigned the next day.

Prosecutors are subject to the laws and ethical codes applicable to Japanese public servants generally In response to criticism of prosecutorial scandals and abuses, in 2011 the Supreme Public Prosecutors Office issued a ten article code of precepts entitled "The Principles of Prosecution."

B. CRIMINAL LAW AND PUNISHMENT

1. Substantive Criminal Law and the Penal Code

The principal source of substantive criminal law is the Penal Code of 1907. It is supplemented by numerous other statutes defining additional specific offenses—the "Act for Controlling the Possession of Firearms or Swords and Other Such Weapons" of 1958, for example—and dwarfed in number by hundreds of regulatory statutes containing criminal penalties for violations, though in many cases these are rarely if ever applied.

The Penal Code nonetheless remains the foundation of substantive criminal law. Structurally it is comprised of two Parts. Part 1 consists of the *sōron* or "general principles" containing rules of general applicability—treatment of offenses committed abroad, accessory, types of punishments, calculation of periods and statutes of limitations, defenses and mitigating factors, intent and other elements of criminal behavior. These principles may also apply to other criminal statutes containing penal sanctions (unless such laws contain provisions to the contrary).

The second Part of the Code contains the *kakuron*, the provisions describing individual categories of offenses which are further broken into specific offenses and the range of possible punishments. While a detailed discussion is beyond the scope of this work, it may be helpful to see how Part 2 is organized to get a sense for the categories of crimes:

Chapter I (articles 73–76)—deleted provisions that prior to post war amendments penalized crimes against the imperial system such as *lese majeste*.

Chapter II (articles 77–89)—Crimes Related to Insurrections

Chapter III (articles 81–89)—Crimes Related to Foreign Aggression

Chapter IV (articles 90–94)—Crimes Related to Foreign Relations

Chapter V (articles 95–96–6)—Crimes Related to Obstruction of Performance of Public Duty

Chapter VI (articles 97–102)—Crimes of Escape

Chapter VII (articles 103–105–2)—Crimes of Harboring Criminals and Suppressing Evidence

Chapter VIII (articles (106–107)—Crimes of Disturbance

Chapter IX (articles 108–118—Crimes of Arson and Fire Caused through Negligence

Chapter X (articles 119–123)—Crimes Related to Floods and Water Management

Chapter XI (articles 124–129)—Crimes of Obstruction of Traffic

Chapter XII (articles 130–132)—Crimes of Breaking into a Residence

Chapter XIII (articles 132–135)—Crimes of Violating Confidentiality

Chapter XIV (articles 136–141—Crimes Related to Opium for Smoking

Chapter XV (articles 142–147)—Crimes Related to Drinking Water

Chapter XVI (articles 148–153)—Crimes of Counterfeiting Currency

Chapter XVII (articles 154–161–2)—Crimes of Counterfeiting Documents

Chapter XVIII (articles 162–163)—Crimes of Counterfeiting of Securities

Chapter XVIII–2 (articles 163–2–163–5)—Crimes Related to Electromagnetic Records of Payment Cards

Chapter XIX (articles 164–168—Crimes of Counterfeiting of Seals

Chapter XIX–2 (articles 168–2—168–3)—Crimes Related to Use of Electronic Records to Give Improper Instructions

Chapter XX (articles 169–171)—Crimes of Perjury

Chapter XXI (articles 172–173)—Crimes of False [Criminal] Complaints

Chapter XXII (articles 174–184)—Crimes of Obscenity, Rape[2] and Bigamy

Chapter XXIII (articles 185–187)—Crimes Related to Gambling and Lotteries

Chapter XXIV (articles 188–192)—Crimes Related to Places of Worship and Graves

Chapter XXV (articles 193–198)—Crimes of Corruption

Chapter XXVI (articles 199–203)—Crimes of Homicide

Chapter XXVII (articles 204–208–3)—Crimes of Injury

Chapter XXVIII (articles 209–211)—Crimes of Injury through Negligence

Chapter XXIX (articles 212–216)—Crimes of Abortion

Chapter XXX (articles 217–219)—Crimes of Abandonment

Chapter XXXI (articles 220–221)—Crimes of Unlawful Capture [arrest] and Confinement

Chapter XXXII (articles 222–223)—Crimes of Intimidation

Chapter XXXIII (articles 224–229)—Crimes of Kidnapping and Buying or Selling of Human Beings

Chapter XXXIV (articles 230–232)—Crimes against Reputation

Chapter XXXV (articles 233–235)—Crimes against Credit and Business

Chapter XXXVI (articles 235–245)—Crimes of Theft and Robbery

Chapter XXXVII (articles 246–251)—Crimes of Fraud and Extortion

Chapter XXXVIII (articles 252–255)—Crimes of Embezzlement

Chapter XXXIX (articles 256–257)—Crimes Related to Stolen Property

Chapter XL (articles 258–264)—Crimes of Destruction and Concealment

Although the Penal Code contains most of the common categories of offense and the range of punishments that may be imposed on those convicted of them, the language will seem sparse to those familiar with codes such as those modeled on the American Law Institute's Model Penal Code. For example, with respect to homicide, article 199 of the Japanese Penal Code says nothing more than:

> [a] person who kills another shall be punished by the death penalty or imprisonment with work for life or for a definite term of not less than 5 years.

One can look to Part1 of the Code for justifications, defenses and some interpretive guidance. Yet the language does not define what it actually means to "kill another," and does not even articulate an explicit requirement of intent (other than as might be implied

[2] 2017 amendments to the Penal Code replaced "rape" with "forced intercourse" and made it applicable to cases involving male victims.

from the word "kill"). Moreover, one finds little in the text of the Code to help distinguish homicide under article 199 and "injury causing death" under article 205, the latter being defined with similar brevity ("A person who causes another to suffer injury resulting in death shall be punished by imprisonment with work for a definite term of not less than 3 years"). Court interpretations, academic theory and prosecutorial practice are necessarily left to fill in many of the gaps.

In addition, although Part 1 contains some general provisions on inchoate crimes, attempt, inducement, preparing and plotting are only offenses covered under the provisions in Part 2 defining specific offenses. For example article 199 covers murder, while article 201 covers "preparation" and article 203 attempted murder. The Code itself lacks a general conspiracy offense, but in 2017 amendments to the Act on Punishment of Organized Crimes and Control of Crime Proceeds of 1999 (the "Organized Crime Act") and other laws came into effect that created a conspiracy-like offense relating to the planning by organized crime groups of approximately 270 specific offenses defined in both the Penal Code and a wide range of other statutes.

Certain offenses such as criminal defamation and other crimes against reputation, are designated as *shinkokuzai*. This means they can only be prosecuted upon a complaint from the victim. Until amendments passed in 2017 changed the treatment of various sexual offenses, rape and other forms of other sexual assault were also *shinkokuzai* and the bravery required of victims in pursing cases was identified as a factor behind the comparatively small number of convictions appearing in criminal justice statistics.

In addition to providing the conceptual foundation for substantive criminal law, the Penal Code covers the offenses that account for the majority of serious crime actually prosecuted and punished in Japan. Leaving aside the 250,000 minor cases resolved through abbreviated proceedings in the summary courts (180,000 of which were offenses under the Road and Traffic Act), of the 54,297 criminal cases initially heard in district courts in 2015, 28,485 were offenses arising under the Penal Code. Of these, "crimes of theft and robbery" (articles 235–245), were most numerous (11,757 cases) followed by "fraud and extortion" (articles 246–251; 4,353 cases). By contrast, homicide cases (article 199–203) were rare (324), a reflection of Japan's famed public safety. However, because judicial statistics are kept in accordance with the categories of crimes under the Penal Code, this number does not capture those of the 3,515 "crimes of injury" that resulted in death (article 204), or those of the 1,305 "crimes of injury through negligence" that also did so.

Of those criminal trials arising under statutes other than Penal Code, violations of the Stimulants Control Act were the most numerous (9,652) followed by the Road and Traffic Act (6,600) and the Act for Punishing Vehicular Homicide (4,265). Trials for violations of the Income Tax Act were surprisingly few—just 24 in 2015.

Arrest statistics confirm a similar picture, with the NPA's White Paper on Crime 2016 essentially addressing crime in terms of "theft and robbery" and "everything else," the former accounting for 73.5% of reported Penal Code offenses. Theft and robbery also accounted for over half (123,847) of the total number of arrests/prosecutions in the same period (239,355).

2. Punishments

a. *Overview*

The Penal Code provides for seven categories of punishment, death, imprisonment with work, imprisonment without work, fines, misdemeanor imprisonment without work, petty fines and confiscation. These are discussed below.

Punishments may be lessened if discretionary or statutory mitigating factors are found to apply (articles 66 and 67) Punishments may also be enhanced in the case of compound offenses or reoffenders (article 72). Beyond that courts have developed their own rules and practices to provide greater guidance to judges so they may impose similar sentences on similarly situated defendants.

Although imposed by courts, prosecutors are responsible for carrying out sentences once they are rendered. As noted in Chapter 3, the MOJ bureaus responsible for corrections and rehabilitation are typically run by prosecutors.

b. *Capital Punishment*

Despite its abolition in much of the developed world, Japan continues to use the death penalty. Nor does this seem likely to change; a 2014 government survey 80% of the population considered it "unavoidable," while less than 10% thought it should be abolished (though some observers have raised issues with the framing of the survey). Although they receive a great deal of attention, death sentences are rarely passed and even more rarely carried out. Only three convicts were executed annually in 2014, 2015 and 2016, despite there being close to 130 people on death row during the same period. In some prior years more convicts on death row died of old age than execution.

This is because years or even decades may pass between an initial conviction and sentence of death and the sentence being carried out. It may take several years for the sentence to be confirmed through the exhaustion of appeals. Motions for new trials are also common and may further drag out the process since, executions are generally not carried out while a motion for a new trial is pending.

In 2011, Hakamada Iwao was certified by the *Guinness Book of World Records* as having spent the longest time on death row of any convict—46 years. Embarrassingly, he was released 3 years later on the grounds that his conviction for multiple murders was based on falsified evidence and confessions derived from torture. Of the 45 confessions he wrote while being brutally interrogated, the trial court refused to adopt 44 of them on the grounds they were not voluntary; somewhat inexplicably the court nonetheless found one confession to be reliable and convicted largely on the basis of it.

Although the long period between conviction and execution may seem like a blessing, some human rights organizations have described it as a form of mental torture. Not only are those sentenced to death housed in isolation from other prisoners, they are not given advance notice of the scheduled date of their execution, meaning they wake up each day not knowing if it will be their last. This is one of several aspects of the death penalty that the UN Committee Against Torture has found problematic, but which as recently as in its 2011 report to the Committee, the Japanese government continues to justify on the ground that "their peace of mind may be negatively affected and the notification could rather inflict excessive pain on them, etc." Prison insider accounts suggest that not announcing executions in advance may also prevent corrections officers from calling in sick to avoid participating in them.

When they are carried out, executions are by hanging (Penal Code, article 11). The procedures followed in conducting them are found in one of the oldest Japanese regulations still in force: Grand Council of State Proclamation No. 65 of 1873.[3] In 1961 the Supreme Court found that carrying out executions using procedures under pre-war laws not passed by the post-war Diet was not a violation of article 31 of the Constitution, which guarantees against deprivation of life, limb or liberty "except according to procedure established by law" (Supreme Court, Grand Bench judgment of July 19, 1961). The court had already found the death penalty did not violate article 36 on torture and cruel punishments in an opinion famous for declaring "life is precious; the life of a single person is weightier than the earth" (Supreme Court, Grand Bench judgment of March 12, 1948).

"Instigation of foreign aggression" (article 81) is the only offense for which the death penalty is mandatory. Instances of prosecutions are non-existent. For a number of categories of other offenses (murder or other specified types of felonious behavior such as arson or rape that result in death) the Penal Code and several other special criminal statutes provide death as an option for sentencing, the other options usually being imprisonment with work for a fixed or indeterminate period.

In a prosecutorial appeal of the overturning by the Tokyo High Court of a death sentence for a 1968 multiple homicide by then 19 yearold Nagayama Norio, the Supreme Court (Supreme Court, 2nd Petty Bench judgment of July 8, 1983), enunciated what became known as the "Nagayama Standards" for evaluating when the death penalty was an appropriate sentence. These include a wide range of objective factors (the age of the defendant, prior offenses, number of victims) and subjective criteria (motive, social impact, etc.). In their simplest interpretation the Nagayama Standards are understood to mean that the death penalty should only be applied in cases where the crime results in multiple deaths.[4]

Trials of crimes for which the death penalty is a possible sentence are now conducted before *saiban'in* panels of lay judges, which are discussed later in this chapter.

Although Japan is sometimes criticized for its continued use of the death penalty, it should also be noted that in 818 A.D., the Emperor Soga proscribed the practice on religious grounds (both Buddhism and Shintō having a dim view of shedding blood). This proscription continued in force for an astounding 338 years until the rise of the warrior class and civil war saw the reintroduction of harsh punishments.

c. *Imprisonment*

The principal form of non-monetary criminal sanction is imprisonment with work (*chōeki*). Article 18 of the Constitution prohibits involuntary servitude but contains a clear exception for its use as punishment. The work schedule helps give convicts a routine and enables them to acquire useful skills for when they are released. Convict

---

[3] Even this is not followed in every detail; the gallows are in the basement of the detention facilities though Proclamation No. 65 calls for hangings to be conducted on the prison roof.

[4] On remand, Nagayama was again sentenced to death and finally executed in 1997. During his time in prison he became an award-winning novelist, donating the proceeds from his writings to family members of his victims.

workers receive a small "work incentive" payment but this is not considered payment for work performed.

Under article 12 of the Penal Code, imprisonment with work may be imposed for a term of term of 1 month to 20 years or for an indefinite term. More detailed ranges of punishment are set forth in the provisions of Chapter 2 of the Code dealing with specific offenses. The mitigation of an offense that might otherwise be punished by death or imprisonment for an indefinite term, or the compounding of punishments for multiple offenses makes it possible to impose a maximum sentence of 30 years imprisonment with work (article 14(2)).

Technically there is no such thing as "life imprisonment" in Japan. Imprisonment with work for an indefinite term (*muki chōeki*) is the second harshest punishment after death. Depending on the age of the offender it may effectively mean imprisonment for life, but those convicted at a comparatively young age and who behave properly can expect to be released after between two to three decades. This means that for those whose loved ones have been killed (usually imprisonment for indefinite term is imposed for offenses resulting in the death of the victim) and their advocates, the punishment may not be harsh enough. Accounts by some prison administrators, however, suggest the introduction of a punishment of true "life" imprisonment would make correctional facilities much harder to manage, since the hope of eventual release is a powerful motivator of good behavior.

Imprisonment without work (*kinko*) can be imposed in the case of certain political and negligence-related crimes, but is comparatively rare. Of the 51,676 convictions resulting in terms of imprisonment in 2017, only 3,103 (6%) were for imprisonment without work. The constitutionality of this form of punishment has been challenged (unsuccessfully) on the grounds that it prevents convicts from exercising their right and duty to work under Article 27 (Supreme Court, Grand Bench judgment of September 10, 1958). In practice those sentenced to imprisonment without work can and do volunteer to work in the prison factory anyways. Imprisonment without work is possible for the same range of terms as imprisonment with work (Penal Code, article 13). Misdemeanor imprisonment (*kōryū*) without work is used to punish minor infractions and is limited to sentences of 1–29 days (article 16).

Within correctional facilities, those convicted of misdemeanor imprisonment are segregated from the longer term prisoners. In the past they might have been detained in jails at police stations, though 2005 amendments to the relevant laws are said to have made this less common. Some commentators have suggested that the distinction between the three forms of imprisonment should be eliminated.

d. Fines

The principal difference between fines (*bakkin*) and petty fines (*karyō*) is the amount; the former ranging from 10,000 yen and above (article 15), with individual provisions establishing the upper limits of fines for particular offenses. While most of the offenses under the Penal Code for which a fine (*bakkin*) is a punishment have a range of 100,000 yen or less, or several hundred thousand yen—comparatively modest amounts in 21st century Japan—penal provisions under other laws such as the Anti-Monopoly Act and the Financial Instruments and Exchange Act may run into hundreds of millions of yen. While many fines may involve insignificant amounts, fines do result in a criminal record, which can be an impediment in areas such as obtaining professional qualifications or maintaining residence status (for non-Japanese).

Bakkin fines accounted for the majority of sentences imposed through the criminal process: close to 278,000 in 2015, according to the NPA's 2016 Crime White Paper. Of these, the vast majority (approximately 275,000) were imposed through uncontested proceedings in summary courts, and most of these (approximately 182,000) were for violations of the Road and Traffic Act.

Possibly because they are such a limited punishment—ranging from JPY 1,000–10,000 (article 17), instances of petty fines being imposed are rare (approximately 2,000 instances in 2015). Commentators have suggested that it should be eliminated as a separate category of punishment.

Those without the means to pay their fines may be sent to a "workhouse" (*rōekijō*) to work off what they owe at a rate per day set by the judge. This can be done for no more than two years in the case of *bakkin* fines or thirty days in the case of petty fines (article 18). Being sent to a workhouse effectively means going to a designated prison the same as someone sentenced to imprisonment with work, since that is where the workshops are. In 2015 4,799 people were sentenced to workhouses for fines, and 17 for petty fines.

Unlike imprisonment, fines can be and are imposed on corporations and other juridical persons.

e. Suspending Sentences, Probation and Parole

Sentences of imprisonment of three years or less or fines below 500,000 yen can be suspended for a period of one to five years (Penal Code, article 25). The suspension can be subject to probation constraints during the suspension period (article 25–2). If during the suspension period the offender commits another offense the suspension can be revoked and the sentence imposed. Of the 51,676 persons convicted in 2017 at an initial trial and sentenced to imprisonment (with or without work), 48,133 (93%)were for terms of three years of less. Of these, 30,974 (59% of the total) were suspended sentences. Provisional release was rare, ordered in only 2,827 (5.4%) cases. Suspension of fines is exceptionally rare.

Successful completion of a suspension period without incident results in the original sentence ceasing to have legal effect. The offender's criminal record is expunged formal legal impediments resulting from the conviction cease.

Note that the widespread discretion courts have to suspend sentences may encourage even defendants who are innocent or do not think they have broken the law to effectively confess. "Failure to show contrition" is reportedly a factor cited by judges as a reason for imposing a sentence of actual prison time.

For those serving custodial sentences, early release through parole with probation is common. Under article 28 of the CCP eligibility begins after 1/3 of the sentence has been served or 10 years in the case of imprisonment for indefinite term (though in practice release in such cases is typically not possible until about 20 years have been served). Parole is administered through the MOJ's Rehabilitation Bureau and parole districts are organized corresponding to district and high court judicial districts.

It is common for western writers to describe Japanese prisons in negative terms. Overall, however, the entire criminal justice system can be said to be operated in a way that, seeks to avoid sending people to prison in the first place, and to get them out of prison expeditiously whenever possible. Prison life is heavily focused on rehabilitation and acquisition of work and life skills.

f. Confiscation

Confiscation of items comprising, used in or resulting from a criminal act can also be imposed as a supplemental punishment (article 29). Confiscation of third party property without giving the owner notice or opportunity to participate in the proceedings has been found to violate articles 29 and 31 of the Constitution (Supreme Court, Grand Bench judgment of November 28, 1962; the *Confiscation Case* discussed in Chapter 6).

g. Non-Penal Punishments and Criminal Records

Japanese law—criminal and otherwise—provides for other sanctions in addition to those described above, though they are not considered "penal" sanctions. These include non-penal fines (confusingly called "*karyō*, a homophone for the petty fines described above) and *hansokukin*—fines—which are imposed on minor traffic violations and non-payment of which can result in criminal penalties. In the world of tax, anti-trust and other financial crimes there are *tsuichōkin* and *kachōkin*—financial penalties imposed by tax authorities or other regulatory agencies for serious violations bordering on criminal behavior, but often committed by corporations.

Violations of electoral laws can also result in the loss of the right to vote and stand for office for a set period of time, in addition to any penal sanctions. This also includes an odd remnant of pre-modern *renza* "collective punishment," whereby violation of electoral laws by family members or certain employees of a candidate for office may result in the candidate's election being invalidated (POEA, article 251–2). The Supreme Court has upheld the constitutionality of this form of collective punishments on the grounds of protecting the integrity of elections as a foundation of representative democracy (Supreme Court, 3rd Petty Bench judgment of November 17, 1998).

As already noted, being convicted of a crime may also result in a disability to qualify for certain professions or roles (such as corporate directorships). Generally, however, the Japanese system makes it very difficult for *individuals* or groups to "punish" (*i.e.*, discriminate against) those convicted of a crime because information about criminal records is extremely tightly-controlled.

Although criminal trials are conducted in open court, as noted in Chapter 5 the records of criminal court proceedings (including judgments) are generally not available to the public. Those judgments that are published have identifying information removed. Therefore, short of searching newspaper archives for arrest records and trial reportage, demanding an individual produce a "police clearance" or hiring a private detective agency (ideally one run by ex-police officers and possibly having a suitable backdoor route to such information), it is very difficult to confirm whether a person has a criminal record or not. This is consistent with the overall rehabilitative goals of the criminal justice system described above.

C. CRIMINAL PROCEDURE

1. Introduction

Japanese criminal procedure may be one of the areas where, in the words of the scholar Carl F. Goodman, "what you see is not (or may not be) what you get."[5] To a U.S.-trained attorney, the constitutional protections accorded defendants and suspects may seem very familiar. Yet the devil is in the details, which turn out to be quite different. This is in part due to the underlying continental foundations of the criminal trial process as well as Japanese variations. The results may also seem different: it is widely reported that Japanese criminal trials have a 99.9% conviction rate, though this is somewhat exaggerated as it includes a large number of cases where the defendants do not challenge the charges.

2. Constitutional Dimensions

The latter half of Chapter III of the Constitution—articles 31–40—contains an extensive set of guarantees applicable not only to access to courts and criminal trials generally, but granting specific protections against deprivations of liberty, property and privacy (with article 21(2) ostensibly protecting the inviolacy of the secrecy of communications). In some ways these extensive protections can be seen as a rejection of the limited protections accorded by the Meiji Constitutional system, under which citizens could be arbitrarily arrested and detained under abusive conditions with few remedies and little recourse.

A brief summary of the constitutional provisions forming the foundation of the criminal procedure follows:

a. Article 31

Article 31 contains the basic prohibition on deprivations of life, liberty or property or "other criminal penalties" except according to procedures established by law. Article 23 of the Meiji Constitution contained a similar proscription.

There is some uncertainty as to whether Article 31 also applies to administrative dispositions. The Supreme Court has upheld administrative prohibitions imposed on the use of property without due process in certain unusual circumstances, but also held that their administrative character does not mean they will never trigger an article 31 violation. (Supreme Court, Grand Bench judgment of July 1, 1992).

b. Article 32

This clause contains the basic guarantee of a right to a trial in a court. Article 24 of the Meiji Constitution contained a similar provision.

c. Article 33

Article 33 requires that arrests be either pursuant to a judicial warrant or for a crime in progress in the presence of the person making the arrest.

---

[5] CARL F. GOODMAN, THE RULE OF LAW IN JAPAN: A COMPARATIVE ANALYSIS (3rd Ed. 2012)

d. Article 34

The full text of Article 34 is worth reproducing in full as it is particularly relevant to the summary of real-world criminal procedure in the pages that follow.

> No person shall be arrested or detained without being at once informed of the charges against him or without the immediate privilege of counsel; nor shall he be detained without adequate cause; and upon demand of any person such cause must be immediately shown in open court in his presence and the presence of his counsel.[6]

The Meiji Constitution contained no corresponding language.

e. Article 35

Articulating rights similar to those of the fourth amendment to the U.S. Constitution, article 35 requires judicial warrants for searches and seizure of homes, papers and personal effects. Article 25 of the Meiji Constitution contained a much more limited protection against unconsented searches of the home "unless in accordance with the law." The secrecy of communications and prohibition on censorship is protected by article 21(2)

f. Article 36

Article 36 prohibits the infliction of torture by public servants and cruel punishments. No corresponding provisions are found in the Meiji Constitution. As has been noted by the UN Committee Against Torture, Japan's penal code and other laws still lack a definition of "torture" for purposes of enforcing this provision. Article 195 of the Penal Code does define the offense of "Assault and Cruelty by Special Public Officials."

g. Article 37

Article 37 sets forth the basic rights of a criminal defendant once brought to trial: the right to a speedy trial, an impartial tribunal, the opportunity to examine all witnesses, have witnesses compelled to appear at trial at public expense, and to procure the assistance of competent counsel, to be provided by the state if the defendant is unable to do so. These rights are also discussed in more detail below.

h. Article 38

To appreciate the discussion that follows, article 38 is also reproduced below in its entirety.

> (1) No person shall be compelled to testify against himself.
>
> (2) Confession made under compulsion, torture or threat, or after prolonged arrest or detention shall not be admitted in evidence.
>
> (3) No person shall be convicted or punished in cases where the only proof against him is his own confession.

---

[6] Note that the English translation is misleading in that the Japanese version only requires that suspects to be informed of the "reason" (*riyū*) for an arrest or detention rather than the more formal sounding "charges against.")

No corresponding provisions existed in the Meiji Constitution.

i. Article 39

This provision sets forth the prohibitions on double jeopardy and ex-post-facto crimes, neither of which were addressed in the Meiji charter. The Japanese term contained in the constitution (*nijū no kiki*) is a direct translation of "double jeopardy," and is rarely used in practice. Instead the more technical *ichijifusairi* (derived from *non bis in idem*, the Roman law doctrine that courts should not revisit a matter already adjudicated once) is used.

j. Article 40

Japan's constitution is progressive in containing a specific guarantee of compensation from the state for persons detained or imprisoned on suspicion of criminal offenses but subsequently acquitted or absolved. This right is distinct from the more general right to seek redress from the state for wrongful acts by public officials contained under article 17 of the constitution. The constitutional guarantee is implemented through the Criminal Indemnity Act of 1950, which provides for compensation in the range of between JPY1,000 and JPY12,500 per day of imprisonment or detention, and up to JPY30 million for wrongful executions, the amount to be determined by a court. Prior to this a limited system of compensation did exist under a 1931 statute, but it was not mandated by the Meiji Constitution.

3. Criminal Procedure in the Real World

a. Introduction

Notwithstanding the seemingly clear protections granted by the constitution, the reality is that these often seem to be treated more like guiding principles that must bend to the needs of the public welfare when necessary. As a result, practical criminal procedure seems much more a creature of the Code of Criminal Procedure of 1948 (CCP) and other relevant laws and regulations than the Constitution.

The primacy of the CCP may also reflect the manner in which law is segmented and studied as an academic subject. Criminal law and procedure typically being taught (and tested on the bar exam) as one field of law, constitutional law as another. In fact, some leading treatises and textbooks on the subject of criminal procedure manage to discuss the subject in great detail with a surprising paucity of references to the Constitution.

The following discussion will go through the stages of the criminal process, starting with investigations by police through prosecution and trial.

b. Criminal Investigations

Most criminal cases start with an investigation. Under article 189 of the CCP law enforcement personnel are supposed to "investigate the offender and evidence" if they believe an offense to have been committed. The CCP authorizes police and other authorities to conduct such investigations as are necessary, but only permits the use of compulsory (*kyōsei*) dispositions in connection with an investigation where specifically provided for in the law (CCP article 197). It is thus necessary to distinguish between *nin'i* (voluntary) investigatory methods which involve voluntary cooperation from suspects, witnesses and other relevant parties, and compulsory (*kyōsei*) ones which involve detention, forcible searches and other uses of state power. The CCP provides for a number of compulsory dispositions—searches of premises, detention and seizure of property, all of which generally require a judicial warrant, unless exceptions apply.

The system of police ranks defined in the Police Act is relevant to the CCP. Somewhat confusingly, the CCP uses the term "judicial police personnel" (*shihō keisatsu shokuin*" to refer to police and certain other categories of law enforcement personnel who are authorized to conduct investigations and make arrests. The CCP further draws a distinction between a "judicial police officer" (*shihō keisatsuin*) and a "judicial constable" (*shihō junsa*; CCP article 39(3)). The distinction depends on rank; NPSC regulations establish which ranks falls into which category, with some variations depending on where within the police organization the officer is posted. Under the CCP, only those police qualifying as "judicial police officers" may conduct investigations (including requesting judicial warrants for search and seizure) or request arrest warrants (e.g., CCP articles 199, 224) and exercise certain other police powers. Judicial constables may arrest offenders for crimes in progress, but must immediately turn the suspect over to a senior officer for further processing. Similarly, under the Wiretapping Act only judicial police officers above a certain rank and designated officers of other law enforcement agencies may request judicial wiretap warrants.

The CCP itself does not use the term "voluntary investigation" though the Criminal Investigation Protocols do (CIP, articles 99–100). As noted in the discussion that follows, "voluntariness" is a highly subjective concept, and it is well known that many supposedly consensual searches, trips to the police station or confessions involve some degree of coercion. Japanese criminal prosecutions still rely heavily on confessions; given the constitutional restraints on formally detaining and procuring confessions from suspects, it is doubtful helpful if as much of the process as possible is "voluntary." This aspect of the system will be discussed in greater detail later in this section.

Many investigations start with "stop and search" approaches by police. Article 2 of the PDEA permits police officers to stop criminal suspects or persons of interest to ask questions or even request that they accompany them to a police facility ("voluntarily," of course). Such questioning may also be accompanied by warrantless searches of pockets, bags, and vehicles, and even urine tests. These may result in the discovery of contraband or other evidence of crimes.

Lower courts have occasionally granted acquittals or overturned convictions of defendants charged based on items found through such police searches, and even awarded largely symbolic damage claims in tort suits against the state arising from them. The Supreme Court has been more circumspect, holding in a 1978 decision that:

> the inspection of belongings that does not reach the level of search and is not conducted on a compulsory basis may be allowable, even without the consent of the person concerned, to a reasonable extent depending on the circumstances in light of the necessity and urgency of the inspection and the balance between individuals' interest to be violated and the public interests to be protected" (Supreme Court, 1st Petty Bench judgment of September 7, 1978).

Article 198 of the Code of Criminal Procedure also empowers prosecutors, *kensatsujimukan* prosecutorial administrators and police officers of suitable rank to "ask any suspect to appear in their offices and interrogate him/her if it is necessary for the investigation of a crime." Article 198 also states that suspects are supposedly free to cooperate (unless they are already under arrest or detention pursuant to a judicial warrant), and must be advised that they are not required to make any statements against their will.

Refusing to cooperate may result in the police seeking (and obtaining) an arrest warrant on the grounds that the suspect may flee or hide evidence. In fact, according to the advice of some lawyers, a request to come to the police station may indicate an arrest warrant has already been issued. Refusing to cooperate may simply result in the warrant being executed.

Even if an arrest warrant is not ready, "voluntary" trips to the police station whether under Article 198 or the PDEA may be coerced—an arrest in all but name only. Someone who refuses such a request may find themselves surrounded by police and unable to move. In 2017 police stopped a suspect and asked him to "voluntarily" submit to a urine test; he refused and sought refuge in the Osaka Bar Association building to consult with his lawyer. A team of eight police officers followed him into the non-public areas of the building and filmed him as he tried to talk to his counsel.

Even if one does go voluntarily, once in the police station the fiction of voluntariness may evaporate when the suspect finds they are not free to leave or even use the bathroom or eat. While not specifically allowing it, of course, the CCP and the PDEA thus offer tremendous scope for police to conduct coercive interrogations and other investigations largely unbounded by the constraints of the constitution or other formal rules of criminal procedure. This enables the police to obtain confessions first, then seek an arrest warrant for suspects who are already in *de facto* police custody.

Article 198 is silent on the subject of lawyers at this stage and whether a suspect can have a lawyer present during this type of voluntary investigation is entirely up to the discretion of the police. A person who voluntarily complies but decides in the course of questioning that he wishes to consult with a lawyer may find it hard to do so.

c. *Arrest (and Further Investigation)*

An arrest is the beginning of the formal criminal justice process for those suspected of a crime. The CCP significantly relaxes the seemingly clear constitutional requirement that *all* arrests be either for a crime in progress or pursuant to an arrest warrant. This is notwithstanding the academic view that "arrest" under article 33 of the Constitution is understood to be a broader concept than as defined under the CCP).

The CCP provides for a very broad application of the concept of a "crime in progress." First, article 213 of the CCP permits "any person" to arrest a "flagrant offender" for a crime in progress. Private individuals who conduct "citizen's arrests" improperly run the risk of committing the offense of "Unlawful Capture" under article 220 of the Penal Code, and those who do so properly are required to immediately turn the offender over to a police officer or prosecutor (CCP article 214). However, specific intent to conduct an arrest does not seem necessary; a woman confronting a man who fondles her on a crowded train, seeks assistance from railway employees who then contact the police may be deemed to have arrested the offender without her ever having used words of arrest.

Second, article 212(2) of the CCP provides for several categories of "deemed" flagrant offenders: (i) a person being engaged in fresh pursuit, (ii) a person carrying the fruits of an offense (stolen goods, etc.) or a weapon, (iii) a person with traces of the offense on his body (e.g., a bloodstained shirt) and (iv) a person who runs away when confronted by police. These exceptions allow police to conduct warrantless arrests of offenders at a time and location significantly removed from the actual offense. In 1996 the Supreme Court upheld the warrantless arrest of suspects almost two hours after the commission of the offense and 4 km from the scene of the crime (Supreme Court, 3rd Petty Bench judgment of January 29, 1998). Such arrests are referred to as *quasi*-arrests in progress (*jun genkōhan taiho*).

Another exception is provided by article 210(1) of the CCP which permits warrantless "emergency" arrests (*kinkyū taiho*) by police or prosecutors "when there are sufficient grounds to suspect" that a serious crime (one punishable by death or three or more years imprisonment) has been committed and the urgency of the situation means a judicial warrant cannot be obtained until after the actual arrest. The Supreme Court has upheld the constitutionality of such arrests (Supreme Court, Grand Bench judgment of December 14, 1955). Some scholars criticize this decision for merely articulating the logic of the CCP provisions permitting warrantless emergency arrests without offering a cogent explanation of how it could be consistent with the Constitution's requirement of a warrant.

Of 76,688 arrests in 2015, 4,141 were emergency arrests, 32,164 were for crimes in progress and the remainder (42,383) were made pursuant to arrest warrants. With respect to arrests by warrants issued in advance by judges, it should be borne in mind that some of these would have involved suspects already in police custody, whether due to arrests for other crimes (as described below) or *defacto* arrest through the supposedly "voluntary" accompaniment to a police facility (as described above).

In 2015 a total of 100,880 requests were made to courts for arrest warrants. Of these, 92,766 were for normal warrants, the remaining 8,114 were for emergency warrants. The great majority of warrants requests (83,280) were made to summary courts, the remainder to district courts. Of all of these requests, judges rejected a grand total of 62, or just 0.06%. A further 1,373 were withdrawn by the requesting law enforcement authorities, some doubtless representing "soft" rejections, it not being uncommon for courts to encourage the retraction of motions and requests they might otherwise be inclined to reject.

Possibly because it involves staying at the courthouse overnight or over weekends, warrant duty is often left up to young assistant judges. In light of the career system described in Chapter 4 this means they may feel direct or unspoken pressure not to rock the boat by upsetting police or prosecutors. The close institutional relationships between the judiciary and the prosecutors means a complaint from the head of the local public prosecutors office to the presiding judge of the relevant court about a young judge rejecting too many warrants can potentially affect the latter's personnel evaluation. The Supreme Court has indicated it is not possible to appeal or otherwise judicially challenge the validity of an arrest warrant (Supreme Court, 1st Petty Bench judgment of August 27, 1982).

Once a suspect has been arrested, the CCP requires that he be informed of the nature of the crime which he has been arrested on suspicion of and his right to appoint counsel, and be given the opportunity to explain (or "justify" *benkai*) himself (CCP article 203(1)). *Miranda*-sensitive American lawyers would likely find problematic a statutory provision actively requiring arresting authorities to invite suspects to make a statement rather than informing them of their right to remain silent (though this is also supposed to happen early in the process).

The CCP (and the constitution) give arrestees the opportunity to engage counsel, and police jails have phones and information necessary to contact the "on-call" defense lawyer provided by the local bar association. However, the right to a state-paid lawyer does not apply at the arrest stage of the process unless it involves a serious crime (one that is punishable by death or 3 years' or more of imprisonment) and the suspect is placed under detention (CCP article 37–2). It is also a comparatively recent right, having been accomplished through legislation that took effect in 2006. Moreover, access to counsel while the suspect is being investigated under detention is highly constrained, as described below. That amendments pending at the time of writing would extend the right of counsel to anyone subject to criminal detention.

Under article 203(1) of the CCP, within 48 hours of arresting a suspect the police must either release him or remand him to the public prosecutors agency. Under the CIP the police have the authority to release offenders in cases involving minor offenses, and even such resolutions must be recorded and reported to prosecutors (articles 198 and 199).

Of those suspects arrested by police in 2015, approximately 6% were released. The remainder were referred to prosecutors for further action. Under article 195 of the CIP, in the report accompanying the remand the police may include a recommendation. Typically there are four standard recommendations: (i) "handle strictly" (a recommendation for prosecution), (ii) "handle as the case deserves" (left to the discretion of the prosecutor), (iii) leniency and (iv) the appropriate disposition, which is the way the police let prosecutors know prosecution is not required. These recommendations are not binding in any way on prosecutors.

Under CCP article 205, within 24 hours of the remand of a suspect the prosecutors must release him, request the issuance of a judicial detention warrant, or initiate a prosecution. Article 205 provides an additional protection for suspects intended to ensure the total time in which a suspect is under the control of police and prosecutors before release or further proceedings does not exceed 72 hours.

The procedure is slightly different if the arrest is made by prosecutors, with prosecutors having 48 hours to make the decision to release charge or detain (CCP article 204). Prosecutorial arrests are rare, however, comprising just 0.2% of the total made in 2015). A savings clause in article 206 offers some flexibility when "unavoidable circumstances" prevent police or prosecutors from meeting the statutory deadlines.

d. *Detention (and Still More Investigation)*

Prosecutors seek detention warrants for approximately 90% of prisoners remanded to them by the police. The detention hearing is the first stage in the process where a suspect appears before a judge, in proceedings held for the limited purpose of evaluating the prosecutor's request to detain him. This request is based on and evaluated on the same grounds for detention recognized by the CCP when a court is deciding whether it is merited *after* charges are brought: *i.e.,* probable cause the suspect has committed the crime and (i) he has no fixed address, (ii) probable cause he will conceal or destroy evidence, or (iii) he is a likely flight risk (CCP article 60(1) and 207). The CCP requires the judge to issue a detention warrant unless there are no grounds for detention (article 207(4)). In 2015, courts received 106,979 requests to detain suspects and rejected just 2,866, a 97.4% success rate for prosecutors. Some individual courts have much higher rejection rates. The initial detention period is ten days, and this can be extended for an additional ten days (article 208).

Together with the initial time in police and prosecutorial custody, a suspect can be kept in jail for over three weeks before a decision to initiate a prosecution is made (and as discussed below there are techniques for extending this period even further). Although detention is sought on the authority of prosecutors, in most cases suspects are detained under the control of the police in police jails (see discussion below) where post-detention interrogations will continue to be conducted by police.

It is important here to appreciate a very subtle but important difference between Japanese and American procedure. Described in superficial terms, the process may seem familiar, with the CCP requiring an appearance before a judge within a few days of arrest. However this is *not* an arraignment proceeding where the suspect is informed of the charges against him, offers a plea and a decision is made for bail. Rather it is a proceeding where the prosecutors seek judicial permission to detain a suspect for the purpose of investigating him in connection with a crime he is suspected of committing *before* decided whether to initiate a prosecution. The grounds for detention in the CCP thus seem to reflect a statutory presumption of guilt before a prosecution is even brought.

As noted above, article 34 of the Constitution prohibits arrests or detentions without informing the suspect of the reason. The arrest and detention proceedings satisfy these requirements, but once the suspect is under detention the police have ample time to investigate him for other crimes, or even crimes committed by other people who may be the real focus of police interest. While not a formal category of arrest, the term *bekken taiho*—arresting someone for a crime that is different from the one police actually want to investigate—is commonly used when desccribing police practices. Most homicide cases begin not with a suspect being arrested for murder, but for "wrongfully disposing of a corpse" (Penal Code, article 190). Once arrested, they are then interrogated until they confess to the killing. It is also possible to keep the detention clock running with *saitaiho*, re-arresting the suspect for a new crime after the detention period for the last arrest has expired. Media reports about arrests often describe the police as continuing to investigate a suspect arrested for one crime in connection with *yozai* (other crimes).

As already noted, a suspect in detention has the right to contact a lawyer. However, under article 39(3) of the CCP, if a prosecution has not yet been initiated police and prosecutors may "designate the date, place and time" of suspects' meetings with their attorneys "when it is necessary for investigation." In other words, police can properly refuse to let a lawyer meet her client on the grounds that they haven't finished interrogating him for the day yet.

CCP article 80 permits suspects under detention to meet and correspond with persons other than their lawyer, subject to the rules of the detention facility. These rules are very restrictive, mandating the presence of guard during a visit, with restrictions on the number and format of letters that can be sent to or received by the detainee and requirements that interpreters be present if discussions will be in a foreign language and translations be available of letters that are not in Japanese (Penal Facilities Act, articles 216 *et seq.* and implementing regulations). However, under CCP article 81, upon request of a public prosecutor or on its own authority a court may prohibit contact and/or censor written communications between a detained suspect and anyone other than their counsel if the suspect "may flee or conceal or destroy evidence" (which would likely already have been established as the grounds for detention).

Combined with detention, an arrest can thus result in the suspect vanishing from their day-to-day lives for a prolonged period, unable to communicate with anyone but their lawyer. For an average person with family commitments, a job to go to, bills to pay and so forth, this can be highly destructive after a few days, let alone a few weeks. The reality is that the detention process provides a powerful weapon by which law enforcement officials, acting with the tacit cooperation of courts, can punish almost anyone severely without even *charging* them with a crime, let alone proving it in court.

That this also makes it difficult for suspects to prepare their defense is hopefully obvious. To comport with the requirements of article 34 of the Constitution that suspects know the reason for their detention, the CCP provides for a procedure whereby a detained suspect or defendant "may request the court to disclose the grounds for detention." (CCP article 82(1). However, it is a procedure that is only used a few hundred times a year possibly because it is meaningless: the judge who issued the warrant is not a necessary participant and the accused or his counsel is only permitted to address the court for ten minutes or less (CCP Rules, article 85). The court likely to merely repeat the grounds articulated when the detention was first approved.

The tight control law enforcement can and does exercise over suspects reflects what some critics refer to as their excessive reliance on confessions. Japan's high conviction rate is sometimes justified on the grounds that prosecutors only bring cases they know they can win. Even if this were usually true (in part due to the heavy reliance on confessions) it would seem to create a potential "moral hazard" on the part of judges who might be tempted to simply rely on this presumption.

It is also common to refer to prosecutors as caring very much about *hansei*, criminals reflecting on and showing remorse for their bad acts. This may indeed be an admirable approach though of course *hansei* presupposes an admission of guilt. It can also make it worse for those who actually innocent, since in the eyes of prosecutors and sometimes judges, who may issue harsher sentences against defendants who persist in asserting their innocence because they have failed to show suitable contrition.

Although the Constitution prohibits convictions based solely on confessions, with a confession in hand it may be easy to develop corroborating evidence, which may sometimes seem added as an afterthought.

This system of prolonged pretrial detention has been highly criticized by scholars, criminal defense lawyers and international human rights bodies such as the UN Committee Against Torture. It is often called a "hotbed" of coerced confessions, and referred to by some in Japanese as *hitojichi shihō*, a "hostage-based system of justice" (with the suspect/defendant being the hostage). It is a system that allows investigators to develop a story of what they think happened, and then coerce suspects until they agree with it. This has been identified as particularly problematic in cases involving corruption or other political elements, where police or prosecutors can only prove their case by getting multiple persons to separately confess to the same storyline. The need for "narrative control" in a confession-based system may also help explain why there is so much focus on limiting contact without the outside world, where potentially competing narratives can be developed both by the suspect and potential witnesses.

A stark example of this was the so-called *Shibushi Case*, which saw a dozen citizens in a small town arrested and prosecuted on allegations of vote-buying in connection with a 2003 prefectural assembly election. Some were detained for months (for crimes that, if confessed to would usually be punished with a fine or suspended sentence). After a trial process lasting four years, all were acquitted despite having confessed to the same version of events that never took place. Some suffered detentions for periods of over a year.

The coercive nature of the pre-charge detention system means that suspects can generally expect their treatment to improve if they confess in the manner required and offer restitution or consolation payments to their victims, if appropriate. If the crime is minor the prosecutors may decide not to prosecute, or to at least defer it subject to the suspect's continued behavior. Access to counsel and friends and family will also improve, since the suspect is no longer under investigation. If the police allegations seem fantastical (as they would to an innocent person) or are pursued in an overly intimidating manner, some suspects might also reasonably conclude a confession is the only way to escape from the very stressful conditions of the interrogation room and police jail and have their explanation heard by a more reasonable actor—a judge, perhaps. Unfortunately, this merely burdens them with the difficult task of convincing a court that their confession was coerced; of proving their innocence.

e. Bail

The Japanese constitution does not contain any guarantees specifically relating to bail. Article 88 *et seq.* of the CCP provide for the possibility of bail, but only after a prosecution has been initiated. This means that suspects who have been arrested and subject to prolonged pre-charge detention may not avail themselves of it (though article 91 does require judges to release or grant bail to persons whose detention has been unreasonably long). A judge hearing a request for bail must hear the views of the prosecutor before deciding (article 92) but must grant it unless certain exceptions apply. These include: (i) the offense charged is serious, (ii) the defendant has a record of prior serious offenses, (iii) the defendant may try to tamper with evidence or threaten witnesses or their family members and (iv) the identity of the defendant is unclear or he has no fixed address (article 89).

These exceptions may have swallowed the general rule. In 2015 bail was granted to only 25.7% of defendants detained pending trial in district courts and 13.6% of those in summary courts. Financial constraints may have also been a factor; the courts generally require bail to be posted in cash and bail bonds do not appear to be well-established financial products; two principal providers exist, one a private foundation, the other a cooperative established by regional bar associations.

f. Prosecutions, Prosecutorial Discretion and Summary Proceedings

Once a prosecution is initiated, whether immediately upon remand from the police or after a period of pre-charge detention, the suspect formally becomes a defendant. This means that more of the constitutional protections come into play; particularly the right to counsel. Yet as shown above, the pre-charge system of detention and isolation is often operated to ensure that as much of the actual process is resolved before trial when fewer constitutional and procedural constraints apply.

Note that not all persons who are arrested and detained are prosecuted and not all persons who are prosecuted are first arrested or detained. In cases involving minor offenses, it may be deemed unnecessary to detain a suspect even if they have been arrested. They may be freed to return home, though still under investigation. In such cases the police may simply refer the crime to prosecutors through paperwork without an arrest. This is sometimes referred to *shorui sōken* ("sending documents to the prosecutor") as distinct from *migara sōken* ("sending the person [of the suspect] to the prosecutor").

A significant number of cases are resolved in summary proceedings (*ryakushiki kisō*) under articles 461 *et seq.* of the CCP. These allow a summary court to impose a fine of JPY 1 million or less through expedited, non-public proceedings, so long as the suspect/defendant clearly consents. The vast majority of criminal trials in summary courts are of this character (281,919 out of a total of 291,261 (over 96%) in 2015). Although the majority of cases resolved in this fashion may involve minor offenses, they may also involve corporations which are not amenable to arrest or detention. In 2017 Dentsu, Japan's largest advertising agency was indicted through this process for violations of statutory overtime restrictionsthat allegedly caused the suicide of an overworked young employee. That decision was noteworthy because the judge refused to allow the case to be resolved through expedited proceedings and instead required an actual trial to take place, even though Dentsu would presumably have preferred to just quietly pay the fine.

One source of the powers of prosecutors is the exceptionally broad discretion they are accorded to *not* prosecute offenders. Under article 248 of the CCP prosecutors do not need to initiate prosecutions if it "*is deemed unnecessary owing to the character, age or circumstances of the offender or the gravity or circumstances of the offense, or situation after its commission.*"

The discretion accorded to prosecutors can be used in several ways. First, some cases do not need to be prosecuted at all. This sometimes leads to criticism when the public feels that the prosecutors are treating politicians from certain political parties more favorably when choosing not to pursue election law violations, or that corporate malfeasance is not being adequately punished.

Second, for certain offenses the ability to refrain from prosecuting—either definitively or tentatively—can be used as a negotiating tool, whether directly in dealings with suspects and their counsel, or indirectly through the *jidan* process discussed later in this chapter. Third, it can be used to convince a minor offender to cooperate in the investigation of a bigger target suspected of more serious crimes.

On a basic level prosecutors make a decision to prosecute (*kisō shobun*) or not prosecute (*fukisō shobun*). However, there are several categories of *fukisō shobun*. Prosecutorial guidelines anticipate a number of circumstances in which a prosecution can be declined. These include because the suspect has not committed the crime (*kengi nashi*), a crime has been committed but there is inadequate evidence to purse it against the suspect (*kengi fujūbun*), the suspect is/was in a weakened mental or physical state (*shinshin sōshitsu*), or a crime has clearly been committed but prosecutors have decided not to pursue it for various reasons.

This last disposition is referred to as a "suspended" prosecution (*kisō yūyo*). The end result may seem the same in terms of what happens to the suspect, but it effectively creates a sort of quasi-criminal official record known at least to prosecutors. They can use it to evaluate how they will handle any future encounters with the same suspect and possibly even de-suspend the prosecution if he behaves badly.

The following table, based on data from the MOJ's 2016 White Paper on Crime, show how prosecutors resolved cases referred to them in 2015. As it shows, prosecutors let a significant number of clearly guilty persons avoid prosecution.

TABLE 8-1 RESOLUTION OF CASES REFERRED TO PROSECUTORS (2015)

Number of cases (persons) referred to prosecutors (2015)	1,191,556	100%
Prosecuted (trial)	92,930	7.8%
Prosecuted (summary proceedings)	278,529	23.4%
No prosecution	69,251	5.8
Remanded to family (juvenile) court	80160	6.7%
SOURCE: MOJ White Paper on Crime (2016).		

g. *Prosecutorial Review Commissions*

The broad discretion accorded prosecutors is mitigated somewhat by the existence of Prosecutorial Review Commissions (PRC). These are established pursuant to the Prosecutorial Review Commission Act of 1948 (PRCA) and represent a compromise between the US occupation authorities who wanted Japan to adopt a grand jury system and Japanese officials who did not.

PRCs are established at district courts and some of their branches, in a total of 149 locations. They are comprised of eleven citizens chosen from voter lists and appointed on a rolling basis for overlapping terms of six months. A chair is elected from their members and they meet on a quarterly basis, though meetings can also be held if called by the chair (PRCA articles 13, 14 and 21). Members are subject to stringent confidentiality obligations.

Crime victims, family members of those killed in an alleged crime, or other concerned parties may petition their local PRC to review a prosecutorial decision not to bring charges. Commissions receiving such petitions may require the prosecutors who handled the case to submit relevant documents and may also call witnesses and seek advice and assistance from outside experts if necessary (PRCA articles 32 *et seq.*). Unlike grand juries, PRC have no ability to *prevent* prosecutions from taking place.

In response to a petition the PRC may issue a verdict that: (i) validates the decision not to prosecute, (ii) indicates the prosecutors should investigate further, or (iii) finding that a prosecution should be brought. Until 2009 the views of a PRC were merely precatory; prosecutors would review their decision but were not required to act in accordance with a recommendation to prosecute. Amendments to the PRCA that took effect in 2009 have established a process whereby a Commission can force a prosecution to take place. If the prosecutors fail to act on a recommendation to prosecute, by a special vote the PRC make a decision to proceed with a prosecution (PRCA articles 41–4 and 41–6). Such prosecutions are conducted by *bengoshi* attorneys acting as prosecutors.

Cases of prosecutions initiated by PRC are rare, with fewer than ten such cases having been brought at the time of writing. Such cases also tend to be high profile—for example executives at Tokyo Electric Power Company, the operator of the nuclear power plant in Fukushima that experienced a meltdown in 2011, were prosecuted through this route. Unlike the infamous 99.9% conviction rate elsewhere in the justice system, however, such prosecutions initiated by the PRC have mostly been unsuccessful.

Some observers have suggested that merely giving the PRC the ability to bypass prosecutors has made them more circumspect about dropping certain types of cases. Others have pointed out PRC actually provide a means for prosecutors to target political enemies without appearing to dirty their own hands. The 2010 prosecution initiated by a commission against leading opposition politician Ichiro Ozawa for violations of political fundingreporting requirements was based in part on a highly misleading account of an interview of his former secretary presented to the PRC by prosecutors. Ozawa was widely known as an enemy of bureaucrats and prosecutors so it has been speculated that they were able to manipulate the commission into putting him on trial, while appearing reluctant to do so themselves. Although he was acquitted, it resulted in his political marginalization and probably prevented him from becoming prime minister.

TABLE 8-2 PROSECUTION REVEW COMMISSION DISPOSITIONS (2015)

Cases Reviewed	By Petition	2,174
	By Commission (*ex officio*)	35
	Total	2,209
Decision	Prosecution warranted*	4
	Decision not to prosecute unwarranted	118
	Decision not to prosecute warranted	1,801
	Other procedural dispositions (venue transfer, etc.)	247
	Total **	2,171

SOURCE: Japan Court Web site (www.courts.go.jp).
* In 2015 3 cases went to the next stage in which the commission decided to initiate a prosecution.
** Total is different from total number of cases because decisions may not be made in the same year a petition is brought.

h. *Jidan—Financial Settlement of Criminal Cases*

One of the lesser-known features of Japan's criminal justice system is that many cases—including some traffic infractions that result in death and even rape cases—are resolved through financial settlements between the (alleged) offender and their victim. This practice is so well-established that some lawyers specifically advertise their expertise in negotiating such settlements, even indicating an unofficial "*sōba*" (range of prices) for different types of offenses and incidents. In some cases an insurance company may even pay for the settlement under a liability policy.

This practice, known as *jidan* is technically a form of "settlement agreement" under article 695 of the Civil Code. It takes place in different forms but will typically start with a serious traffic accident that causes harm, or an incident (such as an assault) resulting in the filing of a police report. The police become involved through an arrest or investigation, and may even encourage the offender to pursue a settlement. Although technically a civil settlement, successful completion of a *jidan* agreement can make a criminal case go away through the victim withdrawing their complaint. An agreement may also serve as evidence of the offender's contrition, and thus support a decision by prosecutors to drop or suspend a prosecution, or a court to grant a lenient punishment.

The payments made pursuant to a *jidan* agreement are usually intended to include both compensatory damages as well as an additional amount of "consolation money." Since these are unofficial resolutions no statistics are available, however it appears that a significant number of criminal cases are actually resolved financially, albeit under the tacit threat of criminal punishment (or more severe punishment) if a settlement is not reached. This may be advantageous to both crime victims and offenders who wish to avoid the bother of a criminal trial; it may further disadvantage those accused of an offense they did not actually commit.

A special law, the Act for Ancillary Measures in Criminal Proceedings for the Protection of the Rights and Interests of Crime Victims (2000) provides a mechanism for having the settlement of civil cases between a victim and an offender reflected in the trial records of the criminal case. It also provides for a mechanism whereby victims of certain types of serious crimes or their surviving family may request an order for civil damages as a derivative of the criminal trial, without having to bring a separate lawsuit.

i. Plea Bargains and Expedited Procedural Regimes

Japanese criminal procedure lacks a general system of plea bargains. Some would say the constitutional prohibition on convictions based solely on confessions prevent them from taking place. Yet such arrangements do exist formally and informally.

The broad discretion granted to prosecutors *not* to prosecute as well as their ability to recommend lenient sentences is said to sometimes be used to make informal plea bargains in certain types of cases. However, these would not be enforceable from the perspective of the suspect/defendant. In any case, there were no means of offering defendants or suspects outright immunity in exchange for testifying against other offenders.

Amendments to the CCP passed in 2016 established a system whereby suspects or defendants in certain types of cases can provide testimonial evidence in the trial of other criminals in exchange for immunity from prosecution or reduced punishment in accordance with a formal agreement (CCP article 157–2, 153). The scope of offenses (by both the suspect/defendant and the offender(s) against whom he will testify against) is limited to economic and drugs crimes, and excludes offenses subject to punishments of death or imprisonment for an indefinite term (CCP article 350–2). Participation of defense counsel is required for such arrangements.

Outside the world of formal plea bargains with potential immunity for helpful testimony, the CCP also offers several other means by which defendants can effectively plead guilty to comparatively minor offenses in exchange for an assurance of lenient punishment, assuming the prosecutors and judges involved agree. Summary proceedings for minor offenses described above and which are punished by fines would fit into this category.

The CCP (article 291–2) also provides for truncated proceedings (*kan'i kōhan tetsuzuki*) whereby a defendant may begin a trial with an admission of guilt and effectively be convicted by hearsay evidence contained in written statements. The

Supreme Court has found this proceeding not to violate the constitutional guarantee to examine witnesses (constitution article 37(2), Supreme Court 1st Petty Bench judgment of February 22, 1962). These proceedings may not be used in trials of serious crimes (those for which the potential punishment is death or imprisonment of greater than one year), and do not contain any clear provisions relating to sentencing.

2006 amendments to the CCP (article 350–2) also added an expedited trial process (*sokketsu saiban tetsuzuki*)). For cases involving crimes that are not serious (the same standard as in the preceding paragraph) the defendant may plead guilty and immediately receive a suspended sentence without further trial proceedings (CCP articles 350–13 and 350–14). Such proceedings may only be held if the defendant is represented by counsel (CCP article 350–9). As with abbreviated proceedings in the preceding paragraph, restrictions on hearsay evidence that would normally apply do not (CCP article 350–12), and the defendant using them loses the right to appeal the result of the trial on grounds of mistake of fact (CCP articles 403–2 and 413–2). In a 2009 decision the Supreme Court rejected a challenge to the effect that the restricted rights of appeal resulting from use of this procedure constituted a denial of the right to a trial guaranteed by article 32 of the Constitution (Supreme Court 3rd Petty Bench judgment of July 14, 2009). Some concern has been expressed that these proceedings may result in cases being resolved without adequate consideration for crime victims.

A plea bargain-like system also exists in the world of antitrust. Companies involved in cartel, bid rigging or other behavior in violation of competition laws can reduce the amount of the fines they would pay by being among the first to voluntarily report such behavior to the FTC.

j. Criminal Trials

(i) Introduction

For the minority of cases not resolved through the summary, abbreviated or expedited proceedings discussed above, a full trial with evidentiary hearings will be held in accordance with the CCP. However, even in many such cases the principal evidentiary proceedings will be about mitigating factors relevant to sentencing rather than the validity of the charge itself. According to statistics published by the Supreme Court, of the 53,247 defendants tried in regular district court criminal proceedings in 2016, only 9.6% contested the charges against them.

For much of the modern era, the vast majority of criminal trials were conducted exclusively by judges. Under article 26 of the Courts Act, a panel of three judges is required for any criminal case where the potential punishment is death or a term of imprisonment of one year or greater. With some exceptions, other cases can be heard by a single judge.

Although there is a distinction between the finding of fact and determinations of law, the Japanese system has lacked the well—established and clearly-segregated "black box" like role of finder of fact accorded to juries in the American and other common law systems. Japanese rules of evidence are correspondingly simpler as a result. This has changed slightly with the introduction of the *Saiban'in* system described below.

(ii) Juries and Lay Judges (Saiban'in)

From 1928 to 1943 juries were used in Japan in trials of serious crimes, though defendants could and did waive this method of trial. Twelve (male) jurors were used as in the traditional Anglo-American jury system but their verdict was not binding; a judge that disagreed with it could procure a different jury. Juries were not popular and only 448 cases were tried by them during the 15 years in which the system was operational. The system of trial by jury was suspended by a special wartime law (the Law for the Suspension of the Jury Act of 1943) that specifically anticipated it would be resuscitated after the war was over. It never was, and although the system is no longer used, the Jury Act of 1923 has never been formally repealed.

Juries were also used in both criminal and civil cases in Okinawa from 1963 until 1972 while the islands were under American administration. The number of cases was not large and the practice was ceased when the islands reverted to Japanese administration in 1972.

Since 2009 particularly serious crimes (those subject to a potential punishment of death or imprisonment for an indefinite term, or intentional offenses resulting in the death of another) have been tried before panels comprised of three professional judges and six randomly-selected citizen *saiban'in* (lay judges), pursuant to a special statute, the Act on Criminal Trials with the Participation of Lay Judges of 2004 (the "*Saiban'in* Act"). This system of trial is commonly called the *saiban'in seido* (the lay judge system)

Unlike the US system, a trial by the *saiban'in* system is not a right of the defendant that can be waived. Upon motion by the parties or on its own discretion, the court may decline to use lay judges if the defendant or his associates make statements indicating that lay judges might feel threatened, or if the complexity of the case is likely to make the trial inordinately long or it is unusually difficult to find enough lay judge candidates (*Saiban'in* articles 3 and 3–2).

Lay judge candidates are selected from voter register information. Interestingly, the law is actually written to exclude almost anyone with any legal knowledge or experience with the court system, starting with *bengoshi* lawyers, patent attorneys, public notaries, judicial scriveners and law professors (article 15). The law also recognizes a number of grounds for being excused from service as a *saiban'in*, including prior service, serious illness, being a student or aged 70 or greater, employment obligations, or need to look after children or infirm family members (article 16).

While it is sometimes described as a "jury system" in western press, a significant difference is that the lay judges do not have the ability to make any decisions independent of the professional judges with whom they sit. Moreover, most of the key interactions between the professional judges and the lay judges—explanations about the law, opinions on the evidence and so forth—take place in a closed room free from outside scrutiny, with lay judges subject to a lifetime confidentiality obligation. This might be disturbing to American lawyers for whom any communication by a judge to the jury that could improperly influence the outcome of the case is potential grounds for appeal. This also means that it is unlikely that the *saiban'in* system will see any "case law" develop out of (for example) incorrect explanations of the law or inappropriate comments on the evidence by judges, as happens in the US system. Criminal cases resolved through *saiban'in* proceedings represent a very small fraction of the total. According to judicial statistics, from its start in the latter half of 2009 through June 2017 a total of 12,010 defendants had been tried by lay judge panels, with robbery resulting in injury, murder, arson, injury resulting in death and drug offenses being the most common offenses on trial. Interestingly, the largest number of cases was not in the Tokyo District Court, but the Chiba District Court. This was due to the large number of cases involving drug smugglers who are arrested on arrival at Tokyo's Narita airport (which is actually located in neighboring Chiba Prefecture). In a 2011 opinion the Supreme Court ruled that trials under the *saiban'in* system were constitutional (Supreme Court Grand Bench judgment of November 16, 2017).

Trials by *saiban'in* panels account for a small minority of the total cases going to full trial—1,126 of the 54,237 cases (2%) in 2016. However, 47.6% of these cases saw the defendants contesting the charges.

TABLE 8-3 INITIAL CRIMINAL TRIALS AT DISTRICT COURTS (2016)

	Total Number of Regular Initial Trials	Those tried by Saiban'in (Lay Judge) system
Number of defendants	53,247	1,126
% of cases where proceedings last for more than 2 years.	0.2%	2.8%
Average number of days of courtroom proceedings (including opening proceedings, evidentiary hearings, and rendering of judgment)	2.7	4.6
Average number of hearings with cross-examination of witnesses*	1.2	2.1
Average number of hearings with questioning of defendant*	1.1	1.7
Percentage of cases where defendant contests the charges	9.6%	47.6%
Percentage of cases in which defendant is represented by counsel	99.6%	100.0%
Percentage of cases in which defendant represented by state-appointed counsel	83.6%	86.1%
Percentage of cases involving non-Japanese defendants (requiring interpreters)	4.9%	5.8%
Percentage of cases involving expert testimony	0.3%	6.1%
Average length of trial (in months)	All cases	3.2
	Cases where defendant confesses	2.6
	Cases where defendant contests charges	8.7

SOURCE: CHIHŌSAIBANSHO NI OKERU KEIJI DAIISSHIN SOSHŌ JIKEN NO JŌKYŌTŌ [Conditions of initial trials of criminal cases in district courts], 2016, published by Supreme Court of Japan.

As the above table shows, the great majority of criminal trials are conducted by panels of professional judges only, with *saiban'in* trials comprising a very small minority of the total. Accordingly, the discussion of trial procedure that follows will be based primarily on bench trials with references to the *saiban'in* system where relevant.

Despite the comparative rarity of criminal trials involving lay judges, the *saiban'in* system appears to have had a disproportionate impact on the manner in which criminal trials are conducted in Japan. Prior to the system's introduction, the lack of a jury-like system meant that there was no particular need to have proceedings over a concentrated period of time. Hearings could be held once a month until the end of time, with the defendant potentially subject to detention for the duration. The case of Matsumoto Chizuo (a/k/a Asahara Shōkō) the Oum doomsday cult leader charged with masterminding the 1995 sarin gas attacks on the Tokyo subway system is instructive, having taken almost nine years to reach a judgment in the initial trial alone.[7] Although the Act on Expediting Trials of 2003 established the goal of concluding initial trials in both the civil and criminal spheres within two years, the procedural regime established for *saiban'in* trials, which is heavily focused on concentrated proceedings that minimize the amount of time required of the lay judges, has had an impact on the conduct of bench trials as well.

This is in part due to amendments to the CCP made in 2004 and anticipating the *saiban'in* system requiring trials lasting more than one day to be tried over consecutive days "to the extent possible" (article 281–6). On the one hand many trials are over in one or two sessions because the defendant freely admits guilt. On the other, trials on consecutive dates do not always happen, particularly if it does not require lay judges. In 2016 the average period between hearing dates was 1.2 months; 1.4 months in cases where the defendant contested the charges.

(iii) Starting the Criminal Trial Process: The Indictment

Once prosecutors decide to bring a suspect to trial, the criminal trial process starts with a *kisojō*, the written indictment or charging sheet (CCP article 256). This document identifies the defendant and specifies the crime being charged as well as the provisions of the Penal Code or other criminal statute. It also contains a summary allegation of the facts of the crime. Prosecutors deliver the indictment to the relevant court which must promptly serve it on the defendant (article 271).

Under the old Code of Criminal Procedure, together with the indictment prosecutors would also submit to the court and the defendant evidence relevant to the case together with the indictment. However, out of concern that this might cause judges to draw conclusions about the evidence before it was considered at trial, the new CCP restricts the documents submitted to the indictment. Somewhat ironically, this means that the defendant and his counsel start the trial process with very limited information about the case against him. The CCP does not contain any provisions clearly requiring the prosecutors to inform the defense of all the evidence in their possession. Nor does the indictment contain many clues of what evidence the defense could ask to be disclosed.

---

[7] In July 2018, immediately before this book was published, he was finally executed together with several of his co-defendants.

(iv) Access to Evidence and Pre-Trial Proceedings

For quite some time, the system worked in a way which required lawyers to anticipate what sort of evidence would likely be in the possession of prosecutors and request that it be provided to the defense in advance. If the prosecutors were actually in possession of the evidence they theoretically had to turn it over, though there have been cases of this not happening and there have been various means of making potentially exculpatory evidence undiscoverable, such as leaving it in the possession of the police. The process by which the defense is able to obtain evidence from the prosecution has developed largely as a matter of practice and precedent derived from the power of the presiding judge to control the trial proceedings (CCP article 294). This was confirmed as including the power to order prosecutors to turn over relevant evidence by a 1969 Supreme Court ruling (Supreme Court, Petty Bench judgment of April 25, 1969).

The situation with respect to defense pre-trial access to evidence and information about the evidence of the prosecutors has improved somewhat at least in trials for serious crimes. 2004 amendments to the CCP introduced formal pre-trial proceedings (*kōhanmae seiri tetsuzuki*) under CCP 316–2 through 316–32. These proceedings were introduced in anticipation of the *saiban'in* system to facilitate the presentation of evidence and issues to lay judges in a concentrated form. The use of these proceedings is mandatory for trials under the *saiban'in* system, but can also be ordered for other trials where the court deems it appropriate, though such instances are rare. In 2016 there were only 1,327 instances of such proceedings being held, of which 1,126 were *saiban'in* system trials.

The purpose of *kōhanmae seiritetsuzuki* pretrial proceedings is to narrow down the factual and legal issues in dispute so that the trial itself can be carried out efficiently. Through the pretrial proceedings, prosecutors and defense counsel are supposed to indicate the nature of the witness testimony and other evidence they will present at trial. This may involve various decisions by the court regarding what sort of evidence will be submitted and who may be called as a witness. Lay judges (if it is a trial under the *saiban'in* system) do not participate in these proceedings, and participation of the defendant is also optional unless required by the court (CCP article 316–9). Once pretrial proceedings are completed it is difficult if not impossible to raise new issues or introduce additional evidence at the trial (article 316–32).

For pretrial proceedings that do anticipate a trial involving lay judges, concern has been expressed that the participation of only the career judges in such proceedings results in an imbalance of information between the career and lay judges when it comes to the actual trial. Some lawyers have also complained that the procedure requires the defense to essentially disclose key aspects of their strategy to the prosecution before trial. Yet many defense lawyers are probably also grateful that the proceedings offer a formal method for requesting the prosecutors to disclose evidence (CCP article 316–14 and 316–15). Supreme Court precedents relating to pretrial proceedings have also expanded the scope of discovery to include documents prepared in the course of investigation and maintained by public servants other than the prosecutors (*i.e.,* the police; Supreme Court, 3rd Petty Bench judgment of December 25, 2007 and 3rd Petty Bench judgment of June 25, 2008).

For the majority of full trials that do not involve the formal pretrial proceedings described above, what preliminary preparations do take place are conducted under the *jizenjunbi ni kansuru kitei* (rules regarding trial preparation) in the Supreme Court's rules of criminal procedure (Rules of Criminal Procedure, Supreme Court Rules of 1948, articles 178–2 through 178–11). These set forth only very rudimentary pre-trial requirements, including not only that defense counsel must meet with the defendant to ascertain the facts before the first trial date, but that the prosecutors and defense should try to cooperate in narrowing down the areas of dispute and identifying witnesses and evidence before the trial begins. The ability of defense counsel to obtain evidence from prosecutors outside the scope of the newer pretrial preparatory proceedings is also correspondingly limited.

(v) The Trial Begins

A full criminal trial begins with the prosecutor reading the indictment (article 291), and the court advising the defendant that they have the right to remain silent. In this respect the CCP is said to expand on the protections afforded by article 38(1) of the Constitution, which only protects against compelled self-incrimination rather than defendants being required to answer questions unrelated to guilt (the defendant can, for example, be compelled to confirm his identity).

Once the indictment has been read the court begins considering the evidence. This starts with the prosecutor's opening statements regarding the facts the state intends to prove with the evidence. Defense counsel may only make an opening statement if approved by the judge (CCP Rules, article 198), unless the trial is conducted before lay judges or has otherwise gone through pre-trial proceedings, in which case defense counsel may also be required to make an opening statement (CCP 316–30).

The investigation of evidence is conducted pursuant to the powers of the court to direct the trial (article 294). Using these powers the court may ask questions of the parties and seek proof of facts. While generally considered a right of the court, it can also be a duty and failure to perform it can be grounds for reversal on appeal (*see, e.g.*, Supreme Court, 2nd Petty Bench judgment of October 16, 2009). Judges have extremely broad discretion to limit the questioning of witnesses on grounds of relevance or in order to protect their privacy, as well as to determine the scope and method of investigating evidence in general (articles 295 and 296). While both the prosecution and the defense may seek to proffer evidence for investigation by the court, the court can also do so *sua sponte* (article 298).

From the start of the trial up to the time when closing statements are made either party can request that the court examine evidence, unless pretrial proceedings were used, in which case the nature of evidence to be considered will generally be set before trial. Typically, however, the prosecutors present their evidence first and the defense then presents theirs. Since the majority of cases involve defendants who are admitting guilt, often the only evidence presented by the defense may be that such as is relevant to establishing mitigating factors justifying a lighter sentence. In fact it is said to be a comparatively recent development that evidence of mitigating factors is formally supposed to be evaluated separately from evidence of guilt, to the extent possible (CCP Rules 198–3).

As in other countries Japan's criminal law has been criticized for the burdens it imposed on victims of certain types of crimes such as rape, at least until the Penal Code was amended in 2017 to make it easier for such offenses to be prosecuted without a complaint by the victim. However, in recent years the criminal justice system has become quite solicitous of the interests of victims as well as third party witnesses, sometimes to the extent of seeming detrimental to the rights of defendants. Under 2005 amendments to the CCP, victims of specified categories of offense (or their surviving family members, since most of the categories are offenses resulting in death) may, with leave of the court, participate in criminal proceedings directly or through counsel (CCP articles 316–33 through 316–39). Victims may ask questions of witnesses or the defendant, as well as voicing their views (though these do not constitute evidence).

The CCP also includes a number of protections to prevent defendants from finding out personal information about witnesses. The appointment of defense counsel is mandatory in serious cases, there being no constitutional right of self-representation or counsel of choice. One ramification of this requirement is that it makes it possible to have a procedural regime where identifying information about witnesses can be disclosed to defense counsel, but defense counsel has a positive obligation to withhold that information from the defendant.

Similarly, courtroom questioning of witnesses and disclosure of evidence held by the prosecutors may also be restricted if it might result in identifying information about the victim or other witness being disclosed inappropriately (e.g., CCP articles 290–2, 295, 299–2, 299–3, 316–23). These provisions reflect an underlying fear that such information will be used by the defendant or his associates to intimidate witnesses or their family members. Finally, closed-circuit video displays or physical barriers erected in the courtroom may be used to allow victims to testify without seeing or being seen by the defendant.

(vi) Evidence

The CCP and CCP Rules establish the scope of evidence that may be introduced and how. Both defense and prosecution may object to evidence and specific questions that the other seeks to put to witnesses. This aspect of the trial process is probably less confrontational than in the United States. Not all objections are formal objections, so it is sometimes necessary to clarify the objection and any exceptions to the court's ruling on them so they are set forth in the trials record.

(a) Standards of Proof

There is no formal provision of the CCP or other Japanese domestic law specifically mandating a presumption of innocence, though it is contained in international human rights instruments such as the Universal Declaration of Human Rights (article 11(1)) which have been ratified by Japan. The related notion that doubts and uncertainties about a case should be resolved in favor of the defendant is considered a fundamental principle of Japanese criminal justice, though again is not set forth in any statute. It has been confirmed by the Supreme Court as applying even to motions for new trials, albeit in a case where it rejected an appeal by a defendant seeking a new trial in a high profile murder case (the so-called *Shiratori* case, Supreme Court 1st Petty Bench judgment of May 20, 1975).

Article 317 of the CCP requires that "[f]acts shall be found on the basis of evidence. Article 318 states that "the probative value of evidence shall be left to the free discretion of the judge," though this may not give judges as much discretion as the language suggests. In fact, as an institution the criminal side of the judiciary appears to have developed a number of rules of fact-finding—establishing intent to kill from the type of knife used or area of the victim's body stabbed, for example—that may seem strangely mechanistic to lawyers accustomed to the black-box fact-finding methodology of the jury system. Mastery of these rules explain why Japanese judges are sometimes portrayed as "experts" at fact-finding.

In serious crimes fact-finding is conducted by a panel of three judges who must agree on the result (or at least not openly object; dissenting opinions only being permitted at the Supreme Court level).

Although not specified in the CCP, the theory and practice of criminal trials recognizes three categories of fact and ascribes standards of proof that apply to each: strict, positive (free discretion) and *prima facie* (accepted as fact unless proven otherwise). Article 317 of the CCP is understood as requiring that all facts relevant to establishing the elements of the crime be established through strict proof, a standard comparable to "beyond a reasonable doubt." This also generally applies to the proof of facts relevant to the compounding of offenses, accomplice liability, mitigating factors and other facts relevant to sentencing.

This does not mean that all such facts need to be proved through direct evidence, but rather that when using indirect or circumstantial evidence to prove such facts, the proof must meet the requirement. In a 2007 case involving a defendant convicted of trying to murder his estranged wife's mother with a home-made mail bomb the Supreme Court upheld a conviction based solely on circumstantial evidence. In doing so it offered a succinct view of the standard of proof used by Japanese courts:

> "In order to find guilt in criminal proceedings, it is necessary to prove it to the extent beyond a reasonable doubt. However, this standard does not require that there is no room at all to have any doubt about the existence of any fact contrary to the charged fact, but it means that even where there is room, as an abstract possibility, to have a doubt about the existence of a contrary fact, if, in light of the sound, social common sense, such doubt is generally judged to be unreasonable, the court may find guilt. This applies equally to the case where findings of fact should be made based on direct evidence and the case where findings of fact should be made based on circumstantial evidence (Supreme Court 1st Petty Bench judgment of October 16, 2007).

In a subsequent decision in a different case the court clarified its views, holding that "when there is no direct evidence, indirect facts found based on circumstantial evidence must include a fact that cannot be reasonably explained (or at least, that would be extremely difficult to explain) if the accused is not the perpetrator." (Supreme Court 3rd Petty Bench judgment of April 27, 2010).

Less significant facts may be established through discretionary or "free" proof. Such facts are those relating to the trial procedure itself, facts on which a court may base an order or a disposition and facts of the case not relating to the crime itself. There is some overlap between this category of fact and others, as well as dispute as to which type of proof is required for a given type of fact, particularly those relevant to the crime that may have an impact on sentencing (such as whether the defendant has paid consolation to the victim). Generally such facts must be proven by the preponderance of the evidence, so that the proof in favor is at least more compelling than the proof against.

There are also facts which may relate to issues in the trial process that only need *prima facie* proof, *i.e.*, the evidence is presumptively true unless contradicted. Examples of such facts are specified in the CCP either explicitly or interpretively, and seem to primarily benefit the prosecution (e.g., when prosecutors must explain to judges why they have failed to timely apply for a detention warrant under article 206, when seeking to obtain the pretrial testimony of a witness critical to making a conviction under article 227).

Finally, there are facts which do not need to be proven at all, such as things that are known to a person of normal intelligence understanding and experience. This is not as clear a standard as it seems, and there are various court decisions on the subject. An interesting example is a constitutional challenge to a traffic conviction where proof of the legal speed limit was never offered by the state. This challenge was rejected by the Supreme Court on grounds that could be paraphrased as 'everyone knows the default speed limit in Tokyo is 40km/h.' (Supreme Court 3rd Petty Bench judgment of June 10, 1966).

For the most part the burden of proof is on the prosecutors, with some exceptions where the defendant is raising defenses or asserting mitigating factors. Some specific offenses may also involve special burdens on the defendant, such as when asserting the truth of a statement as a defense in a criminal defamation prosecution.

(b) Confessions at Trial

As already noted, a common criticism of the Japanese criminal justice is its reliance on confessions, which can be readily produced in the prolonged detention regime described earlier in this chapter. A related criticism is that trials are overly focused on written documents rather than oral proceedings. This was particularly true before the procedural changes wrought by the *saiban'in* system, when all trials were conducted through a series of hearings held every few weeks rather than concentrated proceedings. This meant busy judges were far more likely to favor documents they could read outside of court in order to keep track of multiple cases proceeding in parallel.

In addition to the article 38 constitutional prohibition on convictions based solely on confessions, the CCP (article 319) also prohibits the use as evidence confessions procured through compulsion, torture or threat, after unduly prolonged detention or when there are otherwise doubts about their voluntariness. Article 320 of the CCP also introduces the general prohibition on use of hearsay evidence, which is understood to include any statement made outside of the scope of the trial proceedings. Finally, procedurally article 301 requires other evidence to be considered by the court before any confessions can be introduced.

While the text of CCP article 319 seems to offer a protection against the use of compelled confessions, in practice it effectively places the burden of proving a confession was coerced on the defendant. The initial burden of proof is on the prosecutors, of course, but the Supreme Court held very early on that the voluntariness of a written confession could be established by "appropriate means," meaning strict proof is not required, though it is often sought in practice (Supreme Court, 3rd Petty Bench judgment of June 22, 1954).

Over the decades, the Supreme Court has considered a variety of situations for purposes of evaluating whether a confession was voluntary. Collectively the results suggest certain standards but also what comes across as some odd line drawing. The confession of a 16 year old minor after seven months of unnecessary detention could not be used as evidence, while confessions after two or three weeks of detention have repeatedly been found valid. In one case the Court found a confession procured from a suspect with both hands in shackles questionable, while in another it was held that a confession made with just one hand cuffed was valid, and so forth.

In this and other areas of criminal procedure, the academic and professional literature can make the Supreme Court seem more magnanimous than it actually is. This is because it is not uncommon for a case to be cited as supporting a general rule, while in fact reading the judgments reveals the Court finding the rule not to apply in the case at bar. For example, an October 2, 1956 3rd Petty Bench judgment is cited in academic literature as supporting the notion that a confession may not be voluntary if it was procured in a situation where the defendant had inadequate opportunities to meet with counsel. In its judgment the Court does state this as a general rule but also found it did not apply in the case at bar and rejected the defendant's appeal.

Even when the court *has* found wrongful conduct by investigating authorities, its response may seem surprisingly tepid. For example a May 31, 1957 of the 2nd Petty Bench found it unacceptable that a lower court allowed the use of a confession procured from a defendant who had been denied access to food for six days, but its response was to remand for further proceedings.

It is also noteworthy that two decades before the US Supreme Court's famous decision in *Miranda v. Arizona*, Japan's Supreme Court held that failure to advise a suspect of his right to remain silent or seek the assistance of counsel did *not* invalidate a subsequent confession (Supreme Court Grand Bench judgment of July 14, 1948). That same year the court also issued a decision holding that a confession following an inappropriately prolonged detention would be inadmissible only if there was a clear causal relationship between the detention and the confession (Supreme Court Grand Bench judgment of June 23, 1948). In general, Japanese courts do not appear willing to use their ability to acquit defendants to punish bad behavior by police or prosecutors, at least not when there is other suitable evidence of guilt.

Confessions are procured in interrogation rooms totally under the control of police and prosecutors, without a lawyer present. Since 2007, NPSC rules on detention facilities require logs to be kept in part to provide a record of the treatment of detainees while they are being investigated. However, a more obvious solution would seem to make audio or video recordings of interrogations. Although investigatory authorities have kept such records for their own purposes they have not generally been discoverable or available for use as evidence. Police and prosecutors have also generally resisted efforts to make the full recording of all interrogations mandatory on a number of grounds including: (i) it will make it harder for investigators to share personal information about themselves to suspects as part of developing the rapport necessary to obtain a meaningful confession, (ii) the recordings would be extremely long and burdensome for judges and defense lawyers to review, (iii) it would be difficult for investigators to develop a relationship of trust with suspects they are investigation and (iv) lacking a general plea bargain system, it would be difficult to obtain useful information about other criminals from those being investigated if those discussions were potentially subject to discovery and review in open court.

In part thanks to the *saiban'in* system, police and prosecutors have been forced to become more open to creating video records of confessions and other parts of the investigation. 2016 amendments to the CCP saw the formalization of partial recording of interrogations of suspects in certain serious crimes. However, it is still up to the prosecutors to request the use of such records as evidence in trial, when the voluntariness of a written confession is in dispute.

Finally, it should be noted that while the Constitution does prohibit conviction based solely on the defendant's confession (article 38(2)), it does *not* prohibit convictions based solely on the testimony or statement of a co-defendant or other witness. Depending on the circumstances, such testimony can also be procured in the highly coercive environment described earlier in this chapter, particularly from co-defendants.

(c) Witness Statements and Hearsay

If a written confession or other out-of-court statement against the interests of the defendant is not found to have been involuntary, prosecutors must still overcome the general prohibition on the use of hearsay evidence and use it at trial (CCP article 320). However, the CCP also contains several exceptions to the hearsay exclusions. The principle ones are as follows:

(a) Certain types of prior written statements by a person unavailable to testify at trial due to illness, death or other unavoidable circumstances, or who gives testimony at trial that is inconsistent with such prior statements (article 321).

(b) "A written statement made by the accused or a written statement recording the statement of the accused and which has his/her signature and seal affixed by him/her may be used as evidence, when the statement contains an admission of a disadvantageous fact, or is made under circumstances that afford special credibility . . ." (article 320; such statements are not admissible if they are coerced, as per article 319).[8]

(c) Public documents (e.g. extracts from family or commercial registries) or other official records (article 323)

(d) Statements made by persons other than the accused at trial or during trial preparation that contain statements of the accused or some other person (article 324)

(e) Documents or statements which do not satisfy the requirements of the principle exceptions may still be used to challenge the evidentiary value of statements made by the accused, witnesses or other persons (article 328).

As already noted some of the expedited trial proceedings discussed earlier in this chapter also involve non-application of the hearsay exclusion.

Finally, article 326 of the CCP allows the use of documentary hearsay evidence if both the prosecutor and the defense agree to it. Under article 237 prosecutors and the defense can also agree on submission of a written statement in lieu of testimony if both know the nature of testimony that would be given if the witness appeared at trial. As a result, some trials may end up being mostly about which documents the prosecutors and defense can agree upon using. There are also conceptual disputes about whether

[8] This is the principal exception by which written confessions are introduced despite the hearsay rule. Note that the practice in interrogations is for the investigating officer or prosecutor to write the statement and have the accused sign. This means that most statements are drafted in a way that is convenient for the prosecution, and the accused may not have either the expertise or the ability to negotiate the contents of such statements as they are being drafted and presented to them in the interrogation room (their counsel not being present).

agreeing to admit a written statement also constitutes acceptance its contents, and whether further cross examination of the person making the statement is possible. It is also said that courts sometimes pressure lawyers to accept written statements proffered by the prosecution.

(vii) Summing up and Judgment

Once all of the evidence has been considered, the prosecutors must make a final statement regarding the facts and the applicability of the law, including their views as to punishment (CCP article 293(1)). This is referred to as *ronkoku* and *kyūkei*. The defendant and/or his counsel may also make a closing statement, though this is not required. Since many cases involve defendants who admit their guilt, closing statements by lawyers also often involve a recitation of mitigating factors and a view of what sort of (lighter) punishment is appropriate, though they have needed a different approach for trials under the *saiban'in* system.

The court must then consider the evidence and arrive at a verdict as to guilt (if it is in dispute) and determine a punishment based on the range established for the offenses as set forth in the penal code together with any mitigating or aggravating factors. In the past individual courts were said to have a *ryōkei no sōba*, a "sentencing price range" for different types of offenses that judges at the courts were supposed to follow. More recently the Supreme Court has developed a searchable database intended to help courts impose similar sentences in cases with similar circumstances (a basic requirement of justice), particularly in cases using the *saiban'in* system where lay judges need guidance as to what sort of punishment is appropriate. This system may actually lead to strange discrepancies since it results in decisions being driven by the limited number of searchable terms that generate results relevant to sentencing in any particular case. For example the a search using the term "knife" may generate as a potential reference a prior sentence where a combat knife was used to intentionally murder someone, but which may not be an appropriate exemplar in a case where a wife uses a kitchen knife to defend herself against an abusive spouse.

If the court is comprised of a panel of three judges they will deliberate in secret to arrive at a verdict. Under article 77 of the Courts Act only a majority of the judges on the panel (two out of three) is required to reach a verdict. With respect to sentencing, "the number of opinions most unfavorable to the accused shall be added to the number of opinions next most unfavorable, and so on until a majority is attained. The majority opinion shall be that of the opinion most favorable to the accused." (Courts Act, article 77(2)(ii)). In practice it is exceptionally rare if not unheard of for a verdict to be anything other than unanimous, and the duty of confidentiality regarding judicial deliberations means that there is usually no way for outsiders to learn about dissent within panels regarding guilt or sentencing (Courts Act, article 75(1)). Only on the Supreme Court are dissenting or concurring opinions expressed in the written judgments.

If the trial is by the *saiban'in* system, then in addition to three professional judges there will be six lay judges. The deliberations under the *saiban'in* system are more complicated since the lay judges participate in sentencing and the principal fact finding, but they do not know the law, which must be explained to them by the professional judges. Under the Saiban'in Act, a verdict is reached by "the majority of opinions of the number of persons constituting the panel including the opinions of both the professional judges and the Saiban'in Act, article 67)), a slightly disingenuous way of expressing that the professional judges acting in concert can effectively veto a verdict they find disagreeable. Given the dynamics of the judicial career it is reasonable to expect the professional judges to vote as a bloc.

Although no cases have been reported where the lay judges and professional judges are unable to agree on a verdict, in such a case the defendant would go free based on the principle of resolving uncertainties in favor of the accused (though this is not made clear in the law itself). With respect to sentencing, a method similar to that of judge-only panels is used, with the views of panel members (both professional and lay) being aggregated until there is a majority most favorable to the defendant (Saiban'in Act, article 67). The secrecy involved in the lay judge system means it is impossible to know if a verdict and sentence were arrived at unanimously or through a close split.

The judgment is recited in open court and doing so is what gives it legal effect (CCP article 342). A guilty verdict must set forth the facts of the offense, the evidence and the applicable criminal statute, as well as the judgment on the court regarding any facts asserted that would constitute a defense, or mitigating or aggravating factors, and the sentence, if any (CCP, article 335).

Although the requirements of the CCP are satisfied by the judgment being read out in open court, the written judgment may not be ready for delivery to the defendant and his counsel until several days later. In high profile cases the court may prepareand distribute to the media a summary of the key parts of the judgment, which in a complex or controversial case may be quite extensive. This facilitates reporting on the case by members of the court press club. This document is **not** shared with the defendant, however, and there are occasionally situations where reporters armed with this summary question lawyers for the accused who are less prepared because they only have whatever notes they were able to take when the judgment was read out in court.

(viii) Appeals (Jōso)

Since Japanese criminal trials are not organized around the assumption that a jury will act as finders of fact at the initial trial and there is no right to a jury trial to usurp by allowing findings of fact by appellate courts. The distinction between an initial trial and an appeal has less significance from a procedural and constitutional standpoint. Despite a seemingly clear constitutional prohibition on double jeopardy, it does not attach until all appeals have been exhausted or waived. Prosecutors thus can and do appeal acquittals or even lenient sentences. As early as 1950 the Supreme Court upheld prosecutorial appeals of acquittals, finding that "double jeopardy" did not attach until the trial was complete, including exhaustion of appeals (Supreme Court, Grand Bench judgment of September 27, 1950).

Both defendants and prosecutors can appeal a judgment as well as those dispositions or orders when not otherwise prohibited (CCP article 351). Attorneys or other legal representatives may also appeal on the defendant's behalf (article 353). Appeals by defendants cannot result in a more stringent punishment (article 402), though prosecutors may appeal both convictions and punishments they consider too lenient, neither of which violate the constitutional prohibition on double jeopardy. Persons other than the defendant and the prosecutor who are affected by a court's disposition may also have appeal rights, though not the right to appeal the judgment itself (article 352).

Appeals are one area where Japanese legal terminology demonstrates great precision, since there are numerous terms having a specific meaning within the context of Japanese criminal (and, where applicable, civil) procedure. First there is *jōsō*, the generic term referring to various types of appeal. These are then further categorized as follows:

(a) Kōso Appeals

Kōso is the term used to refer to appeals from the judgment (*hanketsu*) reached in the initial trial at a summary or district court (CCP article 372). Unlike civil proceedings where appeals from the summary court are first heard by the applicable district court, in criminal cases *kōso* appeals from both types of court are made to the applicable high court. *Kōso* appeals must be filed within 14 days of the rendering of the judgment and may be based on a variety of grounds including procedural violations, mistaken application of law, inappropriate sentence, mistake of fact, change in circumstances after closing argument, or grounds that would justify a new trial if the judgment was confirmed (articles 377 through 383).

Appellate courts must examine the claims in the notice of appeal, and may also examine other potential grounds for overturning a judgment that are not mentioned (CCP article 392). They may review the lower court's finding of facts when relevant and may rely on the evidence presented at the first trial, but are limited in their ability to consider new evidence that was not presented at the proceedings below. There is some debate about *how* limited. A 1984 Supreme Court ruling held that with respect to facts in existence at the time of the initial trial, the appellate court may in exceptional circumstances consider evidence that was not submitted at the trial (Supreme Court, 1st Petty Bench judgment of September 29, 1984). To the extent the appeal is based on changed circumstances after final arguments, new evidence must be considered because of the nature of the appeal (articles 382–2, 393(1)).

Although Japanese courts generate a famously high conviction rate at initial trial, what is more shocking is that most of the few acquittals which do occur at the initial trial are overturned on appeal. According to the MOJ's Crime White Paper, of 6,078 *kōso* appeals filed in 2015, 4,321 were rejected and 1,144 withdrawn. Of these 570 were overturned, but 549 saw the appellate court rendering a judgment of full or partial conviction in place of the lower court decision. There were only 21 instances of an initial conviction being changed to an acquittal on appeal.

Judgments rendered under the lay judge system are also subject to *kōso* appeals to high court panels of three judges just like those of other criminal trials initiated at the district court level. There have been several instances of high courts overturning acquittals by *saiban'in* trials, though at least a few of those were subsequently overturned by the Supreme Court.

(b) Jōkoku Appeals

Jōkoku refers to the last stage of the appellate process. Criminal *Jōkoku* appeals are heard by the Supreme Court (usually a Petty Bench), and are made from initial or appellate decisions rendered by high courts. Unlike *kōso* appeals, *jōkoku* appeals can only be made on a limited range of points of law. Article 405 of the CCP only recognizes very narrow grounds for *jōkoku* appeals, *i.e.*, the lower court opinion: (1) was contrary to the constitution or interpreted the constitution incorrectly, (2) was contrary to existing supreme court jurisprudence or (3) was contrary to appellate court precedent in cases where there is no applicable Supreme Court precedent. Under article 406 the court may also grant appeals in cases involving significant matters of interpretation of law.

Most *jōkoku* appeals are unsuccessful. Of 1,891 such criminal appeals in 2015, 82.8% were rejected and 16.8% withdrawn. While many defendants appeal to the Supreme Court, the result for most is a standard form one page judgment stating that their appeal only asserts an error of fact or error of law on the part of the lower court, but fails to state a claim satisfying the requirements of article 405.

Under article 411 of the CCP, courts hearing *jōkoku* appeals may also vacate lower court judgments even if the criteria of article 405 are not satisfied in cases involving various criteria which essentially constitute manifest injustice. Thus, although the Supreme Court does not formally consider appeals regarding factual errors, on rare occasions it will use its discretionary powers to vacate a conviction where it appears the lower court proceedings have been (too) blatantly pro-prosecution.

Once *jōkoku* appeals are completed the judgment in the case is considered confirmed (CCP articles 415 and 418). Further relief can only be obtained through a new trial (see discussion below).

(c) Kōkoku Appeals

Kōkoku appeals are made not against the judgment of the court, but against the decisions (*kettei*) and orders (*meirei*) of the court on procedural and other matters (see explanation at Chapter 5). There are two principal types of *kōkoku* appeals normal (*tsūjō*) and immediate (*sokuji*). Unless otherwise permitted by law, most such appeals are of the "normal" category (CCP article 419). Because of the potential interference with the trial process, the CCP does not allow *kōkoku* appeals against pre-judgment decisions relating to jurisdiction or litigation procedure, except in connection with bail, detention or confiscation (article 420) Most complaints about jurisdiction or process can be dealt with through a *kōso* appeal of the judgment.

Normal *kōkoku* appeals can otherwise be made at any time, but trial proceedings are not suspended pending their resolution unless the trial court decides to do so (article 424). Immediate *kōkoku* appeals are made where permitted by the CCP or elsewhere (for example, certain decisions on the disclosure of evidence in pretrial proceedings under articles 316–26(3) and 316–27(3)). Immediate *kōkoku* appeals must be filed within three days and suspend the trial until resolved (article 422, 425). *Kōkoku* appeals are made to the high court but in order to minimize the burden on the appellate court, the trial court must first review the order or disposition being appealed and either revise it or refer it to the high court with an opinion (article 423).

Additional and further appeals from the decision by a high court on a *kōkoku* appeal are not permitted (CCP articles 427 and 428). However an objection (*igi no mōshitate*) can be filed against the high court's decision, and if a decision or order that cannot otherwise be appealed meets the requirements for a *jōkoku* appeal under article 405 (e.g., constitutional violation, etc.), then a *tokubetsu* (special) *kōkoku* appeal may also be made to the Supreme Court.

(d) Junkōku Quasi-Appeals

While not considered for appeals, an additional remedy for parties alleging error by lower courts are *junkōkoku* (quasi-appeal) proceedings. These can be made against rejections of recusal motions, decisions about bail or detention and certain other dispositions when made by a summary court judge, and are resolved by the applicable district or, if a juvenile case, family court (CCP article 429). Quasi-appeals can also be filed against decisions made by prosecutors or police regarding the time and place of meetings between defendants or suspects and their counsel under CCP article 39(3), or regarding seized items (article 430). Since these latter dispositions are made by executive branch agencies rather than courts, they would normally be decisions subject to challenge through the administrative litigation process, but given their close linkage to the criminal trial process the CCP creates a special exception (article 430).

(ix) New Trials

Once a criminal judgment is confirmed through the exhaustion of appeals, the principal remedy for wrongful conviction is through a motion for a new trial under articles 435–436 of the CCP. Such requests may only be with respect to convictions. Although theoretically a motion could be made for a retrial to seek a reduced punishment, in practice they are only made to challenge the conviction itself.

It is very difficult to successfully obtain a new trial, the grounds for requesting one being limited to circumstances such as fraud or tampering with evidence in the initial trial, fraudulent testimony or other problems, or the discovery of new evidence of innocence or mitigating factor (article 435). That said, in recent years DNA evidence has been used successfully in connection with motions for new trials, including the Hakamada Case discussed earlier in this chapter.

According to a statistical survey published by the Supreme Court, during the five year period leading up to and including 2011, 1151 persons filed for new trials in criminal cases (by comparison, during the same period 367,612 persons were convicted in trial proceedings, and 2.23 million convicted in summary proceedings). Of the new trial motions, 1090 had been resolved within the period, of which 40 resulted in an order to start a new trial. Interestingly in 36 of these 40 successful instances, the motion for a new trial had been requested by *prosecutors* (prosecutors being able to do so under article 439 of the CCP). The majority of these cases were traffic violations or criminal negligence cases where, for example, the convicted person had "taken the fall" for the real offender in summary proceedings.

The number of instances in which a motion for a new trial is successful when made by someone other than the prosecutor (the convict or their legal representative, for example) are vanishingly few. This nicely illustrates how decisions about whether someone will be punished or not are essentially driven by prosecutors rather than the courts through the entire cycle of the criminal trial process.

k. Juvenile Crime

For cases involving offenses by minors (under the age of 20), a very different set of procedures set forth in the Juvenile Act of 1948 are followed. The stated purpose of the Juvenile Act is to "to subject delinquent Juveniles to protective measures to correct their personality traits and modify their environment, and to implement special measures for juvenile criminal cases, for the purpose of Juveniles' sound development" (article 1). Therefore, juvenile proceedings are heavily focused on rehabilitation rather than punishment.

The Juvenile Act draws a key distinction at the age of 14. Offenders under that age are generally not punished for criminal acts, except in exceptional circumstances. Offenders under the age of 14 are typically remanded by police to child welfare offices, which may decide to refer the case to a family court. Those aged 14 and above who commit minor crimes are remanded by police directly to family courts. Those who commit serious crimes are first sent to the public prosecutors officer for referral to the family court as a criminal case. When detention of the minor is necessary pending proceedings, this is done at the order of the family court and carried out at special facilities rather than police jails or adult detention facilities.

Family courts have special investigators (family court investigators, see discussion at Chapter 7) who interact with juvenile offenders and, together with the family court judge, determine the appropriate protective measures (*hogo shobun*) or other dispositions to make. There are three types of protective measures—ordering probation, referral to a children's self-reliance support facility or foster home, or referral to a juvenile training school (Juvenile Act, article 24(1). The court may also decide no action should be taken or that it is more appropriate to refer the child to the local child welfare agency for appropriate action under the Child Welfare Act (articles 18 and 19).

If the family court determines that punishment is more appropriate for a juvenile who commits a serious offense (one punishable by death or imprisonment), it may refer the case back to prosecutors for prosecution through proceedings similar to those for adults, with the offender being appointed to state appointed counsel. As a general rule, offenders aged 16 or older whose crime results in death must be prosecuted. Offenders under the age of 18 at the time they committed the offense are subject to reduced sentences for serious crimes, the Juvenile Act providing for imprisonment for indefinite term in lieu of a death sentence and imprisonment for 10–15 years in lieu of imprisonment for indefinite term (articles 51 and 52).

l. Amnesties

Although not framed in terms of procedural or constitutional rights, Article 7 of the constitution anticipates that "general and special amnest[ies], commutation[s] of punishment, reprieve[s], and restoration[s] of rights" may be conducted as acts in matters of state by the Emperor, upon the advice and consent of the Cabinet. The details of these procedures are provided for in the Pardon Act of 1947.

Amnesties result in the dissolution of a criminal record, while other dispensations in the list simply reduce or prematurely end punishments and/or restore rights otherwise lost due to a conviction. General amnesties are declared by cabinet order and are rare, the last one being in connection with the funeral of Emperor Hirohito. More limited special amnesties have also been declared on special occasions (e.g., the marriage of the current emperor in 1959, the 100th anniversary of the Meiji Restoration in 1968, and the restoration of Japanese sovereignty over Okinawa in 1972) for those meeting certain enunciated standards. There has been some criticism of these amnesties since the standards were defined so that most of those who benefited were persons convicted of electoral law violations.

Requests for special amnesties, reductions of punishment or other special dispensations are handled through the MOJ's National Offenders Rehabilitation Commission pursuant to article 4 of the Offenders Rehabilitation Act of 2007. The

Commission does not seem particularly magnanimous; for example in 2014 it granted only 5 reprieves and 29 restorations.

4. Wire-Tapping, Surveillance and Other Investigatory Tools

The right to the privacy of communications is well-established, being one of the rights enumerated under the Meiji Constitution as well as the current charter (articles 26 and 21(2), respectively). In theory, various constitutional hurdles need to be overcome by law enforcement seeking to conduct investigations that involve intercepting voice or data communications.

Surveillance of private communications in connection with criminal investigations is conducted under a special statute, the Act on Wiretapping for Criminal Investigation of 1999, the existence of which is anticipated in article 222–2 of the CCP, which was added the same year. Prior to this, wiretapping was conducted under the existing generic (at the time) provisions of the CCP allowing searches and seizures for purposes of investigations pursuant to a judicial warrant, notwithstanding article 197(1) of the CCP which states that forcible investigatory measures are not allowed unless specifically provided for in the code.

This was found not to be prima facie unconstitutional by the Supreme Court in a 1999 decision in which one judge dissented (Supreme Court, 3rd Petty Bench decision of December 16, 1999). By the time the decision was issued however, the wiretapping act in the preceding paragraph had already come into force and necessary amendments made to the CCP. That act was originally drafted to allow wiretapping in investigations of a very narrow range of specific crimes. According to MOJ statistics 40 warrant requests were made and all granted in 2016.

An amendment to the Wiretapping Act made the same year dramatically expanded the scope of offenses for which warrants may be requested, and also removed the burdensome requirement that a representative of the telecommunications services provider be present when the wiretapping takes place.

2011 amendments to the CCP (article 99) have also facilitated the seizure by warrant of data on servers connected to a telecommunications circuit through data extraction in connection with criminal investigations. Prior to this, police investigating cyber-crimes had to seize the server itself.

The widespread use of mobile phones and GPS has also made it relatively easy to locate and track the movements of a person holding a device enabled with such technology. While not "communications" such information is considered personal information protected by the Personal Information Protection Act of 2003 and generally requires a warrant to access for purposes of a criminal investigation. Interestingly, the MIC's Guidelines for The Handling of Personal Information by Telecommunications Business Operators (2017 edition) clearly anticipate that location information (and other information about telecommunications service users) can also be provided to authorities in circumstances other than a criminal investigation (e.g., when lives are at risk, etc.; Guidelines, article 35).

In 2017, the Supreme Court held that placement by police of GPS trackers on a suspect's car should require a warrant pursuant to article 35 (Supreme Court, Grand Bench judgment of March 15, 2017). While putatively rejecting the validity of evidence against the defendant, it nevertheless found the remaining evidence adequate to uphold the conviction.

Outside the sphere of criminal investigations, businesses may be subject to administrative investigations by authorities that can require the disclosure of records. Since these usually take place within the framework of a regulatory scheme they are not considered compulsory measures in connection with a criminal investigation, meaning judicial oversight or warrants are not required. Since the regulators conducting the investigations may be the police in some instances, the distinction may seem largely theoretical. For example, article 26 of the Tokyo Prefectural Anti-Violent Crime Group Ordinance of 2011 empowers police to enter premises, demand documents and ask questions to confirm compliance with the Ordinance's restrictions on conducting business with violent crime groups. Paragraph (3) of article 26 helpfully says that the authority given to police should not be interpreted as powers of criminal investigation.

D. PRISONS AND OTHER DETENTION FACILITIES

Shortly after the Meiji restoration Japan started developing western-modeled penal institutions. This culminated in the enactment of the Prison Act of 1908, at the time one of the world's first comprehensive statutes on prisons and the treatment of inmates. After governing Japan's prison system for almost a century, it was replaced by the 2005 Act on Penal Detention Facilities and Treatment of Inmates and Detainees (Penal Facilities Act) and subsequent amendments to that act. The impetus for this legislation was driven in part by abuses resulting in death and injury to a number of inmates of Nagoya Prison. Under this new regime prisons are supposedly subject to greater external oversight.

The Penal Facilities Act governs the treatment of inmates and detainees in all penal detention facilities involved in the criminal justice system (keiji shūyō shisetsu), which includes penal institutions (*keiji shisetsu*) and detention facilities (*ryūchi shisetsu*). Detention facilities are essentially the jails (*ryūchijo*) under the control of the police (or as applicable, the Coast Guard). Penal institutions are under the jurisdiction of the MOJ.

Penal institutions are further categorized as prisons, juvenile prisons and *kōchisho*, a term that is best translated "detention center" even though they are not *ryūchijo* detention facilities of the type referenced in the preceding paragraph. This confusing distinction is important: under article 3 of the Penal Facilities Act *penal institutions* are intended principally for the detention of persons who: (i) have been arrested, (ii) who are being detained for pre-charge investigation pursuant to a judicial warrant, (iii) who are imprisoned with or without work as punishment, or (iv) are awaiting execution of a death sentence. However, under article 15, many detainees—those in categories (i) and (ii) in particular—can be housed in police detention facilities. This represents the recodification of the long long-criticized practice of *daiyō kangoku*, the use of police jails for the prolonged detention of criminal suspects before they are charged with anything and while their trial is pending if they are.

At the pre-charging stage, this means that suspects are being investigated by the same people who, at an institutional level, are responsible for feeding them, giving them medical attention if necessary and protecting their human rights. As discussed elsewhere in this chapter, with the cooperation of prosecutors police can detain suspects for weeks before making a decision to commence a prosecution, during which period access to counsel and contact with family members can be severely restricted. The use of police jails to house suspects before they are formally charged is frequently identified as a hotbed of coerced confessions.

As of 2011 Japan had 62 prisons, 7 juvenile prisons, 8 detention centers, 8 branch prisons and 103 branch detention centers (*i.e.*, penal institutions), including several privately-financed institutions. The number of penal institutions is dwarfed by the approximately 1,200 detention facilities maintained by the police. One of the arguments in favor of using detention facilities for suspects and defendants awaiting trial is that they are numerous and generally more likely to be in a convenient location *vis-à-vis* courthouses.

As for prisons and other detention facilities, they are geographically dispersed across eight administrative districts under the jurisdiction of the MOJ's corrections bureau. Prisons are further categorized into various types, including medical prisons and women's prisons. Most inmates are male, however, and for them the principal distinction is whether they are deemed to have advanced criminal tendencies or not, with another factor being the length of their sentence. In other words a key feature of the Japanese prison involves separating those who may redeemable from those who are hardened criminals.[9]

This is a reflection of the rehabilitative focus of the Japanese criminal justice system, which generally seeks to avoid sending convicted criminals to prison in the first place (as a punishment) whenever possible, and if they do have to be sent to prison to get them out as soon as possible. Prisons have factories or other work facilities (one in Shikoku is connected to a shipyard), where most prisoners must work as part of their punishment. Some prisons have gift shops selling wares made by prisoners. Convicts are intended to learn useful skills as well as develop discipline, routines and other life skills they might have lacked in their lives in the outside world.

Note that the term "juvenile prison" is somewhat misleading. Although intended for the punishment of juveniles convicted of serious offenses and thus even more focused on redemption, it may also be used to house young adults in their twenties or even older who are deemed redeemable. Juvenile prisons may also be used as a *rōekijō* (workhouse), places where those sentenced to penal fines but unwilling or unable to pay them work off their payment obligation.

As of 2015, the daily average population of those confined in Japanese penal institutions was 59,670, a significant reduction from the 80,684 of 2006. Of this 59,670 number, 806 were persons working of fines in prison and 6,456 were suspects under detention pending resolution of their trials, though bear in mind that this number does not include suspects detained in police jails. According to NPA statistics, in 2015 police jails accommodated an average of 9,500 detainees a day for a cumulative annual total of 3,482,190 detainees (doubtless including a significant component of prolonged and frequent visitors).

Of the 59,670 in penal institutions in 2015, 4,981 (8.3%) were women and approximately 5.5% were foreign nationals, with Chinese nationals being the most numerous followed by Brazilians. In recent years, the graying of Japan's prison population is a notable trend. Of those newly entering penal institutions in 2015, 17%

---

[9] Regardless of their criminal tendencies, non-Japanese inmates tend to be concentrated in the small number of prisons that are better equipped to deal with their different dietary requirements and inability to understand Japanese.

were 60 or older, a marked increase from 11.3% in 2006. Stories of ex-convicts shoplifting or committing some other minor offense so they can go back to prison are a recurring story in the news.

The various types of penal institutions are not defined in the Penal Facilities Act, being provided instead under the MOJ Establishment Act of 1999 (MOJEA). In addition to the three categories of penal institutions addressed by the Penal Facilities Act, the MOJEA also anticipates the establishment of other quasi-penal facilities. These include juvenile classification home (*shōnenkanbetsusho*) and juvenile training schools (*shōnen'in*), where young offenders are observed, evaluated and ideally treated for (the former) and sent for more structured, possibly punitive reform and training (the latter) pursuant to the Juvenile Act. Although under the MOJ Bureau of Corrections, these are not "penal institutions" for purposes of the Penal Facilities Act.

In addition to the above, the MOJ also maintains three immigration detention centers (euphemistically called "immigration centers") where non-Japanese who have violated immigration laws are remanded pending deportation. The treatment of detainees in these facilities has been the subject of criticism resulting in a recent review of procedures and policies. Detention in one of these centers may involve a prolonged deprivation of liberty without a criminal trial, but this is not deemed constitutionally problematic in that the guarantee of constitutional rights accorded to non-Japanese is generally preconditioned on their being in the country lawfully.

E. ORGANIZED CRIME GROUPS

Japan is famous for its organized crime groups traditionally known as "yakuza." This is not a legal term though, and most statutes refer to either "violent groups" (*bōryokudan*) or organized crime. A significant part of Japan's criminal law and the efforts that go into its enforcement are devoted to stamping out organized crime or at least keeping it in its place, which has traditionally been in areas such as prostitution, loan sharking, illegal gambling, drugs, guns and other contraband. Organized crime groups expressed a prescient early interest in corporate governance through the institution of *sōkaiya*, the practice of acquiring a few shares in a company and then threatening to expose embarrassing information at the company's annual meeting of shareholders and/or offering to keep other shareholders in line. A whole set of corporate criminal law has arisen around combating this practice, and the assertion of shareholders rights is one example where rights assertion has become associated with a form of extortion.

Yakuza have long been an iconic presence in Japanese popular culture, wearing gaudy white suits, with curly "punch perm" hairstyles, and being about the only people in Japan who drove Cadillacs (before White Mercedes became all the rage). In the past they had identified headquarter buildings, business cards and played a role in society that police seemed willing to tolerate so long as they kept to their turf. The yakuza even provided an alternative dispute resolution mechanism in the form of debt collection, eviction or other services where the civil litigation and enforcement process may have been inadequate. Police authorities still occasionally place posters in train stations encouraging citizens to not fear, pay money to or *use* violent crime groups.

Although somewhat romanticized, Yakuza supposedly lived by a code that minimized the trouble they caused to innocent "civilians" (unless they came looking for it). Strict fealty to senior gangsters was expected, and junior members who ran afoul of the Yakuza code were expected to sever part of their little finger as a sign of contrition. Another aspect of this culture involves younger gang members turning themselves over to the police to be punished for crimes committed by senior members. Being a junior gangster may also involve "renting out" one's *koseki* for visa-related paper marriages to foreign women brought into Japan for prostitution.

In recent years, however, there has been a concentrated effort by law enforcement to eliminate such gangs or at least drive them underground. This includes a number of statutory regimes. The first is the "Act on Prevention of Unjust Acts by Organized Crime Group Members" of 1991. This helped resolve a basic definitional problem by creating a definition of "violent group" and empowering public safety commissions to designate groups as such. It also contained a prohibition on various criminal activities traditionally associated with such groups (protection rackets, debt collection, etc.) and allowed citizens harmed by gang members to sue the gang boss for damages in tort.

Another law is the Act on Punishment of Organized Crimes and Control of Crime Proceeds of 1999. This further expands the scope of definition of organized crime group, forms the basis for Japan's anti-money laundering regime, and established enhanced penalties for certain offenses when committed as part of the activities of an organized crime group. 2017 amendments to this law added a wide range of conspiracy offenses to the corpus of Japanese penal laws.

Finally, each prefecture in the country now has an anti-organized crime exclusion ordinance in place which prevents business from having any commercial dealings with members of organized crime groups or even persons "having a close relationship with them"—effectively rendering gang affiliation a form of status crime. Although these are not laws, because they exist in every prefecture they in many ways have the collective effect of a statute, though not one that has gone through the rigors of the Diet legislative process.

Chapter 9

THE CIVIL CODE, FAMILY, IDENTITY AND THE CIVIL LAW INFRASTRUCTURE

Analysis

This chapter will give an overview of the basic framework for Japan's system of private law, though it involves a number of public law elements as well. The focus of the following pages will be on three basic components of that system: (1) personal identity and family status, (2) property rights and (3) other private rights and obligations outside the business context. Many of these components are derived primarily from the Civil Code of 1896, an overview of which is necessary before dealing with the individual components.

A. THE CIVIL CODE: HISTORY AND STRUCTURE

1. Overview

The Civil Code (*minpō*) is one of Japan's most fundamental statutes. it sets forth most of the basic rules of civil society in Japan, though many of these have been modified or supplemented by special or supplementary legislation, some of which are themselves significant statutory regimes. The Civil Code is thus the foundation on which many other laws are built. For this reason, although *minpō* (literally "civil law") is the name of Civil Code, the same term is sometimes used to refer to the broader universe of Japanese private law generally, with *minpōten* (the "ten" meaning "code") being used when it needs to be made clear that the subject of discussion is specifically the Civil Code alone.

Because it has been the foundation of Japanese civil law for over a century, the Code is hard to amend, since doing so may necessitate conforming changes to countless other laws rooted in or derived from it. When in 2017 Part III of the Code was significantly amended for the first time in 120 years, together with the amendments to the Code itself a separate 200 page bill had to be passed in order to make the necessary conforming amendments to scores of other statutes.

The Code establishes the underlying conceptual framework through which most civil disputes are understood and resolved, and its provisions are usually the starting point for analyzing many legal problems. However simply relying on the Code would be a terrible mistake since many of its often sparse provisions have been supplemented, expanded, subjected to exceptions or effectively amended through other laws and judicial interpretations.

Japan's Civil Code predates the current constitution by half a century. Its older vintage may explain why it sometimes seems more important than the national charter. When provisions of the two basic laws conflict, the Supreme Court has generally allowed the Civil Code to prevail, at least until recently. For example, despite Article 24 of the Constitution appearing to clearly mandate gender equality specifically in the domain of family law, the prohibition on women only remarrying for a certain period after marital dissolution contained in Article 733 survived a constitutional challenge in a 1995 Supreme Court before being found only partially unconstitutional as to the length of the period of prohibition in 2015 (Supreme Court, 3rd Petty Bench judgment of December 5, 1995; Supreme Court, Grand Bench judgment of December 16, 2015). This deference may also be a reflection of a view that the Code is positive law while the Constitution is more a statement of principles to be implemented through further legislation in which the Diet is accorded a wide degree of discretion.

Not having common law roots Japan's civil justice system lacks a distinction between law and equity either substantively or procedurally. The characterization of remedies and the way the flexibility needed to achieve just results in individual cases is built into the Code in a way that may thus seem unusual to common law practitioners.

2. History

As discussed in Chapter 2, the enactment of modern, western-style civil and commercial laws was a pressing matter for the government of Meiji Japan. In order to remove the so-called unequal treaties meant westerners had to be comfortable not only with the criminal justice system, but the manner and rules by which disputes were resolved when they arose in commercial dealings with Japanese counterparts in Japanese courts under Japanese law. This in turn meant developing basic rules of society familiar and acceptable to westerners, particularly those relating to property and contract.

In the late 19th century the French Civil Code was regarded by many jurists (outside the common law tradition, at least) as the epitome of jurisprudential sophistication. It was already the basis for laws adopted in European colonies and developing nations, offering a model that was relatively compact and easy to copy, at least compared to common law alternatives. The government of early Meiji Japan thus naturally looked to Napoleon's code as a source of a basic law that would be acceptable to westerners.

The government also looked to Gustave Boissanade, the French legal scholar who came to Japan in 1873 and ended up staying for 21 years, playing an influential role in the early development of Japan's modern legal system. Involved in developing Japan's first Penal Code, he was not asked to turn to the Civil Code until a draft had already been produced by the government in 1877. That draft was effectively a Japanese translation of the French code, an unsuccessful effort that was abandoned.

Working with Japanese colleagues and taking into account the results of a nationwide survey of Japan's commercial and social practices as well as other European continental codes, Boissanade's draft was completed (in French) in 1886. Political disputes interceded and the Civil Code provisions based on his draft were not approved by the Imperial Diet until 1890, with the relevant laws scheduled to take effect three years later. However almost immediately after its passage the code was subject to criticism that it had been rushed through the Diet too hurriedly in the name of removing the unequal treaties. There was also criticism that parts of it did not adequately account for well-established Japanese practices, particularly with respect to family and inheritance matters. In 1891, a law was passed delaying the Code coming into effect.

By this time the influence of German (Prussian) law was growing among some Japanese scholars and officials and the Civil Code that was ultimately passed into law at the end of the nineteenth century was also influenced by what at the time was still a draft of the German Civil Code (which was not enacted until 1900). Although Boissanade's code did not surivive, it had a lasting influence on what did become the Civil Code. Moreover, Japan's law makers continued to look to the French Code, as well as the laws of Spain, Belgium, Italy and other Western countries as references. Even today, a professor of Civil Code-related subjects would likely be expected to be able to read both French and German (as well as English).

The present Civil Code was enacted in 1896 and took effect in 1898. Despite the complaints about the family and inheritance parts of the earlier draft code, some of those provisions from the earlier draft were incorporated into the version that became law with only minor amendments. While foreign observers may be tempted to regard the family law provisions of the Civil Code as being derived from "ancient" Japanese family traditions, the drafting process reveals it to be the product of more recent imperatives and influences, including an awareness of 19th century Euorpean family law.

As discussed later in this chapter, significant changes to the family and inheritance provisions of Parts IV and V of the Code came later during the post-war occupation period. These took the form of amendments intended to make the Code consistent with the new constitution (particularly the equality provisions of articles 14 and 24), and to eliminate the "head of household" system which the Americans viewed as having facilitated the rise of militarism and totalitarianism.

3. Structure and Composition

The Civil Code is structured similarly to the European Pandectist codes that existed at the time of its enactment. For those who learned law the "American way" through the seemingly random hodgepodge of cases and statutes used at U.S. law schools to teach torts, contracts and other areas of private law as discrete subjects, the structure, organization and completeness of the Code may come as a revelation.

The Code consists of 1044 numbered articles organized across five Parts. However, the actual number of articles is not 1044. A number of provisions have been deleted, and others added. As already mentioned in Chapter 5, in order to avoid needing torenumber cross-references with each such change, deleted provisions have been left in place marked "deleted" and new provisions are added in the appropriate place as additional articles.

A brief summary of each Part follows. More detailed discussions of some of the key areas of law contained in or derived from the Code (such as family law) follow later in this chapter.

a. Part I: General Principles (Articles 1 Through 174–2)

(i) Overview

Part I contains many of the general provisions of interpretation and application that appear to apply to the entire Code, similar to Article 1 of the American Uniform

Commercial Code. However, with some exceptions these provisions are thought to apply mostly only to Part II and III, with different rules applying to the family and inheritance provisions of Parts IV and V. For example, although article 3(1) states that the capacity to enjoy private rights commences at birth, article 886 accords inheritance rights to unborn children by presuming them born.

(ii) Foundational Principles

The foregoing caveat notwithstanding, Part I begins with several statements of foundational principle that do inform not only the interpretation of the entirety of the Code in general, but other laws as well. These can be found in articles 1 and 2, which are reproduced in full below. Both articles were added to the Code when it was amended in 1947, but the substance reflects doctrines that had become well-established through prior court practice.

Article 1

(1) Private rights must conform to the public welfare.

(2) The exercise of rights and performance of duties must be done in good faith.

(3) No abuse of rights is permitted.

Article 2

This Code must be construed in accordance with honoring the dignity of individuals and the essential equality of both sexes.

Paragraph (1) of article 1 is noteworthy due to its use of the term "private rights" and their clear subjugation to the public good, particularly when compared to the French Civil Code, the corresponding provision of which refers to "civil rights" (*droits civil*). It reflects the clear historical distinction between private law and public law, one that saw the judicial courts lacking jurisdiction over administrative law matters under the Meiji Constitutional system. The distinction between private rights asserted as between individuals and public rights asserted against government remains under the current constitution, though claims rooted in Civil Code provisions and concepts still inform the manner in which some claims against the government are brought, particularly tort claims under the State Redress Act.

Paragraph (2) of article 1 establishes a broad duty of good faith applicable to private dealings. There are various theories about whether the provision should be limited to a "gap filling" role in resolving other disputes or can form the basis for claims in specific cases. The principle of good faith (*shingisoku*) has been applied in numerous Supreme Court decisions, and forms the basis for what in Anglo-American law would likely be considered equitable doctrines, such as laches or, depending on the circumstances, estoppel. It has also been used to find pre-contractual liability in cases where the negotiation process results in the reasonable expectation that a contract will be entered into.

Paragraph (3) of the same article introduces the concept of "abuse of rights." This legal doctrine will likely be familiar to those trained in the European continental laws in which Japan's Civil Code is rooted, but may seem alien to Anglo-American lawyers. Yet abuse of rights is another source of what in common law systems would be characterized as equitable rights and principles. One of the classic examples of this doctrine being applied before it was even formally expressed in article 1 is a 1935 case involving a landowner who had purchased land transversed by a pipe supplying hot water to a hot springs resort. The landowner demanded the owner either remove the pipe or buy the land at an astronomical price. Finding in favor of the resort operator, the Supreme Court of Judicature found the landowner's assertion of property rights to be abusive (Supreme Court of Judicature judgment of October 5, 1935).

In the post war period, abuse of rights has been used in a variety of other contexts, including as a means of severely restricting the right of employers to terminate employment contracts and even of litigants to assert the passage of statutory claims periods (Supreme Court 2nd Petty Bench judgment of April 25, 1975 and Supreme Court 3rd Petty Bench judgment of May 25, 1976). The doctrine has also been used to effectively create a "right to sunlight and air," by finding the construction of tall buildings that cast shade and block wind to be an abuse of property rights (Supreme Court, 3rd Petty Bench judgment of June 27, 1972).

Article 2 was added to the Code in 1947 to ensure that private law was consistent with articles 13, 14 and 24 of the Constitution. At risk of oversimplification, the provisions of both article 1 and 2 should be considered applicable throughout the vast body of private law rooted in the Civil Code, subject of course to the legislative discretion accorded to the Diet in protecting and furthering public welfare.

Japanese judges often use the phrase "*shakai tsūnen*"—notions generally accepted by society—to justify some of the conclusions set forth in their judgments. They are also sometimes derided for doing so because their elite status and deliberate isolation from society make them seem particularly unsuited to opine on how society at large views things. However it should be remembered that in some instances the phrase may be serving as a shorthand for the principles encapsulated in the first two articles of the Civil Code, or at least the judge's views of how they are reflected in the "common wisdom."

(iii) The Rest of Part I

The subsequent chapters of Part I set forth in an orderly fashion some of the basic rules of law that some American law students may still have to struggle to derive from court precedents. Chapter 2 (articles 3 through 32–2) deals with natural persons, and sets forth the rules of majority[1] and capacity, as well as the rules of guardianship for those whose capacity is impaired. A basic component of most people's identity—address or place of residence—is also addressed in this Chapter.

Chapter 3 (articles 33 through 84) contain (or contained) many of the basic rules of juristic persons—corporate identity and capacity. However most of these were removed and replaced by the Companies Act when it was passed in 2005 and by the Act on General Incorporated Associations and General Incorporated Foundations. Accordingly, articles 38 through 84 of the Code are now simply marked "deleted."

Chapter 4 (articles 85 through 89) contains just five articles on the subject of "things," defining them as tangible items (article 85). Article 86 establishes land and

---

[1] Article 4 of the Civil Code currently sets the age of majority at 20. This has never been applied consistently with other provisions of the Code allowing for marriage at a younger age, and other ages applying through different statutes for conduct such as driving and criminal liability. In 2016 the voting age was lowered to 18, and immediately before publication the Diet had passed a law changing the age of majority in article 4 to 18.

fixtures upon it as immovable property (*fudōsan*) and everything else as movable property (*dōsan*). The fruits of "things" are further categorized between "natural" and "legal" fruits.

Chapter 5 (articles 90 through 137) deals with juristic or legal acts, and contains provisions relating to expressions of intent, including the impact of fraud, duress and mistake. The rules of agency and those relating to void and voidable acts, conditions precedent, performance deadlines and acceleration of obligations are also contained in this chapter.

Article 90 states that "A juristic act with any purpose which is against public policy is void." Unfortunately the "public policy" in the Japanese government's English translation does not do justice to the nuances in the original; the Japanese might be more accurately translated as "public order and good social mores."

Article 90 has been used to find numerous private law arrangements void, including gambling debts, illegal and abusive contracts as well as subjecting women employees to lower mandatory retirement ages than men (a form of discrimination subsequently remedied by statute). It also forms a basis for possibly finding constitutional norms to be applicable as between private actors, a theory that is supported by many academics but has found less clear acceptance in Supreme Court rulings.

Articles 91 and 92 accord a high degree of autonomy to parties in private law transactions, permitting them to override default rules of law to the extent not contrary to public policy. Article 91 says "If any party to a juristic act manifests any intention which is inconsistent with a provision in any laws and regulations not related to public policy, such intention shall prevail."

Article 92 allows for the possible application of custom in certain circumstances:

> In cases there is any custom which is inconsistent with a provision in any law or regulation not related to public policy, if it is found that any party to a juristic act has the intention to abide by such custom, such custom shall prevail.

Chapter 6 (articles 138 through 143) contains the basic rules for calculating time periods. Chapter 7 (articles 144 through 174) sets forth claims periods (statutes of limitations), their tolling and suspension, as well as prescriptive periods for adverse possession.

b. *Part II: Real Rights (Articles 175 Through 398–22)*

Recall from the immediately preceding discussion that Part I establishes the concept of "things" and further categorizes them as moveable property and immovable property. The Japanese term for thing—*mono*—is expressed using a character that is also pronounced *butsu* and which in combination with the character for right—*ken*—creates *bukken*, the Japanese title for Part II. Thus, although the Japanese government English translation renders this "real rights" this term may confuse because of its similarity to "real property." For consistency, this chapter will use the term "real rights," but it is perhaps more helpful to think of *bukken* as "rights in things." Considering them this way also helps to distinguish them from *saiken* (claims) addressed in Part III of the Code, which are effectively rights in a claim against a person (see subsection c. following).

Part II contains ten chapters setting forth the rules on the creation, transfer, encumbrance and extinguishment of rights in real and personal property. Under article 175, real rights can *only* be created pursuant to the Code or other laws. The Civil Code recognizes ten types of real rights, which are discussed in more detail later in this chapter. Part II also contains various provisions that link real rights to claims under Part III; indeed, a number of categories of real rights are forms of security interest that can exist only in connection with monetary debts, a type of *saiken* claim.

Real rights are concepturalized as being *exclusive* in that they can be asserted against everyone in the world as to the thing in question. Even those real rights that are a form of non-possessory security interest are exclusive as compared to other security interests which will have a higher or lower priority. The rest of the world is also theoretically on notice of the existence of a person's real rights in a piece of real or moveable property either through the fact of possession or the title registry system, though as discussed below this is not always the case.

The exclusivity of real rights is a key difference between *bukken* and *saiken* claims under Part III. The latter can only be asserted against the specific debtor or obligor. There is of course much interaction between real rights and claims. In order to exercise real rights it is usually necessary to assert a claim, and a claim can result in the acquisition of a real right, such as through the performance of a land purchase agreement, or the enforcement of a debt against the debtor's property. In some cases it can be debatable whether a particular asset should be characterized as a real right or a claim. Leaving such cases aside, for purposes of this discussion, however, it is important to understand that the distinction between real rights and claims is basic to the Civil Code and related areas of private law.

c. *Part III: Claims (Articles 399 Through 724)*

With respect to Part III, a basic caveat is necessary. At the time of writing (2017), a wholesale amendment to Part III of the Civil Code was passed by the Diet, though the changes may not take effect until 2020. The bulk of the changes were rendered to the provisions relevant to contract law and represent the first wholesale restructuring of this part of the Code since it was enacted twelve decades ago. While some of these changes codify well established interpretive practices and precedents, others represent a change in approach. Accordingly, it is difficult to write about the *new* contract law and may not be meaningful to engage in an extended discussion of existing contract law either. What coverage is provided on the subject of contract law is contained in Chapter 11.

The Japanese term for claim—*saiken*—is expressed using two characters: *sai,* which means a debt or obligation (usually a monetary one, but not always), and *ken,* which means right. There is also an oppositional term—*saimu*—with *mu* meaning "duty." Together these two terms thus express the concept of a legal obligation (*saimu* being rendered in the government's English translation of the Code as "obligation"), but dependent upon the position of the party. *Saiken* is thus the right of the obligee to demand performance of the obligation and *saimu* the duty of the obligor to perform it. With *sha* (person) added at the end, *saikensha* and *saimusha* mean obligee and obligor or, depending on the context, creditor and debtor.

Yet "claims" may still be the best rendering, since a basic feature of a *saiken* is that it entitles the obligee to demand performance from the obligor and, if necessary, file a claim for such purposes in civil court. Most claims (e.g., arising under a contract) are either for the payment of money or are enforced through a suit for the payment of money damages (tort claims). With some types of claims other remedies are possible, such as an order to deliver a specific item of property or refrain from engaging in a particular type of conduct.

As previously noted, unlike real rights, which can be asserted against anyone, claims can generally only be asserted against a specific person or persons: the obligor(s). Another difference is that while the universe of real rights is limited to those specifically created by the Civil Code and other statutes, the universe of claims that can arise from contracts, torts or other acts or omissions is potentially unlimited, subject only to the bounds of legality, unconscionability, public policy and other similar doctrines.

The nature of a claim ultimately affects how it is pursued in court. While a wide range of claims is possible, all usually have to be characterized in terms of the categories of claim recognized by the Code or other statutes, or acknowledged by court practice and precedent. Claims can be categorized in terms of how they arise, for example through breach of contract, negligence, demand on a guarantee obligation or even unjust enrichment. The type of claim also affects how and if it can be enforced or assigned: a claim for monetary damages can be subdivided or assigned and discharged by receipt of payment from anyone, while a claim against a specific piece of property occupied by a particular person may offer fewer options.

A court order in favor of the plaintiff will itself give rise to a particular type of claim for the plaintiff and an obligation for the defendant (a judgment debt or obligation). How that claim is characterized (*i.e.,* how the *shubun* part of the judgment is expressed; see explanation at Chapter 5) affects its enforcement: an order to pay the plaintiff creates a claim to seek payment that can be satisfied against the defendant's property. By contrast, the claim that arises from an order to hand over a child subject to a custody dispute may be characterized as a claim to the delivery of the child or for *non-interference* by the defendant in the plaintiff taking custody of the child. Either way it obviously cannot be enforced against the defendant's property. The foundation of much of Japanese civil law in the concept of claims means that the anachronistic distinction between tort and contract which still prevails in Anglo-American law is less significant. Similarly, the lack of a distinction between law and equity means the choice of remedies is driven by a fairly rational characterization of the plaintiff's claim rather than the historical divide between the courts of common law and chancery.

Part III contains five chapters. The first (articles 399 to 520) is an extensive chapter setting forth the basic rules by which claims are defined and categorized. It includes rules for the treatment of divisible claims and indivisible claims, joint and several obligations, guarantee obligations, assignment of claims, the various ways in which claims can be discharged, extinguished or voided, how rights of set-off are exercised and so forth.

The second chapter (articles 521 to 696) contain the provisions governing contracts. These are discussed in more detail in Chapter 11. The third chapter (articles 697 to 702) deals with claims arising from the gratuitous management of business or affairs of another person (the Roman law concept of *negotiorum gestio*). Chapter 4 (articles 703 to 708) addressed unjust enrichment, and Chapter 5 (article 709 through 724) comprises the foundational tort provisions, which are discussed in more detail later below.

d. *Part IV: Relatives (Articles 725 Through 881)*

Part IV contains the family law provisions of the Civil Code, though it should be noted that nothing in the Civil Code or any other statute actually uses the term "family law." As its title suggests, Part IV is as much concerned with defining legally significant family relationships and how they are created and terminated as they are with the rights and duties of people within those relationships.

Together with the family register system discussed later in this chapter, the rules contained in Part IV form core components of legal identity and status. Some of these rules were amended substantially during occupation era reforms, but the current system can only be understood within the historical context of family structures that those reforms sought to eliminate and which are discussed later in this chapter.

Part IV is comprised of seven chapters. Chapter 1 (articles 725 through 730) contain general provisions establishing the parameters of what constitutes a "relative" (*shinzoku*) and how degrees of affinity calculated, including through adoptive relationships. Article 725 defines the term as including those within six degrees of relationship by blood, legal spouses, and those related within three degrees by affinity through marriage. The scope of who constitutes a relative is thus extremely broad, and in a large, long-lived family can encompass people who are for all intents and purposes strangers (e.g., the grandchildren of a great grandparent's nephew, uncles-in-law, etc.). Article 730 contains what appears to be a statutory obligation on the part of relatives having a lineal blood relationship or who cohabitate to support each other, though it is instead considered a precatory vestige of older family ideals.

Chapter 2 of Part IV (articles 731 through 771) contain the rules on marriage, annulment and divorce and their effect on property and debts. Chapter 3 (articles 772 to 817–11) deals with the formative aspects of the parent-child relationship (both natural and adoptive) including the rules of paternity and legitimacy. The Civil Code still contains provisions that treat children differently depending on whether a child was born in or out of wedlock. In 2013 the Supreme Court finally reversed prior precedent and found that a proviso in article 900 of the Code which accorded children born out of wedlock a lesser share of a decedent's estate violated the equal protection guarantee of the constitution (The *Legtitmacy-Based Discrimination in Inheritance Case* in Table 6-1 in Chapter 6). However, parents are still required to affirmatively report births out of wedlock, and the Civil Code still treats such children differently for purposes of allocating parental authority and use of legal surnames (e.g., articles 819 and 792).

The Chapter 3 address two types of adoption. The first is the historically more common form of adoption in Japan, which involves the adoption of a child or adult resulting in the creation of a legal parent-child relationship between the adoptive parent and child without terminating the relationship between the natural parent and the adoptee. This form of adoption is sometimes used by families with daughters but no son to adopt the daughter's husband as a son to facilitate continuing the family name and occupation. Depending on the family's religion this may also involve assuming traditional responsibilities such as looking after the family graves. The procedures for entering into and dissolving such adoptive relationships are similar to those used for marriage and divorce and in some cases the Code specifically incorporates by reference provisions on marital dissolution into the dissolution of adoptive relationships (e.g., articles 814(2) and 817).

What westerners typically associate with adoption—a couple adopting a baby or infant in a manner that severs his or her legal relationship with biological parents—is referred to as "special adoption" and procedures for it were only added to the Civil Code in 1987. While some might be tempted to regard this as a lack of a tradition of raising other people's children, it should be noted that when people still had babies at home the family registry system made it possible to register another person's baby as one's own child without any other formal adoption proceedings.

Chapter 4 (articles 818 through 837) sets forth the rights and duties associated with parental authority over minor children, who is vested with such authority and how that is lost. Many of these provisions relate to the exercise of property rights and the conduct of legal acts on behalf of minors.

Chapter 5 (articles 831 through 875) deals with the creation and termination of guardianship for both children and adults, and the rights and responsibilities of a legal guardian. The aging of Japan's population has seen a tremendous increase in both the appointment of adult guardians and disputes arising from such arrangements.

Chapter 6 (articles 876 through 876–10) contains comparatively new (added in 2000) provisions dealing with curatorship and assistance. These provide what are essentially lesser degrees of guardianship for persons with impaired capacity not reaching the levels where guardianship is necessary. Guardianship, curatorship and assistance are all tied to the provisions relating to capacity in Part 1.

Chapter 7 (articles 877 through 881) provide for more specific support obligations between lineal and fraternal relatives (the duty to support spouses and minor children being set forth separately in the chapters of the Code relevant to those relationships). This is a more specific support obligation than the one contained in article 730, with article 877 empowering family courts to order a relative to support another who is within three degrees of affinity. These obligations have received more attention in recent years as more elderly Japanese are forced to rely on public assistance. There may also be a perception in some quarters that the Civil Code provisions on support are inadequate; one of the constitutional amendments proposed by the LDP in 2012 would have made it a constitutional duty for family members to support each other.

e. *Part V: Inheritance (Articles 882 Through 1044)*

The inheritance provisions of the Civil Code were also heavily amended during the occupation. Prior to this the eldest legitimate male child would typically inherit the family property as well as the formal status of head of household, not to mention all the responsibilities that came with it. This aspect of inheritance was excised as inegalitarian, though inheritance rules that discriminated against children born out of wedlock remained until 2013.

Reflecting the constitutional mandate of equality, the Civil Code rules ignore birth order and gender for inheritance purposes. Notwithstanding these egalitarian provisions, the practice of the eldest son (or, in the absence of a son, the husband of a daughter adopted into that status) inheriting a family business, profession and/or assets such as the family home is still prevalent in 21st century Japan. Both individual families and family courts have thus had to bridge the gap between the black letter law and common practice.

Part V of the Code is comprised of eight chapters. The first (articles 882 through 885) contains general provisions, such as the rules as to the time and place at which inheritance begins. Chapter 2 (articles 886 through 895) defines the scope of a decedent's heirs, and the manner in which actual or presumptive heirs can be disqualified or disinherited. Chapter 3 (articles 896 through 914) sets forth how inheritance works; the rules of intestate succession, provisions for accounting for *inter vivos* transfers to some heirs and adjustments for other heirs who (for example) cared for the decedent before death as well as the manner of dealing with divisible and indivisible property and so forth.

Chapter 4 (articles 915–940) deals with the acknowledgement and rejection of inheritance rights by heirs. Rather than having the decedent's debts resolved out of the estate assets, Japanese inheritance rules see heirs step into the shoes of the decedent as to both assets and debts that come with them (article 896). The death of a loved one may thus result in the assumption of a ruinous debt. Under articles 915 and 938, an heir may irrevocably renounce their inheritance rights by making a statement to such effect at the appropriate family court within three months of the decedent's death. This means that some creditors of may prefer to "lay low" for a suitable period, rather than immediately making themselves known to the decedent's administrator.

Chapter 5 (941 through 950) sets forth the procedure by which heirs can have estate property separated for distribution. Chapter 6 (951 through 959) addresses the situation when no heirs can be located, with the default rule being that the property escheats to the state. Article 958–3 allows a family court to award all or some of the estate of such a person to a "person who shared a livelihood with the decedent, a person who contributed to the medical treatment and nursing of the decedent, or any other person who had a special connection with the decedent." Among other things this is one of the ways in which the surviving member of a same-sex couple can make a claim for some or all of the property of a deceased partner, so long as there are no legal heirs.

Chapter 7 (articles 960 through 1027) deals with wills and the manner in which they are executed and retracted. The Code recognizes three types of wills: holographic, notarial and secret. Holographic wills must be fully written by hand as of an identifiable date and bear the name and seal of the testator. In 2016 the Supreme Court ruled that a *kaō*, a highly stylized traditional handwritten signature did not satisfy the article 968(1) requirement that the testator's seal impression (as well as a hand-printed name) be present for a holographic will to be valid (Supreme Court, 2nd Petty bench judgment of June 3, 2016).

Notarial wills are prepared in the presence of a Public Notary (see chapter 7) who makes sure the testator is aware of the contents. A secret will also involves a Public Notary, but only to the extent of confirming that a will has been placed in an envelope and duly sealed with confirmation by the notary, who does not know the contents. The use of formal wills appears to be on the increase. According to the public notary association, 105,350 notarial wills were prepared in 2016, compared to 74,160 in 2007.

Chapter 8 (articles 1028 through 1044) sets forth the statutory portions of a decedent's estate to which certain categories of heirs (spouses and lineal ascendants/descendants) are entitled regardless of a disposition by will. If only lineal ascendants survive then that portion is 1/3 of the entire estate. Otherwise, spouses and children are collectively entitled to 1/2 of the estate, subject to various adjustments. At the time of writing amendments were being considered to give spouses in a long term marriage the right to inherit the residence without including it among the assets subject to the forced share of other heirs.

B. PERSONAL IDENTITY AND FAMILY STATUS

1. Overview

Some laws and regulation refer to a variety of formal indicia of "identity," some of which are in turn linked to Japanese nationality. Japanese nationality is in turn inexorably linked to Japan's *koseki* or family registration system. As a result, some features of Japanese law—family law in particular—involve deeply embedded distinctions (some might call it discrimination) based on nationality that may seem unusual to persons from countries where family law is irrelevant to the passport one holds. Japan is moving in the direction of lessening the distinctions between Japanese and non-Japanese in many aspects of its legal system. However, it is probably still very difficult to understand the system as it exists today without a reasonably detailed explanation of its historical background.

2. Japanese Nationality and the Koseki in Context

As discussed in Chapter 2, during the Edo Period Japanese society was ordered pursuant to a rigorously enforced class system. This has sometimes been described as a four-tier system based on neo-Confucian models, with samurai at the top, followed by farmers, artisans and merchants. In reality the most important disctinction was between Samurai and everyone else.

Most law for most people during this period was local, imposed through the individual domains. Various forms of land and household registers were used in the domains to keep track of people and tax obligations. Buddhist temples were central to the community and provided schooling opportunities as well as other social services. Registration with a temple was mandatory, a requirement which was both intended to help stamp out Christianity but also created a system of recording marriages and other changes in family status.

Marriages (and adoptions) were generally affairs decided between households rather than a decision made between a husband and wife. Different regions and social classes had various traditions for recognizing marriages.

There were virtually no foreigners, other than those permitted to reside at or visit at the enclave in Deshima. At the same time, however, identity for most Japanese at the time was likely tied primarily to membership in an extended family connected to a location within a particular community, which itself was within a *han* feudal domain. This is in contrast to the modern sense of being part of a greater "Japanese" whole. The practical need to distinguish between Japanese and non-Japanese came to the surface in the decade before the Restoration, with treaty rights giving foreigners not only the right to reside in Japan but also enjoying extraterritorial status.

Thus, after the Meiji Restoration, the nation's leaders were charged not only with forging a unifying national identity, but the more basic task of identifying and keeping track of the Japanese people. The family registry (*koseki*) system played a key role in this.

The first modern, national *koseki* system was implemented in 1872 and went through several amendments before it was revamped in 1898 in connection with the adoption of the new Civil Code. A new *koseki* law was passed in 1948 in conjunction with the occupation-era amendments to Part IV of the Civil Code.

As originally implemented by the Meiji government, the *koseki* system served several important functions. First, it provided the government with the demographic information about the Japanese people needed to craft policy. Second, it facilitated implemention of policies that were urgently needed such as national taxation and conscription.

Third, over time the *koseki* system played a role in eliminating the Tokugawa-era class structure. Everyone (other than members of the imperial family) were notionally equal, but Meiji-era *koseki* records still denoted whether a household was aristocracy, former samurai or *heimini* (ordinary people). The denotation *shinheimin* (new ordinary people) was used early on for the former members of the *burakumin* outcast communities. Of course the modern *koseki* no longer contains such information, but even historical *koseki* records have had these class origin notations redacted since they are a source of possible discrimination, particularly for *burakumin* and other disadvantaged communities. Well into the post-war period, *koseki* records also clearly denoted who in a family had been born out of wedlock, and whether someone had been adjudicated legally incompetent, which also facilitated discrimination against people having that status (either themselves or as family members).

Finally, the *koseki* defined who the Japanese people were. The Meiji government essentially started from the proposition that everyone who was already in Japan and clearly hadn't just alighted from the foreign ships that arrived after Perry were Japanese. Having a *koseki* registration became an indicia of Japanese nationality and still is today. Moreover, under the pre-war koseki system, nationality was a family affair; marrying a non-Japanese spouse—after the prohibition on marrying foreigners was abolished in 1873—meant either the Japanese half of the couple exiting the family (and the *koseki*) and losing Japanese nationality, or the non-Japanese half entering the family (and the *koseki* as a member) and acquiring Japanese nationality (which required abandoning other nationalities).

The *koseki* also played a role in Japan's colonial empire, as its non-Japanese subjects with different family practices had to be accommodated as well. This manifested itself in various exceptions and special rules. This came first with the Ainu populations of Hokkaido. Adjustments were also necessary with respect to the population of the Ryukyu Island, which at the time of the Restoration was a kingdom subject to the joint suzerainty of both the Chinese emperor and the lord of the Satsuma domain in Kyushu.

When Japan's empire expanded to Taiwan and Korea, it was necessary to reconcile Japan's *koseki* with existing registration systems in those territories which were based on well-established but different family structures and practices. As a result, both Taiwan and Korea retained separate *koseki* systems as colonies.

This actually facilitated the development of differing forms of citizenship within the Japanese empire. For international law purposes, Koreans Japanese and Taiwanese were all subjects of the Japanese emperor, but which *koseki* they were registered in affected their political rights and their ability to live and work in the Japanese main islands. Those registered in Japanese mainland *koseki* were accorded preferential treatment in a variety of ways.

Under this regime, marriage across *koseki* was similar to marrying a foreigner. A marriage between a person registered in a Japanese *koseki* and one registered in the Korean equivalent would require one (usually the woman) to leave her native *koseki* and enter that of the spouse.

The sudden loss of Japanese nationality experienced by those of Korean and Taiwanese heritage after the war was actually based on the locus of their *koseki*, rather than their actual ethnicity or heritage. The logic was that those registered in non-Japanese (*i.e.*, Korean or Taiwanese) *koseki* at the time the Treaty of San Francisco came into effect in 1952 and extinguished Japanese sovereignty over its foreign colonies were no longer Japanese. This was also not accomplished as a change of law, but by a 1952 MOJ interpretive directive (*tsūtatsu*) to local *koseki* authorities.[2]

Family law under the Meiji-era Civil Code and *koseki* system was based not on nuclear families but on extended family groupings potentially comprised of multiple married couples and three or four generations. Ostensibly they all lived together in the same household or compound, sharing the same last name and all working a family farm, business or trade. The household was under the direction of a head of household. This system was referred to as the *ie* ("household" or "house") system.

Head of household was a heritable, legal status registered in the *koseki*. It generally could not be abandoned or transferred, though the head could retire upon reaching a certain age. The head of household was typically the eldest legitimate male and had authority to dispose of family property. He was also responsible for maintaining family graves, household rites and family traditions. Subject to some exceptions his permission was required for marriages or adoptions involving other members of the household. He could also approve the acceptance into the household of a child born to a family member out of wedlock.

The family registry made it possible for the government to leverage family units as a means of implementing policy. Rather than governing at the individual level, policy could be implemented through the head of household who was both identifiable and accountable for the conduct of the family's members and responsible for supporting them. The trade-off was that a high degree of autonomy was accorded to the head of household in how he managed it, subject to the rigid formal rules of the Civil Code that dealt primarily with how members joined and exited the family rather than the rights of those within it.

Together with various forms of coercion and the ability to participate in government programs of economic benefit (including, for example, the ability to move to the Northern frontier of Hokkaido and participate in its development), marriage and legitimacy and their relevance to property rights were used to make people register in the national *koseki* system when it was introduced. As is still the case today, regardless of what ceremonies or other traditional rites are followed, marriages were only legal if they were registered. Children born to a union that was not legally registered were illegitimate and thus at risk of being ineligible to inherit family property.

This had the impact of relegating the many regional marriage rituals to the realm of quaint tradition. It also triggered a response from the citizenry, who would often use the existing practice of "trial" marriage to circumvent the system. Since marriages were

---

[2] The constitutionality of a loss of citizenship through the combination of the peace treaty and MOJ *tsūtatsu* was upheld in 1961 (Supreme Court, Grand Bench judgment of April 5, 1961).

typically entered into with the expectation of progeny, some families would have a wedding ceremony but wait until the wife was pregnant to register and legalize the marriage. This practice presumably saved the husband's family the trouble of divorcing a barren wife, since she was not legally a wife in the first place (she might have been entitled to damages for a broken engagement). It was also a practice that was continued well into the post-war period. In 1966 a plane crashed at Matsuyama airport, killing everyone on board. The passengers included twelve sets of newlyweds who had been embarking on what at the time was the newly fashionable western custom of taking a honeymoon trip. It turned out that not a single couple had *registered* their marriage, resulting in legal uncertainty that made compensation negotiations complicated and resulted in the MOJ launching a public awareness campaign to encourage the prompt registration of marriages.

Until well into the post-war period family registries could be reviewed by anyone who followed the procedure for doing so, meaning that children born out of wedlock, adoptive status, divorces and other potentially sensitive information was essentially a matter of public record. The early Meiji *koseki* even recorded criminal convictions and pre-Restoration *burakumin* status. The *koseki* thus also provided a source of information for other families, businesses and social actors to evaluate whether to transact with a particular family or its individual members, whether through business or arranged marriages. A male identified through the *koseki* as the eldest legitimate male son of the head of household would be a better credit risk than other members of the family since he could be expected to assume that status and control of the family property.

Together with the Civil Code, the *koseki* system as originally established resulted in individuals being identified by their defined status within a family unit, the *ie*, rather than as individuals with a particular set of family relationships. Moreover, the *koseki* is perhaps best understood as part of a system of family law for government and the rest of society which enables them to identify and structure the dealings with a family and its members. The family relationships registered in the *koseki* and based in the Civil Code identify who is *legally* responsible for whom within the family, as well as who might have rights to property that could affect dealings with it. The *koseki* thus established a set of records that third parties relied upon. For this reason, the rules of the Civil Code on subjects such as paternity, marital status and the locus of parental authority were designed to be unambiguous as to the *legal* status of the family while largely ignoring the emotional and practical realities of individual family circumstance. This subject will be revisited again below.

The Americans who oversaw the democratization of Japan saw the *ie* system as one of the factors that had contributed to Japan's evolution into a totalitarian militaristic nation. It had been common to analogize the Emperor as the head of the national household and thus draw simple parallels between the home and nationalism.

Under American pressure the *ie* system was dismantled, and most inegalitarian provisions, including the concept of a "head of household" were stripped from the Civil Code and the *koseki* system revamped correspondingly. However, the Japanese were able to rebuff American pressure to replace the system of registration of family units with one of registering individuals (arguing at one point that post-war deprivation meant there was not enough paper available to register Japanese people individually). For their part the American negotiators adamantly refused to accept a registration system that allowed three or more generations of family members to appear in a single *koseki*. Some of the quirks of the current two-generational *koseki* system are only comprehensible as an occupation-era compromise between an individual registration system and something closer to the multigenerational system that was possible under the old regime.

By some accounts the Japanese responsible for implementing American demanded changes to family law during the occupation hoped to reestablish some version of the *ie* system after the war. This did not happen, but the general requirement that persons registered in the same *koseki* share the same surname was something that could serve as a foundation for a new *ie* system. Moreover, the actual recompilation of the physical *koseki* into the new format did not take place until the 1950s and 1960s. Today the *koseki* system is computerized, but inheritance cases may still require a review of older records from when it was paper-based in order to search for possible heirs.

3. Law and Identity in Japan Today

With this historical information out of the way, it is possible to turn to how the legal identity of natural persons is structured in the modern Japanese legal system. Corporate (juridical) identity is discussed in Chapter 11.

a. Nationality

Although unity of nationality is no longer a requirement for Japanese families, under the Nationality Act of 1950 citizenship is still based on birth to a Japanese parent rather than place of birth (with an exception for children born in Japan with unknown parents or lacking citizenship elsewhere). Children born to a Japanese parent abroad are eligible for Japanese nationality, so long as their parents report the birth to Japanese authorities within three months (Family Registration Act of 1947, article 49).

Despite the equal protection guarantees of the Constitution, for decades Japanese nationality was transmitted through fathers only. It was only until amendments to the Nationality Act that took effect in 1985 that children born to Japanese wives of foreign husbands also automatically obtained Japanese nationality (a child born to a Japanese mother and an *unknown* father obtained Japanese nationality).

While framed in terms of gender, the pre-1988 law was intended to minimize instances of children having dual nationality. PrIn principle Japanese law still does not permit Japanese adults to have dual citizenship. Those who obtain another nationality as an adult lose their Japanese citizenship. And while it is now not unusual for Japanese children to have two (or more nationalities) due to parentage or birth abroad, the Nationality Act requires them to choose Japanese nationality or their other nationality within two years of reaching the age of majority (Nationality Act, article 14).

Until 2006 the Nationality Act also contained a strange distinction that allowed children born out of wedlock to a foreign mother and a Japanese father to obtain Japanese nationality if the father acknowledged paternity before birth but not after. In 2006 this distinction was found by the Supreme Court to violate the constitution's equal protection guarantee and the law subsequently amended (*The Birth Out of Wedlock Nationality Case*; see Table 6-1 and discussion in Chapter 6).

It is possible for foreign nationals to naturalize as Japanese citizens. The process is not easy, but not as difficult as in the past when applicants were required to adopt "Japanese sounding" names, though adoption of a legal name using approved Japanese characters is still required. The process involves a registration at the appropriate legal affairs bureau and the creation of a *koseki*. A *koseki* extract is one of the documents required when applying for a Japanese passport.

b. *The Koseki System, Residence Registry and Other Components of Japanese Identity*

(i) *The Modern Koseki System*

The modern *koseki* system is based on the Family Registration Act of 1947. Administered by municipal authorities, it is a national system under the jurisdiction of the MOJ which supervises the administration through its network of Legal Affairs Bureaus.

The *koseki* (family registry) refers both to the registrations of individual Japanese person's (his or her "*koseki*") but also to the system as a whole (the *koseki seido*). The *koseki* system is used to register a variety of changes in status. Broadly speaking registrations are of two types. First are those where the registration itself is needed to give legal effect to the change in status. These include marriages, consensual divorces, adoptions, consensual dissolutions of adoptive relationships and voluntary acknowledgements of paternity. Second are those which involve a notification of a factual change that affects the registration details. Examples include notifications of births, deaths, the acquisition or loss of Japanese nationality, and changes in status accomplished through court actions, such as judicial divorces and special adoptions.

An official extract of a person's *koseki,* which can be procured from the relevant municipal office for a small fee, provides the basic form of identification for Japanese persons. It can be used to prove date of birth, parent-child relationships, marital status, death and even extended family relationships (once combined with other *koseki* records).

In many ways it is a superior system of proving identity and family relationships than the event-based systems of birth and marriage certificates and divorce decrees used in some western countries. While an American can use a marriage certificate to prove they married a particular person on a particular date in the past, they would struggle to produce a document confirming they are *still* married to that person today.

By contrast, a *koseki* extract will provide a current snapshot of a person's marital status, since a divorce or marriage is only effective if registered (marriages and divorces abroad of course complicating things if they are not registered in the *koseki*). Similarly, *koseki* extracts obviate a certain amount of probate litigation by making it possible to identify all of a decedent's possible heirs as present or consenting to the disposition of a decedent's bank account or real property. This can involve some significant effort and backtracking through registry records dating to the Meiji Period, since it requires using *koseki* records to start at the beginning of the decedent's life and identify all types of family relationships that might have arisen over the course of it, and thus all possible heirs. In 2017 the MOJ introduced a system whereby it issues a simplified proof of legal heirs based on relevant *koseki* records, sparing heirs the need to produce a bundle of those records for each bank, title registry or other institution requiring such evidence.

Since even changes wrought through judicial action (divorces, for example) are notified to the family registry for recordation, a *koseki* extract serves as proof of the relevant status even in the minority of cases where the change of status results from litigation. For this reason, divorce decrees are not used as proof of status or custody over children the way they are in countries such as the United States. As a result, lawyers from such countries may overestimate the importance of having a custody decree "recognized" in Japan. In fact, recognition of a foreign divorce or decree may be as much about having the key dispositive elements of a foreign judgment (*i.e.,* those which potentially impact third parties; divorce and allocation of parental authority) reflected in the *koseki.*

Notwithstanding the postwar changes the modern *koseki* system still organizes Japanese people primarily in family units rather than as individuals. As noted earlier in this chapter, as a result of occupation era compromises between the American and Japanese authorities, family registries can only accommodate two generations. Marriage or the birth of a child out of wedlock necessitates the creation of a new *koseki.* Typically a person stays on their parent's *koseki* until one of these two events, though childless adults are free to establish their own independent *koseki.* Occasionally it may be necessary to create a separate *koseki* for a child. In the event of divorce, it is possible to return to one's parent's *koseki* but only if one does not have parental authority over children of the marriage (since that would violate the two-generational limit on registrations) or seek to retain the ex-spouse's surname (since the *koseki* is based on the presumption that all members registered in it share the same surname).

While marriages within certain degrees of affinity are prohibited and bigamy is a crime, the *koseki* system generally prevents them from happening in the first place. Registry authorities would not accept a marriage registration if the *koseki* of either party show one of them is already married.

Koseki are still registered with a specific address or location in Japan, which is referred to as the "*honseki*" of the persons registered in it. In the past the *honseki* might have been the actual home where the family lives. Today there is no requirement that the *honseki* be the family's present or past residence, legal residence being a matter dealt with through a separate residence registry (discussed below). Some still use the location of their ancestral home (or even graves) as their *honseki,* and there may even be some pride or cache to having the same *honseki* for generations. However, any location in Japan will suffice. Hundreds of baseball fans reportedly have their *koseki* registered at the location of the famous *Kōshien* baseball stadium, while others use Tokyo Disneyland. People are also free to move their *honseki* as they please, though it complicates procuring *koseki* records and may cause suspicion that they are trying to hide something.

The term *honseki* appears on some Japanese identity documents (though has been removed from driver's licenses). On Japanese passports it is rendered in English as "registered domicile" with a denotation showing the prefecture in which the holder's *honseki* is registered. This is misleading, since the person may never have actually resided in that prefecture. The principal significance of the *honseki* location is it dictates which municipal authority can issue a *koseki* extract when such a document is required. Persons who do not live where their *honseki* is registered can request an extract by post.

Other than the *honseki* of a person being notionally linked to a particular place in Japan, the *koseki* system is essentially borderless. Moreover, since court involvement is not required for most changes of status appearing in the *koseki,* issues such as satisfaction of residence periods or jurisdictional requirements that complicate family law in the United States rarely arise. In fact, Japanese people can conduct many *koseki* transactions from anywhere in the world by filing through the post or with Japanese consular officials. For example, it is possible for Japanese nationals to get married or divorced *for Japanese law purposes* anywhere in the world through *koseki* filings.

The *koseki* system accords a high degree of autonomy to persons, albeit within the rigid framework of family relationships recognized by the Civil Code. Marriages, adoptions of adults (or even minors who are grandchildren or the child of a spouse), consensual divorces (including consensual designations of parental authority over minor children) and consensual dissolutions of most adoptions can be accomplished by merely filing the paperwork with the municipal office in which one resides. It is not even necessary for all the parties affected by such registrations to be present, and it wasn't until 2008 that the person appearing to make such a registration had to provide proof of identity.

There are no jurisdiction-related waiting periods for marriages or divorce (other than the prohibition on women remarrying immediately after marital dissolution discussed in Chapter 6), and Japan is one of the easiest places in the world to get a consensual divorce. In fact, it is so easy that fraudulent filings are a problem, and there is a process for notifying your municipal office *not* to accept a divorce filing if you think there is a danger of your spouse forging your consent on one. A non-Japanese being asked by a Japanese spouse to sign a form that is is described as being a summer school application or some other innocuous document written in Japanese and only later finding it was a divorce filing that gave custody of their children to the Japanese parent is a situation that occasionally arises in international marriages.

The fact that the *koseki* system only registers Japanese nationals means that the entire system of family law is structurally discriminatory at a very basic level. This has been particularly burdensome for the nation's ethnic Korean population, many of whom have lived in Japan for several generations and are generally able to pass themselves as Japanese (if they wish to do so) until it becomes time to produce official proof of identity. Changes in policy have made it easier for members of this population to naturalize (for example, by keeping Korean-sounding names when they do so).

Koseki extracts may also be sought from candidates during the employment process. Some companies might use them to confirm there is nothing "unusual" about the candidate's family situation. This sort of requirement as problematic as it may facilitate improper employment discrimination and is now discouraged by authorities. At the same time, a limited form of extract (or comparable proof) may be necessary in connection with family benefit programs and tax treatment after employment.

Non-Japanese family members appear as notations in the *koseki* of Japanese spouses and children but do not have a *koseki* of their own. Two Japanese seeking to marry in Japan or use the consensual divorce notification process, have to go through a different, more complicated process and in the case of divorce may not be able to use the process at all if their home country law does not permit such divorces.

While in the past *kosekii* were essentially a form of public record, today third party access to *koseki* records is now stringently controlled. *Bengosh)i* attorneys and certain otherlegal professionals have the ability to seek access to records for purposes of litigation or other limited purposes (Family Register Act, article 10–2(3)–(5).

(ii) Addresses and the Residence Registry

Under article 22 of the Civil Code the principal place where a person lives shall be his or her "domicile," though the Japanese term is *jūsho*, which is more accurately translated "residential address" or just "address." Registration in the municipality in which one resides is required and administered through the Residential Basic Book Act of 1967. Although the name of the act suggests a paper ledger, records are of course computerized. The residential registration system is under the jurisdiction of the MIC, which as noted in Chapter 3 oversees local government affairs.

A person's residence registry is linked to their *koseki* (if they have one). However, unlike the *koseki*, it shows (or should show) the actual residence address and the composition of the household living at that address. While a person's *koseki* may show a spouse and children, the registration system may show them to be long estranged and possibly even cohabitating with new partners.

Unless one is a resident foreigner, not being registered in a koseki can be an impediment to obtaining a residence registration and receiving basic government services. Similarly, homelessness can similarly hinder a person's efforts to obtain a residence registration, another basic component of identity in Japan. In an October 23, 2007 judgment that was subsequently affirmed by the Supreme Court, the Osaka High Court rejected a demand by a homeless person that the Osaka municipal government allow the use of the park in which the person lived as a residence address for purposes of obtaining a residence registry.

Until 2012 the residence registry was also for Japanese only, with a separate system of "alien registration" for non-Japanese residents, including the nation's ethnic Korean minority, many of whom were born and raised in Japan. Now, however, foreigners with the appropriate visa status are also registered in largely the same manner. By law, non-Japanese residents are at all times required to carry a card showing their residential status (or if they lack residence status, their passport). Ethnic Koreans residents are categorized euphemistically as *tokubetsu eijūsha* ("special permanent residents") and issued a card reflecting that status by their municipality of residence.

A person's *jūminhyō* (residence certificate) is in many ways now more important than their *koseki* (if they have one) since it is determinative of where they pay local taxes, vote (if Japanese), send their children to school and access a myriad of government health and welfare programs. Official extracts from a residence registry are also a form of identification in that they are proof of residential address, taxpayer status, and "real" (as opposed to legal) family composition. The elimination of the separate registration system for foreigners reflects an effort by the government to move away from the rigid Japanese/not Japanese distinction in various routine aspects of public administration.

Although same-sex marriages are not permitted under Japanese law, some municipal executives have used their administration of the residence registry system to issue certificates that accord same sex couples the same status as legally married couples for purposes of programs developed by that municipality or commercial businesses.[3] For example, mobile phone providers may accept such certificates for purposes of enabling same sex couples to participate in family calling plans.

[3] It has recently also become possible in some municipalities for unmarried cohabitating heterosexual couples to obtain a residence registration with a denotation of "spouse—registration pending" based on what may often be a fiction that they plan to eventually file a marriage registration. This does not create a legal marriage, but may entitle them to receive spousal benefits through public and private benefits programs which recognize *de facto* marriages for such purposes. This reflects the growing importance of the residence registration system in reflecting the realities of Japanese family life as compared to the *koseki* system.

(iii) Birth, Names, Gender, Parenthood and Legitimacy

Although hospitals provide certification of birth, a live birth must be reported (usually by one of the parents) for registration in the *koseki*. *Koseki* extracts showing the date of birth and parents provide all the information typically evidenced in birth certificates, which are rarely used as a form of identification in Japan.

Children whose births are not reported can suffer severe discrimination in that they lack a basic component of Japanese identity and legal existence. In the pre-war period not registering in the *koseki* was a way of avoiding conscription. More recently, it is a problem that sometimes arises because the *koseki* system's connection to the registry residence system means that a woman fleeing from an abusive husband may refrain from registering a birth out of fear that it will enable him to find her. It is estimated that there are approximately 10,000 *mukosekisha*—people without *koseki*—in Japan.

Given names must be reported using characters from one or more of Japan's three alphabets (*hiragana* and *katakana*, the two phonetic alphabets and *kanji* the pictographic characters derived from Chinese). Kanji may be chosen from the official list of "commonly used" Kanji as well as a list of accepted but more obscure or non-standard characters that can be used for personal names. Although a name meeting these requirements must be accepted by the registration authorities, in 1993 Akishima city declined to cooperate with a father who wished to register his new son's name as "*akuma*" (devil). In the ensuing litigation a trial court found the father to have abused his naming rights (Tokyo Family Court, Hachiōji Branch decision of January 31, 1994).

Surnames are more complicated. Children born to married parents take the surname of the parents, which by law must be the same as discussed below (Civil Code article 790(1). A child born out of wedlock takes the mother's surname (article 790(2)).

As noted previously, a premise of the *ie* system was that all members of the same household shared the same surname. A form of this rule is retained in article 750 of the Code requiring either the husband or wife to legally assume the other's surname upon marriage. Returning to one's birth surname is possible upon the termination of the marriage. Only Japanese who marry a foreign spouse have the option of retaining their Japanese surname or adopting their spouse's foreign one.

Although the article 750 unity of surnames requirement is framed in gender neutral terms, in approximately 98% of marriages it is the wife who assumes the husband's name. The requirement has proven an impediment to the growing number of professional working women who have built a reputation and a career on their pre-marital name. It is often possible to continue using a maiden name in work and daily life, but official documents still require the legal name. This can be a problem for women lawyers who go by their maiden name but must submit documents to court under their legal name. Some women deal with the problem by having an unregistered *de facto marriage*. It is possible to petition a family court to be permitted to change one's legal name, but one must articulate a suitable reason for doing so. The unity of surname requirement has been challenged, resulting in a 2015 Grand Bench judgment upholding it, as discussed in Chapter 6.

Gender is reported at birth and recorded in the *koseki*. Since the Special Act on Handling Gender Status for Persons with Gender Identity Disorder took effect in 2004, it is possible to change one's registered gender through a family court proceeding. This requires proving to the court (including through medical certification) that the petitioner is no longer biologically capable of having children. Persons going through this process are entitled to be treated as the new gender for all legal purposes. The procedure under the law is only available to those who are not currently married and do not have minor children.

As already noted, the Civil Code and other laws treat children differently depending on whether they are born in or out of wedlock. Parents are still required to indicate whether a child is born in or out of wedlock when reporting a birth. The constitutionality of this requirement was upheld by the Supreme Court, ironically only a few weeks after it issued its historical decision striking down other legitimacy-based distinctions in the *Legtitmacy-Based Discrimination in Inheritance Case*; Supreme Court, 1st Petty Bench judgment of September 26, 2013).

Legitimacy is closely tied to statutory presumptions of paternity. Under article 772 children conceived during a marriage are assumed to be the child of the husband, and children born within 200 days of the commencement of the marriage and 300 days after its dissolution are also presumed to have been conceived during the marriage. This latter rule has caused problems for numerous women already in relationships with other partners by the time their divorce is finalized, since it results in a child born from the latter union to be registered as the child of the ex-husband. Resolution is possible through family court proceedings but this generally requires the cooperation of the former spouse. This is sometimes another factor that results in a child not being registered at all.

Articles 774 and 775 of the Code allow the husband (only) to rebut the presumption of paternity, but only if he brings an action within a year of birth. The harshness of this restriction has been remediated somewhat through procedural law, with family courts entertaining actions to reach a conciliated result confirming the absence of a parent-child relationship. However, this practice by lower courts involves the consent of the parties in non-litigious conciliation proceedings (discussed in the following chapter); when disputed the Supreme Court has been reluctant to favor biology over the 19th century presumptions of paternity still embedded in the Civil Code (and which were similar to European rules of paternity at the time). In a trio of cases issued on the same day in 2014, the Court declined to allow DNA evidence to be used by parties other than the putative father to overcome the presumptions of paternity embedded in the Civil Code (Supreme Court, 1st Petty Bench judgments of July 17, 2014).

The Civil Code rules on paternity were also a factor in the Supreme Court's oddly precise 2015 ruling that the Civil Code's prohibition on only women remarrying for six months after marital dissolution was unconstitutional as to that part of the prohibition period that was greater than 100 days. The rationale was in part that if a woman remarried on the 101st day after getting divorced a child born within 200 days of the subsequent marriage would benefit from the article 772 presumption of conception during that marriage and thus be considered born in wedlock. This would also avoid overlapping presumptions of paternity arising from the 300 day post-dissolution presumption of paternity contained in the same provision.

The presumptions of the Civil Code have also had an impact on the relationship between parents and children born through assisted reproduction techniques. In 2013 the Supreme Court overturned a municipal authority's refusal to accept a registration of the birth of a child born to the wife of a man who had undergone a legal change of gender on the grounds that he could not possibly be the father (Supreme Court decision of

December 10, 2013).[4] Yet, a few years earlier the Supreme Court had on public policy grounds refused to recognize as legal parents the biological Japanese parents of a child born to a surrogate pursuant to a valid Nevada Law surrogacy contract (Supreme Court, 2nd Petty Bench decision of March 23, 2007). While the Court likely seems very progressive in the former case and misanthropic in the latter[5], in both it was probably just applying very old rules on the presumptions of parentage which the Diet has declined to change.

Children born out of wedlock may be recognized by their father either through the necessary filings in the *koseki* or by a valid will (article 781). Such affiliation takes effect retroactively to birth. An action for affiliation can also be brought in court by a child lineal ascendant or their legal representative (article 787).

(iv) Marriage, Divorce, Adoptions and Children

While marriage is central to the family law system, as already noted, it is easy to get married and easy to get divorced—if both parties agree. The same is true of the creation and dissolution of "normal" adoptive relationships. All can be accomplished by merely filing the necessary paperwork (except for certain adoptions involving minors). The Code also provides for the annulment of marriages and adoptions in certain circumstances (mistaken identity, fraud or duress, etc.).

The Civil Code provides for various rules regarding the division of property on divorce. Outside the sparse provisions of the Code, courts have developed detailed child support guidelines and other rules intended to ensure equitable financial results.

Under article 818 of the Code a minor child is subject to the joint parental authority (*shinken*) of natural parents if born during marriage or of adoptive parents in an adoptive relationship. Article 825 of the Code contains language that specifically protects third parties from conflicting exercises of joint parental authority by parents during marriage. A child born out of wedlock is subject to the sole parental authority of the mother unless the father formally acknowledges paternity and the mother agrees, in which case the father has sole parental authority.

Under the Code parental authority is comprised of a number of components, including the right and duty to care for and educate the child. In a minority of divorces. *Shinken* is occasionally subdivided so that one parent retains "legal custody" (authority to manage the child's property and legal affairs) while the other is accorded "physical custody" (*kangoken*, the authority to make decisions over care and control and education). But this is rare, and *shinken* is usually understood to mean full control and authority over the child.

Although the term *shinken* includes the term *ken* which means "right" (literally "parental right") and parental authority can be removed or suspended if it is abused (as part of the abuse of rights doctrine), most academic commentators and court practices regard *shinken* primarily as a set of parental duties. This makes it hard for parents to assert rights in proceedings over custody and visitation.

---

[4] The registration authorities would have been able to discern from the father's *koseki* that he had been born as a woman and undergone the change of gender procedure described earlier in this section.

[5] As noted in a concurring opinon in the surrogacy case, the Court's decision resulted in the children having no legal parents anywhere.

There are few formal rules regarding what should happen to children when their parents divorce. Visitation was not even mentioned in the Code until 2011, though it had been recognized by family court practice since the 1960s, though primarily as something that the parties could agree to rather than a right. 2011 amendments to article 766 of the Code require parents to make arrangements for visitation and financial support, taking into account the best interests of the child, but the cooperative divorce process offers little scope for ensuring this is done; allocations of parental authority (full custody) over minor children can be made on the divorce filing with no official scrutiny.

One clear rule enunciated by article 819 of the Code is that after divorce parental authority may only be vested in one parent. This is surprising to people from western countries, where joint parenting after divorce has become the norm. However, it has a certain logic within the context of the *koseki* system, where part of the goal is to ensure *koseki* denotations of parental authority are unambiguous, thereby minimizing situations where third parties are subject to conflicting exercises of parental rights as to legal acts or dispositions of property on behalf of the child.

The absence of clear statutory norms and the ability to achieve a divorce and allocation of parental authority without court involvement or oversightmeans that one parent is easily excluded from the lives of their children for most if not all legal purposes through the divorce process, with courts providing limited recourse against a parent stubbornly focused on achieving such a result. Parents in *defacto* marriages who do not have parental authority may also fare badly. Moreover, the easy rules of adoption mean that it is possible for the parent having parental authority to consent to the adoption of the child by a new spouse or a grandparent without the consent of the biological parent/ex-spouse or leave of a family court (article 798).

(v) The Role of Courts in Identity and Family Matters

It is sometimes said that the traditional view of family law in Japan was that the law (or the courts, at least) should not interfere in the household. It is debatable whether that is true, particularly given the *koseki* plays in subtly coercing people into a limited range of family structures.

It may be helpful to think of Japan as effectively having two spheres of family law. The first is the *koseki* system, which is administered by the MOJ and arguably exists largely for the benefit of those outside any particular family by making it possible for outsiders to unambiguously confirm who is *legally* related to whom within that family. The *koseki* system being an administrative system based in public law, judicial challenges regarding the way it is operated generally take place in the realm of administrative litigation, with courts being characteristically reluctant to second guess the operation of highly technical administrative regimes administered by another bureaucracy. In the same manner, "recognition" of a foreign divorce decree may be less a matter of court action as a Japanese party appearing at his or her local municipal office with a copy of their foreign divorce decree (and a translation) and seeking to have the relevant portions (divorce, allocation of parental authority) reflected in the relevant *koseki*. This may involve the municipal authorities consulting with the local Legal Affairs Bureau.

The second systemof family law exists within the sphere of private law, and thus involves disputes between persons within or about family relationships. The courts do play an oversight role in some non-adversarial matters (some adoptions involving minors and changes of gender, for example), but the majority of their time and resources are devoted to disputes involving contested divorces, custody of the children, disposition of marital property and inheritance.

In connection with the resolution of family disputes, when considering the role of Japanese courts—which can seem deceptively familiar to that of their western corollaries—it is is important to remember the greater system of family law in which they operate. First, subject to the constraints of the *koseki* system as to the types of *legal* family relationships that can be registered in it or terminated, parties are generally free to do whatever they want. There is no mandatory involvement of courts in divorces as in some jurisdictions, nor is the system based on parties showing up in a court and asserting rights that are clearly identified in formal law, such as rights to maintain contact with children or even a clear right to a divorce.

The universe of family disputes that do get resolved can be broken into two rough categories: those which will result in a change of status registered in the *koseki* and thus potentially affect third parties, and those which will not and are essentially just disputes between the parties. The former category of disputes includes contested divorces, allocations of parental authority and dissolutions of adoptive relationships (all changes of status which could also be achieved through consensual *koseki* filings). Those in the latter category include most of the things people fight about in divorce and similar situations: who lives with the children, how much visitation and child support there will be (if any) and so forth. The procedural aspects of family court dispute resolution are discussed in the following chapter.

Note that this "two system" characterization is not formally set forth in law or regulations. Rather it is offered by the authors for ease of understanding for non-Japanese readers. Many family cases involve elements of both types of disputes and although often resolved in parallel, depending on how a case proceeds there may be a fork depending on which element of the dispute is at issue. As discussed in the next chapter, family courts may resolve some matters through conciliation or even decrees in lieu of conciliation, but bringing about a change of status such as divorce over the objections of one party is only possible through the formal litigation process. One view holds that parties have a right to *not* be unilaterally divorced, so a prolonged divorce trial may have the effect of giving the party who doesn't want the divorce more bargaining power.

The family courts thus start their involvement in such cases not as a court of law hearing a claim for specific relief, but as an expert authority providing a conciliation services with the aim of encouraging the parties to arrive at a consensual result. Only if this effort fails will the matter proceed to litigation.

Some disputes—such as divorce or allocations of parental authority—do have the possibility of impacting third parties because of the relevance of marital status and parental authority to liability for debts, potential claims over property and legal acts of minors. Possibly for this reason, if the parties are not able to agree upon a conciliated result, the litigation that follows can be arduous and time-consuming. Moreover, there is no absolute right to relief. While a couple is free to get a consensual divorce for any reason at any time, an effort to procure a judicial divorce may be time consuming and end in failure; the Civil Code (article 770) only recognizes five grounds for a judicial divorce: (1) unchastity, (2) prolonged abandonment, (3) disappearance, (4) severe unrecoverable mental illness, and (5) "other grave cause making it difficult to continue the marriage." Even if the grounds in (1)–(4) are proven, the court has the discretion to deny the petition for divorce if it considers it reasonable for the marriage to continue.

A great deal of litigated divorces end up being brought under the "other grave cause" prong of article 770, which means courts have done a significant amount of interpretive "law-making" in this area. For example, during the first few decades of the post-war period the Supreme Court operated on the principle that the spouse at fault for marital breakdown could not obtain a judicial divorce. This was overturned in a 1987 judgment in the case of a husband in his 70s who had been estranged from his ex-wife for three decades and had children with his new partner (Supreme Court, Grand Bench judgment of September 2, 1987). Since then the courts have been moving towards an "irreparable breakdown" standard for granting divorce, but this must be proven by years of separation and which party is at fault in the breakdown is still a factor in some cases. In a 2004 judgment the Supreme Court found that a separation period of two years and four months was not long enough to justify a judicial divorce for a couple who had cohabitated for over six years, despite the husband having had an affair and the wife being a compulsive "clean freak" (Supreme Court, 1st Petty bench judgment of November 18, 2004).

Outside the family structures envisioned by the *koseki*, the courts have also developed a wide range of practices and doctrines for protecting parties in *defacto* marriages. These include using tort and contractual theories to provide financial relief for the economically weaker party in such an arrangement when it is suddenly terminated, particularly if was a long-term relationship where the parties held themselves out as husband and wife and even had children. The difficulty of contested divorces leads to some complex cases where one of the parties in such a long-term relationship is still married to a long-estranged spouse.

The Supreme Court has declined to identify many constitutional dimensions to family relationships. It has never identified a constitutional right to divorce (which would arguably be consistent with the article 13 right to the pursuit of happiness), nor any constitutionally protected dimension to the parent-child relationship. It has specifically refused to find a constitutional right to visitation after divorce, or to identify visitation as anything other than a possible disposition that a non-custodial parent can seek from a court rather than a right of either parent or child (Supreme Court, 2nd Petty Bench decision of July 6, 1984 and 1st Petty Bench decision of May 1, 2000).

Japan's choice of law statute, the Act on General Rules of Application of Laws of 2006 (which replaced the much older international law statute, the Law on the Application of Laws of 1890), mandates that in matters relating to personal status of foreigners in Japan should be governed by their home country law. This becomes complicated when a Japanese party is involved, and may involve legal research that many busy family courts are incapable or unwilling to do, but it is another example of the different treatment accorded non-Japanese.

Family violence is addressed by the Act on Prevention of Spousal Violence and the Protection of Victims Act of 2001 and the Child Abuse Prevention Act of 2000. Article 10 of the former empowers district courts to issue protective orders against abusive spouses. The latter is devoted to empowering child welfare authorities to investigate and, if necessary, take protective steps to protect children from abuse.

c. *Seals*

A small but important aspect of identity in Japan is the personal seal or *hanko*. When individuals execute contracts or formalize government forms, they are typically required to hand write their name and affix their personal seal to the document. A special statute (the Signatures and Seals and Insolvency Certificate in Relation to Foreign Nationals Act of 1899) allows non-Japanese to satisfy such requirements for a seal as are required by law to be satisfied by a signature in the case of foreign nationals. Japanese criminal law also contains special penalties for forgery of a document using a private seal. Most financial institutions also require a seal, and some people may create a separate seal for each bank account. The use of seals in the business and corporate contexts are discussed in Chapter 11.

Seals must identify the surname of the person using them. Stationery stores sell cheap, ready-made seals for most common surnames. A single individual may have multiple seals. It is possible to register one's formal seal impression with the local municipal authorities. Such authorities will in turn issue a formal certificate showing the seal impression. This is used in a manner similar to notarization, confirming that the seal is that of the person identified in the certificate, and providing counterparties the opportunity to compare the impression on the certificate with that being proffered to execute a document.

d. *"My Number" and Other Forms of Identification*

Until 2015 Japan did not have a unified system of tax-payer identification like US social security numbers. In 2015, ten digit identifying numbers were allocated to people (both Japanese and foreign residents) and over time are expected to facilitate greater rationalization in the administration of tax and social welfare systems. Called the "My Number" system, the program may facilitate replacement of more aspects of the *koseki* system with a system of individually-registered identity. The My Number system is new and is subject to great suspicion and protection, so may not become a widely-used component of identification in the way social security numbers have in the United States.

Although financial institutions and cellular phone service providers are now subject to strict customer identity confirmation requirements, many Japanese people do not drive or travel abroad and thus lack a driver's license or passport. Seal registration cards, or the cards issued in connection with national pension, health insurance or other government programs are also used as identification. Foreign residents are issued a residence card that they are required to carry at all times and which serves as a form of identification.

C. PROPERTY AND PROPERTY RIGHTS

1. Overview and Constitutional Dimensions

As already explained, the Civil Code make a clear and important distinction between real rights *(bukken)* and claims *(saiken)*, a distinction that is important to the basic understanding of how private rights are characterized in Japanese law. However, both are included within the broader category of *zaisan* (property), a term that in the Civil Code is used only in the Parts IV and V provisions dealing with subjects such as marital property and inheritance.

Saiken and *bukken* together with other forms of assets (*shisan*) are both also included within the ambit of *zaisanken* (property rights) which are referenced in other laws and protected by article 29 of the constitution. Here they are somewhat clumsily rendered in English as both "the right to own or to hold property" and "property rights." The ambit of this constitutional protection is considered to extend much more broadly than *saiken* and *bukken*, though not to rights to receive government subsidies or welfare benefits.

The language of Article 29 is set forth below.

(1) The right to own or to hold property [*zaisanken*] is inviolable.

(2) Property rights *[zaisanken]* shall be defined by law, in conformity with the public welfare.

(3) Private property may be taken for public use upon just compensation therefor. (*parentheticals added*)

The protection of property rights contained in the Constitution is similar to that of the Meiji Constitution, though under the former charter it was clearly limited to Japanese subjects:

(1) The right of property of every Japanese subject shall remain inviolate.

(2) Measures necessary to be taken for the public benefit shall be provided for by law.

Before even the Meiji Constitution, however, property rights were important and protected. Land reform through the elimination of feudal-era prohibitions on the alienation of agricultural land and the distribution of muniments (certificates of land title) to facilitate both commercialization and taxation of land began in 1872. Yet at the time Japan was still a nation where most people had lived and worked the same land for generations, and one of the challenges of modernizing the property regime was addressing traditional practices such as tenant farming and rights to use communal land such as forests or fishing grounds. As in other countries, electoral rights were also tied to property through a franchise that was limited only to those paying taxes above a certain threshold, until the grant of voting rights to all adult males in 1925.

While it is common to decry the Meiji Constitution's subjecting of all constitutional rights, including property rights, to whatever restrictions might be imposed by law, the very nature of the Meiji Constitution meant that property rights were something bestowed by the Emperor on his subjects. Legislators and other government officials thus had to be circumspect when taking property for the public benefit. While the Meiji Constitution lacked a mandate for compensation for takings of property, the Land Condemnation Act of 1900 did and limited takings to surface rights. Possibly because many takings were in conjunction with essentially public ventures such as railroads conducted by private enterprise, the normal courts were given jurisdiction over disputes. Even during World War II, when the National Mobilization Act of 1938 ostensibly gave the government vast powers to requisition private property and industrial resources, the authorities generally refrained from doing so, instead working cooperatively with companies and paying them to produce items needed for the war.

Today Article 29 is regarded by some as a backwater of constitutional law, with most texts pointing out the conflicted relationship between the first and second clauses:

one declaring property rights (undefined) to be inviolate, and the other then limiting them to the scope of whatever is defined by law in conformity with public welfare.

One of the few instances of the Supreme Court finding a law unconstitutional arises in connection with property rights. In 1987 the court found that restrictions on subdividing forest land imposed by the Forestry Act violated article 29 (Supreme Court, Grand Bench judgment of April 22, 1987; the "*Restriction on Partitioning Forest Land Case* in Table 6-1 in Chapter 6). Though in doing so, the Court appeared to attach as much importance to the logic of article 256 of the Civil Code, which in principal permits co-owners of jointly-owned property to partition it at any time, as it did to the Constitution.

In other cases the court has generally upheld legislative restrictions on property rights, including those imposed through local ordinances and secondary legislation (Supreme Court, Grand Bench judgment of June 26, 1963; 1st Petty Bench judgment of February 1, 1990).[6] Early in the post-war period the court also had to reconcile article 29 with occupation-era policies that involved the wholesale redistribution of land and other wealth through decisions that are no longer relevant.

Despite the seemingly broad discretion given to the Diet to limit property rights in the interests of the public welfare and a number of Supreme Court cases upholding such legislative restrictions, for the most part property rights are accorded great respect in Japan. There is widespread understanding of the basic rules of the Lost Property Act (an 1899 act that was replaced by a new one of the same name in 2006), and the country is almost famous for the reliability with which lost property is turned into the police or other authorities.[7] Despite the existence of condemnation laws, significant negotiations generally go into acquiring land for public purposes. The presence well into the 21st century of a house and a plot of farm land on the apron of Narita Airport near Tokyo—a relic of the poorly executed effort to forcibly acquire the land for what has long been the capital's principal international airport from the 1980s—is evidence of this respect. The Supreme Court finding the confiscation of third party property without due process in criminal proceedings (see discussion at Chapter 6) unconstitutional also presents a useful contrast to the abusive civil asset forfeiture practiced by some law enforcement authorities in the United States.

2. Civil Code Property and Real Rights Revisited

To understand the foundation of property rights, let us now return to a subject introduced earlier in this chapter—*bukken* (real rights). Part II of the Civil Code recognizes ten categories: possession, ownership, superficies, emphyteusis, servitudes, commonage rights, rights of retention, statutory liens, pledges and hypothecs (mortgages). Other statutes establish additional types of *bukken* or deemed *bukken*.

Article 177 of the Civil Code requires that real rights in immovable property must be registered in the commercial registry in order to be perfected as against third parties.

---

[6] The 1990 case involved an MEXT regulation implementing the Firearms and Swords Control Act of 1958. The Act generally prohibits ownership of swords, but allows an exception for swords having artistic or cultural value that are duly registered with the authorities. The implementing rules only provided for registration of Japanese swords, not the Western-style sabre which the unsuccessful appellant in the case was trying to register.

[7] One of the authors has had the experience of stopping by a police box in Tokyo to ask for directions and having to wait while the constable finished bagging a one yen coin that was being handed in by one of the nation's many good Samaritans.

Given that one of the basic features that distinguishes real rights from claims is that they can be asserted against everyone, registration of rights in real property (ownership as well as security interests) giving third parties notice of such rights is a logical extension of this feature. However, registration is not necessary to give legal effect to the creation or transfer of real rights. Under article 176 this is merely a matter of the manifestation of the intent of the parties involved. Since some real rights in real property are security interests whose principal value is their priority over and protection against third parties (*i.e.,* other creditors), registration is essentially required. However, transfers of ownership of real propertydo not need to be registered to be effective as between the parties, resulting in there being significant uncertainty as to who owns a surprising proportion of Japanese private lands, as discussed below.[8]

Taking the real rights provided for in the Civil Code, the first and most basic real right is possession (*senyūken*). Possession may have no legal basis but is often the clearest evidence of the likely existence of real rights of the possessor in the property. Regardless of ultimate ownership and how it was obtained, possession generally entitles the possessor to a legal presumption that the exercise of rights over the property is legal (article 190). It also vests the possessor with rights to enforce his or her possession, thereby discouraging self-help remedies by others (Civil Code, article 190 and articles 197 *et seq.*).

The second *bukken* is ownership (*shoyūken*), the equivalent of common law fee simple absolute. Subject to other laws, ownership of property entitles the owner to freely enjoy the benefits of and dispose of it (Civil Code, article 260). The Code also contains rules regarding co-ownership (joint ownership).

Next there are three categories of *bukken* that entitle the right-holder to *benefit* from property owned by another. These are known as *yōekiken* and sometimes referred to in English as "usufructuary real rights." These include: (i) superfices (*chijōken,* literally "rights above ground" or the right to use the surface of the land), (ii) emphyteusis (*eikyūkosakuken*; the perpetual right to use the land of another for agricultural purposes subject to payment of rent) and (iii) servitudes or easements (*chiekiken*).

Of these, superfices (*chijōken*; articles 265 *et seq.*) may seem functionally similar to long term ground leases, except they can be perpetual, do not need to be derived from a contract and superficiary rightsholders may register them without the assent of the landowner. By contrast, a ground lease has a defined term, is a type ofclaim (*saiken*) and may only be asserted as between the landowner and the leaseholder. Moreover, leaseholders are not formally entitled to have their lease rights registered, and may only request that the landowner do so. That said, over the years laws intended to protect tenants (including owners of houses and buildings constructed on leased land) have resulted in ground leases acquiring a near *bukken*-like quality in practice.

Although the Civil Code (articles 270 *et seq.*) still provides for emphyteusis (perpetual tenant farming rights), these were largely eliminated and rendered unnecessary during the post-war agricultural land reform which resulted in many farmers acquiring the land they worked. In any case, the protection granted to

---

8 Real property taxes are assessed based not on the commercial registry but on records created during the construction permitting process. Thus, although taxable property is identifiable, the inability to identify the true owner/taxpayer through commercial registry records is reportedly becoming a growing issue for local authorities.

leaseholders of agricultural land under the Agricultural Land Act of 1952 is said to be stronger than the real rights granted to tenant farmers under the Civil Code.

Servitudes are dealt with in articles 280 *et seq.* of the Code. Some rights that under the common law would be considered a form of easement, such as the right to use neighboring land to access roads or erect or repair fences or buildings, are considered a component of rights of ownership and addressed under that chapter of the Code (articles 209–238). Unlike these rights, which arise as a matter of law (and in some cases, custom), servitudes as a distinct form of *bukken* arise through the intent of the parties, and entitle the holder of the servitude rights to use the land of another for a particular purpose—drawing agricultural water, for example. Under modern law, many of these goals can arguably also be accomplished through leases or other contractual arrangements. However, together with commonage rights, a broadly defined concept of servitudes are thought to be one of the ways in which the drafters of the Code sought to accommodate various local customs relating to the use of land.

A category of real right that straddles both ownership and servitudes is *iriaiken* (commonage rights). If they include ownership of the underlying land rights, they are a special category of communal ownership that entails using it in a particular way in accordance with local custom (article 263). If they do not include the land, they are essentially a form of easement over the land of another for a specific purpose (article 294). While not defined in such detail, *iriaiken* rights are understood to refer to the customary rights of members of a specific community to use a specific area of forest, field or mountain in a certain way, such as to collect wood or mushrooms.

The remaining four categories of real rights under the Civil Code are those established as security for a debt or other claim. Within this universe, further distinctions can be drawn between possessory and non-possessory rights, and those that arise as a matter of law and those which arise through contract. The four are (i) rights of retention (*ryūchiken*; articles 295 *et seq.*), which are possessory and arise by operation of law (ii) statutory liens (*sakidoritokken*; articles 303 *et seq.*), which are non-possessory and arise as a matter of law, (iii) pledge (*shichiken*; articles 342 *et seq.*), which are possessory and arise through contract and (iv) mortgage or hypothec (*teitōken*; articles 369 *et seq.*), which are non-possessory and contractual.

Rights of retention arise through the delivery of possession where it is clear from circumstances that it will secure related obligations even without an express contractual understanding to such effect. For example, a watch in the possession of a watch repair shop is implicitly held as security for payment of the costs of repair. Additional rights of retention are provided for in the commercial code in the context of specific commercial dealings (e.g., Commercial Code, articles 521, 527, 589 and 753), with Commercial Code rights of retention enjoying greater protection under bankruptcy laws than those arising under the Civil Code.

Statutory liens (*sakidoritokken*; literally, "special preferential taking rights") give their holder a preferential claim on the assets of a debtor. They are an example of a feature of Roman law that was transmitted to Japan through French law models, but were never adopted by German or certain other continental systems. They represent an exception to the general principle that *saiken* (claims) of a creditor should be treated (in bankruptcy, for example), since statutory liens can take priority over contractually-created security interests.

There are several dozen categories of statutory liens, with the Civil Code establishing no less than 15 categories of statutory liens, which are subdivided among those which create a general right against the assets of the debtor, those which apply to specific movable property, and those which apply to specific immovable property. Examples of general preferential rights are those arising in connection with common fees, wages and other amounts owing in connection with an employment relationship, and funeral expenses (article 306). Examples of statutory liens which attach to specific moveable property include rights of a landlord arising in connection with real property leases (e.g., against the lessee's movable property for satisfaction of unpaid rent; articles 311 through 313), and of common carriers as to transported property to the extent of unpaid shipping costs (articles 311 and 318). Example of statutory liens applicable to a debtor's real property include those arising in connection with outstanding costs of construction, repairs to or the unpaid purchase price of the real property (articles 325 *et seq.*). Such liens must be registered to be effective (articles 337–339).

Examples of statutory liens arising under statutes other than the Civil Code include those of the state and local authorities to tax payments and other public duties, as well as special rights arising in maritime, construction and finance contexts. In the case of competing statutory liens, the Civil Code (article 329–330) and other statutes establish the following order of priority (with some exceptions):

1. National taxes
2. Local taxes
3. Payments owed to public authorities and social welfare contributions
4. Common fees
5. Employment-related rights
6. Funeral expenses
7. Cost of necessities
8. Other general collateral

Pledges are possessory rights that can be created contractually over both movable and real property. Pledges of real estate are essentially non-existent today so the relevant provisions of the Civil Code (articles 356 *et seq.*) dealing with them are mostly of historical interest. It is also possible to pledge other property rights (e.g., mining rights or fishing rights) through possession of documentary evidence of those rights, though since many of these rights are created by other statutes, guidance as to the details of security interests in such rights must be sought in those statutes. Some rights (e.g., in bank accounts) may be subject to contractual transfer restrictions which makes pledging them difficult or impossible.

Mortgages (*teitōken*) can be established over land or buildings and entitle the mortgagee to receive payment from the mortgaged property before other creditors, subject to statutory liens. Registration is required and the Civil Code chapter on this form of *bukken* addresses the complexity of mortgages, including priority of claims, joint mortgages, discharge and some rules on disposition of mortgages on auction.

Since the rules on mortgages originally only provided for their use to secure debts in existence at the time the mortgage was established, in 1971 the Code was amended to add articles 398–2 through 398–22, which provide for revolving mortgages (*neteitōken*) that can be used to secure credit facilities for ongoing borrowings. Although banks and businesses had developed practices for engaging in this type of borrowing long before this change, the amendments made the rules clear and dealt with various technical problems from the prior practices that had previously been dealt with through precedent. While regular mortgages require clear identification of the debt they secure, revolving mortgages can be used to secure indeterminate debts that are expected to arise in the future.

As anticipated by the Civil Code itself, a variety of other real rights exist through other statutory regimes, but the rules for their transfer and encumbrance are often governed primarily by those statutes rather than the Civil Code rules. For example, the Fisheries Act of 1949 codifies what were once various traditional fishing rights and "deems" them to be real rights (article 23). This enables them to be readily asserted against infringement, but also generally prohibits them from being alienated or rented out. Similar real rights are crated through laws such as the Mining Act of 1950 (article 12) and the Quarry Act (article 4). A number of commercial laws, starting with the Commercial Code but also including laws such as the Pawn Shop Business Act of 1950, the Railway Mortgage Act of 1905, the Agricultural Moveable Property Credit Act of 1933, the Automobile Lien Act of 1951, the Construction Equipment Lien Act of 1954, the Aircraft Lien Act of 1953 and so forth create real rights in the form of security interests that arise in connection with dealings under those laws. As noted, ground leases with buildings on them have also effectively become a form of *bukken*.

In the world of security interests, those options available through the Civil Code had limitations for many prospective lenders. For lenders wishing to finance the acquisition of moveable equipment or other property for which there was no specific mortgage statute, mortgages were not possible and pledges were not viable since the requirement of possession meant that the borrower could not use the pledged property, defeating the purpose of the arrangement. Even for property such as land where a mortgage could be registered, to benefit from it on default required going through the time consuming and cumbersome auction process.

In response to these limitations, a variety of alternative secured lending practices developed. One was *jōto tanpo* (literally, "transfer collateral") developed. As the name suggests, ownership of the property used for collateral, whether land or equipment, would be transferred to the lender, with the borrower remaining in possession and having the ability to obtain ownership to the property upon payment of the amount of the loan plus interest at the end of the specified period. This had a number of benefits to lenders: on paper they owned the property so in the event of a default or bankruptcy on the part of the borrower, they did not have to do anything and the property was safe from claims of other creditors. Since it was not structured as a loan transaction, the "purchase price" could be set so the economic effect of the transaction was that the borrower paid interest at a rate far above rates prohibited as usury under lending laws. Nor did the lender have to return any surplus to the borrower in the event the value of the transferred property exceeded the value of the loan.

Another practice, one that could be conducted in connection with a *jōto tanpo* transaction, was making a provisional registration of ownership of real property by the lender in the title registry. Some scholars frown on this practice, since it also involves making an essentially false registration in a public registry that third parties are supposed to be able to rely upon. Yet another practice is to "reserve ownership rights" in a seller-financed property until satisfaction of the loan.

Practices such as *jōto tanpo* may sound familiar to an American lawyer from a "title theory of mortgage" jurisdiction, but it should be remembered that it is a practice that developed outside of the bounds of the real rights recognized by the Civil Code or other statutes. Over time courts have addressed many of the problems with the practice so that it is now a form of security interest with known rules. The Provisional Registration Security Act of 1978 also codified a number of protections for borrowers in such arrangements, including a grace period and right to repurchase notwithstanding the default, and an obligation on the creditor/owner to disgorge any surplus value realized upon enforcement.

In addition, in order to facilitate asset-based lending, in 1998 the Act on Special Provisions, etc. of the Civil Code Concerning the Perfection Requirements for the Assignment of Movables and Claims was passed. Under the Act, it has been possible since 2005 to register the transfer of movable property and thereby perfect and clarify the priority of such transfers (whether as collateral or outright transfers) through registration. Similarly, under the same law it is also possible to register the transfer of receivables or other claims in a similar fashion. By providing a means of official notice of assignment of claims, this registration system resolved a problem that existed under the existing Civil Code provisions which required notification of assignment to be given as of a date certain to each obligor, a requirement which made securitization of receivables burdensome or impossible. The system can only be used by corporations and is only available at the Tokyo Legal Affairs Bureau though filings can be made online or by post. It can be used to perfect collateral or actual transfers of moveable property, typically in certificated form such as bills of lading or warehouse receipts.

The development of lease financing has also challenged the existing provisions of the Civil Code, though these are mainly addressed in the context of the Code's contract law provisions.

Finally, it should be noted that trusts have not traditionally been a central feature of Japan's system of property law (or estate planning) in the way they have in common law systems. Trusts are used principally for commercial purposes and administered pursuant to the modern rules contained in the Trust Act of 2006.

3. Land and the Real Property Registration System

The density of Japan's population centers (and thus the magnitude of the growing uncertainty about both ownership and boundaries described below) is hinted at by the fact that 67% of its territory is still forest while another 12% is farmland. Land occupied by houses and buildings comprises only 5.1% of the total, only slightly more than that devoted to roads (3.6%).

According to a 2016 report by the MLIT, of Japan's total land area, 19.9% was owned by the nation (and most of it was forest), 2.8% was owned by prefectures, 5.4% by municipalities, 43.4% was privately owned and ownership of the remainder was categorized as "other." Ownership of privately-owned property was widely dispersed, with over 40 million landowners, the vast majority of whom were natural persons.

Registration of ownership and other real rights (and some contractual rights) in land in buildings is accomplished through the real property registration system, which is administered through the MOJ's nationwide network of Legal Affairs Bureaus and governed by the Real Property Registration Act of 2004. This act replaced an earlier act and modernized the system to provide for computerized and on-line registration.

Japan's registration system has been described as bearing close resemblance to the Torrens system used in some common law jurisdictions. The filings and rules of the system are primarily the domain of a separate legal profession, judicial scriveners (see Chapter 7).

Under the real property registration system, land and buildings are treated as separate items of real property and can be registered separately. Registrations consist of two components, one which describes the land or building, the other the nature of rights (ownership, mortgages, etc.) in it. Nine types of rights can be registered, not all of which are Civil Code *bukken*: ownership, superfices, statutory liens, perpetual farming rights, servitudes, pledges (of real property), mortgages, lease rights and quarrying rights. Unless provided otherwise by law, the order of priority of rights follows the chronological order of their registration.

Since its purpose is to give notice to third parties about the rights in a particular piece of real property, it is accessible to the public. However, there are restrictions on those professions who can make registration filings on behalf of others for a fee.

The bifurcated nature of the manner in which real property is registered reflects the history of the system, which once involved two entirely separate registries, one describing the property and the other describing the rights in it. As noted in Chapter 7, one manifestation of the systems history is two separate professions (judicial scriveners and land and building investigators), whose practices are based on the two different categories of registration information.

As already noted, registration is not necessary to give effect to a transfer of property as between the transferor and the transferee, including transfers by testate or intestate succession. If all the identifiable heirs are present it is possible to register the change in ownership through the registration system without going to court. However this is often not done, either because the heirs are not identified, do not want the real property, or because of the expenses involved in registering a change of title (in the case of mountains or forested land, the costs of the title change may exceed the value of the land in some places). Even with more valuable property the situation may not be different. For example, for a sole heir already living in the house he inherited from his deceased parents, there may be little or no need to undergo the expense and bother of registering the change of ownership, unless to use it as collateral.

Based on a 2014 survey of title records of 100 municipalities, the MLIT estimated that the ownership of approximately 20% of the privately owned land in Japan is indeterminable. Also, 20% of title registrations in the surveyed municipalities showed no new registrations as to ownership being made within the past 50 years!

With Japan's aging and shrinking population, more people are abandoning homes or homeowners are dying without immediate heirs. Somewhat paradoxically, in combination with the *koseki* system this is problematic since it is at least theoretically possible (though often not without tremendous effort in the case of elderly decedents with long and complicated family histories) to identify, though not necessarily *locate* all of the decedent's legal heirs who may have rights in a piece of real property. The inability to confirm ultimate ownership has hindered efforts of local governments to deal with abandoned or empty houses and land. A 2017 book on the subject[9] describes a small municipality that, with great effort, was able to use past real estate title and *koseki* records to identify 150 possible heirs to a 192 m^2 plot of land.

An additional problem is that Japan's national territory has never been fully surveyed. Pursuant to a mandate under the National Land Survey Act of the MLIT has been conducting a survey of lands and trying to establish formal boundaries between plots since the law was passed in 1951. At the time of writing, however, this survey was only 52% complete as to the total land area of Japan, but stalled particularly in densely inhabited municipal areas, where over 75% of the land had yet to be properly surveyed. The entire survey process is estimated to require 120 years to complete, but may become more difficult since the cooperation of landowners is generally required to complete the surveys.

Moreover, in a minority of instances surveys reveal discrepancies between previous map records and the situation on the ground, which requires a notation of uncertainty as to boundaries to be reflected in the land registry. This can impair the value of property or cause disputes among neighbors who previously thought they were certain of the metes and bounds of their properties.

As a result, although article 14 of the Real Property Registration Act anticipates that registration of rights in real property will be based on land survey maps available at the relevant Legal Affairs Bureau, in many areas such maps are still not available. This means that many registrations are conducted through an "exception" under article 14(4) which allows other available maps to be used. In many cases these are still copies of maps prepared by the government for tax purposes as far back as the Meiji Period. Such maps are not always accurate as to boundaries and features.

In any case, the formal boundaries indicated in survey maps are not dispositive of ownership, since land owners are generally free to dispose of such parts of their land as they feel appropriate. Even where the ownership of land is known, there may be disputes over what the actual boundaries are due to discrepancies between possession or the nature of a past transfer and the boundaries indicated on the real estate registry map (which may not be derived from a modern survey in any case). Through its network of Legal Affairs Bureaus, the MOJ offers a system of resolving border disputes or uncertainties without litigation. Land and building investigator professional associations also offer ADR services in this area.

Note that there are no restrictions on foreign private ownership of land in Japan. Non-Japanese have been able to buy real property in Japan since 1925.

4. Other Property-Related Registration Systems

For ships over twenty tons there is a separate registration system administered by the MLIT. Two systems, actually: under the Ship Act of 1899 and the Ship Registration Regulations of 2005 ownership of and other private rights (e.g., mortgages and leasehold rights) in such ships are registered in a system analogous to the real property registration system and which incorporates by reference many provisions of the Real Property Registration Acts (except that registration is mandatory). The second (also

---

[9] SHŌKO YOSHIHARA, *JINKŌ GENSHŌ JIDAI NO TOCHIMONDAI* [Land Issues in the Age of Population Decline] (2017).

under the Ship Act) registers the nationality of the ship as Japanese for international law purposes.

A little-known service offered by the MOJ's legal affairs bureaus is the registration of "marital property contracts" under the MOJ's Spousal Property Contract Registration Regulations of 2005 (which replaced much older regulations dating back to the Meiji Period). Possibly because there is almost no awareness of its existence, this system is rarely used, with only 23 registrations made in 2016, and only 6 in 2015.

Since 2000 the legal affairs bureaus have also been used to register guardianship arrangements under the Civil Code (article 838 *et seq.*), whether resulting from a court decree or a voluntary arrangement pursuant to a notarized guardianship agreement. This replaces the old system whereby notations of legal incapacity were recorded in the relevant person's *koseki* (and used Meiji-era terminology such as *kinchisansha* that literally meant "prohibited from managing property"). Registrations can be made on-line through the Tokyo Legal Affairs Bureau, but certification of the arrangements can be issued by relevant municipal authorities. A guardian can use such certification to prove they have legal authority to manage property and other affairs of the person subject to guardianship. Certifications issued through the system can also be used to prove that one is *not* subject to guardianship and thus not lacking in capacity. Unlike marital property contracts, use of this system is common and growing. Over 168,000 registrations relating to guardianship were made in 2016, compared to just 75,000 ten years earlier.

5. Other Laws Relating to Land

By one estimate there are approximately Japanese 300 laws relating to land. These include a wide variety of urban planning laws and other administrative laws (which may in turn delegate further rule-making to local authorities) of the type that one would see in any modern country and which can have a significant impact on the value and use of private property. Of these only two will be discussed.

The first is the Act on Land and Building Leases of 1991. This act replaced the Land Lease Act of 1921 and the Building Lease Act of the same year. Both laws levelled the playing field between landowners and lessees who either relied on leased land (rather than superfices) for their houses or buildings, or as tenants within a house or building. Since under the Civil Code leases were merely contractual rather than real rights, they were comparatively weak, particularly as against third party transferees of the underlying real property. Japanese courts have further protected lessors, who generally have the right to renew leases indefinitely. Courts have been particularly protective of residential tenants who are hard to remove in Japan, a status that was used abusively by unscrupulous real estate investors to frustrate liquidation of real property collateral after Japan's real estate bubble burst in the 1990s.

In some ways the 1991 law can be seen as levelling the playing field back in favor of lessors. For example, the law makes it possible to enter into fixed term leases that are not subject to automatic renewal rights. However, it still contains a number of provisions highly protective of tenants and which are mandatory in that any contractual terms that seek to modify them are void. It also contains special exceptions to the Civil Code rules on claims that enable lessees to assert their leasehold rights against third parties, even without registration. Law and economics scholars such as Professor J. Mark Ramseyer have argued that excessive protection of tenants by Japanese law and courts is one of the factors that have contributed to a shortage of spacious, affordable, good quality rental housing.[10]

The second is the Agricultural Land Act of 1952. Land reform was a key part of the occupation-era reforms which dovetailed well with the efforts of agricultural bureaucrats to protect tenant farmers from abusive landlords during the pre-war period. In addition, with much of Japan covered by forest and/or mountains, there has long been tension between whether what remains should be used for urban development, residential communities or agriculture. What constitutes good farmland usually also makes a nice location for a house or shopping mall.

The ALA was thus intended to protect both farming and farmers. It did so by creating a special category of land and imposing strict restraints on its alienation and use (including through leases). Agricultural land and rights in it are registered in a separate registry maintained by municipal governments. Agricultural land enjoys various tax benefits. Until amendments to the ALA in 2009 most forms of corporate ownership and long-term use rights in agricultural land were prohibited, as were most transfers to persons other than actual farmers. There was a lot of cheating and with Japan's farming population shrinking and the restrictions preventing the efficient use of farm land (including through industrial farming methods), the 2009 amendments widened the scope of possible use and ownership/usage rights. Many transfers (excluding inheritance) still require the approval of the local Agricultural Committee.

D. TORT CLAIMS

As already described, the other principal category of rights under the Civil Code and related act consist of various types of claims (*saiken*). Tort and contract are two areas where claims are frequently asserted. Contract is discussed in Chapter 11. Accordingly the remainder of this chapter will address how substantive tort claims are addressed under the Civil Code. The related subject of products liability is also covered in Chapter 11.

The principle source of Japanese tort law is article 709 of the Code, which reads:

> A person who has intentionally or negligently infringed any right of others, or legally protected interest of others, shall be liable to compensate any damages resulting in consequence.

This is arguably nothing more than a statement of tort law as it has been applied in most countries for centuries. A great deal of interpretive detail has had to be added to tort law through precedents, court practice and more specific statutes. In that sense there is a certain commonality with common law systems.

Unlike the common law system, there is no general system of separate causes for negligence, strict liability or other forms of tort. Moreover, with both contract and claim being rooted in the same part of the Civil Code, the distinction between those two doctrines may not be as significant as in the common law.

For example, in the medical malpractice context, whether a doctor has committed negligence by breaching a particular standard of care, or breached an implied standard of care in an actual or implicit contract to provide medical services may be a largely notional distinction. Going the other way, article 415 of the current Civil Code (which

[10] JOHN MARK RAMSEYER, SECOND-BEST JUSTICE: THE VIRTUES OF JAPANESE PRIVATE LAW (2015).

imposes on obligors liability for damages from non-performance of obligations, including impossibility of performance due to "reasons attributable to the obligor) effectively adds to breach of contract claims a standard analogous to the article 709 negligence/intentional act tort standard. In a similar vein, liability for defects can be addressed in tort but also by a buyer under article 570 which imposes on sellers a general liability for latent defects (and which article 572 and other statutes limit the ability of sellers to contract out of).

Japanese courts have also long applied the Civil Code provision on recovery of foreseeable special damages on breach of an obligation (article 416, which is primarily a contractual concept) to the scope of damages recoverable in tort (e.g., Supreme Court of Judicature judgment of May 22, 1926; Supreme Court, 1st Petty Bench judgement of June 7, 1973). Japanese law does not provide for punitive or exemplary damages and Japan's Supreme Court has refused on public policy grounds to recognize foreign judgements awarding such damages (Supreme Court, 2nd Petty Bench judgment of July 11, 1997), so the distinction between tort and contract is also not as important for damage purposes as it is in the American system.

What constitutes intentional or negligent infringements for purposes of 709 has been the subject of significant academic debate as well development of judicial doctrines. Again, though, there being no distinct "intentional tort" cause of action as in the common law system, less importance is attached to whether behavior was intentional or negligent. While intentional behavior may have a bearing on the amount of damages awarded in some cases, recover generally does not require negligence or intent. Rather the issue is likely to be one of the degree to which the defendant's mental state is blameworthy.

While intent/negligence is the baseline for tort liability, certain other statutes impose different standards. For example, the Responsibility for Fires Act of 1899 creates a special exception to article 709 of the Civil Code whereby liability only attaches to gross (serious) negligence. On the other hand, there are a number of statutory provisions that provide for what could be called "strict liability" (but which in Japanese simply means "liability without negligence"—*mukashitsusekinin*). Examples include the liability imposed on those in control of defective structures on land or animals under articles 717 and 718 of the Civil Code, liability for workplace injuries under the Labor Standards Act of 1947, liability under the Anti-Monopoly Act of 1947, and perhaps most famously in recent years, the Compensation of Damages from Nuclear Power Act of 1971 (CDNPA). However, it has been pointed out that many laws that appear to apply strict liability to a particular category of harm, are either implemented expressly or implicitly with some sort of negligence-like determination (e.g., through the determination of what constitutes a "defect" or whether a *proviso* allowing a possible defense for liability applies). Even the CDNPA contains a proviso that exempts nuclear plant operators from danages resulting from extreme natural disasters or social unrest.

Absent special pleading requirements in particular cases, as a practical matter the plaintiff must assert the following elements for most tort claims to get anywhere in court require:

1. The existence of a right or legally-protected interest of the plaintiff;
2. The infringement by defendant of such right or interest;

3. The infringement resulted from intentional or negligent behavior by defendant;
4. Injury and the value thereof;
5. A relationship between the infringement and the injury; and
6. If the unlawfulness of defendant's infringement is not self-evident, evidence to such effect.

As originally drafted in 1896, article 709 only recognized tort liability for the infringement of *rights (kenri)*. These were a limited universe of generally known rights derived from statutes. Article 710 also clearly anticipates recovery for infringements of "body, liberty or reputation" or property rights of others, while article 711 establishes claims for wrongful death by surviving kin (which has been extended interpretively to those in *defacto* marriages). Other rights could (and can) be found in other statutes such as those protecting various types of intellectual property rights or corporate names.

The originally limited scope of tort liability is said to have been intended to protect freedom (particularly the economic freedom of businesses) by limiting tort recovery to infringements of clearly protected rights. For example, in 1914, the Supreme Court of Judicature held that the producer of a record of third party *rōkyoku* folk songs could not recover against a defendant who made unsanctioned copies of it on the grounds that there were no copyrights or neighboring rights in "low class" music (Supreme Court of Judicature judgment of July 4, 1914).

The following decade the court reversed itself, however, finding in the so-called *Daigakuyū* case that even without a clearly articulated right at state, tort liability could arise from the infringement of a broader range of "legally protected interest" (in the case at bar the interest was the goodwill associated with a public bathhouse operating under a particular name; Supreme Court of Judicature judgment of November 28, 1925). Since this time courts have gradually expanded the scope of interests the unlawful infringement of which can give rise to tort liability.

The "or other legally protected interest" language of article 709 was added in 2004, though in many ways may have just codified what were already interpretive practices. A narrower sampling of a broader range of interests (which are sometimes characterized as an extension of a recognized right) giving rise to tort liability include privacy (which was found violated, for example, by a university giving to the police a list of students who had applied to attend a speech by a visiting Chinese leader (Supreme Court, 2nd Petty Bench judgment of September 12, 2003), rights to sunlight (Supreme Court, 3rd Petty Bench judgment of June 27, 1972) and freedom from airport noise (e.g., Supreme Court, Grand Bench judgment of December 16, 1981). In a 2004 judgment the Supreme Court even acknowledged that the residents of a particular neighborhood could have a protected interest in it continuing to "look" a particular way (and thus not have the look ruined by the construction of a high rise block of flats), though it declined to find the plaintiffs were entitled to protection in the case at bar (Supreme Court, 1st Petty Bench judgment of March 30, 2004.

In the sphere of family relationships, spousal chastity and the marital relationship have long been protected interests, with tort claims against adulterous spouses or their lovers being a common feature in divorce litigation. The supreme court has even recognized parental interference in a son's *defacto* marriage which resulted in the marriage failing constituted a tort against the ex-wife (Supreme Court, 2nd Petty Bench judgment of February 1, 1963).

As in other systems of tort law, the mental state of the defendant is often an issue. If intentional behavior is alleged as the cause of the plaintiff's harm, then it must be established that the defendant was aware of the possible consequences and acted anyways. If nonfeasance is to be tortious, it must also be established that the defendant had a particular duty to act, though this may be due to the circumstances. In a 1987 decision it was held that when one member of a group of teenagers put a rock on a train track, the other members were tortiuously liable for failing to remove it and thus responsible for the derailment that followed (Supreme Court, 1st Petty Bench judgment of January 22, 1987).

As for negligence, courts generally base findings of liability on breach of a duty to avoid the harm-causing consequences, which assumes foreseeability (this was established in the so called "*Arukari* case" which involved a chemical factory that emitted fumes which damaged surrounding farmland (Supreme Court of Judicature judgment of September 19, 1916). In different types of case (medical malpractice, traffic accident, etc.), courts have developed different doctrines and practices for evaluating foreseeability and thus the standard of care, breach of which constitutes negligence. Note that some statutes, including the Civil Code impose a specific standard of care in certain situations. For example article 298 imposes on possessory lienholders a "duty of care of a good manager" in respect to the property in possession.

Note that pleadings of negligence or intent are not binding on courts; a plaintiff asserting intentional conduct by the defendant does not foreclose a court from finding the defendant negligent. Similarly, a court may not reject a plaintiff's claim on the grounds of lack of intent by defendant without also finding a lack of negligence (Supreme Court of Judicature judgment of September 19, 1916).

Causation and damages are also areas where a great deal has been developed through precedent. In some cases, such as pollution or pharmacological torts where proving causation can be difficult, courts have used evidentiary burden-shifting to lessen the unfairness on plaintiffs.

Monetary damages are the principle remedy for tort claims (article 722), with the Supreme Court generally being hostile to injunctive relief except in special circumstances, though lower courts may issue injunctions in cases which are ultimately settled without reaching the top court. Article 723 allows a court to order "appropriate measures" to remedy reputational torts such as defamation. Famous instances of such remedies include enjoining publication of a defamatory publication and forcing a newspaper to publish an apology over a defamatory article (Supreme Court, Grand Bench Judgments of June 11, 1986 and July 4, 1956).

When damages are of a nature rendering it difficult to prove them in monetary terms, article 248 of the Code of Civil Procedure allows a court to make a finding of "appropriate damages." In a similar vein, contributory negligence is addressed in article 722(2) of the Code, which allows a court to adjust damages to account for the plaintiff's negligence. Not having a civil jury to attach monetary values to tort damages, Japanese courts and practitioners have adopted a variety of practices that make the process seem somewhat mechanistic (which it is). Both courts and lawyers have developed manuals based on court precedents and practices that they use to evaluate damages and, where appropriate, apportion comparative negligence to the plaintiff.

There are, of course, various defenses to tort liability both general ones (such as lack of capacity under article 713 of the code) and those in the form of *provisos* to articles establishing specific grounds for liability. For example, article 715(1) of the Code establishes the master-servant liability of employers for torts committed by employees in the course of conducting employer business, but includes an exception "if the employer exercised reasonable care in appointing the employee or in supervising the business" (a defense which is rarely invoked successfully). There are also defenses that reduce damages, such as comparative negligence or third party conduct.

For damage suits against the state or a public authority, the State Redress Act of 1947 establishes slightly different, and in some cases somewhat broader standards from the Civil Code. However, general tort principles generally apply in such cases, though it must be shown that the damages were caused by a public officer exercising public authority in the course of performing his or her duties. Neither the executive nor judicial branches of government publish statistics on such cases, so it is difficult to evaluate success rates.

In closing it should be noted that tort litigation in particular has been an area where of significant academic debate over the difference in the amount of litigation between Japan and the United States. Various commentators have sought to attribute this to, among other things, a Japanese cultural preference for not resolving disputes through adversarial litigation, the comparative difficulty and expense of bringing successful litigation in Japan, or the comparative predictability of Japanese court decisions, which facilitates out of court settlements by lawyers and insurance companies.

This book will not attempt to consider any of these views. However, it is worth noting that one factor which gets little attention may be Japan's public health insurance system which makes medical care available to the Japanese public at prices which are not ruinous; health-care related personal bankruptcies do not to be a phenomenon the way they are in the United States. This system may also impact tort litigation in another way. As Harvard's J. Mark Ramseyer speculated in a 2015 book, Japan's public health insurance system functions in a way that results in most doctors being compensated by the system for providing scheduled, routine procedures which generate comparatively few malpractice cases, as compared to the United States where innovative but risky new procedures generate a disproportionate amount of cases.[11]

---

[11] *Id.*

Chapter 10

THE CIVIL AND ADMINISTRATIVE JUSTICE SYSTEMS

Analysis

A. INTRODUCTION AND CONSTITUTIONAL DIMENSIONS

This chapter will cover the civil litigation process and other court and administrative proceedings that are available for resolving disputes outside the criminal sphere.

Subjects covered will include: (1) non-litigation matters, (2) civil conciliation and civil litigation, (3) family court civil proceedings (including personal status litigation), (4) administrative claims and litigation. Brief attention will also be given to special procedural regimes such as bankruptcy, as well as ADR mechanisms and institutions. Special dispute resolution bodies provided by national government ministries and agencies (some of which are touched upon in Chapter 3) will also be mentioned.

Article 32 of the Constitution recognizes access to the courts as a basic human right. The charter does not distinguish between cases arising under public and private law in this guarantee, and of course many important rights are protected and enforced through civil and administrative litigation. Thus, while there are not as many clearly relevant constitutional provisions as there are with the criminal justice system, access to civil and administrative justice through the pursuit of remedies in court is clearly a matter of constitutional significance.

As already noted but worth repeating, the English version of article 32 ("No person shall be denied the right of access to the courts.") is somewhat misleading. The Japanese might be more correctly translated as: "No person shall be deprived of the right to a trial in court." This nuance is important to understand because it means in the Japanese version the guarantee only extends to "trials" (*saiban*), a specific term the definition of which in the civil context refers to only a subset of the proceedings which take place in civil courts in Japan.

Both the Supreme Court and academic theory are in agreement that the "trial" in article 32 refers to an adversarial trial conducted in open court (as required by article 82 of the Constitution, which also uses the term "*saiban*") pursuant to litigation proceedings. In 1960 the Supreme Court found unconstitutional the application of a wartime statute that allowed courts to impose a conciliated result achieved through non-contentious proceedings (discussed below) on parties in landlord-tenant disputes without appellate judicial recourse (Supreme Court, Grand Bench decision of July 6, 1960). Article 32 does not, however, guarantee access to the full panoply of appellate proceedings in all cases. For example, the court found there were no constitutional issues with article 394 of the (old) CCivPro, which limited appeals to the Supreme Court (Supreme Court, Grand Bench judgment of September 18, 1950). The court has also upheld the constitutionality of various other rules or dispositions having the effect of severely restricting the ability of parties to pursue litigation or appeals (e.g., a statute that retroactively shortens a limitation period for bringing claims).

With respect to what constitutes a "court," as noted in Chapter 4, article 76 of the Constitution clearly vests the entire judicial power in the Supreme Court and such other inferior courts as are created by law. It also prohibits the exercise by executive branch agencies of *final* judicial power. There are administrative agency institutions that exercise (or have in the past exercised) a form of quasi-judicial "first instance" jurisdiction over certain types of cases, and other hybrid judicial institutions that are not full courts. Some of these are mentioned later in this chapter (see Table 10-5). However in all cases recourse from decisions of such bodies is theoretically possible through appeals to the courts of law.

The following table sets forth some basic statistical information on the civil and administrative caseload of Japanese courts:

TABLE 10-1 SAMPLE HISTORICAL DATA CASES BROUGHT/CLEARED IN JAPANESE COURTS

Year*	Civil and Administrative Cases (other than family cases; Summary, District, High and Supreme Court)				Family Cases (Family Courts and appellate courts in family cases)**
	Total Cases	Litigation**	Conciliation	Other***	
1950	429,853	74,215	56,300	299,338	429,853
	412,603	63,006	53,390	296,607	412,602
1960	970,134	166,518	64,936	738,680	336,057
	960,975	168,720	66,231	726,024	337,138
1970	1,231,321	190,916	53,377	987,028	280,021
	1,218,286	183,417	52.455	982,414	277,662
1980	1,469,848	221,393	64,868	1,183,587	349,774
	1,455,279	216,126	64,084	1,165,069	348,720
1990	1,715,193	229,718	61,007	1,424,468	342,998
	1,779,269	237,985	59,683	1,481,601	340,232
2000	3,051,709	524,884	317,986	2,208,839	560,935
	3,062,459	530,276	298,556	2,233,627	555,455
2010	2,179,355	910,466	87,808	1,181,081	815,052
	2,241,425	947,369	90,888	1,203,168	815,412
2016	1,470,612	539,537	39,191	891,884	1,470,612
	1,482,598	541,562	39,635	901,401	1,482,598

SOURCE: Supreme Court Judicial Statistics.

* For each year given, the upper number is the number of new cases brought during the year, the lower the number represents cases cleared, which includes some cases brought in prior years.

** "Litigation" includes data for: (i) administrative litigation and (ii) divorce and other personal status litigation which, prior to 2004, was under the jurisdiction of district courts but since 2004 is handled by family courts.

*** "Other" includes a broad range of actions brought mostly in district courts, such as corporate litigation and bankruptcy-related actions, domestic violence restraining orders, cases brought in labor tribunals, enforcement actions and preventative dispositions. For example, data for 2016 also includes *shiharai tokusoku* payment demand petitions (a procedure that facilitates prompt enforcement of debts) against a total of 276,030 debtors.

Notwithstanding a healthy body of literature asserting Japanese people are litigation averse, the Table 10-1 shows that a there are still significant volumes of litigation in the civil courts. This is particularly remarkable when one considers the comparatively small number of Japanese judges, as discussed in Chapter 4.

At the risk of stating the obvious, litigation rates are affected by law. For example, courts experienced a significant jump in litigation in the mid-'00s after a series of Supreme Court decision made it possible for consumer borrowers to go to court to recoup from moneylenders interest charged above the civil usury rate; the payment of the excess having previously been deemed voluntary (e.g., Supreme Court, 2nd Petty Bench judgment of January 13, 2006). The resulting spike in litigation accounts for the near-doubling of litigation matters when comparing 2000 and 2010, with the peak appearing to have occurred in 2009 when well over half of the cases brought for initial trial in district courts (144,168 out of a total of 235,508 cases).

The resolution of a large but limited universe of possible excess interest cases also accounts for the similar drop in litigation numbers by 2016, when out of 148,295 total civil cases brought in district courts, only 47,352 were of that type. Similar spikes and drops in litigation or particular types have occurred at other times in modern Japanese history and can often be attributed to specific events or changes in law or practice.

B. NON-CONTENTIOUS CASES

Civil courts play a role in a diverse category of cases known as "non-contentious cases" (*hishō jiken*). These are resolved primarily through procedures set forth in the Non-Contentious Case Procedure Act of 2011 (NCCPA), which replaced an earlier act of the same name dating back to 1898.

The roles courts play in non-contentious cases are often administrative and provided for in various statutes that require court involvement in what are essentially private law relationships in order to further policy goals. As an example, by statute members of a corporate or asset-based foundation may resolve to petition a court to appoint a corporate auditor to examine the records of the foundation (General Incorporated Associations and General Incorporated Foundations Act of 2006, articles 46 and 86).

The role played by the court in such cases does not constitute a "trial," and courts do not issue "judgments" (*hanketsu*) in their resolutions. The proceedings thus do not need to be held in open court. Not being trials, parties to such actions are not being denied their right to a trial under article 32 as the result of some of the procedural restraints the NCCPA imposes. Recourse from unfavorable results in such proceedings is available through the appellate litigation process, satisfying constitutional requirements.

Matters for resolution under the NCCPA are generally provided for in specific statutes. Some are specified within the NCCPA itself, such as petitions to enforce against pledged moveable property (article 93), the appointment of an appraiser in connection with the extinguishing of a right of retention under the Civil Code (article 96) or when giving notice by publication of proposed actions that may affect the rights of indeterminate or unknown interested parties (article 99).

Examples from other statutes are numerous but include petitions to appoint an asset custodian for a trust pending replacement of the trustee (Trust Act of 2006, article 63), and to modify rents or change the terms of ground rights under the Land and Building Leases Act (articles 17–20). The Companies Act of 2005 contains an entire chapter (articles 868 *et seq.*) setting forth rules for resolving "non-contentious" matters arising under it.

Many matters resolved by family courts are also done through essentially non-contentious proceedings, though pursuant to a different procedural statute (the Domestic Relations Case Procedure Act of 2011 (DRCPA), which was passed on the same day as the NCCPA and incorporates by reference some of its penalty provisions (DRCPA article 291(2). Family court matters are addressed in more detail in this chapter.

Of course simply calling a matter "non-contentious" does not make it so. Divorces can be highly contentious as can landlord-tenant and corporate disputes. One criticism of the system of resolving such matters through notionally non-contentious proceedings has been that, depending on the type of action, it can have the same substantive effect as a trial on the rights and duties of a party but without the protections accorded by the rules of civil procedure. Judges are also typically accorded extremely broad discretion in such cases, again without being bounded by clear rules of evidence or procedure.

The passing in 2011 of the new NCCPA (and the DRCPA) represented an effort to address some of these complaints. The new law added provisions for participation by interested parties, provides greater access to case records, and makes the procedures easier by enabling participation through video conference or telephonic means, making resolutions through settlements possible in some cases, and providing for the appointment of expert commissioners in cases where subject matter expertise is necessary or helpful. Yet their basic character as non-trials for procedural and constitutional purposes remains.

C. CIVIL CONCILIATION

Most disputes among private parties are resolved through either civil conciliation or civil litigation. Both involve the courts, with cases typically being brought in either a summary or district court, depending on the nature of the action.

Of the two procedures, civil conciliation (*minji chōtei*) could easily be the most "Japanese," and some commentators suggest that it has roots in well-established dispute resolution practices going back for hundreds of years. In essence, conciliation involves the parties appearing before a judge alone or a conciliation committee comprised of a judge and two civil conciliation commissioners. Representation by a lawyer is not required and the proceedings are non-adversarial, aimed at arriving at a settlement agreeable to both parties rather than a black and white result where one wins and one loses.

In its current form, civil conciliation is conducted under the Civil Conciliation Act of 1951 (CCA). Generally it is up to one of the parties to initiate the proceedings, but judges may also refer cases to conciliation when they deem it appropriate (articles 2 and 20).

Civil conciliation commissioners are appointed by the Supreme Court from *bengoshi* lawyers and other "respectable" members of the local community who have achieved the age of at least 40 (Supreme Court Rules on Civil and Family Court Conciliators of 1974). While the process involves judicial oversight, 2003 amendments to the CCA also made it possible for the Supreme Court to appoint *bengoshi* lawyers with at least five years' practice experience to act as "Civil Conciliators," effectively acting as part-time judges in such cases (though without being called "judges;" CCA, article 23–2).

Most civil conciliation cases unfold at summary courts, which have default jurisdiction under the CCA absent special circumstances (article 3). Of the 39,191 new conciliation cases for 2016, 35,708 were brought in summary courts. Of the 36,138 conciliation cases *cleared* by summary courts in 2016, 12,079 saw formal conciliated settlements reached, 10,334 failed to do so, 6,815 ended with the judge issuing a "decision in lieu of conciliation" (discussed below). In 6,005 cases the petition for conciliation was withdrawn. The CCA also provides special rules for conciliation in particular types of dispute, including commercial, real-estate, farming and pollution (article 24 *et seq.*).

These proceedings are also not "trials" for constitutional purposes and thus do not need to be conducted in open court, privacy being one of their merits for the parties. Article 22 of the CCA also provides for the applicability of the Non-Contentious Cases Act to conciliation proceedings where applicable.

Civil conciliation may seem superficially similar to western mediation (but it is quite different. Among other things, since the conciliation takes place before a judge the clear separation between that part of the process and any subsequent litigation that is expected in western mediation is not as clear. Although parties are not required to accept a conciliated result and can proceed with litigation if the conciliation is unsuccessful, the judges and other court personnel cannot "un-hear" statements made by parties in the process, and there are no evidentiary rules or privileges clearly prohibiting the use of offers of settlement, admissions or other statements made in the course of conciliation at a subsequent trial.

Similarly, while Western mediators tend to stop at facilitating the negotiations between the parties, Japanese civil conciliation proceedings may involve the judge or conciliation committee essentially dictating a proposed settlement. Judges can even issue a "decision in lieu of conciliation," essentially the judge's evaluation of the agreement the parties *should* have reached (CCA, article 17). This becomes binding if neither party files an objection within two weeks (article 18).

D. CIVIL LITIGATION

1. Introduction

Japan's system of civil litigation is rooted in continental models. For over a century disputes between private parties were conducted under the Code of Civil Procedure of 1890, the drafting of which was influenced by the Prussian jurist Eduard Hermann Robert Techow. It was amended significantly in 1926 (this time with influences from the Austrian code of civil procedure), but survived largely intact until it was replaced with the current Code of Civil Procedure of 1996 (CCivPro). The CCivPro is supplemented by the Supreme Court's Rules of Civil Procedure of 1996 (RCP).

Having no civil jury system, both the legal and factual issues in disputes in civil cases are decided by judges, either sitting alone or in panels, usually of three. The absence of a jury means more flexibility as to the timing of evidentiary proceedings, less clear divisions between pre-trial and trial proceedings, and simpler rules of evidence. Finally, although the rules of civil procedure anticipate oral testimony from parties and their witnesses, testimonial evidence is probably less important than it is in American civil trials. In many Japanese trials most evidence is either in documentary form or is reduced to it through the trial record. The judicial career path described in Chapter 4 means that a judge who has heard highly emotional witness testimony in a case may be transferred to another post while it is still in process, leaving his or her successor to render a judgment based on the transcripts.

2. Small Claims Litigation

2003 amendments to the CCivPro (articles 368 through 381) introduced expedited procedures facilitating the resolution of small financial claims in summary courts. At the time of writing such proceedings could be used for monetary claims of JPY 600,000 or less (which amount should not be confused with the overall jurisdictional threshold for civil claims brought in civil court, which under the Courts Act (article 33(1)) is a maximum of JPY 1.4 million). Such proceedings do not require witnesses to be sworn, permit the judge to deliver an immediate oral judgment and are generally not subject to appeal though the defendant can move to have the case governed by the general rules of civil trials, including for purposes of making a counterclaim.

Small claims litigation seems to have achieved limited popularity. Of 845,777 civil actions brought in summary courts in 2016, only 11,030 were brought under the small claims procedure, compared to 326,170 standard civil lawsuits.

3. Standard Civil Litigation

a. *Overview*

Most significant civil litigation is brought in district courts under the CCivPro. Administrative litigation brought under the ACLA and family cases brought under the Personal Status Litigation Act of 2003 (PSLA), both discussed later in this chapter, follow many of the basic rules of the CCivPro but are subject to numerous special exceptions.

In 2016, a total of 148,016 litigation matters were cleared by district courts in Japan. A breakdown of the nature of these lawsuits is set forth in the following table.

TABLE 10-2 BREAKDOWN OF LAWSUITS CLEARED BY DISTRICT COURTS 2016

Type of Case		Number	Average length of trial (months)
Suits for monetary claims	Accounts receivable	1,818	8.6
	Recovery monies owed	7,001	8.9
	Recovery of advances paid	2,923	3.4
	Recovery of construction costs	1,498	16.5
	Damages for defective building	533	25.2
	Damage claims from traffic accidents	14,692	12.3
	Medical malpractice claims	749	24.2
	Pollution-related damage claims	97	11.9
	Other damage claims	28,211	10.5
	Amounts owing under promissory notes	14	8.9
	Objections to promissory notes	38	15.8
	Confirmation of existence (or absence) of payment obligation	1,613	8.4
	Wages	2,441	14.2
	Monies in connection with intellectual property rights	220	13.7
	Other monetary claims	44,357	7.4
Other Civil Suits	Relating to buildings	23,106	3.8
	Relating to land	7,276	9.2
	Relating to boundaries	426	17.2
	Relating to employment (other than monetary claims)	956	14.8
	Relating to intellectual property (other than monetary claims)	318	14.2
	Objections to debt claims	291	8.8
	Third party objections	85	9.0
	Pollution-related injunctions	6	18.3
	Shareholder derivative litigation (etc.)	54	22.7
	Other	9,290	9.5
TOTAL		148,016	8.6
SOURCE: Supreme Court judicial statistics.			

b. Filing, Fees and Service of Process

A civil case begins with a plaintiff filing a complaint against a defendant, ideally in the appropriate court of jurisdiction. The case is docketed by the court and the complaint reviewed to confirm it satisfies the basic requirements to be heard by the court. A complaint must identify the parties, the nature of the plaintiff's claim, the relief sought from the court, the reason for the claim and a description of the relevant facts and possible evidence. If defective, the court may dismiss the complaint or order the plaintiff to amend it.

A complaint filed with a court must also be accompanied by payment of the required filing fees. These generally take the form of revenue stamps that must be affixed to the complaint, though if the amount of fees is very large payment can be separately tendered in cash. Fees are set by the Costs of Civil Litigation Act of 1971 (CCLA) which establishes a nationwide fee table. Fee amounts are based on the type of action. Some filings, such as those in divorce or bankruptcy cases entail a flat fee of a few hundred, thousand or tens of thousands of yen. For suits seeking compensation for damages, fees are based on a sliding scale that at the time of writing ranged from JPY 1,000 for a JPY 100,000 claim to JPY 320,000 for a JPY 100 million claim. Additional, fee schedules also apply at each stage of the appellate process.

Although a plaintiff (or counter-claiming defendant) may be awarded these fees if the court finds in their favor, the high cost of seeking judicial relief has been identified as one possible structural disincentive to litigation in Japan. A 2003 amendment to the CCLA lowered fees generally, and some scholars and practitioners have attributed an increase in shareholder derivative litigation to a 1993 change in the method of calculating filing fees for such actions from a claim based sliding scale to a low fixed amount. Impecunious plaintiffs can petition to have payment of fees deferred to the conclusion of the case (CCivPro article 82).

If the complaint is not defective, the court sets an initial trial date and serves the complaint on the defendant. Service of process is generally conducted by mail, and is the responsibility of the judicial clerk. If efforts to serve the defendant by mail are unsuccessful, service by notice or by court enforcement officers is also possible. Personal service of process is *not* a feature of the Japanese civil litigation system. Japan is a party to the Hague Convention on the Service Abroad of Judicial and Extra Judicial Documents in Civil and Commercial Matters, but Japanese authorities have also indicated that they may not consider service from abroad by post under the Convention valid if the rights of the addressee in Japan are not respected.

A defendant receiving the complaint must file an answer in advance of the initial hearing date. If the defendant does not, the plaintiff receives a default judgment granting all claims in 2015 just over 1/3 of all civil lawsuits ended in defaults.

c. Characterizing the Action

Civil litigation in Japan is conceptualized in terms that seem highly abstract but can be applied to a wide variety of claims without getting caught up with specifics like "the elements of a cause of action for negligence." Such elements must be established in practice, of course.

In their complaint a plaintiff must make one or more claims or demands. Individually or collectively they must constitute a *soshōbutsu* (literally, the "thing litigated"). *Soshōbutsu* is a concept derived from the German *streitgegenstand*, which is commonly translated the "matter in dispute." Although the term is not actually used in the CCivPro, *soshōbutsu* is what the court must ultimately address in the *shubun* dispositive part of its judgment (see explanation at Chapter 5). Narrowly speaking, *soshōbutsu* are legal rights or relationships the existence of which can be adjudicated by a court (occasionally matters of fact may also be *soshōbutsu*). More broadly the term is used to indicate the claims made by the plaintiff.

The prevailing, traditional view (and the one followed by courts) has been that *soshōbutsu* should reflect a specific claim arising under substantive law. Some academic schools of thought believe *soshōbutsu* should more holistically reflect what the case is actually about. For example, as discussed in the previous chapter, a medical malpractice claim will likely be based on both a breach of contract theory and a tort theory. A good lawyer would presumably assert both claims in the complaint, but one could argue over whether it constitutes one *soshōbutsu* or two. The concept of *soshōbutsu* is not merely theoretically since it defines the extent to which a court's judgment has *res judicata* effect, prevents repeat or parallel litigation of the same or similar claims, and is determinative of whether joinder of related claims is possible (CCivPro article 142 and 136). In a 1973 case the Supreme Court held that where a plaintiff sought multiple categories of economic and emotional damages resulting from a traffic accident they should collectively be considered a single *soshōbutsu,* including for purposes of reducing damages for comparative negligence (Supreme Court, 1st Petty Bench judgment of April 5, 1973).

Soshōbutsu or the claims underlying them can be further subdivided into three categories of demand (*uttae*). The most common is a *kyūfu no uttae*, a demand that the court order the defendant to do something: pay money, deliver property, vacate a building or perform (or refrain from) a particular act. As in the common law system, courts prefer to award money damages, with injunctions or orders of specific performance generally only being possible in special circumstances or if anticipated by specific statutes. For example, article 100 of the Patent Act specifically entitles patentees to seek injunctions against infringers, and article 723 of the Civil Code allows a plaintiff in a defamation suit to request the court to order "other measures" (e.g., publishing an apology) in addition to damages.

The second type of demand is a *kakunin no uttae*, a declaratory judgment confirming the existence or absence of a right or legal relationship. Occasionally it may also be used to confirm what are essentially factual matters (the validity of a legal document, for example under CCivPro article 134). Examples of such suits includes those brought to confirm the ownership of property or the absence of a parent-child relationship. Such declaratory judgments are also now common in administrative litigation, as discussed later in this chapter.

The third type of demand is a *keisei no uttae*, a demand that the court issue a judgment that creates, destroys or modifies a right or legal relationship. Unlike a declaratory judgment in the preceding paragraph where the court would find facts relevant to confirming the existence or absence of a legal right or relationship, in this type of suit the court decision itself affects the right or relationship itself. Examples include judicial divorces or suits to invalidate corporate actions.

d. *Capacity, Standing and the Benefit of Suit*

In the course of litigation, one of the things a court must determine is whether it is a lawful suit; that is, whether all the necessary elements of a lawsuit (*soshō yōken*) are present in the case before it. Although not clearly set forth in the CCivPro, court practice is generally based on confirming three categories of elements: those relating to the party, those relating to the court, and those relating to the suit itself.

The party bringing the suit must have the legal capacity either directly or through a suitable representative. Capacity to sue is generally determined by reference to the relevant provisions of Civil Code or other laws or regulations (CCivPro, article 28). The party must also have standing to sue. Generally this means they must be the person whose rights or interests are at issue in the suit. In damage suits this is fairly obvious, but standing can become complicated in suits for declaratory judgments and administrative law cases. Of course the defendant must also be a proper defendant and have been served properly.

Those elements relating to the court are matters of jurisdiction and venue. Whether a court has jurisdiction over a particular case depends on the nature of the case and sometimes the amount claimed. Venue is typically laid in the court having jurisdiction over the address where the defendant is located.

Elements relating to the suit itself include confirmation that the matter has not already been litigated or is not being litigated in parallel elsewhere. Similarly, a pre-existing agreement between the parties to arbitrate or not litigate the matter would potentially result in a necessary element being found missing. Finally, one of the trickier elements required under in this category is that there be a benefit to the suit being heard (*uttae no rieki*). Although similar to standing, unlike standing, which depends on the identity and status of the individual plaintiff, benefit of suit depends on the nature of the suit itself. A suit which lacks *uttae no rieki* will generally be rejected on grounds of mootness, ripeness or judicial economy. For example, a suit seeking payment of a delinquent debt will have *uttae no rieki*, while one seeking payment of a debt that has not yet come due will not, unless special circumstances apply. Similarly, a suit to invalidate a board meeting appointing a certain person as director is moot if the director at issue has already served out his or her term and retired by the time the suit is brought.

A court will generally evaluate whether the necessary elements of a lawsuit are present in parallel with its adjudication of the merits of the parties' claims. Unlike the litigation of the specific case, which is largely shaped by the evidence and arguments of the parties themselves, the court has some authority to independently investigate for purposes of confirming some of these elements, such as jurisdiction (CCivPro, article 14).

If the court finds that all of the elements of the case have not been satisfied, it may resolve the case through what is essentially a judgment on procedural grounds (*soshō hanketsu*) without ruling on the merits. If the court finds the elements of a lawsuit to have been satisfied, it can adjudicate and issue a judgment on the merits of the case. This is called a called a *hon'an hanketsu*, when distinguishing it from a *soshō hanketsu*.

e. *Adjudicating the Case: Doctrinal Concepts*

Most civil litigation is governed by two basic doctrines, though neither is clearly articulated in the CCivPro. The first is called *shobunshugi* ("the doctrine of party disposition, " similar to the German *Dispositionsmaxime*), which refers to the principle that the commencement, advancement and conclusion of civil litigation is driven by the actions of the parties. Under this doctrine, the scope of the trial should be governed by the autonomous decisions of the parties; the court should not enter judgment if the parties have decided to settle or the plaintiff withdraws his case. Notwithstanding the basic principle of *shobunshugi*, the trial itself unfolds under the control of the court, which sets hearing dates and so forth.

The second doctrine is that of *benronshugi* ("the doctrine of argument;" similar to the German *Verhandlungsmaxime*). This term reflects the principle that in civil litigation courts are limited to rendering judgments based on the evidence submitted by the parties and their admissions and stipulations as to facts. Under this doctrine a court should not render judgments that take account of defenses not raised by the party even though the evidence reveals them to be clearly applicable. Similarly, judges may not make findings of fact that have not been asserted by the parties even if they are apparent from the evidence. Nor may they consider evidence relating to facts not in dispute, or base their judgment on such facts. And with respect to facts that are in dispute, courts may only base their judgments as to those facts on the evidence proffered by the parties.

There is some uncertainty about the practical extent of the doctrine of *benronshugi*. Presumably it should not be possible for parties to engage in collusive litigation that results in a judgment contrary to factual reality. There is also an argument that courts are only bound by the parties as to the principle facts of the case, but should have some leeway as to fact finding through inference. And of course, the court is not bound by a party's assertion of what the law is, even if both parties agree on the same interpretation.

Benronshugi means courts are generally prohibited from seeking or examining evidence other than that which has been by the parties, something that was possible under the pre-war practice. *Benronshugi* is sometimes used in opposition to *shokken tanchishugi* ("the doctrine of discovery through *ex officio/sua sponte* authority") which describes instances and procedures where courts have authority to actively seek information. *Shokken tanchishugi* applies in administrative litigation and family court proceedings, where the assertions and evidence of the parties are not necessarily as determinative as they are in regular civil litigation.

f. The Elements of the Case

After getting through the several layers of conceptual foundation described above, we find that plaintiffs must still argue and prove the elements of their cause of action, much as in the common law system. The difference is that while in the common law the elements of a cause of action for negligence (for example) are both part of the substantive law of torts and what a party must assert in order to proceed on the merits in practice, in Japan they are generally only a matter of practice.

The principal elements of a particular cause of action will usually have their roots in the language of a statute which either clearly gives them a cause of action (claim) or has been interpreted as doing so in particular situations (e.g., the tort provisions of Article 709 of the Civil Code as discussed in the preceding chapter). The same is true of many defenses, which often take the form of *provisos* in the same statutory language (Japanese statutes typically do not openly describe defenses as "defenses").

Plaintiffs must prove their case and defendants their defenses. This involves the application of practical knowledge of *yōken jujitsu*, the factual elements of the case (scholars use the term *shūyō jujitsu*—key facts—to express the same thing). Various practice manuals are available for use by both lawyers and court personnel setting forth the facts a party must prove to prevail on a particular type of claim or defense. These are derived not only from statutes and regulations, but court precedents and in some cases training manuals developed by the Supreme Court itself.

For example one of the leading civil practice manuals describes the elements of a cause of action in a suit to enjoin a business or party from behavior that causes bothersome smells as:[1]

1. The business activities etc. of the defendant caused a foul odor;
2. The odor in 1 being worse than what the plaintiff should be expected to endure;
3. Defendant's intentional or negligent act:
4. Damages and their quantum; and
5. A causal relationship between 1 and 4.

The manual also contains a citation to a specific lower court judgment granting relief in a case of this nature.

g. *Trial and Proving the Case*

(i) *Overview*

The factual elements of the case must of course be proven at trial, where any disputes as to interpretation of law must also be resolved. Since this is all done by judges in the Japanese civil justice system, there is no direct corollary to a summary judgment which is used to separate matters of fact from matters of law. Of course a case with no factual issues in dispute may be resolved more quickly.

The absence of a jury system also means there is no need to have concentrated proceedings. The traditional practice was for trials to take place over a prolonged period with hearings on a matter conducted once every few weeks. Now there is a greater effort to concentrate proceedings and conclude cases more rapidly. The CCivPro now calls for the examination of witnesses and parties to be conducted in as "focused" a manner as possible (article 182) and the Expediting of Trials Act of 2003 sets a baseline goal of completing trials of initial instance within two years.

Once the plaintiff's complaint has been accepted by the court, the judge presiding over the case sets an initial hearing date. Assuming the defendant does not default, the parties appear and assert their respective claims and counterclaims. In theory at this hearing plaintiffs read out their complaints and defendants their answer. However, in practice they are more likely to simply orally stipulate they have done so. A similar dynamic applies in subsequent proceedings, with the CCivPro and the RCP giving the impression the proceedings are more orally focused than is often actually the case.

(ii) *Pretrial Proceedings*

For the sake of efficiency, courts have several pre-trial procedural tools at their disposal for narrowing the scope of issues in dispute and relevant evidence before moving

---

[1] KI'ICHI OKAGUCHI, YŌKEN JIJITSU MANYUARU—MINPŌ 2 [Factual Elements Manual—Civil Code Volume 2], at 605–606 (5th ed., 2017)

to trial. Such proceedings are optional and were used in approximately 40% of the cases brought to initial trial in 2016.

The first type of pretrial proceeding is *junbiteki kōto benron* or "preliminary oral arguments (CCivPro, articles 164-167). These are pre-trial oral arguments made in open court and held at the discretion of the court.

The second is *benron junbi tetsuzuki* or preparatory proceedings (CCivPro articles 168–174). These are proceedings where a single judge hears from the parties regarding claims, defenses and proposed evidence. They are not conducted in open court and telephonic participation is allowed.

Finally, the court may order the submission of pretrial written submissions (*shomen ni yoru junbi tetsuzuki*, CCivPro articles 175–178). Again, the goal is to bring clarity to the issues to be resolved and the evidence to be proffered for that purpose.

Once pretrial proceedings are complete, a party seeking to present new allegations or evidence has a positive obligation to explain why they did not do so during pretrial proceedings (CCivPro, articles 167, 174 and 178).

(iii) Evidence and Proof

In civil trials a fact is proved when the judge(s) have certainty of its existence. What this means depends on the circumstances of the case and the court. Taking proof of causation as an example, the Supreme Court has stated that the standard of proof is not "scientific proof that excludes all points of doubt" but rather "a high probability of a relationship between specific facts leading to specific results based on the totality of the evidence as evaluated by a normal person based on rules of experience" (Supreme Court, 2nd Petty Bench judgment of October 24, 1975; translation by Colin Jones).

In order to find facts for purposes of rendering a judgment, there must generally be proof (*shōmei*) of such facts, subject to some exceptions (such as when damages are difficult to prove; CCivPro, article 248). However, for some matters, usually of procedural rather than substantive significance, the CCivPro and other statutes allows a lower standard of proof—*somei* (generally translated "*prima facie* showing;" *see e.g.*, article 92 regarding the standard required for a party seeking confidential treatment of certain information presented at trial).

Facts necessary for the court to reach judgment on the merits of the case must generally be proven using the higher *shōmei* standard, though this can be accomplished through indirect evidence from which such facts can be conclusively inferred. Facts can also be deemed proven through party admissions (*jihaku*). As a general rule, the fact finding of courts is governed by *jiyūshinshōshugi*, the "the doctrine of free evaluation of evidence," which is enshrined in CCivPro article 247. This doctrine permits judges to make their conclusions based on the entirety of the evidence presented. They are not required to favor or disfavor any particular type of evidence or method of proof.

Whether evidence proffered by a party is admitted at trial is at the discretion of the court (CCivPro, article 181). However such discretion cannot be used to prevent a party from proving their case. There is also precedent to the effect that, if proffered evidence is the *only* evidence available it should be allowed (Supreme Court of Judicature judgment of February 24, 1898).

The CCivPro recognizes a number of methods of proof. The first is testimony (examination and cross examination) of witnesses and the parties themselves (articles 190–206, and 207 and 211). Witnesses may be summoned by a subpoena if necessary, must testify under oath and are subject to sanctions for failure to appear or cooperate. They must answer questions presented in court, subject to exceptions such as when answering would subject them or their family members to criminal liability or they are members of a specified protection subject to confidentiality obligations that would be violated by answering. Similar exceptions apply if answering the questions would require disclosing technical or professional secrets (articles 196–197). Public servants have additional protections against being compelled to testify about confidential matters relating to their official duties. It is not uncommon for witness to be submitted first in writing, with cross examination only if necessary.

Parties can also be examined and cross-examined. They are not subject to the same sanctions as witnesses, but a party who fails to appear or cooperate can be punished by finding against them as to all relevant factual matters. Unlike with witness testimony, which must be proffered by a party, the court may question a party *sua sponte* (article 207). In some cases, the testimony of the parties may be the principal or only evidence.

Another method of proof is expert testimony (*kantei*) when special expertise is necessary (articles 212–208). In the Japanese system expert witnesses are chosen by the court (article 213). Of the 2016 cases brought to initial trial in 2016, only 0.6% saw the use of *kantei* evidence, with usage being particularly heavy in medical malpractice cases, but even then in only 7.7% of cases. If court-appointed experts are not available, not appointed, or a different view is desired, parties can introduce their own experts witness testimony or written opinions, just as with any other witness. Such experts are not considered *kantei* for purposes of the CCivPro.

2003 amendments to the CCivPro (articles 92–2 through 92–7) also provides for the establishment within the courts of technical advisers, persons with subject matter expertise appointed by the Supreme Court for consultation on relevant trial matters. Unlike experts who participate through the *kantei* process and give opinions as to facts in dispute in a particular matter, the role of technical experts is more one of explanation and clarification. They may also participate in settlement discussions if appropriate. Articles 92–8 and 92–9 also provide for a special category of judicial research officers with appropriate expertise who may be involved in intellectual property litigation.

A wide variety of documentary evidence is also used as evidence (articles 219–231). Documents must generally be originals or certified copies. Although Japan's civil justice system lacks a US-style system of discovery, the CCivPro does make it possible for parties to request the court to order the other party or a third party to disclose documents likely to have evidentiary value (article 220). Various exclusions apply, including those corresponding to testimonial privileges (e.g., documents that would subject a party or their family to criminal liability), as well as documents relating to criminal trials and documents prepared or internal use.

In the case of corporate or institutional parties, the applicability of this last exception has been the subject of some dispute, particularly in connection with the *ringisho* approval circulars that are commonly circulated by companies as part of their internal decision-making processes. For example the Supreme Court has held that absent special circumstances *ringisho* are internal documents used for corporate decision-making and thus not subject to disclosure orders (e.g., Supreme Court, 1st Petty

Bench decision of December 14, 2000). By contrast, the court has held that internal corporate notices (*tsūtatsu*) are not strictly internal documents subject to the exception and thus are disclosable (Supreme Court, 2nd Petty Bench decision of February 17, 2006).

While there are some exclusionary principles regarding various types of evidence, such as that procured by theft or other unlawful behavior, they are not as rigid as in criminal trials. For example there is no outright prohibition on the use of hearsay evidence in civil trials, though its character may naturally impact its value when evaluated by a judge.

Japanese judges lack the broad contempt sanctions their common law counterparts may use against recalcitrant parties who do not cooperate with document disclosure orders.[2] Since the party petitioning the court to order the counterparty to the action to disclose a document must specify the facts they expect to prove through the document, the court can sanction the counterparty for non-compliance by deeming the fact proved as alleged in the petition (articles 221 and 224). Third parties who do not cooperate with an order are subject to civil fines (article 225).

In the context of gathering evidence, it should also be remembered that *bengoshi* attorneys have statutory powers to seek information from public and private institutions through their bar associations (Attorneys Act, article 23–2). For example, it is reportedly becoming easier to obtain financial information about opposing parties through agreements between some banks and bar associations that now allow a *bengoshi* attorney to find whether a defendant or judgment debtor has an account at any of the bank's branches. Previously an inquiry had to be made as to individual branches. Occasionally courts may directly inspect physical evidence and have the ability to order it made available for inspection (articles 232–233). Instances where such judicial inspections took place are rare, occurring in only 0.1% of cases in 2016.

h. Judgments and Settlements

Many cases that are brought to trial do not end in a judgment. The following table shows the results for initial trials in 2016.

TABLE 10-3 RESOLUTION OF INITIAL CIVIL TRIALS 2016

Total cases brought	148,016
Resolved through judgments *	61,323
Resolved through settlements (*wakai*)	52,957
Case withdrawn (*torisage*)	23,683
Other resolution	10,053

SOURCE: Supreme Court Judicial Statistics.
* Includes default judgments, judgments on the merits (*hon'an hanketsu*) and judgments on other grounds (*soshō hanketsu*).

---

[2] There is a law that enables judges to impose penal sanctions on those who disrupt courtroom proceedings, the Law for Maintenance of Order in Court-Room, etc. of 1952, but it has a limited scope.

(i) Settlements and Other Non-Judgment Resolutions

Under the CCivPro, a judge may encourage the parties to settle at any time (article 89) and anecdotal evidence suggests some even threaten to rule against a party (or both parties) if they refuse to do so. A judicially-sponsored settlement (*wakai*, articles 264–267) will have its terms entered into the trial record and has the same effect and enforceability as a confirmed court judgment.

It is also possible for parties to settle out of court, which may often result in the case being withdrawn by the plaintiff, though of course a case may be withdrawn (*torisage*) for other reasons as well. Withdrawing a case has no *res judicata* effect, so the same claim could theoretically be brought again by the plaintiff, though presumably the terms of the settlement would likely prevent this in practice.

Cases can also end by the plaintiff formally abandoning their claim (*hōki*) or the defendant conceding the case (*nindaku*). Such actions may also result from a negotiated settlement, the difference between these and *torisage* being that *hōki* and *nindaku*: (i) require more effort because the party must appear in court and acknowledge the disposition while withdrawing an action can be done simply through paperwork and (ii) have *res judicata* effect, barring re-litigating the same claim and, like in-court settlements are entered into the trial record and have the same effect and enforceability as a confirmed judgment.

(ii) Judgments

Those cases which are pursued to the end by the parties (or in which one party defaults) end in a judgment (*hanketsu*). A default judgment entered against a party who does not answer or fails to appear at the initial hearing is called a *chōsho hanketsu*, since it is based principally on the plaintiff's pleadings rather than adjudication by the court. As noted earlier in this chapter, the two principal types of judgment are *soshōhanketsu* (procedural), and *hon'an hanketsu* (judgment on the merits). In complex litigation the court may also issue interlocutory judgments (*chūkan hanketsu*) as to specific allegations or evidence (article 245). Please refer to Chapter 5 regarding the types and structure of judgments and other dispositions.

A court judgment, once confirmed through the waiver or exhaustion of appeals, has a number of legal effects. First, it has *res judicata* effect on the parties as to the dispute between the parties and cannot be litigated again. Second, it is binding on the court. Third, it is enforceable through the mechanisms discussed later in this chapter, though these can depend on the nature of the judgment. Fourth, if it is a judgment in a *keisei no uttae* (such as a divorce suit), the judgment changes the applicable legal status as per the terms of the judgment (e.g., the previously married parties are now divorced).

i. Complex Litigation and Consumer Actions

Japan does not have a general system for conducting class action suits. In fact, the prospect of lawyer-driven mass litigation which could turn Japanese lawyers into ambulance chasers and Japan into a horrible American-style *soshō shakai* (litigious society) is a perpetual bogeyman reliably trotted out whenever enthusiasm about legal system reform needs to be moderated.

The CCivPro does contain provisions for "joint litigation" (*kyōdō soshō*; articles 38 through 41) as well as intervention by third parties (articles 42–53). It is also possible for either a plaintiff or defendant group to have one or more representatives act as "appointed party" (*sentei tōjisha*) to pursue the group's common interests in the litigation. Either method becomes complex because the larger the group the more likely it is that members will leave, join midway or object to the course of litigation resulting in questions as to the extent to which the ultimate result of the case binds both the parties in the groups and other similarly-situated potential plaintiffs. The Companies Act provides some additional rules for certain types of derivative lawsuits (article 847 *et seq.*). However, other types of large scale litigation involving widespread harm to numerous potential plaintiffs such as pharmacological or environmental torts can be very complicated to deal with under the existing Code of Civil Procedure.[3]

As with other countries, Japan has to struggle with the problem of businesses engaging in deceptive or other wrongful practices that harm large numbers of consumers very slightly, so that it is profitable for them but not worth any individual consumer bringing an action. Depending on the regulatory regime in which the business operates, regulators may perform a role in policing such misconduct.

To facilitate judicial policing of such behavior, rather than adopting a US style class-action litigation process, Japan has adopted a European-modelled system. This involves allowing "Qualified Consumer Organizations" that have been approved by the Cabinet Office to bring injunctions to force businesses to stop improper behavior when authorized under specific statutes. The first such statute was the Consumer Contract Act of 2007 and this has been expanded to other consumer protection statutes including the Prizes and Labelling Act, and the Food Labelling Act. More recent amendments to the system have made it possible for a subcategory of Qualified Consumer Organizations—Specific Qualified Consumer Organizations—to bring actions against business to obtain financial redress on behalf of consumers injured by wrongful business practices. Special abbreviated court proceedings are provided for such actions under the Act on Special Measures Concerning Civil Court Proceedings for the Collective Redress for Property Damage Incurred by Consumers of 2013. Many of these changes had only taken effect at the time of writing, so not much can be said about their substantive impact. As of June 2017 there were 16 Qualified Consumer Organizations and two Specific Qualified Consumer Organizations.

j. Labor Tribunals

Since 2006 Japan has had a system of labor tribunals intended to provide prompt resolution to disputes between employers and individual employees. Labor tribunals fall under the jurisdiction of the district courts. Note that they are one of a variety of means of resolving employment disputes, including the Labor Commissions (see Chapter 3) in the case of disputes involving unions, but also mediation programs offered by Labor Bureaus and other formal and less formal mediums offered by labor regulators and local governments.

Under the Labor Tribunal Act of 2004, the tribunals are conducted by a panel comprised of a judge and two other standing members chosen by the courts for two year terms based on their experience in employment issues. In practice, one member is chosen from labor unions or other organizations representing employees, and the other from

[3] In the case of some mass torts the government response has been to establish certification and compensation systems, such that under the Law Concerning Compensation for Pollution-Related Health Damage and Other Measures of 1974.

organizations representing employers (the vast majority of both are men in their 60s). The tribunals conduct a maximum of three sessions Historically the system has resulted in mediated (conciliated) results in approximately 70% of cases.

Proceedings before the tribunals are not "trials" and are intended to resolve the dispute expeditiously and may examine evidence as they deem necessary. The proceedings may lead to a conciliated settlement or a decision (*shinpan*) by the tribunal. Either party filing an objection within two weeks of a decision results in it being void and a lawsuit reflecting the claim originally brought before the tribunal having been filed in the court.

E. FAMILY COURT LITIGATION AND OTHER PROCEEDINGS

1. Overview

Family court is often the first and only time many Japanese people experience their country's judicial system. For those who learn about courts through textbooks and movies the experience may be surprising, since these courts work very differently from the regular civil and criminal courts. This surprise may even extend to *bengoshi* lawyers, whose formal training does not include very much family law but who may find upon being licensed that the most immediate demands for their services arebe in this area.

Family matters are resolved under two procedural regimes. The first is the Domestic Relations Case Procedure Act of 2011 (the "DRCPA," which replaced the less procedurally robust Domestic Relations Adjudication Act of 1947), and the Personal Status Litigation Act of 2003 (the "PSLA" which replaced an earlier act of the same name). Note that "personal status" refers to those aspects of identity (marital status, parental authority, adoptive relationships, etc.) which potentially affect other people and which are likely reflected in the family register (see discussion in Chapter 9). This is a much narrower universe of disputes than those which may actually be brought in family court.

The following table sets forth the breakdown of matters brought and cleared under these two procedural regimes in 2016:

TABLE 10-4 FAMILY COURT CASES IN 2016

DRCPA Cases				PSLA Cases (Personal Status Litigation)	
Family Court Decree Proceedings		Family Court Conciliation Proceedings			
Brought	Cleared	Brought	Cleared	Brought	Cleared
835,716	838,530	140,641	138,685	10,003	9,951
SOURCE: Supreme Court Judicial Statistics.					

2. Resolutions Under the Domestic Relations Case Procedure Act

In order to appreciate family court procedures, it may help to have first read the description of substantive family law in the preceding chapter.

The great majority of family court matters arise under the DRCPA. Technically matters under this act are a special category of non-contentious case (see discussion earlier in this case), though to the extent they involve divorce, child custody or inheritance they may be highly contentious in practice. Procedurally, however, this means they are not "trials" (*saiban*) and if resolved by the court this is accomplished through a *kettei* (decision) rather than a *hanketsu* (judgment), which has various implications for the appellate process.

Family courts did not even handle civil litigation matters until the passage of the new PSLA moved jurisdiction over such cases from district courts to family courts, effective from 2004. As Table 10-4 shows, litigation under the PSLA still accounts for a very small part of family court dockets. Most cases arise under the DRCPA, which establishes two methods of resolution: conciliation (*chōtei*) and decrees *(shinpan)*.

The DRCPA includes two schedules. Schedule 1 sets forth a list of matters that may be resolved through a family court decree. Most of these are matters that are unlikely to be disputed and may not even involve an adverse party, but nonetheless potentially affect third parties and thus require judicial oversight. The current Schedule 1 contains 134 categories of matters, many arising under the Civil Code (e.g., commencement of guardianship, petition to change a child's surname, confirmation of a will executed in exigent circumstances, articles 7, 791, 976 and 979) or other statutes, such as a change of legal gender under the Act on Special Cases in Handling Gender Status for Persons with Gender Identity Disorder.

Schedule 2 sets forth matters which are potentially adversarial. These can also be resolved through a court decree, but under the DRCPA family courts work on a "conciliation first" *(chōtei zenchi)* principle with respect to Schedule 2 matters and those which can be ultimately pursued through litigation (articles 244) and 257). Conciliation is thus mandatory before parties can avail themselves of more adversarial decree or litigation proceedings. Schedule 2 includes various matters relating to divorce, dissolution of adoptive relationships and contentious inheritance matters. Judges also have discretion to refer such matters to conciliation (article 274).

Schedule 2 matters are a small minority of those handled by the courts, though likely consume more of its time and resources than Schedule 1 matters. Of the 835,716 conciliation matters brought before family courts in 2016, only 19,498 were Schedule 2 matters.

The two DRCPA schedules are intended to establish a *limited* universe of matters under the jurisdiction of the family courts, and are thus much more extensively and concretely defined than under the pre-DRCPA process. Yet to the extent a slightly different matter can be characterized or analogized to something on the list, it can probably be brought into court. For example, Schedule 2 only refers to conciliation in connection with marital relationships, but the proceedings can also be used by parties in *defacto* marriages. Similarly, though not clearly on the list it is still possible to seek an *enman chōtei*, a conciliation proceeding intended to resolve marital discord rather than pursue a separation.

Family court conciliation takes place before a panel of conciliators under the direction of a family court judge. Theoretically a conciliation panel is composed of one judge and two part-time conciliators, usually a male-female pairing, one of whom is a lawyer. In some courts the judge may be too busy to participate in all individual conciliation proceedings, leaving the family court conciliators and court personnel to lead the process. *Bengoshi* attorneys with suitable experience may also be appointed to lead the conciliation panel in lieu of a judge.

Conciliation proceedings are usually conducted once every 4–6 weeks until either a settlement is reached or further efforts are deemed futile. Parties do not need to be represented by counsel and the costs of bringing a conciliation action are nominal. The presence of a *bengoshi* lawyer or other legal expert on the conciliation panel is intended to ensure parties have the opportunity to be informed of legal issues in the course of the proceedings despite not being represented by counsel. Now it is not uncommon for one or both parties to have lawyers. This may make the proceedings more adversarial and "trial-like" even though their purpose is to reach an amicable settlement.

Intended to help the parties reach an agreement they could not otherwise reach out of court, these proceedings are not a "trial" (*saiban*) but may include trial-like elements. The presiding judge or committee members may examine evidence (article 261 and 262) and a family court investigator may also be involved and conduct factual investigations at this stage, particularly if children are involved. Preservative dispositions may also be ordered by the conciliation panel (article 266), though have limited enforceability.

One aspect of the conciliation proceedings that is decidedly *not* trial-like, is that the standard practice in most family courts is to conduct the proceedings so that the parties never encounter each other in the courthouse, let alone sit in the conciliation room at the same time and hear each other talk. Each party takes turns talking to the conciliation panel, which then relays only what they consider the cogent information to the other when it is their turn. Thus neither party has the opportunity to hear let alone challenge factual assertions made by the other.

A successful conciliation results in a written conciliation protocol which, once executed, has the same effect as a confirmed judgment or decree (depending on the matter). Similar to civil conciliation, a family court may also issue a "decree in lieu of agreement"—effectively ordering the result the parties should have agreed to—with respect to matters of personal status (e.g., divorce). However, these are rendered ineffective if an objection is filed within two weeks (article 277, 279). Similarly, a "decree in lieu of conciliation" may be issued in respect of other matters brought for conciliation, again subject to party objections (article 284, 286).

When conciliation in a matter brought under Schedule 2 of the DRCPA is unsuccessful, the law deems a petition to have been brought to resolve the matter through a decree (article 272(4)). This ensures that, for example, the interests of children are protected through a determination of physical custody and child maintenance despite the parties' inability to agree to a conciliated result. However, if a divorce conciliation fails, one of the parties must actively pursue the matter further by filing for a judicial (*i.e.*, litigated) divorce under the PSLA.

At the same time, numerous other matters relevant to a contested divorce (division of marital property, custody, visitation, etc.), *are* on schedule 2. Thus, a conciliation that is unsuccessful respect to such matters will result in an automatic progression into decree proceedings as to those matters, things such as who has custody of the child and child support obligations do not go undecided for a prolonged period of time while the divorce itself is pending. This reflects a policy choice and means that the principal of *shobun shugi* applicable to regular civil trials—the proceedings being subject to the control of the parties—is much less applicable than in civil trials outside the family sphere.

Decree proceedings under the DRCPA leading to a decree in a Schedule 2 matter are more trial-like, but still do not involve the same level of due process as trials (*saiban*) under the CCivPro or PSLA. Decree proceedings are non-public and even the parties themselves may not have full access to the records of them. Moreover, to the extent there are evidentiary proceedings leading up to a decree in a Schedule 2 matter, the court may have already informally gathered much of the impressions and information it needs to reach a decision as to the decree through the conciliation process.

As to matters affecting personal status—such as the divorce itself—if the conciliation fails, typically one of the parties must proactively bring an action under the PSLA to move ahead, as the court cannot deem a petition for a decree to have been made as it can for ancillary matters. Although the court can issue a decree in lieu of agreement as to the divorce this is rare since it can be readily nullified by a timely objection.

Depending on the matter, a court may hear the views of a counselor, the unfortunate translation of the term "*sanyo'in*" which suggests a mental health professional. In fact it refers to a respectable member of society appointed on a part time basis by the family court to opine on matters to be adjudicated by the court. Such persons may perform a "juror"-like role providing an "average person" perspective to the court, though their involvement is optional at the court's discretion (DRCPA, article 40). This was another innovation of legal system reform intended to get citizens more involved in the judicial system (like the *saiban'in* system described in Chapter 8), but at the time of writing it had not become particularly widespread.

One of the special features of family courts is their specialist staff, particularly family court investigators (see discussion at Chapter 7). A court may order a family court investigator to participate in the proceedings or conduct an investigation, and report to the court on his or her findings (article 58, 59). For example in child custody or access disputes it is common for a family court investigator to investigate the child's living environment, interview parents and teachers and issue an evaluative report.

The role of family court investigators in preparing reports for the courts means that what is often the most significant piece of evidence evaluated by the court in making its decision is prepared by a court employee. This makes it very difficult to challenge, and a parent may not even be given full access to the investigator's reports, sensitive parts of which may be redacted when disclosed.

The DRCPA also provides for the formal investigation of factual matters in connection with the adjudication of matters by decree, including special proceedings for ascertaining the intentions of minor children when involved (articles 61–65). However, family court proceedings also represent another exception to the principle of *benronshugi*, since the court itself takes an active role in fact-finding and is not necessarily bound by the evidence, or by assertions or admissions of the parties. This reflects the broader interests involved in family court proceedings, which can involve the interests of children, unidentified heirs, and other persons not directly involved in the dispute.

The DRCPA does provide for appointment by the court of a representative for children or other persons of limited capacity in proceedings where appropriate (article 23). Anecdotal evidence suggests such appointments are only being made in a minority of cases involving disputes about children. This is due in part because it is only possible when a child is of sufficient age to have some capacity to express intent (generally around the age of ten or above).

3. Resolutions Under the Personal Status Litigation Act

For family disputes that cannot be resolved through conciliation or decrees and which involve a potential change of personal status such as a divorce, the process shifts to litigation under the PSLA, if a party files a suit in order to do so. Litigation under the PSLA is handled by the family courts. Although many inheritance-related disputes may be resolved in family courts through the DRCPA conciliation and decree processes, litigation over such matters must be brought in the district courts under the CCivP.

The PSLA provides special rules to supplement the CCivP for "litigation related to the following actions and other actions seeking the formation, or a declaration of the existence, of family relationship" (articles 1 and 2). The PSLA enumerates a limited range of cases that fit within this rubric (article 2(i) through (iii)), and including essentially matters that would affect marital status (including the validity of a divorce), paternity, or adoptive relationships. In marital cases, the PSLA also empowers the court to make ancillary dispositions as to child custody, visitation, property, division of pension assets and so forth, even if the marital action itself is ultimately resolved through other means (articles 32–36).

As with adjudicatory (decree) proceedings under the DRCPA, a court hearing cases under the PSLA may use *san'yo* "counselor/jurors" as a source of disinterested opinions (articles 9–11). Utilization has been limited, however, with *san'yo* participating in just 4.3% of PSLA cases in 2012, most of these being divorce trials.

Although unequivocally trial litigation, proceedings under the PSLA are still subject to restrictions on the *benronshugi* and *shobunshugi* principles governing other civil litigation and discussed earlier. Article 20 specifically authorizes the court to engage in fact-finding and examine evidence outside the scope of party assertions and submissions. As with proceedings under the DRCPA, family court investigators are available to conduct factual examinations and effectively produce key evidence (article 34). Finally, despite the "open court" requirement generally applicable to trials under article 82(1) of the Constitution, a court conducting litigation under the PSLA may close the hearings to protect the privacy of the parties. This is justified under the "dangerous to public order or morals" exception under paragraph (2) of article 82 (though this seems to acknowledge that rights guaranteed under Chapter III of the constitution are never at issue in PSLA cases, since the constitution requires such cases to always be conducted in open court).

4. The Hague Child Abduction Convention

Many non-Japanese people also experience Japan's court system for the first time through divorce or custody disputes. For those from countries where joint custody and frequent and continuous parent-child contact after parental divorce or separation are taken for granted, the Japanese system can be frustrating. Even after courts become involved, the prolonged period of conciliation proceedings during which one parent may have little or no contact with his or her children can be extremely frustrating. Japanese parents in strictly domestic cases also find this frustrating, and it is commonly asserted that failure to protect the parent-child relationship after relationship breakdown constitutes a breach of Japan's obligations under the UN Convention on the Rights of the Child, which among other things recognizes the right of children to know and retain contact with both parents.

Recurring instances of Japanese parents residing abroad bringing their children back to Japan (or retaining them there under the pretense of a "temporary" visit which then became permanent) against the wishes of the other, often non-Japanese parent, have sometimes been a minor source of diplomatic friction in Japan's relations with other countries. With great regularity Japanese courts ratified these abductions (which is what they often were under the laws of the jurisdictions of the countries in which the children had been living), and the non-Japanese parents found it difficult to even see their children let alone obtain their return, despite sometimes having full custody rights under their home country law. Japan thus developed a reputation as a "black hole" of parental child abduction, a place where once a child was taken they might never return. While such cases received a great deal of attention, for the most part they were arguably just a reflection of how the family court system functioned in domestic cases.

In 2014 Japan acceded to the Hague Convention on the Civil Aspects of International Child Abduction, which is intended to facilitate prompt returns of children removed from a signatory nation in violation of rights of custody there. Japan adopted an entire new procedural regime just for cases arising under the convention, the "Act for Implementation of the Convention on the Civil Aspects of International Child Abduction" of 2013. Under this Act the Tokyo and Osaka family courts are designated as the courts of jurisdiction for all cases arising under the Convention. The Act also enables extremely broad interpretation of the exceptions to the principle of return recognized by the Convention, and also enables a losing party to file for reconsideration—effectively a new trial—after losing initially on appeal. Moreover, mechanisms for enforcing the return of a child remain weak even if a return order is issued, just as they are in domestic child custody disputes.

The Convention is also intended to facilitate the cross-border exercise of rights of access (visitation). At the time of writing the results of Japan's implementation of the Convention were mixed. The MOFA, the designated Central Authority, had put significant efforts into assisting parents in cases going both ways and in facilitating the establishment of ADR systems for the amicable resolution of such cases in accordance with the tents of the Convention. However, there has been little sign of cross-border access being any more successful in the face of an intransigent custodial/taking/residential parent than in domestic cases. In December 2017 the Supreme Court issued its first decision under the Convention and the implementing legislation, upholding a high court reversal of a return order in favor of the American father (which the taking Japanese mother had refused to comply with) on the grounds that he no longer had the financial means to look after the children if they were returned to the United States (Supreme Court, 1st Petty Bench decision of December 21, 2017). At the time of writing the MOJ had proposed amendments to the law to enhance enforcement of return orders in cases arising under the Convention.

F. ADMINISTRATIVE PROCEDURE, REMEDIES AND LITIGATION

1. Overview

Administrative law is an extremely dense and specialized area which can only be summarized briefly in a book such as this. With that caveat aside, the starting point for understanding administrative disputes is the Administrative Procedures Act of 1993, which establishes common rules administrative agencies are supposed to follow when making dispositions, conducting administrative guidance, giving notifications and issuing orders in connection with their statutory mandates. The APA is intended to bring transparency and fairness to administrative processes and to counter the long-standing practice of "administrative guidance" that could sometimes be used by regulators to impose on the regulated requirements outside the scope of their statutory authority. Subsequent amendments to the APA specifically empower parties to formally demand a stop to unlawful administrative guidance (article 36–2).

The APA requires administrative agencies to establish clear standards for the applications for permits, licenses or approvals and for their rejection. It is a statute of general applicability, but was preceded by more limited statutes establishing administrative procedural requirements and remedies in specific contexts, such as land condemnation. Some of these are discussed below to the extent still applicable.

In an administrative hearing process in which an agency considers a license application or has discretionary authority, the APA generally requires the applicant or affected party be given the opportunity to be heard, to be assisted by licensed professionals, and to be informed of the reasons for any unfavorable decisions or other dispositions. The APA also establishes the requirement and process for soliciting public comments in connection with proposed rule-making and other administrative actions (articles 39–43).

The APA includes a long list of contexts in which it does not apply. These include the criminal justice process, actions by courts and the Diet, actions taken by schools, measures taken by authorities in the interests of public health, and dispositions and administrative guidance under immigration laws and regulations (article 3).

Once administrative action has been taken (including a decision not to take action), there are three general ways in which an aggrieved party can seek relief. If the party has suffered damages, the first is a claim for state compensation under the State Compensation Act. The second is the filing of objections under the Administrative Complaint Review Act of 2014 (ACRA). The third is litigation under the Administrative Case Litigation Act of 1962 (ACLA). Each of these statutes will be discussed shortly. The Administration Case Litigation Act, the ACRA and the State Compensation Act are collectively referred to as the *kyūsai sanpō*—the "three laws of [administrative] recourse." Together they embody one of the significant differences between the post-war and pre-war legal systems: the availability under the latter of a comprehensive regime of formal recourse against government action. To the extent that some of the administrative remedies discussed below are available through procedures and dispute resolution bodies under the direct or indirect jurisdiction of an administrative agency, it should be remembered that article 76(2) of the constitution requires that courts must have final judicial power over all resolutions.

2. State Compensation

Tort claims can be brought in court against the state or state entities under the State Redress Act of 1947, which implements article 17 of the constitution. Note that the Japanese term for state compensation—*kokka baishō*—actually refers to compensation by the *nation* state (*kokka*). However, it applies to lawsuits brought in connection with prefectural and municipal government actors as well.

Interestingly, the government does not keep uniform statistics on actions brought under the State Redress Act It is thus not possible to confirm how many actions are brought each year, how frequently plaintiffs prevail in them, and how much money is paid out on judgments or settlements. Anecdotal evidence suggests plaintiffs prevail in only a small minority of cases, but multiple administrative information disclosure requests filed by one of the authors before the time of writing failed to produce any useful responses or statistics.

As discussed in Chapter 8, another compensation regime exists under the Criminal Indemnity Act of 1950, which provides compensation for the deprivation of liberty suffered by criminal suspects and defendants who are ultimately acquitted.

3. Administrative Complaints Review Act

The Administrative Complaints Review Act (ACRA) establishes a standard process for challenging administrative actions where other procedures do not apply. The ACRA was also significantly amended in 2014, such amendments taking effect in 2016 and including corresponding amendments to hundreds of other laws. Accordingly, at the time of writing the full impact of these changes was yet to be seen.

The ACRA establishes two principal means of objecting to administrative action or inaction. The first is a request for review with respect to dispositions or inaction (articles 2 and 3). This is an objection made to a higher level of the administrative agency than the one responsible for the challenged disposition or inaction, which may be the responsible minister in the case of national government institutions. The review must also be conducted by a reviewing officer within the institution who was not involved with the original disposition (article 9). The ACRA provides for an adjudicatory, albeit document-based process for conducting reviews. The ACRA requires complainants and intervenors to be given the opportunity to participate in the process directly or through agents, to submit pleadings and even make oral statements. They must also be informed of the results of the process in writing (procedural requirements in this paragraph are set forth at articles 9 through 53 of the ACRA).

Subject to a number of exceptions, the opinion of the reviewing officer must also be submitted to an independent complaints review board which is established at the municipal or prefectural level (for requests for review made at those levels) or, if a national government agency, to the Administrative Complaint Review Board within the MIC. Once the feedback of the review board is received the reviewing agency must make a determination, but is prohibited from modifying its original determination in a way that would make it even more adverse to the complainant than the one challenged (article 48). A petition for suspension of implementation of the disposition in question can also be filed (article 25) pending the review, or the agency can decide to do so of its own accord. If allowed by specific statutory regimes, a further review—an administrative appeal—can also be requested (article 6).

Article 5(1) of the ACRA also makes it possible for aggrieved parties to request that the relevant agency to reconsider the basis on which a decision is made, *if* permitted by the relevant regulatory regime (e.g., article 75 of the Act on General Rules for National Taxes of 1962). A process is set forth for this type of action as well (articles 54 through 62).

It is generally not mandatory to use the procedures under the ACRA. It is possible to seek immediate judicial recourse through the ACLA as discussed in Section 5 of this chapter. However, under the ACLA courts are only able to invalidate unlawful administrative acts. The ACRA procedures allow for greater flexibility in results, particularly where the exercise of administrative discretion is involved in the disposition at issue. ACRA proceedings are also generally considered to be faster and simpler than full-blown trials. Particularly since the 2014 amendments, the ACRA is designed to provide a higher degree of procedural protections within the administrative dispute process before anyone has to go to court.

The ACRA includes a number of exceptions where it does not apply, many of which correspond to those in the APA—the criminal justice system, actions taken within the framework of judicial administration and Diet procedures and so forth.

4. Administrative Tribunals and Decrees

There are several statutory regimes that establish tribunals under administrative committees or agencies of the national government. Some of these tribunals are mentioned in Chapter 3. Such tribunals conduct quasi-judicial proceedings in connection with areas within their regulatory remit. While the majority conduct post-facto reviews in connection with objections by parties to administrative dispositions by related administrative bodies (an appellate function), others engage in trial-like proceedings that impose sanctions or find fault.

The details depend upon the governing statute and the body, but although these tribunals are generally under a national government institution, they are structured to be highly independent. Proceedings are conducted before experts and may involve evidentiary hearings and such tribunals usually render decisions in the form of a decree (*shinpan*). Collectively decisions by these bodies are called *gyōsei shinpan* to distinguish them from judicial decrees such as those rendered by family courts.

The following table lists the principal tribunals of this type.

TABLE 10-5 ADMINISTRATIVE TRIBUNALS

Name of tribunal	Affiliation	Role	Statute
National Tax Tribunal	National Tax Agency (MOF)	Review taxpayer requests for review of unfavorable determinations made by national tax authorities	Act on General Rules for National Taxes of 1962.
Japan Patent Office (Trial and Appeal Department)	Japan Patent Office (METI)	Review appeals from initial JPO determinations in connection with patents and trademarks	Patent Act, Trademark Act, Design Act, Utility Model Act (all of 1959)
Eminent Domain Council	Prefectural governments (MLIT)	Review of decisions regarding expropriation	Compulsory Purchase of Land Act of 1951*
Labor Relations Commission	Prefectural Labor Relations Commissions, Central Labor Relations Commission (MHLW)	Determinations and orders in connection with labor practices/	Labor Union Act of 1949
Radio Regulatory Council	MIC	Initial review of objections to dispositions in connection with licensing matters	Radio Act of 1950
FSA Administrative Law Judges	Financial Services Agency (Prime Minister)	Ruling on financial penalties imposed for violations of securities regulations	Financial Instruments and Exchange Act of 1948
Marine Accident Tribunal	MLIT	Initial findings of fault in marine accidents	Marine Accident Inquiry Act of 1947
Environmental Dispute Coordination Commission	MIC	Objections to the grant of mining permits	Act on Adjustment Procedures for Utilization of Lands for Mining and Other Industries of 1950

SOURCES: Government web sites and relevant statutes.

* The Compulsory Purchase of Land Act also provides mechanisms for mediating and arbitrating condemnation disputes.

Recourse from the dispositions or findings of such tribunals can be had to the court system, as is required by the Constitution. Appeals from the decrees of such tribunals are generally made directly to the high court(s) designated as having jurisdiction, though this depends upon the specific law. In some instances, a court may be bound by the tribunal's findings of fact, but not the law or its application (e.g. Act on Adjustment Procedures for Utilization of Lands for Mining and Other Industries, article 52).

5. Administrative Case Litigation Act

a. Historical Background

In the early Meiji Period such administrative litigation as was possible had to be brought in the ordinary courts, subject to whatever specific laws or regulations allowed such actions at all. Under the Meiji constitutional system the Administrative Court Act of 1890 established a single administrative court in Tokyo. Based on Prussian models, this court existed outside the scope of the regular judiciary and its decisions could not be appealed (article 19). The scope of claims that could be brought under it was limited to those provided under specific laws or ordinances, and it was specifically precluded from hearing damage claims (articles 15 and 16). Litigants were also required to petition with the relevant government authority for relief before filing suit, and were prohibited from filing suit while such petition was pending (article 17).

It is common to make a sharp distinction between the administrative litigation regime of the post-war period and that of the Meiji Constitution. However, some Japanese scholars have noted that proposals to amend the system were already being considered in the Taisho Period, and that these formed the basis for the Special Law for Administrative Litigation passed in 1948 as a special set of rules under the Code of Civil Procedure. This was then replaced with the current ACLA.

b. Scope

The ACLA is a special form of civil litigation. Article 7 makes it clear that matters for which the ACLA does not contain relevant provisions, "shall be governed by the provisions on civil action." This means the rules for matters such as appeals and filing fees generally fall under the rules of civil litigation.

Conceptually, the ACLA anticipates two types of action: objective lawsuits (*kyakkan soshō)* and subjective lawsuits (*shukan soshō*), though the law does not use these terms. Objective lawsuits are those which are provided for in a specific statute. They consist of two types: citizen actions (*minshū soshō*; article 5) and interagency actions *(kikan soshō*; article 6). Examples of citizen actions include challenges to the validity of elections under articles 203 and 204 of the Public Offices Election Act and suits challenging the legality of the disbursement of public funds under article 242–2 of the Local Autonomy Act. Examples of interagency actions include suits by ministries against prefectural governments in connection with unlawful conduct relating to national administrative functions that have been delegated to them, or in connection with a prefectural government's failure to perform legally-required acts. Such actions appear to be exceptionally rare with examples of actual cases almost non-existent.

Subjective lawsuits are more common and are called this because they do not need a specific statutory basis. They can be brought by individual plaintiffs with specific cases arising from their personal, subjective interactions with the administrative process. The ALCA anticipates two broad subcategories of this type of lawsuit: public law-related actions (*tōjisha soshō;* literally "party lawsuit") and judicial review of administrative dispositions (*kōkoku*[4] soshō). These are discussed in the following section.

c. *Public Law-Related Actions*

A public law-related action is one:

> relating to an original administrative disposition or administrative disposition on appeal that confirms or creates a legal relationship between parties, wherein either party to the legal relationship shall stand as a defendant pursuant to the provisions of laws and regulations, an action for a declaratory judgment on a legal relationship under public law and any other action relating to a legal relationship under public law (ALCA, article 4).

Such cases have traditionally arisen either (i) in connection with administrative acts that affect the legal relationship between private parties or (ii) when a government agency is a party but in a way that is not particularly different from civil litigation between private parties.

The former are called *keishikiteki tōjisha soshō*—formal public law-related actions—and are in substance a different type of administrative litigation but fall into this category because of the involvement of another private party. The most commonly given example is that of a condemnation of private land for the benefit of a private developer carrying out public works where the challenge is not the taking decision by the government, but the amount of compensation awarded.

The latter are called *jisshitsuteki tōjisha soshō*—substantive public-law related actions—where a government body is involved but in a capacity similar to that of a private party. Examples include cases involving tenants in government housing or certain types of claims by public servants in connection with their employment. Some scholars have criticized public-law related actions as pointlessly creating a separate litigation protocol for cases that could readily be handled through the existing civil litigation system.

2004 amendments to the ACLA added to article a variety of what is essentially a standard form of civil litigation "*an action for a declaratory judgment on a legal relationship under public law and any other action*." This greatly expanded the scope of possible litigation, making it possible for parties to, for example, confirm the interpretation of a regulation or their entitlement to a license or take other proactive steps without first going through the process of filing and being rejected. This procedure was used, for example, to confirm that Japanese national living abroad had the right to vote in *future* House of Representatives elections in the *Overseas Voting Rights Case* (See Table 6-1 in Chapter 6).

d. *Judicial Review of Administrative Dispositions*

Traditionally, however, the focus of administrative litigation under the ALCA has been judicial review of administrative dispositions (*kōkoku soshō).* These may take many forms, and article 3 defines most of the key categories: (i) actions for the revocation of an administrative disposition (*torikeshi soshō*; article 3(2) and 3(3)), (ii) actions for the declaration of nullity (*i.e.,* that an administrative disposition is *void ab initio*—a *mukō*

---

[4] Confusingly this is the same *kōkoku* that in a separate context is used to describe a particular type of judicial appeal: see discussions at Chapter 8 and later in this chapter.

kakunin soshō under article 3(4)), (iii) suits for a declaration of illegality of inaction (*fusakui ihō kakunin no uttae*; article 3(5)), (iv) actions for mandamus (*gimutsuke soshō*; article 3(6)) and (v) actions for injunctive orders (*sashidome soshō*; article 3(7).

Other types of action not specified in the ACLA may also be possible and are referred to as *hōteigai kōkokusoshō* (challenges of a type not specified in the law), and are considered to arise under the general language of ACLA, article 3(1) of which defines judicial reviews of administrative dispositions generally as actions "to appeal against the exercise of public authority by an administrative agency." The details of the requirements of each type of action for judicial review of an administrative disposition and how they proceed are beyond the scope of this summary.

Regardless of the type of action, much jurisprudence and academic theory has developed around the issue of what sort of official acts are "dispositive." An interesting early example of this arose under the Graveyards and Burials Act of 1948, which prohibits the operators of graveyards, crematoria and ossuaries from refusing to accept requests to inter the remains of a deceased person "without good reason." Since many such facilities were operated by Buddhist temples, elder care homes or other facilities, issues arose when requests for interment were received in connection with the remains of "outsiders"—whether sectarian or otherwise. What constituted a "good reason" was dealt with through an interpretive directive (*tsūtatsu*, see explanation at Chapter 5) from the Ministry of Health. When this interpretation was changed by the ministry in 1960 so as to prevent Buddhist temples from refusing remains on sectarian grounds it was challenged. However, the Supreme Court found that the directive did not affect the rights or duties of the people, meaning it was not "dispositive" and thus not amenable to judicial review (Supreme Court, 3rd Petty Bench judgment of December 24, 1968).

Similarly, the issue of who has standing to challenge government actions even if they are dispositive has been another significant hurdle, particularly before the 2004 amendments to the ACLA. So has the related issue of whether a plaintiff would actually benefit from a successful challenge, which might not be the case if, for example, the permitted construction being challenged is already under way by the time the court rules.

For example, some early legal challenges to the grant of construction permits for the first generation of Japanese nuclear power plants in the 1960s were rejected on the grounds that only the applicant for the permit had standing to bring litigation in connection with it. Over time courts became more flexible in acknowledging standing, but until the turn of the century it was often difficult to bring suits merely on the grounds that one would be affected by an administrative decision—because they lived in the affected neighborhood, for example; one needed to be a land owner or have some other more concrete traditional form of legal right that was threatened with infringement. The 2004 amendments to the ACLA sought to remedy this by added admittedly tortuously circuitous language to the article 9 provisions on standing allowing courts to grant standing to a wider category of plaintiffs. This was quickly used by courts to recognize standing to bring suit in the residents of a Tokyo neighborhood that would have been negatively affected by a plan to elevate a section of a commuter rail line (Supreme Court, Grand Bench judgment of December 7,2005).

Once an administrative disposition has been made, the government agency proceeds accordingly. However, it is possible to petition a court to suspend execution of the disposition pending resolution of the trial (article 25). In such situation the ACLA allows the Prime Minister to file an objection to suspending execution of the disposition or to provisional injunctions ordered against the government (articles 27 and 37–5). This was added to the previous administrative litigation act on the instructions of GHQ during the occupation. Some scholars find the existence of this provision highly problematic from a separation of powers perspective, but instances of it being used are essentially non-existent.

e. *Future Outlook*

Although both the law and the courts can be said to be moving towards greater acceptance of judicial oversight of administrative behavior, for all the attention it gets administrative litigation is comparatively rare. While district courts cleared 148,016 civil cases in 2016, they cleared only 2,375 administrative cases. Moreover, the likelihood of winning a case under the ACLA is low. Of the 1,845 cases in 2016 that were cleared through full trials ending in judgments, only 179 saw courts issuing judgments in favor of plaintiffs. Recall from the discussions in Chapters 3 and 4 that in administrative litigation government defense counsel may be a judge on secondment to the MOJ,

There also remain numerous hurdles to bringing a successful administrative lawsuit and prevailing all the way through appeals. Some of these depend on the type of action under the ACLA, while others may depend on the specific statute being challenged. In this respect the ACLA could also be seen as merely granting courts greater discretion in the way they avoid ruling against the government. For example, regular (non-family) civil litigation, where courts may only resolve cases within the bounds of arguments and evidence presented by the parties, article 24 of the ACLA permits the courts to examine evidence that has not been presented by either party, though this does not permit them to simply make such decisions as they feel are appropriate.

Another very basic hurdle to administrative litigation is the ability to fund the litigation against a government defendant having massive resources. It has already been noted that the *hōterasu* legal aid system—funded by the government—will generally not provide assistance with administrative claims. A related issue is that most lawyers have little or no experience with administrative litigation. Cases are rare and there are no statutory regimes that enable recoupment of attorneys' fees if the plaintiff prevails.[5]

6. Petitions

Before there was any sort of administrative redress, people aggrieved by official action or inaction could petition the government. This was a traditional means of recourse well before the Meiji Period, and there were established protocols for submitting petitions to authorities. Violating these protocols could result in punishment.

The first Meiji-era rules on petitions (*seigan*) were established in 1882. Petitioning government was also one of the rights enshrined in the Meiji Constitution at article 30, though was limited to limited to petitions that observed "the proper forms of respect" and complying with the rules established for that purpose. Article 40 of the Meiji Constitution also made it possible for the Imperial Diet to submit petitions. These are referred to as "representations [*kengi*] to the government as to laws, or any other subject," but in the Legislature Act of 1890 the term *seigan*—petition (article 35) was

[5] At the time of writing the Japanese court system's official web site offered useful explanations directed at the general public regarding the procedures followed in criminal (including juvenile), civil and family cases but did not appear to offer any guidance on administrative proceedings.

also used. Rules for petitions by Japanese subjects were established through an Imperial Edict, the Petition Edict of 1917.

Article 16 of the current constitution also guarantees to every person "right of peaceful petition for the redress of damage, for the removal of public officials, for the enactment, repeal or amendment of laws, ordinances or regulations and for other matters" and further protects those who exercise this right from discrimination. The Petition Act of 1947 requires petitions to be in writing, and prevents them from being presented directly to the Emperor. It is common to see people gathering signatures for various causes in Japan and some of these are ultimately submitted as petitions.

Petitions made with the Diet must be introduced through a member of one of its chambers (Diet Act, article 79). These are submitted to the appropriate committee and may be adopted and referred to the Cabinet, which must report annually on action taken in respect of such petitions (articles 80–81).

Another form of petitioning can also be accomplished by lobbying municipal and prefectural assemblies. Under Article 99 of the Local Autonomy Act, such assemblies can submit opinions to the Diet or other national government institutions.

7. Informational Justice

One other aspect of the administrative justice system is access to information held by government institutions. This includes both information *about* government, as well as personal information about specific information maintained by government institutions.

The development of rules for disclosing information held by government is an interesting example of law-making that started at the grass roots level. The first such rules were established in 1982 by a town in Yamagata Prefecture, followed the next year by the adoption of prefectural ordinances. Today all prefectures and virtually all municipalities have information disclosure ordinances.

It was not until 1999 that similar rules were adopted by the national government. Under the Act on Access to Information Held by Administrative Organs of 1999, anyone can file a request for the disclosure of information maintained by executive branch institutions. The general principal of the Act is that documents containing the requested information must be disclosed subject to specific exceptions (e.g., personal information, commercial information, etc.; article 5) as well as a general "public interest" grounds for not disclosing where exceptions do not apply (article 7). Although technically applicable only to administrative institutions, the judiciary also generally follows the law as to requests for information relating to judicial administrative affairs (the rules relating to disclosure of case records being different).

In some cases government agencies appear to have dealt with the increased scrutiny by either not creating "official" documents or destroying those that have been. For example, when in 2014 the Cabinet Legislation Bureau changed its longstanding interpretation of Article 9 of the constitution as it applies to collective self-defense requests for documents relevant to the decision-making process were met with the response that no official documents had been prepared. Similarly, in 2017 the Kinki Finance Bureau of the MOF asserted that it had destroyed all records of meetings in connection with the sale of national land at a deeply discounted price to a school reportedly having close ties with the Prime Minister's wife.

The Act on Protection of Specially-Designated Secrets of 2013 also permits government agencies to designate various types of government information as secrets. This naturally removes such information from the scope of disclosure through the above law, and also subjects those who do disclose information so designated to criminal penalties.

With respect to personal data held by government institutions there is the Act on the Protection of Personal Information Held by Administrative Organs (APPIHAO). Passed in 2003, the same year as the Personal Information Protection Act (which provides for protection of personal information gathered by *private* institutions), the APPIHAO imposes various restrictions on national government institutions relating to the gathering, use, accuracy and disclosure of personal information. Those persons to whom the information pertains have certain rights to seek the disclosure of information about them and request it be amended if mistaken.

The Personal Information Protection Act imposes general obligations on prefectural and municipal governments regarding the protection of personal information in a manner consistent with the Act. By 2016, all prefectures and municipalities had passed ordinances relating to the protection of personal information held by them.

There are special procedures for raising objections regarding the handling of personal information or information disclosure requests by government bodies to the Personal Information and Information Disclosure Committee of the MIC. Further objections can be pursued in the courts through the administrative litigation process.

8. Liability for On-Line Content

A different form of "informational justice" is available through the Limitation of Liability for Damages of Specified Telecommunications Service Providers and the Right to Demand Disclosure of Identification Information of the Senders Act of 2001 (commonly called the "Provider Limitation of Liability Act"). As its title suggests, it immunizes ISPs and other telecommunication services providers from liability for infringing content posted on the Internet or otherwise distributed through specified telecommunication services.

The law provides for a "notice and takedown" mechanism for removing infringing on-line sources, cooperation with which is tied to the limitation on liability for service providers. The law also provides a means for aggrieved parties to obtain identifying information about the infringing party, which can then be used to take further action such as a suit for defamation of copyright infringement.

G. BANKRUPTCY AND OTHER INSOLVENCY PROCEEDINGS

1. Historical Background

Insolvency proceedings are an interesting example of American concepts being interposed into Japan's European-modeled system of civil procedure. Before the Meiji period there were procedures for liquidating the assets of a bankrupt and distributing them to creditors, including variations based on local customs and practices. In modern terms these would generally be considered a form of negotiated ADR, either with or without official oversight. Because of their specialized and extremely complex nature, only a brief overview of this aspect of Japan's civil justice system will be given.

Japan's first "modern" (*i.e.,* western-style) bankruptcy law was a chapter in the Commercial Code of 1890. Although the Code was influenced significantly by German models, the bankruptcy chapter was based on the French law of insolvency at the time. Being set forth in the Commercial Code meant that only those qualifying as "merchants" under it could avail themselves of the bankruptcy provisions.

It wasn't until 1923 that a more generally-applicable, stand-alone law was passed, the Bankruptcy Act, which was replaced by the current law of the same name in 2005. The Bankruptcy Act of 1923 was heavily influenced by German and Austrian models and then substantially amended under the US occupation, particularly with the addition of the concept of debts being discharged through the process, even for individuals. The occupation period also saw the adoption of the Corporate Reorganization Act of 1952, which was heavily influenced by Chapter 11 of the US Federal Bankruptcy Code, and completely revised in 2002.

2. Statutory and Informal Insolvency Regimes

Japan currently has four general insolvency regimes; two are liquidation regimes, and two rehabilitative regimes. The former are (i) the former consist of the Bankruptcy Act of 2004, which may be used by both natural persons and companies of any size, and (ii) court-supervised "special liquidation" under articles 510 *et seq.* of the Companies Act, which by its nature is only available to companies, and even then only for joint stock companies. The latter consist of: (iii) the Corporate Reorganization Act described above, which can only be used by joint stock companies and (iv) the Civil Rehabilitation Act of 1999 which can be utilized by both natural and legal persons.

Other statutes apply to the insolvency or liquidation of particular types of entities, such as the Act on Special Treatment of Corporate Reorganization Proceedings and Other Insolvency Proceedings of Financial Institution of 1996. There is also a special statute providing for the recognition and enforcement of foreign insolvency proceedings that have an impact in Japan, the Recognition of and Assistance for Foreign Insolvency Proceedings Act of 2000. At least one Japanese municipality (the town of Yūbari in Hokkaidō) has also gone bankrupt, though this was a special case outside of the judicial process. Now the fiscal health of prefectural and municipal governments is addressed through a special statute: the Local Autonomous Body Fiscal Enhancement Act of 2007, which addresses such insolvencies without court involvement.

By some estimates approximately 60% of insolvencies are resolved outside the formal judicial insolvency regimes through private negotiations or various types of ADR-like proceedings. However some cases are resolved through what is referred to as a form of *judicial ADR,* under the Special Conciliation for Expediting Arrangement of Specified Debts Act of 1999. This creates special rules enabling insolvency-type debtor-creditor cases to be handled through the Civil Conciliation system discussed earlier in this chapter. Of the 35,708 new civil conciliation cases brought in summary courts in 2016, 3,084 were of this character.

The prevalence of non-judicial negotiated insolvency-type restructurings and liquidations is evidenced by the existence of a set of "Private Restructuring Guidelines" established in 2001 by key financial industry stakeholders. While ostensibly "private" guidelines, it is worth noting that the study group that created them included "observers" representing the FSA, BOJ, MLIT, METI and Development Bank of Japan, and that they are posted on the NTA website. In 2011 similar guidelines were established by the

Management Committee of Individual Debtor Guidelines for Out-of-Court Workouts, an (ostensibly) private foundation.

Even if judicial and other forms of ADR and other private resolution systems may account for the majority of resolutions in the majority of insolvency cases, the negotiations involved take place in the shadow of the available court-based formal insolvency proceedings and the substantive law they reflect. Accordingly, the importance should not be underestimated. The following table gives an indicator of the frequency of the cases cleared by Japanese courts under the four principal procedural regimes described above:

TABLE 10-6 INSOLVENCY CASES FILED/CLEARED IN JAPANESE COURTS IN 2016, BY CATEGORY

Procedure	Category	Number	Total
Bankruptcy (Bankruptcy Act) *	Personal	64,871	71,838
	Corporate	6,967	
Special Liquidation (Companies Act)	Corporate	305	305
Civil Rehabilitation (Civil Rehabilitation Act)	Personal	8,981	9,177
	Corporate	196	
Corporate Reorganization (Corporate Reorganization Act)	Corporate	4	4

SOURCE: Supreme Court Judicial Statistics.

* Numbers given are for new cases filed during the year; statistics show 71,316 bankruptcy cases being cleared in 2016 but do not give a personal v corporate breakdown. Numbers for other categories are the number of cases cleared.

Of those resolved in courts and reflected in the above table, the dominance of Bankruptcy Act cases explains why this overview will focus primarily on that procedural regime, with supplemental discussion of the others where appropriate.

That said, the relatively small number of corporate reorganization cases (which reflects a significant reduction from the over 80 cases brought in the year the relatively new procedure was introduced) may understate their importance or the amount of judicial time they consume. Whereas corporate civil rehabilitation cases leave management in place and see a rehabilitation plan approved by the court within six months, corporate reorganizations involve replacing management and a long drawn out process that may take years before a plan is approved. This may still be preferable or necessary in the case of large, possibly public companies with large numbers of creditors. Corporate reorganization proceedings have greater power to restrict the exercise of rights by secured creditors, and are more likely to allow for, the sale of subsidiaries, business unites or other types of M&A activities as part of the restructuring.

In 2003 the government established the Industrial Revitalization Corporation of Japan for the purpose of assisting large struggling Japanese companies with public financial support. It was established for a limited time and dissolved in 2007, but the unrelated global financial crisis that immediately followed saw the establishment in 2009 of another government institution, the "Regional Economy Vitalization Corporation of Japan," owned by Japanese Deposit Insurance Corporation and the MAFF (but with directors from the MOF and METI) which also provides financial and other support to struggling companies. Originally established to help SME's (which are the remit of METI), its first significant mandate was the restructuring of Japan Air Lines, one of the nation's two major airlines. It also helps medical corporations, schools and other special corporate forms that may not fit into the judicial insolvency regimes, as well as commercial corporations. METI's Small and Medium Enterprise Agency also provides various forms of support for struggling SMEs.

3. Procedural Overview

All judicial insolvency cases come under the initial jurisdiction of the district courts. Typically this is the court having jurisdiction over where the debtor resides or has its head office (if a corporation). In the case of bankruptcy or civil rehabilitation proceedings where there are 500 or more creditors, the case may be filed in the district court in the location of the high court for its appellate district (e.g., if such case could be brought in the Fukushima District Court, it could also be brought in the Sendai District Court, since the Sendai High Court has appellate jurisdiction over and administrative responsibility for the Fukushima court; see discussion at Chapter 4). Cases involving over 1,000 or more creditors may be filed in either the Tokyo or Osaka District Courts. The Corporate Reorganization Act also allows for filing in those courts, and the concentration of companies in Tokyo and Osaka would suggest that the majority of special liquidation filings are handled in those courts as well (Bankruptcy Act, article 5; Civil Rehabilitation Act, article 5; Corporate Reorganization Act, article 5; Companies Act, article 868).

The statutory preference for filing complex insolvency cases in a limited number of courts, particularly Tokyo or Osaka reflects the specialized nature of these proceedings and a policy decision to have them handled in large courts that have specialized divisions devoted specifically to insolvency. Insolvency proceedings are for the most part considered *shōji hishō jiken*—commercial non-contentious cases, rather than trials. Oral arguments—mandatory for a trial—are optional in insolvency proceedings (Bankruptcy Act, article 8; Civil Rehabilitation Act, article 8; Corporate Reorganization Act, article 8)). Given the zero sum nature of bankruptcy, this may seem counterintuitive, but the reality is the courts are playing a largely administrative role that even in complex proceedings is likely to involve the oversight of a trustee or other form of executor who will make most of the dispositive decisions. In other words, the civil division of a smaller district court lacking a division specializing in insolvency cases is more likely to do a disservice to both debtor and creditor by treating a bankruptcy case as a specialized form of civil litigation rather than a complex administrative process.

The administrative character of insolvency proceedings is also illustrated by the important role played by judicial clerks (*saibansho shokikan*; see discussion at Chapter 7). Clerks are empowered by the applicable insolvency statutes and court practice to make many of the dispositive orders or decisions needed to move a case along, including, for example, approving the final distribution of assets from the bankruptcy estate (Bankruptcy Act, article 195(2)) or filing notices with the commercial registry of preventative dispositions (Civil Rehabilitation Act, article 12).

Insolvency proceedings are generally triggered by an individual or company falling into a condition known as *shiharai funō* or "inability to pay, though civil rehabilitation proceedings can be commenced before that point is reached. "Inability to pay" is defined as being "generally and continuously unable to pay his/her debts as they become due" (Bankruptcy act, Article 2 (xi). The vast majority of petitions to commence proceedings are initiated by debtors themselves, but creditors or corporate directors can also trigger the process.

Insolvency filings are noticed in the official gazette (*kanpō*). In the case of corporate insolvencies, the courts are supposed to notify the appropriate Legal Affairs Bureau when orders to commence the relevant proceedings are issued (Bankruptcy Act, article 257, Civil Rehabilitation Act, article 11).

A filing for bankruptcy usually results in the appointment by the court of a trustee (*kanzainin*),[6] who takes control of the debtor's assets for the purpose of liquidating them and distributing the proceeds to creditors. In many small consumer bankruptcies, however, where the debtor's assets are not sufficient to even pay the bankruptcy costs (at the time of writing the court website gave an indicative value of such assets as JPY 200,000 or less), a trustee is not appointed and effectively the commencement of the process and the discharge of debts take place at the same time (Bankruptcy Act, article 216). Approximately 41,000 of the bankruptcies cleared by courts in 2016 were of this character.

In civil rehabilitation proceedings, where the debtor is left "in possession" of a business and/or assets, a trustee can be appointed upon motion or *sua sponte* by the court, but such a trustee would then assume effective management control. The more common practice is to appoint one or more "supervisors" (*kantokunin*) to ensure the company is not operated by existing management in a way that causes further detriment to its creditors. Corporate reorganization proceedings also involve the appointment of a trustee (in practice a team working under one), who works closely with management to implement the reorganization effort. Abbreviated proceedings for small-scale restructurings or personal debt restructurings for individuals with salaries are also available, in which case little or no supervision is required.

Trustees and supervisors are typically lawyers, though there is no a requirement that this be the case; accountants may also be appointed and occasionally a doctor may be appointed if the insolvency involves a medical corporation. Juridical persons can be supervisors. There is some grumbling among lawyers about the opaque process by which these roles are allocated, as some can be quite lucrative. Trustees and supervisors are subject to further supervision by the courts that appoint them.

The powers of trustees and supervisors vary and may depend on the nature of the debtor or the terms of their appointment. Bankruptcy trustees are generally empowered to sell assets. They can also void post-bankruptcy preference transactions and suspend contractual relationships. Supervisors may take such steps as are necessary to preserve the assets of a business so it survives as a going concern and to restructure it in accordance with a restructuring plan. Both trustees and supervisors also have the powers necessary to obtain information about assets and businesses in order to perform their roles.

Japan's insolvency laws are based on the underlying principal that all unsecured creditors should be treated equally. In general the debtor is prohibited from making preferential payments to specific creditors. Unsecured creditors at least are generally

---

[6] Note that despite being commonly translated as "trustee," the term *kanzainin* literally means "person who manages assets," and has no linguistic or legal connection with Japanese trust law.

prohibited from exercising self-help remedies or availing themselves of the civil enforcement process described in the next section. This principal of equal treatment has in the past hindered efforts to establish sophisticated multi-tiered financing structures with subordinated and senior classes of debt. The validity of contractual agreements between a borrower and different creditors as to their relative seniority entered into before the bankruptcy process is now recognized by the bankruptcy process (Bankruptcy Act, article 99(2)). In addition, certain types of claims are also relegated to inferior status by statute, such as interest on debts arising after the bankruptcy process begins, or costs incurred by debtor in order to participate in the bankruptcy process (article 99).

In contrast, certain types of claims are entitled to priority of payment out of the bankruptcy estate. Of course the term "claim" is *saiken*, the same as established in in Part III of the Civil Code and discussed in Chapter 9. Some claims are accorded statutory priority, including trustee fees and other expenses of the process itself, as well as pre-filing tax obligations and amounts due to employees. However, employees are only protected as to that that portion (including bonus and lump-sum retirement allowance) relating to the three months prior to the filing.[7]

In theory secured creditors (*i.e.*, those having some of the non-ownership *bukken* property rights described in Chapter 9) exist outside the insolvency process and can enforce their collateral when entitled to do so through default or other circumstances. The reality is more complex. First, the collateral may not be sufficient to satisfy the full amount of the secured debt, leaving the secured creditor in the same situation as other creditors as to the amount of any shortfall. Second, the trustee or supervisors have some powers to seek restrictions on the exercise of security rights, particularly as to those assets necessary to maintain the business as a going concern in the case of a civil rehabilitation proceeding. Similarly, the trustee in a corporate reorganization plan can often also effectively force even secured creditors into the reorganization plan. Third, certain types of collateral (most rights of retention under the Civil Code) are rendered ineffective by the bankruptcy proceedings (Bankruptcy Act, article 66).

The old Bankruptcy Act anticipated that an integral part of the process would involve a meeting of creditors who would discuss and agree upon the basic approach. In practice this rarely happens. The current Act makes this optional upon petition by the trustee or creditors meeting a certain threshold (article 135 *et seq.*), and creditors are presumably protected by giving adequate notice of the progress of the case, particularly once they have submitted notice of claims.

Upon petition the court may also appoint a committee of creditors who can represent all the creditors by, for example, expressing opinions on the process to the court and the trustee, and requesting information from the trustee (Bankruptcy Act, article 144 *et seq.*). This is a feature of insolvency proceedings that was first included in the Civil Rehabilitation and Corporate Reorganization Acts, and then introduced to the Bankruptcy Act when it was revised.

---

[7] The treatment of amounts owed to employees was reportedly highly controversial when the replacement for the Bankruptcy Act of 1923 was being deliberated. In a typical Japanese regular employment relationship, a significant portion of an employee's compensation is deferred compensation that accrues over the term of employment (which for some workers may be decades) and is paid out as a lump sum upon leaving the company's. Paying out the full value of such amounts to employees first would in many cases leave little or nothing in the bankruptcy estate for other creditors.

At the appropriate juncture in the bankruptcy process, the debtor may apply to the court for a discharge of remaining debts that have not been satisfied out of the estate, except for certain types of claims (taxes, certain tort claims, child and spousal support obligations, etc.; article 253) which are not discharged. A similar discharge takes place in civil rehabilitation proceedings as to claims not covered by the rehabilitation plan (Civil Rehabilitation Act, article 178).

An individual going through the bankruptcy process is named on a "Register of Bankrupts" (*hasansha meibō*) kept in the municipality where they have their *honseki* (see Chapter 9). Being on this register is an impediment to registering as or practicing under a wide range of professional qualifications, including most of the legal professions discussed in Chapter 7, as well as numerous roles involving the handling of money. This only applies so long as a discharge has not been granted (article 255). Since most personal bankruptcies involve an immediate discharge this is not an issue for most people. Notice of the commencement of bankruptcy proceedings—and discharges—including the names of those involved—are given in the official gazette.

H. CIVIL ENFORCEMENT

1. Overview

The enforcement side of the civil and administrative justice system seems to get surprisingly little attention, even though without enforcement or enforceability, everything leading up to a judgment or order may end up being nothing more than legal theory. Other than the very limited powers to keep orders within the court room (Court Act, article 71), to impose limited penal sanctions on disruptive parties under the Act in Connection with the Maintenance of Order in Courtrooms (etc.) of 1952, and such other generally limited and specific sanctions as may be available under specific procedural statutes (and rarely used), Japanese judges lack general contempt powers to summarily sanction parties who refuse to comply with court orders. This includes with respect to the enforcement process.

There is nothing particularly cultural or traditional about this state of affairs. Before the adoption of western-style laws and procedural regimes, those who failed to comply with the orders of judicial authorities were subject to a variety of sanctions including being put in chains, confined to their homes, expelled from their communities or subject to criminal punishments. More likely it is the case of the primacy of continental European rather than common law models underlying the Japanese judicial system.

Some western scholars have suggested that the comparative weakness of civil court orders in Japan has led some parties to seek help from so-called *yakuza* organized crime groups to help collect debts or get rid of persistent tenants. Police authorities occasionally conduct public awareness campaigns using posters and other notices encouraging citizens not to *use* such groups, suggesting such situations may still occur.

However, others point out that in comparative terms Japan is unusual in having a system for enforcing civil judgments that is much more under the control of the courts than in many other countries. This is also a recent development; until the 1960s enforcement was left to court outsiders who could hire assistants who were sometimes unsavory, threatening or aggressive. The Court Enforcement Officer Act of 1966 brought court enforcement officers (*shikkōkan*; see Chapter 4) under greater control of the court through the selection process and physically locating them within district court buildings.

Various efforts have been made in the spheres of both legislation and practice to improve the enforcement of court judgments and other dispositions through greater enforcement. This is discussed more below, but since it is a highly technical subject that few foreign readers will likely never have to deal with first hand, coverage will be suitably circumspect. A similarly brief description of preventive and preservative dispositions that can also be ordered by courts while proceedings are pending is also given. First, however, a brief discussion of non-judicial *administrative* enforcement mechanisms is necessary.

2. Administrative Enforcement

Public authorities generally have a wide range of enforcement tools available. One often includes criminal sanctions, though it is impossible for the police and other law enforcement personnel to address all regulatory violations even if they are theoretically crimes. Moreover, as noted in Chapter 8, the police are organized on a national/prefectural basis, and may have limited resources to devote to offenses incurring in a particular regulatory sphere or at a municipal level. The police also have a well-established policy of *minji fukainyū*; not becoming involved in civil matters.

To the extent the violations take place within a regulatory regime the regulatory body may have other enforcement tools, such as the suspension or revocation of a license or other privilege. In some areas—such as employment or fire safety regulation, for example—there may be a "naming and shaming" regime that allows regulators to publish the names of companies or buildings that violate the applicable laws or regulations.

Overdue taxes and other public duties may also be collected by authorities by seizing and selling property through a process known as *tainō shobun* (delinquency disposition) under the National Tax Delinquency Act of 1959 and other revenue or similar laws that apply the same or similar provisions.

As for the multitude of other rules and orders of administrative authorities at all levels of government, as well as municipal and prefectural ordinances, the Administrative Enforcement by Substitute Performance Act of 1948 (the post-war replacement for a Meiji-era law of the same name) provides default rules for their enforcement against recalcitrant parties. Certain orders and rules of administrative agencies and municipal or prefectural government institutions may be enforced by those authorities in lieu of the person or people who are obligated to follow them.

The procedures under the Act are used in a variety of contexts including dealing with environmental violations and the nation's growing problem of abandoned houses. The costs of enforcement may be charged to the obligor and enforced in the same manner as tax delinquencies.

The courts are not involved in this process and, in fact, one of the interesting aspects of the Japanese system is the comparatively limited use by government agencies of the courts to resolve disputes outside the criminal sphere. In a well-known case, Takarazuka City sought judicial enforcement of an order by its mayor against a company that was continuing construction of a *pachinko* parlor in violation of the order which prohibited it. In a 2002 decision the Supreme Court rejected the lower court judgments in favor of the city, holding that the matter was not a "legal dispute" under article 3 of the Courts Act and the ACLA did not specifically provide for such cases (Supreme Court, 3rd Petty Bench judgment of July 9, 2002).

3. Enforcement of Civil Court Judgments

Article 414 of the Civil Code provides the substantive foundation for enforcement, by providing that if an obligor fails to voluntarily perform an obligation that is owed, the obligee may request court enforcement. Procedurally, enforcement of civil court judgments and other dispositions is dealt with primarily under the Civil Execution Act 1979 (CEA). This replaced the enforcement provisions of the old Code of Civil Procedure of 1890, as well as a now-defunct act that provided for forced auctions anticipated under the Civil and Commercial Codes.

As noted above, compared to some other countries Japanese courts are heavily involved in the enforcement process. However, enforcement is typically handled by a different *part* of the court. In professional and academic literature it is common to see the term *shikkō saibansho* (court of enforcement) used to distinguish this part of the court system from the part that conducts trials and renders judgments. The term is also used in the CEA (article 3) and refers to any court that is to make a disposition for execution. However, most civil execution actions are the province of the district courts, as they are the only courts which have court enforcement officers, and the CEA requires an action for execution by such officers to be brought in a district court.

Enforcement proceedings are very different from trial proceedings, since in many cases the trial is already over and much of what happens is largely administrative. Judgment debtors (and sometimes judgment creditors) are largely passive in the process, and generally limited to objecting to technical aspects of the process, the substancive result having already been decided.

Large district courts such as those of Tokyo and Osaka have entire sections staffed with numerous judges who deal with enforcement matters full time. In the past a posting to the enforcement division of a court might have been considered bad for a judicial career, but this may no longer be the case. In any case, the civil enforcement process is another area of the judicial system where judicial clerks play an extremely important role.

Civil enforcement actions can be divided into two main categories: compulsory execution and enforcement of security interests. The civil enforcement process may also be used in certain other ways, such as compelling the disclosure of assets. These are not discussed in detail.

a. *Compulsory Execution*

Compulsory execution (*kyōsei shikkō*) is what most people probably associate with "enforcement of judgments," though a judgment is not always required, as discussed in the following paragraph. Execution may be of either a monetary or non-monetary character. Monetary enforcement involves the seizure of real or movable property or other assets to satisfy the judgment debt or other qualifying obligation. In the case of compulsory execution against real property it may be either sold through compulsory auction or occasionally placed under management, in either case with the proceeds or income going to satisfy the judgment or obligation. Compulsory execution of a non-monetary character can be required if the judgment orders the delivery or surrender to a party of a piece of movable or real property, to do or refrain from doing something, or to make an expression of intent.

A basic requirement for compulsory execution is a *saimu meigi* or "title of obligation" fitting one of the categories listed in article 22 of the CEA. These include: a final judgment of a court, certain other judgments subject to only limited appeals or including declarations of provisional execution, final and binding foreign court orders (which have been confirmed by a judgment of execution by a Japanese court), final and binding arbitral awards, various types of orders for provisional execution, notarial deeds containing a promise to pay money, and documents that have "the same effect as a final and binding judgment."

While most of these reflect a type of court order, the last two require some explanation. Money borrowed pursuant to a notarial deed attested by a public notary (see Chapter 7) has the same enforceability as a final court judgment and can be enforced as such without first bringing a suit for the debt. Other documents having the "same effect" as a final judgment include court-sponsored settlement agreements reached in civil trials (*wakai chōsho*) and family court conciliation protocols (*chōtei chōsho*).

Whatever form the *saimu meigi* takes, to be enforceable it must be accompanied by or include a *shikkōbun* (execution certification), which serves as official proof of its enforceability. This certification is usually provided by the clerk of court, but can also be done by a public notary in the case of a notarial deed of indebtedness.

Enforcement is usually performed in one of three ways: (i) direct compulsory execution (*chokusetu kyōsei*), which typically involves a court enforcement officer taking direct action in furtherance of enforcement, (ii) indirect compulsory execution (*kansetsu kyōsei*) which involves imposing financial levies against the judgment debtor that accrue (and are payable to the judgment creditor) until he performs and (iii) execution by substitute (*daitai shikkō*), which involves the court enforcement officer taking the action the judgment debtor has been ordered to perform.

The nature of the *saimu meigi* and the way it is expressed is relevant to how (and if) it can be enforced. Those of a monetary character (e.g. an order to pay damages) can usually be enforced by direct compulsory execution against the assets of the judgment debtor (or through garnishment of the judgment debtor's salary, if any). Those of a non-monetary character are more complicated. For example, an order to hand over moveable property can either be directly enforced by having the court enforcement officer seize the property or through indirect compulsory enforcement. Orders to perform certain acts depend on the nature of the act. Those that can be performed by another person can be enforced through indirect compulsory execution or execution by substitute. Those that cannot and orders *not* to act in a certain way can only be enforced through indirect means, if at all.

b. Enforcement of Security Interests

Enforcement of security interests can be accomplished through the court and, where appropriate (e.g., when enforcing a mortgage against real property) with the assistance of a court enforcement officer. There are some key differences between this and enforcement of a court order. First, unlike enforcement of and monetary judgment where multiple creditors would share equally in the proceeds, the benefit of the security interest only accrues to the secured creditor. Second, only the secured property is subject to enforcement. Third, enforcement of a security interest only requires the document evidencing the security interest (in the case of real property) or possession (in the case of movable property). There is some practical complexity depending on the nature of the security interest and the property.

4. Provisional Remedies

In trials or other court proceedings, it may be necessary for the court to order provisional remedies (*hozen shobun*) to protect a party pending the resolution of those proceedings, or to prevent a party from transferring or destroying the value of assets and thus making the proceedings meaningless. The principal law governing such proceedings is the Provisional Remedies Act of 1989, which is incorporated by reference into other procedural regimes, such as those under the various insolvency laws and the DRCPA.

Provisional remedies consist of three basic types: (i) provisional seizure (*karisashiosae*) against a party's assets to ensure the ability to satisfy a judgment against them, (ii) provisional disposition of disputed subject matter (*keisōbutsu ni kansuru karishobun*), an action against *specific* property that prevents its transfer, and (iii) provisional disposition of provisional status as to rights under a private law relationship (*kari no chi'i wo sadameru kari shobun*). The provisional remedies in (i) and (ii) anticipate compulsory execution upon conclusion of the trial or other proceedings, while that in (iii) does not, but includes a wide range of actions including prohibitions on enforcement of security interests as well as provisional confirmation of employee status pending a termination dispute. In practice there are numerous other types of provisional dispositions, but most can be conceptualized in these terms. *Karishobun* may also be used in proceedings under the DRCPA to make provisional determinations regarding physical custody of children, for example.

As the name suggests, provisional remedies are intended to be temporary. They may be requested and granted on an expedited basis, and the burden of proof is lower than in the underlying action itself. To the extent a disposition may interfere with the property rights to the detriment of the other party, the party requesting it may be required to post a bond to compensate any damages suffered in the event the disposition is proved unmerited by the result in the underlying case.

In some types of actions a provisional disposition may ultimately be determinative, despite the lesser procedural protections. For example, in child custody disputes the court may simultaneously issue provisional dispositions and decrees regarding physical custody of a child in a divorce-related dispute. Although the ultimate issue of parental authority over the child may not be resolved until the divorce is fully litigated (which may take several years), the issuance of a provisional disposition over physical custody often indicates the court has already made the decision long before the formal process for making it has been followed.

I. RECOGNITION OF FOREIGN JUDGMENTS

A particular area of interest to foreign practitioners dealing with Japan-related matters is whether a judgment from a court in their jurisdiction can be recognized in Japan. As suggested elsewhere in this book, whether a judgment is recognized may not be as important a question as whether it will be *meaningful*. This may be due to the different value accorded to judgments as proof of personal status (in the case of foreign divorce or custody decrees), or their enforceability, as described elsewhere in this chapter.

Article 118 of the Civil Code provides the basic rules for recognition of foreign judgments, which are set forth below:

> A final and binding judgment rendered by a foreign court is valid only if it meets all of the following requirements:
>
> (i) the jurisdiction of the foreign court is recognized pursuant to laws and regulations, conventions, or treaties;
>
> (ii) the defeated defendant has been served (excluding service by publication or any other service similar thereto) with the requisite summons or order for the commencement of litigation, or has appeared without being so served;
>
> (iii) the content of the judgment and the litigation proceedings are not contrary to public policy in Japan;
>
> (iv) a guarantee of reciprocity is in place.

Japan's Supreme Court has refused to recognize foreign judgments on public policy grounds in the case of an order from an American court to pay punitive damages, and in a case involving the parenthood of a child born in the United States pursuant to a surrogacy arrangement (Supreme Court, 2nd Petty Bench decision of March 23, 2007; 2nd Petty Bench judgment of July 11, 1997).

Note that as to the "contents of the judgment and the litigation proceedings" lower courts asked to recognize foreign judgments may potentially struggle with those rendered through jury verdicts and thus lacking the extensive enumeration of judicially-found facts that typically form the basis of a Japanese civil judgment. Note also that for a foreign judgment that affects personal status of a Japanese person in Japan (a divorce decree, for example), for many practical purposes "recognition" may consist of taking a translation of the judgment to the appropriate municipal office and having the relevant portions reflected in that person's *koseki*.

J. JUDICIAL APPEALS

1. Overview

Parties may appeal unfavorable results in judicial proceedings in civil, family, administrative or other court proceedings. As with the description of criminal appeals in Chapter 8, in civil cases too the overall general term for an appeal to a higher court is *jōso*. The basic structure of the appellate process is similar to that as set forth in the criminal trial process.

In the case of non-final dispositions, the first line of recourse may be to file an objection (*igi no mōshitate*) with the same court that made the ruling being challenged. The rest of this section, however, will deal with appeals to courts higher up the judicial food chain.

2. *Kōso* Appeals

Initial appeals from a final trial court judgment (*hanketsu*) are known as *kōso* appeals (CCivPro, article 281), except when a high court is acting as court of initial instance under special statutory provisions (e.g. challenges to elections under the Public Offices Election Act). *Kōso* appeals from summary court civil judgments are made to the relevant district court, while those from judgments of district courts having initial jurisdiction are made to the high courts (Courts Act, articles 16 and 24. *Kōso* appeals are generally heard by panels of three judges, though appeals in matters relating to intellectual property made to the Intellectual Property Branch of the Tokyo High Court are heard by panels of five (CCivPro, article 310–2).

Kōso appeals must be filed within two weeks of the judgment being issued (article 285). Such appeals are filed with the court of first instance, which serves as gate-keeper for defective filings and may reject those that do not satisfy the formal requirements (articles 286, 287).

The right of appeal may not be abused. Courts may and occasionally actually do impose financial sanctions on parties who appeal "exclusively for the purpose of delaying the conclusion of the litigation" (article 303). This does not appear to present any constitutional issues.

Only about 20% of *kōso* appeals are successful. An appeals court may reverse or modify a lower court judgment, though is limited in its ability to do so by the scope of the appellant's objection (articles 304 to 306). The appellate court may also remand the case to the lower court for further proceedings if additional oral arguments are necessary (articles 307 and 308).

Kōso appeals can be made as to both the trial courts finding of facts and conclusions of law. In theory, the *kōso* appeal is a continuation of the trial and parties are free to present new evidence and introduce new arguments. In addition some writers have suggested that in the past when there were few *bengoshi* lawyers and many people brought suit *pro se*, the initial appeal was the opportunity to bring a case again properly, this time with counsel. Finally, since trials in the past involved fewer concentrated proceedings, with a hearing held every few weeks over a prolonged period of time, the fact finding and arguments might be a moving target anyways, particularly in something like a divorce case.

The ability to re-argue a case and submit new evidence in *kōso* appeals appears to be increasingly constrained. Whereas in 1983 high courts hearing *kōso* hearings heard testimony from an average of 1.1 witnesses per case (*i.e.,* hearing new evidence or revisiting old evidence), in 2014 this had dropped to 0.02 witnesses, with courts not hearing any witness testimony in 98.7% of cases. Of the 13,264 *kōso* appeals heard by high courts in 2016, 10,264 were concluded after a single hearing and 2,239 after a second hearing, collectively accounting for almost 95% of such appeals.

Kōso appeals can thus be seen to have moved away from being a continuation of the trial to a post-facto, primarily documentation-based review of lower court findings, with appellate courts reluctant to entertain new arguments or hear new evidence at least in the form of testimony or oral arguments. This may reflect both a desire by high courts to reduce their burgeoning case load, but also an expectation that parties should do a better job at trial, particularly now that there are more *bengoshi* lawyers available.

3. *Kōkoku* Appeals

As in criminal appeals, initial appeals from decisions that are *not* judgments are known as *kōkoku* appeals. As is suggested by the translation of *kōkoku*—"appeal against a ruling"—such appeals are made in respect of decisions (*kettei*) or orders (*meirei*) of courts made in the course of a trial, such as rulings on evidence or other procedural dispositions. In the case of family proceedings in particular, however, *kōkoku* appeals also are made against the decrees (*shinpan*, which are typically issued as *kettei* decisions) made by family courts under the DRCPA. Appeals from *judgments* issued in family cases resolved through litigation under the PSLA would be handled as above through *kōso* appeals. *Kōkoku* appeals are also the principal form of relief from rulings made by courts in insolvency, civil enforcement or preservative proceedings.

The general rules for *kōkoku* appeals are set forth in articles 328–337 of the CCivPro, with additional rules set forth in articles 85 through 98 of the DRCPA, as well as where relevant in other statutes. *Kōkoku* appeals can be broken into two categories; general and immediate. Immediate *kōkoku* appeals (*sokuji kōkoku*) are interlocutory appeals which are resolved during the course of the litigation during which they are raised on an urgent basis since they may impact the result of the trial itself. Matters subject to normal *kōkoku* appeals may also affect the trial itself (if there is one), but are dealt with subsequently. As a general rule, immediate appeals are only possible when specifically permitted by statute. For example, article 85 of the DRCPA provides that family court decrees can generally be immediately appealed, and article 93 makes many of the appellate rules of the CCivPro applicable to such appeals.

4. *Jōkoku* and Other Final Appeals

As in the criminal appeals process discussed in Chapter 8, a final appeal of a judgment, whether a further appeal from a *kōso* appeal or from an initial trial at the high court is called a "*jōkoku*" appeal (often translated as "final appeal" but really meaning just "to appeal upwards"). A difference between civil appeals and criminal appeals is that the court of final appeal for civil judgments issued by summary courts is the relevant high court, while that of trial court judgments is to the Supreme Court. A "special" jōkoku (*tokubetsu jōkoku*) appeal on constitutional grounds is also possible from an unfavorable ruling in a *jōkoku* appeal to a high court (*i.e.*, in a case that originated from a summary court; article 327).

Jōkoku appeals may only be filed with the Supreme Court if the ruling of the lower court "reflects an error in the interpretation of the Constitution or that it is otherwise unconstitutional" (CCivPro article 312(1)) or if there were other very fundamental defects in the jurisdiction or composition of the court or basic procedural violations ((312(2)). That the lower court erred in the application of law or regulation is only grounds for a *jōkoku* appeal when it is made to a high court (312(3)), after amendments to the CCivPro taking effect in 1998 removed such errors from the scope of civil appeals to the Supreme Court in the interests of reducing its docket. At the same time as this amendment, however, the Supreme Court was empowered to grant discretionary *jōkoku* appeals in "case[s] in which a prior instance judgment reflects a determination that conflicts with Supreme Court precedent . . . or to accept any other case that is found to involve matters of material import in the interpretation of laws and regulation" (CCivPro, article 318(1))". Thus, if the Supreme Court wants to amend prior precedents in non-constitutional cases, or otherwise clarify the interpretation of laws or regulations when necessary it still has the ability to do so through the discretionary *jōkoku* appeals process.

Approximately 30% of *kōso* appeals are followed by a further *jōkoku* appeal. The following table sets forth the categories of *jōkoku* appeals received by the Supreme Court in 2016.

TABLE 10-7 NUMBER OF *JŌKOKU* APPEALS TO THE SUPREME COURT (2016)

TYPE OF MATTER	Special *Jōkoku* Appeal	*Jōkoku* Appeal	Discretionary *Jōkoku* Appeal
CIVIL LITIGATION			
Personal Status matter	–	181	222
Suits relating to money	42	1,010	1,333
Suits relating to buildings	–	65	81
Suits relating to land	2	198	244
Other Civil suits	2	414	474
ADMINISTRATIVE LITIGATION	–	420	501
TOTAL	46	2,288	2,855
SOURCE: Supreme Court Judicial Statistics.			

As this table shows, notwithstanding the greater control the Supreme Court acquired over its docket at the end of the 20th century with the adoption of the new Code of Civil Procedure, it still deals with a large number of cases. However, it is exceptionally rare for *jōkoku* appeals to be *successful*. Of the 4,523 *jōkoku* appeals in civil and administrative cases resolved by the Court in 2016, only five resulted in the lower court judgment being vacated in *jōkku* appeals, 22 in discretionary *jōkoku* appeals and none in special *jōkoku* appeals. Most applications for discretionary appeals cleared in that year (2,436 out of 2,506) were simply not accepted. Of the 1,970 regular *jōkoku* appeals cleared that year, 1,920 were dismissed with prejudice (*kikyaku*; *i.e.*, because they failed to state adequate grounds for an appeal) and 29 were dismissed without prejudice (*kyakka*, *i.e.*, because of procedural defects). All 49 special *jōkoku* cleared that year were dismissed with prejudice.

Other types of further appeals—*i.e.,* from *kōkoku* appeals (which, at risk of repetition, are appeals against rulings or other lower court dispositions that are not "judgments" issued after a trial) consist of: (i) *tokubetsu kōkoku* ("special" *kōkoku)* appeals on constitutional grounds from rulings, orders or decisions of summary or trial courts, as applicable (CCivPro, article 332), (ii) *tokubetsu kōkoku* appeals from family court decrees or decisions of high courts in connection with family cases on constitutional grounds *or* on the grounds of mistake in law (DRCPA article 94) and (iii) permissive *kōkoku* appeals (*kyoka kōkoku*), where a high court permits the appeal to the Supreme Court on constitutional grounds, or because it is inconsistent with prior Supreme Court precedents ((CCivPro, article 337, DRCPA article 97); essentially parallel to the grounds for discretionary *jōkoku* appeals.

In 2016 the Supreme Court cleared 1,291 appeals of this type. As with *jōkoku* appeals, such *kōkoku* appeals were rarely successful, with most (1,258) being dismissed with prejudice (*kikyaku*). Interestingly, while there were only 38 *kyoka kōkoku* permissive appeals, they accounted for *all* of the 18 instances where the appeal resulted in the lower court ruling or decision being vacated. This may indicate the Supreme Court regards the views of the high court judges certifying such cases for further consideration by the top court as far more persuasive than party arguments.

As in criminal cases, once a judgement has been confirmed by exhaustion of all appeals, it is possible to move for a retrial. Grounds for retrial in most civil cases are very narrow, and include subsequent identification of defects in the composition of the court, the discovery that fraudulent testimony was proffered at the original trial and so forth (CCivPro article 338). A retrial can also be sought once a final family court decree is confirmed by exhaustion of all appeals (DRCPA article 103). There are some conceptual issues here, since not being "judgments" resulting from a trial, family court decrees do not have *res judicata* effect, and the DRCPA itself provides various means of revisiting family court decisions (including on grounds such as changed circumstances). Since at the time of writing the DRCPA was still comparatively new, this is an area of practice that will likely continue to evolve.

K. ALTERNATIVE DISPUTE RESOLUTION

Western readers are likely to associate alternative dispute resolution (ADR) with modalities such as mediation and arbitration which are intended to *avoid* involving the courts if possible. Although the English acronym "ADR" is now commonly used in Japan, it can be confusing because it is often used synonymously with the more formal term: *saibangai funsō shori*, which means "non-trial dispute resolution." As shown earlier in this chapter, Japanese procedural laws and court practice involve devoting significant resources to non-trial resolutions of disputes that nonetheless take place under court supervision, in the courthouse. Examples are the civil and family conciliation regimes described earlier in this chapter.

Although it is sometimes described as as "mediation," the principal form of ADR used in courts is *chōtei*, which is more commonly translated as "conciliation," since it is conducted by a court that will ultimately decide the matter if the parties do not agree to a resolution.

Government bodies and private associations also offer conciliation (*chōtei*) and mediation (*assen*) services. In many cases they are limited to handling specific types of disputes (e.g., the MIC's Telecommunications Dispute Resolution Committee, which resolves disputes between telecom business operators). The Promotion of Use of Alternative Dispute Resolution Act of 2004 (the ADR Act) make it relatively easy for private institutions to establish an ADR center, and many bar and other professional associations have done so.

The principal arbitral body in Japan is the Japan Commercial Arbitration Association (JCAA), a private foundation. There is also a public interest foundation, the Japan Association of Arbitrators (JAA).

Possibly because the expense dynamics are different or because Japanese courts themselves devote significant energy to resolving cases without completing, or even starting a trial, arbitration is not widely used in Japan. For 2016 the JCAA reports just 16 arbitration actions being brought. At the time of writing, the Japanese government was trying to make the nation a center for international dispute resolution, with the JAA announcing plans to establish an international media center in Kyoto.

The principal laws governing ADR outside the courts are the ADR Act and the Arbitration Act of 2003. Japan is a party to the New York Arbitration Convention on the Recognition and Enforcement of Foreign Arbitral Award.

At the time of writing there was a growing interest within the Japanese legal professional community in western-style mediation techniques. Facilitative-style mediation, where the mediator focuses on assisting parties in arriving at a resolution without telling them what to do is a new concept in Japan, where most existing forms of mediation and conciliation involve an official or *defacto* authority figure listening to the parties and then indicating what the appropriate resolution is. Possibly to distinguish it from existing Japanese forms of mediation, the western style is often referred to using a Japanization of the English term; *medieshon*. *Bengoshi* attorneys and court personnel whose primary experience is with family court conciliation are also surprised by mediation where both parties sit in the same room, as that has rarely been the practice in Japan.

One possible hurdle to wider acceptance of mediation and other private ADR in Japan is the lack of evidentiary rules or privileges segregating them from court proceedings. This is perhaps understandable given the prevailing nature of court-sponsored ADR.

Chapter 11

THE LEGAL FRAMEWORK OF THE BUSINESS ENVIRONMENT

Analysis

A. INTRODUCTION AND CONSTITUTIONAL DIMENSIONS

1. Opening Remarks

To truly do justice to the subject of business law in Japan would require a lengthy separate book drawing on the expertise of a number of contributors. Moreover, business law and regulation is an area where there is a comparatively large body of reference material available in English. These include not only books and law review articles, but client memos published by leading Japanese and global law firms as well as the web sites of Japanese regulatory bodies and other organizations. For example, at the time of writing the Japan Patent Office had on its website a good English description of the types of patents and the procedures for applying for them, suggesting a detailed description is unnecessary here. There is also a large and constantly growing body of work on the subject of corporate governance in Japan, a significant amount of which is available on the Internet.

That being the case we feel coverage in this book can be correspondingly brief. Accordingly, the principal goal of this chapter will be to give readers a sense of the framework of the business regulation in Japan by focusing on a limited number of core areas. These will include contract, employment regulation, the Commercial Code, corporations and other legal persons, intellectual property, consumer protection and a few areas where Japan has a particular way of doing things that merits attention.

In addition, based on the experience of the authors, for many foreign business or legal practitioners in Japan, the principal issue in the field of business regulation (other than employment regulation and corporate formalities) is most likely to be who the primary regulator of their business is. Once that is understood, a great deal of "business law" is likely to involve understanding the regulatory regime. The next most likely issue will be communicating with local legal and other advisors with an understanding of the contextual environment. The vertically-integrated nature of much Japanese industry regulation and the limits of practical recourse to the judiciary when regulators are unreasonable in their demands or interpretations means that for many businesses (particularly those engaged in activities requiring a specific license or registration), the legal environment is primarily a matter of complying with regulatory dictates.

In some cases, these may include very detailed instructions as to how a business should be conducted. Depending on the industry, other businesses may also be expected to conduct their business in accordance with detailed formal guidance far below the level of actual law and secondary legislation, or even informal guidance. In the past informal guidance was common in the form of *gyōsei shidō* (administrative guidance). Although this practice was supposed to have been stopped, or at least more readily challenged by the administrative procedural regime described in the previous chapter, regulators may still be able to exercise considerable control through informal guidance in some situations. Accordingly, it may be helpful to have read Chapters 3 and 5 first in order to get a flavor for which ministry, agency or other central government institution regulates a particular area of business and how.

2. Constitutional Dimensions

Article 29 of the Constitution protects property rights, while articles 27 and 28 refer to organized labor and employment regulation. Apart from these the key constitutional provision relevant to the regulation of business is probably paragraph 1 of article 22, which protects, *inter alia*, the right to choose one's occupation so long as it does not interfere with the public welfare.

This part of article 22 was the grounds for second instance in which the Supreme Court found a statute to be unconstitutional, the *Pharmacy Proximity Restriction Case* discussed in Chapter 6. While famous as a rare finding of a statutory constitutional violation, the case may have been an outlier in terms of business regulation. Although numerous other regulatory restrictions on trade, the conduct of business, entry to professions and other aspects of commerce have been challenged in the courts, virtually all have been upheld, at least on constitutional grounds.

In fact, a basic, recurring theme of Japanese business regulation is that excessive competition is bad, even destructive. Thus, a certain amount of regulation is devoted to limiting competition through entry barriers, quantitative licensing restrictions, market allocation and other practices which are, on a certain level, incompatible with supposed "free" market economic theory. The segmentation of the legal services industry described in Chapter 7, including the seemingly arbitrary number of persons permitted to pass the NBE is an example of this type of regulation.

Although the right to "choose" an occupation is interpreted broadly, and thus extends to the right to engage in it as a business, the "public welfare" qualifier to the article 22 guarantee means that restrictions having a rational basis will generally survive constitutional challenges. Moreover, courts have usually been willing to find regulations intended to restrict competition to be a policy goal in furtherance of the public welfare. There are a number of other Supreme Court cases upholding regulations, some of which seem difficult to distinguish from the *Pharmacy Proximity Restriction Case* discussed in Chapter 6. Even prior to that decision the court had already upheld the constitutionality of geographical (proximity) restrictions on the licensing of public baths and public markets (Supreme Court, Grand Bench judgments of January 26, 1955 and November 22, 1962), as well as taxi licensing requirements (Supreme Court, Grand

Bench judgment of December 4, 1963). In 1989 the Court again upheld restrictions on public bathhouse licensing (Supreme Court, 2nd Petty Bench judgment of January 20, 1989), perhaps confirming that the Pharmacy Case had been an anomaly. In 1990 it rejected challenges to a prohibition on silk garment makers from procuring silk thread directly from abroad; they were required to purchase it at much higher prices through what was essentially a government-sponsored import cartel (Supreme Court, 3rd Petty Bench judgment of February 6, 1990). The court also upheld regulations giving discretion to local tax authorities to refuse to grant a license to operate a liquor license based on the applicant's financial standing (Supreme Court, 3rd Petty Bench judgment of December 15, 1992). In 2000 the court upheld the criminal conviction of an administrative scrivener for conducting corporate registry filings in violation of the Judicial Scrivener Act (Supreme Court, 3rd Petty Bench judgment of February 8, 2000).

B. CONTRACT LAW AND THE COMMERCIAL CODE

1. Contract Law and Practice

a. *The Foundations of Contract Law: The Civil Code*

The basics of Japanese contract law are covered in Part III, Chapter 2 of the Civil Code (articles 521 through 696). Readers should read Chapter 9 first to familiarize themselves with the structure of the Code and the concepts it uses to characterize claims (*saiken*) and other concepts relevant to contracts. As also noted in that chapter, at the time of writing the provisions of Part III had been drastically amended for the first time since the Code was enacted at the end of the 19th century. However, these amendments had not yet taken effect at the time of writing. Accordingly, the discussion in this section will be limited to a broad outline of contract law as it has existed up to these amendments followed by a brief summary of some of the key changes. References to the Civil Code are to the articles as in force at the time of writing rather than as amended.

For the benefit of readers from common law jurisdictions it may be helpful to first identify what Japanese contract law *lacks*. As with continental legal systems, there is no doctrine of consideration and thus issues such as the enforceability of gift contracts" do not present as many conceptual difficulties as in the common law. Nor is there a parol evidence rule or legal provisions comparable to the "statute of frauds" that require particular types of contracts to be in writing or limits courts to considering only a particular type of evidence. Some contracts may in fact need to be in writing, though this will be a matter of consumer protection and/or regulation of a particular type of business rather than a general principle.

Contracts are formed through offer and acceptance, with acceptance on different terms constituting a counter-offer and the possibility of a "battle of the forms," though there is surprisingly little jurisprudence on the subject. Offers that do not specify a deadline for acceptance remain open for a "reasonable" period of time. The Civil Code's "mailbox rule" (article 526(1) and 527)) date back to the 19th century and deems acceptance to be effective when mailed. It has been superseded in certain types of e-commerce consumer transactions by the Act on Special Provisions of the Civil Code Concerning Electronic Consumer Contracts and Electronic Acceptance Notice of 2001.

Remedies for breach of contract are essentially those established for other claims under the Civil Code: damages due to default under article 415, or court-ordered specific performance under article 414, though subject to potential limitations depending on the nature of the default. Another way in which Japanese contract law is different from the common law is that it contains no general prohibition on contractual penalties. In a context where a US-law contract would have to justify and define "liquidated damages," it is not uncommon to see Japanese contracts containing a clause providing for *iyakkin*—literally, "amounts payable for breach." Excessive damages of this type would be mitigated through doctrines such as unconscionability or public morals.

Courts are generally very strict in requiring performance of contractual obligations. The Supreme Court has acknowledged that a change of circumstances may be grounds for modification or non-performance if the possibility of such change is both unforeseeable at the time of contracting and not attributable to the fault of the contracting parties. At the same time, however, it has virtually never recognized a situation in which the doctrine applies. In the seminal case, the Court describes the doctrine without finding it applicable to the case at bar (Supreme Court, 3rd Petty Bench judgment of July 1, 1997).

Recall from Chapter 9 that article 1 of the Civil Code infuses the exercise of rights and performance of duties with a duty of good faith in all areas of private law, including contract. An undertaking by the parties to resolve issues and uncertainties is often the last clause in a Japanese contract. Pre-contract negotiations and memoranda of understanding or other preliminary agreements to negotiate toward a more substantive definitive agreement may result in greater liability than American lawyers might expect.

A dramatic example of this was illustrated in litigation between two mega-banks, The Sumitomo Trust Bank ("Sumitomo") and The UFJ Financial Group ("UFJ"). In 2004, the two banks had entered into a preliminary agreement regarding the possibility of Sumitomo selling to UFJ its trust banking business. The agreement contained an "exclusivity clause" intended to prevent either party from negotiating the same deal with other prospects. Later the same year UFJ terminated this preliminary agreement and announced it was merging with another mega-bank, The Mitsubishi-Tokyo Financial Group. Sumitomo immediately brought suit seeking to enjoin UFJ from negotiating with Mitsubishi-Tokyo. On appeal the Supreme Court found that UFJ and Sumitomo were still subject to the exclusivity provisions of the preliminary agreement, but that Sumitomo would not suffer irreparable harm from its breach such that an injunction was merited. The subsequent suit for damages was settled with UFJ (merged to form Tokyo Mitsubishi UFJ Bank) paying Sumitomo JPY 2.5 billion.

It should also be remembered from Chapter 9 that courts may use the doctrine of "abuse of rights" to prevent the exercise of contractual rights that may seem clear on paper. This doctrine has been used to protect one party, particularly when there is an imbalance in the bargaining power (such as in the employment relationship) and/or expectations as to the duration of the contract, such as in long term distributorship relationships, which, on paper, can be terminated after a fairly short notice period.

b. Types of Contracts

Another way in which Japanese contract law is quite different from the common law is that the Civil Code identifies 13 specific categories of contract: (1) gift (*zōyo*), (2) sale (*baibai*), (3) exchange (*kōkan*), (4) loan for consumption (*i.e.*, of funds; *shōhi taishaku*), (5) loan for use (without compensation; *shiyōtaishaku*)), (6) lease (*chintaishaku*), (7) employment (*koyō*), (8) contract for work (*ukeoi*; e.g., a construction or outsourcing project), (9) representation/agency or mandate (*inin*), (10) bailment (*kitaku*), (11) cooperative partnership (*kumiai*), (12) life annuity (*shūshin teikikin*) and (13) settlement (*wakai*).

Having been established over a century ago, some of these types have become archaic or obscure (e.g., life annuities). Others have been largely superseded by other statutory regimes (e.g., statutory employment law). Nonetheless, the distinctions between some types of contracts may be important due to different rules that apply either through provisions of the code or practice and precedent. In addition, how a contract is categorized may also affect the applicability of stamp taxes (see discussion later in this chapter).

c. *The 2017 Civil Code Amendments*

In 2017 the MOJ's decade-long project of amending Part III of the Civil Code was brought to fruition, though not without some parts of the business and legal communities questioning whether changes to the well-established rules and precedents were actually necessary. The amendments are expected to take effect in 2020.

In broad strokes, the following is a partial summary of some of the salient aspects of the amendments.

- ***Unifying and simplifying claims extinction periods.*** Under current law, the statutory period after which contractual or other civil law claims expire varies from one to ten years depending on the type of claim and when it arose or when the claimant became aware of it. Under the amended Code, most contractual claims will expire five years after they are known and ten years from when they could have first been exercised if known, with tort claims being similarly unified at five and twenty years. The rules for calculating and tolling these periods have also been rationalized.
- ***Establishing greater protections for personal guarantees of business debt.*** Guarantee undertakings by individuals will be subject to numerical thresholds and other protections. Persons giving personal guarantees of third party business debts will now only be able to do so through a notarized promissory note, and will be entitled to receive certain information about the business they are guaranteeing.
- ***Addition of provisions the assignment of rights to receive payment.*** Under the language and interpretation of the current Code, contractual provisions restricting assignment of the right to receive payments are generally enforceable and may even invalidate attempted assignments. This had made many forms of financial obligation less liquid than they could be and hindered restructurings, securitizations and other transactions. The amended Code will make such assignments easier.
- ***Addition of provisions governing adhesion contracts.*** The current Civil Code contract provisions generally assume equal bargaining power between two contracting parties and ignore the reality that most contracts that are executed are standard forms between a large company and an individual consumer or smaller company with no ability to negotiate the contents. While some protections have been developed through specific laws such as the Consumer Contract Act or other statutes dealing with

particular types of contracts, there have not been any core principals dealing with contracts of adhesion. The amendments add a new type of contract—*teigata yakkan* (standard terms and conditions) that are used by one party without modification for dealings with large numbers of counterparties. On the one hand, unexpected or unreasonable terms in such contracts will be more easily invalidated. On the other, it will be easier for the businesses using such contracts to modify them unilaterallyby providing for the possibility in on-line terms of service.

- ***Clarifying the rules on impossibility of performance.*** Article 415 of the currentCode provisions state that an obligor breaching their obligations is liable to compensate the resulting damages of the obligee, even if performance has "become impossible to perform due to reasons attributable to the obligor." This means that only an obligor who is not responsible for the impossibility can escape liability. Responsibility for impossibility of performance is currently evaluated by courts based on the specific circumstances, resulting in more flexibility than the text implies. The amended provisions will add greater clarity and codify some of this practice.
- ***Codifying rules as to when a party can terminate a contract without the other party being in breach.*** Under the current (old) Code provisions, it is not clear that a party can terminate if the other party cannot perform for reasons beyond its control (e.g., *force majeure*). This is clarified in the amendments.
- ***Clarifying the rules on seller's liability for defects.*** The amended Code will codify existing rules on Buyer's remedies and establish clear rules as to the period in which Seller can make claims.
- ***Codifying some of the basic principles of contract.*** Subject to requirements and limitations of other applicable statutes, these include the freedom to contract (or not contract), freedom to choose who one contracts with, freedom to decide on the contents of the contract one signs, and the method of contracting (oral vs. written). Prior to the amendments (through their incorporation into new articles 521 and 522), these principles were widely accepted as part of contract theory but not reflected in the Code.
- ***Clarifying the rules on residential and commercial leases.*** As anyone who has rented in Japan is likely to have noticed, there is a certain amount of fuzziness around entitlement to refund of security deposits and the contractual obligation to restore the premises to their original condition. The amended Code provides greater clarity based on existing best practices.

d. *Other Sources of Contract Law*

There are a wide variety of other laws that address contracts used in specific contexts. The Consumer Contract Act of 2000 gives consumers the right to rescind contracts with businesses on the basis of misrepresentations or other grounds. The Land and Building Lease Act of 1991 contains mandatory provisions governing the renewal and termination of real estate leases.

Various regulatory regimes also include mandates regarding the inclusion or prohibition of certain terms in contracts within those regimes. For example, article 19 of the Telecommunications Business Act of 1984 requires terms of service used by licensed carriers to provide basic telecommunications services include provisions that *inter alia* clearly indicating the manner in which charges are calculated and prohibit terms that discriminate against specific persons or would result in "improper competition with other carriers." Some contract law rules and other variations to the Civil Code involving transactions by merchants are also created by the Commercial Code discussed below.

In 2008 Japan joined the United Nations Convention on Contracts for the International Sale of Goods, which took effect in 2009.

e. The Use of Seals

The use of engraved seals (also called "chops") is very common in Japan and forms a component of personal identity as discussed in Chapter 9. Contracts and other legal documents are usually executed by individuals by hand writing their name and then affixing the sale. Most contracts or documents requiring a seal include the Chinese character for seal (印) to indicate where the seal impression should be affixed.

There is, however, no general legal requirement that contracts be executed using seals, though statutes may require it in other contexts. The Commercial Code refers to the execution of documents by signatures in a number of places, but also contains a provision permitting the use of the combination of a written name and seal impression to be used in lieu of signature (e.g., Commercial Code article 32).

While seals are not mandatory for individuals, corporations must have them and the impression of the corporate seal is registered with the Legal Affairs Bureau. As with individual seals, a certification of the validity of that seal impression may be issued and is another common document required for various transactions.

The process by which corporations approve the execution of contracts or other significant actions may also involve seals. A common practice is for a *ringisho* (approval circular) to be circulated to all the responsible department heads for approval, which is typically indicated by their seal, approval effectively being given when all the necessary seals have been affixed. A similar use of multiple seals as part of paper-based compliance systems is also common.

It is also common to use tape to bind contracts, corporate minutes and other documents and then have the relevant parties affix their seal across the binding. This makes tampering with the document difficult. Seal impressions are also used to acknowledge key terms or manual corrections, similar to the way initials are used in western contracting practice.

f. Contract Documentation

Traditionally commercial contracts between companies have often been quite brief—a few pages of relatively sparse articles, the last of which is a standard undertaking to engage in good faith discussions to resolve uncertainties about interpretation, gaps and other discrepancies. This may reflect the higher degree of trust between parties that some corporate managers feel is necessary before they will enter into a formal contract with another company. It may also reflect the lack of a need to address the applicability of various contract doctrines and interpretive precedents that drives boiler plate in American-style contracts. In other words, there is no need for language justifying the applicability of equitable remedies or liquidated damages, ensuringthe applicability of the parol evidence rule, properly waiving the right to a jury trial and so forth. Nonetheless, a recent trend appears to be towards the use of more extensive contract documentation, sometimes with clauses and language that suggest American models.

g. *A Note on Stamp Taxes and Contracting*

In Japan the use of revenue stamps (*shūnyū inshi*) as a form of taxation/public duty is common in Japan. Revenue stamps look like postage stamps and are affixed to documents that require them. Sold at post offices, legal affairs bureaus and other authorized locations, they can be used to pay litigation fees, fines, government application fees and other amounts due to national government institutions.

Under the Stamp Tax Act of 1967, revenue stamps must be affixed to a wide variety of contracts, negotiable instruments and other documents with a value above a certain threshold (currently JPY 10,000 or 50,000 for most types). The amount of revenue stamps required depends on the value and type of contract or instrument. Failure to affix revenue stamps to a contract when necessary does not affect the validity of the contract, but asserting rights under such a contract heightens the risk of being subject to penalties for non-payment of taxes. For contracts such as a real estate purchase agreement, failure to attach the required revenue stamps will prevent the transfer of title from being registered in the real property registry.

Of course, revenue stamps can only be affixed to physical paper contracts (or other physical media containing electronic records of such contracts). The NTA appears to still be struggling with the question of how to tax contracts that are of a type subject to stamp taxes but are executed entirely on-line.

h. *A Note on Contracting and Organized Crime*

As noted in Chapter 8, organized crime groups have in the past played a surprisingly open role in Japanese society. More recently law enforcement have put significant efforts into driving them out of business, as well as suppressing other "anti-social forces" a term that can also include political radicals and other troublemakers. One result of these efforts can be seen in laws and prefectural ordinances intended to prevent commercial dealings with organized crime groups.

One manifestation of these rules has an impact on contracting. It is now very common for consumer and commercial contracts and real property leases to contain extended representations and warranties assuring that at least one party to the contract, usually the consumer, is not affiliated with organized crime groups or a long list of other problematic groups. These provisions can be long, sometimes running to almost a page.

2. The Commercial Code

a. *Overview*

It would be remiss to discuss business law without mentioning the Commercial Code (*Shōhō*). The Commercial Code of 1899 is one of the original "Six Codes" (see Chapter 5), but the term *shōhō* is often used as a broader reference to commercial law in general, and as an area of study and one of the core subjects tested on the NBE. As we shall see, however, over time the Commercial Code itself has gradually declined in importance over time. At the time of writing, parts of the Code remained in the original *kanamajiribun* classical Japanese reflecting its 19th century provenance. A bill to modernize both the language and the content of the Code had been submitted to the Diet but had not yet been passed.

b. *History*

Japan entered the Meiji Period with a large merchant class and well-established, sophisticated rules for doing business. The first futures contracts (for rice) are said to have been invented in Edo-Period Japan. However, with the Meiji Period and the unequal treaties came the need to develop rules acceptable to foreign trading partners. Japan's first Commercial Code was drafted with the assistance of the German legal scholar, Karl Friedrich Hermann Roesler, and adopted in 1890. However, it quickly became tied up in the more famous dispute over the Civil Code (see Chapter 9). Complaints from scholars and commercial organizations arose about there being too much overlap between the French-influenced Civil Code and the German Influenced Commercial Code, as well as the latter's incompatibility with existing Japanese commercial practices. The result was the adoption of the present, still heavily German-influenced Commercial code less than a decade later.

Since its enactment, the Code has gone through numerous amendments. These include the incorporation of certain American corporate law concepts and practices during the occupation.

Perhaps the most significant trend affecting the Commercial Code has been its gradual dismantling through the removal of key chapters and sections and their replacement with separate statutory regimes. The most important of these is the 2005 removal of the Part II provisions on company law and their replacement by the massive Companies Act of the same year. In the past, bankruptcy and negotiable instruments were also part of the Code, but have long been separate statutes. The law of insurance was also part of the Code until the Insurance Act of 2008 resulted in the removal of all the provisions, except those on marine insurance.

These changes demonstrate the increasing volume and sophistication of Japanese commercial law. For the Commercial Code, however, they mean that the majority of its articles—several hundred of them—simply read "deleted."

c. *The Commercial Code Today*

Following the same structure as other codes, Part I contains general principles and definitions. Definitions include terms that are no longer used in normal business parlance, such as merchant (*shōnin*). Chapter 3 of Part I establishes the basic requirements of registering a business, though the details are left to the Commercial Registration Act of 1963. Chapter 4 of the Code introduces the still-important concept of trade name (*shōgō*), and covers some of the protections associated with having one.

Part II deals with commercial conduct (*shōkōi*), and establishes special rules for offer, acceptance and sales transactions as between merchants, joint liabilities for commercial obligations and other variations from the rules laid down in the Civil Code. Article 521 creates a special *bukken* security interest (a right of retention) in objects or negotiable instruments subject to a commercial transaction between merchants.

One section of Part II that has retained importance in the context of financial transactions is the provisions of articles 535 through 542 on silent (or anonymous) partnerships (*tokumei kumiai*—often referred to in practice as "TK"). These are often used as tax-efficient passive investment vehicles.

Part II also establishes some of the basic rules for specific types of commerce-related businesses: warehousing, brokering, freight forwarding and freight and passenger transportation. Many of these businesses are subject to further regulation through more detailed industry-specific laws and regulations (e.g., the Warehouse Business Act of 1956, the Railway Business Act of 1986).

Part III of the Code establishes the foundation of Japan's laws of maritime commerce, and together with the Civil Code is the starting point for what would elsewhere be called the substantive laws of admiralty. Japan is also a party to the United Nations Convention on the Carriage of Goods by Sea.

C. COMPANIES AND OTHER LEGAL (JURIDICAL) ENTITIES

1. Historical Background and Overview

a. History

In the world of business, continuity between the pre- and post-Meiji era can be seen in the numerous businesses that survived the transition, some even to the modern day. The two oldest businesses in the world are Japanese hot springs resorts. *Kongō Gumi*, a construction company tracing its roots back to Korean artisans invited to Japan by Prince Shōtoku Taishi in 578 was the world's oldest continuously operating family business until it became a subsidiary of Takamatsu Construction Corporation in 2008. Ancient cities like Kyoto in particular are rich with businesses that have existed for centuries. Some of Japan's global businesses also have similarly deep roots. For example, the Sumitomo Group of companies traces its roots back to a pharmacy established in the 17th century.

Business organizations—many of them based on the extended family structures discussed in Chapter 9—existed long before the Meiji Restoration. The first joint stock corporation—the Daiichi Kokuritsu Ginkō—was established in 1873 under a special banking law, the "National Banking Ordinance" of 1872. However, the legal framework for modern corporations was not laid until 1890 with the enactment of Japan's first Commercial Code, which contained a chapter on corporations. As already discussed, this was replaced with the new (and current) Commercial Code of 1899, which served as the principal source of corporate law for over a century. Until recently, the Civil Code also contained provisions providing for basic rules governing the capacity of legal persons and the establishment and governance of certain types of not-for-profit corporate entities. These latter rules were deleted and replaced by a separate act in 2006, as discussed below.

After the Meiji Restoration many areas of commerce came to be dominated by family-owned or other forms of conglomerate known as *zaibatsu*. The most famous of these were the Sumitomo, Mitsubishi, Mitsui and Yasuda *zaibatsu*, but there were a numerous other national and regional concentrations of wealth and industry as well. This effectively included the Emperor and the Imperial Household Ministry, which came to control vast holdings of land, shares and other property independent of the national treasury.

The Americans who administered the occupation believed excessive concentrations of wealth were undemocratic, and devoted significant energies to breaking up the largest of the *zaibatsu* (which effectively included the imperial family) and established laws to prevent the resurgence of similar corporate groupings. Occupation-era reforms dedicated to this end include the adoption of the Anti-Monopoly Act of 1947 which prohibited holding companies (one of the hallmarks of many family-owned *zaibatsu*) until its amendment in 1997.

The occupation era also saw extensive amendments made to the Commercial Code in 1950. These resulted in the primarily German-influenced corporate law provisions of the Code taking on a distinctly American twist, with provisions added that were modeled on the Illinois Business Corporations Act of 1933 and the Uniform Stock Transfer Act of 1909.

Just as the occupation-era land reform resulted in a vast expansion of land ownership, the dismantling of the *zaibatsu* resulted in widespread share ownership. The American reforms were directed at strengthening shareholder rights and thus, supposedly, shareholder *democracy*.

For example it was at this time that the ability of shareholders to file derivative lawsuits was added to Japanese corporate law. Restrictions on share transfers were also abolished in order to enhance the value of shares, though the ability to impose restrictions on share transfers was subsequently reinstated after the occupation ended. These reforms also saw the decision-making powers of the board of directors enhanced. While previously many important management decisions could be made at the *zaibatsu* shareholder meetings due to the limited number of shareholders, this was no longer possible at companies with larger, diffuse shareholder communities.

The post-war period saw some of the former *zaibatsu* regrouping in corporate groups known as *keiretsu*, or new forms of *keiretsu* developing. Some *keiretsu* are or were organized horizontally and centered around a major bank serving as the "main bank" for the group. Group companies would have shareholdings in each other. The Sumitomo, Mitsui and Mitsubishi Groups are examples of this type of *keiretsu*.

Others *keiretsu* developed vertically, with a large manufacturer at the top and numerous suppliers and subcontractors underneath, again with interlinked shareholding relationships. Car manufacturers such as Toyota and Honda are leading examples. There are debates about whether *keiretsu* are or ever were as relevant as commonly suggested.[1]

Since the occupation, the company law provisions of the Commercial Code were subject to frequent amendments, experimentation and innovations, not all of which have proved successful. For example, amendments taking effect in 2003 made it possible to have U.S.-style boards with committees, though comparatively few companies have chosen to do so.

---

[1] That they are still relevant is suggested by the fact that one aspect of Japanese business etiquette entails serving the appropriate brand of beer based on which large brewery is a member of the same *keiretsu* or otherwise affiliated with the company whose employees or executives are being entertained.

In 2005 corporate law was excised from the Commercial Code and completely reorganized in the form of the massive new Companies Act. Since its enactment the MOJ has continued to tweak the Companies Act with frequent amendments. These have been accompanied by corresponding efforts to modify the corporate governance of non-commercial juridical entities, a subject covered briefly later in this chapter.

b. Corporate Existence and Registration

A basic distinction in Japanese corporate law—broadly defined—is whether an organization (business or otherwise) has status as a legal/juridical person separate from its human constituents (*hōjinkaku*). Legal persons can own property, acquire rights and assume obligations in their own names. There are a range of organizations that have a collective nature but lack formal status as legal persons. These are collectively referred to as "*jinkaku no nai shadan*" (associations without personality), but have little importance in business and will not be discussed further.

There is a great deal of academic theory about juridical personhood. However, in practice a key factor in establishing it under any of the corporate forms recognized by law and discussed below is registration in the commercial/corporate registry (*shōgyō/hōjin tōki*) maintained by the appropriate Legal Affairs Bureau. The criteria that need to be registered depend on the type of legal entity and are specified by law, but generally include the corporate/trade name, address of head office and any branches, person responsible or having representative authority, location of branches, capitalization and so forth.

For joint stock corporations (*kabushiki gaisha*) the list of things that must be registered is substantial, including filing the necessary updates such as changes in directors and branch relocations. Publicly accessible (including through on-line systems) the registration system is part of legal personhood in that it makes it possible for the rest of the world to confirm some of the basic, legally-significant details about a particular corporate entity. A great deal of enforcement of basic corporate law thus takes place at the incorporation stage, with the Legal Affairs Bureau refusing to accept non-conforming applications. An extract of a company's corporate registry is a commonly-required document in corporate transactions and used to confirm the "identity" of the corporate person, in the same way a *koseki* extract is used to confirm the identity of a natural one (see Chapter 9).

Some of the characteristics of the corporate body that must be registered are also be required to be set forth in the entity's articles of incorporation (*teikan*) or other charter document. The requirements of a corporate charter depend on the specific law under which the corporate entity is established. Moreover, some provisions are mandatory and others permissive. However, the articles of incorporation of virtually all corporate entities must at a minimum include the corporate name, a statement of corporate purpose and address of principal office or place of business.

Information about corporate bodies relevant to creditors and other third parties (including the fact of their establishment and registration) must also be disseminated through public notices. The default means of doing so is through the *kanpō* official gazette, but the Companies Act permits companies to provide for other means of notification (including through approved electronic means) in their articles of incorporation. The method of giving public notice must be specified in the corporate charter and is recorded in the company registry.

The combination of the company registry and the notice requirements are intended to ensure that basic information about all companies is available to those who need it. The disclosure requirements applicable to publicly listed companies are far more extensive and provided for in the Financial Instruments and Exchange Act.

c. *Corporate Size and Regulations*

Before the Companies Act was passed, the corporate law provisions of the Commercial Code distinguished between three types of joint stock corporation: large (*dai*) medium (*chū*) and small (*shō*), based on capitalization and other metrics. These distinctions have been eliminated, though sections the Companies Act still makes a number of important distinctions in the rules applicable to joint stock companies that fit the definitions of "large" or "public" companies and those that do not, as discussed later in this chapter.

Apart from these rules relating to joint stock corporations specifically, the distinction between "large enterprises" (*daikigyō*) and small- to medium-sized enterprises (SMEs, in Japanese *chūsho kigyō*) is used in a range of other regulatory contexts, without reference to a particular corporate form. These are rooted in the Small and Medium-sized Business Enterprise Basic Act of 1963 (SMBEBA).

Note that "SME" is a single category of business. The definition of SME itself is based on a combination of the nature of the enterprise's business, and its capitalization *or* the number of its "regularly used employees" (*jōji shiyō suru jūgyōin*). A manufacturing, construction or transportation business with fewer than 300 *or* a capitalization of less than JPY 300 million is an SME. For a retail firm to fit the definition, however, it must have a capitalization of JPY 50 million or less or 50 or fewer employees. Different statutes establish other thresholds for specific types of businesses. The SMBEBA does not further delineate between "small enterprise" and "medium enterprise," but does establish a special category of "small scale entrepreneur" (*shōkibo jigyōsha*), who operate businesses with a small number of employees (20 or fewer or five, depending on the business).

Among other things, being an SME puts companies under the jurisdiction of the METI's Small and Medium Enterprise Agency, which offers various programs to assist them, as does the Organization for Small & Medium Enterprises and Regional Innovation, an IAA also under METI. This IAA makes available to SME's group provident funds and other benefit programs. SME's also enjoy numerous tax advantages.

d. *A Note on Trusts*

Trusts (*shintaku*) have been a feature of Japan's business world for a long time, with a 1905 act enabling the use of trusts in connection with the issuance of collateralized corporate bonds. The first general Trust Act was passed in 1923 and replaced in 2006 by a new act of the same name.

The basic components of trusts—trust property, trustee, and beneficiary—are the same as in the Anglo-American system. However, trusts have never achieved the widespread use or applicability as they have in the common law system. Trusts are generally only used for business purposes and are essentially a service provided by trust banks. The Trust Act now allows the use of a special form of trust the limited liability trust as a financial structuring vehicle.

2. The Taxonomy of Business Organizations and Other Legal (Juridical) Persons

a. *Non-Profit (Sharing) Corporations*

(i) Overview

The Companies Act and other laws provide for a variety of corporate forms and business organizations. Before we can turn to them, however, we must look to the larger universe of legal entities.

Prior to the Companies Act, the Commercial Code (old article 52) actually defined a Company as a for-profit (*eiri*) collective enterprise. The "for profit" nature of companies is not clearly spelled out in the Companies Act, but article 5 of the Act does declare that any act by a company in furtherance of its business is a "commercial act" (as defined in article 501 of the Commercial Code). Through this provision the Commercial Code (article 4) in turn renders all companies "merchants." Profit is thus implicitly still part of the corporate mandate. This is also reflected in the ability of Companies Act entities to distribute profits to their members or shareholders.

For corporate entities that are not engaged in merchant behavior but may still be relevant to business and its regulation, it is necessary to look elsewhere than the Companies Act. For the sake of brevity the countless *public* corporations such as national universities or the Bureau of Printing (for example) will not be addressed.

With respect to the private corporate entities, it is still common to distinguish between *eiri hōjin* (for profit legal entities) and *hieiri hōjin* (legal entities that are not for profit). The use of the term "for profit" may be misleading, since for many such institutions there is no prohibition on engaging in profit-making activities, only restrictions on the distribution of profits to their members. So "profit sharing" vs. "non-profit sharing" may be a better translation.

(ii) Incorporated Foundations and Associations

Companies Act business organizations (*eiri hōjin* for profit entities) are discussed in greater detail below. In the not-for-profit category, first there are General Incorporated Associations (*ippan shadan hōjin*) and General Incorporated Foundations (*ippan zaidan hōjin*), which are provided for under the General Incorporated Associations and General Incorporated Foundations Act of 2006 (GIAGIFA), though they were previously provided for in the Civil Code.

General Incorporated Associations are established by one or more members to pursue a particular purpose. This may involve commercial activities, but the association is not permitted to pay dividends to its members. This corporate form is commonly used for industry associations or other quasi-public service activities. A general incorporated foundation is established for similar purposes but is focused on accumulating assets for a particular purpose rather than members. Special governance structures are provided for such entities and centered on a board of directors (*riji*, a different term from that used for company directors).

Some General Incorporated Associations (GIA) and General Incorporated Foundations (GIF) are ostensibly private but have actually been directly or indirectly established in furtherance of a governmental purpose or to benefit from a relationship with a particular aspect of governance. For example, the Japan Traffic Safety Association is a GIA that acts as an umbrella organization for similarly organized prefectural traffic safety associations which have traditionally been heavily staffed by retired police officials and, through no-bid contracts with police authorities, is said to have a virtual monopoly on providing the periodic training required by law to renew driving licenses.

The quasi-public character of many such entities is illustrated by the fact that the MOJ courts are required to seek the opinion of the Minister of Justice when considering liquidating them under the (GIAGIFA, article 261). In addition to governing these two types of entities, the GIAGIFA (and, in some cases the Companies Act as well) provide default rules that are incorporated by reference in various statutes providing for more specialized or different types of corporate entity discussed below.

The "general" in the name of incorporated associations and foundations distinguishes them from "Public Interest" (*kōeki*) associations or foundations. It is possible to apply for certification for such status; those who meet the rigorous standards under Public Interest Association and Public Interest Foundation Certification Act of 2006 enjoy tax benefits, such as the ability to accept tax-deductible contributions. They are also subject to numerous restrictions on engaging in for-profit activities.

In the past, public interest entities could only be established if approved by the government. The GIAGIFA takes away government discretion over the establishment of general foundations and associations, but the requirements for establishing a Public Interest Association and Public Interest Foundation remain rigorous, and it is probably very difficult to do without the support of a governmental backer or a large corporation. The near monopoly enjoyed by the government over the establishment of such tax-advantaged entities means the public interest sector of Japan's economy and society has been primarily dominated by government-affiliated bodies that have enjoyed the benefits of most funding available for such purposes. It also means the emergence of entities devoted to openly challenging or questioning government policies has been limited.

(iii) NPO Corporations

A 2008 law, the "Act for the Promotion of Specified Non-Profit Activities" now makes it very easy to establish a corporate non-profit organization (commonly referred to with the slightly tautological "*NPO hōjin*" (Non-Profit Corporation). Such organizations may be established to pursue a wide (but specific) range of public interest activities, and also enjoy various tax benefits.

(iv) Area-Specific Entities

Moving into specific areas of public interest (and regulation), there are also a wide range of other special corporate entities that enjoy certain special privileges and tax advantages but are also subject to restrictions, including the general prohibition on distributions of surplus. Most are a form General Incorporated Association or General Incorporated Foundation under the GIAGIFA, but with an additional layer of regulation and requirements specific to the area in which they operate. They are also often eligible for government subsidies within the regulatory domain they occupy.

For example most private schools and universities take the form of "school corporations" (*gakkō hōjin*), essentially a special form of incorporated foundation (but established under the Private School Act of 1949) that is primarily under the jurisdiction of MEXT. Similarly, the majority of clinical medical practices are likely to be *iryōhōjin* (medical corporations) under the Medical Care Act of 1948, with a variety of subcategories based on governance structures and regulatory criteria. Large hospitals, elder care or other medical institutions (that are not public institutions) may be "social welfare corporations" *shakai fukushi hōjin*, a special category of public interest corporation established under the Social Welfare Act of 1951 (and under the jurisdiction of the MHLW).

Institutions of a public character that fall under the category of *hieiri hōjin* corporate entities also include bar associations and other professional associations that have a separate legal personality. Various private or public pension funds and mutual aid associations are also included in this category (though of course they try to make profitable investments and to distribute funds to pensioners).

(v) Commercial Non-Profit Sharing Entities

There is also a large universe of institutions engaged in a wide range of business activities under corporate forms that prohibit the distribution of profits. The most common are what known as cooperatives (*kyōdō kumiai*). There are a wide variety of types and subcategories of cooperative, generally each existing within a specific industry or economic space. For example university bookstores and cafeterias are often run by cooperatives. Some local supermarkets also take this form of organization.

Banding together in a cooperative enables weak individual members sharing common interests or requirements in specific sectors such as farming or fishing. Cooperatives are membership based, and by jointing members can enjoy access to bulk purchasing discounts, shared benefit programs and access to credit. Some cooperatives function as financial institutions, as discussed later in this chapter.

Despite their number and variety there is no single law governing cooperatives, possibly because different types fall under the jurisdiction of different ministries. Instead there are type-specific laws, such as the Small and Medium Enterprise Act of 1949 (administered by METI), the Agricultural Cooperative Act of 1947 (administered by MAFF) and so forth. Labor unions (*rōdō kumiai*) are also a form of *kumiai* and may or may not have legal status depending on how they are formed.

Such cooperatives are a more advanced and purposeful version of one of the most basic corporate forms, the simple contractual *kumiai* (partnerships) under article 667 of the Civil Code. The difference is that the Civil Code partnerships are merely a contractual arrangement with no separate legal personality. The *kumiai* may be recognized as a single actor for certain purposes, but externally all members of the partnership have unlimited liability. The TK silent partnerships provided for under the Commercial Code are a similar type of *kumiai* that lacks separate legal entity status, but which limit the liability of the "silent" partners to the amount of their investment.

Hieiri not-for-profit corporations also technically include mutual companies, which are the corporate form that used to be required of insurance companies until the Insurance Business Act of 1995 permitted joint stock companies to conduct the insurance business. Five of Japan's leading insurance companies remain in the form of mutual companies. Many of the requirements applicable to joint stock companies also apply to mutual companies. They are still considered *hieiri* corporations because their goal of providing mutual insurance through policy holders means they are structured so as to prevent the distribution of profits in the form of dividends, as opposed to using them to pay policy benefits.

(vi) Religious Corporations

The *hieiri* category of corporations also includes *shūkyō hōjin* religious corporations. A visit to the shrines and temples of Kyoto will demonstrate the continuing dominance and wealth of some religious corporations. Established under the Religious Corporations Act of 1951 (which is administered by MEXT), religious corporations enjoy various tax benefits in connection with their devotional and spiritual activities.

b. Companies Act (Profit-Sharing) Companies: An Overview

The Companies Act (article 2(i)) recognizes four types of "for profit" (*eiri*) company (*kaisha*). These are: (1) general partnership companies (*gōmei gaisha*), sometimes abbreviated using the English acronym "GMK", (2) limited partnership companies (*gōshi gaisha;* or "GSK"), (3) limited liability companies (*gōdō gaisha,* or "LLC") and (4) joint stock companies (*kabushiki gaisha*, or "KK").

There is also a legacy category of company that predates the Companies Act, the *yūgen geisha* ("YK") or Limited Company. Used primarily by small businesses, a large number of them existed at the time the Companies Act was passed. Implementing legislation passed at the time of the Companies Act provides for their continued existence but also makes it easy to convert such entities into KK stock companies. Prior to this change, when YK did exist they were generally regarded as inferior to KK, and considered unsuitable to bid for large contracts or obtain certain types of business licenses simply because of their corporate form.

Companies are required to specify the type of company they are in their corporate name (Companies Act, article 6). The three types of company other than *kabushiki gaisha* are sometimes collectively referred to as "membership companies" (*mochibun gaisha*), and in many areas the Company act provides regulations for all types of membership companies with the same provisions. Unlike stock companies whose owners have "stock" (*kabushiki*) and are called stockholders (*kabunushi),* membership companies have "members" (*shain,* a term which confusingly is also more commonly used to refer to employees of companies, as well as the members of the general incorporated associations and foundations discussed earlier). A member's interest in a membership company is called a *mochibun* ("the portion they old" or "equity").

The Companies Act (article 2(ii)) also recognizes the existence of "foreign companies" (*gaikoku gaisha)* doing business in Japan. Such companies are recognized to the extent they are cognates of Japanese for-profit corporate forms, *i.e.,* "any juridical person incorporated under the law of a foreign country or such other foreign organization that is of the same kind as the Company or is similar to a Company."

Of the four native types of companies provided for in the Companies Act, *kabushiki gaisha* joint stock companies are by far the most numerous and receive the most attention. Such companies also comprise the vast majority of public companies whose shares are listed on Japanese stock exchanges. Accordingly, after a brief description of the three other types, the remainder of this section will focus on *kabushiki gaisha.*

c. *General Partnership Companies (Gōmei Gaisha, GMK)*

The GMK is a corporate form that predates the Companies Act. As the name suggests, GMK's are roughly analogous to general partnerships in the common law system. They are also similar to *kumiai* partnership under the Civil Code, but having separate legal personality through registration in the corporate registry.

GMK members are jointly and severally liable to the company's creditors (Companies Act, articles 576(2); 580(1)). All members generally participate in the management of the Company and can bind it and unless the articles of association provide for "managing members" and/or members who act as representative (articles 590, 591 and 599). Interests in a GMK must be financial; "sweat equity" (labor) or the provision of credit may not be used to become a member.

Although some members may contribute far more to the GMK than others, decision making is generally made on a "one member one vote" basis. GMK are often used for small family businesses meaning the identity of other members is important. Membership interests are not freely transferrable without the consent of all other members, and the death of a member results in a pay out to his or her heirs rather than succession to the membership interest, unless otherwise provided in the articles of incorporation (articles 585, 607 and 608).

During the twenty year period from 1996 to 2015, almost twice as many GMK were liquidated as were newly established (1218 versus 628).

d. *Limited Partnership Companies (Gōshi Gaisha, GSK)*

The GSK also existed under the Commercial Code, and was the form taken by some *zaibatsu* holding companies. Limited partnership companies are similar to general partnership companies, but may establish distinctions between limited liability and unlimited liability members. The former are only at risk as to the amount of their financial investment, but cannot acquire equity through other means. Unlimited liability members have unlimited liability to creditors, but may become members through "sweat equity" or other means besides the contribution of assets. The distinction between limited and unlimited liability members must be set forth in the articles of incorporation (article 576(1)). Limited liability members and unlimited liability members, together with the amount of financial contribution made by the former must be registered in the Corporate Registry (article 913).

Limited liability members are not prohibited from participating in or being primarily responsible for management or representing the company unless the articles of incorporation provide otherwise. The transfer of membership interests as between limited or unlimited members is more complicated than in general partnership companies, and similarly restricted.

As with GMK, liquidations of GSK during the 1996 to 2015 period outstripped new incorporations (6915 to 3099).

e. *Limited Liability Companies (Gōdō Gaisha, LLC)*

LLCs are corporate form that was newly established by the Companies Act and was based on the American model of the same corporate form, though without the benefit of pass through tax treatment. All members have limited liability but can only become members through financial contributions. The amount of capital contributions must be registered in the corporate registry. Management is similar to the other membership companies, but managing members are liable for any shortfall if they authorize dividends that result in a shortfall at the end of the fiscal year (article 631).

Due to the absence of any members having unlimited liability, in the interests of protecting their creditors, LLCs are subject to greater restrictions on the distribution of assets than GMKs and GSKs. For example, LLCs are limited in their ability to demand a payout of their interest, even upon leaving the company (article 632). LLCs also may not be voluntarily liquidated (restricted in their ability to have their interest paid out (article 638).

23,787 LLCs were established in 2016, an impressive number given the corporate form's relatively short history.

f. Joint Stock Companies (Kabushiki Gaisha, KK)

(i) Overview

Joint stock companies are the principal corporate form used to conduct business in Japan. In 2016, 90,405 new KK companies were established. The KK is the principal focus of a significant portion of the Companies Act, which necessarily anticipates its use by small family businesses, large family businesses, and public (listed) companies. The prevalence of this corporate form is illustrated by its use to refer to the Japanese political economy as a whole—*Nippon kabushiki gaisha* or *Kabushikigaisha Nippon* or, "Japan, Inc."

The governance rules on KK are more complex than those for membership companies. While the rules for membership companies assume significant overlap between those who invest in the company and those who manage it, the KK format anticipates the possibility of the almost complete separation of management from ownership. In the case of publicly-listed companies the law must also address the likelihood that many or even most shareholders will have acquired their shares through anonymous transactions on exchanges that bring no direct benefit to the company or management, but are entitled to the rights and benefits of shareholder status nonetheless.

Because of the scope of use, the Companies Act anticipates a variety of KK types, with different and governance structures that involve a variety of roles for persons involved in governance. These are described in the following subsections.

(ii) Distinctions Between Types of KK

The Companies Act establishes two fundamental bases for distinction which serve as the basis for further categorization. The first is size. Although in the past the Commercial Code established three categories of company—large, medium and small, based on defined financial metrics, the Companies Act only draws a distinction between KK that are "large companies" (*daigaisha*) and those that are not. Large KK are those that have either JPY 500 million in capital or liabilities of at least JPY 20 billion (article 2(vi)). The principal significance of being a large company comes in the type of governance structures that are required as discussed below, but these vary depending on whether the company is "public" or not.

The second basis for distinction is in whether shares of the company are subject to transfer restrictions. The Act distinguishes between KK that are "public companies" (*kōkai gaisha*) and those that are not (article 2(v)). Somewhat confusingly, in this context "public company" does not mean having shares traded on an exchange. Rather it refers to a company that has any shares or class of shares that are freely transferrable. Of course, this means that all KK companies whose shares *are* traded on an exchange would necessarily need to be public companies.

A KK company whose article of incorporation subjects all of its shares to transfer restrictions is referred to as a non-public company, closed company or company subject to share transfer restrictions. For convenience the discussion that follows will refer to them as "closed companies").

Whether a KK company's shares are subject to transfer restrictions and thus whether it is a public company is apparent from its registration details. The great majority of KK are closed companies, including the many KK that were converted from YK limited companies.

Public companies must have a board of directors. The exercise of some rights of shareholders in public companies may be limited to those who have been shareholders for at least six months (or a shorter period if set forth in the articles of incorporation; e.g., article 297(2)). Public companies may not have directors or corporate auditors who are appointed by a single class of shareholder and may not issue 50% or more of their equity in the form of shares with restricted voting rights (articles 108(ii) and 115). When a public company is required to give notices to its shareholders, it may do so through whatever means of giving public notice it has adopted rather than the individual notices generally required for closed companies.

Public companies are further subject to restrictions that prevent them from doing things that only closed companies can do. These include, *inter alia*: (i) having articles of incorporation that permit only shareholders to become directors or executive officers, (ii) not having company auditors (*kansayaku*), (iii) if establishing a company audit board (*kansayakkai*), limiting its role to accounting audits, (iv) having an authorized number of shares that is more than four times greater than the number of issued and outstanding shares, and (v) having articles of incorporation that treat shareholders unequally with respect to dividends and distributions (articles 331(2), 402(5), 327(2), 389(1), 37(3), 113(2), 109(1), and 105(1)).

(iii) KK Company Governance Structures

Note that the corporate governance requirements discussed in this subsection are only those arising under the Companies Act. With respect to companies with shares publicly-traded on an exchange, exchange listing requirements, the Financial Instruments and Exchange Act and other rules impose additional governance requirements. These are discussed briefly later in this chapter. Directors of companies in specific regulated businesses may also be further subject to additional requirements imposed by the applicable regulatory regime.

All KK must have one or more directors (*torishimariyaku*; article 326). The powers of the director(s) may be defined by the articles of incorporation or a shareholder resolution, but this is not required. A simple KK with just directors and shareholders may not require further governance structures if it is to be managed primarily by its shareholders.

Many KK may go further and establish a board of directors (*torishimariyakukai*). This may be necessary if it would be bothersome to have a shareholders meeting every time a corporate decision is to be made. It is also *required* for public companies. If a board of directors is established, it must have at least three directors at the time of incorporation and, unless it is a company with board committees, one of the directors must be a representative director (*daihyō torishimariyaku*) (articles 39(1) and 47(1)).

A KK company that establishes a board of directors must also have a company auditor (*kansayaku*), unless: (i) it is a closed company, in which case it can elect to appoint an accounting advisor (*kaikei san'yo*) in lieu of having a company auditor, or (ii) it is a large company or has a board with committees, in which case more complicated requirements apply as described below (articles 327 and 328).

The Companies Act imposes more stringent requirements on a company that is both a large company and a public company. Companies meeting both of these criteria must have an accounting auditor (*kaikeikensain*). In order to ensure the board is subject to suitable oversight, they must also have either have a board of directors with committees (particularly an audit committee) or a company auditor board (*kansayakukai*).

The board of directors combined with a company auditor board is the "traditional," German-modeled governance structure used by most major Japanese companies. The company auditor board must be comprised of at least three company auditors (*kansayaku*), the majority of whom must be outside company auditors (*shagai kansayaku*) (articles 39 and 335). One must also be a full time (*jōkin kansayaku;* article 390(3)).

Companies with (board) committees are either: (1) "companies with committees" (*iin setchi gaisha*) or, since 2015 amendments to the Companies Act, "companies with nominating committees, etc. (*shimeiinkaitō setchi gaisha*, article 2(xii)) or (2) companies with an audit committee (etc.) (*kansatōiin setchi gaisha*, article 2(xi–2).

The concept of a "company with committees" predates the Companies Act, having been introduced to the Commercial Code in 2003. Now under the Act, a KK which adopts this form of governance does not need to have a separate company auditor board, but must establish three board committees: (i) a nominating committee that nominates director candidates for approval by the meeting of shareholders, (ii) an audit committee that oversees the performance by the directors of their duties and appoints the accounting auditors, and (iii) a compensation committee that decides the compensation of directors and executive officers. Each committee must be comprised primarily of outside directors (*shagai torishimariyaku*). A company with committees must also have executive officers (*shikkōyaku*). An effort to transpose "American-style" corporate governance on Japanese companies at a time when many were struggling, this governance structure proved unpopular with few large Japanese companies adopting it.

2015 amendments to the Code made it easier to have a board with committees by effectively allowing such companies to only have an audit committee comprised of at least three directors, the majority of whom are outside directors.

(iv) KK Corporate Governance Actors and Accourtements

(a) Overview

The following is a brief description of the key corporate governance actors described above and their roles and responsibilities and related features. Before doing so, it is necessary to introduce the slightly confusing term "*yakuin.*" This is generally translated "officers." However Japanese corporate law does not distinguish between "officers and directors" as is common in the Anglo-American governance model. Rather, *yakuin* (literally "person with a role") is a collective reference to directors, company auditors and (if applicable) accounting advisors. Similarly, when referring to a Japanese company's "board" it includes the company auditors who also sit in board of directors meetings but do not vote.

(b) Directors (Torishimariyaku)

Directors are chosen and removed by the shareholders by a simple majority vote, unless the articles of incorporation establish a higher voting threshold (articles 339 and 341). If multiple director positions are being filled, the Companies Act provides for cumulative voting unless disallowed by the articles of incorporation, which is the common practice (article 342). Directors do not need to be shareholders but closed companies may include such a requirement in their articles. Only natural persons may be directors. Persons subject to guardianship or having other capacity constraints, and persons with criminal records from certain types of criminal violations—particularly those relating to corporate offenses—may not be directors (article 331).

Director appointments are for a term of two years or one year for companies with board committees, though these terms can be shortened by a resolution of the shareholders or the articles of incorporation. Closed corporations may provide for terms of up to ten years in their articles of incorporation. Directors can be removed at any time by a regular shareholder resolution unless the articles of incorporation establish a higher voting threshold for removal.

When sitting as a board, directors make decisions by a simple majority unless the articles provide for a higher threshold (article369). Except for closed companies that do not have accounting auditors and have limited the powers of company auditors, company auditors attend board of director meetings and may voice opinions but do not vote. Minutes of meetings must be kept in the form specified by MOJ regulations and signed by all members.

Under article 362, the board of directors of a "traditional" company is responsible for the execution of corporate operations, supervising the execution of duties by individual directors, and appointing and removing representative directors. In most companies it is common that most or all directors are insiders who also perform executive roles within the company.[2]

In Japanese companies using the traditional governance model, the board of directors is generally responsible for actually managing the company, rather than providing an oversight role over a separate management group as in their Anglo-American counterparts. KK companies with committees are closer to the Anglo-American model. For such companies, the Companies Act anticipates a narrower role for the board of directors, requiring it to appoint at least one executive officer (*shikkō yaku*) to whom is delegated a broad range of operational authority. This in turn narrows the range of matters where a board decision is required. Executive officers do not need to be directors but can also sit on the board.

---

[2] For this reason, depending on the company it may be helpful to think of an appointment to the board as being akin to a promotion within its employment track as much as anything to do with corporate governance.

Japanese law does not have an equitable context of "fiduciary duty" applicable to directors. Article 330 of the Companies Act does make it clear, however, that the relationship between a director and the company is that of a "representation" (*i'nin*) contract under articles 643–653 of the Civil Code. This means directors are subject to the "duty of care of a good manager" (*zenryō na kanrisha no chūi gimu;* Civil Code, article 644). Under article 355 of the Companies Act, directors are also subject to a duty of loyalty (*chūjitsu gimu*), which requires "compliance with laws and regulations, the articles of incorporation, and resolutions of shareholders meetings." Directors are also subject to restrictions on completion and conflict of interest transactions, and have a positive duty to report to the company about potentially detrimental facts (articles 356–357). The end result of all these obligations is probably analogous to a fiduciary duty for most practical purposes, though experts would likely quibble about the details.

Directors are jointly and severally liable for the decisions of the board of directors (unless the minutes show they objected to a decision), and for the actions or malfeasance of other directors or executive officers. Directors are primarily liable to the company and its shareholders, but may also be liable to third parties for harm caused by gross negligence or willful misconduct (article 429). This provision is often used by creditors or other third parties in lieu of "piercing the corporate veil" of companies that go insolvent.

(c) Representative Director (Daihyō Torishimariyaku)

A company with a board of directors must have at least one representative director who is formally empowered to represent the company. Frequently the representative director is also the president or CEO, though these are not titles of legal significance. In the past it was necessary that at least one representative director be a resident of Japan but this is no longer required. The representative director is registered in the commercial registry. In a company with board committees representation is through a representative executive officer (*daihyō shikkō yaku*).

(d) Outside Director (Shagai Torishimariyaku)

For Companies Act purposes, outside directors are only required for companies with committees. As noted above, the majority of directors on the committees in such companies must be outside directors. Article 2(xv) of the Companies Act establishes a long list of conditions a director must satisfy in order to qualify as an outside director. Greatly oversimplified, a person who has been an employee, director company auditor or auditing adviser of the company or its subsidiary or parent during the previous ten years will not qualify as an outside director. A director's outside status is a registration matter.

(e) Company Auditor (Kansayaku)

Possibly because of the use of "auditor" for this role's English translation, but also likely because it has no corollary in Anglo-American corporate governance, Japanese company auditors (also in the past referred to in English as "statutory auditors") have been a source of confusion to many western observers of Japanese corporations.

Unlike directors, company auditors are not an absolute requirement for KK companies. However, if the company has a board of directors (but is not a company with board committees, or a closed company that has appointed an accounting advisor) and or has appointed accounting auditors, it must have a company auditor.

To give them greater independence, company auditors are appointed for a period of four years. Closed companies can provide for periods of appointment as long as ten years in their articles of incorporation. The company auditor(s) must also consent to any proposals regarding the appointment of company auditors to be made by the directors to the meeting of shareholders.

Company auditors are responsible for auditing the company's accounting, but this will usually involve overseeing the outside auditors and receiving the audit report. In order to preserve the independence of the accounting auditors (*i.e.,* the outside audit firm), their appointment and dismissal by the board of directors is subject to the consent of the company auditor(s) (article 344). If the company has a board with committees instead of company auditors, this role is performed by the audit committee (and in fact a company with board committees may *not* have company auditors; article 327(4)).

Except for closed companies whose articles specifically divest them of this role, company auditors also audit the performance by the directors of their duties for legality and propriety. Company auditors are thus expected to conduct a form of compliance oversight, and in this capacity are entitled to participate in board of directors meetings and voice opinions as to proposed actions. Company auditors also have extremely broad powers to seek and obtain information about the company and its affairs (article 381). They must report to the directors and, if necessary meeting of shareholders on any serious violations they discover (article 381 and 384). Company auditors are empowered to bring suit to enjoin the directors from engaging in unlawful acts (article 385). However one would struggle to find examples of large company corporate auditors actually using their significant (theoretical) powers of oversight or acting in a manner openly adversarial to the directors.

The majority of company auditors for large public companies must be outsider company auditors (*shagai kansayaku*) a term that is defined in terms similarly stringent to those applicable to outside directors (article 2(xvi)). Because of the compliance oversight role of company auditors, it is now common to see lawyers or retired prosecutors or judges serving as company auditors for listed corporations.

(f) Executive Officer (Shikkō Yaku)

Under article 418 of the Companies Act, companies with board committees may formally delegate more corporate decision making and executive functions to officers (who may also be board members, though this is not necessary), as is common in American companies. These are called executive officers. In such companies one or more officers may also be vested with representative powers (even without being directors) in which case they are called *daihyō shikkō yaku.* Confusingly, it is common in some corporations without a board committee governance structure to use the similar-sounding term *shikkō yakuin* (also typically translated "officer") to refer to high-level managerial personnel who are not board members. This is simply a matter of corporate usage and, unlike *shikkō yaku*, the term has no legal significance under the Companies Act.

(g) Auditing Advisor (Kaikei San'yoin)

Auditing advisors are a comparatively new role in Japanese corporate law having been added to the pantheon by the Companies Act when it was adopted in 2005. Intended to be adopted by SME's, a KK company that provides for the appointment of an auditing advisor in its articles of incorporation does not need to have a company auditor. The auditing advisor must be a chartered accountant, tax accountant or a firm practicing either profession and, if individuals, may not be employed by the company or also sit as a director. The auditing advisers assist the directors with the preparation of the company's financial statements, and participate in board meetings where those statements are approved (articles 374 and 376).

(h) Accounting Auditors (Kaikeikensanin)

A KK company's accounting auditors must be chartered accountants (see description at Chapter 7) or an accounting firm. They are required to be independent from the company they provide services to in order to ensure that they provide an unbiased view of the company's financial statements. However, for legal purposes they are considered an organ of the company and as such may be sued by the shareholders of the company in derivative litigation for harm caused to the company by their failure to adequately perform their duties (articles 423, 847).

(v) KK Shareholders and Shareholder Litigation

Together with director(s), a basic requirement of a KK is it must have at least one shareholder (*kabunushi*). As a basic stakeholder in a KK company, shareholders and their interests are directly or indirectly the focus of a great deal of the requirements of the Companies Act, particularly with respect to large public companies with a diffuse shareholder population and a significant lack of overlap and imbalance in access to information between management and shareholders. It has long been fashionable on the part of western foreign investors and other observers to decry the state of Japanese corporate governance and its apparent lack of attention to the interests of shareholders. Defenders of the Japanese system hold it up as a model of "stakeholder capitalism," with large, publicly-traded companies supposedly being managed for the benefit of a broader range of stakeholders than just those owning stock; employees, vendors, customers, and so forth.[3]

Such criticism is ironic when coming from American observers, since compared to the more lax (or "management friendly") corporate law regimes in the United States, Japanese shareholders enjoy far more firmly-defined statutory rights. However, the exercise of these rights is subject to the ability of KK companies to specify in their articles of association a minimum number of shares (a "unit" or *tangen*) that is entitled to a vote in a shareholders meeting (article 188). The maximum size of a unit is 1,000 shares (or 0.5% of the total issued shares (Companies Act Enforcement Ordinance, article 34)). Since listed company shares are typically only traded in units, the ability of companies to have different numbers of shares in a unit is a source of potential confusion. Accordingly, Japanese exchanges have made a concerted effort to encourage listed companies to unify their units into 100 or 1,000 shares. Exchange requirements for new listings require companies to have 100 share units.

---

[3] In the views of the authors, the government may often be the most important stakeholder, particularly with respect to companies involved in heavily regulated industries or those that are core to national industrial policies (*e.g.,* export driven automobile and electronic manufacturers). Pointing this out has long seemed impolitic, though now with the government now indirectly becoming the largest shareholder in dozens of listed companies and holding significant stakes in hundreds of others through Japan Pension Investment Fund and Bank of Japan holdings of Exchange Traded Funds invested in equity shares, it is even true in the more traditional sense.

Holders of shares not constituting a full unit are still entitled to participate in dividends and other distributions in respect of their shares (Companies Act, article 189(2)). Such shareholders also have the right to demand the Company purchase their shares (article 191).

Holders of a unit are entitled to participate in management of the company by voting in shareholders meetings. Recall from the preceding discussion that a public company may limit the exercise of such rights of participation to those who have been shareholders consecutively for a period of six months or less. Shareholders who have held at least 1% of the voting shares of the Company consecutively for the preceding six months may demand the board of directors include specific proposals to be voted on at the shareholders meeting. Those who have held at least 3% for the same period may demand the convocation of a shareholder meeting.

The list of matters that must be approved by a shareholders meeting is long, and includes, *inter alia*: (i) appointment and removal of directors, statutory auditors, liquidators and accounting advisors (articles 329 and 339), (ii) appointment of representative for company in suits between company and directors (article 353), (iii) approval of officer consideration (articles 361, 379 and 387), (iv) approval of competing/conflict of transactions by officers (articles 356 and 365), (v) approval of the company's financial statements (article438(2)), (vi) allotments of shares without contribution (article 186(3)), (vii) reductions in stated capital (by setting off against a loss) or of capital reserve and reductions or distributions of surplus (articles 447, 448, 450, 450–2 and 454), and (viii) appointment and removal of the accounting auditors (article 338–2).

Unless otherwise provided for in a company's articles of incorporation, the above matters can be decided by a simple majority of the required quorum of shareholders attending or represented. However, the Companies Act also requires that a number of matters be approved by a supermajority vote of shareholders. For these the threshold is at least 2/3 (or greater, if provided for in the articles of incoropration) of the shareholders constituting the required quorum. A partial list of such matters includes: (i) removal of a company auditor before the end of his/her term (article 339(1), 309(2), (ii) most significant corporate transactions including securities offerings, reorganizations, mergers of various types, sale or other disposition of all or a material portion of corporate assets, and spin-offs, (iii) winding up, (iv) amendment to articles of incorporation, (v) waiver of rights to be indemnified by directors, and (vi) substantive reductions in stated capital (articles 309(2), 180(2), 309, 199, 200, 309(2)(vii), (xi) and (xii), 467(1)(i)–(v), 471, 783, 795, 804, 776(1), and 425).

Shareholders are also empowered to use the courts in a variety of ways to remedy unlawful behavior by the company or its officers. These include bringing actions to enjoin corporate behavior in violation of the law or its articles of incorporation (article 360). Shareholders may also bring suits against the company's officers, liquidators, accounting auditors, or in some cases, even other shareholders for wrongful behavior that harms the company. Such derivative suits are brought by shareholders on behalf of the company and are one of the innovations to Japanese corporate law introduced by the Americans in 1950 during the occupation. Shareholders must first demand that the company file the suit, and may only bring the suit if the company does not do so within 60 days (article 847).

Although derivative litigation has resulted in some famous precedents, until recently the system was not widely used. From 1950 to 1985 there was less than one derivative action brought per year and none of them were successful. It wasn't until 1986 that a plaintiff first scored an initial win in a derivative lawsuit against a company that paid of a greenmailer resulting in a loss to the company (the so-called "Mitsui Mining Derivative Lawsuit Case," the ruling in which was ultimately affirmed (Supreme Court 1st Petty Bench judgment of September 9, 1993).

One reason may have been that unlike derivative litigation in the US, the shareholder plaintiffs did not benefit from any recovery except to the extent of their shareholdings, meaning there was little incentive to bring suits. Moreover, until the 1990s the filing fees for such actions were based on the amount of damages sought, meaning that bringing suit to remedy wrongful conduct that significantly harmed the value of the company was an expensive proposition. There was thus little financial incentive in bringing such suits.

Amendments made in the 1990s and early 21st century (including a dramatic lowering of the filing fees) have made the system somewhat easier to use. Derivative litigation is now; writing in 2012, Professors Puchniak and Nakagishi could claim that "*Japan now competes with Delaware for the title of the jurisdiction with the highest frequency of derivative litigation in the world*."[4] Puchniak and Nakagishi also question whether derivative litigation is even driven by economically-motivated shareholders and lawyers, noting their research indicated many cases were being brought by social activist lawyers using the derivative litigation to affect corporate behavior in areas such as gender equality or environmental protection. Whatever the motive, most shareholder derivative litigation is unsuccessful, but not reliably so.

Although the Companies Act theoretically vests in shareholders an extensive catalog of legal rights, various doctrines and techniques have developed to limit their exercise, particularly in large public listed companies. This includes the practice of limiting the exercise of rights through the unit share requirements described above, as well as the common requirement that shares be held continuously for six months before the holder can exercise many rights. In part because the great majority of Japanese companies close their books on March 31 (the same as the government) and thus report their financial results around the same time, it has also become common practice for most publicly-traded companies to have their annual shareholders meeting on the same day, usually in late June.

Some Japanese companies may maintain cross-shareholding relationships with other companies, typically those they have other business relationships with, such as financial institutions, customers, vendors, subcontractors and so forth. Cross shareholdings mean that management of the companies in such relatonships can rely on each other for support at shareholders meetings. Some observers are critical of this cozy arrangement on the grounds that it helps entrench management at the expense of shareholders, or at least those shareholders who are not in a position to benefit from the company through other business dealings. A counterargument might be that cross-

---

[4] Dan Puchniak and Masafumi Nakahigashi, *Japan's Love for Derivative Actions: Irrational Behavior and Non-Economic Motives as Rational Explanations for Shareholder Litigation*, 45 VAND. J. TRANSNAT'L. L. 1, 32 (2012).

shareholdings help protect companies from fickle, short term financial investors seeking a quick return at the expense of the long term welfare of the company.

Basic principles of the Civil Code described in Chapter 9 also apply to shareholder rights; they cannot be exercised abusively. In fact a category of shareholder most commonly associated with the exercise—and abuse—of shareholder's rights are *sōkaiya*. *Sōkaiya* often had underworld connections and practiced a form of extortion that involved purchasing a few shares in a company and then threatening to expose embarrassing information or engage in disruptive behavior at the annual shareholders meeting. Various legal responses were developed against this type of extortion, including article 120 of the Act which prohibits a company from giving benefits to a shareholder for the exercise of their rights. *Sōkaiya* appear to have been driven into other lines of business, but remain as a conceptual reminder of where shareholders rights and their abuse.

A more recent example of the view that shareholder rights can be abused is the famous Bulldog Sauce case involving the foreign investment fund group Steel Partners in its attempt to acquire 100% of the shares of Bulldog Sauce KK, a famous maker of brown sauce. In upholding the defensive measures adopted to protect the company from Steel Partners, the Supreme Court indicated it was willing to entertain the possibility that an acquirer of a company might be "abusive." However, it decided it did not need to reach that issue because the defensive measures adopted by Bulldog Sauce to frustrate Steel Partners (a rights offering given to all shareholders but the fund group, which was paid the equivalent value in cash) had been approved by the company's shareholders (Supreme Court, 2nd Petty Bench decision of August 7, 2007).

The Bulldog Sauce case highlighted both a basic principle of Japanese corporate law; that shareholders should all be treated equally (article 109) as well as its limitations. The court held that treating Steel Partners differently from other shareholders was permissible "*in order to prevent the harm to the corporate value and the violation of the common interest of shareholders*" that would have resulted from Steel Partners taking the company over. In doing so, the court effectively green-lighted what at the time was the relatively new practice of adopting "poison pills" defenses against hostile take-overs, and numerous companies subsequently presented such plans for approval to their shareholders. As of 2015, approximately 20% of companies comprising the Topix index of leading Japanese firms had adopted such plans, compared to under 6% for S&P 500 companies. This practice has made it further difficult to engage in hostile takeovers of Japanese companies and helps keep management entrenched.

The Supreme Court's rationale in the Bulldog Sauce case illustrates, or perhaps confirms, that corporate law in Japan is not just about shareholders. After all, what "common interests of shareholders" or "corporate value" of concern to shareholders would have remained if Steel Partners had acquired 100% of the company's shares as proposed? The Tokyo High Court decision in the case was more explicit on this point, expressing concern that a storied Japanese company manufacturing a well-known household condiment (which the court even described as "delicious") might be dismantled if it were taken over and put under new management.

(vi) Financial Statements

All KK Companies must prepare and maintain basic annual financial statements (balance sheet, statement of profit and loss, statement of shareholders equity and notes, together with a business report as to items that cannot be expressed in numerical terms). These must be prepared in accordance with the MOJ's Rules of Corporate Accounting and preserved for a period of ten years (Companies Act, article 435). These accounts may be prepared in electromagnetic form. The requirements for the financial statements of publicly listed companies are much more extensive.

(vii) Third Party Committees

A common practice that has developed in response to scandals in organizations, particularly corporations, is the appointment by its management of a "third party committee" to investigate and report on the cause of the scandal. The committees are often comprised of lawyers and other outside experts, but often suffer from the fact that they are appointed for and paid by the same management that may be partially responsible for the problem. In 2010 the JFBA published guidelines for the composition and operation of such committees.

g. Other For-Profit Business Organizations: Professional Corporations and Other Miscellaneous Entities

(i) Professional Services Corporations

Before moving on to the next subject, it should be briefly noted that in addition to the various forms of *eiri hōjin* provided for in the Companies Act, another category of for-profit ventures exists. These are particularly relevant to the legal system, since they consist of the sundry types of professional services corporations through which *bengoshi* attorneys, chartered accountants and many of the other legal professions discussed in Chapter 7 are permitted to conduct business; if they decide to practice through a corporate form at all. There is no single form of professional service corporation; the governing statute for the applicable profession contains rules for the establishment and governance of the specific type of the corporate entity for that profession. The rules appear generally similar, however, being designed to ensure only those with appropriate professional qualifications can be members, and that the corporate form is not used to enable fee sharing with non-professionals.

(ii) Limited Liability Partnerships

In what may be an interesting example of the continuing "territorial" nature of regulation in Japan, at the same time the Companies Act was passed under the auspices of the MOJ, METI was able to push through the Limited Liability Partnership Act of 2005. This act makes possible the establishment of limited liability partnerships (*yūgen sekinin jigyōkumiai*, or "LLP"), another entity that can be used to conduct business. While it has various tax advantages and protects members from liability, it lacks separate legal personality. Nonetheless, the law requires various details about the LLP to be registered with the corporate registry.

(iii) Special Purpose Vehicles

Although vehicles like T.K. silent partnerships were amenable to use as investment vehicles, the formal requirements applicable to KK and other forms of companies made them inappropriate as limited purpose entities for complex financing transactions. The Asset Securitization Act of 1998 permits the establishment of special purpose companies (*tokutei mokuteki kaisha* or "TMK") to use as asset-securitization vehicles.

(iv) A Note on "Agricultural Corporations"

In the context of agriculture and agricultural regulation it is not uncommon to see references to *nōgyō hōjin* or "agricultural corporations." This is not a particular type of corporate form, but rather a general description of corporate entities (which may include cooperatives, non-public KKs or other types of companies) that qualify as "judicial person qualified to own farmland" under article 2(3) of the Agricultural Land Act of 1952. To qualify requires *inter aliai,* being engaged in the business of using farmland for agriculture, being majority owned by farmers or persons who transfer or make the land available to the company (which itself generally requires some connection to farming).

h. *Foreign Ownership Restrictions*

There are no general legal restrictions on non-Japanese owning or acquiring shares in Japanese companies. Within certain regulated industries the applicable laws establish maximum foreign ownership thresholds (e.g. 1/3 or 20%, depending on the statute) intended to prevent foreign control. Examples include airlines and broadcasters, as well as the communications giant NTT. The Foreign Exchange and Foreign Trade Act of 1949 (discussed later in this chapter) also imposes a notification and waiting period on certain investments by foreign parties in Japanese companies.

D. FINANCIAL INSTRUMENTS AND EXCHANGES

1. Statutory Framework

Another area of commercial law in which American ideas have had a big influence is in securities regulation. A new Securities and Exchange Act was passed in 1948 during the occupation, and influenced heavily by the then still new American regime for federal securities regulation. Japan's law was substantially updated and amended in 2006 and renamed the Financial Instruments and Exchange Act (FIEA).

The FIEA addresses three principal areas of regulation: (i) timely and accurate disclosure of necessary information about publicly-traded shares and other securities and the companies or other entities issuing them; (ii) regulating businesses that deal in financial instruments (including the licensing of securities companies) and (iii) the governance of stock exchanges and other bourses where financial instruments are traded. The FIEA also provides the rules for tender offers and the disclosure requirements applicable to tender offer statements (article 27–2 *et seq.*) Customer disclosure requirements and other practices that must be followed are separately provided for in the Financial Instruments (etc.) Sales Act of 2000.

Subject to various exceptions (such as for qualifying private offerings) an issuer or underwriter engaged in a primary or secondary public offering of securities must file a registration statement with the Prime Minister's office (through the FSA) setting forth the required information about the securities and their issuer (article 5 *et seq.*). Information in the registration statement must be reflected in a prospectus that must be distributed to prospective investors.

Once a registration statement has been filed and becomes effective, the company filing it is generally required to file with the Financial Services Agency annual, quarterly and other reports providing the required information to investors and the FSA (article 24 *et seq.*). Most of these documents are available on-line through EDINET, the FSA's disclosure database. Publicly-listed companies also typically also disclose their own filings in an "IR room" on their corporate websites. Most of this information is primarily or exclusively in Japanese, though many large companies produce an English annual report that includes at least some of the required information.

Pursuant to article 193 of the FIEA, the financial statements required in registration statements and periodic reports must be prepared in accordance with the MOF's Ordinance on Terminology, Forms, and Preparation Methods of Consolidated Financial Statements.[5] Rules 21 *et seq.* of the FIA contain the extensive provisions defining the liability of companies, officers and other parties responsible for misleading or false statements in disclosure filings under the act and correspond roughly to the famous American Rule 10b–5, but using a lot more words. The FIEA imposes stringent liability on persons using prospectuses containing material misstatements or misrepresentations to deal in securities, establishing a rebuttable presumption of negligence/intent and damages (articles 16 through 19). Similar presumptions apply to material misstatements or misrepresentations contained in reports filed with the FSA under the Act (article 24 *et seq.*).

The FIEA also contains prohibitions on trading by corporate insiders. Under article 163 corporate officers and significant shareholders are required to report trades in the company's securities to the FSA. Articles 164–165–2 provide rules for disgorging profits from short-swing sales by insiders, while article 165 prohibits both officers and significant shareholders from short-selling the company's shares. Finally, the prohibition on insider trading on material information (defined at great length) not yet disclosed to the public is set forth in article 166.

The FIEA is also a source of governance requirements for registered companies. The principle means is through an Internal Control Report (article 24–4–4, *et seq.*) which reporting companies must file annually, and which contains the required information about the internal controls it has to ensure the accuracy of its financial information. The firms accounting auditors must audit and report on the company's internal controls.

2. Exchanges and Listing Standards

Japan's principle stock exchange is the Tokyo Stock Exchange (TSE). The TSE is part of the Japan Exchange Group (JPX), a KK Company that acquired the Osaka Stock Exchange in 2013 (which had in 2010 acquired JASDAQ, another established exchange). It has a variety of shareholders including financial institutions, individuals and a surprising number of foreign institutional shareholders.

JPX also includes, Japan Securities Clearing Corporation, which is the clearance organization for all securities exchanges in Japan and TOKYO PRO Market, an exchange targeted exclusively at professional investors. Finally, it includes Japan Exchange Regulation, a special corporate entity established under the FIEA (articles 102–2 *et seq.*) to carry out the self-regulation the law requires of exchanges. Since the exchanges are controlled by KK entities and therefore *must* pursue profit, the Japan Exchange Regulation entity (whose only members can be financial exchanges or their holding companies) can provide this functionality without the burdens of KK status.

---

[5] Since they contain official definitions of terms such as "subsidiary" and "affiliated company," these rules are sometimes relevant to the interpretation of other regulatory regimes outside the sphere of financial regulation.

After its incorporation into the JPX group, the Osaka Stock Exchange changed its name to the Osaka Exchange and has come to become the nation's principal derivatives exchange. Japan has three other stock exchanges, the Sapporo, Nagoya and Fukuoka Stock Exchanges, which account for so little activity that one wonders why they still exist. For this reason, the remainder of this discussion in this section will focus on the JPX and the TSE.

The TSE is comprised of multiple bourses, eligibility for listing/trading on which is dependent upon on satisfying the respective eligibility requirements. These consist of a combination of threshold number of shareholders, market capitalization and other metrics. The First Section of the TSE is the most prestigious. It has the most stringent eligibility requirements and is where most large companies are listed. The Second Section is for smaller but still substantial companies. The Mothers Section is for high growth, emerging companies. JASDAQ and TOKYO PRO have much looser standards for smaller, riskier companies.

The TSE is a source of a significant amount of soft law particularly in listing standards it requires of companies on the First Section. These are used to impose an addition layer of corporate governance requirements on leading publicly-traded companies. Listing rules accord the exchange broad discretion to delist companies.

In 2015 JPX adopted a Corporate Governance Code (CGC) intended to ensure listed companies accorded equal treatment for shareholders, cooperated appropriately with non-shareholder stakeholders, provide appropriate information disclosure and transparency, established suitable governance structures and communicated appropriately with shareholders. For example, the CGC calls for companies having cross shareholdings to enunciate a policy for doing so and reevaluate it annually. It also establishes a number of principles that should guide corporate boards in their management of the company and its relationship with shareholders, including director training, having multiple independent directors, proactive disclosure and other suggested "best practices".

Perhaps the most illustrative norm advocated by the code is Principle 2.1, which says: "Guided by their position concerning social responsibility, companies should undertake their businesses in order to create value for all stakeholders while increasing corporate value over the mid-to long-term. To this end, companies should draft and maintain business principles that will become the basis for such activities." Of course, it is all very well to talk of "other stakeholders" but who they are and what legal rights or entitlement they might have to "value creation" they might have in companies (and why) is left unexplained.

Compliance with the Code is optional for TSE listed companies. However substantial companies (those listed on the major sections) that choose not to must disclose the fact and their rationale for declining to do so (TSE Listing Rule 436–6). Most companies now comply.

TSE listing rules also require companies to have at least one "independent" director *or* company auditor (article 436–2) and impose numerous other requirements in areas such as establishing anti-takeover defenses and the appropriate conduct of business. A similar "appoint or explain why not" rule is imposed on large publicly listed companies by the Companies Act (article 327–2). Again, most companies appear willing to satisfy the requirement.

A separate KK company owned by leading financial institutions, Japan Securities Depository Center, Inc. (JASDEC), serves as the sole depositary for Japanese share certificates and book entry securities.

E. FINANCIAL INSTITUTIONS AND PAYMENT SYSTEMS

1. Overview

Japan has a surprising variety of financial institutions. The use by individuals of cash to make even large payments is still not uncommon and the widespread penetration of credit cards (and subsequently, debit cards) has been a recent phenomenon compared to countries such as the United States. Amazon and many other e-commerce sites find it necessary to offer alternatives to the use of credit cards for settlement Cash-based borrowing at high interest rates through ATM-like facilities where one can enter into a consumer borrowing contract without the embarrassment of interacting directly with a human being have long been a driver of consumer spending in Japan.

Many Japanese individuals will go through life without ever writing or receiving a check. This is thanks in part due to the highly developed and efficient domestic interbank payment system, which made direct payments to another bank account through teller or ATM transactions and long before Internet banking. As with many Japanese systems, it is closed and works less well in conjunction with the rest of the world, meaning making and receiving payments across borders has been more expensive and complex than seemed necessary. The Payment Services Act of 2009 facilitates the development and regulation of on-line and cloud-based payment and settlement systems, and has led to the expansion of electronic payment systems. Stored value railway cards and mobile phones can now be used to make many purchases necessary in daily life.

Checks and other forms of negotiable instrument do exist but their use is rare and it is now difficult if not impossible to open a personal checking account. The Check Act of 1933 remains on the books but its principle significance seems to be as a pointless subject law students still have to study because questions on negotiable instruments still occasionally feature on the NBE.

A separate Negotiable Instrument Act (of 1932) governs other types of negotiable instruments. The principle type is a *yakusoku tegata*, which is commonly translated as "bill" but is essentially a negotiable promissory note. Such instruments have a long history dating back to the Edo Period at least, and in their more modern iteration have long served as a common form of short-term financing. Used as a form of payment, such bills may have a maturity of up to three months. If the payee recipient wants cash sooner, they may sell the bill at a discount through a clearing house, of which there are approximately 200 nationwide. A payor who fails to pay a note when due may have their paper suspended from trading at all trading houses, being effectively shut out of this important source of short-term liquidity. For this reason "suspension of trading" is a common insolvency-type event of default in Japanese contract boilerplate. The availability of other forms of financing and liquidity support now make this type of deferred payment system seem archaic, yet it persists.

Crypto-currencies have been embraced by some Japanese investors and at the time of writing Japanese regulators were still coming to grips with them. There had already been two highly-publicized incidents of security flaws at two crypto-exchanges resulting in large losses.

Foreign exchange transactions are subject to the Foreign Exchange and Foreign Trade Act of 1949 (FEFTA), the history of which is mostly of amendments gradually removing restrictions on conversion and payments in foreign currencies. Currently cross-border payments and currency conversion can be done freely, subject to reporting requirements, restrictions in certain contexts and the Ministry of Financing retaining the ability to exercise greater control.

2. Financial Institutions

a. *Overview*

For a unitary legal jurisdiction, Japan has a surprisingly diverse menagerie of financial institutions. Although now subject to broadly similar regulation by the FSA, they are a reminder of the historical vertical integration of Japanese regulation, with different types of institution having a past or present jurisdictional association with a particular ministry.

There are a number of governmental financial institutions. These include policy-related institutions established under specific statutes. Examples include the The Bank of Japan (the nation's central bank), The Japan Bank of International Cooperation and Japan Finance Corporation. There is also a quasi-public bank serving SME's, the The Shoko Chukin Bank, Ltd., whose principal shareholder is the Minister of Finance, with numerous small financial institutions as the remaining shareholders.

Most private banks and other depository and financial institutions are regulated notionally by the Prime Minister, substantively (and strictly) by the Financial Services Agency.[6] There are some exceptions or areas of overlapping regulation. Since the collapse of Japan's economic bubble at the end of the 1980s, Japanese bank regulation has been heavily focused on getting banks and other lenders to remove the huge volume of non-performing loans from their books. Some have observers have suggested that the resulting prolonged period of stringent bank oversight aimed at preventing smaller banks from making new bad loans has strangled availability of credit to small businesses and resulted in a generation of bank managers who no longer know how to evaluate businesses for purposes of making unsecured loans to them. At the time of writing the FSA was reportedly introducing initiatives (manuals!) aimed at forcing banks—particularly smaller regional banks—to be more entrepreneurial.

The following sections contain brief descriptions of the principal types of financial institutions.

b. *Banks*

Banks (*ginkō*) are established under the Banking Act of 1981. The "banking business" is defined as accepting demand or term deposits, extending credit and foreign exchange (article 2(2)). They must be licensed by the Prime Minister (effectively the FSA), and be KK companies with the most stringent governance structures applicable to such companies. Many banks are publicly traded companies. As in most countries, they are subject to restrictions on their non-banking activities whether directly or through subsidiaries.

---

[6] An interesting illustration of the degree to which banks and other financial institutions are regulated is the fact that until the 1990s they were prohibited from advertising on television.

Banks must use the term *ginkō (*bank) in their corporate name and all other businesses are prohibited from doing so. This terminology is important; although many other financial institutions are called "bank" in English, they are *not* in Japanese either legally or by name.

Though not provided for in the Act, there is a clear hierarchy of banks. First there are several large "megabanks" that are amalgamations of what were once called "city banks." These have their headquarters in Tokyo or Osaka and a nationwide presence. There are also two tiers of what are called "regional banks" (*chihō ginkō*), smaller banks which are active principally within a single prefecture. Financial deregulation has also seen a variety of "new" banks, such as "Seven Bank," which is established and regulated as a bank but focuses principally on operating an extensive network of ATMs in Seven Eleven convenience stores. Finally, the recently privatized banking arm of Japan Post is also a bank in the form of in the form of *Yūchō* Bank, K.K. However, having long been a separate form of publicly-owned depository institution (under MIC jurisdiction) the postal banking system still retains its own legacy payment and account numeration system that is different from that used by other banks and depositary institutions.

Foreign bank branches in Japan are also regulated under the Banking Act.

c. *Trust Banks and Trust Companies*

In the past banks that provided trust-related services were a discrete category of financial institution. Now under the Act on Engagement in Trust Business Activities by Financial Institutions, banks and certain other financial institutions that have obtained the appropriate license may also provide trust services. There is also a separate category of Trust Companies (*shintakugaisha*) who are licensed by the Prime Minister to provide trust services under the Trust Act.

d. *Cooperative Organization Financial Institutions*

(i) Overview

A variety of financial institutions exist under the rubric of "cooperative organization." This type of financial institution is usually a special type of *kyōdō kumiai*, corporate entity (see discussion earlier in this chapter) and involved in a particular sector of the economy (SME's, fishing, fish processing, farming, labor unions etc.). Such entities are able to engage in financial businesses under the Financial Businesses by Cooperatives Act of 1949, subject to licensing by the Prime Minister. Unlike most banks these are not listed companies and have different governance structures, though the Act incorporates various provisions (including governance provisions) of the Companies Act to cooperatives engaging in financial businesses.

Although many of these financial institutions are individually small, collectively they form a substantial network with a private "central bank" entity that provides guidance, oversight and financial support. The principle categories of institutions are as follows:

(ii) Shinkin Banks

Shinkin Banks (*shinyōkinko*) are only called "banks" in English. The Japanese term meaning literally "credit safe" and "credit union" may be a better translation. Most retail banking customers would find them offering the same services as a "real" bank—taking deposits and making loans. They are established under the Shinkin Bank Act of 1951, which provides many of the details of their required governance structures. The Act also incorporates by reference many of the provisions of the Banking Act (article 89). The central entity for Shinkin Banks is the "Shinkin Central Bank," which as of 2017 had 264 member shinkin banks and over JPY 37 trillion in total assets.

(iii) "Shinkumi" Credit Cooperatives

Shin'yo kumiai or *shin'yo kyōdō kumiai* are similar to Shinkin Banks, offering the same basic banking services, but are restricted in their ability to take deposits from customers who are not also members of the applicable cooperative. They are organized under the Small and Medium-Sized Business Cooperative Act of 1949. Their "central bank" entity is the The Shinkumi Federation Bank (which despite the English title, is technically not a bank). As of 2017 it had total assets of almost JPY 9 trillion.

(iv) Rōkin Labor Banks

Rōkin labor banks (*rōdō kinko*) are another form of cooperative financial institution whose membership is derived principally from labor unions. Although they provide basic banking services to all customers, credit is generally limited to those who are actually cooperative members. Established under the *Rōkin* Labor Bank Act of 1953, unlike other financial cooperatives, Rokin Labor Banks must be licensed by both the Prime Minister and the Minister of Health Welfare and Labor (article 6). It's central institution which, again, is not a bank but a general incorporated association is simply called "The Rokin Bank."

(v) Agricultural Cooperatives (JA)

Now commonly (and collectively) going by the English acronym "JA" (for Japan Agricultural Cooperative), *nōgyōkumiai* or "*nōkyō*" play a central role in many of Japan's farming communities. Formal voting membership and governance roles in agricultural corporations is limited to farmers or farming corporations (one of the seemingly numerous ways in which status as a "farmer" confers special privileges), but non-voting associate membership for non-farmers is possible. Agricultural cooperatives provide "one-stop shopping" to agricultural communities, providing farming supplies and a distribution network for agricultural produce. Under Article 22 of the Act on Prohibition of Private Monopolization and Maintenance of Fair Trade of 1947 (or "Anti-Monopoly Act," JA cooperatives enjoy exemptions from some of the Act's basic prohibitions. Nonetheless, in those areas where they do not, JA has sometimes been the subject of FTC cautions regarding unfair trade practices and restraints of trade, practices such as overcharging members for farming necessities such as fertilizer being a common accusation directed at JA.

Advertising under the name "JA Bank," agricultural cooperatives provide a wide range of financial services, having been one of the few institutions that could provide both banking services and sell life insurance before financial deregulation in the 1990s. It is also one of the few financial institutions able to make loans with farmland as collateral.

As of 2016, there were approximately 650 JA cooperatives around the nation, based on a prefectural-national organizational structure with around 4.5 million full members. JA presents an interesting study in corporate governance, since in around 2014, the number of non-voting associate members exceeded the number of voting (*i.e.*, farmer) members, opening up a debate about for whose benefit they should actually be operated.

Collectively JA also constitutes a powerful political lobbying force and are a key demographic for politicians seeking votes in over-weighted rural constituencies. JA cooperatives are one of the reasons why Japan's market for agricultural products continues to offer limited access to foreign imports, at least of products that are produced in Japan.

JA also represents a significant segment of the financial services industry. JA's central banking organization, the Norinchukin Bank (again, technically not a "bank" under Japanese law), one of Japan's elite companies and a significant institutional investor, which as of 2017 had total assets of approximately JPY 113 trillion.

JA are subject to regulation by the MAFF as well as the Prime Minister (through the FSA).

e. *Insurance Companies*

The Insurance Act of 2008 effectively establishes three types of insurance: life, casualty and "other." Under Article 3 of the Insurance Business Act of 1995 insurance companies must be licensed by the Prime Minister (effectively the FSA). It is prohibited for a company to have a license to engage in both life insurance and casualty insurance businesses.

f. *Financial Instrument Business Operators (Securities Companies)*

The FIEA is the principal law governing the securities business. While many companies in this business still have "Securities" in their corporate title, the FIEA now regulates them as Financial Instrument Business Operators (FIBOs). The FIEA (article 28) establishes four categories of financial instruments business activities: (i) Type 1 (dealing in and underwriting liquid securities and bonds), (ii) Type 2 (dealing in more complex financial instruments), (iii) investment advisory services, and (iv) asset management. FIBOs (including branches or subsidiaries of foreign securities companies) must register with the Prime Minister (the FSA) depending on the type of business the engage, with some requiring additional authorizations.

The securities industry association is represented by the Japan Securities Dealer Association (JSDA). JSDA issues guidelines regarding business practices that form a type of "soft law" in this industry.

g. *Leasing Companies*

Leasing companies provide lease financing for expensive equipment or other capital investments. The principal sources of regulation are the tax rules and accounting standards relating to treatment of the lease arrangement.

h. *Credit Companies and Moneylenders*

Credit companies (*shinpan gaisha*) finance the purchase of goods and services. Among other things, this category encompasses providers of credit card services. Companies in this business must register as "comprehensive purchase credit intermediaries" with METI under the Installment Sales Act. METI is the primary regulator of this industry, with the Prime Minister retaining some oversight functions that are delegated to the Consumer Affairs Agency. To the extent credit cards can also be used at ATMs to obtain cash advances, registration as a moneylender is also required.

Moneylenders (*kashikingyōsha*) have long been a feature in the Japanese economy and go by various names such as the euphemistic *sarakin* (payday financing for salarimen) or *shōhisha kinyū* (consumer finance) depending on their target market and degree of respectability. Those who target small businesses are sometimes called *shōkō rōn* (commercial and industrial lenders).

Shady or criminal moneylenders are stock figures in popular fiction and loan sharking continues to be a profitable business for organized crime groups. Usury and aggressive collection activities by moneylenders have long been a problem, and in 1999 a collector from a major, now defunct industry player was recorded hectoring a debtor: "*sell your house, sell your eyes, sell your kidney!*".

Under the Money Lending Business Act of 1983 moneylenders must be registered with the Prime Minister (FSA), unless they only do business within a single prefecture, in which case registration is with the governor of that prefecture. Registrations must be renewed every three years, and police authorities provide some oversight in the form of opinions to the Prime Minister or Governor regarding licensing, and the ability to question moneylenders about collection activities.

Significant legislative and regulatory effort has gone into driving aggressive, disreputable money lenders out of the industry and preventing those that remain from driving consumer borrowers into a debt spiral. Since 2010, moneylenders have been restricted from lending an individual borrower more than 1/3 of their annual income (article 13–2). This odd requirement applies to credit card cash advances but not credit card purchases.

Moneylending has been one area where the judiciary could be described as playing an "activist" role in favor of debtors. As described in Chapter 10, Supreme Court decisions at the beginning of the 21st century in favor of debtors charged interest over the civil usury rate triggered a wave of litigation seeking to recover excess payments.

i. Pawn Shops, Ticket Shops and Pachinko

As in other countries, pawn shops offer a form of secured lending based on the pledging of property. Pawn shops are regulated by the Pawnbroker Business Act of 1950. Pawnbrokers must obtain a license from the applicable Public Safety Commission (article 2), which puts them under the jurisdiction of the police. Since they also sell used goods that have been pawned, they are generally also subject to the Secondhand Article Dealers Act of 1949.

The universe of secondhand articles dealers includes antique dealers and junk shops. An interesting and common derivative of this business is what are called "ticket shops" (*kinkenshoppu*). Gift certificates and stored value cards of various types are widely used in Japan, so there is a vibrant secondary market in such items, as well as stamps, train tickets and other documents that are not negotiable but still have a defined value and can thus be bought and sold at a discount.

For individuals who have reached their borrowing limit under the Moneylenders Act, using a credit card to purchase designer goods that can then be pawned or train tickets or gift vouchers that can be sold at a Ticket Shop is a common desperation play for cash. For this reason, the purchase of many gift vouchers with credit cards is not possible.

Ticket shops (and pawn shops to the extent they resell pawned goods) are regulated under the Used Goods Business Act of 1949, which requires dealers in such goods to be licensed by the prefectural Public Safety Commission (*i.e.,* the police).

Second hand dealer licensing also play an important role in maintaining the fiction that *pachinko* is not gambling. *Pachinko* is a form of "entertainment" (also regulated by the police) that involves going to a casino-like establishment and buying tokens or balls to feed into slot machines or other devices in the hopes of winning more balls or tokens. These balls or tokens can be exchanged for prizes such as chocolate bars or trinkets. However, the prizes can also be sold to a used goods dealer conveniently located near the *pachinko* parlor for cash at a set rate. The prizes eventually make their way back to *pachinko* parlors. This complex process has enabled Japanese authorities to assert that *pachinko* is not gambling and that *pachinko* parlors are thus not "casinos" for purposes of anti-money laundering regulations, including international protocols.

j. Convenience Stores

While not formally financial institutions, the vast and growing number of Japanese convenience stores should be noted as part of the financial system. Most have an ATM that can be used to conduct basic financial transactions, and convenience stores can also be used to make many common payments such as utility bills.

3. Anti-Money Laundering and Related Regulations

In the past it was relatively easy to open accounts at financial institutions, particularly the postal savings system. Opening a savings account required the use of a seal and some form of identification. However, many Japanese people lacked a picture ID, and cards such as health insurance cards that show name, birthdate and other identifying details but no picture would commonly be used. While opening multiple accounts at different branches of the same bank, or even at the same branch once involved a separate pass book for each account, it is now possible to have accounts without passbooks or association with a particular branch (other than as part of the application process).

Many banks and other institutions are making it harder to open accounts in locations distant from where the prospective account holder lives or works. Opening an account in an obscure location has long been a common way of hiding assets from judgment creditors (or family members), one facilitated by the lack of a widely used system of unified taxpayer identification number. This may change with the gradual implementation of the "My Number" identification number system, as well as arrangements making it easier for lawyers to find assets on behalf of judgment creditors.

Japanese banks do not offer joint accounts, so in a traditional family, merely having the passbook and bank seal would enable a wife to transact out of an account in her husband's name (and into which his salary might be direct-deposited). This is no longer true, with the Prevention of Transfer of Criminal Proceeds Act of 2007 (PTCPA), Japan's first comprehensive anti-money laundering statute imposing stringent identification confirmation requirements on financial transactions.

In the past, taking possession of the trinity of ATM card, pass book and seal associated with the account were an easy way of establishing a *defacto* security interest over a bank account. However, this meant that it was also possible to "sell" bank accounts that could be used for criminal purposes without the criminals ever being identified. Making bank and other accounts available to others for wrongful purposes was first criminalized in 2004 and is now proscribed by the PTCPA (article 28).

The PTCPA also imposes "Know Your Customer" and Suspicious Transaction Reporting obligations on most of the financial institutions described above. KYC requirements are also imposed on some of the legal professions described in Chapter 7.

F. THE ANTI-MONOPOLY ACT AND RELATED LAWS AND REGULATIONS

The Prohibition of Private Monopolization and Maintenance of Fair Trade Act of 1947 (Anti-Monopoly Act or AMA) was part of the occupation-era American effort to break up the *zaibatsu* conglomerates and disperse their excessive concentrations of wealth and monopolistic power. The AMA is administered by the Fair Trade Commission (FTC). For several decades after the end of the occupation the FTC was considered a "toothless watchdog," and the AMA saw limited enforcement. Cartel-like behavior was effectively a part of Japan's industrial policy, often implemented through informal administrative guidance since cartel-like behavior by MITI (now METI), and other bureaucracies.

The FTC (and the prosecutors who have a symbiotic relationship with the body) did start to make their mark in pursuing *dangō*, the bid-rigging cartels that have long plagued the nation's public works projects. Bid-rigging has even sometimes been organized or facilitated by procurement-side bureaucrats. In recent years the FTC has taken an aggressive approach with respect to anti-competitive behavior, though there remains a basic tension between their mandate and the underlying theme of much Japanese regulatory policy that "excessive" competition is bad and thus needs to be limited by appropriate regulation.

The AMA prohibits three broad categories of behavior. First: private monopolies, which are business activities by one or more businesses that have the effect of excluding or controlling other business operators and thereby causing a detrimental and substantial restraint on competition in a particular field of trade. Second: unreasonable restraints on trade, *i.e.*, when businesses acting in concert to "mutually restrict or conduct their business activities in such a manner as to fix, maintain, or increase prices, or to limit production, technology, products, facilities, or counterparties" in a manner that has an anti-competitive effect (articles 1 and 2(5)(6)).

The third category of behavior is "unfair business practices," designated by the FTC: (i) that is unjustly discriminatory against other business, (ii) involves unfair consideration, (iii) improperly induces or coerces customers of a competitor to deal with oneself, (iv) dealing with a party on terms that unduly restricts their business, (v) improperly using one's bargaining position, and (vi) unjustly interfering in the dealings between a competitor and their transaction counterparties (article 2(9)). The FTC has further clarified (and seemingly expanded) this statutory definition through a directive identifying over a dozen types of unfair business practices, including: refusal to trade, discriminatory treatment in a trade association, unjust low price sales, unjust high price purchasing, deceptive or unjust customer inducement, tie-in-sales, trading on exclusive or restrictive terms, interference with the corporate governance of a transaction counterparty and interference with a competitor's transactions or internal operations (FTC Public Notice no. 11 of 1953).

As this directive illustrates, a great deal of the detail of the AMA is filled in by rule-making and guidance from the FTC. The FTC has issued an extensive range of guidelines and standards relating to specific industries, practices and situations. Many of these are available in English on the FTC's website. Examples include guidelines for proper practices in distribution networks, proper conduct in trade associations (natural venues for anti-competitive activities), the applicability of the AMA to medical association activities and so forth. Although not formally being law, they probably should generally be regarded as such for compliance purposes. A possible indicator of the FTC's growing power is their growing willingness to issue guidelines in areas of the economy under the regulatory authority of other agencies, such as energy and telecommunications. The FTC may also pursue cross-border anti-competitive behavior.

The principal tools used by the FTC to enforce the AMA are: (1) cease and desist orders, (2) orders to pay administrative fines (surcharges), (3) civil injunctions of anti-competitive behavior and (4) referral to prosecutors for criminal violations (e.g., articles 7, 7–2, and 74. The availability of these tools depends on the nature of the violation and its severity. When imposing fines (surcharges), the FTC has a leniency program intended to encourage members of cartels to self-report; those doing so first or relatively early are entitled to a reduction in the amount. Articles 25 and 26 of the AMA also give businesses harmed by anti-competitive behavior the subject to final cease and desist or surcharge payment orders to sue the offending parties for damages under a strict liability theory. Until 2015 amendments to the AMA took effect, the FTC also played a quasi-adjudicatory role in evaluating the facts of claims of AMA violations. This role is now performed by a division of the Tokyo District Court.

Corporate mergers and acquisitions are also prohibited if they have a significant anti-competitive effect. The FTC oversees a system of reporting and, if applicable, authorizing such transactions (articles 9 through 16).

The FTC also administers the Act against Delay in Payment of Subcontract Proceeds, Etc. to Subcontractors of 1956 (commonly called the "Subcontractor Act"). This law protects small subcontractors by preventing larger general contractors from using their superior bargaining position to force subcontractors to accept disadvantage terms. The "small subcontractor" and "general contractor" categories are based on a combination of capitalization thresholds and nature of business. Once a party is a subcontractor under the Act, then the general contractor may not impose oppressive terms on it, such as payment terms of greater than 60 days or forced participation in discount or rebate programs.

G. EMPLOYMENT

1. Overview

Employment law is one of the most basic elements of the Japanese business environment. Anyone conducting a business of even a modest size is likely to need employees and thus deal with employment regulation.

Work is also one of the few aspects of the business environment specifically addressed by the constitution. Article 27 of the constitution establishes work as both a right and obligation of the people, and mandates the creation of legal standards for wages, working hours, rest and other conditions. Article 28 guarantees the rights of workers to organize and engage in collective action.

Japan is well known for its "lifetime employment" system. While usefully descriptive of the long-term nature of this type of employment, the term is a misnomer (as is a common alternative, "permanent employment"). The mode of employment describes is neither for life nor permanent. Among other things, most corporate and other employers have a mandatory retirement age of 60, subject to recent legal requirements extending that in a limited fashion and described below.

This chapter will subsequently use the term "regular employment" (*seiki koyō*) to describe this type of employment relationship, and "regular employees" as those in it. "Non-regular employment" (*hiseiki koyō*) is the term used to describe other types of modes of employment.

2. "Regular" Employment vs. Irregular Employment

a. A Conceptual Framework for Understanding "Regular Employment"

It is important to understand some basic features of the regular employment system and the general landscape before turning to other modes of employment and the key statutes governing them.

First, there is nothing "traditional" about regular employment in Japan. It developed during the "high economic growth" period of the mid-1950s to the mid-1970s as a response to both labor shortages and highly political labor movements. In essence many workers were enticed into trading job security for mobility.

Second, although lateral hiring into regular employment positions is not unusual, the system is still based primarily on hiring young graduates straight out of high school or college and employing them continuously until they reach retirement age. The employment period is thus potentially three decades or more. Regular employees just out of college are not hired because they have a particular set of skills or to fill a particular role in the institution; they are hired because of their pedigree and potential. There is clearly an employment contract in the relationship, but it is not defined either by skills or a job description; it is defined on a basic level by the worker being told what to do by the employer and getting paid to do that. This relationship is rooted in the Civil Code (article 623). Among other things, this means there should be a unity between the two sides of the equation (employer/employee). This can cause problems in other types of employment or business relationships, as discussed below.

Third, there is no concept of "employment at will" in Japan, even with respect to many of those not in regular employment jobs. Thanks to both court practice and statutory law discussed later in this chapter it can be particularly difficult to terminate regular employees. Not only is it difficult, but unpredictable since there are no clear rules about how much an employer should pay to terminate someone with regular employee status even if they are willing to do so. Thus, once hired and past the provisional employment period of a few months, employees hired into this status effectively become fixed costs that cannot be reduced very easily. For management there is thus an incentive to both minimize the number of regular employees hired and maximize the effort that can be obtained from them. Uncompensated and excessive overtime have long been a common and problematic feature of some permanent jobs.

Fourth, the regular employment model means regular employees should go where they are needed by the employer. A regular worker who is transferred, promoted or retires usually must be replaced from internal resources, and the same will apply for his or her replacement. Personnel decisions thus necessarily have a knock-on effect within the employing institution. Periodic rotations through different departments and roles are thus a feature of life for most regular employees. For a large company with offices throughout Japan or even abroad, this can mean geographic disruption as well.

These transfers can be very disruptive for an employee's family life, particularly once an employee has purchased a home in a particular location and has children in school. *Tanshin funin*—the practice of the employee living alone apart from his family (sometimes in company-provided housing) for several years because of an assignment to a different geographical location from his or her family home is a common feature of life in a regular employment position.

The resulting unpredictability and disruption (including the expectation of working overtime on short notice) is likely one of the many factors that has made regular employment roles particularly difficult for women who act as the primary caregiver of their children. *Tanshinfunin*—the practice of one working family member (traditionally the father) moving to a new and distant location to live alone for months or years because of a posting to a different geographical location in order to avoid disruptions to a child's schooling or other aspects of family life—is a common feature of regular employment.

Large employers may have more than one "regular employment" track. For example one may require the employee to work at a variety of locations in the course of his or her career, while the other may be limited to a particular geographical location. In the past different but ostensibly gender neutral career tracks were commonly used to perpetuate the different treatment of female employees.

Fifth, permanent employment has the benefit of making regular employees extremely familiar with the company, its operations and workforce. It may also have a limiting effect on employee development. Large companies invest significant sums in employee training, and regular employees may acquire particular skill sets or professional qualifications during their careers (including an LL.M. from a US law school in the case of those staffed to the legal department). They may thus come to circulate through a particular subset of job categories within the company (e.g. technical as opposed to financial). However, their principal area of expertise may be the company and its business. This necessarily means they may not be useful to other companies and in any case, there is limited liquidity in regular employee jobs. Someone who has worked at a large company for ten or twenty years would have limited expectations that they could both increase their compensation and continue to enjoy the same job security by moving to another large company. This appears to be changing in recent years, and foreign companies establishing businesses in Japan and more recently a general labor shortage appear to have acted as a catalyst for increase competition for lateral hires. In general, however, job-hopping is not as common a practice as in some countries.

Although not required by law, employees typically receive a lump-sum payment upon leaving the company, the amount of which is based on years of service and can be a significant sum at the end of a full career. This also encourages staying with the company rather than leaving mid-career.

Sixth, regular employees are far more likely to share a common motivation to see the company succeed, or at least a powerful and common interest in it not failing. In a 2008 LLD Thesis, Dan Puchniak (now a renowned scholar of Japanese and comparative corporate law), posits that Japan's lifetime employment system rather than its systems of corporate or bankruptcy law are the key reason why investors (both debt and equity) have had a high degree of trust in Japanese management compared to many other countries.[7]

The long-term character of employment relationships also makes employees a significant consideration in corporate governance. Depending on the company it would be easy to conclude that the company is run more for the benefit of employees than shareholders.

Seventh, the regular employment system makes the link between pay and a regular employee's particular job description at any time in their career much less clear than in employment regimes based primarily on skills, roles/job-titles or contract terms. While some regular employees may have an incentive/performance-based component to their pay, the bulk of their compensation is likely to be based on their age and/or years of service to the employer. As a result some Japanese workplaces may take on an "everyone does everything" atmosphere that is based more on senior people telling junior people what to do when necessary.

Eighth, the regular employment compensation system was essentially designed (if that much thought can be attributed to it) to support families—a "family allowance" being a common component of compensation for those with spouses and children. Other forms of employment are more likely to be based on the immediate market value of the worker's services. At the time of writing the government was moving towards an "equal pay for equal work" regime, and it has become common in both the western and Japanese press to point out the disparity in compensation between regular workers (who have traditionally primarily been men) and non-regular workers (who are often women) despite performing substantially similar tasks. The underlying assumptions about family embedded in the compensation system for regular employment as opposed to other forms is rarely mentioned in these discussions but is certainly a factor in the disparities.

Ninth, the regular employment system has resulted in companies and other employers that have it (including most government employers) effectively becoming a part of the social welfare system for the households that benefit from it. This should be born in mind any time policies affecting large companies and their workforce are discussed. The famed difficulty of terminating Japanese employees, particularly those regular employees, is also a reflection of this reality. Some social welfare programs may even discourage employment. For example, the eligibility of one spouse to participate in some of the other spouse's family benefits programs gained through regular employment may be conditioned on *not* having independent employment income above a surprisingly low threshold.

Tenth, much of the rigidity of employment has been initially driven by courts, with law and regulation often following well-established judicial practices and simply adding greater definition. In this respect some of the "black letter" employment law described

[7] Dan Puchniak, *Rethinking Comparative Governance: Valuable Lessons from Japan's Post-Bubble Era*, Kyushu University LLD Thesis (2008).

below can be misleading, For example the default provisions in the Civil Code (article 627) appear to require only two weeks' notice for terminating an employment contract not specifying other terms, and the Labor Standards Act (article 20) establishes a 30 day notice requirement. The reality, however, is that courts have long used the notion of "abuse of rights" (*i.e.*, the right of the employer to terminate the contract) and other "equitable" notions to make termination of employees—particularly those in regular employment—both difficult and unpredictable. One of the most famous cases involved an employee of a commercial radio station operator whose responsibilities included reading the morning news. He overslept not once but twice in a two week period, resulting in static instead of news being broadcast not once but twice, and then compounded the failure by falsifying information in the subsequent incident report. Terminated by his employer (though not for cause), he challenged the action and the Supreme Court found that his dismissal to be an abuse of right (Supreme Court, 2nd Petty Bench decision of January 31, 1977).

Employees challenging a termination of employment through litigation may also seek *karishobun* provisional remedies such as confirmation of their continuing status as employees and/or requiring continued payment of salary until the dispute is resolved. If such a remedy is granted it can gives the employee additional leverage in obtaining a more favorable settlement than originally offered, though if they are simply seeking a better financial result that can sometimes be more easily sought through a labor tribunal.

Judicial remedies are not necessarily limited to permanent employees. To the extent part of the consideration in such cases is the extent to which employee expectations should be protected, more may be at stake in cases in those involving permanent employees.

On the other hand, the nature of regular employment may make it more difficult to pursue judicial remedies in situations where an employee is not terminated. When employees are overworked, subject to abusive or discriminatory behavior by superiors, not paid for overtime or otherwise enjoying the full benefit of the rights ostensibly guaranteed by some of the statutes described below, the pursuit of judicial remedies or other external recourse must be balanced with the likely effect doing so will have on institutional and personal relationships that may be expected to continue for decades. Unpaid overtime and *karōshi* (death by overwork) remain prominent themes in Japanese employment, and lawmakers and regulators alike devote significant efforts to improving the quality of the Japanese workplace. A recent example of this is the concept of *pawahara*—power harassment—the use of a dominant position to engage in abusive or hurtful behavior in the workplace. This concept is so broad that it can even be asserted by senior employees against their juniors if, for example, the junior has technical skills that the senior does not and uses that power imbalance in an abusive manner. The long-term nature of regular employment is a likely factor in the solicitude accorded to protecting workplace harmony by labor regulators and judges.

b. Non-Regular Employment

(i) Overview

Non-regular (*hiseiki*) employment is a term used to describe most other forms of employment that are not "regular." Western observers sometimes refer to such jobs as "precarious" or "contingent" employment, though some may still offer more job security than in countries such as the United States. These terms – together with "irregular employment"—are often misnomers in any case, as some employees having such status may work for many years at the same place either by choice or out of necessity.

Unlike regular employment, these jobs involve compensation for the individual rather than the assumption of a family life that underlay the compensation of regular employees. In that sense some can be viewed as having originally offered a source of *supplemental* income by family members (children in school or spouses) of a person in a regular employment job. Of course is often not the case for those in such jobs, which are often associated with poverty, particularly demographics such as single mothers.

(ii) Fixed Term Contract Employees

Formal employment contracts are often used by employers to limit an employment relationship to a fixed term. Not having such a contract may actually be the indicia of regular employment status. Courts have restricted the abusive use (or termination) of repeatedly renewed fixed term employment contracts, restrictions that were recently codified in the Labor Contract Act discussed below.

(iii) Arubaito

Derived from the German term "arbeit," *arubaito* is the description given to loose short-term, often part time jobs filled by students; working at convenience stores or restaurants, for example.

(iv) Pāto

Derived from the Japanized English term "*pāto taimu jobu*" (part time job), such jobs may actually be full time jobs but without the pay or benefits of regular employment. The trade-off is that working hours and location of work are subject to greater certainty.

(v) Dispatched Workers

Commonly called *haken* (dispatched), dispatched workers are employees of a company licensed to provide dispatched workers under the Worker Dispatch Act of 1985 (WDA) discussed below. When dispatched to a client needing "temporary" workers, they are employed by the dispatching company but instructed and supervised by the client—an exception to the basic structure of the employment relationship envisioned by the Civil Code (*i.e.*, the person or company actually utilizing the workers in this relationship is not the person or company that pays their salary).

(vi) Technical Interns

Due to significant resistance from part of the Japanese populace and policymakers, Japan has yet to open itself to widespread immigration from other countries as a solution to the growing shortfall in its worker population. However, for several decades now it has been able to satisfy some of its needs for lowly-paid manual workers through immigration rules that allow people from specific developing countries to come to Japan under the aegis of being paid "trainees" rather than "employees." The system assumes that while engaging in various types of manual, labor such technical trainees will acquire useful skills in Japan that they can then take back to their countries of origin, which the immigration rules ensure they must do. The system was ripe for abuse, however, with limited recourse for the "trainees." In 2017 the "Act for the Protection of Foreign Technical Interns and the Proper Implementation of Technical Training Programs" was passed to provide for greater protection and oversight of trainees, and to make it more likely that they would actually receive the promised training.

3. Key Statutes

The following is an incomplete and brief summary of some of the key statutes constituting the main body of Japanese employment law. For the most part, these statutes are supplemented by a further suite of implementing and interpretive regulations and directives issued and administered by the MHLW.

a. The Labor Standards Act

(i) Overview

Although pre-war Japan had a variety of statutes intended to protect workers in specific limited contexts, it was the Labor Standards Act of 1947 (LSA) that first established widespread rules intended to protect the interests of workers. The historical experience at the time of its passage included debt-servitude (including as prostitutes in the case of women), and labor bosses effectively keeping workers in prison-like conditions, renting them out while keeping most of the fruits of their labor.

The Act rejects such arrangements, mandating"[w]orking conditions shall be those which should meet the needs of workers who live lives worthy of human beings" (article 1). It does so by establishing minimum standards for employment and workplace safety, which may not be lowered by contract or other arrangements, and seeks to maintain an equal bargaining position between workers and employers in deciding the other aspects of the employment relationship. It also prohibits employment discrimination based on nationality, religious faith or social origin, prevents brokers or other intermediaries from benefiting from the labors of others, and protects workers exercising their voting rights (articles 3, 6 and 7).

The LSA establishes the basic requirements of employment contracts and renders a variety of oppressive contractual terms void. It requires employees to be paid on time, in cash, without offset or withholdings other than those required by law. Workers are protected by a statutory maximum number of working hours per week (subject to numerous exceptions), requirements for overtime pay, mandated break times and paid days off.

Various articles of the LSA permit employers and unions or a majority of employees to enter into collective agreements that exclude the applicability of some of the basic standards established by the LSA relating to working hours, working offsite, working on holidays, time off and so forth. These are collectively referred to as *rōshi kyōtei* (labor-management agreements), though specific types of agreements refer to the article of the LSA containing the standard to which they create an exception. The existence of such an agreement prevents penalties from accruing to violations of the applicable article, but may also have private law effect as to the contractual employment relationships.

The LSA (article 20) requires that at least 30 days notice be given before termination of employment. As discussed earlier in this section it may be difficult to actually do so.

The LSA is enforced by local Labor Standards Bureaus whose officials have broad powers to investigate violations and even arrest egregious employers.

(ii) The LSA and Rules of Employment

One of the first things a business may need to do after incorporation is establish Rules of Employment (*shūgyō kisoku*) which establish the basic working conditions (working hours, rules for supplemental payments of various types, safety, training and so forth) for employees. These must be filed with the local Labor Supervision Bureau (Labor Standards Act article 89). The establishment or amendment of the Rules of Employment requires the employer to seek the views of a labor union or representative representing at least a majority of employees (Labor Standards Act, article 90).

Since regular employees may never have an employment contract with their employer, the rules of employment may play a similar role, except that they apply to all employees or categories of employees addressed by the Rules of Employment. These also establish minimum standards even if there is an employment agreement; any provision of an employment agreement (including a collective agreement under the Labor Standards Act) that does not meet the standards set forth in the Rules of Employment is void (Labor Contract Act, article 12). They are also binding on employees, even those who object to their contents.

There are a multitude of academic theories as to the legal character of Rules of Employment—that they are a collective agreement, a form of adhesion contract, a type of positive law, a simple contract, and so forth. The Supreme Court has essentially described them as a form of custom that should be accorded status of a legal norm to the extent they are factually derived from the working conditions as between management and labor (Supreme Court, Grand Bench judgment of December 25, 1968). Courts have also acknowledged that management and workers can through further customs develop terms of employment that are inconsistent with the Rules of Employment and that these may become binding as contractual rules between the parties (e.g., Osaka High Court judgment of June 25, 1993).

The Rules of Employment are also important in that they can be used to set forth the standards and procedures for discipline and termination.

b. The Labor Union Act

The Labor Union Act of 1949 helps implement article 28 of the Constitution, which guarantees the rights of workers to organize and bargain collectively. It provides for the rules for establishing unions—something which is easy to do and employers can neither prevent employees from forming a union or joining an external one. Article 1 of the Act provides that strikes and other non-violent labor activities are exempt from criminal liability under article 35 of the Penal Code.

The formal requirements for establishing a union are not rigorous, but to obtain the full protection of the Act it is necessary to be recognized as such by the Labor Relations Commission. This entails having supervisory personnel, having a written charter, accepting all qualified workers on a non-discriminatory basis and satisfying certain other requirements.

Although there are various sector-wide unions, some of which are very powerful, it is not uncommon for companies to have what is essentially a "company union," though it is prohibited for a company to form or control unions. Company-specific unions may facilitate workers and management working cooperatively and work cooperatively towards improving employment conditions. Some companies also establish "employee associations" which can perform some of the functions of a union. The existence of single-company unions does not mean the company can prevent some employees from forming a separate union or joining an external one.

The Labor Union Act also prohibits various acts by employers in connection with union membership, such as firing or disadvantaging a worker for joining one. Recourse for such actions can be had to the Labor Relations Commission.

Union-driven mass strikes and political protests were once a common feature earlier in post-war history. Now it is rare to see or hear of strikes of any significance taking place.

c. *The Labor Relations Adjustment Act*

The Labor Relations Adjustment Act of 1946 (LRAA) provides a counter-balance to the Labor Union Act by providing multiple layers of mediation and arbitration through the Labor Relations Commission with the aim of preventing large scale disruptive strikes or lockouts. It also requires that prior notice be given to the authorities at least ten days in advance of strikes by workers in "public welfare" jobs, which include the transportation, post and telecommunications, utilities and health care sector (article 37). With the shift in focus during recent decades from union *vs.* industry collectivist disputes to employee vs. employer individual disputes, the LRAA seems less important than it was in the past. That said, together with LSA and the Labor Union Act it is still counted as one of the *rōdō sanpō*, the "three labor laws."

d. *The Labor Contract Act*

The Labor Contract Act of 2007 (LCA) is a comparatively recent but important act which codifies many rules that were developed by courts over decades of employment litigation. While the LSA is essentially a regulatory law that involves oversight by the MHLW and contains penal sanctions for violations, in substance it is concerned primarily with the private law relationship between employer and employee; it is thus a special law built on the foundations of the Civil Code.

The LCA is based on five basic principles that should be reflected in labor contracts: (i) they should be based on an equal bargaining position between employer and employee, (ii) similarly situated workers should be treated similarly in accordance with their jobs, (iii) contracts should strike a balance between work and private life, (iv) employer and employee must perform the contract based on the principle of good faith, (v) abuse of rights is prohibited.

Fixed-term employment contracts have long been one of the means by which employers were able to increase their workforce as needed without taking on additional regular employees. In the use of repeatedly-renewed fixed term contracts could be used abusively to keep employees for a prolonged period without giving them all the benefits of regular employee status. Courts have protected the expectations of workers in such situations by preventing employers from abusing their rights *not* to renew contracts, a practice known as *yatoidome* (cessation of employment). 2013 amendments to the LCA effectively codified some of this jurisprudence by establishing clear rules entitling any employee in a fixed term contract relation that lasts more than five years (or any combination of shorter consecutive contract renewals) to demand regular employment. These provisions took effect in 2018.

e. The Equal Employment Act

The Act on Securing, Etc. of Equal Opportunity and Treatment between Men and Women in Employment ("Equal Employment Act") began life as the Working Ladies Welfare Act of 1972. After Japan acceded to the Convention on the Elimination of all forms of Discrimination Against Women in 1985 its name was gradually changed over the course of several amendments until reaching its current form.

The Equal Employment Act contains broad prohibitions on discrimination against women in employment, as well as protections against unfair treatment of women workers on the grounds of pregnancy. Prohibitions on gender-based discrimination in compensation are also included in the Labor Standards Act. Many would likely say that these efforts have not been as effective as the statutory text would suggest, since the predominance of men in regular employment positions, particularly in managerial and senior positions continues to be a frequent criticism of the Japanese work environment. It was not until 1999 amendments to the law that treating women equally in hiring, promotion, compensation and other aspects of employment were changed from precatory statements of ideals to enforceable prohibitions on discrimination.

f. The Worker Dispatch Act

The sesquipedalian Act for Securing the Proper Operation of Worker Dispatching Undertakings and Improved Working Conditions for Dispatched Workers Act of 1985 (the Worker Dispatch Act or WDA), essentially legalized what was an already existing business of providing temporary workers. An employment arrangement where the employer of the worker (the dispatching agency) and the business giving instructions to the worker (the client using the dispatched worker) is at odds with the basic characterization of the employment relationship in the Civil Code. In addition, for a dispatching agency to take a margin on the labor of the dispatched worker is also a violation on the LSA prohibition on intermediaries profiting from the labor of others, absent an approved arrangement such as that permitted under the WDA.

Dispatched workers fulfilled a special need. It was also an arrangement that originally enabled women driven out of companies by discriminatory rules requiring them to leave at a certain age or upon marriage to be gainfully redeployed to workplaces that needed their skills. The WDA thus started out as offering a way for companies to temporarily procure workers with specific skills, such as the ability to type in English or operate "Office Automation Equipment. In its original form, the WDA only permitted the dispatch of workers having such enumerated skills. Gradual expansions resulted in the WDA providing a means of procuring general workers on an as-needed basis without assuming the risks and potential long-term costs of taking on regular workers. However even now the "skill-based" roots of the WDA regime are reflected in continuing prohibitions on the use of certain categories of workers on a dispatch basis, including attorneys, dockworkers, security guards, and construction workers. The addition in 2004 of manufacturing workers to the category of workers who could be used on a dispatch basis was one of the ways in which Japanese manufacturers were able to continue competing with lower cost foreign competitors.

Many companies are willing to pay a premium for dispatched workers since they are still cheaper than regular employees and can be terminated on relatively short notice. This is one of the reasons why the worker dispatch business has grown substantially in Japan. However as a business it is heavily dependent on the *inflexibility* of regular employment.

It was possible for dispatched workers to spend years or even decades being employed by one company (the licensed provider) but actually working for another (the client). Such workers have often been women, who may find themselves paid substantially less than the regular employees at their workplace. At the same time, since dispatched work arrangements are based on hourly pay, they may offer greater certainty as to where they will work and what time they will be able to go home as compared to regular employment jobs. Dispatched workers arrangements are subject to the LCA provision entitling them to permanent employment (with the provider) if they are deployed for more than five years. 2015 amendments to the WDA also prohibited dispatching the same worker to the same client workplace for more than three years. An underlying goal of the WDA is to encourage employers who need dispatched workers for a long enough period to convert the role into one of direct and regular employment.

The WDA requires that such worker dispatch arrangements only be conducted by companies holding a suitable license from the MHLW. It protects dispatched workers by ensuring that the statutory obligations applicable to employers are clearly allocated between the dispatching company and the receiving client. The worker dispatch business is byzantine and highly regulated.

As their proportion in the workforce increases, improving the status of dispatched worker has become a policy goal of the MHLW and some poiticians. The WDA is intended to encourage conversion to regular employment, and recent amendments also impose on providers of such workers an obligation to provide training and other opportunities to advance their careers.

The WDA represents a potential compliance minefield for companies offering outsourcing or contracting services. Contracting or outsourcing arrangements whereby a company sends workers to work with a client (for example an IT service provider sending employees to a client site for a prolonged project) in which client managers begin giving those workers detailed instructions as to what tasks to perform and how to perform them risks being viewed as an unlicensed worker dispatch arrangement. Disguising what was essentially a dispatch arrangement as an "outsourcing" or other similar arrangement was a common practice, particularly prior to 2004 when manufacturing was a category in which the use of dispatched labor was prohibited. Accordingly, there is a significant and complex body of MHLW rules and guidelines devoted to evaluating whether outsourcing and contracting arrangements are legitimate.

g. *The Employment Security Act*

The Employment Security Act of 1947 (ESA) provides the regulatory framework for public and private employment intermediaries, specifying the type of information that must be made clear in solicitations of employees. It imposes licensing requirements on private recruiting businesses.

h. *Other Employment-Related Laws*

A few other statutes bear brief mention. First itshould be remembered that the Civil Code still forms the foundation of the rules of employment contracting, and also offers the possibility tort remedies in cases of malfeasance by employers.

The Unemployment Insurance Act of 1974 and the Industrial Accident Compensation Insurance Act of 1947 establish the basic safety net for terminated and injured workers. The Act on Improvement of (etc.) of Management of Part-Time Workers of 1993 is intended to protect workers in short-term or part time roles that may not otherwise be able to avail themselves of all of the protections of the LSA or other laws.

The Act on Succession of Labor Contracts upon Company Split of 2000 protects workers from degradation or loss of employment through spin-off transactions. Essentially the Act mandates that workers stay with whatever part of the company they have been working for, unless they agree otherwise.

The Act for Promotion of Employment of Persons with Disabilities of 1960 prohibits employment discrimination based on disabilities, and requires companies with more than 50 full time employees to have 2.0% or more of their workforce comprised of certified disabled persons a combination of financial payments and "naming and shaming" are imposed on companies that do not comply. Finally, the Elderly Person Employment Stabilization Act of 1971 seeks to extend the availability of employment opportunities to senior citizens. 2013 amendments to this act required employers to give employees the opportunity to work past the standard retirement age of 60 to continue working to the age of 65 (or higher), albeit for reduced compensation and in non-managerial positions. As some of these examples illustrate, employment law is used to coopt companies into acting as part of the social welfare system by ensuring broad and long-term employment opportunities for as many people as possible.

At the time of writing the government was pushing ahead with further broad amendments to the way Japanese people work, including an "equal pay for equal work" regime, and potentially wide-reaching advances in employment flexibility.

H. INTELLECTUAL PROPERTY

1. Overview

Japan's intellectual property regime has a long history and is rooted in a number of statutes. Each statute essentially establishes the rules for a particular type of intellectual property. For those types that require registration with the Japan Patent Office in order for the intellectual property right to be effective, the first to file is entitled to the registration absent special circumstances.

Remember that just as is the case with other rights in Japan, overly aggressive or unreasonable assertion may be found abusive. For example in a February 28, 2013 judgment in a case between Samsung and Apple involving assertions of infringement, the Tokyo District Court found Samsung to be abusing its patent rights. In a June 30, 2016 case, the same court also found the assertion of trademark rights by the heirs of the founder of the Kyokushin school of Karate against other former members of the school abusive.

Japanese intellectual property law does not appear to have a clearly developed "public domain;" there is no commonly-used Japanese term for the concept. Nor does there appear to be a clear linkage of fostering creative behavior through limited-term monopolies to the eventual enrichment of the public domain at the end of the monopoly period. Individual statutes speak in more general, utilitarian terms, such as "encourage inventions, and thereby to contribute to the development of industry" (Patent Act) or "contribute to the development of culture" (Copyright Act).

Many of the categories of intellectual property rights described below involve registration with the Japan Patent Office. The JPO has a well-developed English website describing the legal requirements and processes involved in applying for the various types of registration.

2. The Civil Code

In the past the tort provisions of article 709 of the Civil Code were used as a remedy for unfair competitive behavior that infringes protected rights (as well as other business torts). This would include the use of the same or similar corporate name as an existing business that caused customer confusion or other harm. The same claims can be made under current tort law, but some of the other more specific statutes described below may offer more specific remedies.

3. The Unfair Competition Prevention Act

In connection with Japan's accession in 1934 to the Paris Convention on the Protection of Intellectual Property, Japan also passed its first Unfair Competition Prevention Act. This law was completely revised under the same name in 1993. It prohibits (by defining as "unfair competition") the use of identical or similar trademarks, similar goods, trade names, corporate titles or domain names or other means likely to confuse consumers, as well as providing for the protection of trade secrets. Injunctive relief is available to aggrieved parties (article 3).[8] In addition to civil remedies, the Act imposes criminal sanctions on serious violations, as do other intellectual property statutes.

4. Trademark

Trademarks were granted specific legal protection early in the in the Meiji Period with the passage of the Trademark Order in 1884. The first Trademark Act was passed by the Imperial Diet in 1899, and replaced with the current Trademark Act in 1959. Japan's trademark laws have reflected Japan's efforts to be consistent with the various international trademark conventions to which it is party, including the Paris Convention (which Japan joined in 1899) and the Madrid Agreement and its more recent Protocol.

Trademarks (*shōhyōken*) are administered by the JPO, which maintains the trademark registration system. Registration with the JPO is necessary for a trademark to be effective (article 18). In order to be registered the trademark must be letters, signs, symbols, shapes and color in a combination that is distinct and otherwise registrable (article 2) and used in connection with a business or service. Since 2015 it has also been possible to register trademarks in holograms, unique colors, moving marks and even sounds.

Marks that cannot be registered include those that are similar to already well-known marks or names (whether names or not), infringe the rights of personality of others, flags or symbols of other countries, marks that would contravene good public morals and so forth (articles 3 and 4). Trademark rights have a ten year term but can be renewed indefinitely. The holder of a trademark right has the exclusive right to use

[8] The Unfair Competition Prevention Act is also the locus of Japan's minimalist version of the U.S. Foreign Corrupt Practices Act, with article 18 containing a prohibition on the bribing of foreign officials in connection with international commercial transactions. Immediately before the publication of this book a case arising under this provision of the Act saw the first use of the new plea-bargain system described in Chapter 8, with a company implicating its employee in a violation.

them. The registration system is also used to perfect transfers of and security interests in trademarks, as well as exclusive licenses to their use.

Trademark registrations can be challenged at the application stage and after issuance actions can be brought at the PTO for a decree of invalidation (articles 43–2 and 46). Failure to use a registered mark for three years or more entitles other persons to bring an action for a decree of cancellation due to non-use. Decrees issued by the PTO can be appealed to the Intellectual Property Branch of the Tokyo High Court (article 63).

Remedies for infringement include injunctions, damages and other measures that may be needed to restore the reputation of the business whose trademark it is (articles 36 through 39). Damages are based on the general tort provisions of article 709 of the Civil Code, but the Trademark Act contains a presumption of negligence on the part of the infringer (article 106).

5. Copyright

Japan's first modern copyright law was the "Publication Ordinance" of 1869 which was as concerned with controlling the publication of content as it was in establishing exclusive rights for the publisher. When Japan joined the Berne Convention for the Protection of Literary and Artistic Works in 1899, it passed a Copyright Act the same year. This was replaced in 1970 with the current act of the same name. In addition to the Berne Convention, Japan is a party to other principal conventions relevant to copyright. Japanese copyright law is based on European, rather than American models.

The Copyright Act protects the rights of authors in "work" (*chosakubutsu*), which is defined as "a production in which thoughts or sentiments are expressed in a creative way and which falls within the literary, scientific, artistic or musical domain" (article 2(1)). Court decisions have dealt with whether specific categories of creative effort fall under this rubric. For example, private diaries do, but new fonts do not. Databases, translations and other derivative works having "creative" element are separately protected as works of authorship (articles 11, 12, 12–2).

Copyright (*chosakuken*) confers several non-transferrable moral rights on the author, including the rights to make the work public, to have attribution of authorship in it, and to preserve the integrity of the work (articles 18–20). The Act also establishes in the work a bundle of rights that can be transferred or licensed. These include the rights of reproduction, performance, broadcast, recitation, distribution, exhibition, transfer, rental, and translation (articles 21–28).

Japanese copyright law lacks a general concept of fair use, but contains a large number of exemptions permitting limited use of copyrighted works for specific purposes. These include private copying, various uses by libraries and educational institutions (including use in entrance exam questions), rendering into braille or other media for people with sensory impairments, quotations, and certain other public interest uses, subject to attribution of authorship and such use not affecting the moral rights of the author (articles 30 to 50). There is also an arbitration-based system of acquiring compulsory licenses through the Cultural Affairs Agency but it is rarely used.

The term of a copyright is generally of 50 years from the death of the author or, if the author is corporate or pseudonymous, from the date of creation. Copyrights in cinematographic works last for 70 years from creation (articles 53 and 54).

The Cultural Affairs Agency has jurisdiction over copyright and maintains a copyright registry. Registration is not relevant to the existence of copyrights in creative works, but is necessary in order to perfect transfers or security interests in them (articles 75–78). Registration of copyrights in software is conducted through a foundation designated by the Director of the Cultural Affairs Agency pursuant to a separate act, the Act on Special Rules for the Registration of Copyrights in Computer Programs of 1986.

6. Patents

The western concept of patenting inventions was first introduced to Japan by the intellectual Fukuzawa Yukichi in his 1867 book, "Things Western." The Meiji government tried to develop a system of monopoly patents to encourage innovation—by Japanese. However, it struggled with the conflicting goals of making it difficult or impossible for foreigners to obtain patents) while at the same time not making it too difficult for Japanese inventors to obtain them either.

Modern patent law has its roots in an "exclusive right of sale" ordinance passed in 1885. The current Patent Act was passed in 1959. Japan is also a party to key international conventions relating to patents, including the Paris Convention and Agreement on Trade-Related Aspects of Intellectual Property Rights (TRIPs Agreement).

The Patent Act defines an invention as a "highly advanced creation of technical ideas utilizing the laws of nature" (article 2(1)). Patents (*tokkyo*) can be obtained for inventions pursuant to the requirements and procedures of the Act. Article 29(1) also requires the invention to have novelty, though expresses the requirement in terms of the invention having "industrial applicability" and *not* already being publicly-known or used or described anywhere (subject to certain exceptions). Inventions that would harm public order, morals or health also cannot be patented (article 32).

The JPO has built on the relatively sparse statutory requirements for patentability and developed a number of additional requirements through practice. The "utilizing the laws of nature" requirement in particular has resulted in challenges but means it is difficult to get "business method" patents or patents on things like arbitrary rules of a game, computer programs or mathematical models (unless they somehow utilize a law of nature). The industrial applicability requirement also limits the patentability of things that may be fun or interesting but which are not commercially useful. Surgical techniques and other medical procedures are also not patentable, though medical devices are. The novelty requirement is also strictly applied, so that prior publication of the idea is fatal to patentability.

For the past decade the JPO has received at least 300,000 applications for patent registrations every year, and the process of obtaining a decision can take several years. There is a claims procedure, including a quasi-judicial adjudicative process within the JPO which is appealable to the Tokyo High Court. If granted, a patent has a duration of 20 years subject to a possible extension of five years for certain pharmacological patents (articles 67 and 67–2).

Even if a patent is granted it is subject to challenge by someone claiming to have invented the same thing independently. The same claim can essentially be made in infringement actions brought in court. These must be brought in the Tokyo or Osaka district court. For decades the Patent Act only anticipated a patent being invalidated only by a decree of the JPO. In a 2000 ruling, however, the Supreme Court held that a court could refuse to enforce rights in a patent that it found to be invalid (Supreme Court. 3rd Petty Bench judgment of April 11, 2000). This was codified in a 2004 amendment to the Patent Act (article 104–3).

Remedies for infringement include injunctions, damages and other restorative measures (article 100 and 102). There is a presumption of negligence once infringement is established (103). There are also criminal penalties for egregious violations.

Holders of patents have the exclusive right to exploit the patented invention for the exclusive period. As with trademarks, the registration system is also used to record transfers, security interests and licenses. There is also a compulsory licensing regime for unused patents (article 83).

A recurring issue with patentable inventions is when they are created by employees of companies. The most famous case is that of Nakamura Shūji who invented the blue LED (an invention for which he also subsequently shared in the award of the 2014 Nobel Prize for Physics). Having been awarded a paltry sum of JPY 20,000 (around $200) for his contribution to Nichia Corporation, his employer at the time, he went to court and in 2004 was awarded by the Tokyo District Court the astounding (for Japanese court-awarded damages) sum of JPY 20 billion. On appeal, the Tokyo High Court made it clear that he should settle for JPY 600 million. He did so but held a press conference to express his disgust with the Japanese judicial system. He now lives in America.

The case nonetheless caused alarm in corporate Japan and an amendment to the Patent Act was quickly passed requiring employers to remunerate employees for "the reasonable value" of patents they invent on behalf of the company (article 35). Remuneration is presumed to be reasonable if it is based on consultations between employer and employee, which are now a part of the employment and compliance systems of many companies.

7. Utility Models

Utility models (*jitsuyō shin'an*) are a form of "petty patent," usually on incremental improvements on existing technologies or inventions that have not been made public before the application. They are administered by the JPO, but not subject to the same rigorous substantive examinations as patent applications.

Utility models are covered by the Utility Model Act of 1959, which replaced a 1905 act based on a German law at the time. Utility model registrations are effective for ten years from application (article 15). Significant amendments to the Act in 1993 appear to have had the effect of making utility model registrations less attractive. While in the past there was a time when the number of applications for utility model registrations exceeded those for patents, in the decade ending in 2016 annual applications consistently stood at about 10,000 or less.

Remedies for infringement of utility models are more limited. An enforcement action may only be brought after applying for and receiving a technical evaluation from the JPO (article 29–2) and may be required to reimburse the alleged infringer for damages if the infringement claim is unsuccessful. The burden of proof remains on the rights holder.

8. Design Rights

Design rights (*ishōken*) are a form of design patent that in Japan are provided for under a separate statutory scheme. Unlike the Utility Model Act, the Design Act of 1959 traces its roots back to an 1888 law based on British models. It is similar to the Patent Act in structure and based on a registration system administered by the JPO.

The stated goal of the Act is to "contribute to the development of industry" through the promotion and protection of designs (article 1). Designs must be "novel" and registrations are not permitted for designs injurious to public order or morality, would cause confusion with an article pertaining to another person's business, or which are based solely on functional requirements (article 5).

Design rights are valid for 20 years from application and give their holder the exclusive right to exploit them. At the time of writing amendments were pending that would extend the period of protection to 25 years and expand the range of designs eligible for protection.

Remedies for infringement are similar to those for patents and include a presumption of negligence (articles 37–40). In recent years the annual number of applications for design rights has ranged between 30,000 and 35,000.

9. Other Intellectual Property Regimes

Two other forms of registered intellectual should be mentioned. First are semiconductor integrated circuit layouts, which are protected for a ten year period under the Semiconductor Layout Law of 1985. Registrations are made with METI rather than the JPO.

Seeds and seedlings are protected under the Seed and Seedlings Act of 1998, which is drafted in reference to the requirements of the International Union for the Protection of New Varieties of Plants. Registrations are effective for 15 or 18 years depending on the plant and are filed with the MAFF.

10. Cultural Properties

While not really intellectual property or directly relevant to business, this seems the appropriate juncture to mention Japan's extensive system for designating culturally significant buildings under the Cultural Properties Protection Act of 1950. The Act enables the Cultural Affairs Agency or, where applicable prefectural governors, to designate buildings or other tangible artifacts, intangible artifacts customers or other aspects of culture as important, with various levels or types of designation depending on the cultural artifact or practice. For example, many famous temples or other tourist attractions are "Important Cultural Artifacts."

Designation may create an entitlement to government funds in support of maintenance of the cultural artifact. However, it may also result in severe restrictions on the property rights of the owner, if allowed to remain in private hands.

I. CONSUMER PROTECTION

1. The Consumer Affairs Agency

Historically, consumer protection has been achieved primarily through piecemeal industry-specific regulation under the jurisdiction of whichever ministry or agency is responsible for a particular area of business. Financial services regulated by the FSA, telephone and Internet services by the MIC, food safety by the MAFF and so forth. Since the regulators are also generally charged with advancing the interests of the industries they regulate, there is a difficult balance to be achieved when it comes to protecting consumers.

A great deal of business and industry regulation relevant to consumer protection remains vertically-integrated. It may now just be more complicated with the advent of the Consumer Affairs Agency, in 2009. While the CAA now has primary jurisdiction over some consumer protection acts, the older ministries appear jealous of their territory and for many laws they still retain some form of concurrent jurisdiction. For example, with respect to the Food Sanitation Act of 1947 and the Health Promotion Act, the CAA has control over labelling standards applicable to products regulated by the act, but must do so in consultation with the MHLW, which originally had sole jurisdiction over other aspects of the law. Similarly, with respect to laws such as the Travel Agency Act, the Moneylending Act or the Installment Sales Act (discussed above), the relevant ministries and agencies overseeing those statutory regimes have retained primary jurisdiction, with the CAA empowered to make recommendations and conduct investigations for the purpose of doing so. The CAA has also been given jurisdiction over a wide range of miscellaneous laws, including the Personal Information Protection Act, the Whistleblower Protection.

Three key areas of focus in consumer protection regulation are: (1) ensuring proper disclosure of information to consumers, (2) preventing abusive contracting practices that harm consumers and (3) product safety. These coincide with three of the key acts under the jurisdiction of the CAA: the Unjustifiable Premiums and Misleading Representations Act of 1962, the Consumer Contract Act of 2000 and the Product Liability Act of 1994. These are summarized briefly below.

2. Unjustifiable Premiums and Misleading Representations

The Unjust Premiums and Misleading Representations Act is broadly applicable to most types of misleading or false advertising or labelling. The CAA may issue remedial orders or impose civil fines on violators. Within specific industries, there may be detailed guidelines. For example, a real estate agency advertising a home and describing it as a walk of so many minutes from the nearest station would have to follow guidelines for arriving at that number of minutes.

The Act is interesting in that it also restricts the value of prizes or "free gifts" that can be offered to entice consumers to buy something. The CAA has set specific thresholds that prohibit the prizes/gifts from exceeding the value of the goods or services being sold. For example, the value of a prize (a chance to win a trip to Hawaii, for example) cannot exceed 2% of the expected sales that are being promoted through the prize.

3. Consumer Contracts

As noted earlier in this chapter, one of the features of the 2017 amendments to the contract provisions of the Civil Code is the establishment of special rules for form contracts that are generally non-negotiable and are entered into between parties with vastly disparate bargaining power. Many contracts signed by consumers are of this character.

In the past, protecting consumers from predatory contracting practices was largely a piecemeal approach involving specific statutes addressing particular practices. The concept of a "cooling off" period was adopted in the context of laws like the Specified Commercial Transactions Act of 1976 or the Act for the Improvement of Golf and Other Club Membership Contracts of 1992 and gave consumers a right to cancel a contract within a specific period. These were intended to protect consumers subject to high pressure sales tactics, often by visiting sales personnel who could take advantage of the politeness of many Japanese people. The "cooling off" period under these acts was generally quite short—8 days and only applied to the types of transaction specified in the laws.

The Consumer Contract Act of 2000 applies to consumer contracts generally, and provides three basic protections. First, it allows consumers to rescind contracts if they were misled about or provided with key information relevant to their contracting decision, or subject to other improper pressure (article 4).

Second, the CCA renders certain consumer contract provisions void, including excessive exclusions or limitations of the business party's liability for negligence, torts, willful misconduct or defects (article 8). Third, it makes it possible for a Qualified Consumer Organization to bring a suit for an injunction in and establishes the criteria for such organizations (articles 12 et seq.; see discussion at Chapter 10).

4. Product Liability

Until the passage of the Product Liability Act of 1994 the tort and contract provisions in the Civil Code were the principal grounds for making claims in connection with defective products. The Act itself is very short, comprised of just 6 articles.

The Act defines "product" as movable property (as defined in the Civil Code) that is "manufactured or processed."). [9] Potential liability for defective products falls on "manufacturers, etc." which includes manufacturers, producers or importers of the product, any party that puts its name, logo or trademark on the product or could otherwise be reasonably considered a manufacturer, importer or producer. "Defect" means "a lack of safety that the product ordinarily should provide, taking into account the nature of the product, the ordinarily foreseeable manner of use of the product, the time when the manufacturer, etc. delivered the product, and other circumstances concerning the product" (article 2).

The scope of liability for defective products is harm to "life, body or property of others." The Act creates a special exception to article 709 of the Civil Code, essentially establishing strict liability for defects, subject to proof of causation and damages, where the rules of the Code remain applicable (articles 3 and 6).

There is a defense if the defect is of a type that "could not have been discovered given the state of scientific or technical knowledge at the time" of manufacturer or delivery, but there are appear to be virtually no instances of the defense being found applicable. There is also a defense for subcontractors providing parts or raw materials

[9] Japanese has two categories of terminology commonly translated as "product." One (*shōhin*) refers to an item that is sold. The other (*seihin*) refers to something that is manufactured or produced. As the article 2 definition shows, "product" in the Product Liability Act refers to the latter, but uses the more legalistic term *seizōbutsu* ("thing that is manufactured").

under specifications provided by the manufacturer of a product into which they are incorporated (article 4(i)–(ii)).

GLOSSARY

ACLA	Administrative Case Litigation Act
ACRA	Administrative Complaint Review Act of 2014
Amakudari	"Descent from heaven"—the practice of government officials retiring into lucrative jobs in the public, quasi-public and private sectors
APA	Administrative Procedure Act of 1993
Bengoshi	Attorneys who have passed the NBE and are licensed to represent clients before all courts in Japan
Benronshugi	The principle governing most civil litigation that limits courts to considering arguments and evidence presented by the parties
Bukken	Real right
BOA	Board of Audit
BOAA	Board of Audit Act of 1947
CAA	Consumer Affairs Agency
CCA	Civil Conciliation Act of 1951
CCivPro	Code of Civil Procedure of 1996
CCLA	Cost of Civil Litigation Act of 1971
CCP	Code of Criminal Procedure
CGC	Corporate Governance Code
CIP	The NPSC's Criminal Investigation Protocols of 1957
CLB	Cabinet Legislation Bureau
DRCPA	Domestic Relations Case Procedure Act of 2011
Edo Period	1603–1868 (sometimes also called the "Tokugawa Period")
FIEA	Financial Instruments and Exchange Act (formerly "Securities and Exchange Act") of 1948
FSA	Financial Services Agency
Fukukenji	Assistant Prosecutor
GIA	General Incorporated Association (*ippan shadan hōjin*)
GIAGIFA	General Incorporated Association and General Incorporated Foundation Act of 2006
GIF	General Incorporated Foundation (*ippan zaidan hōjin*)
Han	A feudal domain within the system of government predating the Meiji Restoration of 1868.
Hanji	Judge (with at least 10 years experience)

Hanjiho	Assistant judge
Hanketsu	Judgment of a court resulting from a trial
Hanrei	Judicial precedent
Heisei Period	The period of reign of the Emperor Heisei (Akihito) (1989 to present, subject to planned abdication on May 1, 2019)
HOC	House of Councillors
HOR	House of Representatives
Hōrei iken	A court finding that a provision of a law or regulation is unconstitutional
Hōsō	The collective reference to the three legal professions (judges, prosecutors and *bengoshi* attorneys) who have passed National Bar Exam.
IAA	Independent Administrative Agency
IAC	Independent Administrative Commissions
IHA	Imperial House Act of 1947
JCP	Japanese Communisty Party
JFBA	Japan Federation of Bar Associations
JIA	Judicial Impeachment Act of 1947
Jimujikan	Administrative vice minister; the top public service official at a particular ministry
Jōkoku	A final appeal (usually to the Supreme Court)
Jōso	The generic term for appeals
JPY	Japanese Yen
JSA	Judicial Status Act of 1947
Kabushiki gaisha (KK)	Joint stock corporation, the most common form of corporation; abbreviated "KK"
Kanpō	The Official Gazette, published by the MOF's Bureau of Printing, and which is used to promulgate laws and regulations and used to give public notices required by law
Kanpō	The official gazette
Ken	Right, authority
Kenji	Prosecutor
Kenri	Right
Kensatsukan	Prosecutors (all categories)
Kokkai	The Diet, the national legislature
Kōkoku	An appeal from a decision or other disposition that is not a judgment

Koseki	The system of family registration in which births, marriages, divorces, deaths, adoptions and other changes in personal and family status are recorded, and documentary extracts of which function as a basic form of official proof of status and identity
Kōso	An appeal from a judgment
LAA	Local Autonomy Act of 1947
LCA	Labor Contract Act of 2007
LDP	Liberal Democratic Party
LSA	Labor Standards Act of 1947
LPSA	Local Public Service Act of 1950
LRTI	Legal Research and Training Institute
LSEE	Law School Equivalency Exam
MAFF	Ministry of Agriculture, Fisheries and Forestry
Meiji Constitution	The Constitution of the Empire of Japan of 1889, which was replaced (through amendment) with the current constitution
Meiji Period	The period of reign of the Emperor Meiji (1869 to 1912)
METI	Ministry of Economy, Trade and Industry
MEXT	Ministry of Education, Culture, Sports, Science and Technology
MHLW	Ministry of Health, Labor and Welfare
MIC	Ministry of Internal Affairs and Communications
MLITT	Ministry of Land, Infrastructure, Transport and Tourism
MOD	Ministry of Defense
MOE	Ministry of the Environment
MOF	Ministry of Finance
MOFA	Ministry of Foreign Affairs
MOJ	Ministry of Justice
NBE	National Bar Exam
NBEA	National Bar Examination Act of 1949
NCCPA	Non-Contentious Case Procedure Act of 2011
NGOA	National Government Organization Act of 1999
NPA	National Police Agency
NPSA	National Public Service Act of 1947
NPSC	National Public Safety Commission
NTA	National Tax Agency
PAA	Patent Attorney Act of 2000
PDEA	Police Duties Execution Act of 1948.
POEA	Public Offices Election Act of 1950

PPOA	Public Prosecutors Agency Act of 1947
PRC	Prosecutorial Review Commission
PSLA	Personal Status Litigation Act of 2003
RCP	Rules of Civil Procedure of 1996
Ritsuryō	The per-modern imperial criminal and administrative rules based on Chinese models
Roppō	"Six Laws;" commonly used to refer to the various statutory and regulatory compilations used by students and practitioners
Saiban	A criminal or civil trial in accord under a procedural regime that results in a judgment (*hanketsu*)
Saiban'in	Lay judges
Saibansho shokikan	Judicial clerk
Saiken	Claim (against someone)
Saikensha	Obligee; creditor
Saimu	Obligation (to someone); debt
Saimu meigi	The character of an obligation being enforced through the judicial enforcement process
Saimusha	Obligor; debtor
SDF	Self Defense Forces
SDFA	Self Defense Force Act of 1954
SDFA	Self Defense Force Act of 1954
Shihō	The judiciary; the administration of justice
Shihōken	The judicial power; the power to administer justice
Shinpan	Decree (judicial or administrative)
Shobunshugi	The principle that the commencement, advancement and conclusion of civil litigation is driven by the actions of the parties
Shōwa Period	The period of reign of the Emperor Shōwa (Hirohito) (1926 to 1989)
SME	Small to Medium Sized Enterprise
SOFA	The "Agreement under Article VI of the Treaty of Mutual Cooperation and Security between Japan and the United States of America, Regarding Facilities and Areas and the Status of United States Armed Forces in Japan of 1960" or "Status of Forces Agreement"
Taishō Period	The period of reign of the Emperor Taishō (1912 to 1926)
Tekiyō iken	A court finding that the application of a law or regulation or other government act
TMP	Tokyo Metropolitan Police

Tokubetsu kōkoku	A further appeal from a *kōkoku* appeal, usually to the Supreme Court
Tsūtatsu	Directives issued by a higher level regulatory authority (including the Supreme Court administration) to lower level authorities regarding how to interpret rules or address specific types of situations
WDA	Worker Dispatch Act of 1985

Index

References are to Pages